Map Index

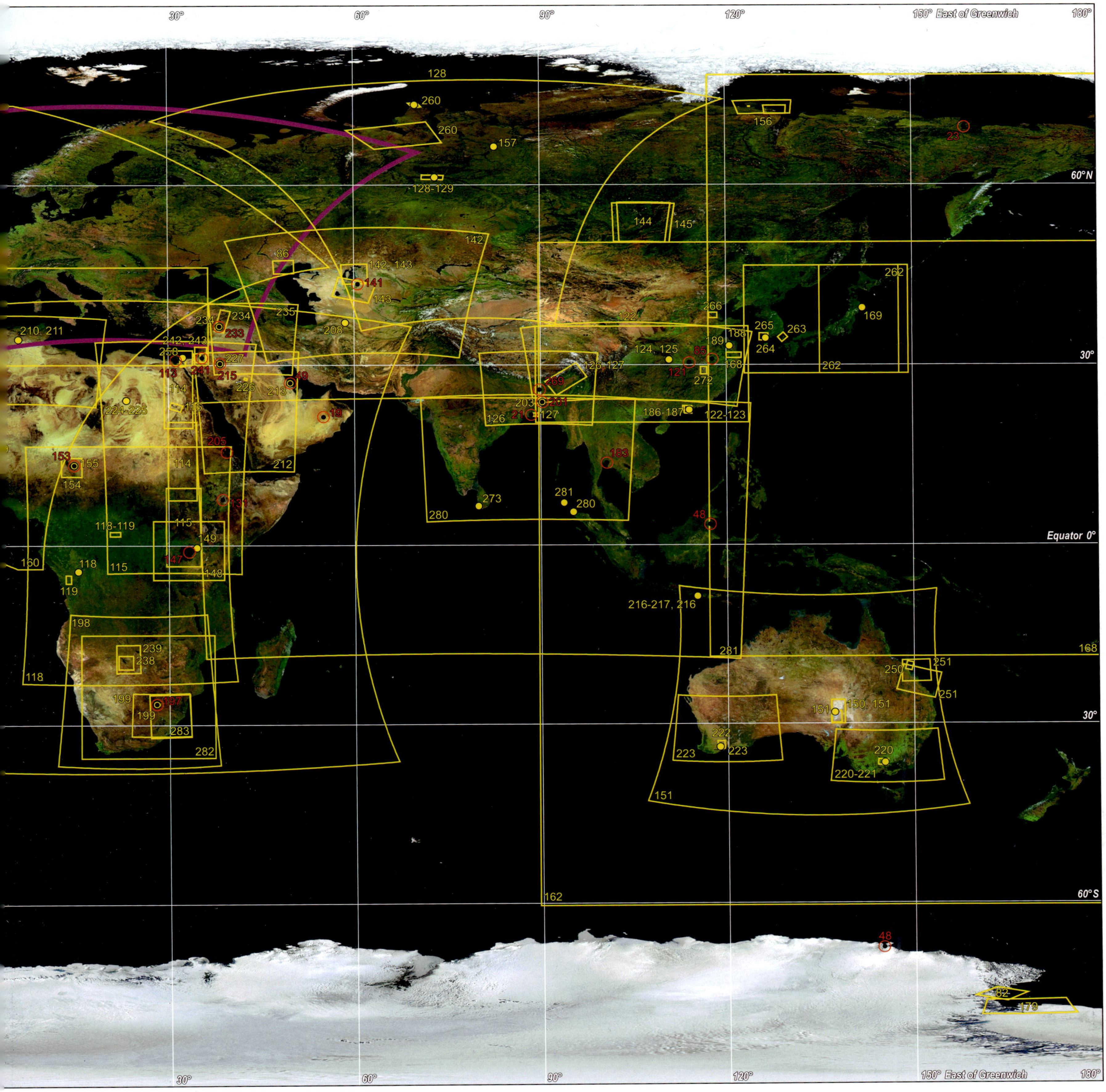

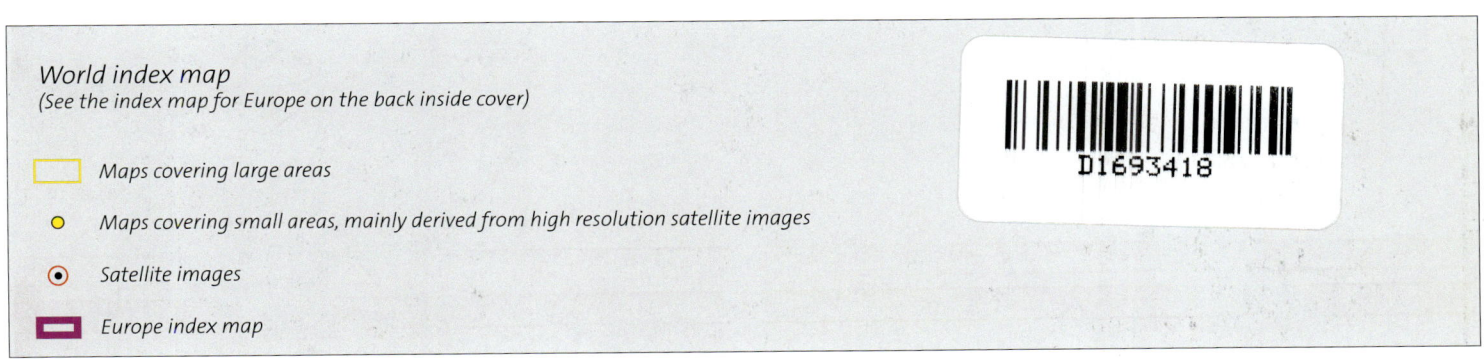

World index map
(See the index map for Europe on the back inside cover)

- ☐ Maps covering large areas
- ● Maps covering small areas, mainly derived from high resolution satellite images
- ⊙ Satellite images
- ▬ Europe index map

D1693418

© **Copyright**
2015 ESA/ESRIN, Frascati, Italy.

All rights reserved. No part of this work may be reproduced in any form (photocopy, microfilm or any other method) without the prior written consent of ESA/ESRIN, Frascati, Italy or processed, reproduced or distributed using any electronic system.

© **Satellite image data**
- BlackBridge AG (formerly RapidEye), Berlin, Germany
- Canadian Space Agency (CSA), Longueuil, Canada, Defence Research and Development Canada (DRDC and MacDonald Dettwiler and Associates Geospatial Services Inc. (MDA GSI), Richmond, Canada
- Centre National d'Études Spatiales (CNES), Distribution Astrium Services/Spot Image, France
- CNES, distributed by VITO, Mol, Belgium
- DigitalGlobe, Longmont, USA
- e-GEOS - TELESPAZIO, Rome, Italy
- Earth Resources Observation and Science (EROS) Center, U.S. Geological Survey, Sioux Falls, USA
- EUMETSAT, Darmstadt, Germany
- European Space Agency ESA-ESTEC, Noordwijk, Netherlands
- European Space Agency ESA-ESRIN, Frascati, Italy
- European Space Agency (ESA, HQ), Paris, France
- EUROPEAN SPACE IMAGING (EUSI), Munich, Germany
- NASA, Goddard Space Flight Center, USA

Notes:
This atlas is not to be used as a reference work for political borders.
Unless specified differently, all maps in this book are oriented north.
Please use the map index in the front and back covers to locate the individual maps.

Contributors in alphabetical order

Originator
ESA/ESRIN

Concept
Lothar Beckel, Markus Eisl, Mario Fest

Project management
Markus Eisl, Mario Fest, Martin Unterdechler

Satellite image processing
Marco Fröhner, Judith Grubinger, Gerald Mansberger, Gerald Ziegler

Cartography
Markus Daichendt, Manfred Egger, Marko Fröhner, Astrid Köpf, Hannes Krause, Daniela Kühnlenz, Helmut Perl, René Pfahlbusch, Andrea Spannring

Layout and typesetting
Mario Fest, Hannes Krause, René Pfahlbusch

Authors (if not stated differently)
Nicolas Ackermann, Markus Daichendt, Markus Eisl, Mario Fest, Hannes Krause, Kerstin Peuker, Michael Rast, Francesco Sarti, William White

Editing
Nicolas Ackermann, Fabiano Costantini, Mathieu Depoorter, Reinhold Drazansky, Markus Eisl, Diego Fernandez, Mario Fest, Mario Hernandez, Benjamin Kötz, Juerg Lichtenegger, Antonios Mouratidis, Michael Rast, Ute Rosner, Roberto Sabia, Francesco Sarti, Peter Brøgger Sørensen, Chris Stewart, William White

Translation
Toptranslation, Germany

Print
Ueberreuter, 2015, Austria

1st English Edition, 2015
ISBN 978-3-903073-00-5, Globe View press, Austria

Web resources:
http://www.world-of-water.org
https://earth.esa.int/web/guest/ESA_World_of_Water

WORLD OF WATER

A contribution of the
European Space Agency
towards a better understanding
of a global challenge

CONTENTS

6	**PREFACE**	**51**	**WATER — THE GLOBAL PERSPECTIVE**	117	A precious resource for many countries
6	Synoptic View from Space			117	Egypt – a gift of the Nile
7	Global Responses to Global Challenges	**53**	**THE BLUE PLANET**	**119**	**Congo**
		54	Water in the geological eras	119	The Congo Basin
9	**WORLD OF WATER**	55	Water – the essence of life	**121**	**Yangtze**
11	The Blue Gold of the 21st century	56	Topography and bathymetry	121	The Yangtze Delta
11	The physical states of water	58	Precipitation distribution	124	The Yangtze Dams
12	The hydrosphere	60	Temperature distribution	**127**	**Brahmaputra**
12	The water cycle	61	Evapotranspiration	127	The Ganges Delta
12	The Sun as a driving force	63	Climate zones of the world	**129**	**Ob**
13	Water reservoirs	65	Land cover and land use	129	Industry on the banks of the Ob
13	Freshwater resources	66	Population distribution	**131**	**LAKES OF THE EARTH**
		69	Natural hazards	**133**	**Great Lakes**
		70	Availability and consumption of water	133	Saint Lawrence Seaway – the link to the North Atlantic
25	**PERSPECTIVES FROM SPACE**	**73**	**WATER TREATIES**	135	Niagara Falls – natural wonder and energy source
27	**EUROPE IN SPACE**	74	International water resources	135	Welland Canal
28	The European Space Agency (ESA)	74	Water conflicts and hydro-diplomacy	**137**	**Lake Titicaca**
28	The concept of Geographic Return for Europe	75	"Water for Peace"	137	The floating islands of the Uros people
29	The European Environmental Satellite (Envisat)	75	Development of international water resources norms and institutions	**139**	**Lake Garda**
30	The Copernicus Programme	76	International water agencies	**141**	**The Aral Sea**
30	The Sentinels			142	The slow poisoning of the Aral Sea and its effects
31	The Earth Explorers	**79**	**WATERS OF THE EARTH**	142	Climate change and the shrinking lake
31	GOCE			143	Possible solutions
31	SMOS	**81**	**GLACIERS**	**145**	**Lake Baikal**
31	CryoSat-2	82	Malaspina Glacier	**147**	**Lake Victoria**
32	Swarm	82	David Glacier	148	Population density
32	ADM-Aeolus	83	Aletsch Glacier	148	The invation of water hyacinths
32	EarthCARE	**85**	**RIVERS OF THE EARTH**	148	The Nile perch – a voracious predator
32	Biomass	86	The end of the journey – the river's mouth	148	Water pollution
32	Earth Explorer 8	86	Deltas	149	Falling water levels
33	Navigation and telecommunication satellites	87	Estuaries	**151**	**Lake Eyre**
34	What's the weather like?	**89**	**Colorado**	151	A lake in Australia's outback
37	Water for Africa – the ESA TIGER initiative	90	Agreements for the Colorado River	**153**	**Lake Chad**
37	TIGER projects	90	Large-scale projects on the Colorado	154	Significance of Lake Chad for the local populations
39	**WATER AND SATELLITES**	91	Water management with satellite data	154	Why is Lake Chad shrinking?
40	Milestones in Earth Observation from space	**93**	**Mississippi**	155	Lake Chad Basin Commission
40	Satellite orbits	93	Mississippi River Delta	**157**	**Tundra lakes**
41	Characteristics of satellite data	94	Flooding as a recurring event	157	Is the tundra drying out?
43	Satellite image resolution	**99**	**Amazon**	157	Life on the tundra
43	From the global to the local scale	101	The Amazon Basin	**159**	**OCEANS**
44	What can maps reveal?	101	The mouth of the Amazon	160	Global ocean currents
44	"We own the Night"	102	Impact of population and industry in the Amazon Basin	160	The Gulf Stream and its formation
45	From satellite images to maps	**105**	**Danube**	161	The Gulf Stream and the climate
46	Geographic Information Systems	105	Danube Delta – World Heritage site	161	Currents in the Mediterranean Sea
46	Data and Information	105	The exploitation of the Danube	162	El Niño, La Niña and ENSO
47	Representing our world and predicting its future	107	The Iron Gate 1 hydroelectricity plant	162	Coupling between currents
48	Satellite image applications	107	Gabčíkovo hydroelectric power station	163	Far-reaching consequences
		108	The Danube as a waterway	163	The future of El Niño
		111	**Rhine**	164	Phytoplankton
		111	The Rhine as a waterway	164	Algal bloom
		113	**Nile**	166	Low and high tides
		113	The Nile Delta	167	Global rise in sea levels
		115	The Aswan Dam	167	Effects of sea level rise on coastal regions

167	Coastal protection measures	
168	The rubbish dump of developed and developing countries	
168	Great Pacific Garbage Patch – a new continent?	
169	Treat the cause or the effect?	
169	The Seventh Continent and satellite technology	

171 POLAR REGIONS
171 Floating ice in the oceans and ice on land
171 Differences between the Arctic and Antarctica
172 Satellites and ice monitoring

173 Arctic
173 Living conditions in the Arctic
173 Arctic sea ice extent
174 Arctic sea ice thickness
175 Permafrost
175 Greenland and Petermann Glacier
175 Sea level rise

177 Antarctica
178 The ice sheet of Antarctica
178 Ice thickness in Antarctica
179 Antarctic ice streams
179 Ice sheet movements: the Ross Ice Shelf

181 WATER FOR HUMANITY

183 CITIES
185 Cities built on water
185 Major cities – the proximity to water
186 Land reclamation and prosperity
189 Spatial patterns of rural settlements in the Jiangsu Province
189 The Grand Canal in China

191 Mexico City
191 Water availability
192 Main sources of water for Mexico City
195 Wastewater management

197 Johannesburg
197 Urban development
198 Water supply
198 The Lesotho Highlands Water Project
199 The Vaal Dam
199 Wastewater treatment in Johannesburg

201 Dhaka
201 Monsoon floods
203 Drinking water supply and wastewater disposal

205 WATER ACCESS
206 The fog-harvesting technique
206 Eritrea project: the success of fog-harvesting
207 Fog-harvesting in Morocco – providing water to villages
207 The future of fog-harvesting
208 Transporting water

211 Groundwater in the Sahara
211 AQUIFER project
211 Monitoring of subsidence using radar satellites
213 Water supply in Saudi Arabia – a challenge
213 Seawater desalination plants

215 IRRIGATION
217 Paddy field farming
217 Rice terraces in Bali
217 Rice and methane
218 Inner Niger Delta
218 Agriculture around the Inner Niger Delta
219 "Office du Niger"
219 Desertification in the Sahel
221 Irrigated farming in the southeast of Australia
221 Shepparton Irrigation Region
221 Barossa Valley
223 Dryland salinity in the southwest of Australia
225 The Al Kufra oases
225 The Great Man-Made River project
227 Irrigation in Saudi Arabia
227 Centre-pivot irrigation systems

229 WATER-USE COMPETITION
229 Hypoxia in the Gulf of Mexico
231 The Caribbean – a paradise whose days are numbered

233 UTILISATION CONFLICTS
233 Water usage rights on the Tigris and the Euphrates
237 Bilateral water management between Spain and Portugal
237 The Albufeira Drought Management Agreement
238 The Okavango Delta
239 Biodiversity in the Okavango Delta
239 Utilisation conflicts in the Okavango Delta

241 INDUSTRY AND TRANSPORT
242 Salt from the Dead Sea
243 Characteristics of the Dead Sea
243 The Red Sea-Dead Sea Conduit – "Two Seas Canal"
244 Oil pollution in the seas
245 The sinking of the 'Prestige'
245 Oil slicks: impacts and clearance
245 Tracking oil spills from space
246 Deepwater Horizon – oil spill in the Gulf of Mexico
246 The chronology of the disaster
247 Oil slicks and ocean currents
247 The oil slick below the sea surface
247 Countermeasures and consequences
249 Cyanide and heavy metal mining accident in the Tisza basin
249 Cyanide in gold mining
249 Damage from the cyanide disaster in 2000 at Baia Mare
251 The Great Barrier Reef
251 Coral bleaching – a worldwide threat to reefs
251 Nature and business on the Great Barrier Reef

253 The Kaprun hydroelectric stations
253 The hydroelectric power stations and the Kapruner Ache
254 Lake Powell
254 Itaipu Reservoir
255 Iguaçu/Iguazú Falls
257 Lake Maracaibo
257 Oil underneath Lake Maracaibo
257 Lemna minor
258 Global shipping
258 The Suez Canal
259 The English Channel
259 The Port of Rotterdam
261 Sea ice navigation in the Arctic supported by satellite images
261 The danger of icebergs
263 The fishing industry
263 Fishing techniques
265 Aquaculture
267 Aquaculture – a blessing or a curse?
267 Squid fishing at night
267 Do we have to stop eating fish?

269 NATURAL HAZARDS
270 Causes of floods
270 Storm surges
271 River floods
271 Flash floods
272 Tsunamis
273 Increasing impact of worldwide floods
274 Prevention strategies against floods
275 The potential risks for the future
276 Central European floods in 2002
276 The Elbe floods in Saxony and Czech Republic
276 Flood damage along the Elbe and Danube
277 The Danube floods in Austria
277 Flood mapping using radar
279 Hurricane Katrina
279 Katrina's course
279 Katrina´s damages in New Orleans
281 The Sumatra-Andaman earthquake
281 Propagation speed of the tsunami
281 Mapping tsunami damages using satellite images
281 GITEWS – The German-Indonesian Tsunami Early-Warning System
283 Droughts and soil moisture monitoring
283 The rainy season in southern Africa

284 EXTERNAL AUTHORS

285 INDEX OF GEOGRAPHICAL NAMES

291 SUBJECT INDEX

294 IMAGE CREDITS

296 GLOSSARY

299 REFERENCES

PREFACE

Synoptic View from Space

From space our planet appears as a 'blue marble' – a phrase coined back in 1972 by astronauts on Apollo 17 looking back at their homeland. It's the watery surface that, of course, gives Earth its bluish hue and allows life to exist. Uniquely, water can exist naturally as a gas, liquid and solid within a relatively small range of temperatures and pressures and it is continually being circulated between the oceans, the atmosphere and the land.

This cycling of water leaves just three per cent of the water budget as freshwater – and most of this is inaccessible. The vast majority of freshwater is locked up in the huge ice caps that blanket Antarctica and Greenland and underground. In fact, only about 0.3 per cent of Earth's freshwater is found on the surface in rivers and lakes and wetlands – relatively, a mere trickle.

Moreover, this precious resource is not evenly distributed, with some of us desperate for an adequate supply and others at times coping with inundations. And, as our climate continues to change and a growing global population places more pressure on supplies, it is expected that this disparity is likely to widen.

These pressures edge us ever closer to a global crisis with major implications for agriculture, the economy, the environment, sustainable development and human health. Understanding the complexity of this resource and learning how best to manage it are among the most difficult challenges of the 21st century.

In order to be able to respond with any degree of adequacy, accurate and timely information is imperative. Satellites orbiting Earth have the ability to view our planet with unparalleled spatial and temporal scales, and over inhospitable and inaccessible regions. Organisations such as the European Space Agency (ESA) are entrusted with providing accurate space-based information to serve science and an increasing array of practical applications.

ESA's Earth Explorer satellite series are designed to support such research priorities: they measure the salinity of the oceans, a driver of ocean circulation; they provide input to estimate the thickness of continental ice sheets and sea ice, to improve our understanding of the impacts of global warming; and they deliver regular global maps of moisture in continental soils, also vital component of the water cycle.

The series of Sentinel satellites from the European Commission's Earth Observation Programme Copernicus are designed to supply a myriad of measurements for services that are related to caring for the environment and improving everyday lives, as well as for responding to disasters such as floods and drought.

Observations and measurements provide input to improved models and forecasts resulting in better information. Enhanced information, in turn, leads to more informed decisions by leaders and policymakers responsible for proposing solutions that best benefit humankind. The continuation and improvement of the quality of observations is therefore an essential foundation upon which to construct a sustainable and secure future.

Maurice Borgeaud
Head of EO Science, Applications & Future Technologies Department
Directorate of Earth Observation Programmes, ESA

Michael Rast
Head of Science Strategy, Coordination & Planning Office
Directorate of Earth Observation Programmes, ESA

PREFACE

Global Responses to
Global Challenges

The beginning of the 21st Century confronted humanity with challenges that were previously unknown to us on this global scale. Inevitably, we have become aware of the importance of retaining Earth's fragile ecosystems, of reducing our negative impacts on the environment, and also of handling our finite natural resources with care.

Space technology can assist us in two ways. On the one hand, satellites are tools that deliver global remote sensing data irrespective of political boundaries; they enable unimpeded communication with even the remotest corners of our planet and they give us reliable coordinates for navigation whenever we need them. On the other hand, technology transfer has led to space technology being applied in other economic areas in order to improve products and their production processes, simultaneously decreasing the environmental footprint.

Therefore, the use of space technology for resolving global issues, particularly those conveyed by the United Nations, presents an alliance that benefits both sides. To attract the attention of a wide audience, the European Space Agency ESA has supported the production of this book, "World of Water", the second volume of a series of satellite image atlases, like the ESA School Atlas and the ESA Mega-Cities Atlas. It will be a further contribution to the promotion of Earth Observation from Space in schools and for the general public.

The Atlas "World of Water"

Following on from the World Summit on Sustainable Development in Johannesburg in 2002, the "World of Water" atlas aims at raising people's awareness of the importance of water and its management. Using up-to-date satellite data, the atlas highlights a number of the most crucial aspects of the resource, whether exemplifying global dimensions or revealing regional or local effects.

The atlas does not attempt to be a scientific publication but strives to appeal to everyone and deliver background knowledge. It implies that sustainability is better attained by us joining forces with the environment rather than by us fighting against it.

As information technology has become more widely distributed, water issues have also come under closer focus in IT research and development activities. Now, Earth observation through satellites can be considered an indispensable tool to capture and visualise water issues on a larger scale. In doing so, space technology has revealed a lack of institutional structures in the water industry. These are more vital than ever today, as water management ought to pursue an integrated approach forming the basis of multiple benefits and sustainability. If water resources were conceived as one big system together with Earth's other reserves, they could be used far more economically. Satellite data provide a practical gateway for this approach.

The production of a complex book like 'World of Water' requires contributions from many sides. We would like to thank our partners from ESA for their commitment to this project and for providing support whenever requested. In particular we would like to thank Michael Rast and Francesco Sarti and their team at ESRIN for backing our project, but also Juerg Lichtenegger and Peter Brøgger Sørensen for their valuable efforts in optimising the content of this book. Last but not least, we would like to thank our teams at Globe View and eoVision too for the enjoyable collaboration with us on this project.

Lothar Beckel

Markus Eisl
CEO eoVision GmbH Salzburg

Mario Fest
Head of geoscientific department
CEO GlobeView GmbH

WORLD OF WATER

Ἄριστον μὲν ὕδωρ
"Best is water"
(Pindar, 522–443 BCE)

Over the entire evolution of life, from the beginning of the formation of biomolecules more than three and a half billion years ago all the way up to the current technological era, water has always been the most vital element for survival. Compared with the air or soils, it is distributed highly unevenly both in spatial and in temporal respect — droughts alternate with floods, and well-watered strips of land border parched, arid zones that pose a threat to life itself. No wonder water has, throughout history, often been personified in gods of rivers, seas or other forms that water takes, to dominate myths that tell of ceaseless battles against the elements.

The rise of great civilisations, whether in Mesopotamia, Egypt, China or Central America, was reliant on the ability of man to tailor the water supply to his needs. Building and maintaining extensive irrigation systems, like those of the Euphrates and Tigris, demanded planning and coordination efforts that were adventurous and the first of their kind. These accomplishments coincided with the rise of other cultural abilities, such as writing systems, mathematics and astronomy.

Satellite images show how water naturally leaves traces on the Earth's surface, ranging from the expanses of the oceans and glaciated areas to landforms shaped by water erosion, natural vegetation distribution, and the incredible variations in the cloud forms that carry atmospheric water. The images also concisely portray man's impact on these areas. This is reflected in irrigation systems, reservoirs and shipping canals, and also in indirect changes caused by man's influence on climatic conditions, as shown by the retreat of ice bodies, the rise in sea levels, and the increasing toll taken by natural hazards.

◁
1 – View of Earth from the International Space Station (ISS).

◁
1 – The Italian Alps and adjacent regions taken by Envisat MERIS on 19/02/2003. Both clouds and snow show up in white.

▷
2 a-e – Everywhere in the world, water follows gravity. Here, water is shown as a single drop (2a, reflecting the Großglockner massif), a creek (2b), rivers and waterfalls such as the Yellowstone River in Yellowstone National Park, USA (2c), sediment-laden rivers (2d, coastal plain east of Denpasar, Bali) and open sea such as on the Cabo da Roca at Portugal's Atlantic coast (2e).

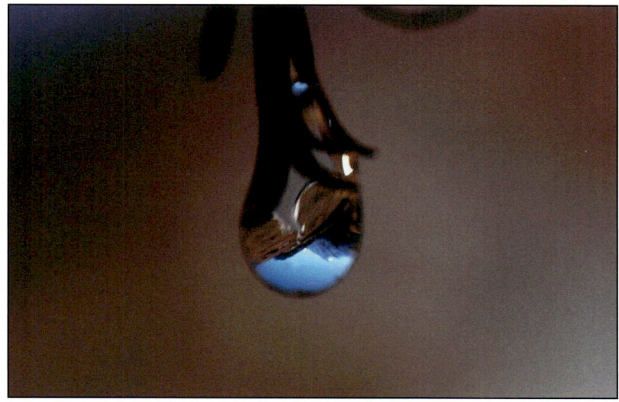

The Blue Gold of the 21st century

The tremendous social and economic relevance of water supply and wastewater management is becoming increasingly evident all over the world. This comprises challenges posed by the infrastructure of growing metropolises, agricultural productivity, and energy supply. Overuse of the resource is the consequence of population growth as well as increasing standards of living. Hence, water can today be perceived as the "Blue Gold" of the 21st century.

It is therefore hardly surprising that water issues have become increasingly significant within scientific and political debates. International conferences provide platforms where, based on consensus, decisions are made locally regarding the requirements and options of companies or towns; but they also deal with issues on an international scale.

In this context, remote sensing has become an indispensable technological tool. It is ideal for both inventories and for carrying out change analyses. Together, both forms of data analysis furnish a detailed picture of developments on a global or local scale, such as when the compliance of international contracts on water-use is being monitored or when water pollution caused by marine oil spills is being controlled.

The physical states of water

Water plays a special role on our planet. The main reason for this is that water has very special physical properties: at standard pressure, the freezing point and the boiling point are at 0 degree Celsius and 100 degrees Celsius, respectively; water has a high surface tension and, due to the anomaly that ice has a lower density than water, ice floats on water.

These properties become important when considering the temperature conditions on Earth. The average surface temperature of 15 degrees Celsius lies between the extremes that can prevail on the surface of Earth due to differences in geography and the seasons and range from almost -90 degrees Celsius to +60 degrees Celsius. As a consequence, water appears in the environment in its solid, liquid and gaseous states, and is therefore either fixed or mobile (Fig. 1, page 12). Hence, large amounts of energy can be absorbed and stored or carried over long distances, where this energy is then released once more. Irradiated solar energy is thus distributed more evenly across the planet, resulting in a more balanced temperature distribution globally.

The conversion of water vapour into a liquid state is known as condensation and occurs permanently in the formation of clouds, fog, and dew. In that change of state, the latent energy contained in the water vapour is released, resulting in a noticeable warming. The opposite process to condensation is the evaporation of water – a process that absorbs energy.

The processes by which water alternates between the solid and liquid states are known as melting and freezing. Among others, these processes are important as they efficiently contribute to erosion, thus shaping the landscapes of Earth. However, it is also possible for water to directly change from the solid state to the gaseous state without passing through the liquid phase. By this process, the water changes from the lowest-energy state – ice – to the highest-energy state – a gas. This transition of ice into water vapour is known as sublimation. The opposite process, known as deposition, is found e.g. in the formation of hoarfrost.

The hydrosphere

Around 71 per cent of the Earth's surface is covered with water and just 29 per cent by the continents. When seen from space, the Earth looks like a big blue ball. This fact came to light for the first time in 1968 during the Apollo 8 mission, when the first colour photo of the entire planet was taken by astronauts from a distance of 30,000 kilometres. This is where the term 'the Blue Planet' comes from. If we look at the Earth from above the Pacific, it becomes obvious that the water of this Ocean covers almost half of the Earth's surface (Fig. 2).

All the liquid water in the global water cycle is called the hydrosphere. The Earth's water resources consist of around 97.4 per cent saltwater, in the oceans and seas, and of only 2.6 per cent fresh water, of which around 99.4 per cent is stored in the ice sheets and glaciers of the cryosphere, mostly in the polar regions (Fig. 3), and deep groundwater layers. These reservoirs, which are difficult for humans to access, represent 2 per cent of the entire water reserves. Less than 0.6 per cent of the world's fresh water is available in the form of soil moisture, rivers and lakes. This water is easily accessible by man and is known as surface water.

Although it only makes up 0.001 per cent of the total volume – or one litre out of a hundred thousand – the water vapour contained in the atmosphere is still of major importance to humans and the biosphere, since all the freshwater reservoirs on the continents are fed by the precipitation that falls from it. This relatively small amount of water plays a hugely significant role in climatic energy transfer on a regional to global level. Moreover, water vapour plays an important role as a greenhouse gas involved in maintaining the energy balance on Earth.

The water cycle

Although at first glance it seems simple, the water cycle is actually a highly complex system in a constant state of flux (Fig. 3). The basic principle of the global water cycle was described in poetry by Johann Wolfgang von Goethe in his poem "Song of the spirits over the waters" from 1779:

It comes from heaven,
It ascends to heaven,
And earthward again it must descend,
Eternally changing.

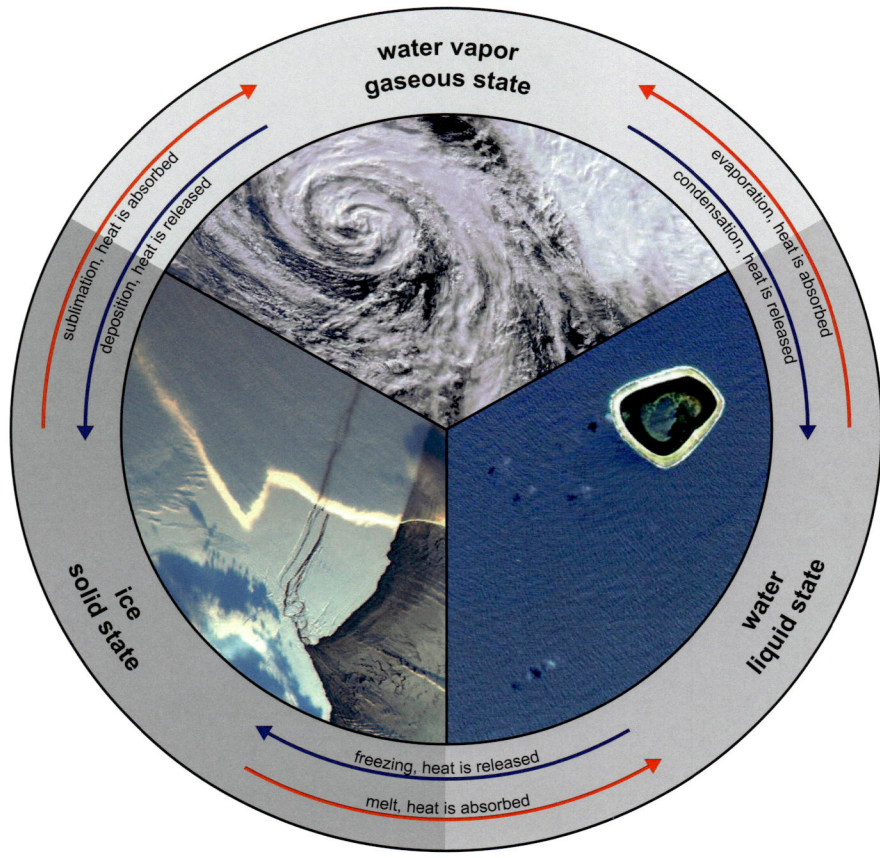

This simplified description of the water cycle may be ideal for the intentions of the poet and philosopher Goethe, but it does blur the intricate detail. To this day, the media and specialist literature still often oversimplify or misrepresent the water cycle.

In reality, the enormous global water cycle consists of several independent sub-cycles which are nonetheless interlinked in manifold ways (Fig. 3) and which differ widely in duration. The largest and, in some respects, simplest of these sub-cycles takes place above the surface of the oceans. Water evaporates from the oceans' surface, rises into the atmosphere, condenses into clouds and falls as rain to the surface of the ocean.

However, there are also several complex ocean/atmosphere/land relationships that cause the water that evaporated from the sea to rise and fall on the continents as rain, which then re-enters the atmosphere via evapotranspiration processes, e.g. at surfaces of plants, and falls back onto the land surface or into the ocean as rain or snow.

A third cycle is the ocean/atmosphere/land/ocean relationship, where the water falling over the land drains through the soil and is carried back by groundwater streams and surface rivers to the oceans, where it can once again evaporate.

The Sun as a driving force

But what keeps this never-ending cycle going? The driving force behind the Earth's water cycle is the Sun, whose heat maintains the endless cycle of melting and evaporating. That heat drives the constant exchange of water between the biosphere, pedosphere, lithosphere and hydrosphere on the one hand and the atmosphere on the other.

Over a given year, a total of 577,000 cubic kilometres of water are transported within the global water cycle. The oceans are by far the most important source of water in the atmosphere. Around 502,800 cubic kilometres of water evaporate from the seas, while only 74,200 cubic kilometres evaporate from the land surface. At the other part of the cycle, 458,000 cubic kilometres of precipitation fall over the seas and 119,000 cubic kilometres over the land.

△
1 – Water occurs on Earth in all three physical states: solid, liquid and gas. When transferring from one state to another, energy is either released or absorbed.

◁
2 – The blue planet: The Pacific ocean covers almost half of the Earth's surface. Derived from data of the Blue Marble: NASA next-generation mosaic.

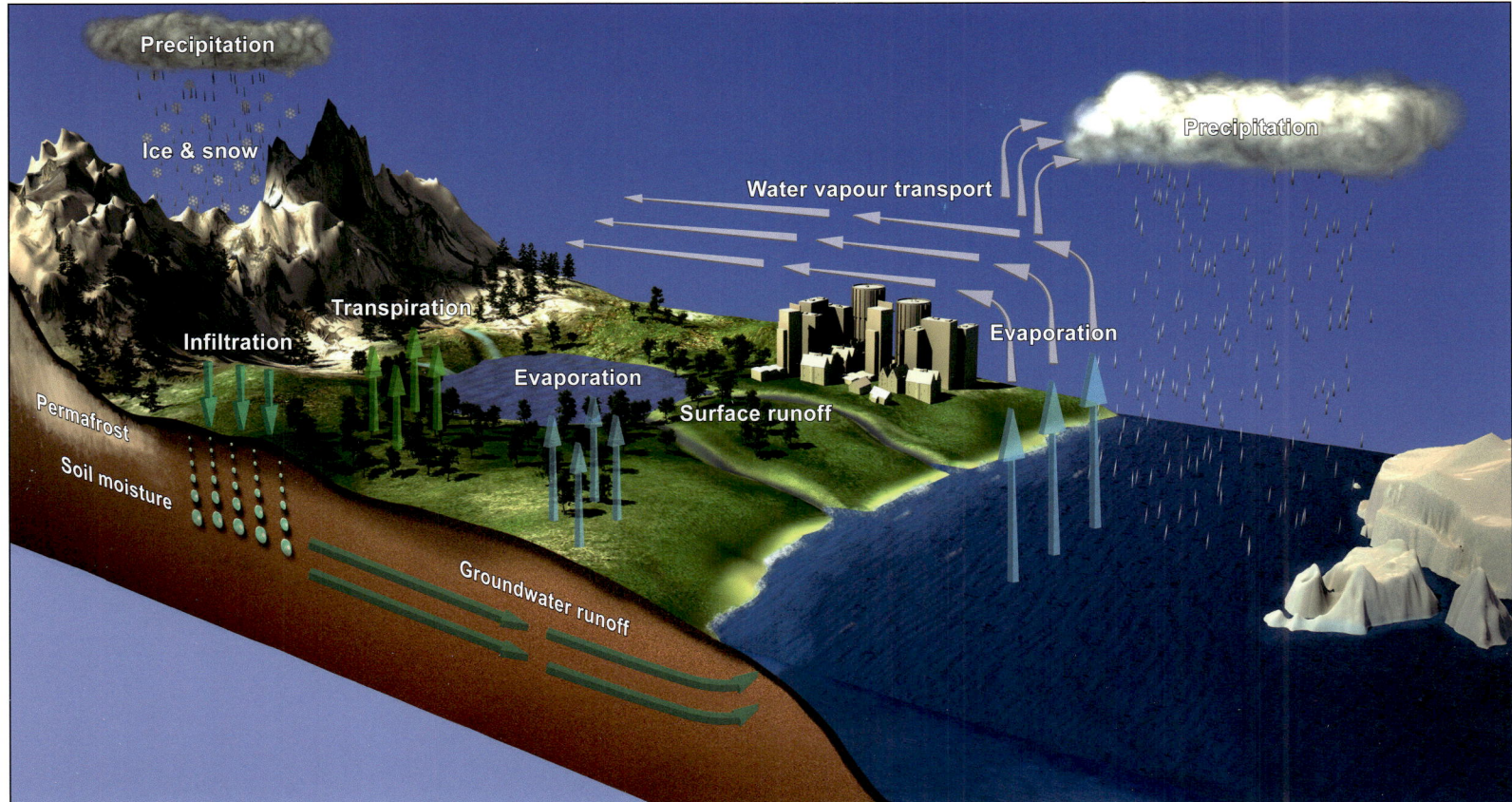

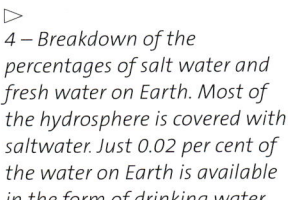

3 – The global water cycle: Driven by the energy from the Sun, it disperses around 577,000 cubic kilometres of water every year.

Almost two-thirds of the precipitation that falls on the land surface returns to the atmosphere via evapotranspiration. The difference between evaporation and precipitation over the land is made up of surface run-off of 42,600 cubic kilometres and groundwater flow of 2,200 cubic kilometres per year. These are the main sources of fresh water human consumption.

Water reservoirs

The global water cycle is a closed circulation system that comprises three main components, namely evaporation, precipitation, and run-off. All three physical states of water play a major role in that cycle. Water moves between the different reservoirs (Fig. 4), which also make up part of the water cycle. By far the largest reservoirs of water are the oceans, with a volume of around 1.3 billion cubic kilometres. The glaciers and polar ice caps contain a total of 24 million cubic kilometres, and the groundwater supply has almost 11 million cubic kilometres.

The most important water reservoirs for humans – standing water (lakes and swamps) of 102,000 cubic kilometres, groundwater of 16,500 cubic kilometres and running water of 2,100 cubic kilometres – add up only to a very small proportion of the total volume. The proportion of water that is contained in the atmosphere in the form of water vapour and water droplets in clouds, in total 12,900 cubic kilometres, is also astonishingly small compared to the total volume of water on Earth.

Freshwater resources

The amount of fresh water available to the worldwide water cycle in a certain place and at a given time, usually one year, is known as 'water resources'. For example, in the Federal Republic of Germany, the potential water resources are around 188 billion cubic metres per year, of which 38.1 billion, or around 20.2 per cent, are used by consumers.

Here, the largest consumers of freshwater are thermal power stations, which use 24.8 billion cubic metres, followed by industry and mining (7.8 billion cubic metres), private households (5.4 billion cubic metres) and agriculture (0.1 billion cubic metres). The data on water resources show that there is a significant surplus of water in Germany. For every citizen, 2,286 cubic metres of freshwater are available per year.

A water shortage is defined as under 1,000 cubic metres of freshwater available per year per person. Extreme water shortages primarily occur in the arid zones of the subtropics.

On a country base, Kuwait experiences the most severe water shortage at only 10 cubic metres of water per person per year, followed by the United Arab Emirates (61 cubic metres) and Libya (107 cubic metres). Here the natural fresh water resources have to be significantly expanded by technical solutions such as desalination plants and the exploitation of deep groundwater layers in order to make these regions habitable.

4 – Breakdown of the percentages of salt water and fresh water on Earth. Most of the hydrosphere is covered with saltwater. Just 0.02 per cent of the water on Earth is available in the form of drinking water.

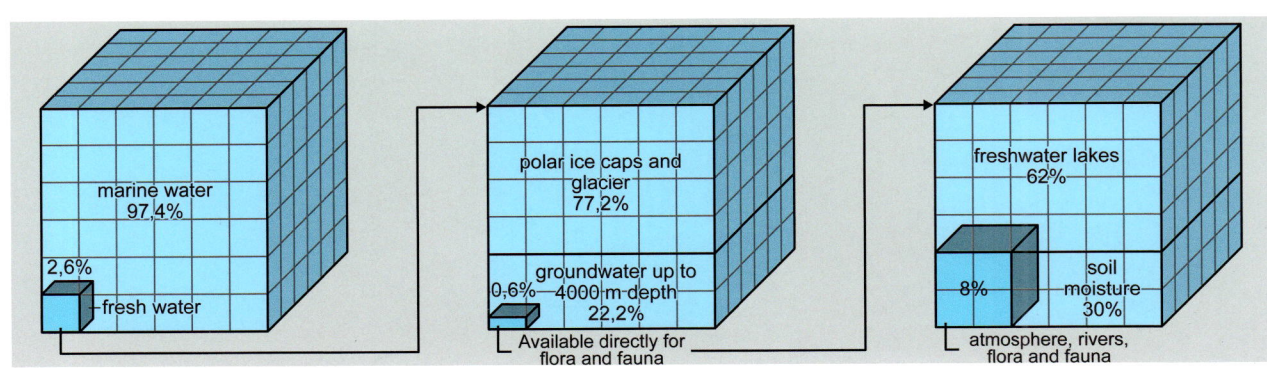

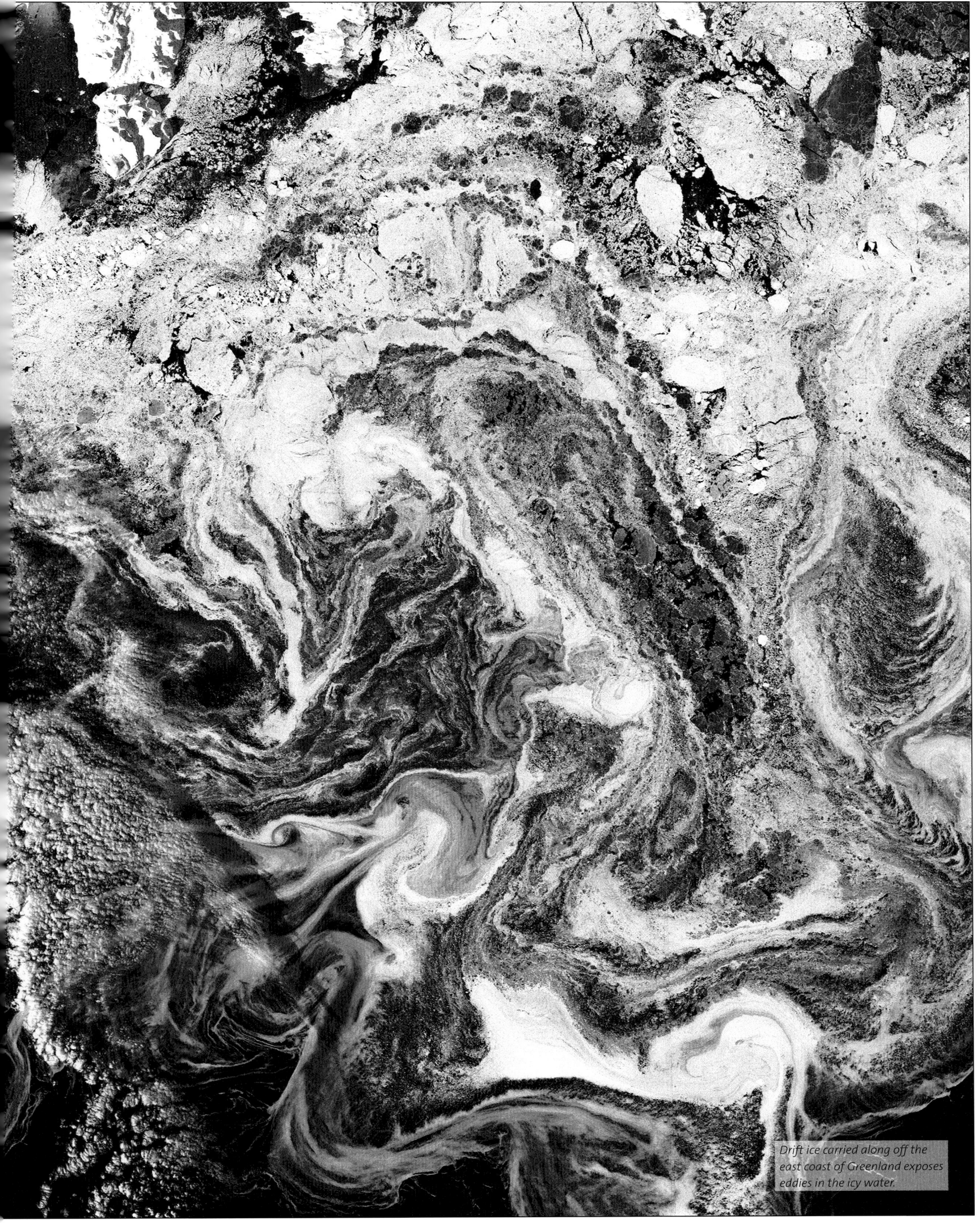

Drift ice carried along off the east coast of Greenland exposes eddies in the icy water.

Near the city of Manaus, the Rio Negro and Rio Solimões, coloured brown due to its sediment load, merge to form the River Amazon.

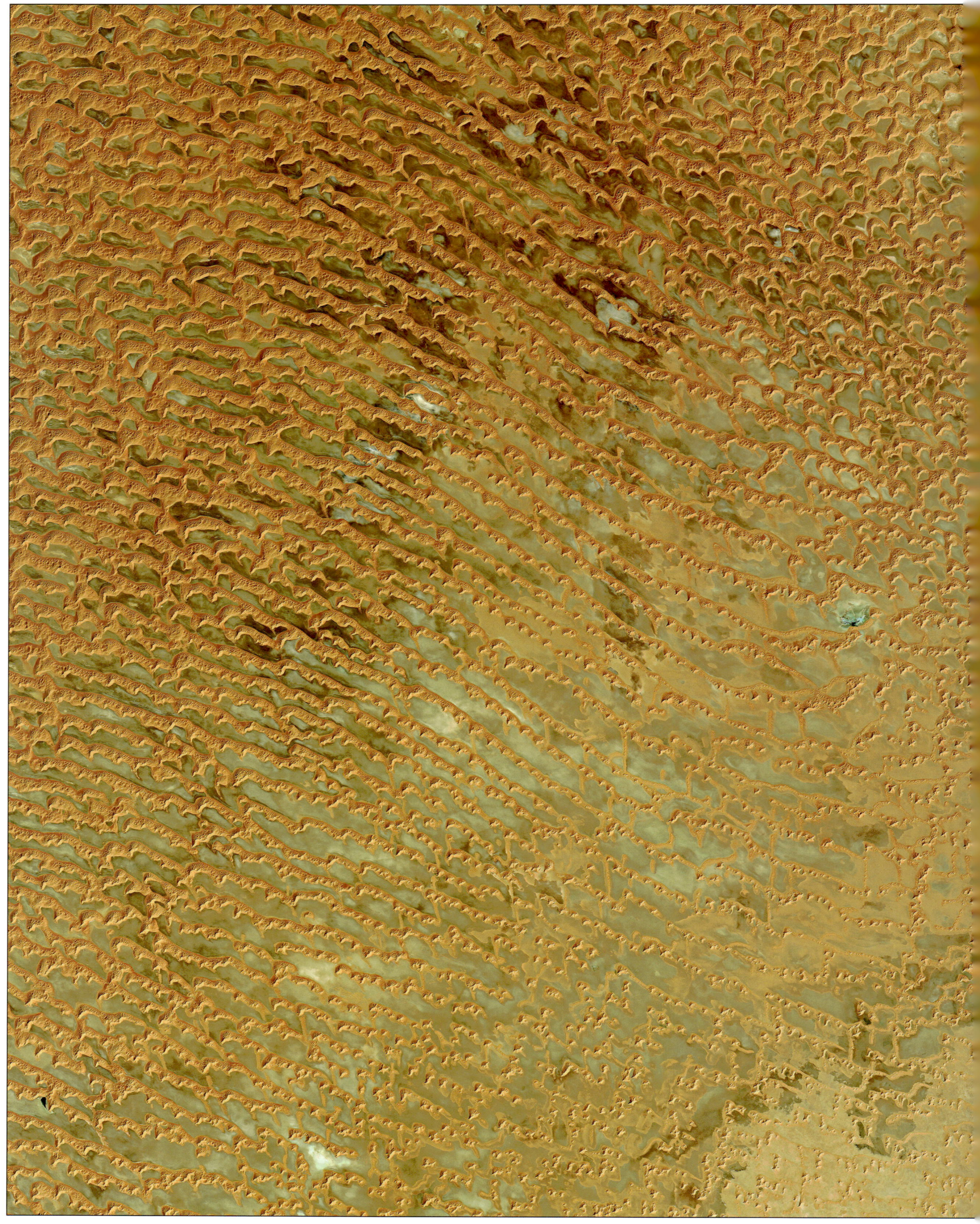

Between the dunes of the Rub' Al Khali, shown here on the border between Oman and Saudi Arabia, sabkhas (salt marshes) sometimes form, drawing moisture year-round from the shallow groundwater table. They also fill up with rainwater, though seldom.

The two great rivers, the Ganges and the Brahmaputra, flow together to form the biggest river delta on Earth.

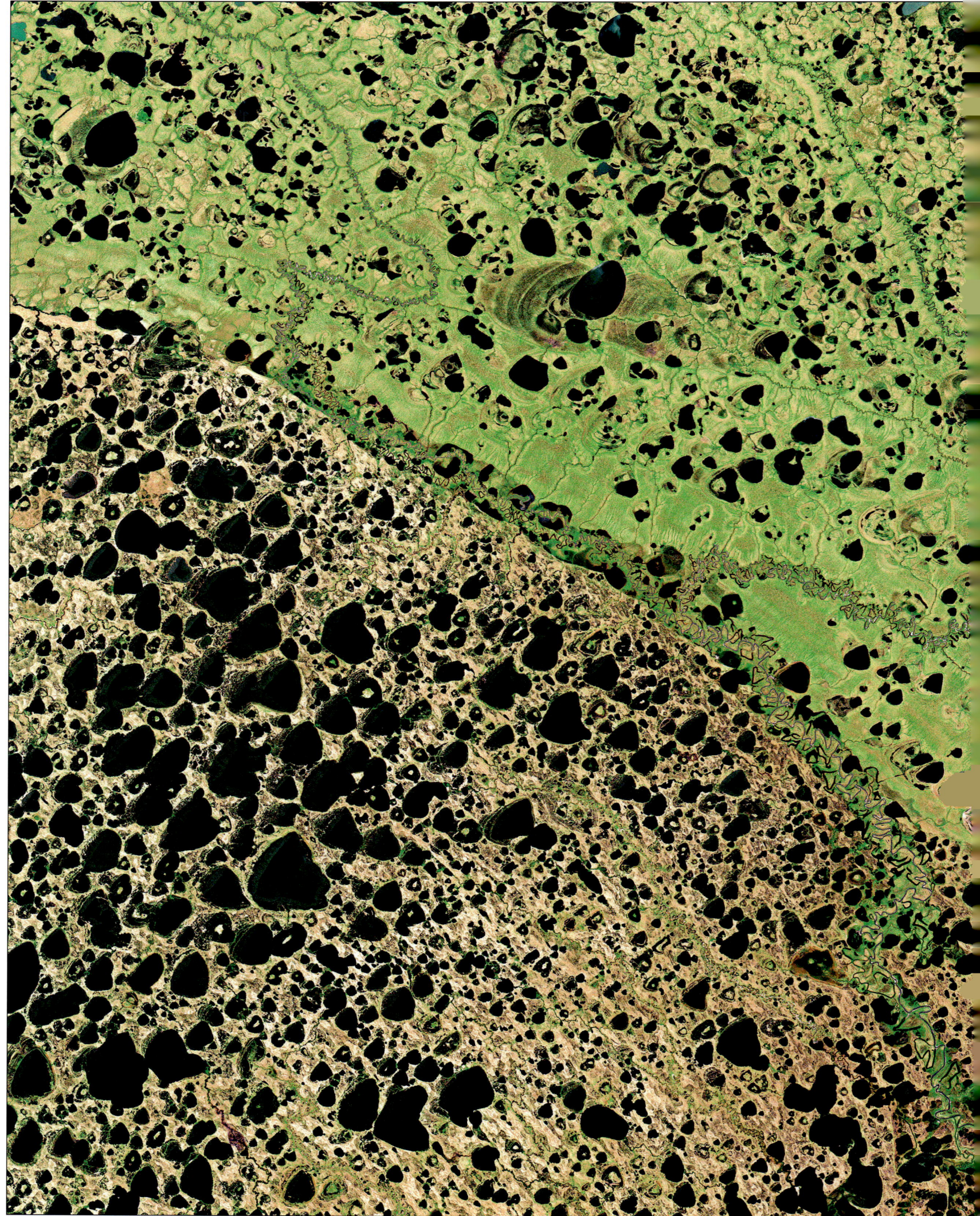

Every year thousands of small lakes in the tundra, such as here in east Siberia, offer a home to many millions of migratory birds.

PERSPECTIVES FROM SPACE

Earth observation satellites and geographic information systems (GIS) deliver high-quality data – a basis for numerous applications supporting efficient water management.

△
1 – Launchers:
Launch of Ariane 5, flight 164, from the European spaceport in French Guiana.

◁
2 – Space exploration:
The Venus Express space probe has been sending information about our neighbouring planet back to ESA since 2006. It primarily aims to explore the thick and cloudy atmosphere of Venus.

EUROPE IN SPACE

The European Space Agency (ESA) – Europe's gateway to space.

◁
3 – Navigation and communication: GSTB-V2/A, the first satellite in the new Galileo navigation system, is already orbiting the Earth.

▷
4 – Earth observation: The ERS-1 and ERS-2 satellites, active between 1991 and 2011, provided weather and daylight independent images, worldwide. Moreover, in all seas their scatterometers allowed wind speeds in strong storms to be measured.

The field of satellite Earth observation involves numerous technological challenges, making the aerospace industry one of the most expensive enterprises. In this context, international collaboration is a fundamental necessity. Established in 1975, the European Space Agency (ESA) supports and promotes cooperation among European states in space research and technology, exclusively for peaceful purposes, with a view to that technology being used for scientific purposes and for operational space application systems. Today, 20 European countries are Member States of ESA.

ESA plays a leading role in all areas of European aerospace. It contributes to this field through exploring spacecraft (Fig. 2), telescopes and manned space missions, through research and Earth observation satellites (Fig. 4), and also through the development of systems in telecommunications and satellite navigation (Fig. 3).

For the 21st century, ESA has set out four main goals. These encompass expanding research findings, improving quality of life on Earth, successful collaboration within Europe and advancing the European industry. Although ESA is an independent organisation, it pursues a common European space strategy with the European Union, leading to the joint development of European space policies. But ESA also works closely with other international space agencies, letting the whole world benefit from its research and inventions. Furthermore, it is vital for the general public to be informed of current developments within the space industry and to understand the role of ESA programmes.

Most importantly though, potential young research and technology recruits need to be inspired by and attracted

1 – ESA headquarters in Paris, France.

2 – ESOC, Darmstadt, Germany.

3 – Launch pad of Ariane 5, Kourou, French Guiana.

4 – Satellite receiving station at ESRIN, Frascati, Italy.

to the space sector. This is supported by activities organised for specific age groups and with the use of captivating resources. A typical example of this effort is the educational website "Eduspace" for Earth observation applications. It includes a wealth of teaching material and exercises, as well as the open-source image processing and Geographical Information Systems (GIS) software LEOWorks, designed specifically for educational purposes. These tools and resources help teachers and students enhance their learning process, while getting involved in space technology and its applications.

The European Space Agency (ESA)

ESA deals with practically all space-related activities, ranging from human spaceflight, space research and Earth observation to navigation and telecommunications. These activities encompass the development and maintenance of launchers and satellite systems, as well as the collection and distribution of retrieved data.

ESA's headquarters are based in Paris (Fig. 1). Due to its extensive and diverse fields of activity, ESA establishments and facilities are spread across Europe and the world.

The European Space Research and Technology Centre (ESTEC) in Nordwijk, the Netherlands, is responsible for preparing and managing space projects, while the European Space Operations Centre (ESOC) in Darmstadt, Germany, ensures the smooth in-flight operation of the spacecraft (Fig. 2).

The coordination of over 20 ground stations and ground segment facilities in Europe and the administration of data are handled at ESA's centre for Earth observation – the European Space Research Institute (ESRIN) in Frascati, Italy (Fig. 4).

ESA astronomy projects are managed by the European Space Astronomy Centre (ESAC) in Villafranca, Spain.

ESA's Redu Centre in Belgium is responsible for controlling and testing a range of satellites as part of ESA's ground station network. It is also home to the Space Weather Data Centre (as part of ESA's Space Situational Awareness Preparatory Programme).

ECSAT, the European Centre for Space Applications and Telecommunications, in Harwell, Oxfordshire, United Kingdom, supports activities related to telecommunications, integrated applications, climate change, technology and science.

The European Astronaut Centre (EAC) in Cologne, Germany, selects astronauts and prepares them for their missions to the International Space Station ISS.

Additionally, ESA operates the Guiana Space Centre (CSG) – Europe's spaceport in Kourou, French Guiana, while maintaining offices in Brussels, Moscow and Washington (Fig. 3).

The concept of Geographic Return for Europe

Direct or indirect, ESA's contribution to the European job market is significant. In 2014 ESA employed 2,200 highly qualified scientists, engineers, IT specialists and administrators from all member states. In total, the number of people directly employed in the space industry is estimated at 40,000. An additional 250,000 jobs are indirectly associated with the business.

ESA's activities can be financially subdivided into mandatory programmes and several optional ones. Mandatory programmes are financed by all participating Member States and incorporate the space research programmes and the general budget. Each country's contribution depends on its gross domestic product. As the name suggests, each individual Member State can decide whether it wishes to participate in the optional programmes and, if so, by how much.

In 2014 ESA had a budget of almost 4.1 billion euros. The budget is distributed according to a so-called "geographic return". This means that ESA invests in each member state by means of industrial contracts for space programmes, with the sums roughly corresponding to each country's contribution. The European investments per capita in aerospace are comparatively low. Each citizen of an ESA member state pays about ten euros in tax for aerospace every year. Investments in the USA for civil aerospace are nearly four times as high.

5 – With its wide variety of sensors on board, Envisat was one of ESA's most important satellites. Launched in 2002, the satellite was retired on 8 April 2012 after having more than doubled its scheduled life-time of five years. A new generation of Earth observation satellites, the Sentinels, are replacing Envisat as part of the EU's Copernicus Programme from 2014 onwards.

6 – The Envisat MERIS sensor, with a resolution of 300 metres, captures forest fires in Greece. Taken on 20 August 2004.

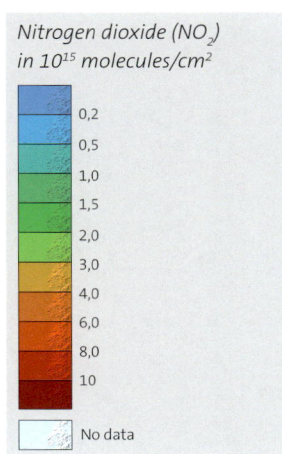

7 – Image from the SCIAMACHY Envisat sensor: nitrogen distribution across Europe, annual average 2003.

Nitrogen dioxide (NO_2) in 10^{15} molecules/cm^2

0,2
0,5
1,0
1,5
2,0
3,0
4,0
6,0
8,0
10
No data

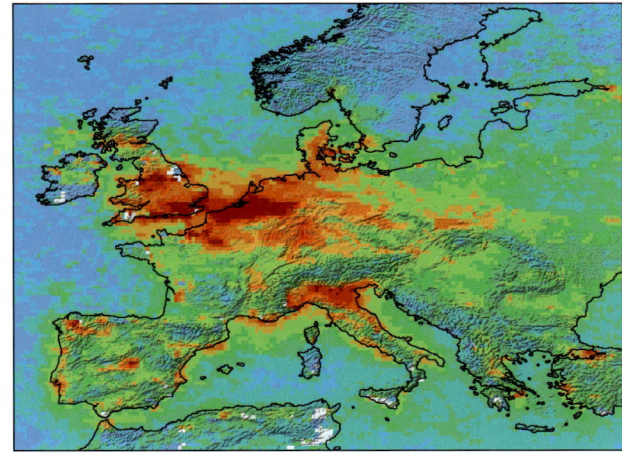

The European Environmental Satellite (Envisat)

Water resource issues and their potential impact on humans are fundamental to ESA. To support decision-makers and improve the quality of life on Earth, ESA has established several Earth observation missions. Within the Living Planet programme, the long sequence of ESA Earth observation satellites reached its climax with Envisat (Environmental Satellite), which was launched in March 2002 (Fig. 5).

Envisat is an extremely powerful tool for ESA, serving a broad spectrum of scientists. The instruments of the satellite are used for a large number of highly diverse Earth observation tasks. These comprise measurements of the composition of the atmosphere, ocean colour and surface temperature, the mapping and monitoring of Earth's vegetation, and the determination of sea ice cover. Areas affected by floods or forest fires can also be quickly identified. Weather and sunlight-independent radar systems monitor the sea in particular with respect to the detection of ships and oil spills. Additionally, cultivated areas and forests in cloud-covered regions, as well as ocean winds and wave heights, are measured operationally and worldwide. Apart from scientific research, Envisat data are also used for a range of commercial services.

Envisat covers this broad spectrum of applications, thanks to its ten different instruments. The best-known sensors are MERIS (an optical and infrared sensor for regional to global studies, with a ground resolution of 300 meters per pixel, Fig. 6), AATSR (a thermal infrared sensor) and ASAR (a C-band synthetic aperture radar). Other important sensors are GOMOS, MIPAS and SCIAMACHY (Fig. 7), which focus on atmospheric measurements, e.g. the concentration of trace gases such as ozone, nitrogen oxides and methane.

After 10 years of successful operations, the Envisat mission ended on 8 April 2012 following the unexpected loss of contact with the satellite, which had already by far exceeded its expected lifetime. The catalogue of all Envisat data is available on-line and the data can be downloaded free of charge.

The Copernicus Programme

The European Union's response to environmental monitoring is the European Earth Observation Programme Copernicus, previously known as Global Monitoring for Environment and Security (GMES). Within Copernicus, ESA is responsible for the space component and coordinates data delivery from upwards of 30 satellites (including the Sentinels), while the European Environment Agency (EEA) is responsible for developing the in-situ component and coordinates the gathering of data coming from both European and non-European organisations.

Copernicus contributes to the Global Earth Observation System of Systems (GEOSS), intended to advance a sustainable development of environmental and security policy. Among the number of services that are prepared within Copernicus, some are related to water. They deal with diverse problems, including irrigation and water consumption, water supply for refugees, and flood as well as sea ice mapping.

The Sentinels

Starting from 2014, the series of Sentinel satellite missions are continuing the legacy of Envisat as well as SPOT and Landsat. These missions carry a range of technologies, such as radar and multispectral imaging instruments for land, ocean and atmospheric monitoring:

Sentinel-1 (Figs. 1 and 2) is a polar-orbiting, all-weather, day-and-night radar imaging mission for land and ocean services. The first Sentinel-1 satellite was launched on 3 April 2014 on a Soyuz rocket from Europe's spaceport in French Guiana.

Sentinel-2 is a polar-orbiting, multispectral high-resolution imaging mission for land monitoring, collecting images, for example, of vegetation, soil and water cover, inland waterways and coastal areas. Sentinel-2 also delivers information for emergency services.

Sentinel-3 is a multi-instrument mission to measure sea surface topography, sea and land surface temperature, ocean colour and land colour with high-end accuracy and reliability. It supports ocean forecasting systems, as well as environmental and climate monitoring.

Sentinel-4 is a payload devoted to atmospheric monitoring that is mounted on a Meteosat Third Generation-Sounder (MTG-S) satellite in geostationary orbit.

Sentinel-5 is a payload that monitors the atmosphere from a polar orbit aboard a MetOp Second Generation satellite. A Sentinel-5 Precursor satellite mission is developed to reduce data gaps between Envisat, in particular the SCIAMACHY instrument, and the launch of Sentinel-5. This mission is dedicated to atmospheric monitoring.

1 – Launched on 3 April 2014, the radar satellite Sentinel-1 is the first satellite in the Sentinel family, which will take over the operational observation of the Earth as part of the European Copernicus Programme.

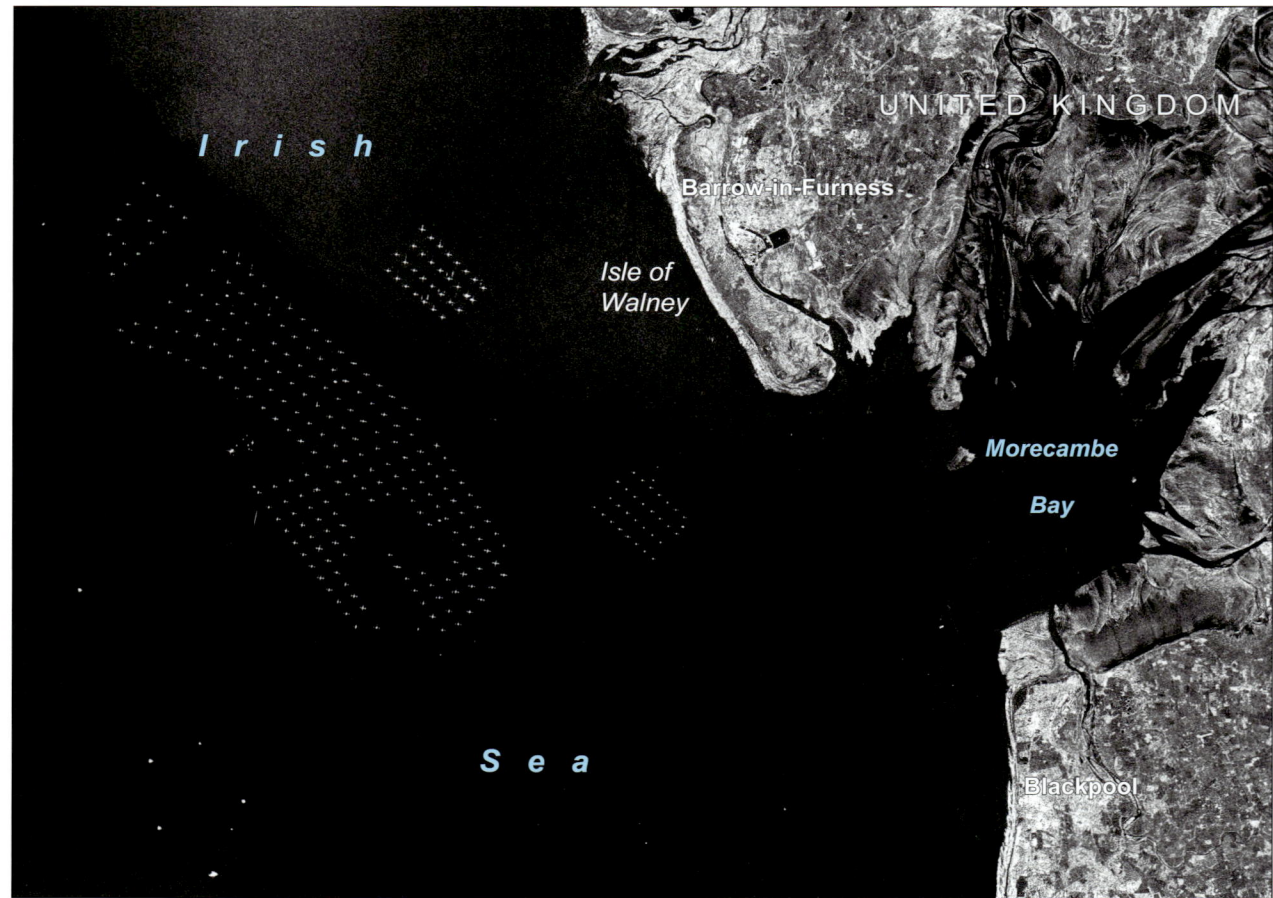

2 – The Barrow offshore wind farms (UK) and effect of wind on sea surface shown on a Sentinel-1 image acquired on 12 July 2014. Imaging radar instruments are sensitive to water surface roughness such as waves produced by wind on open oceans or lakes. This information is used to retrieve wind estimates which are essential to the management of wind farms and to weather forecasting.

▷ 3 – Launched in 2009, GOCE provided highly precise data of the gravity field and models of the geoid, before burning up in the atmosphere on 11 November 2013 after having consumed all the fuel on board.

▷ 4 – SMOS measures the soil humidity and the salinity of the oceans. These data allow the global water cycle to be examined in detail, leading to improvements in climate predictions and weather forecasts.

The Earth Explorers

Earth Explorer missions form the science and research element of ESA's Living Planet Programme. They are divided into two categories: 'core' and 'opportunity'. Core missions respond directly to specific areas of public concern. Opportunity missions are smaller, low-cost satellites that are relatively quick to implement to address areas of immediate environmental concern. To date, four core missions and three opportunity missions have been selected for implementation.

GOCE

The Gravity Field and Steady-State Ocean Explorer (GOCE, Fig. 3) is a core mission launched on 17 March 2009 and ended on 21 October 2013. This satellite is dedicated to measuring the Earth's gravitational field (Fig. 5) and to modelling the geoid with unprecedented accuracy and spatial resolution to improve scientific knowledge of ocean circulation, which plays a crucial role in energy exchanges around the globe, sea level change and Earth's internal processes. GOCE leads to significant advances in the field of geodesy and surveying.

SMOS

The opportunity mission Soil Moisture and Ocean Salinity (SMOS, Fig. 4) was launched on 2 November 2009. SMOS is observing soil moisture over the Earth's land masses and salinity across the oceans using a passive microwave radiometer in the L-band (1.4 GHz). Soil moisture data are highly necessary for hydrological studies and ocean salinity data are vital for improving our understanding of ocean circulation patterns.

CryoSat-2

Launched on 8 April 2010, the opportunity mission CryoSat-2 acquires accurate measurements of the thickness of floating sea ice to allow seasonal to inter-annual variations to be detected. CryoSat-2 also surveys the surface of continental ice sheets to detect small elevation changes. Data from CryoSat-2 will help to find regional trends in Arctic perennial sea ice thickness and mass and determine the contribution that the Antarctic and Greenland ice sheets are making to mean global rise in sea level. This satellite replaces the original CryoSat, which was lost in a launch failure in 2005.

▽ ▷ 5 a/b – Map and geoid model (EIGEN 6C2) of the global gravity field as measured by GOCE.

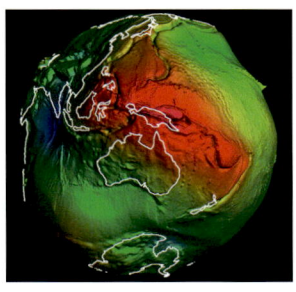

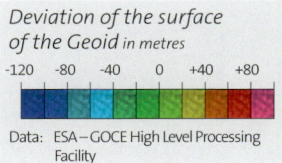

Deviation of the surface of the Geoid in metres
-120 -80 -40 0 +40 +80

Data: ESA – GOCE High Level Processing Facility

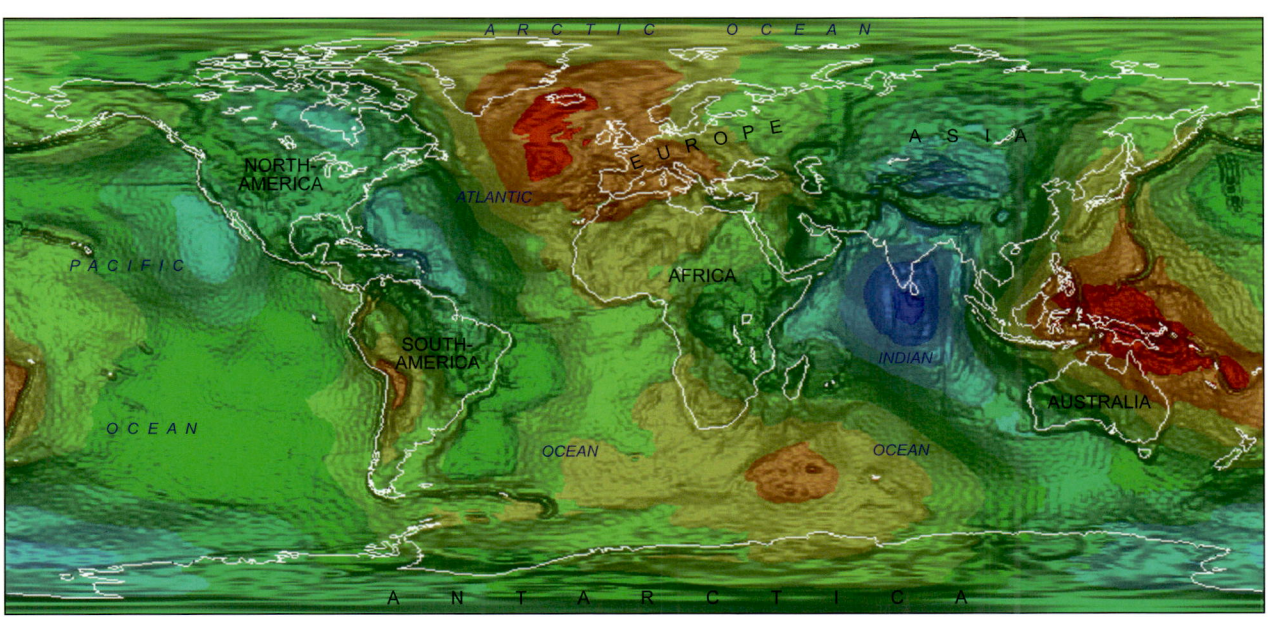

1 – The satellites of the Swarm constellation. Combining the data from the three satellites allows to measure the magnetic field of Earth with unprecedented accuracy.

Swarm

The opportunity mission Swarm was launched on 22 November 2013. Swarm is a constellation of three satellites (Fig. 1) that provides high-precision and high-resolution measurements of the strength and direction of the Earth's magnetic field as well as its development over time (Fig. 2). The resulting geomagnetic field models provide new insights into the structure and the dynamics of Earth's interior, extend our understanding of atmospheric processes related to climate and weather, and will have numerous practical applications in areas such as space weather and radiation hazards.

ADM-Aeolus

The core mission Atmospheric Dynamics Mission Aeolus (ADM-Aeolus) is scheduled for launch in 2015. ADM-Aeolus is the first space mission to measure wind profiles on a global scale. It improves the accuracy of numerical weather forecasting and advances our understanding of atmospheric dynamics and processes relevant to climate variability and climate modelling. The sensor is based on a lidar, measuring runtimes and frequency shift of short laser pulses reflected by the atmosphere.

EarthCARE

Earth Clouds, Aerosols and Radiation Explorer (EarthCARE) is a core mission scheduled for launch in 2016. EarthCARE is implemented in cooperation with the Japanese Aerospace Exploration Agency (JAXA), and addresses the need for a better understanding of the interactions between cloud, radiative and aerosol processes that play a role in climate regulation.

Biomass

Following ESA's Call for Ideas, the Biomass mission has been selected as ESA's seventh Earth Explorer. Biomass aims to provide, for the first time from space, P-band radar measurements that are required for estimating the amount of biomass and carbon stored in the world's forests with greater accuracy than ever before.

Earth Explorer 8

Two missions are being evaluated as candidates for the Earth Explorer 8 selection: the Fluorescence Explorer (FLEX) and CarbonSat missions. Both FLEX and CarbonSat aim to provide key information on different aspects of the carbon cycle.

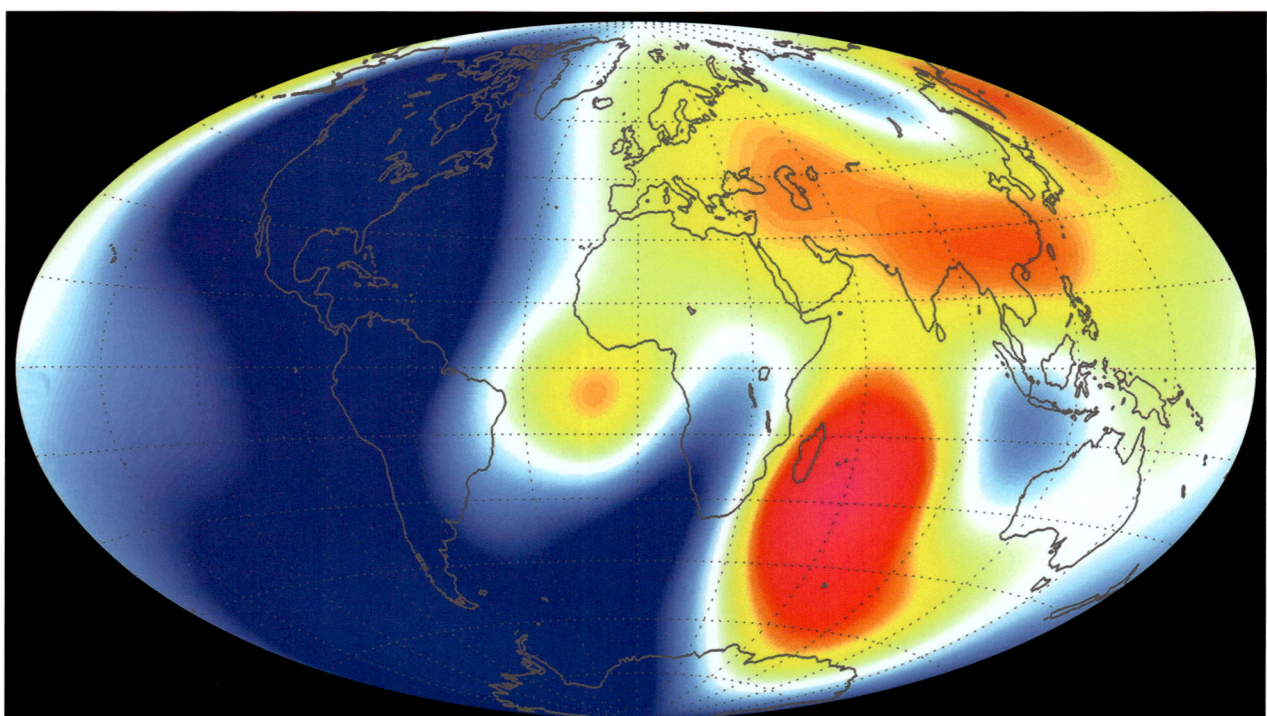

2 – Changes in the strength of the Earth's magnetic field between January and June 2014 as measured by the Swarm constellation.

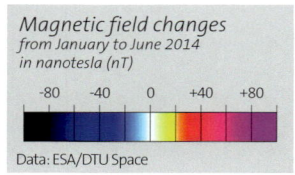

▷
3 - Table of Earth observation satellite missions developed and launched by ESA since 1977 and planned to be launched until 2021.
• blue: Meteorological missions
• yellow: Pre-operational and Technology missions
• red: Earth Explorer missions
• green: Sentinel missions
(The asterisks * denote dates in the future as planned at time of print).

Satellite	Launch date	End date	Mission	Technology status
Meteosat-1	1977	1979	Meteorology	Pre-operational
Meteosat-2	1981	1988	Meteorology	Pre-operational
Meteosat-3	1988	1995	Meteorology	Pre-operational
Meteosat-4	1989	1994	Meteorology	Operational
ERS-1	1991	2000	Earth observation radar	Pre-operational
Meteosat-5	1991	2007	Meteorology	Operational
Meteosat-6	1993	2011	Meteorology	Operational
ERS-2	1995	2011	Earth observation radar	Pre-operational
Meteosat-7	1997	2016*	Meteorology	Operational
Proba-1	2001	2012	Earth observation	Experimental
Envisat	2002	2012	Earth observation	Operational
MSG-1 (Meteosat-8)	2002	2019*	Meteorology	Operational
MSG-2 (Meteosat-9)	2005	2021*	Meteorology	Operational
MetOp-A	2006	2013	Polar meteorology	Operational
GOCE	2009	2013	Gravity field and geoid	Experimental
SMOS	2009	2013	Soil moisture and ocean salinity	Experimental
CryoSat-2	2010	2015*	Ice monitoring	Experimental
MetOp-B	2012	2017*	Polar meteorology	Operational
MSG-3 (Meteosat-10)	2012	2022*	Meteorology	Operational
Proba-V	2013	2016*	Vegetation monitoring	Experimental
Swarm	2013	2016*	Magnetic field	Experimental
Sentinel-1 A-B-C-D	2014	2027*	Earth observation radar	Operational
ADM-Aeolus	2015*	2019*	Atmospheric dynamics	Experimental
MSG-4 (Meteosat-11)	2015*	2025*	Meteorology	Operational
Sentinel-2 A-B-C-D	2015*	2027*	Land monitoring	Operational
Sentinel-3 A-B-C-D	2015*	2027*	Marine monitoring	Operational
Sentinel-5 Precursor	2016*	2020*	Atmosphere monitoring	Operational
EarthCARE	2017*	2020*	Radiation and cloud interaction	Experimental
MetOp-C	2018*	2021*	Polar meteorology	Operational
MTG-I 1-2-3-4	2019*	2039*	Meteorology	Operational
Biomass	2020*	2025*	Forest biomass mapping	Experimental
Sentinel-6 A-B	2020*	2030*	Marine monitoring	Operational
MetOp-SG A-B	2021*	2030*	Polar meteorology	Operational
MTG-S 1-2	2021*	2037*	Meteorology	Operational
Sentinel-4 A-B	2021*	2037*	Atmosphere monitoring	Operational
Sentinel-5 A-B	2021*	2028*	Atmosphere and marine monitoring	Operational

▷
4 – The Advanced Relay and TEchnology MISsion (Artemis) satellite was used to demonstrate a wealth of telecommunication technologies, including laser data transmission between satellites and data links between satellites and aircraft.

Navigation and telecommunication satellites

Directly related to Earth observation is the existence of a reliable Data Relay Satellite system, precise satellite orbital control and precise positioning on the ground. Data relay satellites are placed in geostationary orbit to relay information to and from non-geostationary satellites, spacecraft, other vehicles and fixed Earth stations, which otherwise are unable to stay permanently in touch with each other. This has been well demonstrated by ESA's Advanced Relay and Technology Mission (Artemis, Fig. 4), a communication satellite that provided high-quality – and on an operational basis – relay services between Envisat and the ESA/ESRIN satellite communication antennas. The European Data Relay System (EDRS) will be an independent, European satellite system designed to reduce time lags in the transmission of large quantities of data.

EDRS will fulfil the need for a European telecom network that is fast, reliable and seamless, and through this will contribute to Europe's independence. It will make on-demand data available at the right place and at the right time.

Despite present telecommunication capabilities, a number of limitations still delay the delivery of time-critical data to users. With the implementation of the Copernicus programme, it is estimated that the European space telecommunication infrastructure will need to transmit 6 terabytes of data every day from space to ground.

The present telecom infrastructure is challenged to deliver such large data quantities within short periods, and conventional means of communication may not be sufficient to satisfy the quality of service required by users of Earth observation data. In addition, Europe currently relies on non-European ground station antennas being available to receive data from Earth observation satellites. This poses a potential threat to the strategic independence of Europe, since these crucial space assets effectively may not be under European control. EDRS offers a solution to these issues.

With respect to space-borne navigation, Europe will have its own and independent global satellite navigation system in the near future – Galileo. The fully deployed Galileo system will consist of 30 satellites (27 operational + 3 active spares), positioned in three circular Medium Earth Orbit (MEO) planes at 23,222 kilometres altitude above the Earth, and at an inclination of the orbital planes of 56 degrees to the equator. Each orbital plane will be occupied by ten satellites. The satellites will be dispersed evenly around each plane and will take about 14 hours to orbit the Earth. One satellite in each plane will be a spare on stand-by for the case one of the operational satellites in its orbit plane fails.

In December 2013, the four satellites already deployed were successfully tested, while the full system made up of 30 satellites will be ready by 2020.

What's the weather like?

Since the launch of the first Meteosat satellite by ESA in 1977, images of clouds and eddies from weather satellites have become familiar through their everyday use in weather forecasts in television and newspapers. It would be difficult nowadays to imagine any visual forecast without this simple but effective portrayal of weather, which is often combined with animation and meteorological symbols such as high and low pressure systems and weather fronts.

Weather satellites make up a very specific and at the same time an extremely important part of ESA's Earth Observation Programme. They complement the much more detailed images of Earth observation satellites through their more frequently recorded data from the whole planet. This enables them to meticulously follow the temporal development of the weather, giving the basis for weather forecasts.

The reliability of weather forecasts has improved continuously due to the advances in the quality and number of satellite images, as well as the refinement of weather models and related computing systems. This has led to hundreds of millions of euros in savings each year, for example in farming, where crop losses have been prevented thanks to better weather forecasts.

Geostationary weather satellites are placed in orbit directly above the equator, relatively far above the Earth's surface (at about 36,000 kilometres). That means their orbit speed coincides with that of the Earth's rotation, which allows them to 'hover' over a particular area, hence remaining 'attached' to a point in the sky. They are capable of frequently acquiring data for large areas of the Earth, as almost half of the planet's face can be captured in one image and only a few images are needed to cover the entire globe. This is the case with the Meteosat satellites.

Apart from cloud-cover data, the current satellites of the Meteosat series operated by ESA in cooperation with the European Organisation for the Exploitation of Meteorological Satellites (EUMETSAT) deliver data on coastal winds, aerosol concentrations, atmospheric motion, cloud analysis, temperature, radiation, precipitation index, water vapour, trace gases, volcanic ash and much more. A spatial resolution of down to one kilometre is possible.

On the other hand, meteorological satellites in a polar orbit are at a lower altitude – typically 800 kilometres – and can observe Earth in closer detail. Moreover, they are also able to acquire data over the poles, which are not accessible to the geostationary weather satellites. This global observing system delivers meteorological data to the world within two hours and fifteen minutes of the measurements being taken, and in real time to regional users with their own receiving stations.

The Meteorological Operational satellite programme (MetOp) is a European project providing services based on weather data to monitor the climate and improve weather forecasts. The programme was jointly established by ESA and EUMETSAT, forming the space segment of EUMETSAT's Polar System (EPS).

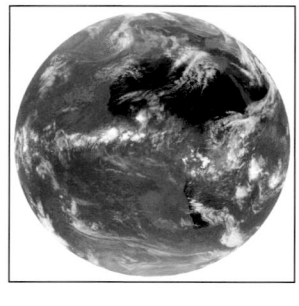 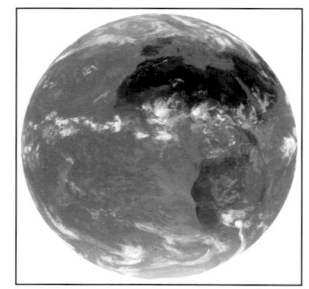  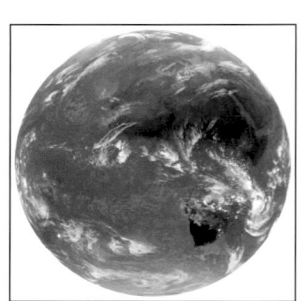

◁
1 a-d – Meteosat-7, infrared, seasonal change.
31/03, 30/06, 30/09 and 31/12/2004, all at 12:00 UTC.

◁
2 a-d – Meteosat-7, visible light – shown in greyscale, diurnal change.
30/06/2004, at 6:00, 12:00, 18:00 and 24:00 UTC.

▷
3 a/b – Meteosat-7, visible light, combined with an infrared channel on 30/06 and 31/12/2004 at 12:00 UTC.

▷
4 a/b – Meteosat-7, water vapour, on 30/06 and 31/12/2004 at 12:00 UTC.

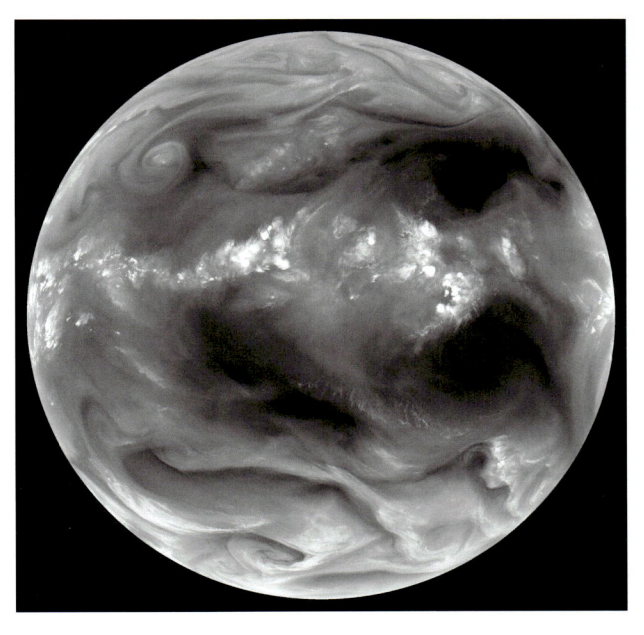

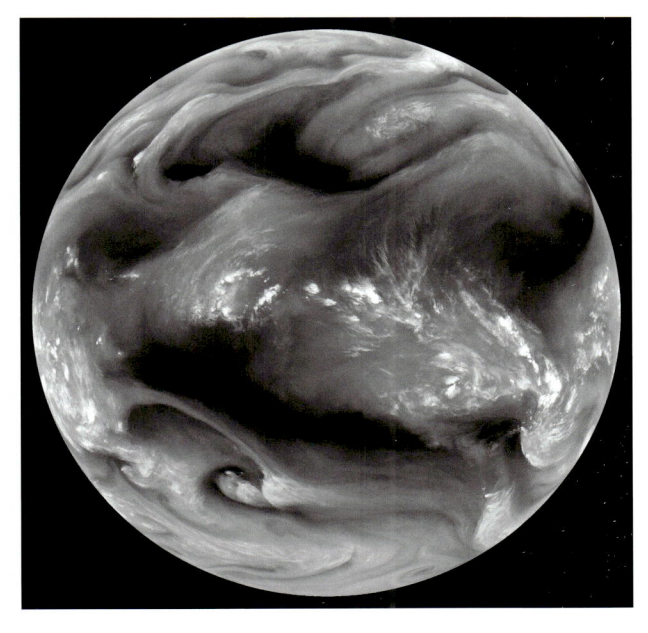

▷
5 – Meteosat-9 is geostationary at 0° longitude and latitude. It plays a major role in weather observation in Europe.

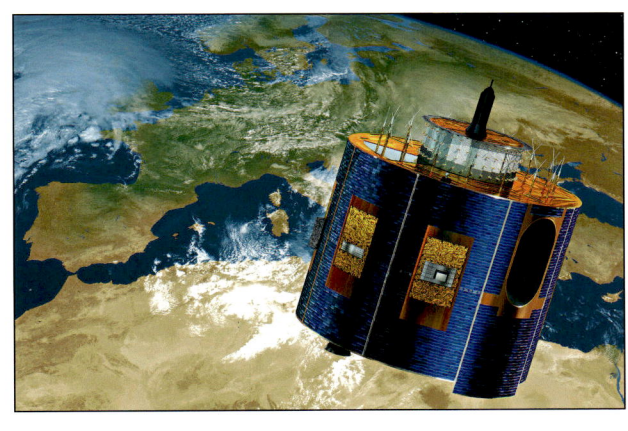

▷
6 – Weather map of Europe on 18/02/2003.

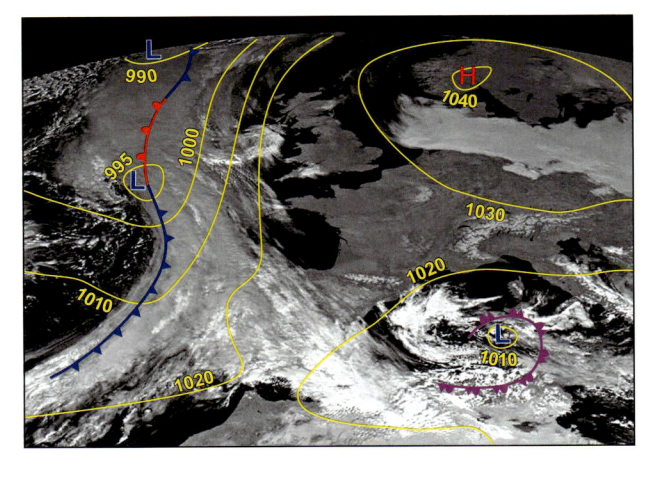

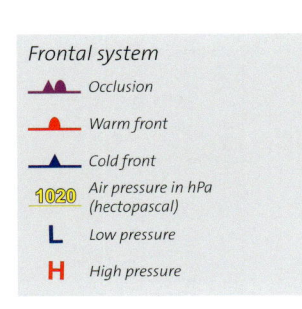

Frontal system
- Occlusion
- Warm front
- Cold front
- 1020 Air pressure in hPa (hectopascal)
- L Low pressure
- H High pressure

The programme also represents the European contribution to a cooperative venture with the United States' National Oceanic and Atmospheric Administration (NOAA), which for the last 40 years has been delivering meteorological data from polar orbit, free of charge, to users worldwide.

Launched in October 2006, MetOp-A, the first satellite in the series of three, replaced one of two satellite services operated by NOAA. MetOp-A is Europe's first polar-orbiting satellite dedicated to operational meteorology. MetOp-B, launched on 17 September 2012, operates in tandem with MetOp-A, increasing the wealth of data even further. The third and final satellite of the series, MetOp-C, will be launched in 2018.

Carrying an array of sophisticated instruments, the MetOp satellites can provide data of unprecedented accuracy and resolution on a wealth of different variables relevant for our weather, such as temperature and humidity, ocean surface wind speed and direction and concentrations of ozone and other trace gases – thus marking a major advance in global weather forecasting and climate monitoring capabilities.

In addition, this new generation of weather satellites provide imagery of land and ocean surfaces and carry instruments that can support search and rescue operations to aid ships and aircraft in distress. A data relay system is also on-board, linking up to buoys and other data collection devices.

35

36

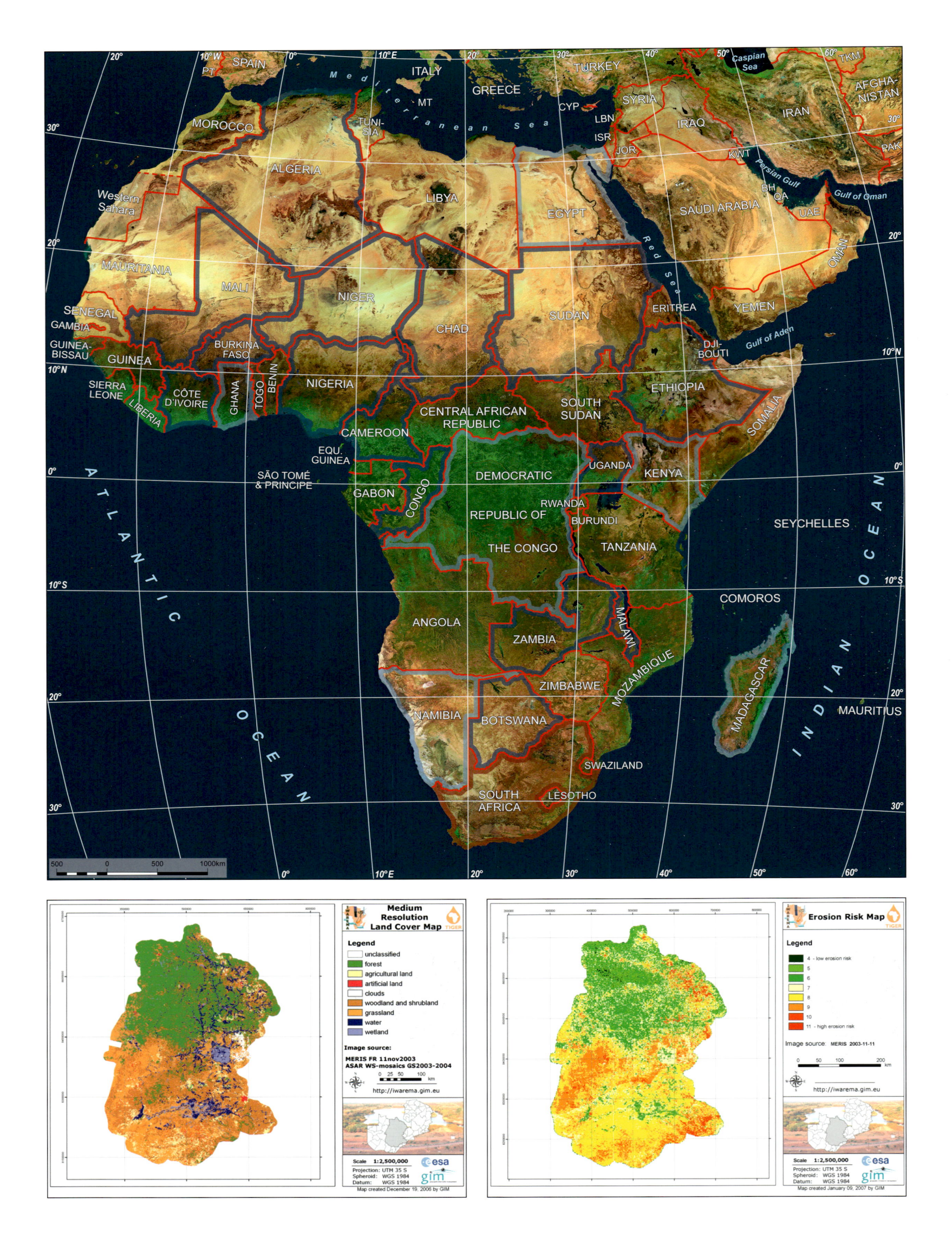

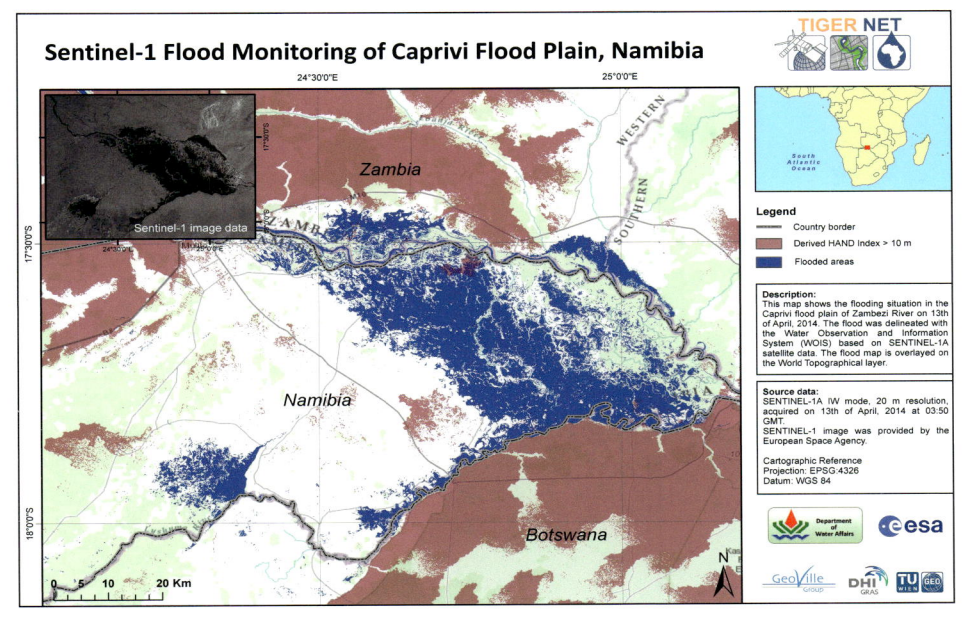

Sentinel-1 Flood Monitoring of Caprivi Flood Plain, Namibia

◁ 1 – Most countries in Africa are home to one or more ESA TIGER project. Used abbreviations for country names are ISO coded, see list in the glossary section.

◁▽ 2a/b – Land use (left) and erosion risk maps (right) based on satellite data were produced for the Kafue Basin as part of the IWAREMA TIGER project.

△ 3 – Data acquired by ESA's Sentinel-1 is used to produce and distribute flood maps within the TIGER programme.

▽ 4 – International workshops in the TIGER programme support knowledge transfer.

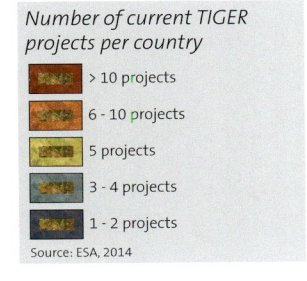

Number of current TIGER projects per country
- \> 10 projects
- 6 - 10 projects
- 5 projects
- 3 - 4 projects
- 1 - 2 projects

Source: ESA, 2014

Water for Africa – the ESA TIGER initiative

Progress in the area of Integrated Water Resource Management (IWRM) is of great importance for sustainable development and for the fight against poverty in Africa as everywhere in the world. One prerequisite is the existence of efficient information systems that can respond to the information needs of participating authorities, organisations and consumers. The development of such complex systems is a challenge even for the more developed countries of Africa and Europe, due to the linked demand for expertise and resources.

The water information systems of most African states are presently in a poor state, meaning that decisions made in politics and water management are based on unreliable information. With this in mind, an innovative approach is needed, so that Africa can participate in a world of rapidly developing Earth observation systems and have access to efficient methods to collect, administrate and distribute water-related information. Without rapidly assisting the African partners with information technology, integrated water management will remain a dream and the water-related Millennium Development Goals (MDGs) will not be met in Africa.

Many examples from other parts of the world have proven the usefulness of satellite data for IWRM. Because of this and as an answer to the urgent need for action in Africa, stressed by the Johannesburg World Summit on Sustainable Development (WSSD) in 2002, the European Space Agency (ESA) launched the TIGER Initiative within the context of the Committee of Earth Observation Satellites (CEOS). The goal of TIGER is to assist African states in handling issues concerning the acquisition, analysis and distribution of water-related geoinformation, using the advantages of Earth observation.

To achieve these ambitious objectives, a long-term strategy is needed. This was broken down into pursuing results in three main categories. First, a contribution should be made towards improved governance and decision making for enhanced IWRM on regional, national and local scales by using space-based technology to overcome the water information gap in African countries.

Another contribution of TIGER is related to the improvement of institutional, personnel and technological capacities. For these purposes, the establishment of a critical number of water authorities, technical centres and universities in Africa is to be supported. These institutions will have the know-how and equipment to derive water-related information from satellite data, share and use this information with relevant regional, national and decision makers for IWRM. Finally, sustainability should remain an objective, by developing a long-term strategy for strengthening and supporting the use of information based on Earth observation data for the IWRM and decision support systems.

The TIGER programme has been established as an international partnership that has been endorsed by the African Ministerial Council on Water (AMCOW), contributes to the strategy (e.g. as part of AfriGEOSS) of the Group on Earth Observation (GEO) and involves the contributions from the space agencies organised under the Committee on Earth Observation Satellites (CEOS). The founding partners consisting of the United Nations Educational, Scientific and Cultural Organisation (UNESCO), the Canadian Space Agency (CSA) and the South African Council for Scientific and Industrial Research (CSIR) have been joined by a growing number of organisations such as UNDP Cap-Net and the World Bank.

TIGER projects

TIGER is split into four action lines. The focus of the first action line is to facilitate access to Earth observation data and derived information to African researchers and water experts. The second area concerns training and capacity building, to ensure on a long-term basis that the critical knowledge of experts from African states is improved, enabling them to extract water-related information from remote sensing data and prepare it for water management. The third area is the creation of efficient networks enhancing information flow and the collaboration between participating individuals and organisations. The fourth and overarching action line of the initiative is the development of geoinformation services based on Earth Observation for IWRM – starting from research projects, and leading towards operational information systems and services.

Recent achievements of the TIGER Initiative are focused to support the satellite-based assessment and monitoring of water resources from watershed to cross-border basin level, delivering information for IWRM through:

1. Developing an open-source Water Observation and Information System (WOIS) for monitoring, cost-effectively assessing and taking stock of water resources;
2. Capacity-building and training of African water authorities and river basin organisations to exploit the observation capacity of current and upcoming generations of satellites, including the ESA Sentinels.

38

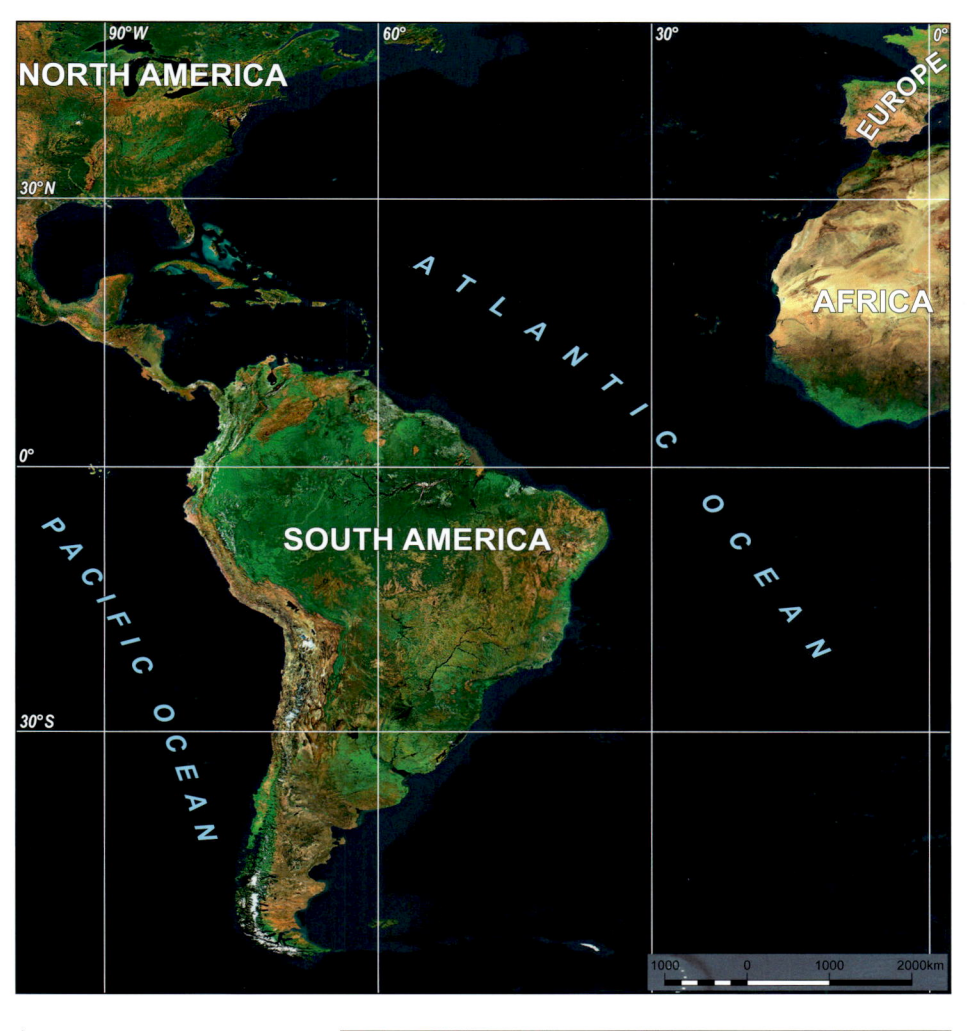

WATER AND SATELLITES

With the help of sophisticated technologies, Earth observation satellites acquire data that is essential for a sustainable use of water resources.

△
2 – Using modern satellite technologies, a complete image of the Earth can be taken from several hundred kilometres up and mapped precisely.

◁
1 – The oldest known map showing the continent of America, was drawn by Turkish geographer Piri Reis in the 16th century. This portolan map on parchment was used to navigate the seas.

▷
3 – Historic nilometer dating back to the golden age of Egyptian civilisation.

▷
4 – Today, the water levels in the Nile are measured by satellites too, such as this one, part of ESA's River and Lake project, which uses data from the ERS and Envisat satellites. The levels upstream of the Aswan Dam show variations of several metres depending on the time of year.

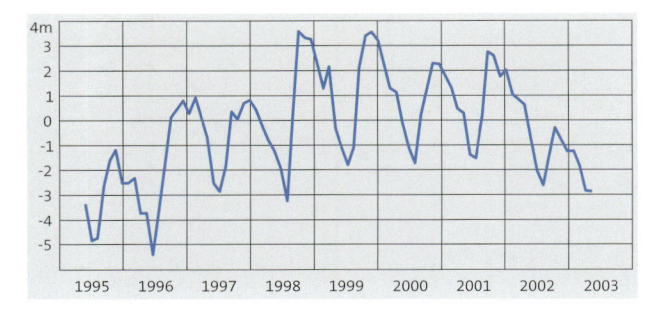

Being knowledgeable about the whereabouts of water and of its changes has always been a requirement in order for man to survive in an often hostile environment. It was natural for the aboriginal population of Australia who lived in remote areas, for instance, to have a mental map of the water sources of their living space. With it they could use concealed water resources. Explorers and navigators needed information on the expanse of the oceans and of the location of coasts, without which they could be doomed. These examples easily explain the significance of cartography. Early maps were schematic illustrations, but with the onset of ocean voyages in the 14th century more detailed sea charts were required for navigation. The mapping of the world was almost completed towards the end of the 19th century. During this process it was necessary to travel to unknown regions, which coincided with the conquest of these areas in the era of the colonial powers. The legendary quest for a sea route to the Far East led to the circumnavigation of South Africa and to the discovery of America. The exploration of Earth's major rivers was also ground-breaking.

The start of civil satellite remote sensing with the launch of Landsat-1 in 1972 marks a milestone for surveying Earth's surface. Irrespective of the observer's location, remote areas can be exactly recorded and mapped. The high acquisition rate of the satellites allows the maps to be kept up to date. Traditional mapping also benefits from space technology due to the exact positioning of the Global Navigation Satellite System (GNSS) such as GPS and Galileo.

39

Milestones in Earth Observation from space

The prelude to our conquest of space came with the launch of Sputnik-1, which was the first satellite to orbit the Earth, in 1957, and sent back information on Earth's upper atmosphere. This event was the start of unmanned space flight, which soon was complemented by the development of technologies for human spaceflight, climaxing with the missions to the moon and the International Space Station ISS; it was also the start of the exploration of our solar system with space probes and of our planet with Earth observation satellites. About 10 years after the launch of military reconnaissance satellites, the era of civil satellite remote sensing began with the first images of Landsat-1 in 1972, giving mankind a truly new perspective on their living environment.

From then onwards, several hundred Earth observation satellites with a wide variety of data acquisition instruments and tasks have been launched into orbit, transmitting ever increasing amounts of data to receiving stations all over the globe. These are then forwarded to institutes and companies to be evaluated and integrated into products to be delivered to their customers. Satellites with imaging sensors play a special role, as their data have the advantage of being graphic. The images can be analysed thematically by an array of methods, and so offer exhaustive information of wide areas of Earth's surface.

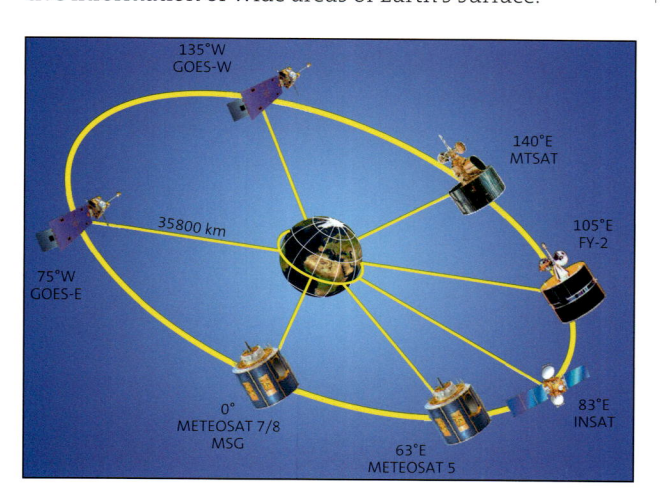

Satellite orbits

Depending on the task at hand, two specific orbits have proven to be suitable for routine tasks in Earth observation – geostationary and Sun-synchronous, polar orbits. Geostationary satellites circle the Earth at a height of about 35,800 kilometres above the equator, where their matching speed of orbit allows them to 'hover' above a specific point on the Earth's surface. In this way, frequent images of the same area can be made. Weather satellites are important examples of geostationary satellites (Fig. 2). Images of the Earth's hemisphere are sent every quarter of an hour to meteorology institutes for weather forecasts. Other examples of satellites in this type of orbit are television and telecommunication satellites that need to stay at a fixed position within the reception area of private satellite dishes at home.

Earth observation satellites with Sun-synchronous, polar orbits have entirely different tasks (Fig. 3). They are built to assess smaller sections of the Earth's surface with a higher degree of detail. They are also designed to be able to take images of all points of the Earth recurring at the same time of day. Only by doing this two images from different years can be directly compared with respect to real changes to Earth's surface such as the state of vegetation, forests or lakes. Otherwise mainly the differences in illumination following the time of the day would be seen.

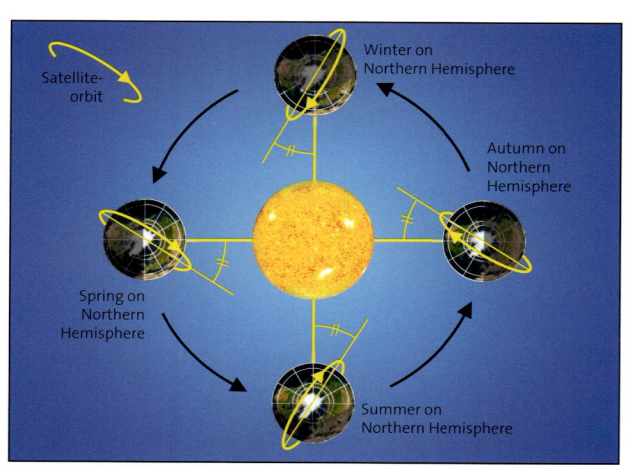

△
1 – Land cover determined by Envisat MERIS over one day. The satellite passed over the same point at 10 a.m. local time every day, recording images of the Earth's surface in continuous strips.

◁
2 – Many weather satellites are placed in a geostationary orbit 35,800 kilometres above the Earth.
This lets them make large-scale observations of the weather and of the Earth with a high repetition rate.

◁
3 – Satellites with a Sun-synchronous polar orbit can take images of Earth's entire surface within a certain time (repeat rate).

4 – Overview of typical spectral reflections of materials, electromagnetic spectrum, transmittance of the atmosphere, and recording channels of various satellites. Reflectance curves of a selection of types of surfaces and their appearance (see below).

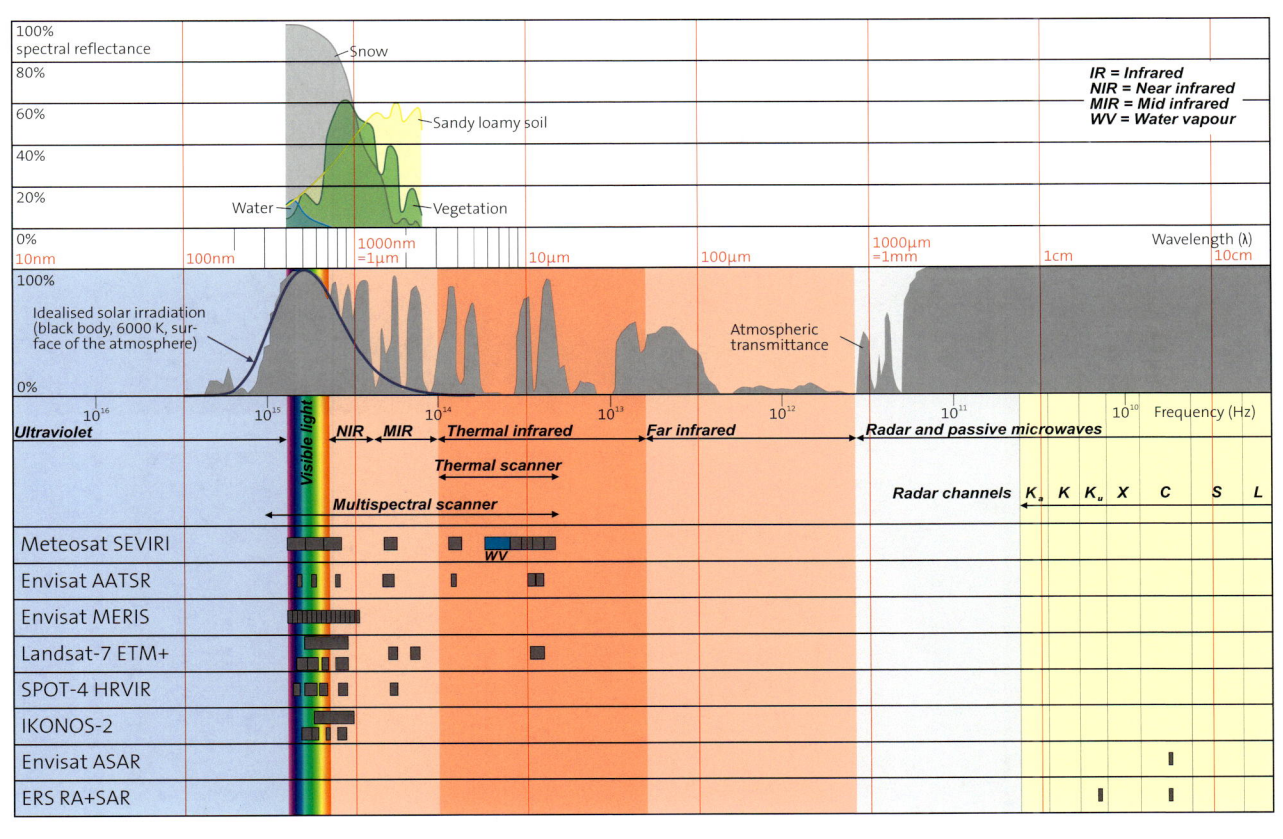

5 - False-colour infrared image acquired by an optical sensor. The intensity of the reddish colours correlates with the intensity of vegetation, which makes it easy to distinguish vegetation classes.

6 a/b/c/d – Near-natural colour images from optical sensors:
a – Snow and ice,
b – Water,
c – Vegetation,
d – Sand and rock.

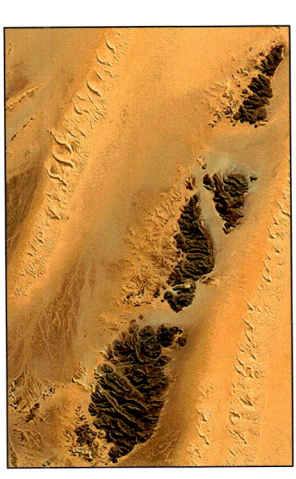

These orbits typically lie between about 450 and 800 kilometres above Earth's surface. A satellite at this altitude takes about one and a half hours to complete an orbit, which means that 15 swaths can be covered every day (Fig. 1).

The swaths have different widths, which depend on the camera system as well as on the altitude of the satellite. The widths of images at higher resolution are typically narrower so that the data size can be restricted, but this means the gap between the swaths is large. The gaps are closed during the following days, and so take longer to close for satellites with higher resolutions. Nevertheless, these satellites are often capable of steering their camera systems, letting them image regions otherwise not captured from that orbit and record data from the same areas more frequently. In this way, also high resolution satellites can achieve revisit times of a few days.

Characteristics of satellite data

Like the human eye, most satellite instruments 'see' the environment in different wavebands of the electromagnetic spectrum (Fig. 4). Unlike many animals that are able to see ultraviolet and infrared, we humans are restricted to the spectral region between blue and red (400 to 700 nanometres). Satellite sensors, though, can cover all wavebands starting from ultraviolet through visible and infrared wavelengths to thermal radiation (approximately 10 micrometres; Fig. 4) and microwaves, which allows determining the nature of the material more accurately. Images acquired in the near-infrared are particularly important for analysing vegetation, as green plants reflect these wavelengths especially well, yielding a strong signal in satellite images. In contrast, water surfaces absorb these wavelengths very well and are represented in infrared images by dark areas.

For effective visualisation of satellite images the collected data acquired at different wavelengths are frequently combined to create colour images – in a way similar to television pictures, which are put together by overlaying individual images of red, green and blue. A specific data combination is chosen depending on which one is most suitable for the task at hand. Data acquired in the visible band can be transformed into near-natural colours (Figs. 6 a-d), providing a realistic view of our planet. On the other hand, the condition of the vegetation cover is often analysed by combining visual and infrared data into false-colour images (Fig. 5). The vegetation in these images then mostly appears in a more or less intense red, which depends on the vitality of the plants. Many band combinations can result in strangely coloured images, but they enhance specific objects of interest to be detected and analysed.

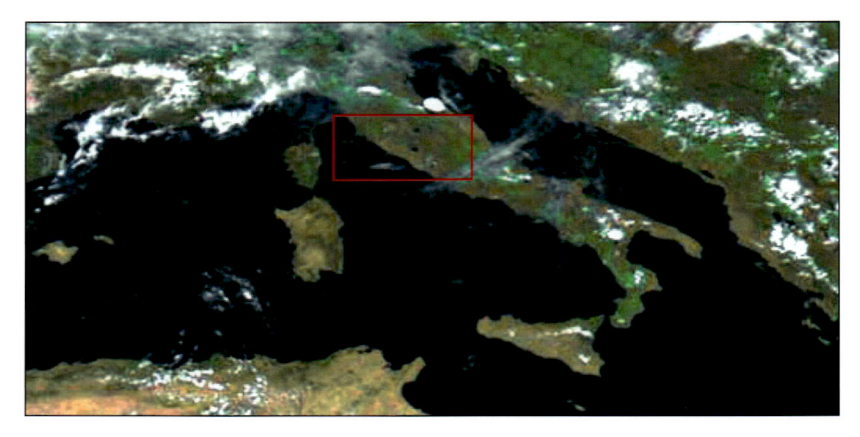

Earth observation satellites are used for various purposes which require different ground resolutions.

◁◁
1a – Meteosat-8 MSG-1 SEVIRI, full scene.

◁
1b – Meteosat 8-MSG-1 SEVIRI, ground resolution approximately four kilometres in the middle of the picture.

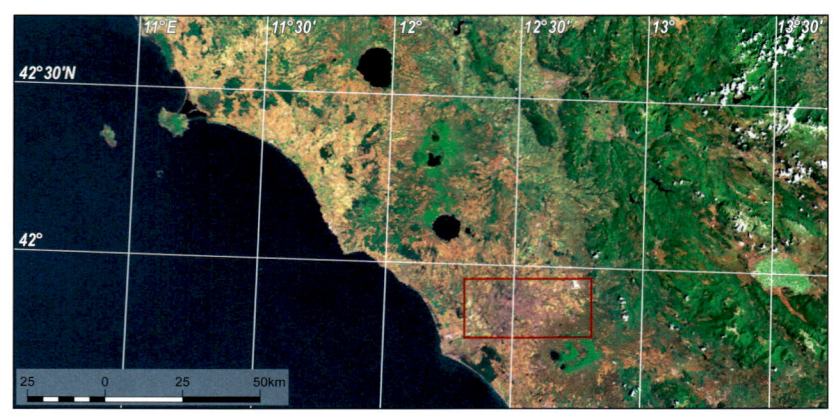

◁◁
2a – Envisat MERIS, quarter scene, 575 x 575 kilometres.

◁
2b – Envisat MERIS, ground resolution 300 metres.

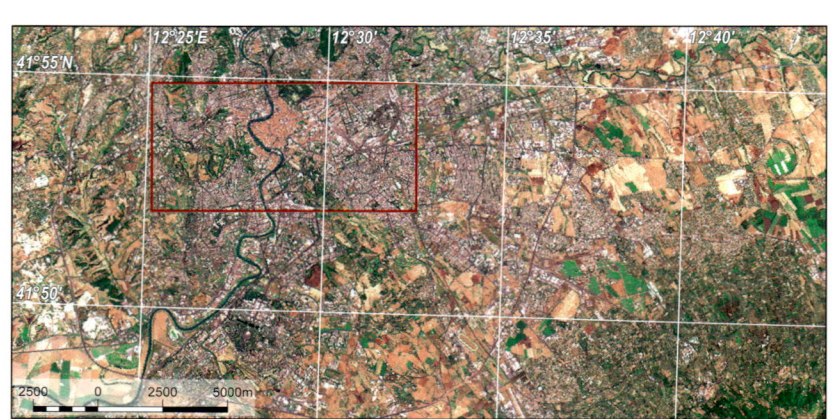

◁◁
3a – Landsat ETM, full scene, 185 x 185 kilometres.

◁
3b – Landsat ETM, ground resolution 30 metres.

◁◁
4a – SPOT-3 HRV, full scene, 60 x 60 kilometres.

◁
4b – SPOT-3 HRV, ground resolution 10 metres.

◁◁
5a – IKONOS-2, full scene, 10 x 10 kilometres.

◁
5b – IKONOS-2, ground resolution 1 metre.

Satellite	Startup operations	Orbit			Sensor	Ground resolution (m)	Number of spectral channels			
		Altitude (km)	Orbit	Repetition rate (days)			Visible light	Near/Middle infrared	Thermal infrared	Microwaves
MetOp-A, -B, -C	2006	820	Sun-synchronous	30–50 min	AVHRR/3	500–1100	1	3	2	
Meteosat 1–7	1977–1997	35 800	Geostationary	30 min	MVIRI	2500–5000	1	2	1	
Meteosat 8–10 MSG	2004	35 800	Geostationary	15 min	SEVIRI	2500–5000	2	7	3	
Envisat	2002	780–820	Sun-synchronous	35	MERIS	260–1200	10	5		
Envisat	2002	780–820	Sun-synchronous	35	AATSR	1000	2	3	2	
Terra/Aqua	1999, 2002	705	Sun-synchronous	16	MODIS	250–1000	10	17	9	
Landsat-1, -2, -3	1972, 1975, 1978	900	Sun-synchronous	18	MSS	80	2	2	1 (Landsat-3)	
Landsat-4, -5	1982, 1984	705	Sun-synchronous	16	TM	30–120	3	3	1	
Landsat-7	1999	705	Sun-synchronous	16	ETM	15–60	4	3	1	
Landsat-8	2013	705	Sun-synchronous	16	OLI, TIRS	15–100	5	4	2	
RapidEye (5 sats.)	2008	630	Sun-synchronous	1	REIS	6.5	4	1		
SPOT 6	2012	695	Sun-synchronous	1–26	NAOMI	1.5–6	4	1		
IKONOS-2	1999	681	Sun-synchronous	1–14	OSA	0.82–3.2	5			
QuickBird-2	2001	450	Sun-synchronous	1–20	BGIS 2000	0.61–2.44	5			
GeoEye-1	2008	681	Sun-synchronous	2–3	GIS	0.41–1.65	5			
WorldView-2	2009	770	Sun-synchronous	1.1	WV10	0.46–1.80	6	2		
TerraSAR-X	2007	514	Sun-synchronous	11	SAR	1–16				1 (X-band)
ERS-1, -2	1991, 1995	780	Sun-synchronous	35	SAR	30				1 (C-band)
Envisat	2002	780–820	Sun-synchronous	35	ASAR	30–1000				1 (C-band)
Sentinel-1 A–D	2014–2023	693	Sun-synchronous	1–12	SAR	5–40				1 (C-band)

△
6 – Some important Earth observation and meteorological satellites and their characteristics.

Satellite image resolution

There are a great number of Earth observation satellites that orbit the Earth (Fig. 6). This variety of satellites is needed because each task requires purpose-built camera systems. These differ in number and range of wavelength regions sensed (spectral bands) as well as in the spectral resolution. The level of spatial detail of the data acquired by the instrument is called the spatial resolution and corresponds with the area of the Earth's surface represented by one pixel of the image data.

For an image acquired at the normal altitude for Earth observation satellites, between 450 and 800 kilometres above the Earth, a spatial resolution down to half a metre can be obtained. A newspaper would be recognised as a light dot, but its headlines would not be legible, contrary to what some movies suggest. Even military satellites would not be capable of this, although they can achieve a spatial resolution of down to about ten centimetres due to their special optics and orbits.

From the global to the local scale

Because of the enormous amounts of data that accumulate during constant acquisition of data about Earth's surface, a fine balance must be found between expanse of the surveyed area and spatial resolution. A medium resolution of 300 metres with swath widths of about 1,200 kilometres (e.g. Envisat MERIS) suffices for large-scale overviews and the global evaluation of surface and atmospheric effects. The properties of extensive ocean areas in particular, such as sea-surface temperature, chlorophyll concentration or ocean flow conditions, as well as various atmospheric properties, can be analysed with this type of data. The large swath width allows each point of the Earth to be covered in intervals of up to one day, which is ideal for many monitoring tasks aiming at detecting short-term changes and at compiling long-term average values.

Spatial resolutions from five to thirty metres with swath widths of around 100 to 200 kilometres (RapidEye, SPOT, Landsat) are perfect for regional analysis and representation. This combination of resolution and spatial coverage is appropriate for farming analysis, but also for studying hydrological problems such as along rivers, coastlines and flooded areas. Many projects dealing with the monitoring of conservation areas are also based on this combination, as it is a good compromise between spatial detail and coverage. On top of this, it is worth mentioning that data of this type have been recorded for about 40 years already. This enables the monitoring and evaluation of long-term developments such as the shrinking of rainforests due to human activities or the growth of urban areas in developing countries. Such regular, long term monitoring at large spatial scales is not practical with other techniques.

Systems offering the most detail, such as GeoEye-1 and WorldView-2, are designed for local analyses and have swath widths of around 10 kilometres at spatial resolutions of about half a metre. This data can compete with aerial photography and supports local planning measures (e.g. river engineering) with high-quality visualisation of changes effected by such projects. The higher the spatial resolution, the higher is the data volume to be transmitted to the ground receiving station. For colour images this volume can be reduced by acquiring a special high resolution panchromatic image (similar to black and white photography) additionally to the spectral bands (infrared, red, green, blue). Combining the panchromatic with the colour bands results in a colour image of the same resolution as the panchromatic image. Similar to the human eye: it combines the blurred colour image of the retina's cones with the more focused black and white image of the rods.

Weather satellites with their much coarser resolution mark the other end of the scale. From a distance of 36,000 kilometres, satellites such as Meteosat acquire information over almost half the globe every quarter of an hour. MetOp, another satellite system, covers the high latitudes twice a day from an orbit 800 kilometres high. The spatial resolutions of both systems range from several kilometres to down to 500 metres. They deliver information on the atmosphere, such as cloud movement, temperature and humidity distribution, but also dust storms, volcanic plumes, and ozone concentration. Measurements of wind and surface temperature over the oceans and soil moisture, precipitation and vegetation over land deliver vital information for weather forecasts and climate models.

What can maps reveal?

Maps can be produced from image data as a simple representation of pixels (Fig. 1) to visualise terrain, or to serve as a background for additional information such as roads or geographic names. There is a broad range of maps that comprise a wide variety of thematic information, either directly measured by the acquired data or derived from it by applying specific evaluation procedures.

One example of a map produced directly from satellite data is the surface temperature of water or land (Fig. 2). Scaling the thermal infrared data assigns intensity values to temperatures in a map, for instance coded by the familiar representation of temperatures by a colour scale from blue to red. Similar depictions are used for visualising the concentration of trace gases in the atmosphere, phytoplankton in water bodies and vegetation-intensity maps.

Maps based on the evaluation of data require an additional interpretation of the image content — as for instance in the case of land-use maps where the colours and structures of the satellite image are assigned to the corresponding utilisation classes (Fig. 4, 5 p. 189). It may be necessary to analyse data from different seasons for farming areas to allow grass and cultivated fields to be told apart. Due to the overwhelming complexity of our environment, which in addition is subject to manifold influences such as weather and seasons, more detailed interpretations almost always need interactive processing integrating additional background knowledge. This means that although obvious progress has been made in image processing, a fully automatic compilation of such maps often only provides unsatisfactory results.

"We own the Night"

Radar satellites are based on physical and technical principles completely different from those of the optical systems. Optical satellite sensors record sunlight reflected or radiation emitted from the Earth's surface. Radar satellites, in contrast, use active sensors. They 'illuminate' the surveyed area with very weak microwaves and record the backscattered signals. Their intensity depends on the roughness and humidity of the ground cover (vegetation, man-made constructions), and on the waves on water surfaces. Additionally, distances to the ground and signal phases are evaluated to derive digital height maps and small movements of the terrain (e.g. soil subsidence or creeping, earthquake induced displacements).

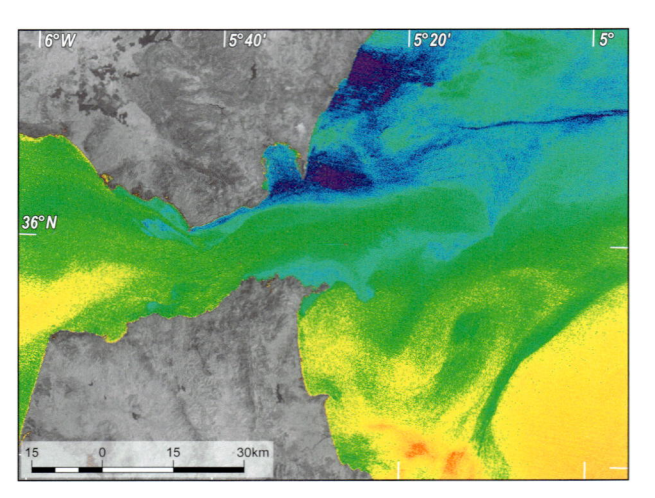

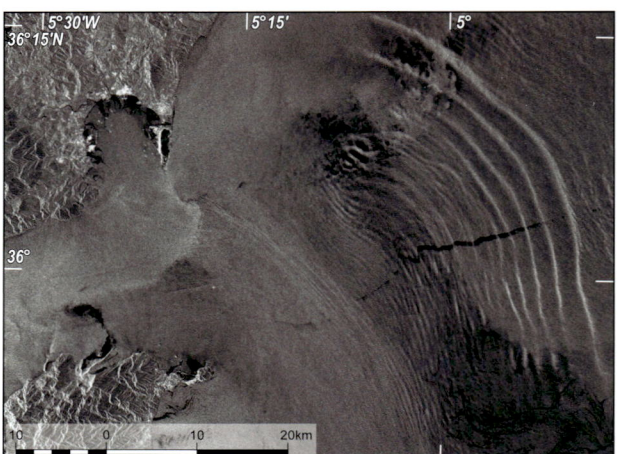

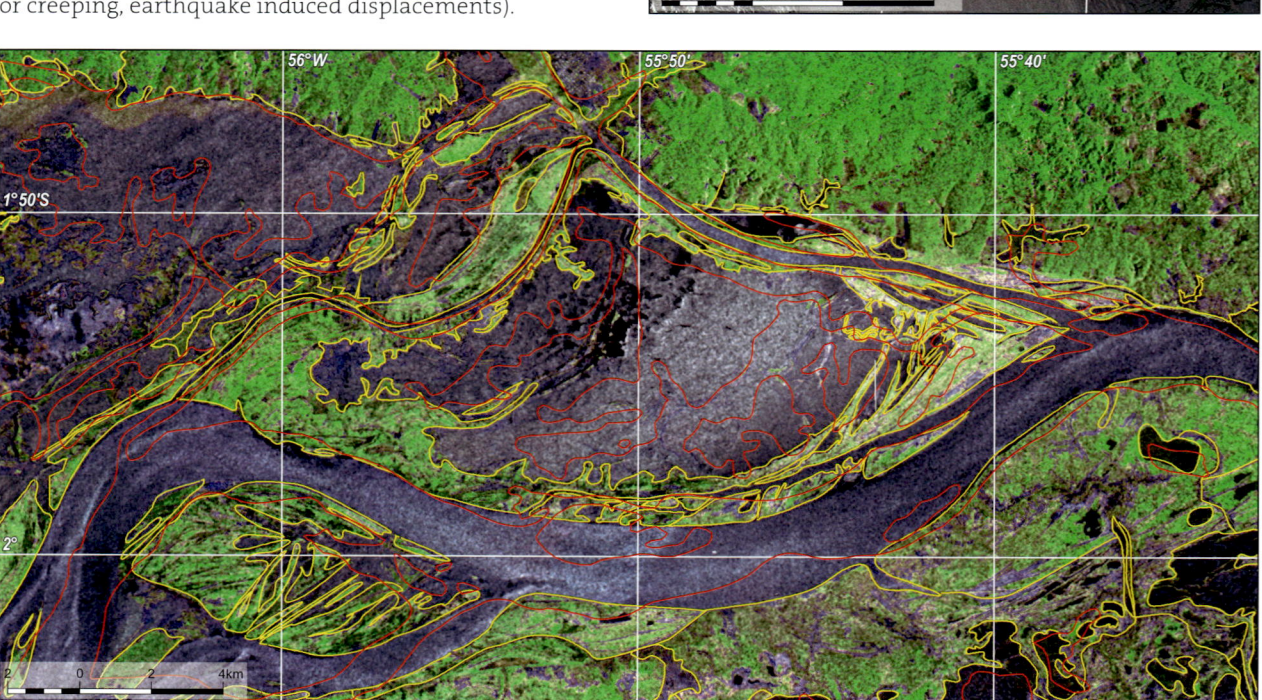

1 – A map derived from satellite images contains, apart from high-quality processed satellite images, a projection, a map grid, a scale bar and cartographic annotations.

5 – A mosaic of Europe created from MERIS quarter-scenes – a puzzle for experts.

2 – The surface water temperatures are made visible and interpretable by the scaling of the information contained in the thermal infrared channel (Landsat TM band 6).

Temperature on sea surface
cold — warm

3 – Using radar images, local currents in the sea here at the Strait of Gibraltar can be made out, as can oil pollution, due to its influence on the choppy water.

6 – Finishing a satellite-image mosaic needs much work and patience. A near-natural colour image of Europe has been created from MERIS raw data.

4 – Satellite-image data are also used to update maps. The Amazon, west of Santarém in Brazil.

Comparison of Operational Navigation Chart (ONC) from 1992 with maps using satellite data
ERS-SAR from 07/06/1992 overlaid with Landsat TM from 06/09/1992
— Riverbed according to ONC
— Riverbed as delineated from satellite image

Compared to near-real colour data from optical sensors, radar data represent the Earth in an unusual and often visually less intuitive way. On the other hand radar sensors have the huge advantage of being able to work during any time of day or night and of operating under any kind of weather conditions, as clouds are penetrated by radar microwaves. This might explain the slogan of the US radar satellite Lacrosse: "We own the night". Radar data is therefore ideal when reliable and up-to-date images are required within a short time. One prime example is the possibility to rapidly map flooded regions to provide a basis for emergency management. The detection of oil spills on water surfaces is another important application of radar satellites, which can locate them and trace them directly to the cause. Radar is also used in navigation when sea ice must be identified and located and wave height and currents must be determined (Fig. 3). Active radar systems are also important for mapping tasks, especially in tropical regions, where frequent cloud cover means that high-quality optical data is difficult to get hold of (Fig. 4).

From satellite images to maps

Satellite data are often used to create large-scale maps. Apart from revealing the aesthetics of satellite images, these maps also make use of the high technical quality of satellite data. This includes exact geographical positioning of the data, high-quality detail and a homogenous reproduction of similar surface categories over large areas, such as dark-green coniferous forests or pale-green meadows and pastures.

What then makes a map out of a satellite image? The essential aspect is the unambiguous relation between a point in the image and the area on the Earth's surface represented by this point. The process of geocoding establishes this relation by identifying points with precisely known geographic coordinates, so-called ground control points, in the image. The next step transforms the image into a map projection, which allows coordinates and distances to be determined. If high accuracy is needed, the topography needs to be considered in order to eliminate the distortion in perspective.

If a very large area needs to be covered, a single satellite image in most cases is not sufficient. This particularly also applies to digital maps that are meant for zooming in for greater detail. The number of assembled satellite images can easily reach over one hundred (Fig. 5). Here it is especially important that suitable satellite data are chosen. Apart from ensuring that the whole area is covered, data from the same season need to be used to avoid sudden changes of the vegetation between images and to keep the brightness homogeneous. Additionally, the images should be free of clouds as far as possible. Parts of images blurred by clouds need to be replaced by sections of other images.

The chosen sections of the geocoded images then need to be colour-matched. Remaining differences in the vegetation or atmospheric haze are eradicated. A uniform image is then left, with no detectable edges in the transition areas (Fig. 6). These processes are partially carried out automatically, but in some cases additional interactive processing steps are necessary to achieve high-quality.

The process of producing a large-scale satellite image map from several hundred individual satellite scenes is comparable to putting together a jigsaw puzzle, the difference being that the pieces of this kind of jigsaw first need to be selected from a large pool of images and shaped in order to fit together.

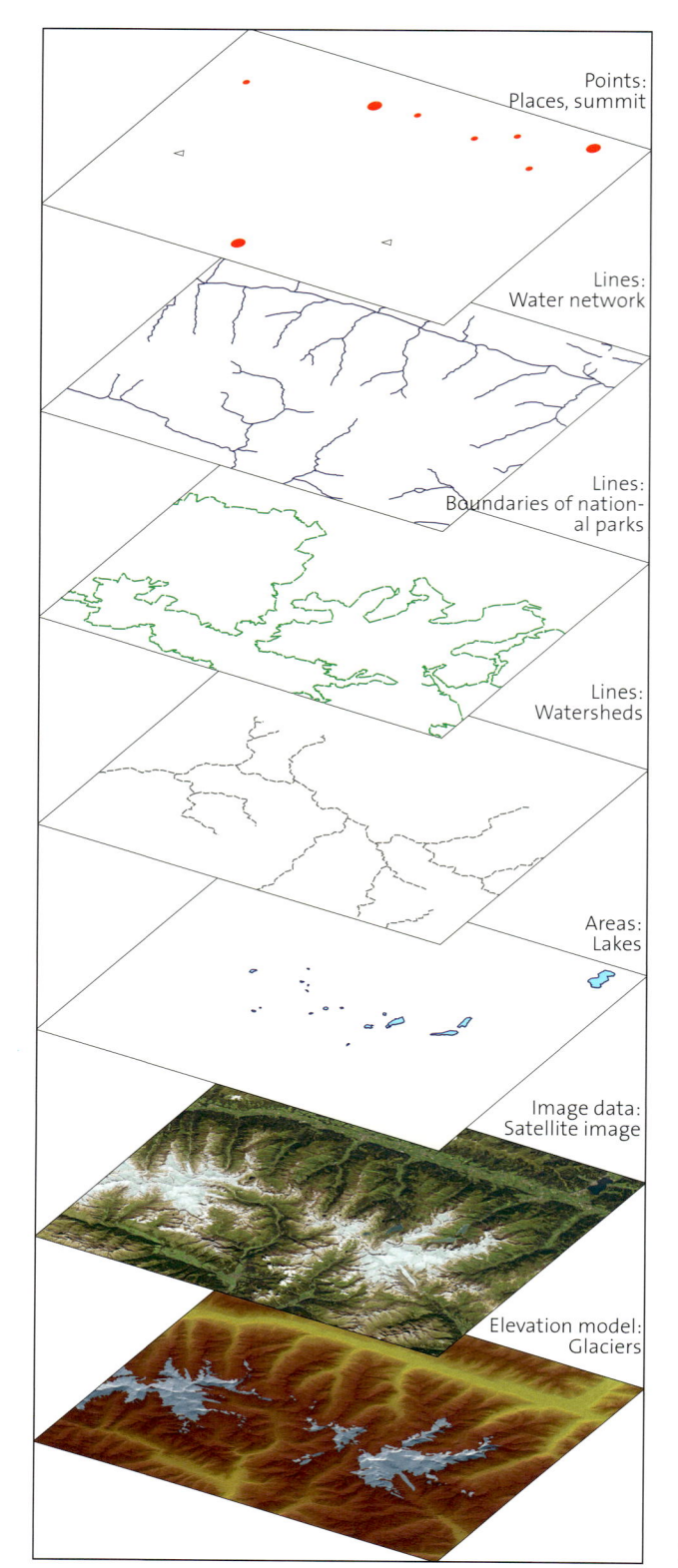

Geographic Information Systems

The surface of Earth is home to an amazing diversity of natural and man-made structures and phenomena. The phenomena are interrelated, and the structures' sizes are characterised by a broad range of scales. Because of this and depending on the analysed problem, the type of information, its spatial resolution, the area to be covered and the method in which these are related to each other need to be carefully selected and coordinated. The success of geographic information systems certainly was triggered to a large part by the development of stable high-performance computer systems that met the needs for processing power. While efficient computers are important, well-designed processing algorithms and methods bundled in software packages with user-friendly interfaces are essential as well to be able to cope with large amounts of incoming data.

So-called geographic information systems (GIS) are software systems that specialise in spatial information. They have established themselves as indispensable aids for the organisation, visualisation and particularly the further processing of geodata. Using GIS combined with efficient databases allows results tailored to the demands of the specific investigation area to be produced – for instance, for flood-risk areas following longer periods of rain in a specific administrative region.

Data and Information

The most important component of a GIS, even more so than computers and software, is the data. All the data used in a GIS must have a spatial reference. This means that it is related to corresponding points or areas on the Earth's surface. The system usually includes a number of different information layers, such as elevation models or aerial photos and satellite images, individual two-dimensional polygon elements (e.g. lakes or settlements), one-dimensional elements (e.g. rivers, roads, boundaries) and point information (e.g. mountain summits or triangulation points). Not only the location and shape of the objects are stored, but also additional attributes, such as elevations, population densities or noise emission values at a measuring station. This information is organised in the GIS in a layered data structure. The information layers can be interconnected using mathematical methods, which allows new information to be produced from the existing layers and visualised as a separate information layer (Figs. 1 and 2). When needed, GIS can make also the step from the plane to a three-dimensional description of our world, as for instance in the case of many geological or hydrological problems.

◁
1 – Structure of a geographic information system (GIS) – the topics are organised into their own levels that can be combined if required.

◁▽ ▽
2 a/b – Geographic information systems (GIS) are often linked to extensive data bases and work stations.

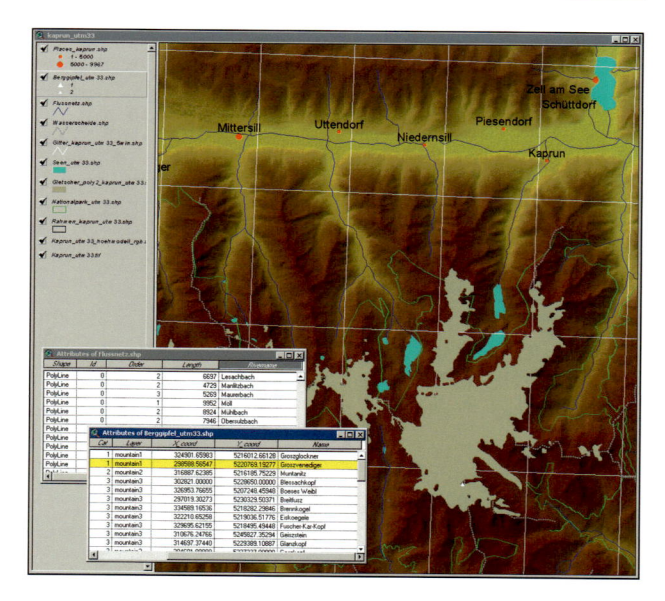

▷
3 – SPOT image stereo pair taken from two overflights.

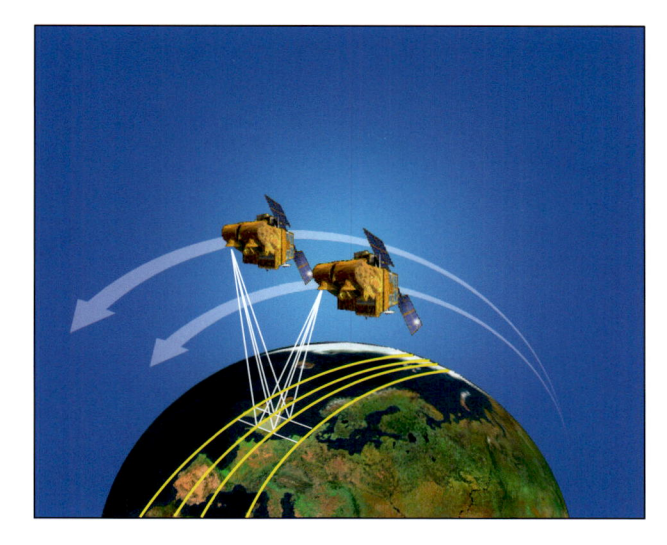

▷
4 a/b– SPOT image stereo pair. The relative positions of points at different elevations are shifted due to the different viewing angle. This shift is exploited to derive elevation models.

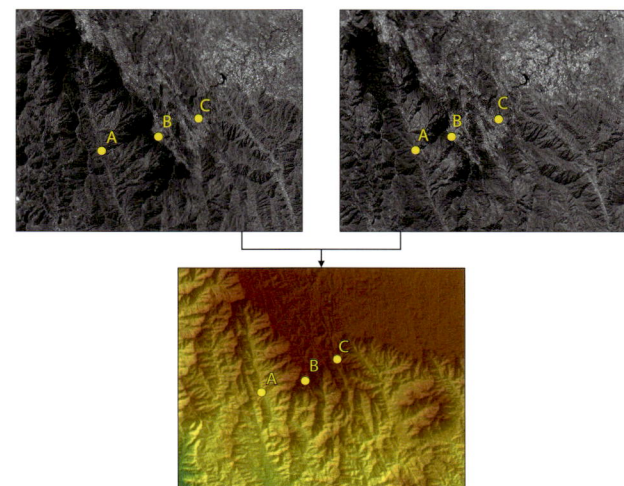

▷
5 a/b – Elevation model with coloured and shaded surface relief.

▷
6 – SRTM acquiring a stereo pair of images with X-SAR.

▽ ▷▽
7 a/b– Satellite image and map used for the example of Salzachtal, Austria.

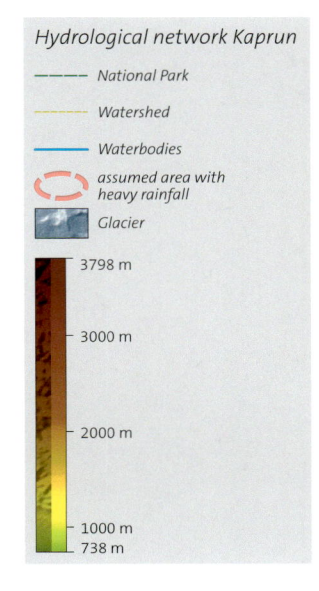

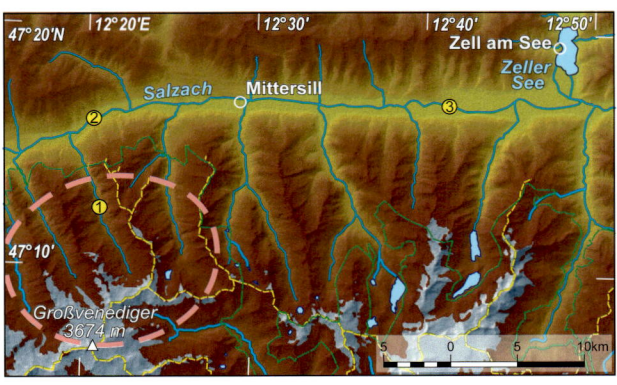

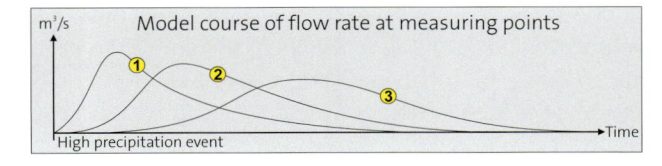

Geodata is acquired from diverse sources that range from basic data such as digital elevation models (DEM) or boundaries to digitised historical maps or atmospheric data transmitted automatically on a regular basis. One increasingly important source of geodata comes from Earth observation satellites that continuously survey the state of the Earth's surface and send the acquired data to the receiving stations. This is a major contribution with respect to up-to-date data, and together with data from other sources it allows creating thematic maps, such as for temperature, land use or pollutant dispersion in air or water.

If reliable data sources are used, GIS act as indispensable tools for the analysis of the location and the planning of measures. The Decision Support System (DSS) for emergencies such as floods or earthquakes is a prime example of the application of a GIS. The tasks carried out range from disaster prevention (creation of suitable land development plans and flood retention plans), to the support of emergency action plans and to the surveying and assessing of damage after the event. GIS invariably help to carry out these tasks more quickly and more precisely, making disaster management both more effective and more efficient.

Representing our world and predicting its future
On top of visualising current conditions, geographical information systems can be applied to simulate temporal developments using appropriate computer models, as is done on a large scale for weather forecasts and, on a longer timescale, for calculating climate scenarios. A good understanding of the processes and a sufficient database are both important for this. Many management tasks dealing with water rely on models reflecting the dynamics of the element. Good examples are the estimation of discharge following heavy rainfall, pollution dynamics in rivers, and the planning of energy production with water dams.

Accurate elevation models play a significant role for many of the models related to water because the discharge properties hugely depend on the terrain. Elevation values are derived frequently from optical (e.g. SPOT, Figs. 3–5) or radar data acquired from space, such as those from the Shuttle Radar Topography Mission (SRTM) of the space shuttle Endeavour performed in 2000 (Fig. 6), reaching a spatial resolution of one arc second, or about 30 metres. The twin radar satellite constellation TerraSAR-X and TanDEM-X attains a horizontal and vertical accuracy of about five metres. The elevation data is ready to be used for a whole range of derived datasets, such as slope, exposition, water divides, gullies, and hollows. These are then all used further in additional hydrological models (Fig. 7).

1 – Radar image of the
Antarctic, George V Land.

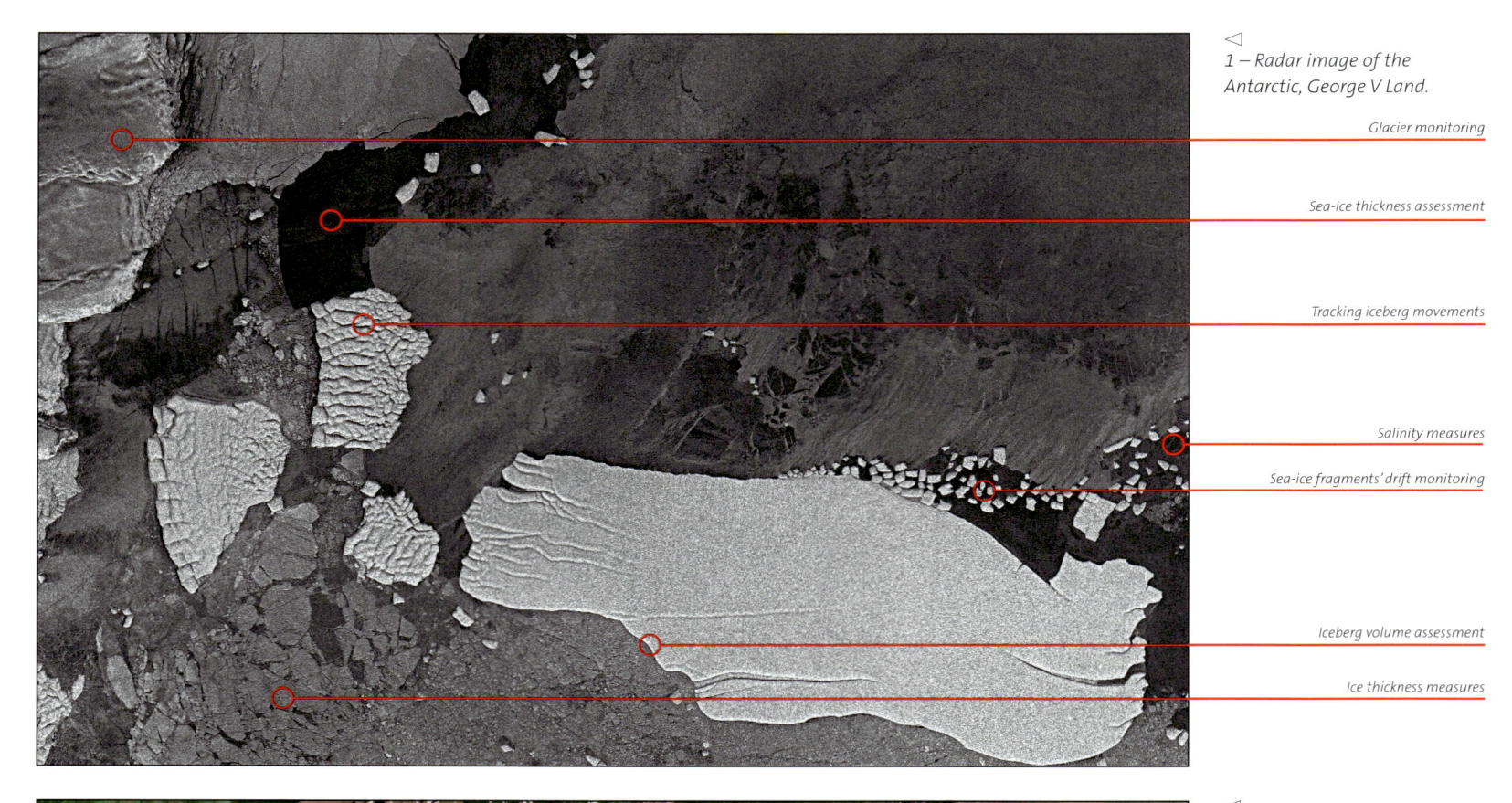

Glacier monitoring

Sea-ice thickness assessment

Tracking iceberg movements

Salinity measures

Sea-ice fragments' drift monitoring

Iceberg volume assessment

Ice thickness measures

2 – Rainforest in Borneo.

Sediment load assessment

River course mapping

Land cover change assessment

Cloud cover estimation

Forest biomass estimation

Monitoring of land use changes

Conservation status assessment

Rain estimation

Coastal erosion mapping

Mapping for infrastructure projects

Logging control

Satellite image applications

Data acquired by the growing fleet of Earth observation satellites is used in an ever-increasing number of different applications. Even the most remote regions of the globe, from the poles to the temperate zones to the tropics, are monitored on a regular basis to provide specific information for a wide variety of applications.

Satellite data is used as an indispensable source of information for a vast array of scientific disciplines dealing with geo-related issues as well as for other fields. This can range from cartography and geodesy to the description of the water cycle in hydrology and the description of short and long-term developments in meteorology and climatology. Combined and applied in a sensible manner, the data contributes towards a significantly better understanding of our planet in a way that was impossible to imagine only a few decades ago.

Important economic benefits can be derived through the many applications of Earth observation developed for agriculture and forestry. They can simultaneously optimise the harvest while maintaining sustainable farming. Management of farmed arable and forestry areas can be improved by monitoring water supply and irrigated fields, supporting precision farming, measuring soil moisture and soil salinity, and determining the state of the vegetation cover. All this helps to develop a basis for an efficient use of the resources of Earth, be it soil, water or the atmosphere.

▷
3 – Mountain and lake landscape in the central latitudes of Austria.

Water quality assessment

Water level monitoring

Crop yield estimation

Flood risk assessment

Assessment of shoreline changes

Landslide mapping

Monitoring of silting

Assessment of wetland health

Monitoring of sealed surfaces

▷
4 – Desert climate: Saudi Arabia's east coast near Al Jubayl.

Sea surface temperature monitoring

Assessment of desertification

Monitoring marine and coastal areas

Mapping for navigation safety

Monitoring fisheries activities

Mapping of new infrastructure

Assessment of soil salination

Monitoring irrigation activities

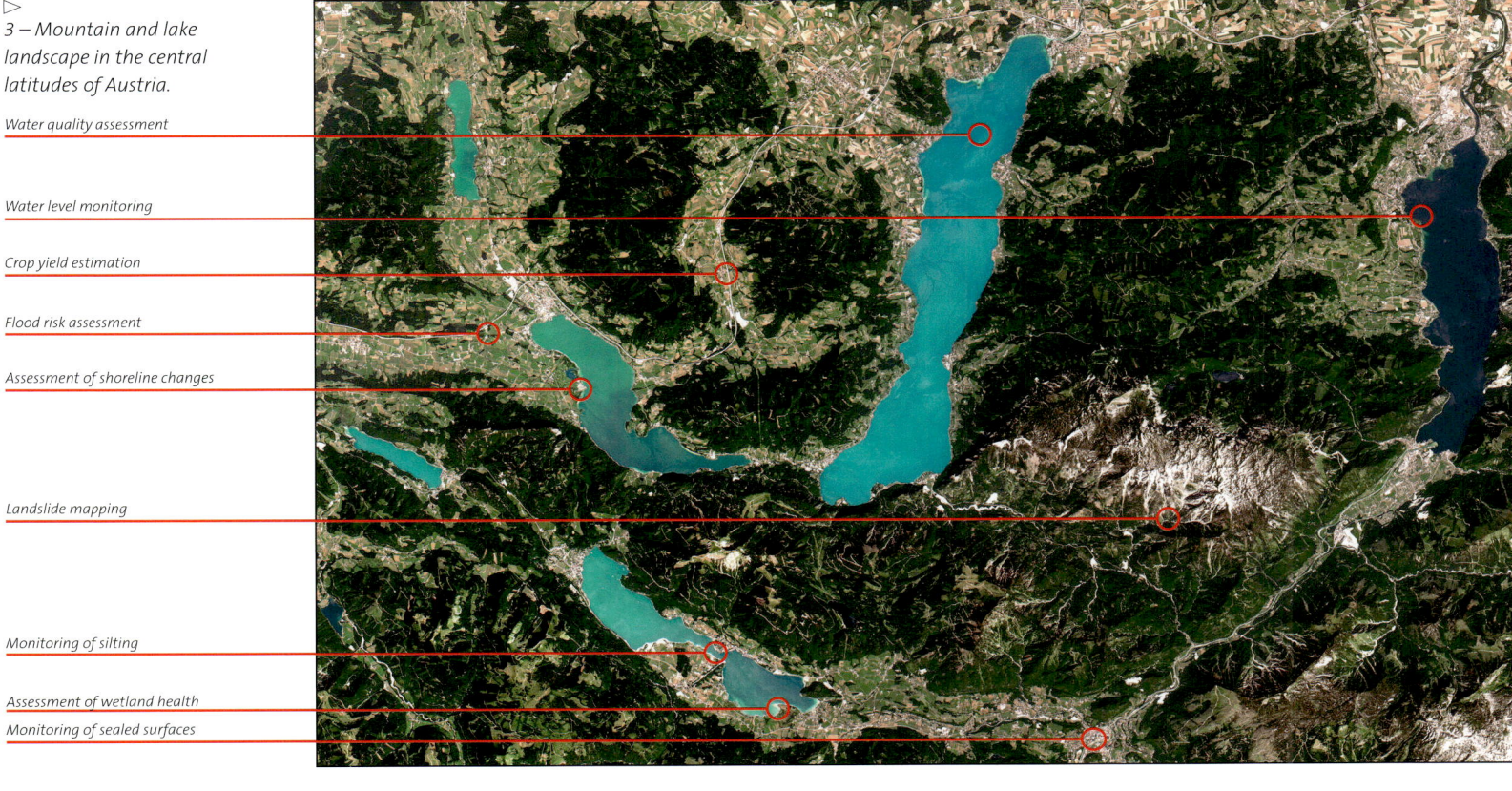

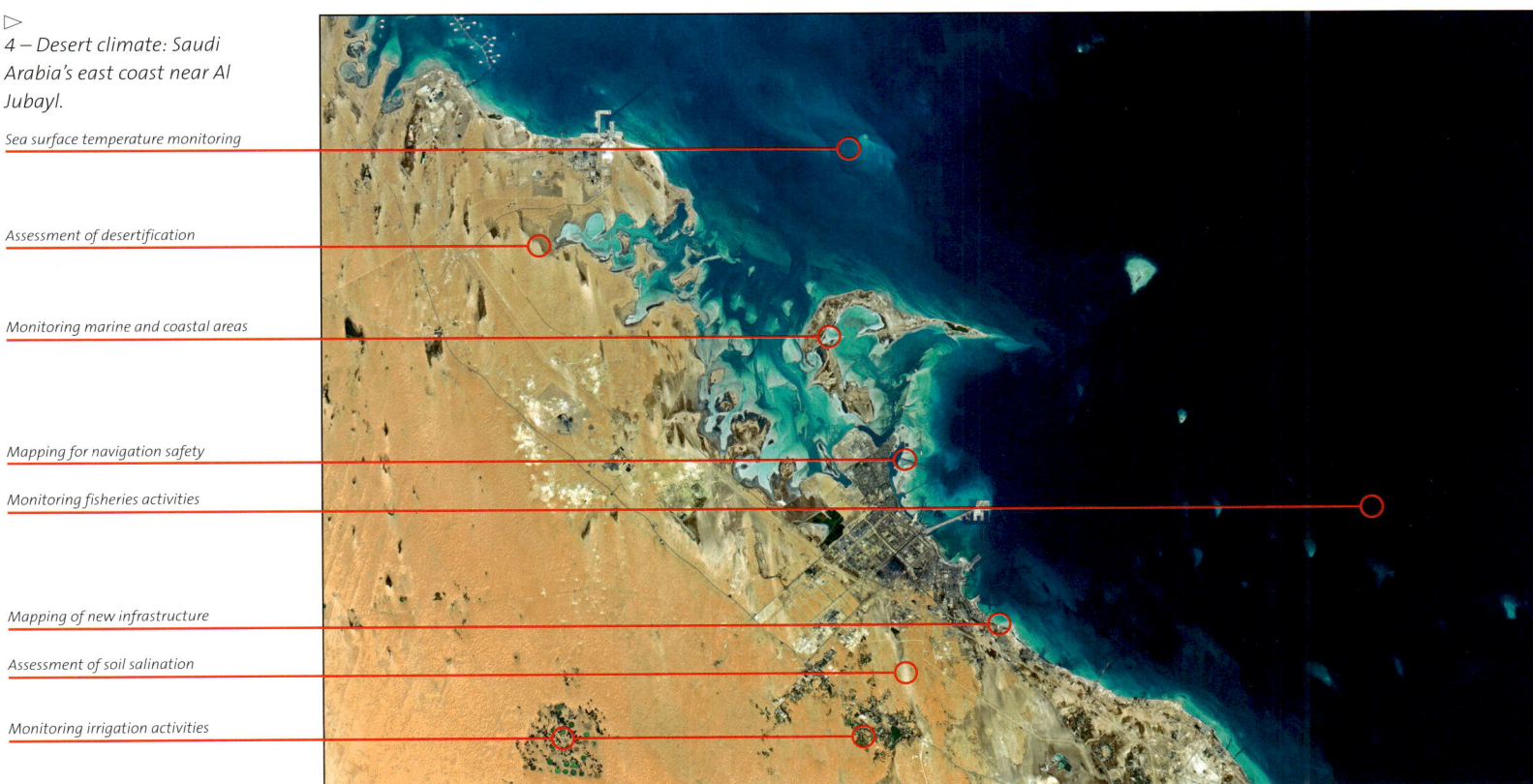

The situation is similar for urban development. Satellite data helps survey the current situation of built-up areas, to draw up plans for future settlement and infrastructure and to assist in water supply issues. The application of information derived from satellite data is also important in the case of natural hazards, particularly for urban areas, where tasks stretch from measures for disaster prevention to emergency plans, action plans, and damage surveys following events.

Jointly with navigation and communication satellites, Earth observation satellites play an ever-increasing role for traffic and logistics. Important contributions to better traffic safety include helping ships navigate treacherous sea ice, monitoring water pollution, and supplying timely weather information along trade routes. Recent developments include even surveilling sea traffic with respect to piracy and migration.

Remote sensing data is of course used also in ecology and environmental protection, such as for monitoring the quality of air and water in order to detect pollution events at an early stage, measuring soil salinity and desertification, and monitoring wetlands, conservation areas and coastal ecosystems.

Last but not least, Earth observation data is also an increasingly important information source for leisure and tourism. Examples of this are data about expanse and thickness of snow cover, water quality and water temperatures, and weather data and forecasts.

49

WATER – THE GLOBAL PERSPECTIVE

An extensive cartographic presentation of the topic of water
helps in understanding the various complex interrelations of issues
that are of major significance to sustainable development

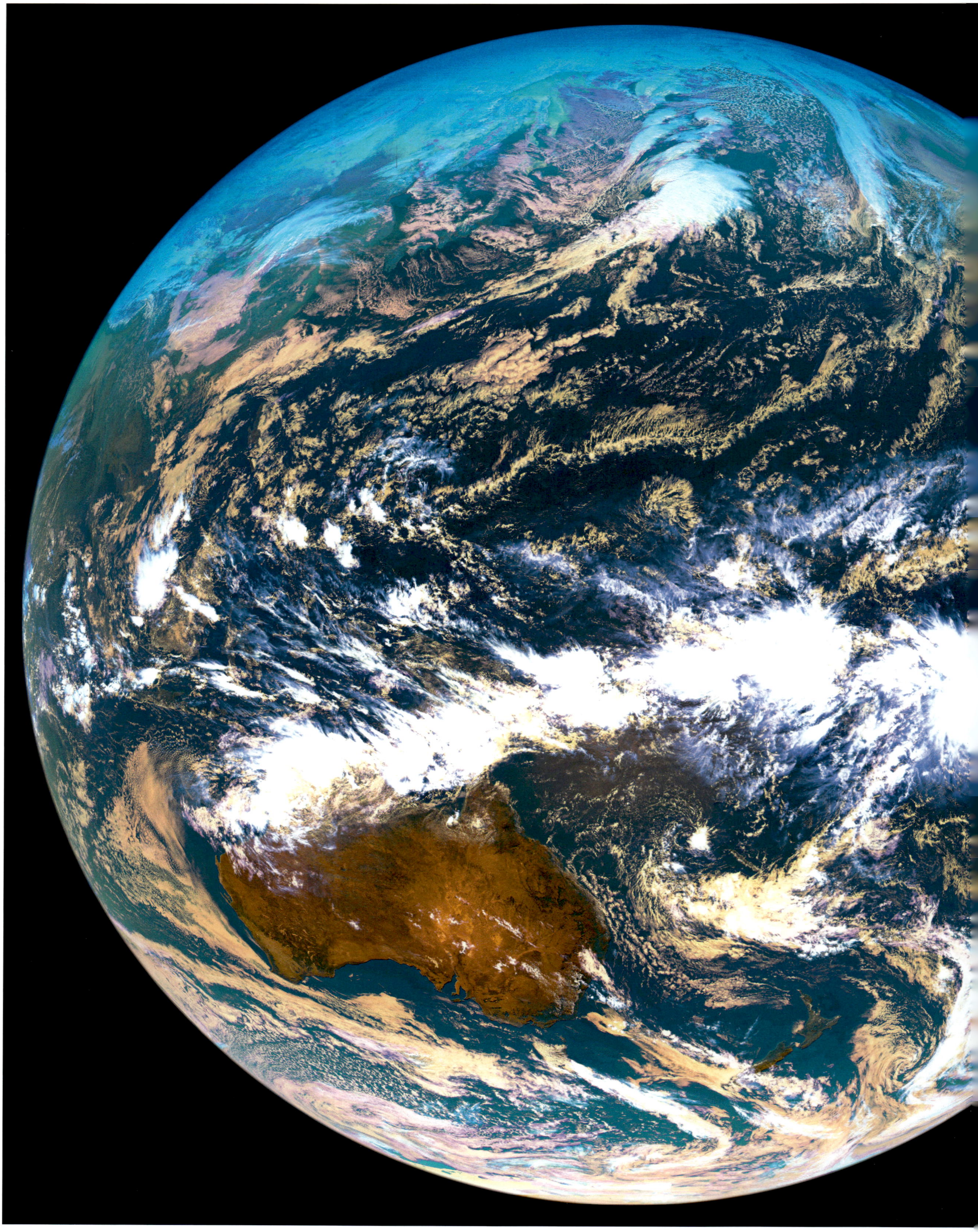

THE BLUE PLANET

The view from space justifies this term, because water determines the appearance of Earth.

△
2 – The GOES 12 image taken on December 31, 2004 reveals South America's position between the Atlantic and the Pacific. Large areas of the hot and humid Amazon basin are covered by clouds.

△
3 – Meteosat image on 18/07/2003. The Mediterranean region is free of clouds, while tropical storms show up north of the Equator.

▽
4 – Meteosat 5 image of the Indian Ocean on 30 June 2004. The Arabian Peninsula is cloud-free and India is hit by the monsoon.

According to current knowledge, other than on Earth, water only exists in the solar system as ice on Mars, on our moon and on Saturn's moon Titan. At a distance from the Sun of 150 million kilometres, Earth is the only celestial body of the solar system with a significant part of its surface covered by water – it has been a water planet for billions of years. Mercury orbits the Sun at a distance of only about 58 million kilometres. Venus, Earth's cosmic twin sister, maintains a distance of around 108 million kilometres, resulting in temperatures far above 400 degrees Celsius. This makes the existence of water in its fluid state impossible. Consequently, also the existence of life elsewhere in our solar system is very unlikely.

Earth's total water resources are estimated at around 1.38 billion cubic kilometres, more than one thousandth of Earth's volume. The oceans make up about 96.5 per cent of this amount. The estimations for the proportions of other water reservoirs vary. They include ice, snow, groundwater bodies, the volume of all fluvial bodies and the volume of all lakes. The average annual discharge from the entire terra firma is estimated at about 47,000 cubic kilometres.

Earth's freshwater resources comprise between 35 and 40 million cubic kilometres. The figures are much lower, when only economically available fresh water for currently seven billion people is taken into account. Significant restrictions are imposed by the fact that much of the water is stored as ice and snow. Antarctica is home to 90 per cent of all ice, more than half of the entire planet's fresh water. Another example of the restricted availability is the current distribution of humid and arid climate zones.

◁◁
1 – The GOES 9 image shows the Pacific Ocean on 1 July 2004 during the southern winter. A high-pressure cell over Australia keeps the sky cloud free.

53

Climatic conditions cause water-abundant regions, such as northern Canada and Siberia, to be only sparsely populated. On the other hand, in Egypt about 60 million people squeeze into the densely populated region along the Lower Nile, which comprises under one-tenth of the country's total surface area (about one million square kilometres). Most of Egypt's agriculture, as well, almost completely relies on irrigation water from the Nile and Lake Nasser.

Apart from large parts of Australia and the USA's Southwest, the arid and hyper-arid zones of our planet are scattered mainly amongst the developing countries of Latin America, Africa and Asia, of which 30, 85 and 60 per cent, respectively, are covered by areas with water deficit. Mankind has also substantially influenced the expansion of arid environments.

The fact that Lake Chad (see also page 148ff) in the Sahel Zone has shrunk from 25,000 square kilometres in the 1960s to less than 1,000 square kilometres today cannot be blamed solely on climate change. The same applies to Lake Aral (see also page 182ff), which was once 68,000 square kilometres in size but is now only around a fifth of that, while salinity has risen from ten grams to, at times, over 75 grams per litre within the South Aral Sea. The change in volume is to a large degree due to human mismanagement of an ambitious irrigation project for cotton that draws water from both tributaries, the Amudar'ya and Syrdar'ya. The effects have been disastrous: a desert and salt-dust storms where there was once a lake, an alarming rise in illnesses triggered by dust storms carrying pesticides over the wide plane, and the end of lake fisheries and transport by water across the former lake. These factors are hardly compensated for by the economic gain from the production of second-class cotton.

Other large-scale projects, such as the plan to supply water to the arid Asian southwest of the former Soviet Union from Siberian rivers or the southwest of the USA with water from the north, proved to be uneconomic and had to be abandoned. More recent and highly controversial large-scale diversions have been planned in South Africa. They are the fruits of serious water scarcity in the region. At least a preservation plan for the Northern Aral was agreed upon, and now fisheries, and people, are returning to the convalescing ecosystem.

The current water scenario on our planet is, on the one hand, marked by the spread of arid regions (especially in Africa and Asia) and on the other by the retreat of glaciers following the Little Ice Age (16th century to 1850/60) in the Alps, Caucasus and in tropical high mountain ranges.

Here it must be mentioned, though, that glaciers are growing strongly in other regions such as Norway, Alaska and in eastern Antarctica. Greenland's ice is more or less in balance, although its mass has been decreasing more rapidly in recent years, with the result that this island, largely comprised of ice, is playing a major role in rising sea levels. Those levels have risen 19 centimetres in the last one hundred years.

Water in the geological eras

The Holocene, which by definition began 10,000 years ago, has been witness to moderately changing climate scenarios, some of which were warmer and wetter and with fewer arid regions than now, especially in the northern hemisphere. The temperature is believed to have peaked between 5,000 and 6,000 years ago. At this time, there dominated a pluvial period in today's savannah and desert regions of Africa, which was particularly decisive for the temperate and sub-polar regions. Countless lakes and rivers covered the vast area between Mauretania and the plains just south of Khartoum. The famous samples of Saharan rock art found e.g. in the Tibesti massif testify to the habitable conditions that prevailed in this now inhospitable region in earlier millennia.

North of the Tropic of Cancer, this humid period may have extended back to 20,000 years ago, leading to the creation of the artesian groundwater that is being exploited especially in Libya today. Regarding the warmer historical periods, it is worth mentioning that the Alps were almost free of glaciers during the Roman era, leading into a Late Medieval warm period in Europe that brought malaria and wine cultivation up to Scandinavia.

Reaching back further to older periods of Earth's history, it can be expected that the hydrological contrasts were far more marked. The first Precambrian ice age cooled our Earth about two billion years ago. Its scale can only be roughly estimated to be like that of the ice age in the Ordovician/Silurian period (420-450 million years ago). The later Permian-Carboniferous ice age (25-30 million years long) during the early development of Pangaea was extremely expansive in the southern hemisphere and gradually ended whilst Pangaea drifted further north from the South Pole.

Plate tectonics and the subsequent ocean currents were far more apparent thereafter during the Pleistocene, but also before then. Temperatures dropped after the Eocene, when the Pacific Ocean stretched from pole to pole, the Atlantic was narrower, and tropical ocean currents could reach the poles without any barriers. Important developments included the movement of Antarctica to the South Pole, its splitting off from South America, and the creation of an Antarctic Circumpolar Current, as well as an almost complete isolation of the northern Polar Basin.

Eastern Antarctica may have had its first ice in the Oligocene and expansive ice-cap development towards the end of the Miocene, before any ice development reached the northern hemisphere, which marks the beginning of the Quaternary period and Pleistocene, around 2.5 million years ago. Up to then the temperatures in Europe had dropped about 15-20 degrees Celsius since the Eocene.

The causes of the ice ages and interglacial periods during the Pleistocene are still debated. More recently fluctuations of the solar activity have been included, and Milankovitch cycles, or variations in eccentricity, axial tilt, and precession of the Earth's orbit, all of which shape climatic patterns, have come under scrutiny. However, there is no clear consensus here, nor is there consensus regarding the climate of tomorrow. Extreme scenarios may have domi-

◁
1 – The Earth's water is subject to various uses and threats – such as here, through the discharge of mud from a gold mine in Johannesburg.

nated hydrological events on our planet: extreme aridity of the terra firma (as may have marked parts of the Devonian and Permian periods) and ice ages, with wide-ranging effects on the global climate and sea level. During the last glacial period 20,000 years ago, for instance, the sea level dropped at least 90 metres, which dried out the Persian Gulf and cut the Red Sea off from the Indian Ocean. This led to a subsequent massive rise in salinity of the remaining seas, which was fatal for numerous microorganisms. There were also periods of global humidity, however, that saw inland waters expand to their greatest extent ever. Postglacial periods and mountain formation may have contributed to this, and Carboniferous coal, as well as Tertiary lignite, are proof of the vast wetland areas that once existed.

Knowledge about the development of the climate in the past does not allow the three mentioned scenarios to be precisely reconstructed, even though the fluctuations of Tertiary climates are partially known and those of the Quaternary climate, especially in the northern hemisphere, are known even better. However, one thing is certain: the current climatic situation, in the midst of the ongoing exponential population growth, is particularly critical for the future of mankind, but also for that of numerous other species on our planet.

Water – the essence of life

On top of a water supply restricted by being locked up in ice and by the global climate zoning, other large-scale limits are caused by a poor water quality brought about by humans. In the ancient world, water pollution was merely a local or perhaps regional issue, but today it is on a global scale. Up until the Industrial Revolution, the main problems that arose were deforestation, erosion and wastewater produced by people working and living in the settlements (see e.g. the "cloaca maxima" in ancient Rome) as well as the salinisation of arable land caused by early irrigation methods.

The last centuries have been influenced to a larger degree by eutrophication due to phosphorous and nitrogen nutrients. Starting about fifty years ago there has been an exponential increase in harmful substances (heavy metals, pesticides, atmospheric entry of nitric oxides NO_x, sulphur oxides SO_x, etc.) entering the Earth's waters.

Poland serves as an example. In 1967, more than a third of the country's rivers had water good enough to drink. This has dropped to less than one river in twenty, and the contamination levels have reached values that are so high that half of the rivers are not even suited to industrial use.

Another example is the March River in former Czechoslovakia whose pollution is caused in equal measure by farming and by wastewater from settlements and industry. The river is the most polluted in its country, and more than half of its course is categorised as having the highest degree of contamination. These are only two examples of thousands of other minor to major rivers with similar conditions, especially in Eastern Europe and in many developing countries. Restoring these rivers is entirely a financial issue and has highest priority in countries with seriously diminished water resources, as it is in Europe the case with Poland.

Of the 139 largest fluvial systems in North America, Europe and the former Soviet Union, 77 per cent of the waters are influenced to a medium to high degree by reservoirs, river diversions, irrigation and dams. The number of large dams multiplied globally by a factor of seven between 1950 and 1986, and today there are more than 40,000 all around the world. These global technological measures have caused an estimated six per cent of discharge to disappear worldwide, caused mostly by evaporation from reservoirs and irrigation networks. Inside the Colorado River catchment 64 per cent of the water is lost to irrigation and an additional 32 per cent to evaporation from man-made lakes; only a small fraction finally reaches the Gulf of California.

In the ancient world salinisation was caused by irrigation (e.g. in Mesopotamia), and the waters of tributaries of endorheic lakes (without an outflow) have been ruthlessly exploited to irrigate large areas of farmland for decades (e.g. Lake Aral).

Regionally, there is another pollutant that has been more and more apparent over the last fifty years. This is acid rain, carrying SO_x and NO_x from industrial emissions, domestic combustion etc., which has caused numerous lakes in eastern North America, Scandinavia and in some parts of Central Europe to acidify. Some examples can be traced back to the last turn of the century, but people have only been fully aware of the problem since the 1970s. This acidification, with accompanying pH values of four, or even less than that in some cases, causes heavy metals to dissolve – especially aluminium, which causes high fish mortality. Due to this, frequently neither water use nor fishing use has been possible.

Emissions of SO_x have been greatly reduced in many industrial countries, but not those of NO_x. At the same time, recovery technologies, such as the treatment of lake sediment with sodium carbonates, have contributed to an immensely improved condition of many smaller and medium-sized lakes in these countries. The acidity situation will most likely be mastered in western countries by lowering emissions and proceeding with treatment of the affected lakes. But now an ever-increasing number of areas are being affected in India and China due to population growth and the rapid economic development in these countries, and pollution in Eastern Europe is ongoing, although at a decreasing rate.

The total amount of economically useable water that is currently available to mankind is estimated at between 7,000 and 10,000 cubic kilometres. As mentioned, this is restricted by the huge amount of water stored as ice (increased by an additional 36 cubic kilometres during the last ice age), by the geographical distribution of humid and arid zones, and lastly, but increasingly important, by pollution. On top of these factors, social and political processes lead to additional inequalities in the distribution and availability of water.

Text: Heinz Löffler

▷
2 – Water as the essence of life – in Nubian Sudan, the Nile is the lifeline of the people.

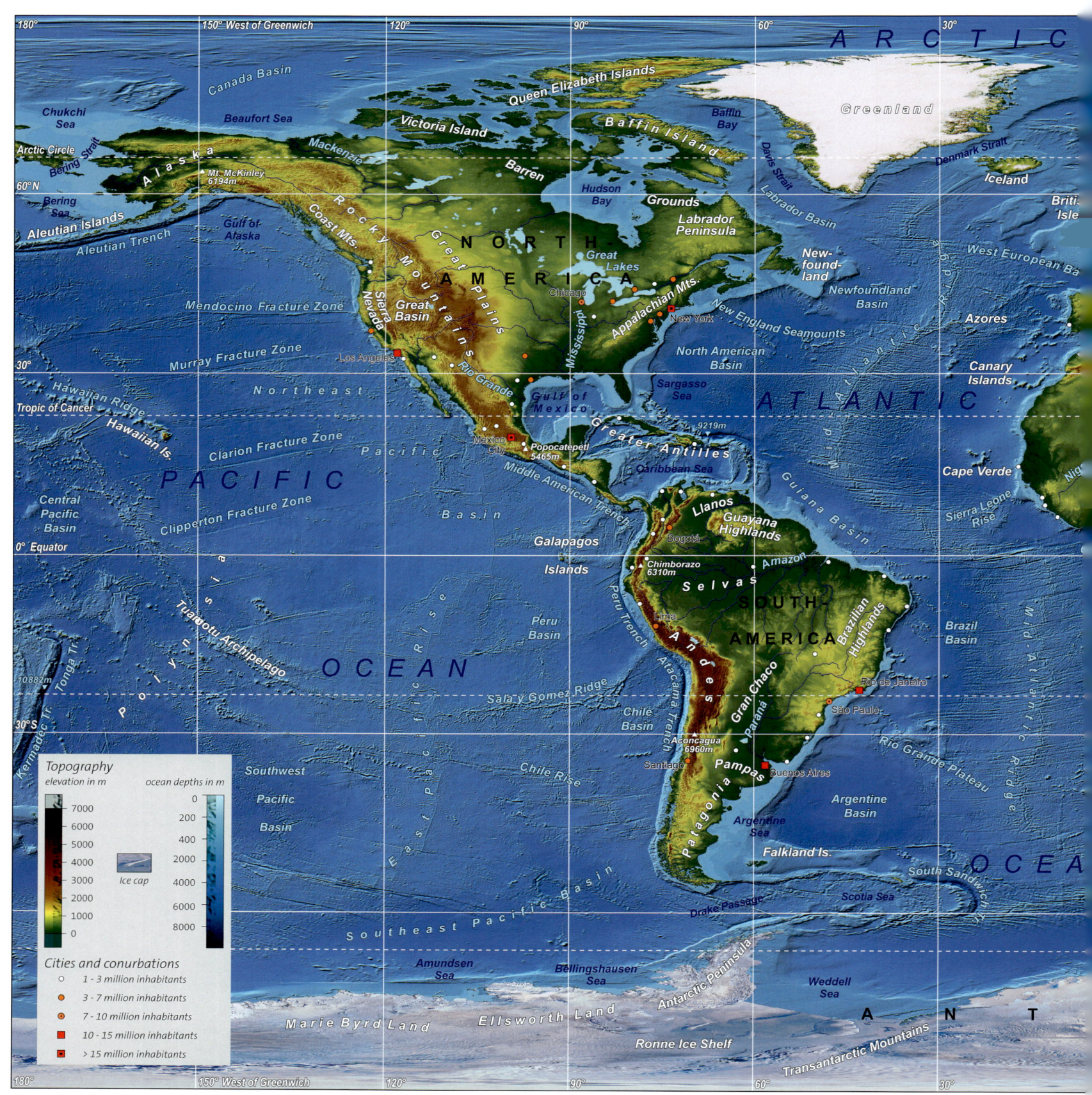

Topography and bathymetry

About two thirds of the Earth's surface is covered with water, that is 360 million square kilometres, with the southern hemisphere having the larger portion. The total amount of water on Earth lies at around 1.38 billion cubic kilometres. But this enormous wealth of water mostly exists as saltwater (97.4 per cent), which is useless for farming, and not as freshwater, which accounts for 2.6 per cent only. More than two thirds of the freshwater is stored as ice in the polar regions and glaciers, as snow or is bound as permafrost in the earth. The rest can be split into groundwater, water bodies and water in the atmosphere.

The Sun's energy acts as a motor keeping water in a constant cycle of evaporation, precipitation and drainage. Water evaporates due to the energy irradiated by the Sun on the ocean and land surfaces and rises as a gas. The water vapour cools at altitude and condensates, forming tiny droplets and leading to cloud formation and to precipitation. This brings the water back to the Earth's surface as rain, snow, hail or dew. Part of the precipitation is picked up by the plants, but the largest portion falls on the water and land surfaces. The latter means that the water reaches the ground where it penetrates the soil and advances to the groundwater store or flows to the nearest tributary.

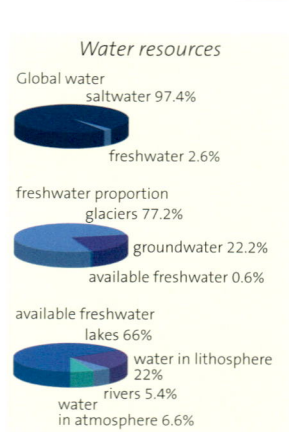

Water resources

Global water
- saltwater 97.4%
- freshwater 2.6%

freshwater proportion
- glaciers 77.2%
- groundwater 22.2%
- available freshwater 0.6%

available freshwater
- lakes 66%
- water in lithosphere 22%
- water in atmosphere 6.6%
- rivers 5.4%

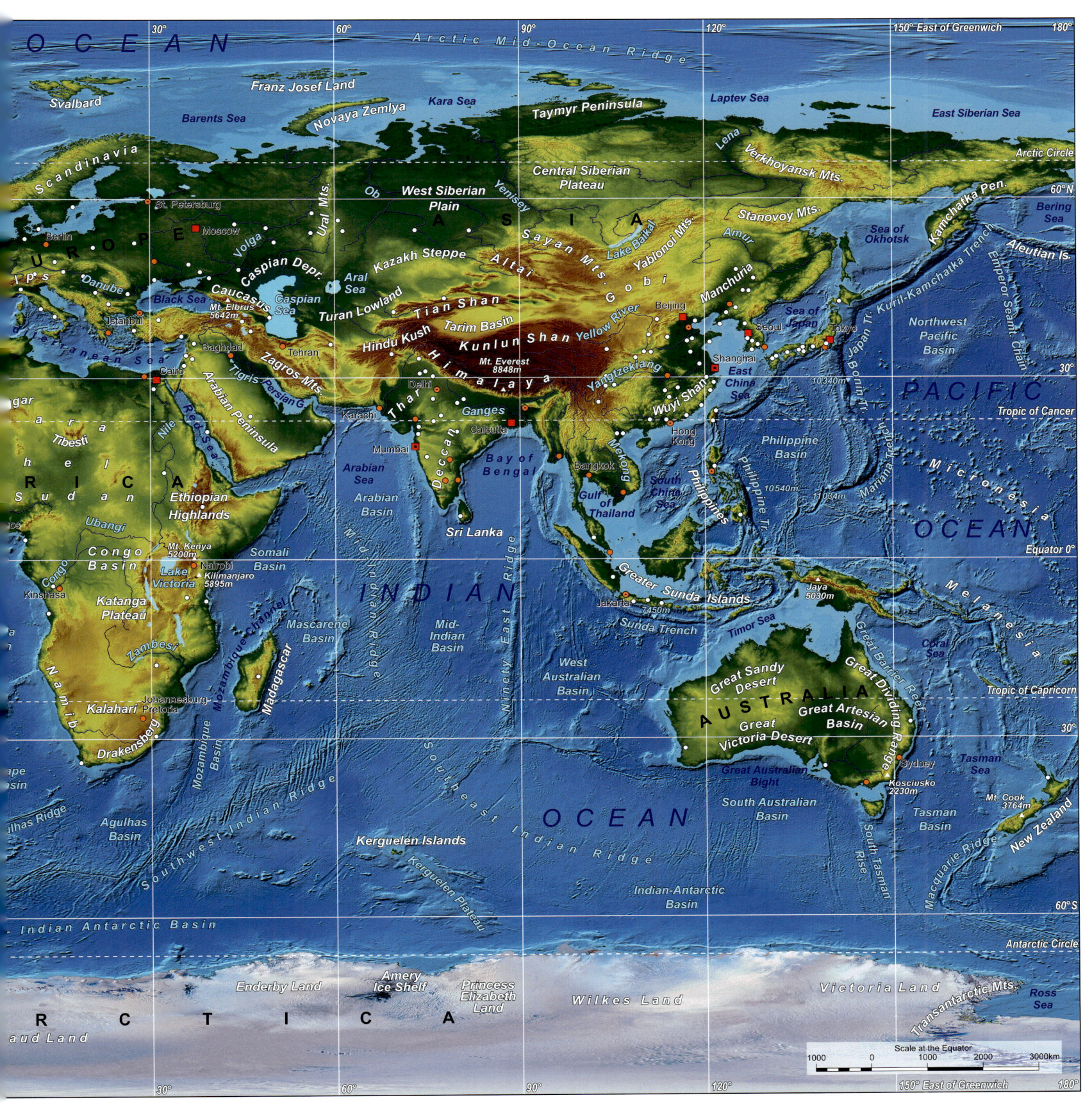

△
1 – Topography and bathymetry.

Front-runners
- Maximum depth: Mariana Trench, 11,034 m
- Biggest ocean: Pacific Ocean, 181 million km²
- Warmest ocean: Indian Ocean, 22 - 28°C average yearly temperature of the sea surface
- Longest river: Nile, 6671 km
- Biggest lake: Caspian Sea, 371,000 km²
- Deepest lake: Baikal, 1640 m

The rivers lead the precipitation back to the lakes and oceans where the water cycle begins from scratch.

The oceans of the Earth can be split into three major basins that are interconnected: the Pacific Ocean, the Atlantic Ocean and the Indian Ocean. It is also possible to distinguish between different parts of the ocean floor: the continental rim, the so-called ocean shelf which acts as a transition zone from the continents to the deep sea, and the deep sea itself with the systems of the mid-ocean ridges and trenches. The topography (surface form) of the Earth is constantly changing. The motor of this change is plate tectonics, which is responsible for the drift of the seven large continental plates.

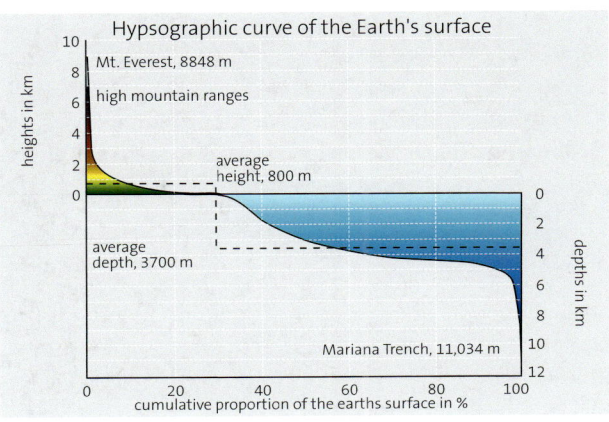

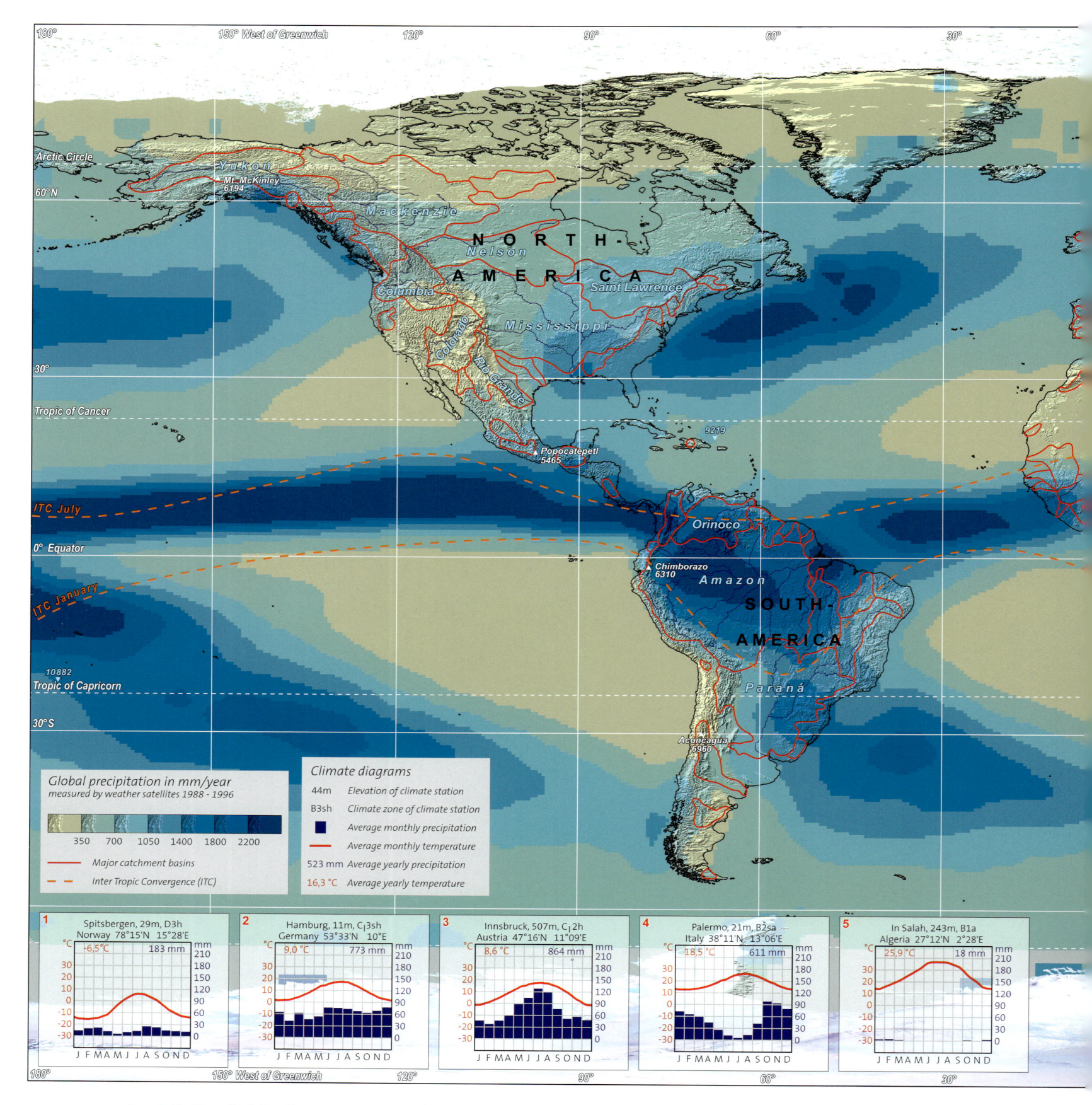

Precipitation distribution

Water can be found in the atmosphere as water vapour. The amount of water that can be taken up by the air is limited by the saturation point, a result of temperature and air pressure. If the saturation point is passed, water condensates on dust particles or other condensation nuclei, and the growing drops precipitate, either as a fluid (rain) or a solid (snow or ice).

The frequency and amount of precipitation varies strongly and characterises a geographic region and its climate. At the equator and in temperate zones, rainfall amounts are high compared to the often extremely low amounts in deserts and polar regions. The heterogeneous distribution of precipitation is caused by the circulation of the atmosphere. One important factor is the location of the Inter Tropic Convergence (ITC). This is a zone near the equator at which northerly and southerly airflows meet at ground level and are forced to rise due to high solar irradiation at this latitude, taking with them large amounts of water vapour received at the Earth's surface. This determines cloud formation and subsequent strong precipitation. That is why regions within the range of the ITC are characterised by high-intensity rainfall. The location of this equatorial trough is by no means consistent – it underlies significant seasonal changes, depending on the position of the Sun.

△
1 – Global distribution of average annual precipitation.

Extremes of precipitation
- place with lowest average annual precipitation of 0 mm/year is the Atacama Desert in Chile
- place with highest average annual precipitation of 12,000 mm/year is Cherrapunji in India
- place with most measured consecutive rain days in one year (325 days) is the Campbell Island (New Zealand).

58

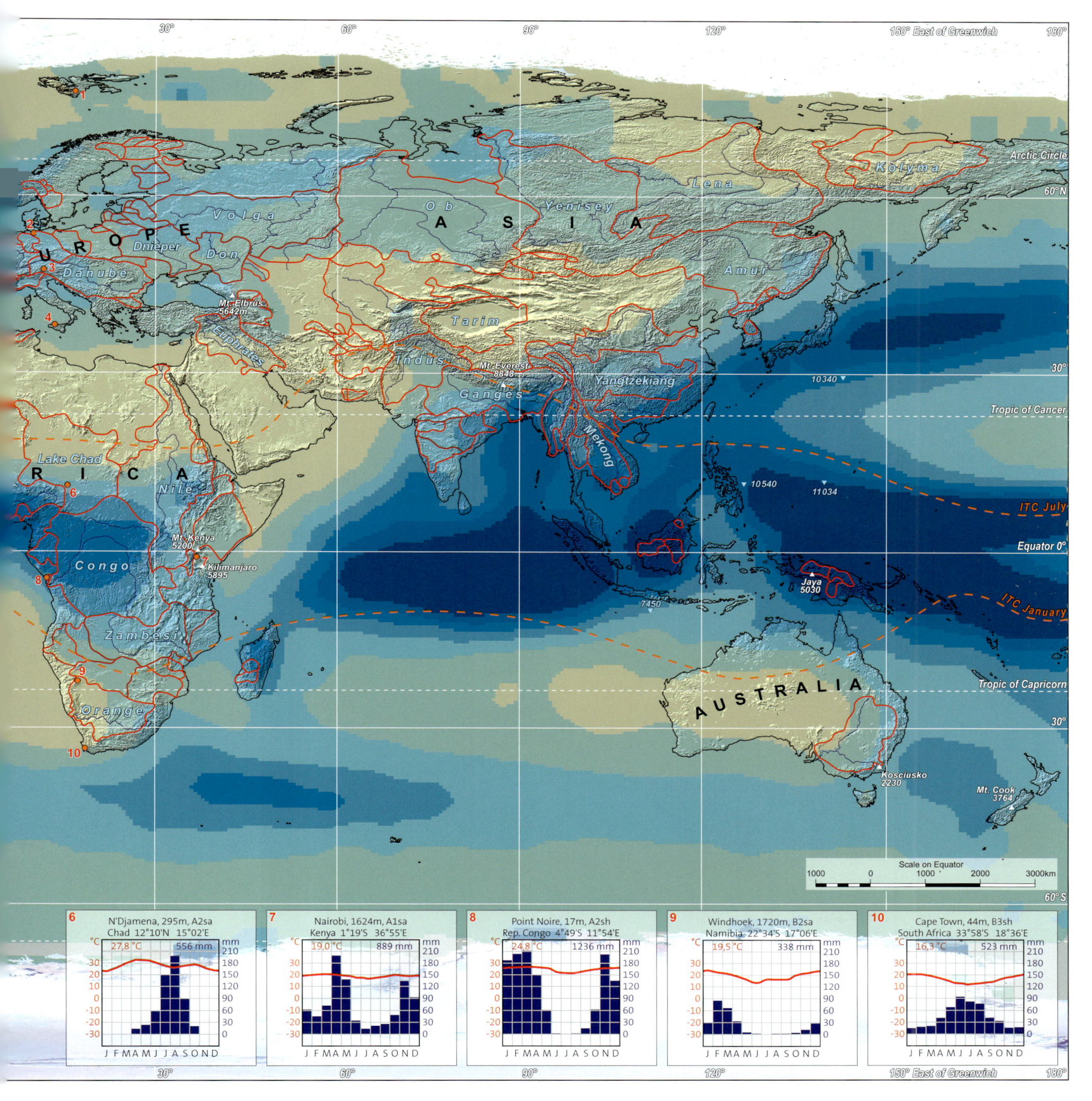

Other factors influencing the distribution and amount of precipitation are the proximity to the sea as well as the surface relief. Coastal regions generally have more rainfall, due to the higher water-vapour amount building up over the oceans and larger lakes. A mountain barrier forces air masses to rise. This cools the air, causes condensation and produces precipitation on the windward side of the ridge. As a rule, leeward sides usually receive little rainfall.

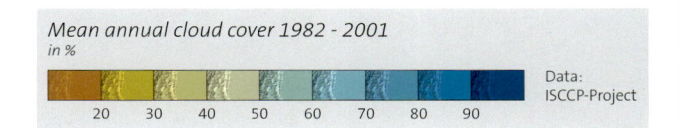

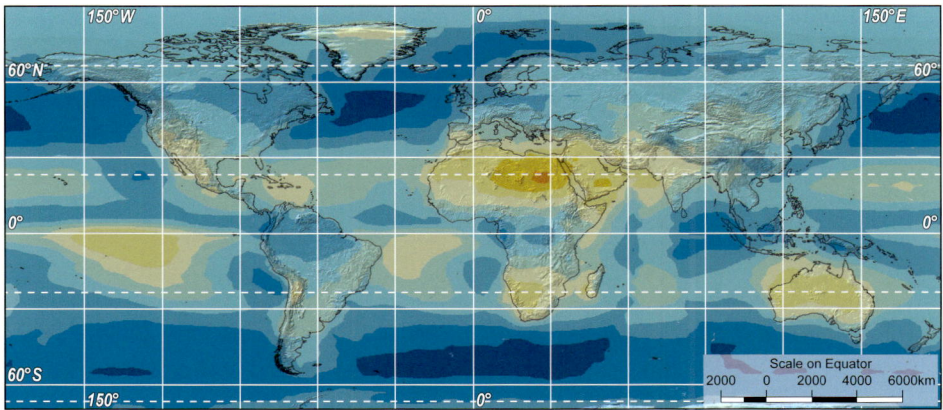

Mean annual cloud cover 1982 - 2001
in %

Data: ISCCP-Project

20 30 40 50 60 70 80 90

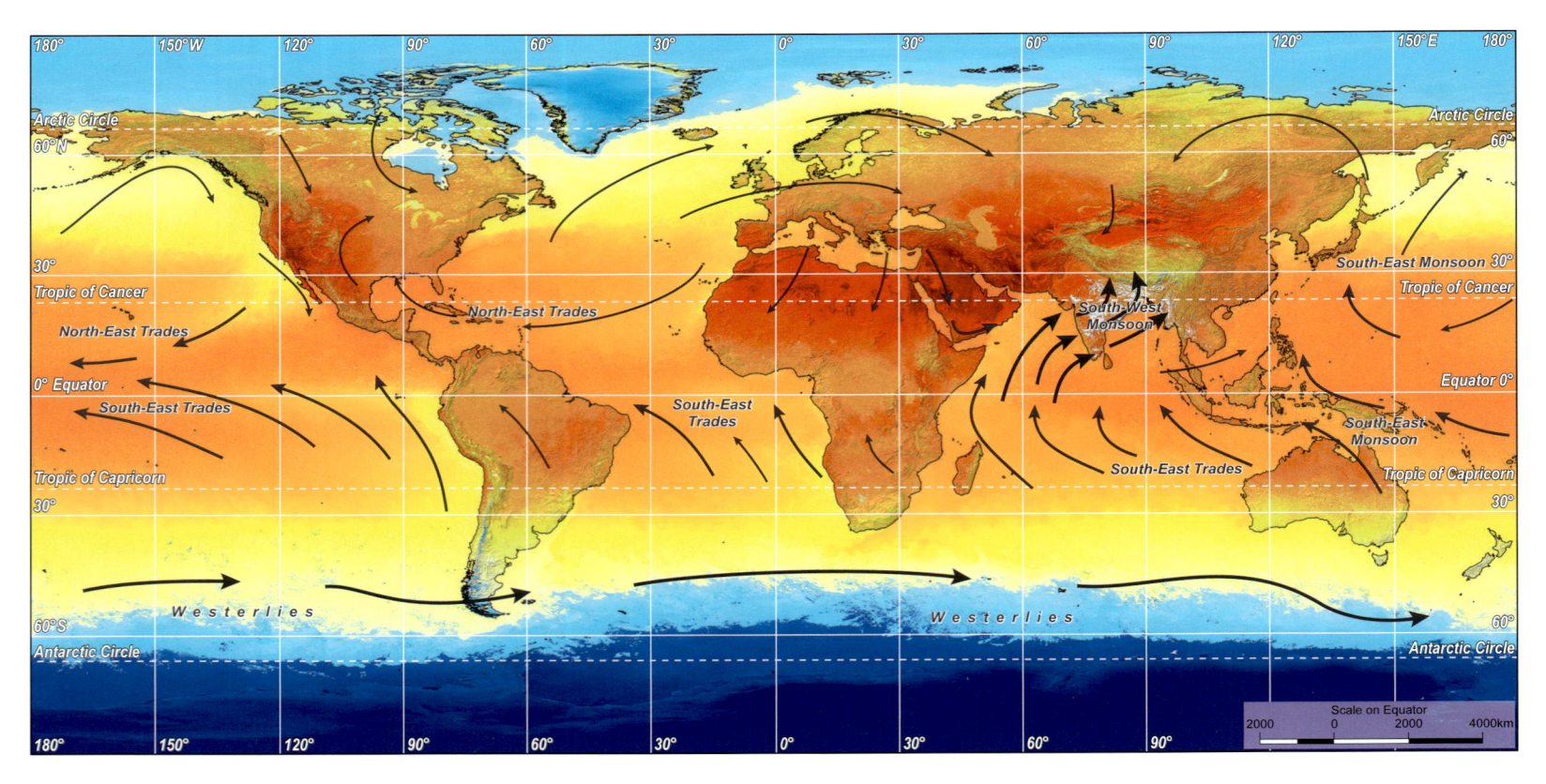

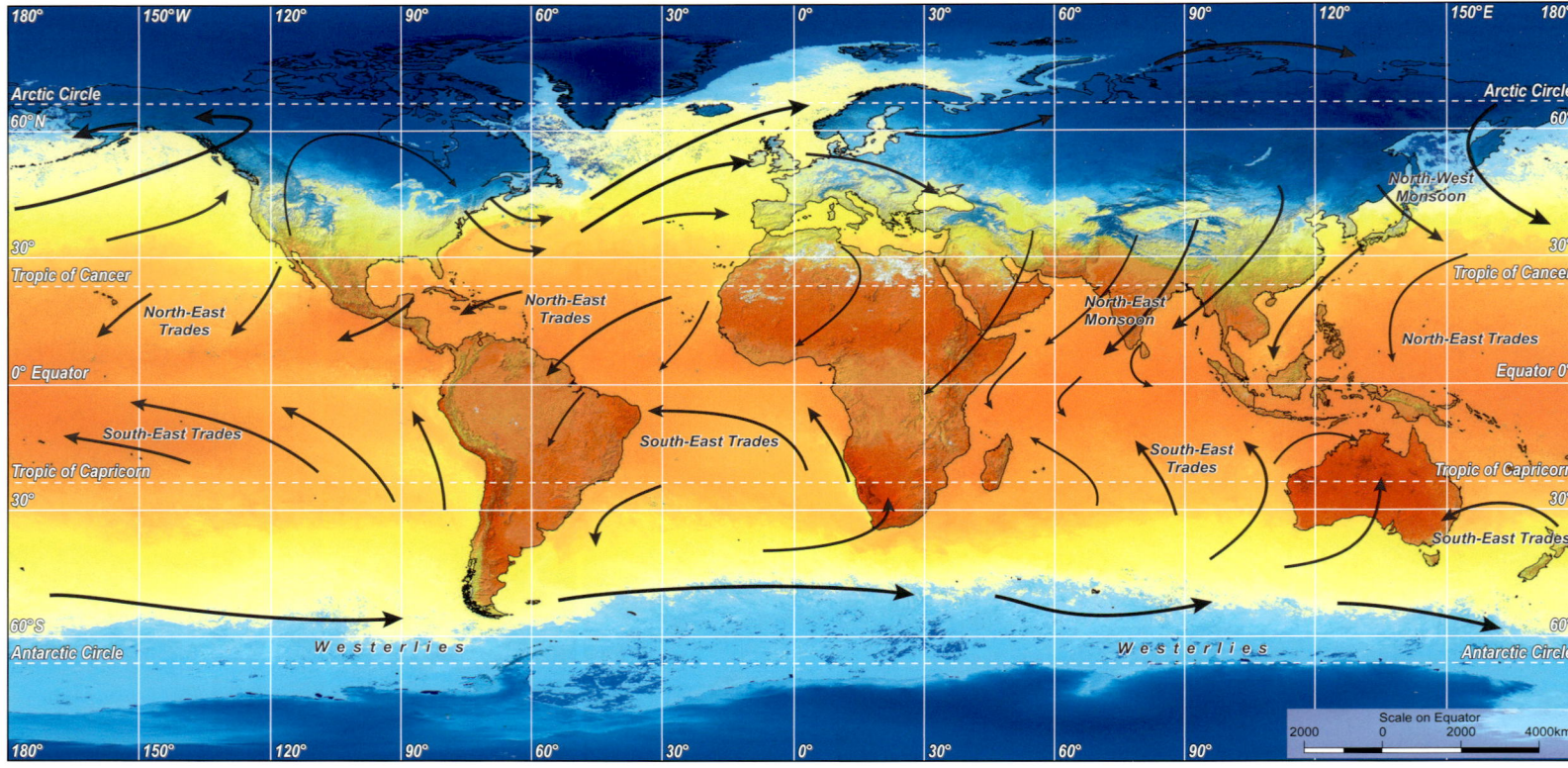

Temperature distribution

The temperature of the Earth's surface is determined by the balance of solar radiation transferred through the atmosphere to the ground and thermal radiation emitted from the surface. The surface temperature influences many processes involving energy transfer, and so plays an important role for all kinds of terrestrial life. The temperature varies seasonally and is influenced by latitude (length of day) as well as cloud and vegetation cover. Geographic relief causes temperature differences due to elevation as well as the diversion of energy transport through air and ocean currents.

The average land surface and sea surface temperature maps (Figs. 1 and 2) reveal large seasonal differences. The inclination of the Earth axis causes the length and intensity of solar irradiation to change during the year. This produces seasonal climates either side of the tropics that are defined by low temperatures in the winter and higher ones during the summer months. The tropics have a diurnal climate. Here, solar irradiation is fairly constant throughout the year so that the variation is larger between day and night than between seasons. The largest amplitudes can be found in the deserts where daytime temperatures of 50 degrees Celsius contrast with nighttime temperatures that can drop below freezing point.

The maps also show that sea surface temperatures are more homogenous. Land surfaces can warm up quickly but also lose warmth more easily. Water surfaces increase their temperature more slowly, but they can also store warmth for longer. This explains why ocean currents, such as the Gulf Stream, play a significant role for the temperatures of bordering land surfaces.

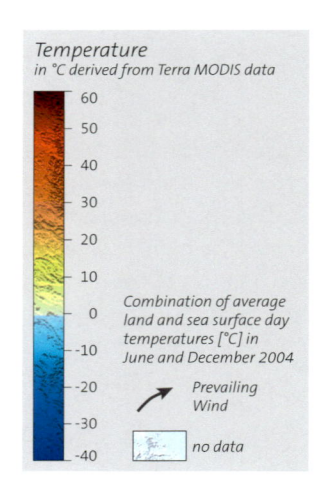

Temperature in °C derived from Terra MODIS data

Combination of average land and sea surface day temperatures [°C] in June and December 2004

Prevailing Wind

no data

1 – June 2004.   2 – Dec. 2004.

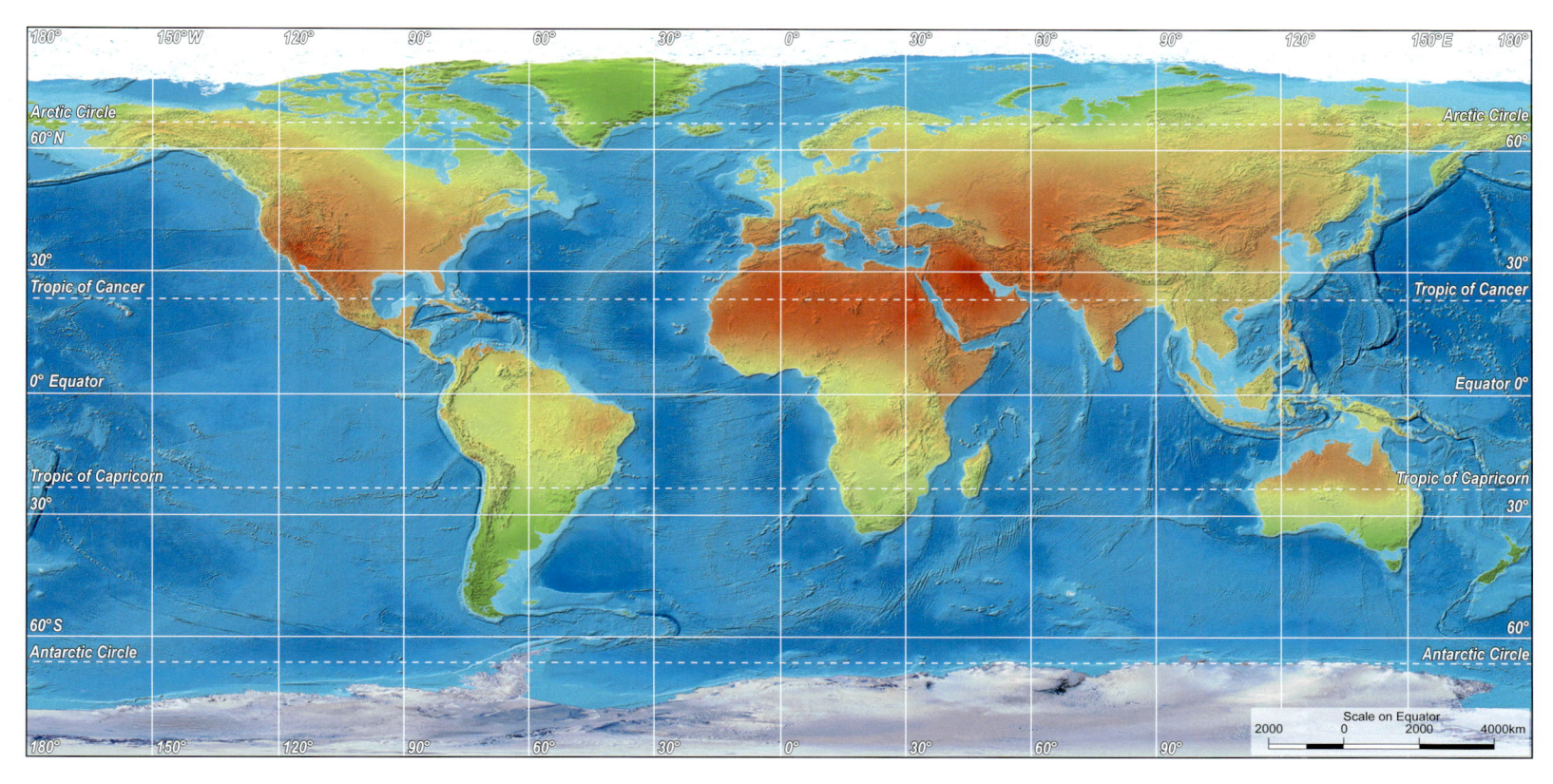

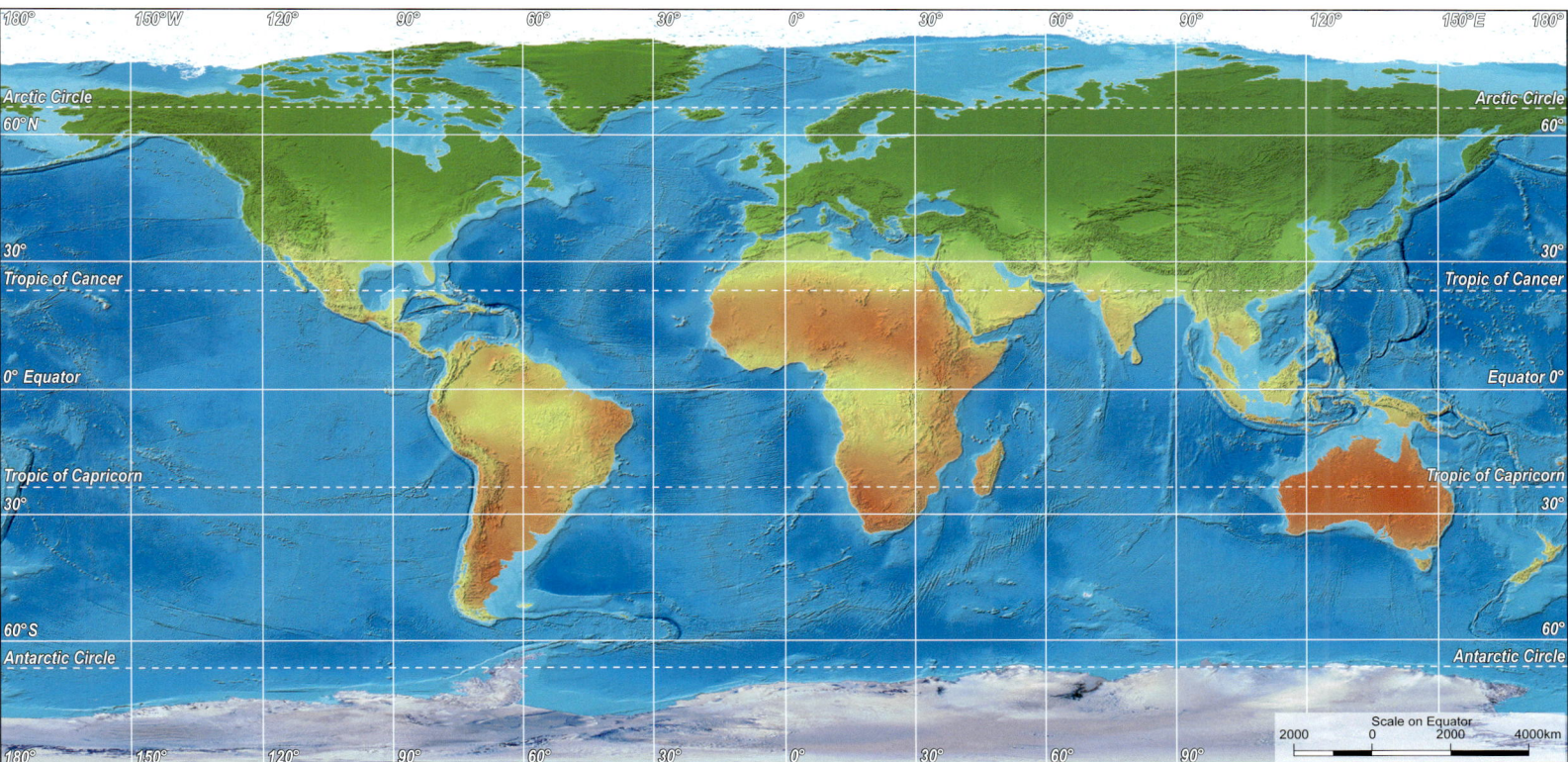

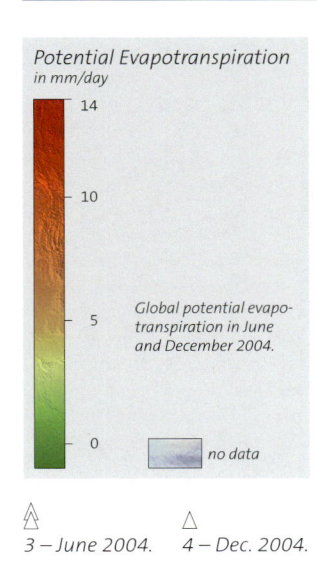

Evapotranspiration

Evapotranspiration is the sum of the evaporation from flora and fauna (transpiration) and of the evaporation from water surfaces. In general terms, evapotranspiration is the opposite of precipitation. The encompassing air takes up the water released by evapotranspiration, later on this water comes back to Earth by rainfall. The most influential factors are water content of the ground, vegetation intensity and its species composition, near-surface temperatures, the temperatures of the ground and water surfaces, air moisture, wind conditions at ground level, and the intensity of solar irradiation.

Evapotranspiration is a significant variable of the water cycle and of global climate. Water can only be precipitated if it has been taken up by the atmosphere via evaporation before. Evaporation is also important on a local level, especially for farming. In addition to the larger amounts of water needed for irrigation, also salinity is a problem in many arid areas where evaporation is more intense. Evaporation removes only water, causing minerals and salts dissolved in the water to remain in the ground and increasing their concentration.

The potential evapotranspiration, as depicted in the two global maps on this page (Figs. 3 and 4), shows the theoretical evaporation potential assuming a ground fully saturated with water. The highest potential evaporation rates can be found in the world's deserts, as vegetation is lowest here and solar irradiation is particularly high. High potential evaporation does not everywhere lead to high evaporation. Only water that exists can be evaporated, therefore low precipitation in arid regions results in much lower evaporation than the potential evaporation allows for.

Potential Evapotranspiration in mm/day

Global potential evapotranspiration in June and December 2004.

3 – June 2004.　　4 – Dec. 2004.

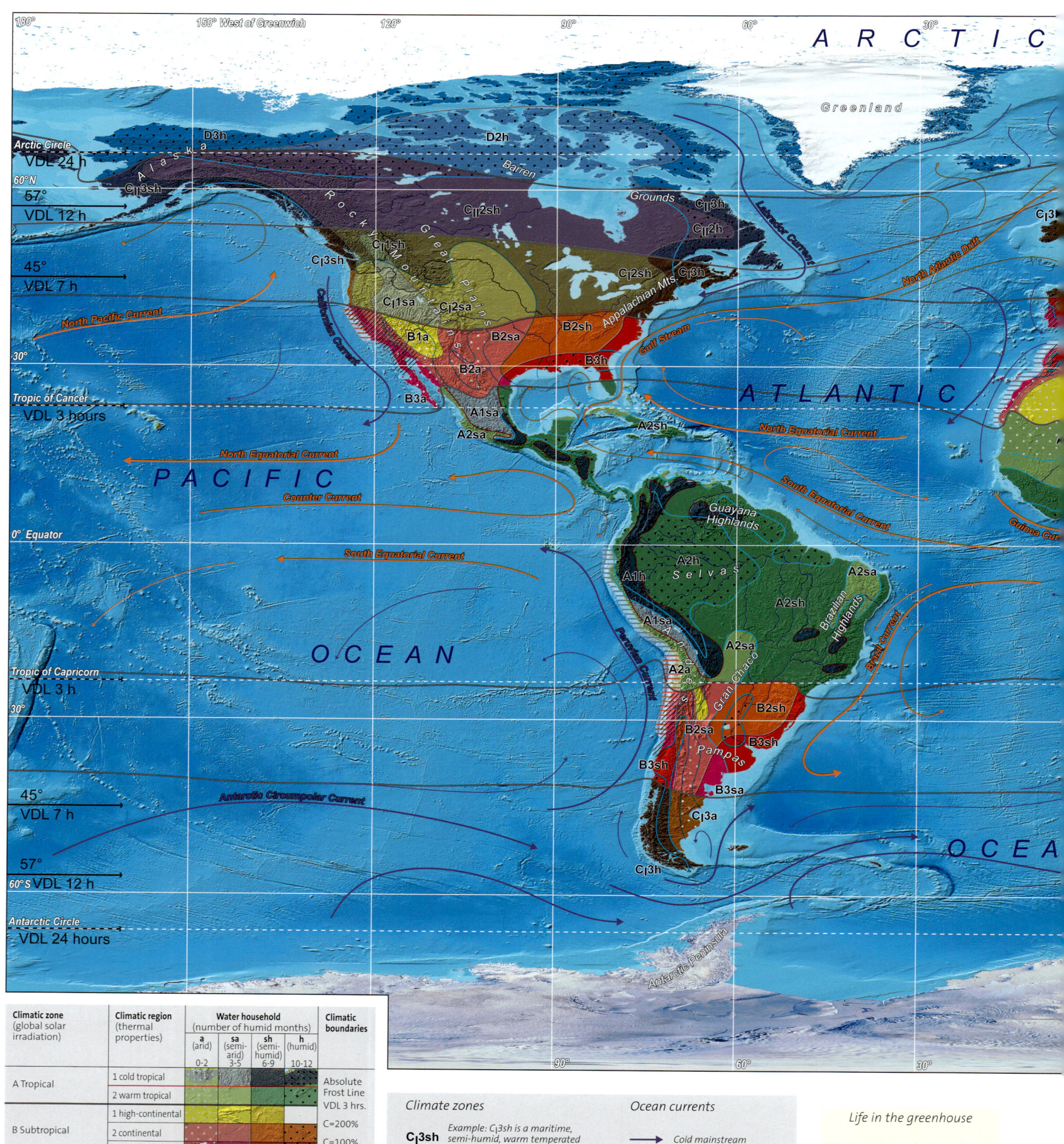

1 – Global climate zones acc. Lauer/Frankenberg with the main ocean currents.

Climatic zone (global solar irradiation)	Climatic region (thermal properties)		Water household (number of humid months)				Climatic boundaries
			a (arid) 0-2	sa (semi-arid) 3-5	sh (semi-humid) 6-9	h (humid) 10-12	
A Tropical	1 cold tropical						Absolute Frost Line
	2 warm tropical						VDL 3 hrs.
B Subtropical	1 high-continental						C=200%
	2 continental						C=100%
	3 maritime						VDL 12 hrs.
C Temperate	warm temperate I	1 high-continental					C=200%
		2 continental					C=100%
		3 maritime					VDL 12 hrs.
	cool temperate II	1 high-continental					C=200%
		2 continental					C=100%
		3 maritime					VDL 24 hrs.
D Polar regions	1 high-continental						C=200%
	2 continental						C=100%
	3 maritime						Snow Line
	Glaciers						

Climate zones

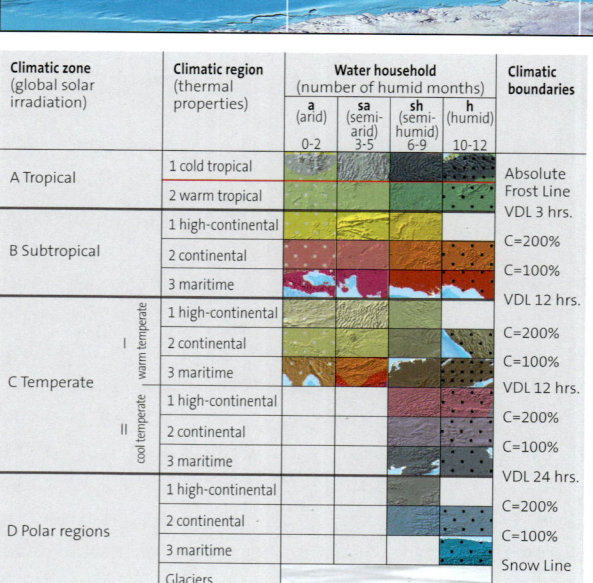

C₁3sh Example: C_I3sh is a maritime, semi-humid, warm temperated climate

$\frac{57°}{VDL\ 12\ h}$ Yearly variation of day length (VDL) in hours (solar climatic boundary)

― Thermally adapted climatic boundary with influences of mountains and sea currents taken into account

C Degree of continentality (in %) as measure of the annual temperature variations

--- Humid months: precipitation > evaporation from the landscape

▧ Region of subtropical winter rain

≡ Coastal fogs (winter/summer)

Ocean currents

→ Cold mainstream
→ Cold current
→ Warm mainstream
→ Warm current

Life in the greenhouse

The term 'greenhouse effect', which now seems to be used with negative connotations only, was what made life possible on our planet in the first place. Without the greenhouse effect, the average temperatures on Earth would be around -18 °C. However, humans have boosted the effect by burning fossil fuels and clearing the

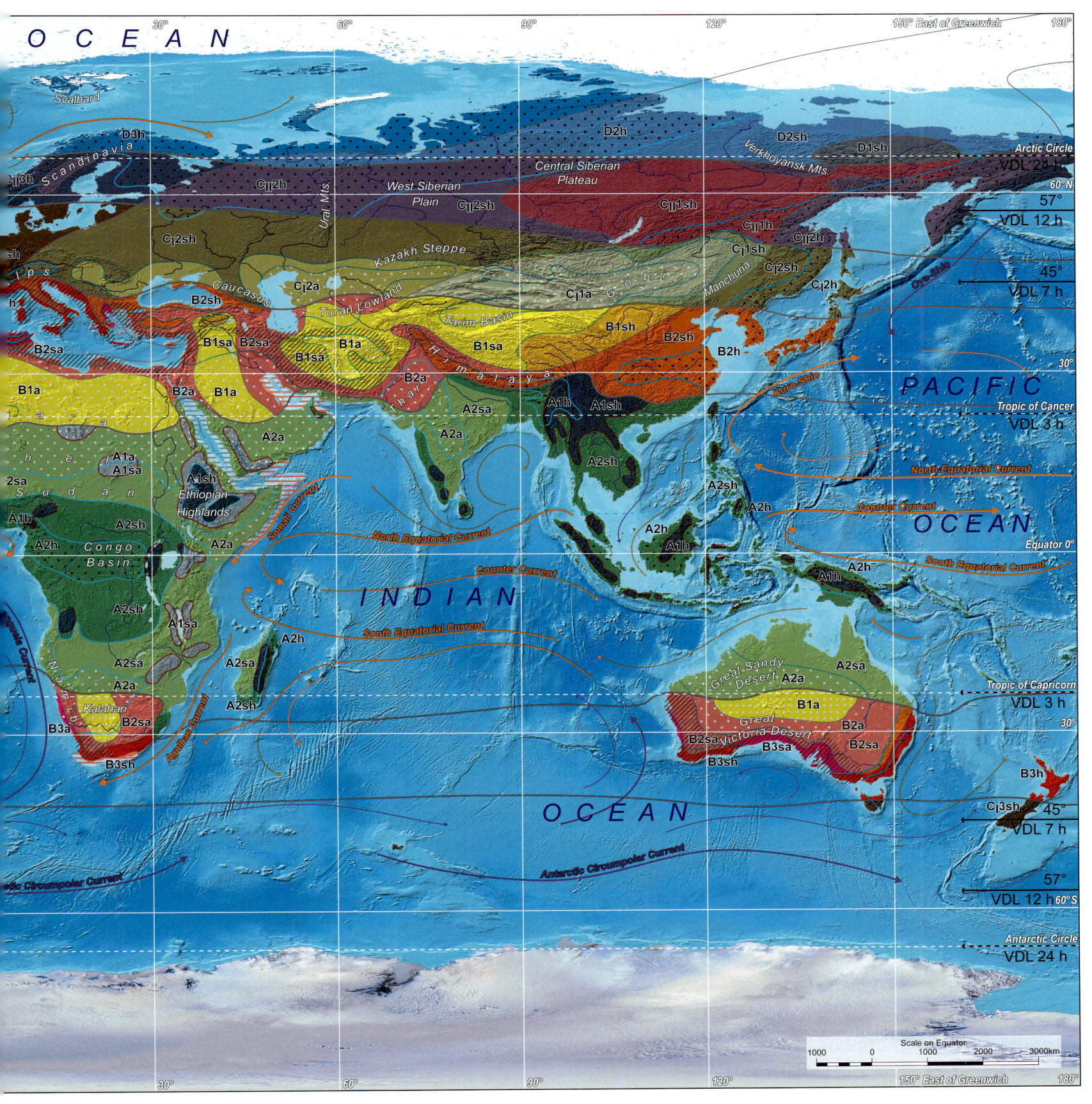

Climate zones of the world

The Earth's climate is influenced by a large number of factors. Latitude is one parameter that has a considerable influence on temperature. The further a location from the equator, the lower its average temperature. The distance from large water bodies (continental climate) has an additional strong effect on climate. Land surfaces warm up and cool down more quickly than seas, which in turn store heat better. This explains why coastal regions have a smaller temperature amplitude than areas in the centre of a continent. Summers are colder and winters milder along the coast, and summers are hotter and winters colder further inland.

Areas with similar climatic conditions are grouped together as being in the same climate zone. Lauer and Frankenberg (1987) split the Earth up into four basic climate zones: the tropics, the subtropics, the mid-latitudes and the polar regions.

Mountain ranges (e.g. Himalaya, Andes, Alps) act as climatic barriers and have a strong effect on the zoning of individual climate zones. Ocean currents that are driven by wind systems, e.g. the Gulf Stream and the Humboldt Current, play a crucial role for the global climate. They store and transport energy. Their influence causes deviations in an otherwise parallel arrangement of climate zones along the latitudes.

forests that reduced the concentration of carbon dioxide by converting it to oxygen. The Intergovernmental Panel on Climate Change (IPCC) calculates that if carbon dioxide emissions double, temperatures will increase by 4.5 °C. This would make much of the planet uninhabitable – either as a result of coastal flooding due to the melting polar ice caps or as a result of increased desertification.

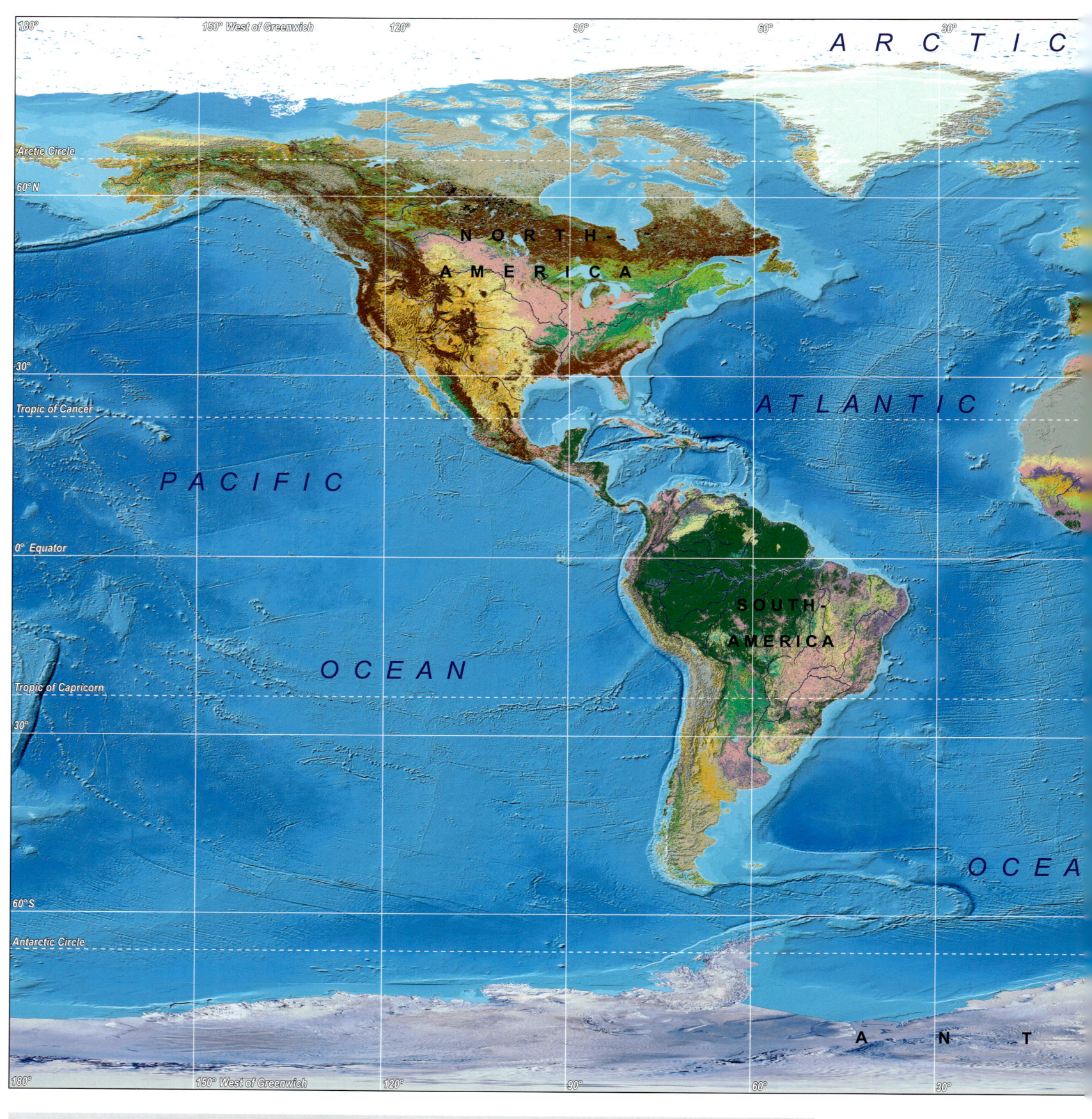

Global land cover and land use

- Snow and ice
- Water surface
- Sparse herbaceous or sparse shrub cover
- Tree cover, conifer, deciduous
- Tree cover, mixed-leave type
- Tree cover, broad-leaved, deciduous, closed
- Tree cover, conifer, evergreen
- Tree cover, burnt
- Mosaic: tree cover / other natural vegetation
- Bare ground
- Artificial surface and associated area
- Cultivated and managed area
- Herbaceous cover, closed-open
- Regularly flooded shrub and/or herbaceous cover
- Tree cover, broad-leaved, deciduous, open
- Tree cover, broad-leaved, evergreen
- Mosaic: cropland / tree cover / other natural vegetation
- Mosaic: cropland / shrub and/or grass cover
- Shrub cover, closed-open, evergreen
- Shrub cover, closed-open, deciduous
- Tree cover, regularly flooded, saline water
- Tree cover, regularly flooded, fresh water
- no data

1 – The global distribution of land cover and land use largely depends on climate zones and altitudes.

Water consumption

The types of crop not only depend on the climatic conditions but also on the amount of water available. Incredible amounts of water are required to grow the products we consume in our daily lives.

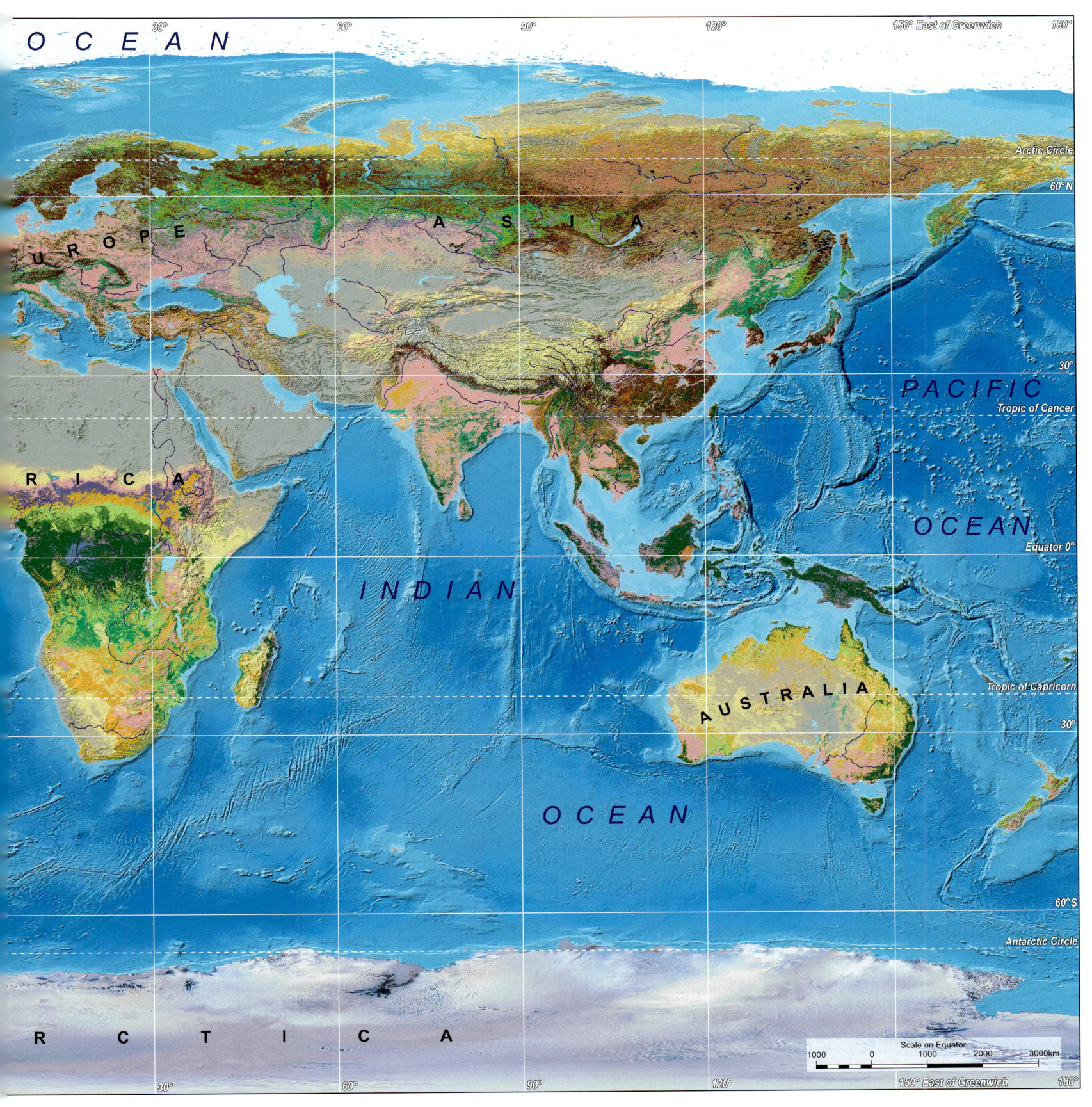

Land cover and land use

The vegetation zones of the Earth are arranged in zonal bands that run almost parallel with the lines of latitude. They are primarily determined by climate, topography and the distribution of land mass. In this context, also the distribution of temperature and precipitation plays a major role. Each zone has a characteristic composition of vegetation types and plant species. Generally speaking, we distinguish between eight different vegetation zones. Working towards the Equator from the poles, we cross tundra, boreal coniferous forest, deciduous broadleaf forest, steppes, Mediterranean scrub, deserts, savannah, and rainforest.

The natural land cover and type of land use have long been closely linked. Areas that are actually naturally well-suited to agriculture are rare. As a result, humans have progressively tried to reclaim more and more land for agriculture. As such, deserts are irrigated, forests are cut down and wetlands are drained. Many of these areas are threatened by soil degradation, desertification and nutrient depletion, making it necessary to clear more and more land for agriculture.

The scarcity of agricultural land will require the strict long-term use of sustainable methods and practices in order to protect the soils, the forests, and, more generally, the Earth's climate.

Amount of water required to grow various foodstuffs

- *1 kg rice: 3,000 l*
- *1 kg bread: 2,400 l*
- *1 kg maize: 900 l*
- *1 orange: 500 l*
- *1 cup of coffee: 124 l*

In arid regions, the land must be irrigated if it is to be used for farming. This method often harms the soil quality.

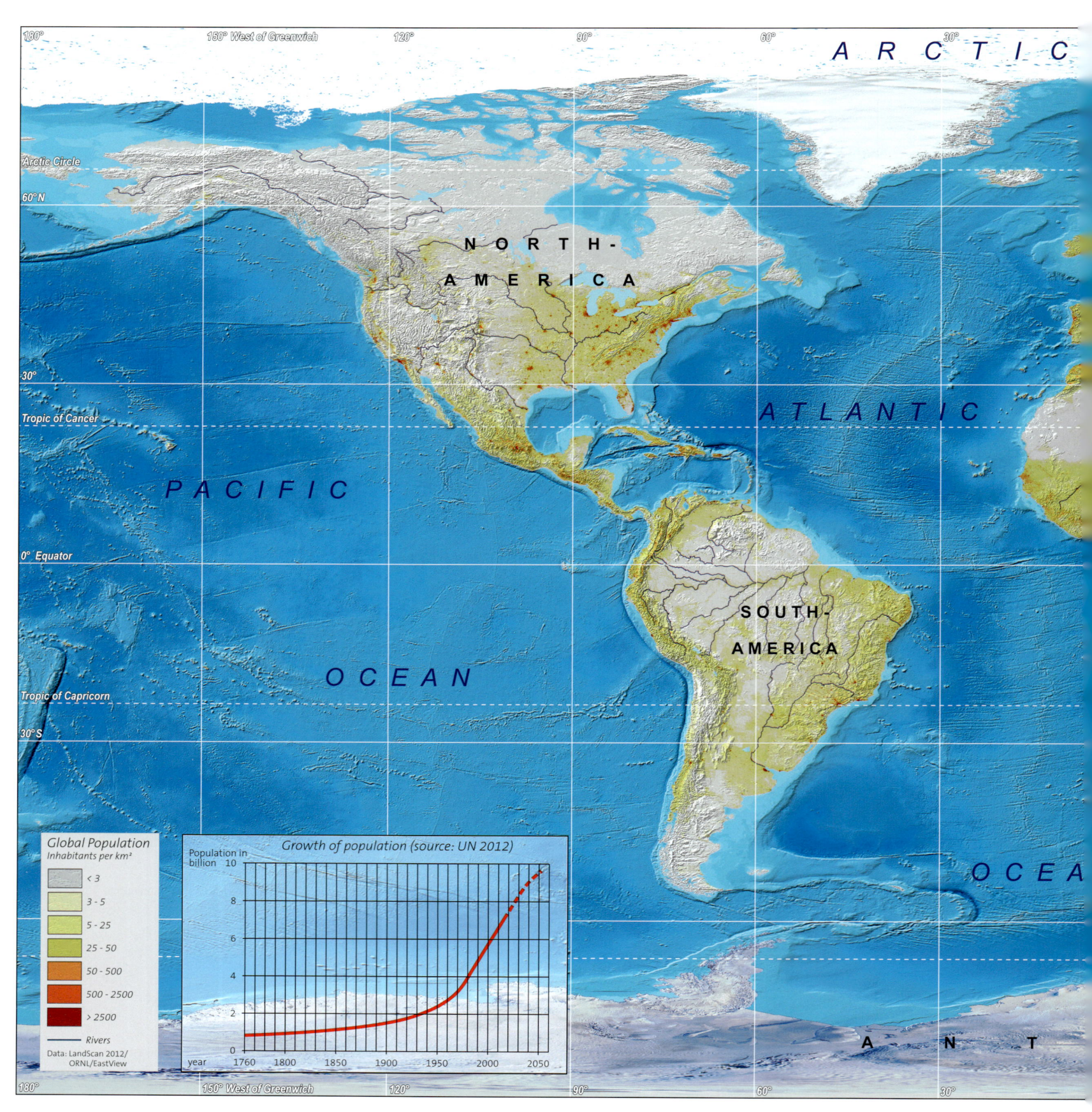

Global Population
Inhabitants per km²
- < 3
- 3 - 5
- 5 - 25
- 25 - 50
- 50 - 500
- 500 - 2500
- \> 2500
- —— Rivers

Data: LandScan 2012 / ORNL/EastView

Growth of population (source: UN 2012)

Optimal population development	Declining population	Strong demographic increase
New Zeeland 2003 U.S. Census Bureau	**Germany 2003** U.S. Census Bureau	**Nigeria 2003** U.S. Census Bureau
male 1.962.310 / female 1.988.997	male 40.368.387 / female 42.029.939	male 62.106.476 / female 60.689.562

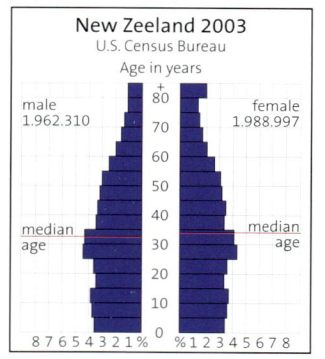

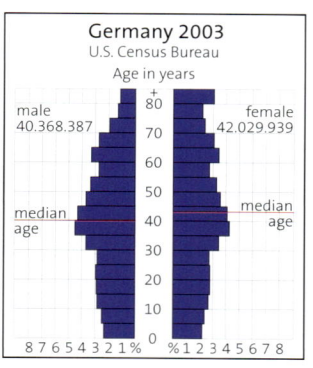

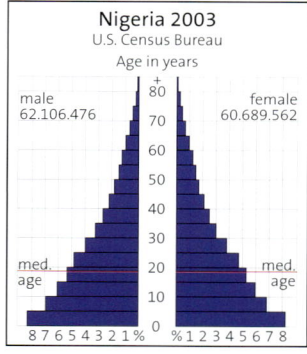

△
1 – Global population distribution and growth trend.

◁
2 – Age distribution pyramids, 5-year age groups in per cent.

▷
3 – The world at night – light sources as seen by DMSP.

Population distribution

Within a period of just a few thousand years, humans have dispersed across the entire surface of the Earth, making homo sapiens in a sense the most successful species on the planet. However, population distribution and population density show huge local differences depending on the cultural area and habitat (Figs. 1 and 2).

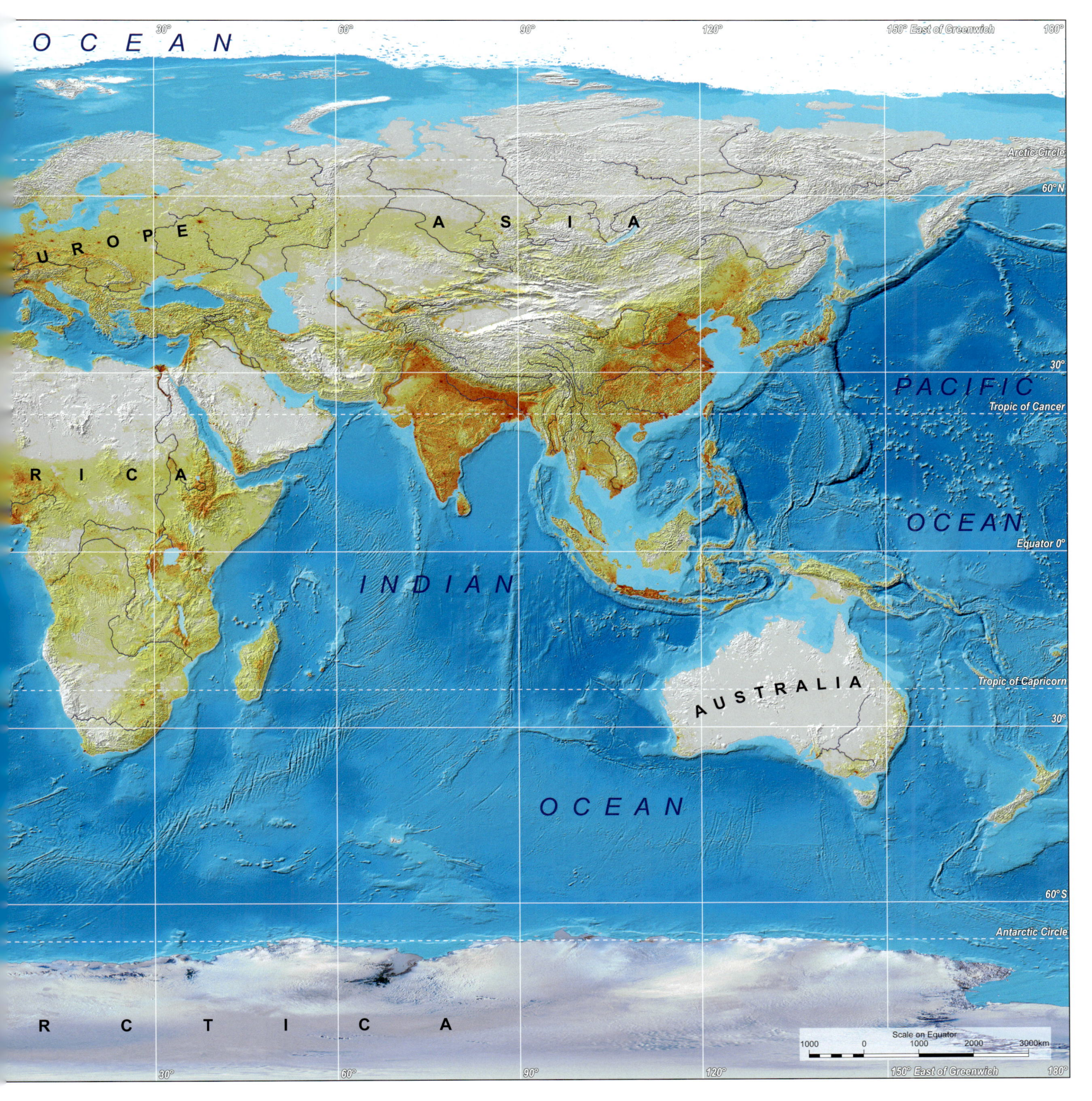

People are dependent on water and, as a result, have often built their settlements near water. Even today, the most densely populated regions are to be found within a strip measuring 80 to 150 kilometres wide along coasts, and along rivers, such as the Indus, Ganges or the Yangtze. while the inhospitable polar regions, tundra and deserts are generally unpopulated. It is interesting to compare the map of population distribution with a satellite image of the Earth at night (Fig. 3). The lights are not only related to the population density but also to the level of development of a region, with whole areas left in the dark.

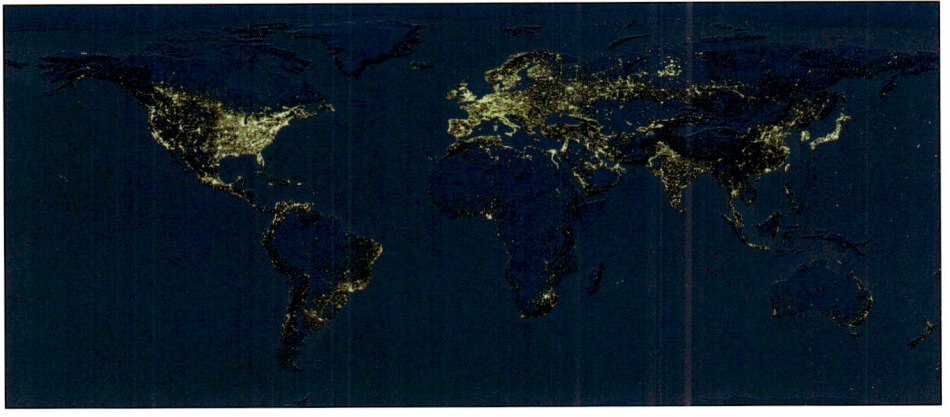

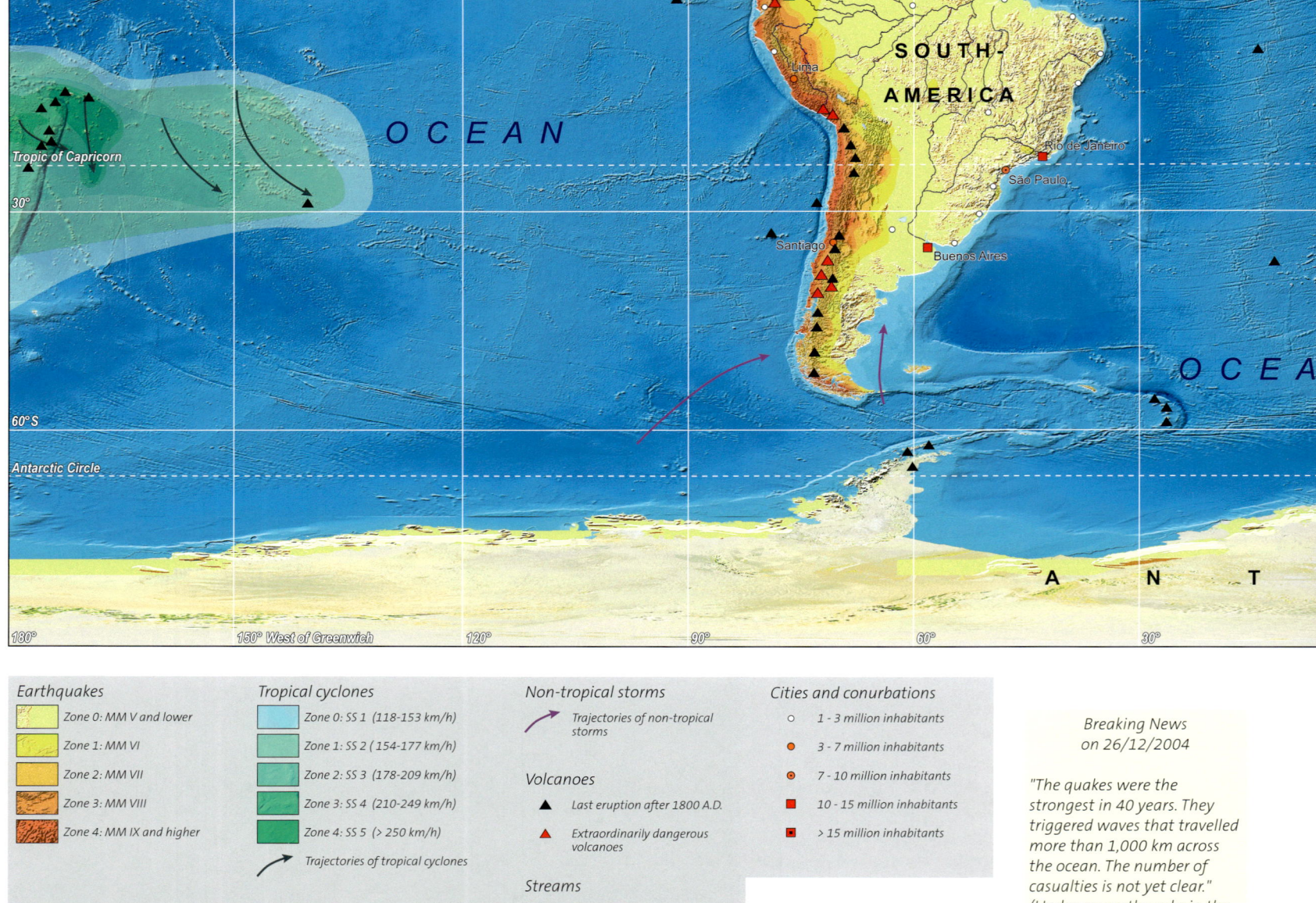

Earthquakes
- Zone 0: MM V and lower
- Zone 1: MM VI
- Zone 2: MM VII
- Zone 3: MM VIII
- Zone 4: MM IX and higher

Tropical cyclones
- Zone 0: SS 1 (118-153 km/h)
- Zone 1: SS 2 (154-177 km/h)
- Zone 2: SS 3 (178-209 km/h)
- Zone 3: SS 4 (210-249 km/h)
- Zone 4: SS 5 (> 250 km/h)
- Trajectories of tropical cyclones

Non-tropical storms
- Trajectories of non-tropical storms

Volcanoes
- Last eruption after 1800 A.D.
- Extraordinarily dangerous volcanoes

Streams
- Main rivers

Source: Münchener Rückversicherungs-Gesellschaft

Cities and conurbations
- 1 - 3 million inhabitants
- 3 - 7 million inhabitants
- 7 - 10 million inhabitants
- 10 - 15 million inhabitants
- > 15 million inhabitants

Maximum intensity of earthquakes (MM: Modified Mercalli scale) with a excess probablility of 10% within 50 years (corresponds to a repetition period of 475 years at average substrate conditions).

Maximum intensity of tropical cyclones (SS: Saffir Simpson hurricane scale) with a mean excess probability of 10% within 10 years (corresponds to a repetition period of 100 years).

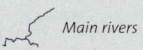

1 – Global map of natural hazards.

Breaking News on 26/12/2004

"The quakes were the strongest in 40 years. They triggered waves that travelled more than 1,000 km across the ocean. The number of casualties is not yet clear." (Undersea earthquake in the Indian Ocean, which caused the Indian Ocean Tsunami).

Natural hazards

In many regions of the Earth, natural disasters are a major and often also frequent risk to the population (Fig. 1). Tropical storms are the most common risk, often going hand-in-hand with major flooding, and they can devastate large populated areas. They appear in summer and early autumn both north and south of the Equator. From there, they initially travel from east to west until they are diverted to the north or south by the Coriolis effect. The frequency of tropical storms has increased significantly in recent years. One reason for this is global warming, as the higher water temperatures mean that more energy is available to feed these storms.

The risks of earthquakes and volcanoes depend on the movements within the Earth and on plate tectonics. Both earthquakes and volcanoes primarily occur at the weak spots of the Earth's crust, with seismic and volcanic events being particularly frequent around the Pacific Ring of Fire. Underwater earthquakes sometimes result in tsunamis, which threaten the coastlines. Tsunamis can also be triggered by landslides into the sea.

Major natural disasters aside, also local catastrophes such as landslides, mudslides, avalanches and floods frequently occur in many regions of the world. Although the high-risk zones are usually well known, they still put people and their property at risk.

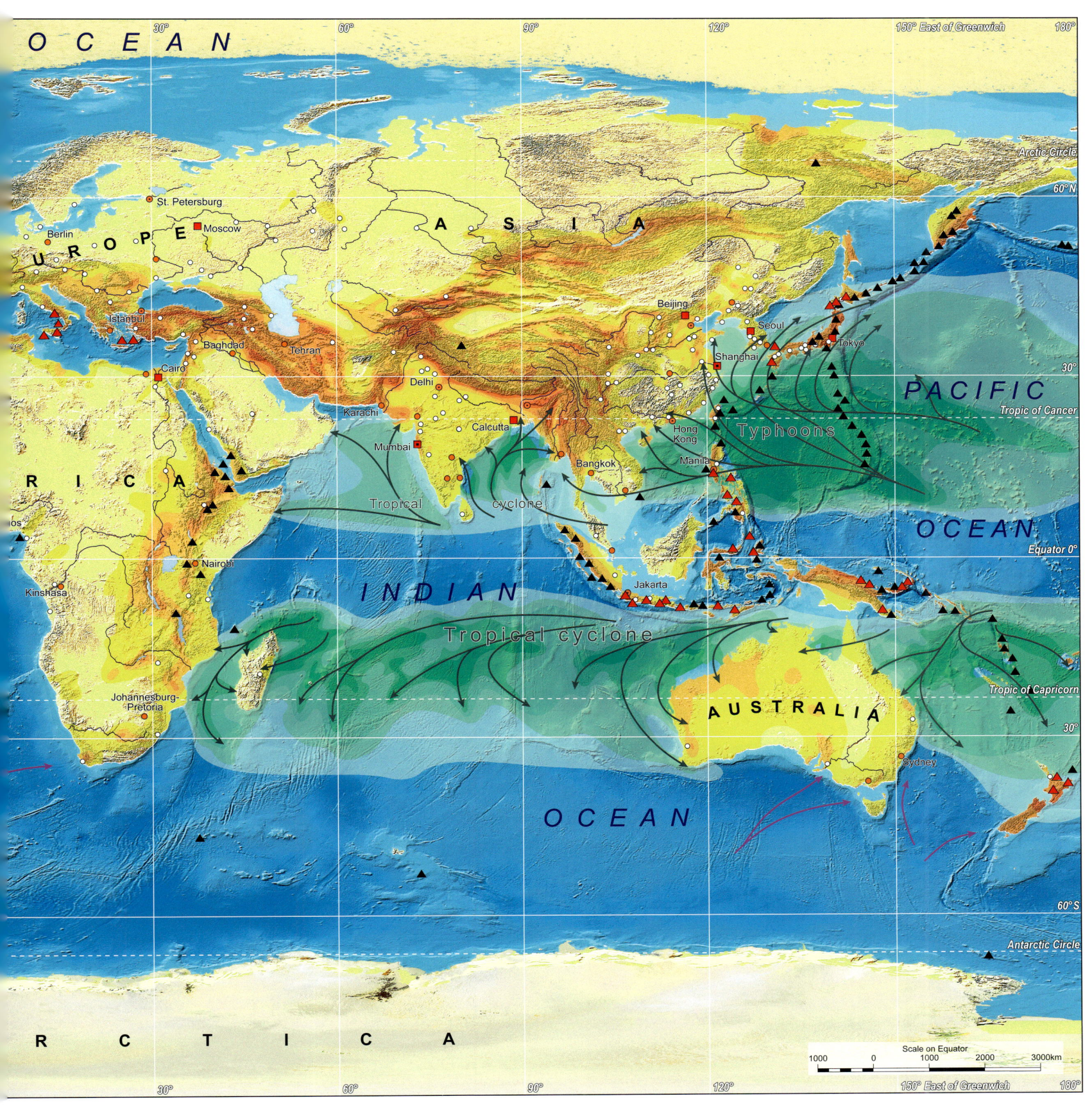

Breaking News on 01/09/2005

"The devastating conditions in the crisis-hit region of the US are worse than anyone expected. In the wake of Hurricane Katrina, the South has been plunged into chaos. The people have no food, anarchy rules the streets and fears of the spread of disease are growing."

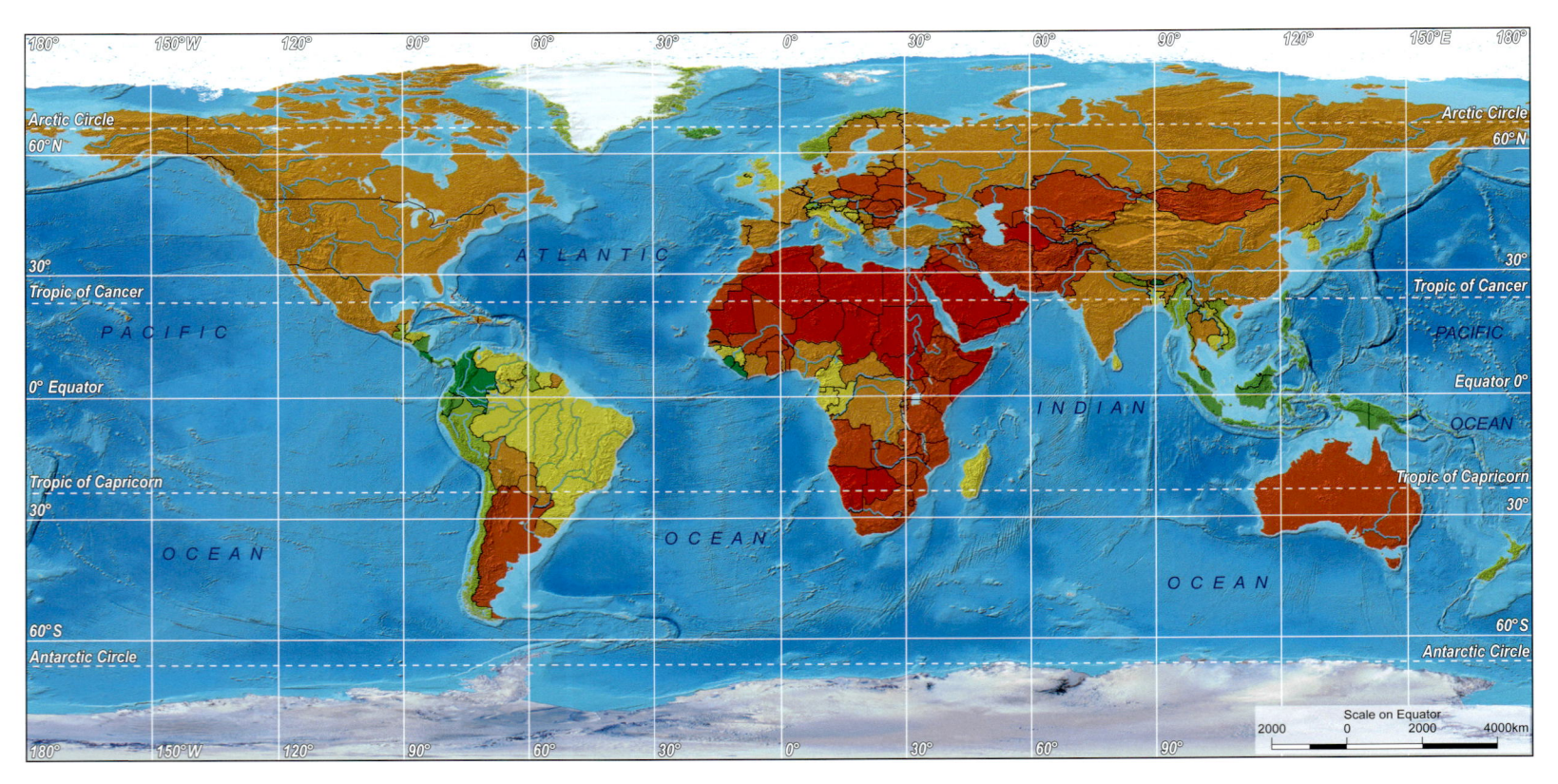

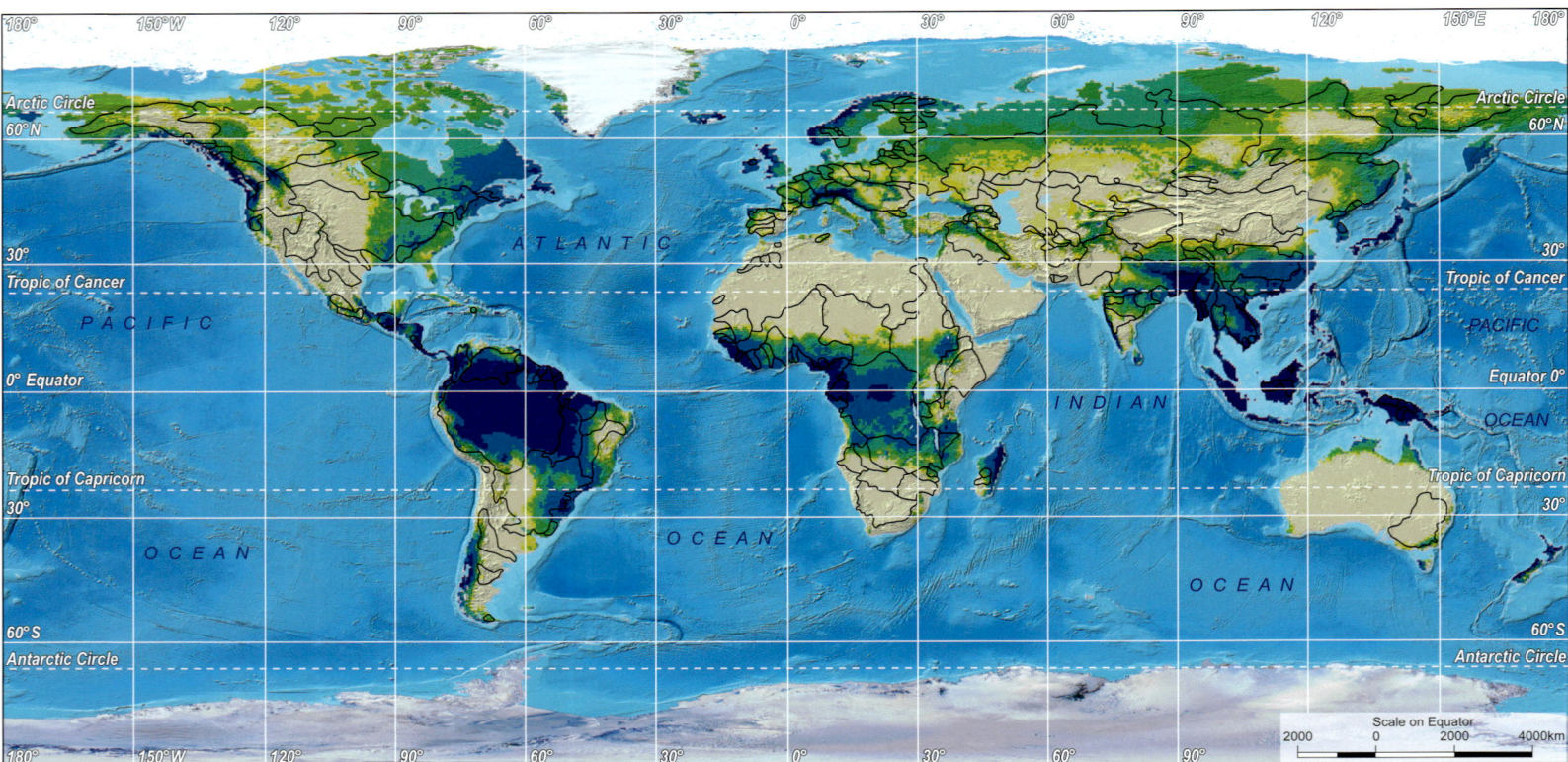

Availability and consumption of water

The enormous variations in climatic and geological conditions in the Earth's different geographical regions have a huge impact on the amount of freshwater available. The range extends from largely arid expanses in the great deserts to large surpluses of water in the tropical rainforests. When compared on a country basis, the amount of annual precipitation ranges from 30 litres per square metre in Libya to almost 3,000 litres per square metre in the equatorial island state of São Tomé and Principe (Figs. 1 and 2).

When it comes to extracting water, we distinguish between renewable resources, which are constantly topped up by rainfall or other inflow, and resources that are cut off from this kind of replenishment. Important examples of these kinds of non-renewable resources are fossil water aquifers in dry regions, and also some lakes and inland seas and glacial ice bodies. Not only does water have to be available in the first place; its quality is of decisive importance. That quality can be degraded by bacteria, acidity and salinity, or by high concentrations of chemicals such as pesticides and fertilisers. Often, water can only be made usable by complex processing.

For long periods of time, human development depended on water being directly available. Only later were engineers of the first great civilisations able to provide settlements located at a distance from natural water sources with a sufficient supply of a suitable quality. In doing so, they laid the foundations for the development of larger cities. Today's major cities and extensively irrigated farmland would not be viable without the various and

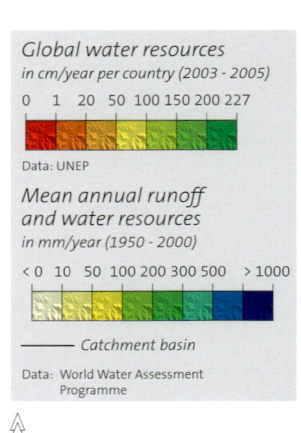

Global water resources
in cm/year per country (2003 - 2005)
0 1 20 50 100 150 200 227

Data: UNEP

Mean annual runoff and water resources
in mm/year (1950 - 2000)
< 0 10 50 100 200 300 500 > 1000

—— Catchment basin

Data: World Water Assessment Programme

1 – The uneven distribution of freshwater resources

2 – Overground water runoff

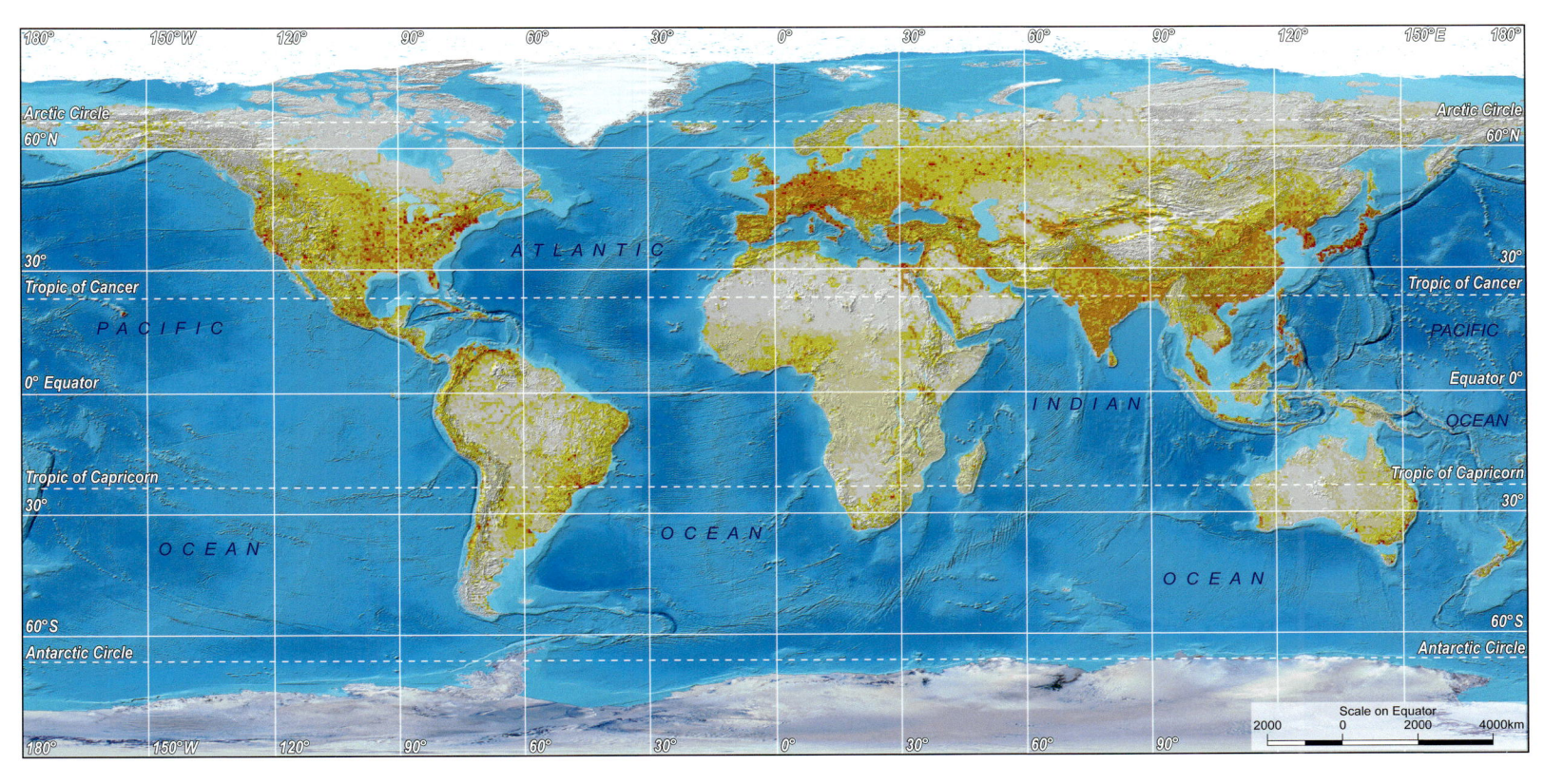

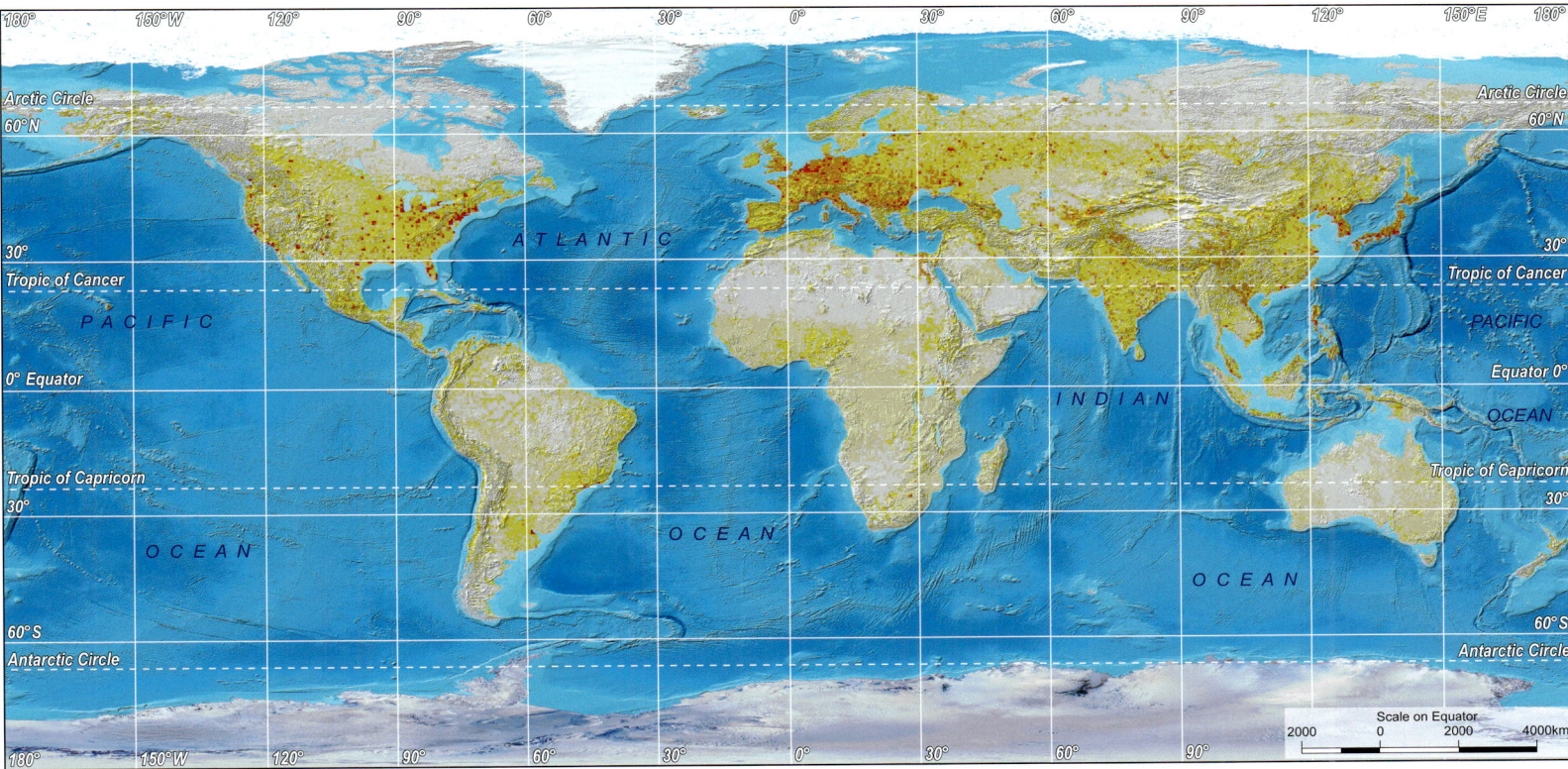

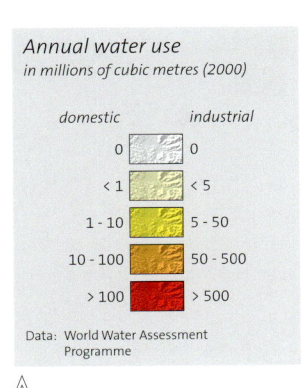

Annual water use
in millions of cubic metres (2000)

domestic	industrial
0	0
< 1	< 5
1 - 10	5 - 50
10 - 100	50 - 500
> 100	> 500

Data: World Water Assessment Programme

3 – Annual private water consumption

4 – Annual industrial water consumption

complex facilities required by our water infrastructure, such as efficient water mains and wastewater treatment plants. It would be just as impossible to sustain them without tapping into new water resources, such as through seawater desalination plants.

The major geographical differences in the availability of water are reflected in the distribution of the population and thus in its use of water resources, although the level of economic development of a region also plays a role, in addition to population density. Areas that are more economically developed have significantly higher per capita water consumption than less economically developed regions. This goes for both industrial and commercial water consumption (Fig. 4) and private water consumption (Fig. 3), as higher standards of living generally go hand in hand with higher water consumption for hygiene, gardening and similar purposes, and the water can also be distributed via a more efficient infrastructure. On the other hand, water scarcity is a serious problem in many conurbations with growing populations, restricting the quality of life for the people who live there and the chances for development of that region.

An important concept for the evaluation of water resources and consumption is known as 'virtual water'. Virtual water consumption takes into account not only water that is used directly but also the water used to manufacture imported goods. While virtual water consumption in Asia is around 1,400 litres per person per day, it amounts to 4,000 litres per person per day for Europe and North America. Rather like the global trade in CO_2 emissions, virtual water will in the future form the basis for offsetting the consumption of natural resources.

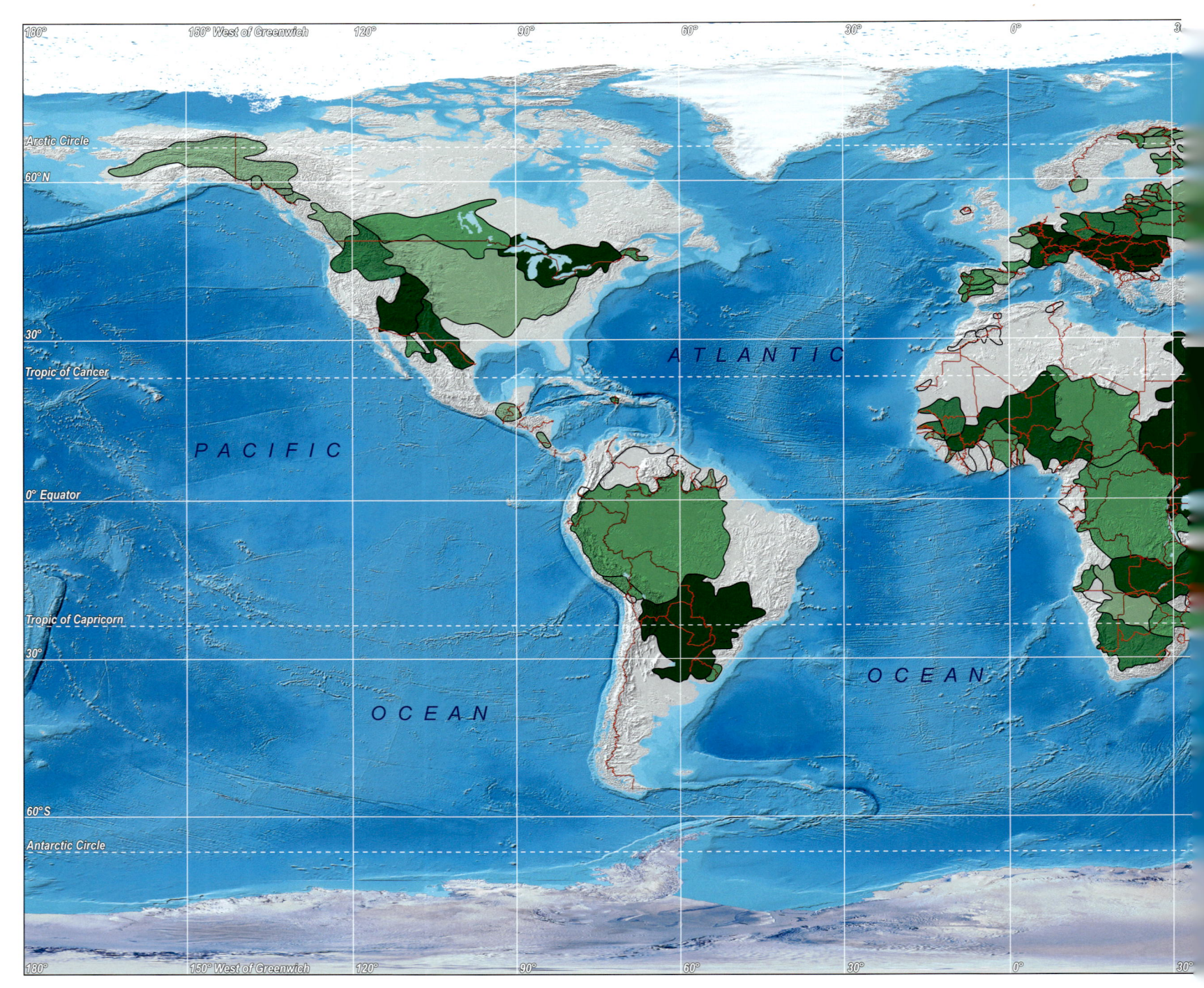

	Area of the catchment basin (in km²)	Average population density (per km²)	Neighbouring countries	Number of agreements
North and South America				
Amazon	6,145,186	3.66	7	6
Colorado	703,148	9.32	2	23
Columbia	657,501	9.06	2	8
Mississippi	3,202,185	21.27	2	1
Rio Grande	607,965	17.76	2	8
Lake Titicaca	193,090	8.19	3	6
Europe				
Danube	795,656	102.02	18	45
Duero	98,258	41.74	2	6
Elbe	148,919	168.99	4	7
Garonne	53,540	62.14	3	3

	Area of the catchment basin (in km²)	Average population density (per km²)	Neighbouring countries	Number of agreements
Europe				
Oder	124,164	120.35	3	4
Rhine/Meuse	198,735	318.61	8	46
Vistula	180,156	137.08	5	3
Volga	1,410,951	43.02	2	1
Africa				
Congo	3,730,881	14.88	9	4
Lake Chad	2,497,738	11.49	8	3
Niger	2,261,741	31.4	10	14
Nile	3,254,853	46.2	11	25
Okavango	721,258	1.95	4	2
Orange	941,351	9.95	4	8

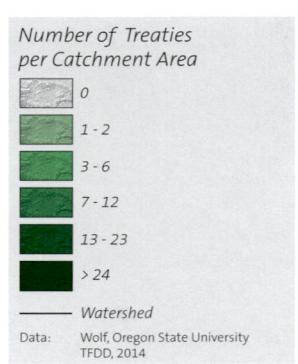

Number of Treaties per Catchment Area
- 0
- 1 - 2
- 3 - 6
- 7 - 12
- 13 - 23
- > 24
- Watershed

Data: Wolf, Oregon State University TFDD, 2014

△
1 – Number of international treaties per catchment basin

◁▷
2 – Information on a selection of river catchment basins with the number of international treaties assigned to them (source: International River Basin Register, TFDD, 2014).

WATER TREATIES

The demand for water resources and supply facilities has shown a dramatic rise during the past century.

	Area of the catchment basin (in km²)	Average population density (per km²)	Neighbouring countries	Number of agreements
Africa				
Senegal	419,575	9.54	4	11
Zambezi	1,332,412	18.03	8	13
Asia				
Brahmaputra	651,335	181.61	4	-
Euphrates/Tigris	765,742	57.17	4	7
Ganges	1,016,124	401.18	4*	16
Yellow River	944,970	156.43	1	-
Indus	1,138,800	802.57	5	9
Yangtze	1,722,193	214.09	1	-
Mekong	805,604	71.19	6	5
Ob	2,972,493	9.73	4	3

The demand for water resources and for water-related benefits has seen dramatic developments during the past century. While the world population has tripled, the demand for water has increased sevenfold. The water needs of growing cities for basic water supply and sanitation and the input needs of industry have entered into a difficult competitive relationship with more traditional water uses, especially agriculture, which, under pressure from growing populations, also needs more water for irrigation to meet growing demands for food in many regions of the world. At the same time, massive wastewater disposal has had serious consequences on the quality of surface waters and groundwater, and so have reduced their usability.

The waters of the Aral Sea in Central Asia and of Lake Chad in West Africa, shrinking for lack of adequate cooperation among the co-basin countries, exemplify the drama of the water crisis.

Unsustainable exploitation of water-related natural resources, in particular in the watershed areas in upstream countries, are causing serious problems of water runoff, in particular floods, groundwater recharge, the suspended load of soils and sands and, related to that, to the use of storage facilities in downstream countries. Climate change is altering evaporation and precipitation patterns and increasing the number of natural disasters, and having major impacts on the patterns of water availability and use. The past forty years have seen a growing awareness of the significance of the institutional framework for water resources management, focusing on reforming water law and water administration.

1 – As part of the 4th World Water Forum in Mexico in 2006, the then President of France, Jacques Chirac, emphasised via satellite link that a lack of access to drinking water and wastewater disposal may not only cause health crises but also political crises.

International water resources

Almost half of the Earth's land surface is covered by river basins, lakes and shallow groundwater aquifers shared by two or more sovereign states. Forty per cent of the world population lives within such basins. The UNESCO report, "Water for People – Water for Life", counts 263 major transboundary river basins, 59 in Africa, 53 in Asia and Oceania, 73 in Europe, 61 in Latin America and 17 in North America. A report of the United Nations Economic Commission for Europe, for instance, counts as many as 150 major transboundary rivers in Europe alone that form or cross borders between two or more countries. Added to those rivers are some 25 major transboundary and international lakes. Of the 192 member countries of the United Nations, 145 – representing more than 90 per cent of the world's population – share international water resources.

All major rivers of the world, such as the Nile, the Niger, the Senegal, the Indus, the Ganges, the Mekong, the St. Lawrence, the Colorado, the Amazon, Rio Paraná, the Rio de la Plata, the Rhine and the Danube flow across international boundaries. The international dimension of water may thus well be considered an issue for all of humankind. Of the 145 countries sharing transboundary waters, 21 lie entirely within the hydrologic boundaries of one or more international basins, while 33 countries have more than 95 per cent of their territory lying within one or more international basins. About two-thirds of the 263 transboundary basins are shared by only two countries. Nineteen river basins, however, are shared by five or more sovereign states. The Danube basin, for example, now takes in the territory of 18 countries.

The significance of the international dimension of water resources becomes very evident when the dependency of countries and their economies on those resources is considered. Egypt is known to be dependent on the waters of the Nile, 87 per cent of which rises in the Ethiopian highlands. The growing scarcity of water has also led to an increased use of groundwater resources. A recent report of the UN Economic Commission for Europe recognises more than 100 transboundary aquifer systems in Europe. Especially in countries with low precipitation, aquifers are vitally important. The interrelationship between surface and groundwater and the impact of upstream surface water management on downstream groundwater availability has now been included in the conceptualisation of international water law.

Water conflicts and hydro-diplomacy

Freshwater has, in fact, become central to national and regional development. Competition for these scarce resources will continue to grow, both with regard to the quantity as well as the quality of shared water resources. The question is how interstate relations can be structured and developed towards cooperation and how possible water-related conflicts can be avoided.

The issue of water wars has been discussed internationally in recent years. In 2001, UN Secretary General Kofi Annan stated that "fierce competition over fresh water may well become a source of conflict and wars in the future". Former World Bank Vice-President Ismail Serageldin said that while wars in the 20th century were over oil, wars of this century would be over water.

In fact, three cases have become known in recent years in Africa, Central Asia and in Latin America of countries considering military action against upstream countries or of even articulating threats of war against co-basin countries in order to underline the seriousness of their water claims. Water has no doubt become a potential element in and for conflicts. However, while water has been part of some conflicts during the recent past, the last "water war" took place more than 4,500 years ago, between the Mesopotamian city states of Lagash and Umma.

An empirical study of Oregon State University covering the second half of the 20th century identified a total of 1,831 water-related international interactions between sovereign states, both conflictive and cooperative. The statistics reveal an overwhelming record of cooperation: Between 1950 and 2000 there were 37 cases where violence was involved, while in the same period 150 new water treaties were negotiated and signed. Characteristic of the 21 incidents of extensive military acts between co-basin countries has been the fact that they primarily concerned quantitative aspects of water use or issues of water use infrastructure.

Dam Density

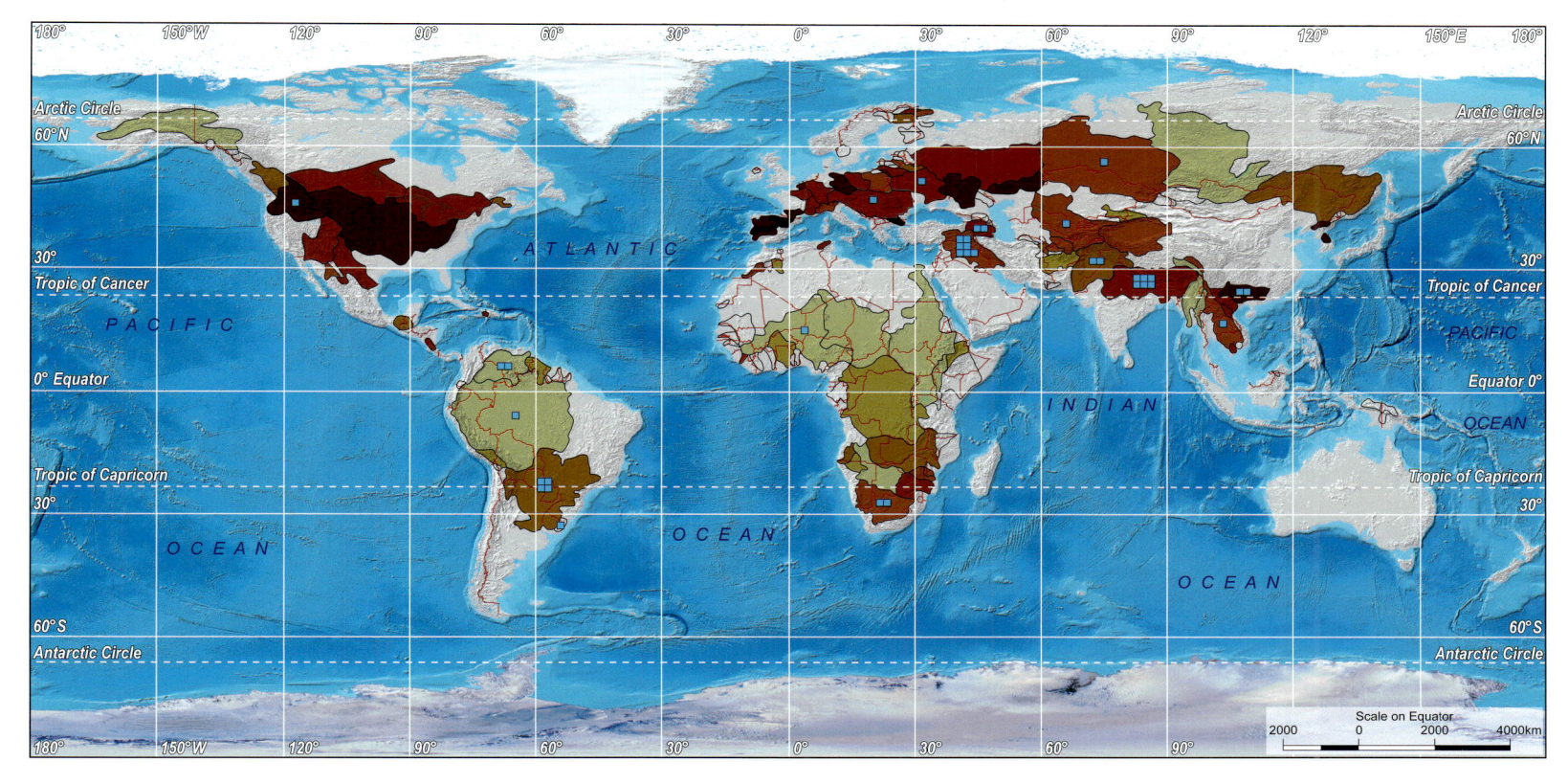

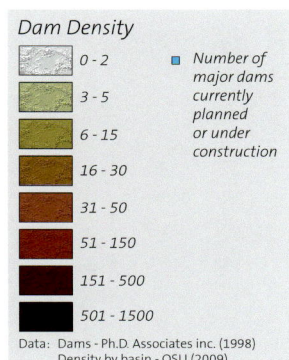

- 0 - 2
- 3 - 5
- 6 - 15
- 16 - 30
- 31 - 50
- 51 - 150
- 151 - 500
- 501 - 1500

■ Number of major dams currently planned or under construction

Data: Dams - Ph.D Associates inc. (1998)
Density by basin - OSU (2009)

△
2 – Number of existing dams as well as those planned and under construction for international river catchments.

The study concluded that in certain bilateral relations, such as between Israel and Jordan, India and Pakistan, Canada and the United States, water may act both as an irritant and as a unifier. Interestingly enough, water issues may be solved even among bitter enemies, and even while conflicts continue over other issues. Conflicts related to water also have tended to be bilateral only, without getting a broader scope involving other riparian countries.

"Water for Peace"

As studies in the development of international institutions and legislative norms have shown, common interests and the potential benefits of cooperation furnish strong motivation for the states involved to take action. Reciprocity is a necessary element in setting common norms and in creating institutions and establishing international cooperation.

Water resources have always been a very specific and difficult field when it comes to ensuring cooperation. Because there are no overarching legal regulations or institutional structures that would facilitate cooperation between countries neighbouring on water resources, the United Nations Educational, Cultural and Scientific Organisation (UNESCO) together with Green Cross International, created the initiatives 'From Potential Conflict to Cooperation Potential' and 'Water for Peace'. The initiatives aim to promote cooperation and dialogue between neighbouring countries to overcome social and political conflicts. The project also aims to set up mutual institutions for water resources management as a means of overcoming these obstacles.

Development of international water resources norms and institutions

National and international law will be used to create institutional guidelines to enable the safe and effective use of water resources. The public interest in a peaceful solution to water conflicts is also reflected in the important contributions made by the World Bank, the United Nations with its regional commissions and by the United Nations Development Programme (UNDP). The role of the World Bank in the agreement between India and Pakistan with regard to usage rights along the Indus river goes back to the 1950s. The Mekong River Commission also resulted from major mediation efforts by the United Nations. Water agreements for the catchment basins of the Senegal, Niger and Kagera rivers and Lake Chad were also concluded with the help of the UNDP.

The UN Secretariat launched its international water resources programme in 1968 to coordinate the activities of the various UN institutions in this field. In 1972 the International Law Commission, a subsidiary body of the UN, was commissioned with drafting a UN convention to regulate the development, use and management of international water resources. However, it was over 25 years before the International Law Commission presented the international agreement known as "The Convention on the Law of Non-Navigational Uses of International Watercourses" and for this to be passed by the UN. Until now, the agreement has been ratified by only a few members and has therefore not yet entered into force. Nonetheless, the convention is a major contribution towards the international practices that enshrine many of the necessary principles for the management of water resources. Some of these include: the internationality of shared water resources; the legal and proper use of water, taking into account basic human needs; the avoidance of damage; duty of care; the provision of information and negotiations with regard to planned measures; the duty to cooperate with the regular exchange of information, and environmental protection. It also contains the fundamentals for exchanging information and regulations regarding conflict resolution.

In past years, the UN's Conference on Environment and Development in Rio de Janeiro in 1992 and the International Conference on Water and the Environment in Dublin both boosted public awareness of the need to evaluate the world's water reserves as the basis for integrated water resources management. Ten years later, the World Summit on Sustainable Development in Johannesburg highlighted the inequalities in the global distribution of water resources. This was also the first time that the significance of space technology for water management became clear. This aspect was also incorporated into the agenda of the United Nations Committee on the Peaceful Uses of Outer Space (COPUOS) based in Vienna two years later.

UNESCO's contribution to strengthening international cooperation in the management of shared water resources has been most significant. The first International Hydrological Decade between 1965 and 1974 provided the first global survey of hydrological data on shared resources.

The United Nations World Water Development reports, published by UNESCO, have been able to contribute to the issue of the definition of water and of internationally shared water resources. The first report of 2003 emphasised the critical importance of freshwater, including the issues of transboundary water management in every region of the world. The second edition of the report, issued in 2006, places international water sharing into the broader political context of geopolitical developments and includes a special focus on transboundary aquifers.

In the follow-up to the Rio Conference of 1992, the World Water Council offered the most valuable platforms for articulating the shared challenges of international water resources. So far four World Water Forums, convened every three years, have taken place since 1997.

International water agencies

The first international organisation that dealt with water resources, the Central Commission for Navigation on the Rhine, was agreed upon at the Congress of Vienna in 1815. In this context one cannot but remember the theory relating the first creation of state structures to the organisation of irrigation in the historic societies of the Nile and in Mesopotamia. And it has been water resources that have been at the root of the first international multilateral institutions. However, institutionalised cooperation on international water resources has been rather slow in developing compared with other areas of international integration.

In 1963 there were only 263 international agreements for the shared development and use of water resources. Forty years later, the number of agreements has increased to beyond 400. These recent developments have also seen the establishment of joint water agencies with increasingly independent powers for data collection, planning and even for the construction and management of shared water works. Yet 157 international river basins have no framework for co-operation at all. Of the 106 river basins with shared institutions, 70 have three or more co-riparian countries, yet only 20 international water agencies are multilateral. With regard to internationally shared groundwater there is still a general lack of interstate agreements and joint institutions.

Contiguous rivers offered easier agreement on principles and modes of sharing the use of the resource than successive rivers. Bilateral agreements were easier to reach than multilateral treaties. In fact, several international river basins, such as the Nile with a multitude of co-basin countries, have historically seen institutionalised cooperation often limited to the bi-lateral level. In recent years, however, new initiatives have been taken and cooperation on water has changed from the competitive zero-sum situation to the more positive approach of an integrated river basin development, where the sharing of water has been replaced by a sharing of benefits for the international water system.

Historically, cooperation on international water resources began with agreements on single-purpose non-consumptive uses of water, such as navigation and fisheries, or with regard to the concrete sharing of water quantities to be withdrawn from the system. The Danube Commission and the Rhine Commission are examples of institutionalizing cooperation on international river navigation. The agreement between Mexico and the United States on the waters of the Colorado or the agreement between Egypt and Sudan of 1927 on the use of the waters of the Nile are examples of cooperation on the quantitative aspects of water sharing.

In functional terms, joint institutions initially disposed of rather limited responsibilities, such as monitoring joint regulations and collecting and exchanging data. Joint planning and the joint execution of projects are a higher level of functional integration. Only in the recent past has international water cooperation moved on to a broader spectrum of water uses and conservation.

The institutional development concerning the Danube and the Nile are interesting examples in this regard. Stimulated by the UNECE (United Nations Economic Commission for Europe) work on water quality protection and multipurpose uses, the co-basin countries of the Danube agreed in 1994 to establish a new framework of cooperation – the International Commission for the Protection of the Danube River, headquartered in Vienna. Its functions focus especially on flood protection and flood prevention, river basin management, pollution control, water quality management and accident prevention and control. Members are not only the 18 co-basin countries but also the European Commission. The European Union has made special efforts to support and guide water-related cooperation in Europe, including through the EU Water Framework Directive.

The challenges of coping with the growing water needs of the co-basin countries of the Nile led to the creation of the Nile Basin Initiative. The Nile Basin is one of the biggest watershed areas in the world and the river has strategic importance to all its co-basin countries. Until recently, cooperation on the Nile has been limited to the two downstream countries Egypt and Sudan which agreed on the sharing of the river's water flow.

New levels of cooperation were initiated in 1992 by Egypt, Sudan, Uganda, Rwanda, Democratic Republic of Congo and Tanzania with the creation of a "Technical Cooperation Committee for the Promotion of the Development and Environmental Protection of the Nile Basin" (TECCONILE), the elaboration of the Nile River Basin Action Plan, and a Conference of Ministers, which in 1999 formalised the newly founded multilateral cooperation as the "Nile Basin Initiative" (NBI). The upstream countries, especially Ethiopia, are now participating in the NBI. The partnership has now also been extended to Burundi, Ethiopia, Kenya, South Sudan and, with observer status, Eritrea.

One of the most advanced international water agencies in terms of delegated empowerment is the Organisation for the Development of the Senegal River (OMVS) with broad responsibilities for managing the shared resources among three (Mali, Mauritania, Senegal) of the four co-basin countries. The water works of Manantali and Djama are even the property of the OMVS, which acted as the multilateral recipient of the international credits for the construction of these dams.

The development of cooperation on the Mekong River, which is of fundamental importance for the economies of the downstream countries of Laos, Cambodia, Thailand and Vietnam, exemplifies the relevance of the broader political context within which international water resources cooperation takes place. The Mekong Committee

▷
1 – Fishermen on the Mekong casting their nets. The river is the lifeblood of the entire region. The people use it as a source of food, a place to work, a transport route and a place to live.
Treaties aim to regulate water usage from the Mekong by the neighbouring countries of Laos, Cambodia, Thailand and Vietnam.

▷▷
2 – Table of international water events and conferences.

established in 1957 by the four downstream co-basin countries took a very broad approach to the development of the river basin, at some time, through the South East Asian Development Advisory Group, and even dealt with archaeology and the historical and cultural identity of the region. In 1995 the Mekong Committee was transformed into the Mekong River Commission, with a significantly broader focus of activities.

In Latin America the Treaty of the River Plate Basin created a multifunctional platform which included but was not limited to cooperation on the development and use of water resources. In fact, the co-basin countries have concluded a broad spectrum of bi-lateral and multilateral treaties that deal with concrete issues of border disputes, the construction of major water works (e.g. Itaipu) and the regulation of navigation and the prevention of pollution of the river. Its broader political objectives are reflected also in the institutional framework, including the annual meetings of foreign ministers, an approach which eventually led to the creation of the MERCOSUR, the free market of the River Plate Basin countries.

Contemporary approaches to international water resources management have also increasingly recognised the importance of participatory opportunities for civil society and local governments.

In conclusion it must be recognised that coping with the sharing of transboundary water resources is and will become an ever more important element in the further development of regional cooperation and integration among co-basin countries. Benefits of successful cooperation will not be restricted to water user interests only but will enhance the general quality of relations between countries and societies and hence to international peace, security and development. International waters may turn out to be a lynchpin in the achievement of humankind's future agenda.

Text: Walther Lichem

Year	Event	Location	Organiser
1972	UN Conference on the Human Environment	Stockholm	UN
1977	UN Conference on Water	Mar del Plata	UN
1981–1990 International Drinking Water Supply and Sanitation Decade			
1990–2000 International Decade for Natural Disaster Reduction			
1990	Global Consultation on Safe Water and Sanitation for the 1990s	New Delhi	UNDP
1991	World Water Week	Stockholm	Stockholm International Water Institute (SIWI)
1992	International Conference on Water and the Environment	Dublin	WMO (World Meteorological Organization)
1992	UN Conference on Environment and Development	Rio de Janeiro	UNCED Earth Summit
1993	World Water Week	Stockholm	SIWI
1994	UN International Conference on Population and Development	Cairo	UN
1995	World Summit for Social Development	Copenhagen	UN
1996	UN Conference on Human Settlements (Habitat II)	Istanbul	UN
1996	World Food Summit,	Rome	FAO
1997	1st World Water Forum	Marrakesh	World Water Council
1997	World Water Week	Stockholm	SIWI
1998	World Water Week	Stockholm	SIWI
1999	World Water Week	Stockholm	SIWI
2000	World Water Week	Stockholm	SIWI
2000	2nd World Water Forum	The Hague	World Water Council
2001	International Conference on Freshwater	Bonn	Government of the Federal Republic of Germany
2001	International Water Conference	Porto	CEA (Centro de Estudos de Águas)
2001	Youth World Water Forum, Hogeschool Zeeland	Vlissingen	YWWF (Youth World Water Forum)
2001	The Role of Water in History and Development: 2nd International Conference of the IWHA	Bergen	University of Bergen
2001	Rainwater International	Mannheim	IRCSA (International Rainwater Catchment Systems Association)
2001	River Basin Management	Cardiff	Wessex Institute of Technology, UK
2001	The National Urban Watershed Conference	California City	NWRI (National Water Research Institute)
2001	International Water Conference	Pittsburgh	ESWP (ENGINEERS' SOCIETY OF WESTERN PENNSYLVANIA)
2001	Water and Wastewater Management for Developing Countries	Kuala Lumpur	IWA (International Water Association)
2002	World Water Week	Stockholm	SIWI
2002	World Summit on Sustainable Development, Rio+10	Johannesburg	UN
2003 International Year of Freshwater			
2003	3rd World Water Forum	Kyoto	World Water Council
2003	World Water Week	Stockholm	SIWI
2005–2014 Decade of Education for Sustainable Development			
2005–2015 International Decade for 'Water for Life'			
2005	4th International Water History Association Conference: Water and Civilization	Paris	IWHA (International Water History Association)
2005	World Water Week	Stockholm	SIWI
2006	4th World Water Forum	Mexico City	World Water Council
2006	World Water Week	Stockholm	SIWI
2007	World Water Week	Stockholm	SIWI
2007	International Water Conference	Orlando	ESWP (ENGINEERS' SOCIETY OF WESTERN PENNSYLVANIA)
2007	International Conference on Sustainable Water Resources Management	Kos	Wessex Institute of Technology, UK
2008	World Water Week	Stockholm	SIWI
2009	5th World Water Forum	Istanbul	World Water Council
2010	World Water Week	Stockholm	SIWI
2010	International Water Conference	San Antonio	ESWP
2011	Forest and Water Week	Geneva	UNECE/FAO
2012	6th World Water Forum	Marseille	World Water Council
2014	World Water Week	Stockholm	SIWI
2014	3rd International Conference on Water Resources and Environmental Management	Antalya	GIWEH (Global Institute for Water, Environment and Health)
2015	7th World Water Forum	Gyeongju	World Water Council

WATERS OF THE EARTH

Bodies of water of various kinds are the source of life on Earth and the cradle of civilisations. As natural transport routes and boundaries they are links and barriers at the same time.

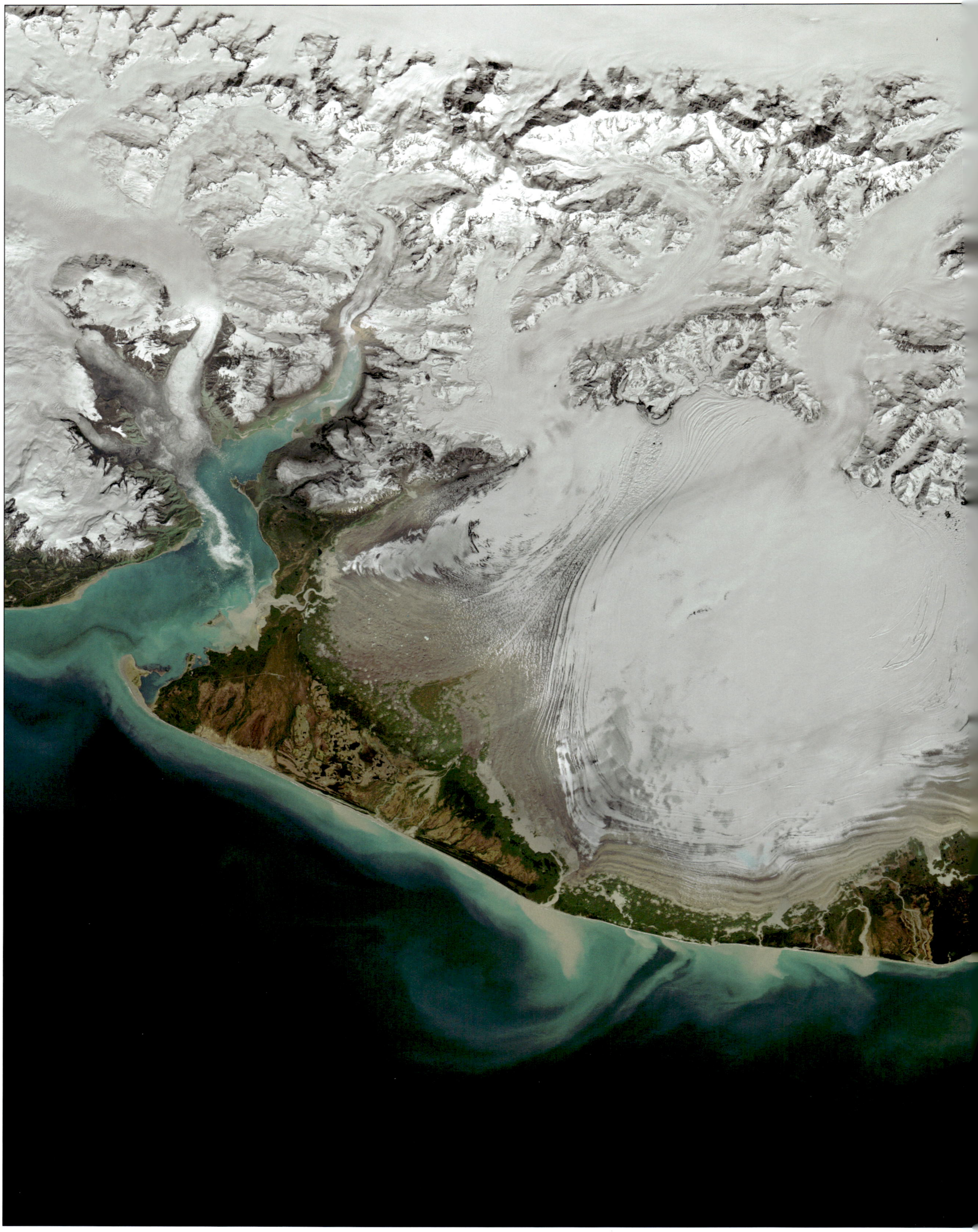

GLACIERS

Around three quarters of all the world's freshwater is stored in glaciers and in the polar sea ice. Glaciers are the most reliable indicators and archives of climate change.

Glaciers are large deposits of snow, ice, sediment, rock and water. On high ground at higher latitudes, precipitation can fall as snow almost all year round. This area is known as the accumulation zone (in the glacier's head area). As a result of pressure and temperature variations, the snow is changed into firn snow (névé), then firn ice, and finally into glacier ice. Glaciers are in no way motionless blocks of ice, but slowly flow down mountainsides, tugged by gravity. In the ablation zone, the glacier loses mass due to melting or calving. Glacial movements leave clear marks on the landscape. Among these formations are nunataks, cirques, U-shaped valleys, roches moutonnées ('sheepbacks') and lakes, as well as a sequence of landforms created by glacial advances (moraines and broad glacial valleys), along with smaller drumlins, tunnel valleys, kames and eskers. Ground moraines and glacier forelands are characterised by extensive, highly eroded gravel terraces.

The size of a glacier and the speed of its movement are determined by temperature, precipitation and topography. The bed of the glacier also plays an important role. When the bed is frozen, the speed is slower than across a thawing bed that has been penetrated by meltwater.

Currently, around 10 per cent of the Earth's surface is covered with glaciers, while in the ice ages this figure was somewhere around 32 per cent. Glaciers are highly important for the water balance because they store three-quarters of the world's freshwater supply (along with the polar sea ice). Changes in the mass balance of glaciers, particularly as a result of melting, affect the microclimate, ecological habitats, drinking water supply and also energy generation via hydropower. Moreover, glacial retreat can cause natural hazards such as rockslides and glacial lake outburst floods, and contributes to sea-level rise.

Satellite images can be used to monitor the size and movement of glaciers and can ascertain changes in the mass balance before they happen. In some cases, like that of the Malaspina Glacier, Greenland and the Antarctic, the glaciers are so large that satellite images are the only way to monitor the full extent of their sizes and status.

◁
1 – The Malaspina Glacier in Alaska is a typical example of a piedmont glacier. It reaches a width of up to 65 km after it has left the mountains.

Malaspina Glacier

Measuring 45 kilometres in length and 65 kilometres in width and with a total area of around 3,900 square kilometres, the Malaspina Glacier in the south-east of Alaska (pp. 80/81, Fig. 1) is one of the biggest piedmont glaciers in the world. Piedmont glaciers are valley glaciers that have flowed down from a mountainous region and spread out laterally on the flatter ground, where there are no barriers to hold them back. The Malaspina Glacier's lobe-like formation is the result of the convergence of several glaciers in the Saint Elias Mountains, primarily the Agassiz and Seward Glaciers.

A terminal moraine in front of the glacier prevents it from flowing into the sea and calving, which forces it to spread out laterally and results in the ice building up to 600 metres thick. In the past 20 years, the Malaspina Glacier has also been affected by global glacial retreat and is thinning by around one metre every year.

David Glacier

The David Glacier is the largest and fastest-flowing outlet glacier in Antarctica's Victoria Land. With a north-south width of 14 to 24 kilometres, it flows into the McMurdo Sound, tipped with the Drygalski Ice Tongue, which measures over 48 kilometres in length and is 300 metres thick (Fig. 1). The surface of the Ice Tongue is split by countless fissures and rifts. The glacier calves into the Ross Sea, where currents then carry the icebergs into the open sea.

The Drygalski Ice Tongue made the headlines in 2005 when Iceberg B-15A, which at that point was still 115 kilometres long and covered an area of 2,500 square kilometres – a part of Iceberg B-15, which broke off from the Ross Ice Shelf in March 2000 – rammed into the tip of the Ice Tongue and broke off a piece five kilometres in length. ESA documented this event with the ASAR sensor on board its Envisat satellite (Fig. 2) and continues to track the movements with the SAR instrument on board Sentinel-1.

1 – The Drygalski Ice Tongue of the David Glacier (Antarctica) extends into the Ross Sea.

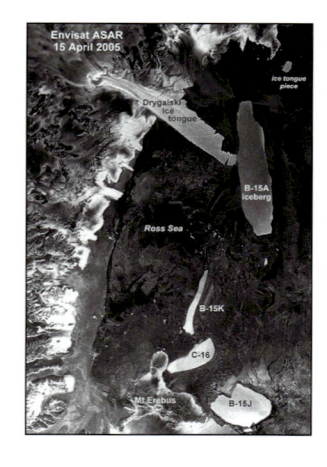

△
3 – The "Aletsch" is the largest glacier in the European Alps.

◁
2 – Tabular icebergs in the Ross Sea, section measuring 240 x 360 km, Envisat ASAR, 15/04/2005.

▷
4 – Map of the Aletsch Glacier showing the glacial extent in 1850 and today.

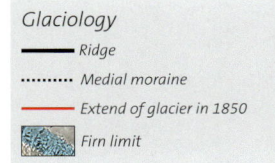

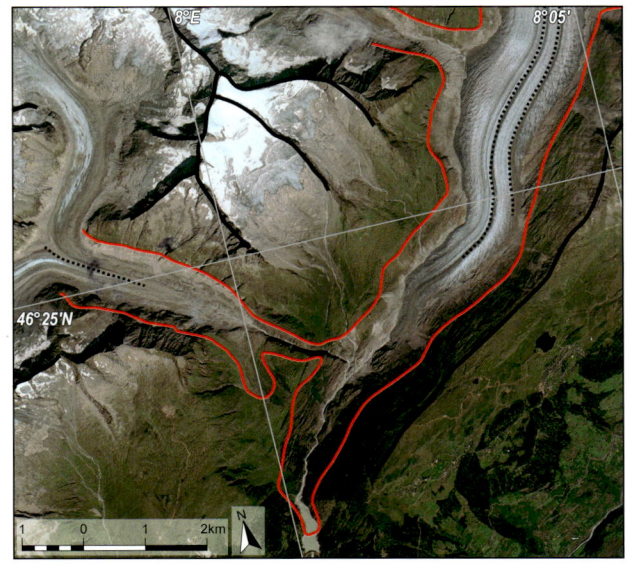

Glaciology
— Ridge
····· Medial moraine
— Extend of glacier in 1850
▒ Firn limit

Aletsch Glacier

Measuring 23 kilometres long and with an area of 82 square kilometres, the Aletsch Glacier (Fig. 3) in the Upper Valais region of Switzerland is the longest and largest glacier in the Alps. It originates in the Jungfrau region at an altitude of around 4,000 metres. It is made up of the Aletschfirn, the Jungfraufirn, the Ewigschneefeldfirn and the smaller Grüneggfirn. The convergence of the firns results in two distinct medial moraines.

The glacier has gone through periods of change since the last ice age – in the Middle Ages and around 1850 it was around three kilometres longer than it is today (Fig. 4). Advances of this kind can be established by the presence of fossil wood in the glacier foreland and by the age of the lateral moraines. During the past few decades the Aletsch Glacier, like many other Alpine glaciers, has gone through a massive retreat. In recent years it has been particularly affected, retreating up to 50 metres per year.

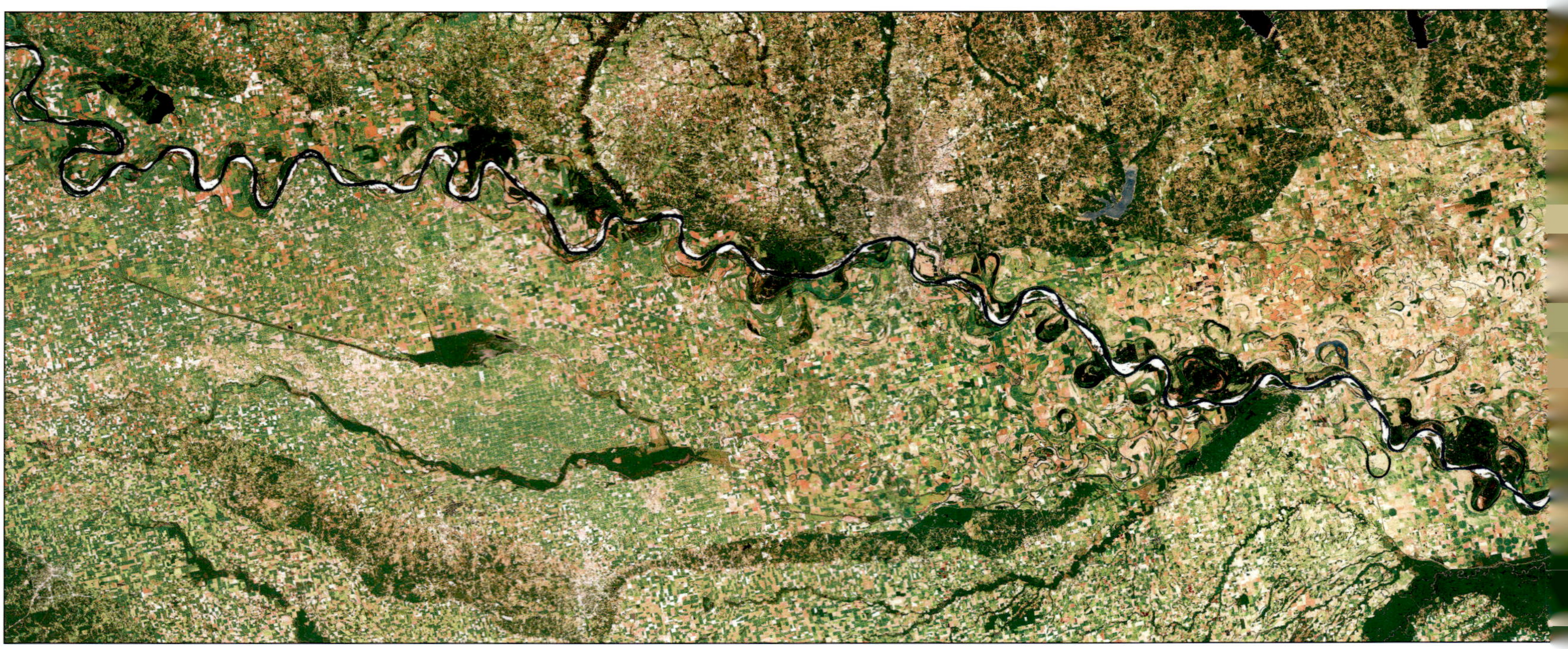

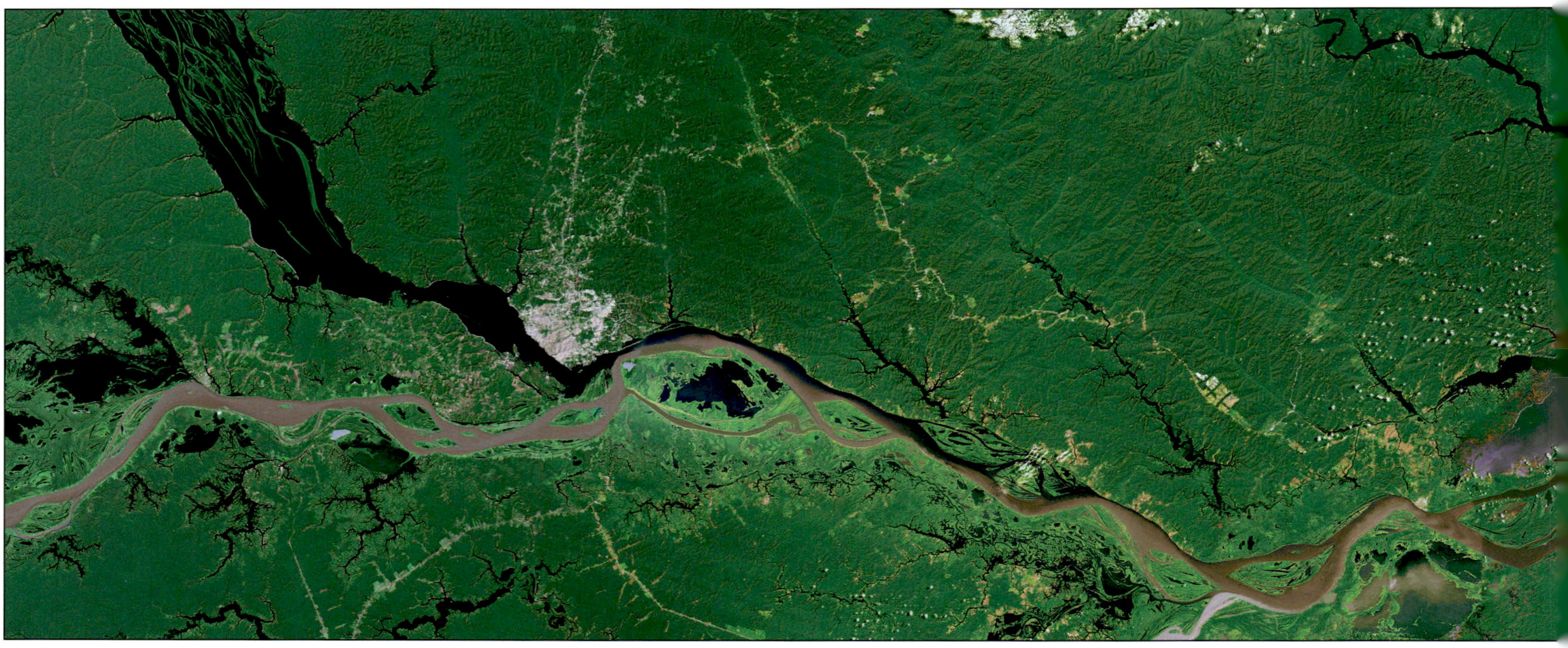

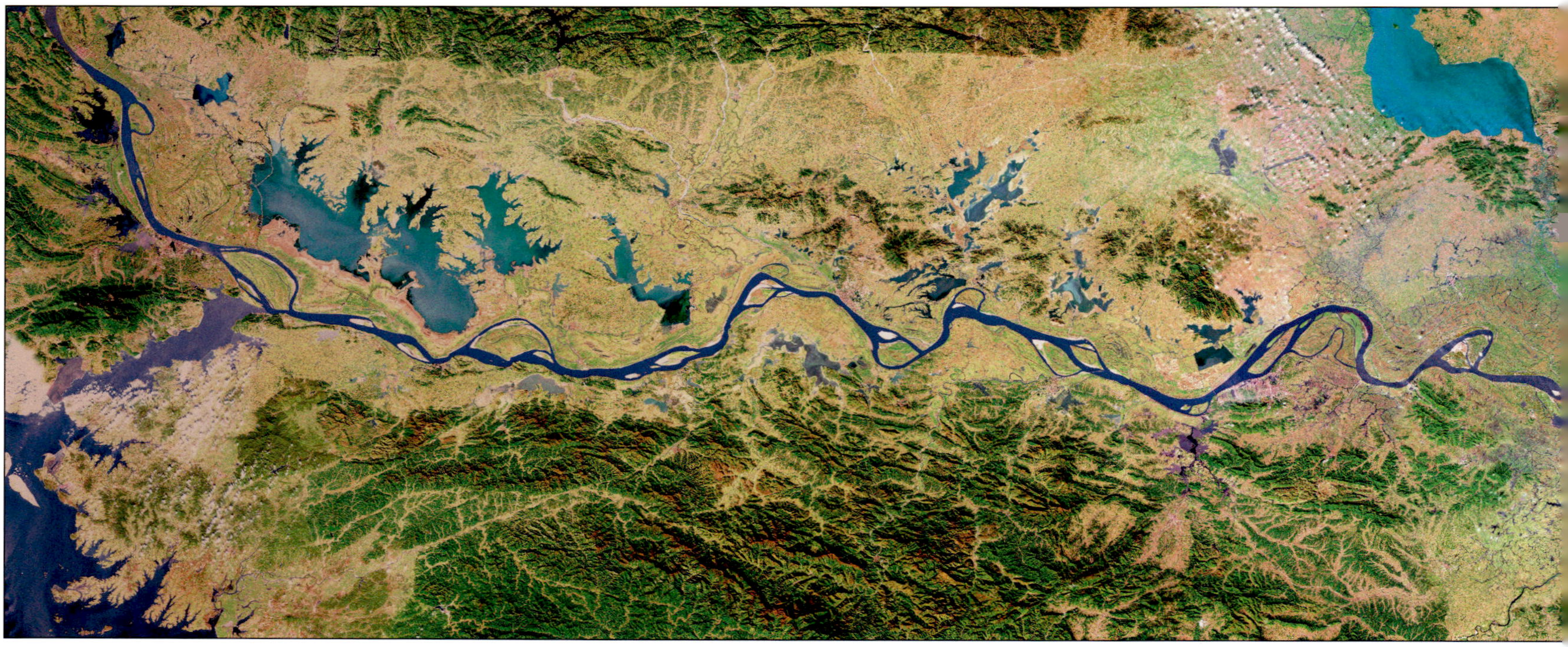

RIVERS OF THE EARTH

Rivers are the lifeblood of our planet. They transport water from inaccessible mountain regions to the oceans and enable the landscape to bloom along their path.

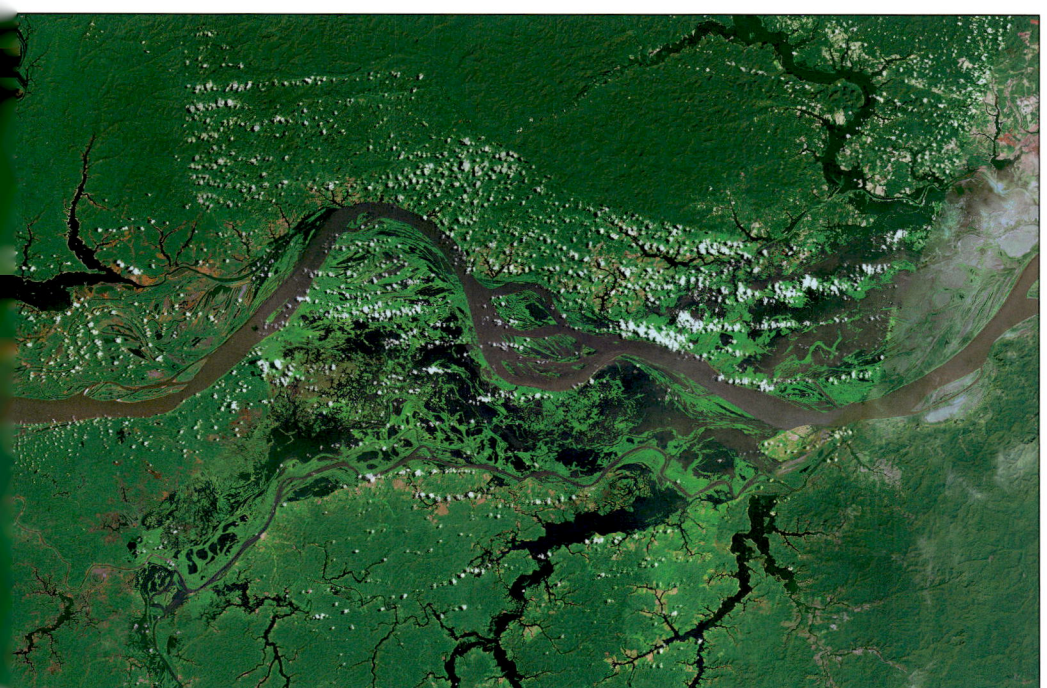

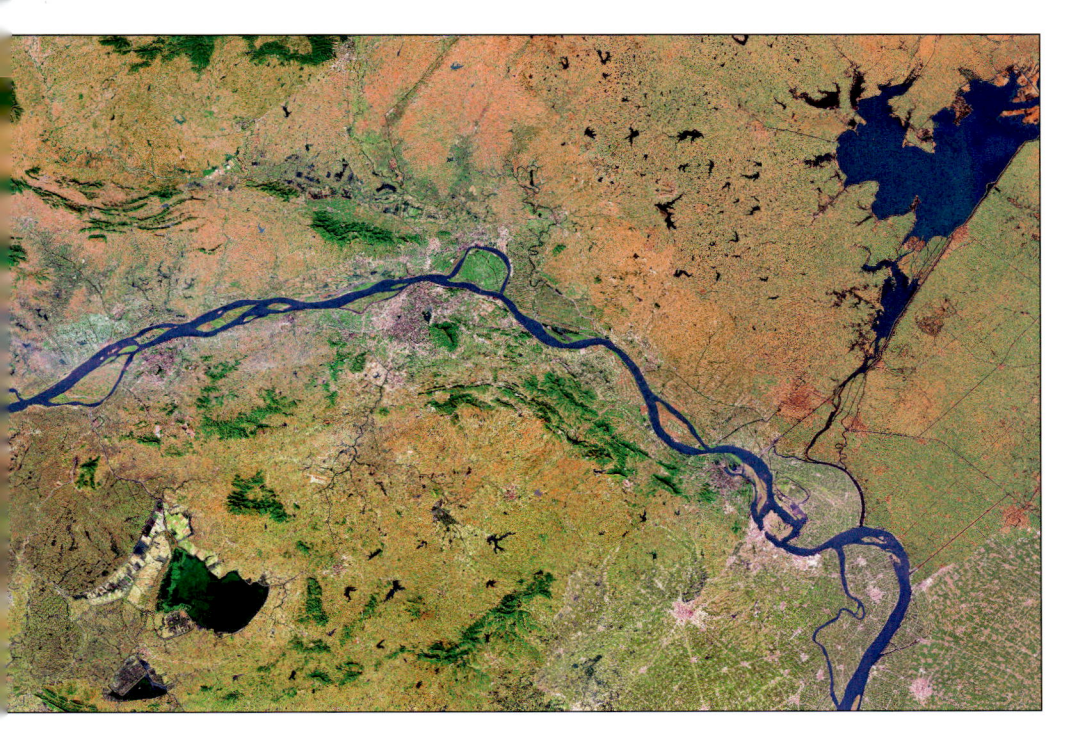

River systems play an important role in every region of the Earth. Since water first appeared on our planet, the landscape has been shaped by its perpetual movement. Running waters wear away slopes in some places, deposit gravel banks in others, and create deltas and estuaries at their mouths. Together with the surrounding natural habitats, they support life for countless species of animals and plants.

Rivers are essential for humans, too, as evidenced by the history of very early settlements located along their banks. River landscapes have also become popular for local recreation and leisure. From an economic point of view, rivers are primarily used for transportation, to generate electric power, for irrigation and to extract drinking water.

The morphology of a river (Figs. 1, 2 and 3) is primarily shaped by the predominating tectonic, climatological and topographical conditions, as well as the geological substratum, which in turn influences the surface processes that shape the land.

Only very few of our planet's rivers are completely unspoilt. Direct effects on the river system are, for example with dams, straightened watercourses and the introduction of wastewater. In addition to this, rivers are also shaped indirectly by interventions upstream in their catchment basins. Some such effects include de-forestation as well as the soil sealing as a result of urbanisation and the creation of infrastructure.

◁
1 – *The Mississippi passes through a number of states on its way to the Gulf of Mexico. This section shows a high number of oxbow lakes.*

◁
2 – *The Amazon and its rainforest between Manaus in the west and Parintins in the east.*

◁
3 – *The lower course of the Yangtze between Jiujiang in the southwest, past Nanjing down to Zhenjiang in the northeast.*

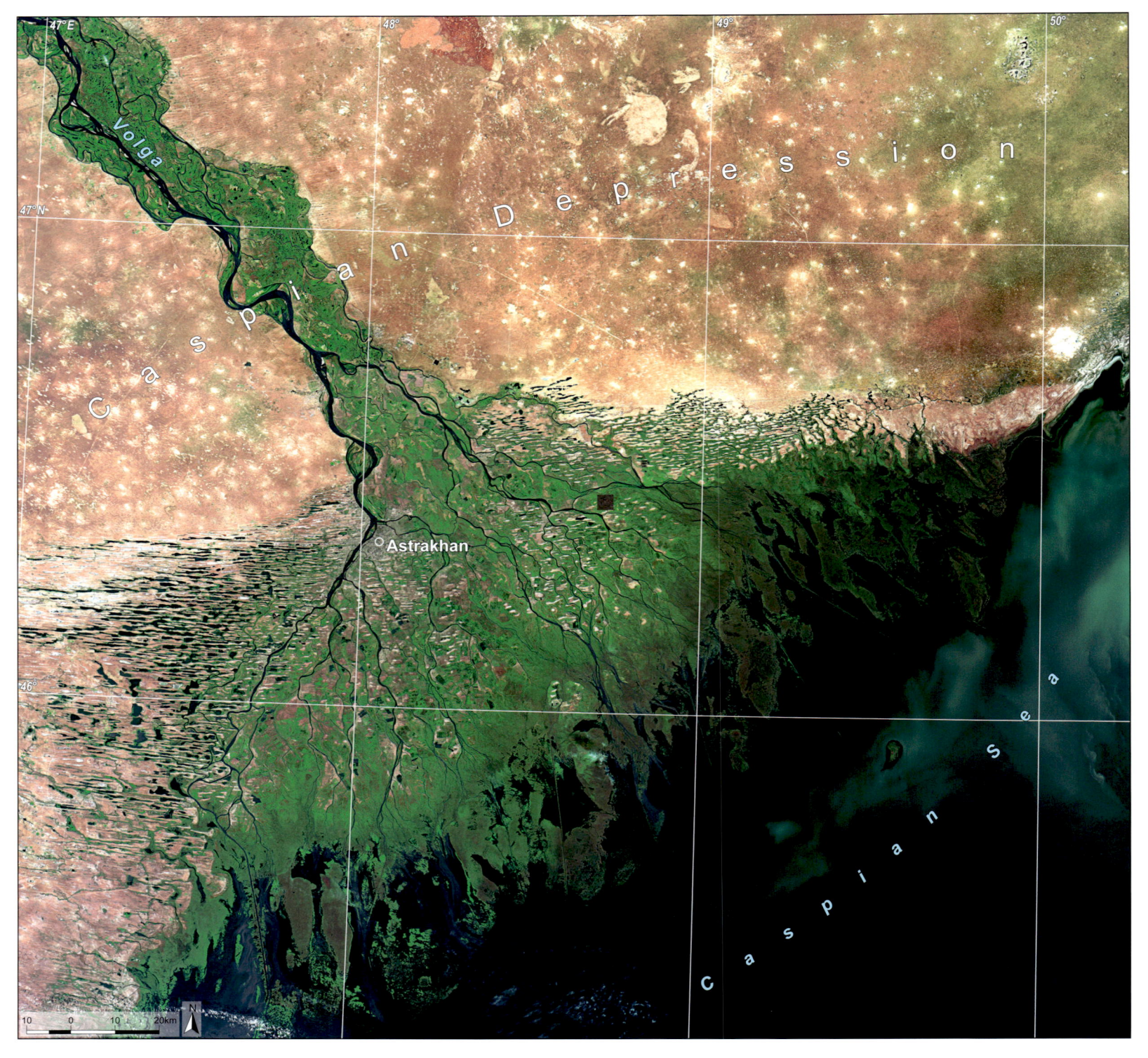

The end of the journey – the river's mouth

Most rivers on our planet end their journeys in a lake or in the sea. Only very few of them form an inland delta. The best-known example of an inland delta is probably the Okavango Delta, which is situated in a closed basin in the desert of the western Kalahari in Botswana. The area of the Okavango Delta can cover up to 20,000 square kilometres, depending on the seasonal variations of the river's water level (Fig. 1, p. 238).

River mouths that end in lakes or seas vary enormously in appearance and extent. The river mouth is largely determined by the geology and topography of the area, the sediment load and the tidal activity of the river mouth. On a general level, river mouths are categorised as deltas (Fig. 1) or estuaries, (Fig. 2). In some cases, a river may simply flow into another body of water without forming a delta or estuary. This generally happens when a river flows into another river, as in the case of the Main and Neckar flowing into the Rhine.

Deltas

Deltas are formed by sediment settling out from a river. When the river broadens at the mouth, its currents slow down, the force of the flowing water decreases, and islands of sediment form. These obstacles to the waterflow divide the river into several arms and create a labyrinth of flowing and non-flowing watercourses. Over time, the delta extends into the lake or sea. The shapes of these alluvial fans in many cases also very closely resemble that of the Greek letter delta, or Δ, giving name to this geographic feature, as the Volga Delta (Fig. 1) nicely shows.

One of the most impressive examples is the Mississippi River Delta (Fig. 1, p. 93), whose lobes stretch out into the Gulf of Mexico by up to 100 metres every year. It is also an excellent example of a river-dominated delta. As a result of the weak currents in the Gulf, there is hardly any transport of sediments off from the delta and the sediments remain deposited at the river mouth. This accumulation of material results in a huge alluvial fan with its intricate pattern of streams and branches.

△
1 – The Volga opens out into the Caspian Sea in a broad alluvial fan. The delta is the largest wetland area in Europe and has been protected by environmental conservation law in its entirety since 1997. When flooded with snowmelt, the meadows are home to over 300 species of birds.

△
2 – The Rio de la Plata is the estuary of two major rivers: the Uruguay and the Paraná. The water at the river's mouth is turned brown by the sediment load of both rivers. Argentina's capital, Buenos Aires, is on the southern bank of the Rio de la Plata.

The high tidal range in the Gulf of Bengal determines the appearance of the Ganges Delta (Fig. 5, p. 127), which is strongly influenced by the tides. This delta, the largest on Earth, is split up by the effect of the tide. The banks of the delta are shifted towards the sea, forming long sandbars. The sediment brought down by the river, however, is deposited parallel to the coast.

As a result of the currents flowing along the coast, the sediment load is deposited parallel to the coast also in wave-dominated deltas. This type of delta is characterised by its asymmetric shape, another example of which is the Rhône Delta in the Mediterranean.

Estuaries

Estuaries are created primarily on tidal coasts when the sediment load deposited by the river is lower than the amount eroded by the tidal currents. The effect of the tides results in the river mouth expanding into a funnel shape (Fig. 2). The estuary results from the fact that erosion occurs on one side of the river mouth during high tide and, at low tide, on the opposite side. As a result of the Coriolis effect, in the Northern Hemisphere, the high tide affects the left bank of the river whereas the low tide affects the right bank, and vice versa in the Southern Hemisphere. One example of an estuary is the Elbe river mouth in the North Sea at Cuxhaven. The river carries very little sediment, which is deposited before it reaches its mouth. This is because the river flows slowly. The Hamburg Wadden Sea, into which the Elbe empties, has been shaped by the tides more than almost any other sea in the world. The tidal range of three metres is what gives the river mouth its estuary-like appearance.

In general, the areas around river mouths, primarily deltas, have highly fertile soils. As a result, they are some of the most densely populated areas in the world and are heavily farmed. This is certainly the case in the Ganges and Nile deltas. The verdant Nile Delta is visible from space, striking in the barren landscape of the desert, making it probably one of the most spectacular in the world and certainly one of the best-known.

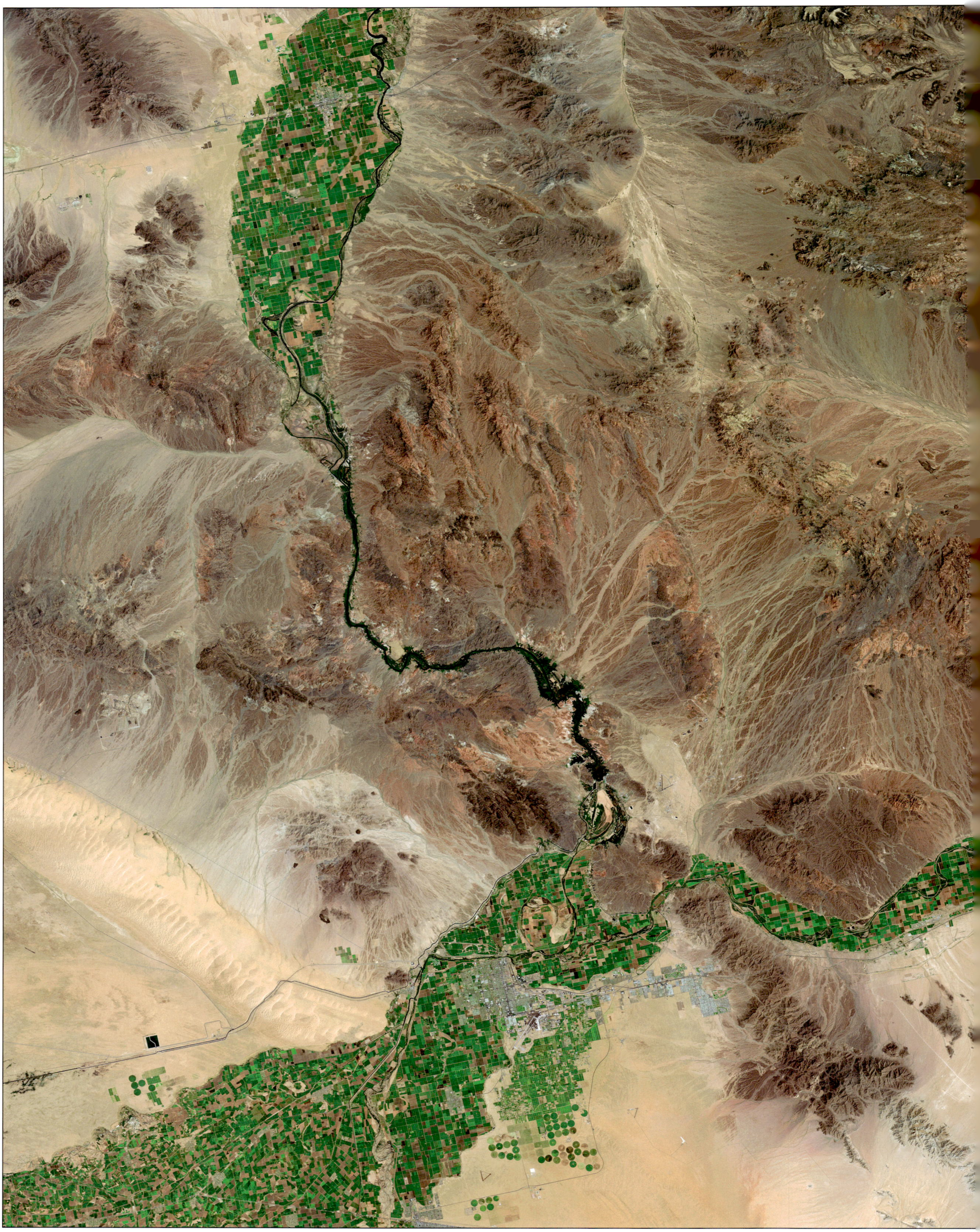

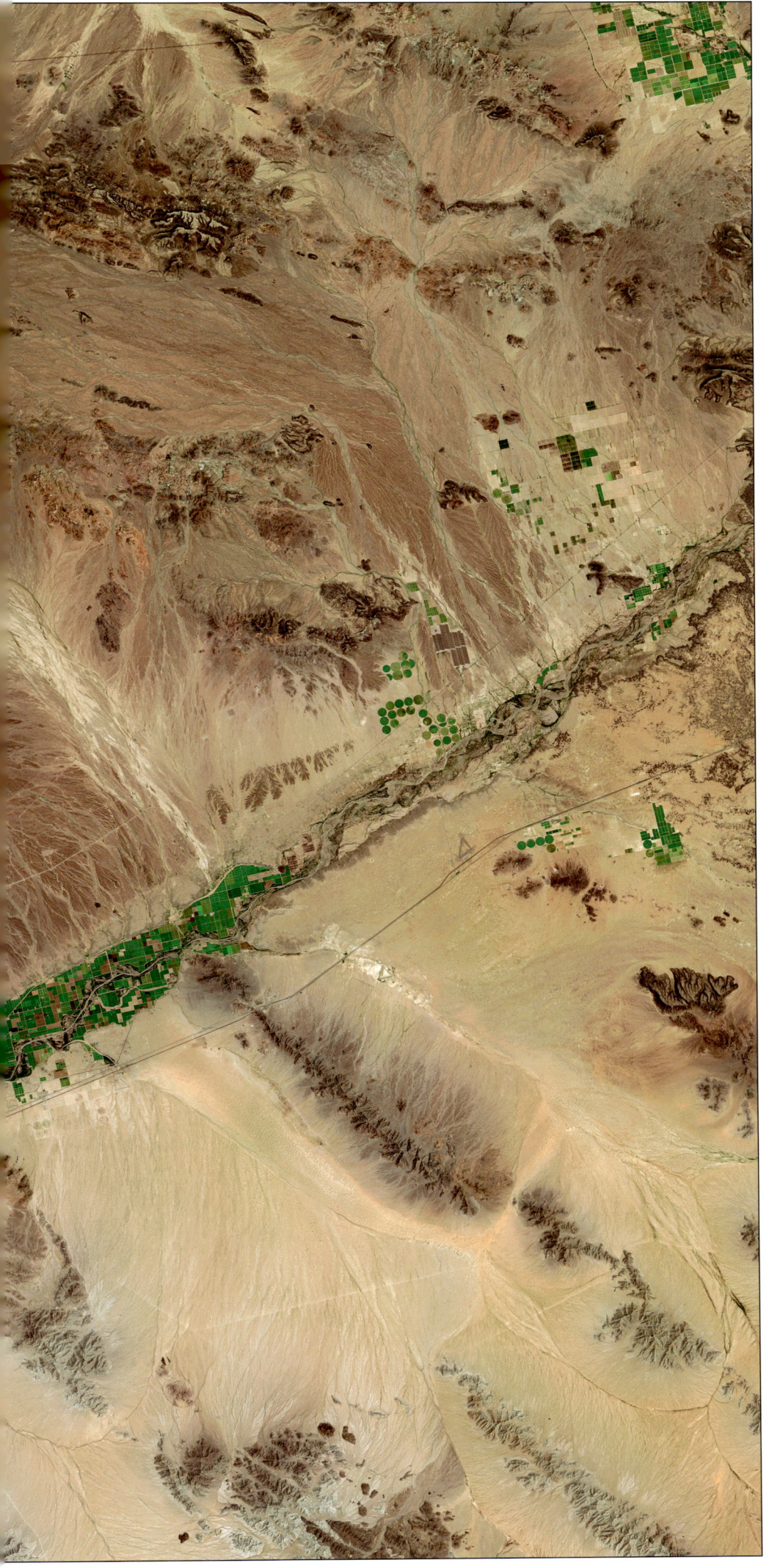

COLORADO

Plunging from frozen heights of 4,000 metres on the continental spine, the Colorado writhes for 2,300 kilometres to the sea. It has shaped the Rocky Mountains and carved out the Grand Canyon.

The explorers heading west thought the land the Colorado River flowed through was good for nothing. "Ours has been the first and will doubtless be the last party of whites to visit this profitless locality," wrote Lt. Joseph C. Ives of the Army Engineers in 1858, after steaming upriver to the present site of Hoover Dam in search of a navigable route between the Rockies and the Pacific. "The Colorado River, along the greater portion of its lonely and majestic way, shall be forever unvisited and undisturbed."

In comparison with other rivers, the Colorado merits only a few superlatives: Its drop in elevation is the greatest in North America; it is one of the siltiest (before the dams, it carried an average load of 380,000 tons a day); and it is one of the saltiest, carrying nine million tons a year. Although it ranks seventh in length in the U.S., its water volume has averaged only 18.5 cubic kilometres of water yearly since 1905. (The Columbia discharges 237 and the Mississippi more then 493 cubic kilometres per year).

The Colorado and its waters are the source of life for major parts of the Southwest: Southern Nevada, Arizona, Southern California – a semi-arid 637,000 square kilometres drainage area (larger than France). It has earned a reputation as the most legislated, litigated over, and debated river in the world.

In the northwest of the Colorado catchment basin, in the Rocky Mountain range, the Colorado River and its main tributary, the Green River, rise (Fig. 1, p. 90). In the centre of the image runs the Grand Canyon, cutting the Colorado Plateau into northern and southern sections, with Lake Powell to the East and Lake Mead to the West. At Lake Mead the Colorado turns south, heading towards Baja California. The irrigated land along the river course (Fig. 1), but also in the Salton Sea region shortly before the river reaches Baja California, contrasts sharply with the desert-like surroundings.

The river's headwaters are in the Rocky Mountains of Colorado and parts of Utah, where the annual precipitation may reach 2,500 mm. Further downstream the river flows through an arid region, lying in the rain shadow of the Sierra Nevada mountain range, where less than 250 mm of rain falls. This rainfall is seasonal and highly unpredictable.

◁
1 – The irrigated fields stand out from the barren sands of the Sonoran Desert at the confluence of the Colorado and Gila rivers at Yuma, Arizona. The pattern of the Mexican fields in the bottom left of the image differs from the homogeneous shape of the plots of land in the US.

The Colorado River system supplies water for seven western US states: Arizona, California, Colorado, Nevada, New Mexico, Utah and Wyoming, and also Mexico as well. Dams, canals and other structures collect the river water for this thirsty region.

Agreements for the Colorado River

The river is divided among the seven states according to the 1922 Colorado River Compact, known as the Law of the River. The Law of the River is a complex body of laws, court cases and regulations that rules the use of Colorado River water and the operation of its dams.

In the 1800s, states diverted water from the Colorado River and its tributaries without restrictions. As the diversions increased, a long battle over apportionment was joined. Today, the Colorado River is probably the most institutionally controlled and controversial river in the world.

In 1922, the states negotiated the Colorado River Compact, which divided the states into two basins (upper and lower) and apportioned 9.25 cubic kilometres per year to each basin. The Compact also referred to Mexico's right to the Colorado. In 1944, the United States signed a water treaty in which it agreed to deliver an annual quantity of 1.85 cubic kilometres of water to Mexico.

The rule of `first come, first served´ (prior appropriation) was agreed – meaning that, if a state downstream, for example California, already had a dam providing irrigation water, this water could not be removed by a state upstream, for example Utah, building a dam at a later date.

While Compact negotiators estimated the flow of the river to be at least 21 cubic kilometres per year, today's records indicate a flow of 18.5 cubic kilometres, just below Lake Powell. Consequently, in most years, the sum of the Compact apportionments and the Mexican treaty exceed the actual flow of the river. From 2000 to 2002, the Colorado River system flows averaged about 12 cubic kilometres per year – the lowest three-year average since record keeping began in 1906.

Therefore in some years the allocations cannot be fulfilled, causing major water stress to the consumers and requiring drastic conservation measures. Due to those low flow rates, there is often not enough water left to support irrigation for agriculture in Mexico and no water at all reaches Baja California (Fig. 6). These problems lead to intergovernmental disputes over the water rights.

Still, there is little support in the seven basin states for renegotiating the Compact. A new agreement would require approval from each state's legislature and the U.S. Congress.

The Colorado River Aqueduct (CRA) was completed in 1941 with the aim of bringing water to the metropolitan areas on the coastal plain of southern California from north of Los Angeles to San Diego. The quantity of exported water ranged from 0.38 cubic kilometres to 1.57 cubic kilometres between 1939 and 1985. Explosive growth in California has caused the state to overdraw on its quota set by the Compact for many years. In a 1991 drought, California officials asked for the right to take 0.5 cubic kilometres more than the state's allotment; Colorado Governor Roy Romer agreed, under the condition that interstate talks begin to meet individual needs but still uphold the Compact.

Large-scale projects on the Colorado

The 1922 Colorado River Compact also provided the legislative stimulus to harness the river. After much debate, Congress passed legislation to authorise the construction

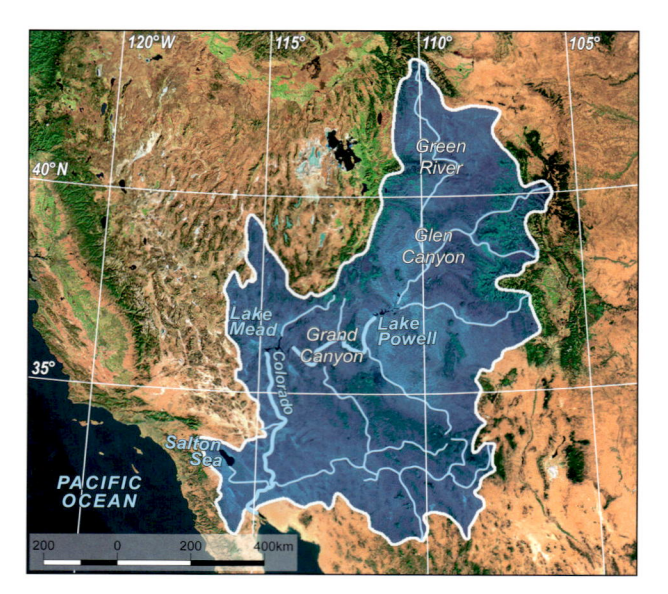

1 – Colorado catchment basin.

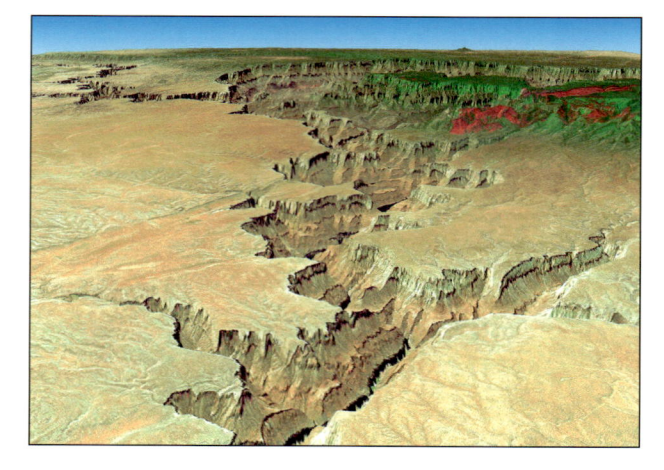

2 – The sharp clefts of the Grand Canyon, captured in a 3D view calculated from satellite data.

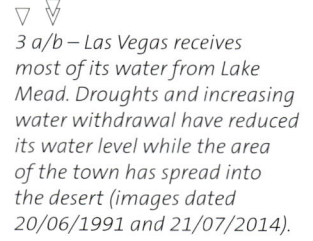

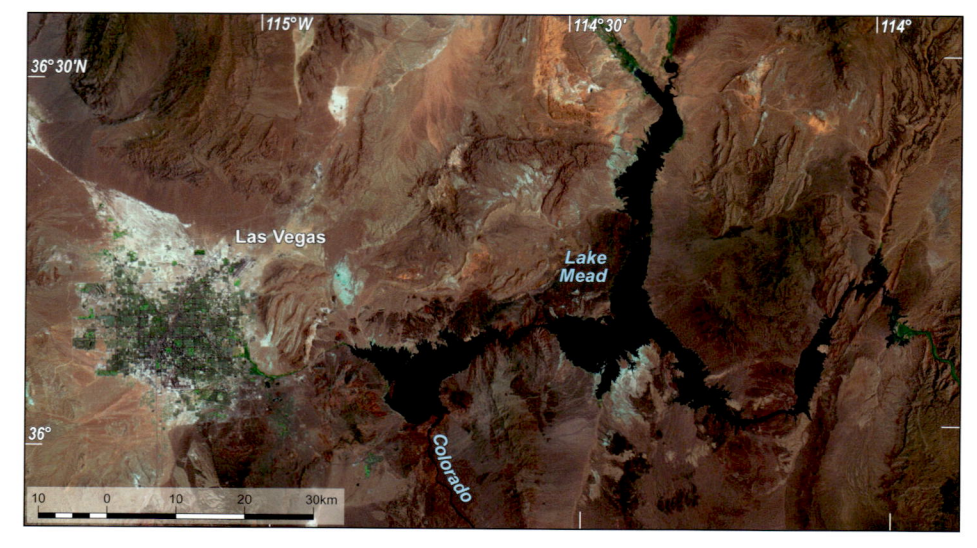

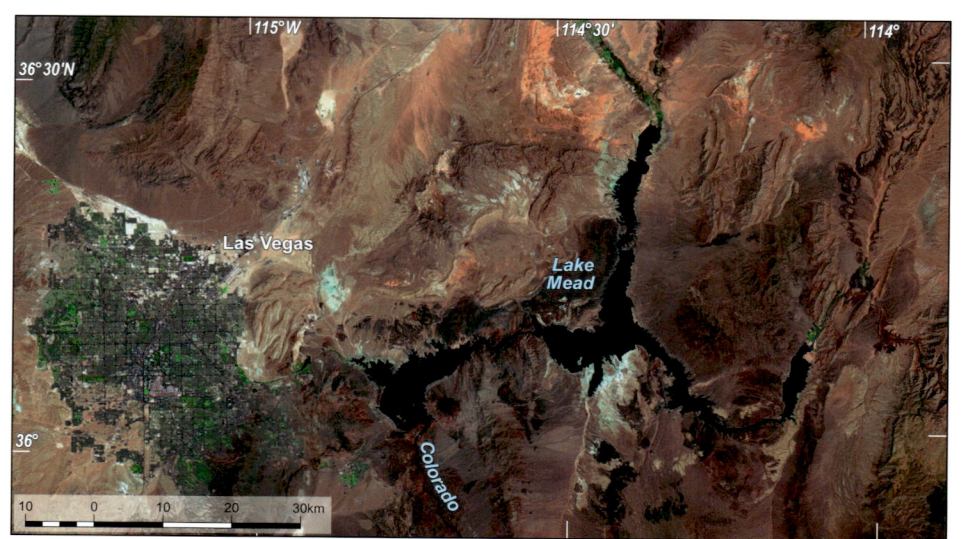

3 a/b – Las Vegas receives most of its water from Lake Mead. Droughts and increasing water withdrawal have reduced its water level while the area of the town has spread into the desert (images dated 20/06/1991 and 21/07/2014).

▷ ▷
4 a/b – The Salton Sea on the 27/02/1989 (left 6 a) and on the 15/05/2013 (right 6B). Directly north of the State border runs the All-American Canal, which brings the water taken from the Colorado at Imperial Dam to the irrigated fields and into the Palm Springs area. The border city of Mexicali is situated between the intensive and less intensively irrigated fields. The increasing population density clearly reveals the region's dependence on water from the Colorado

▷
5 – Palm Springs is almost entirely dependent on water from the Colorado.

▽
6 – The lower reaches of the Colorado, with its mouth on the Gulf of California.

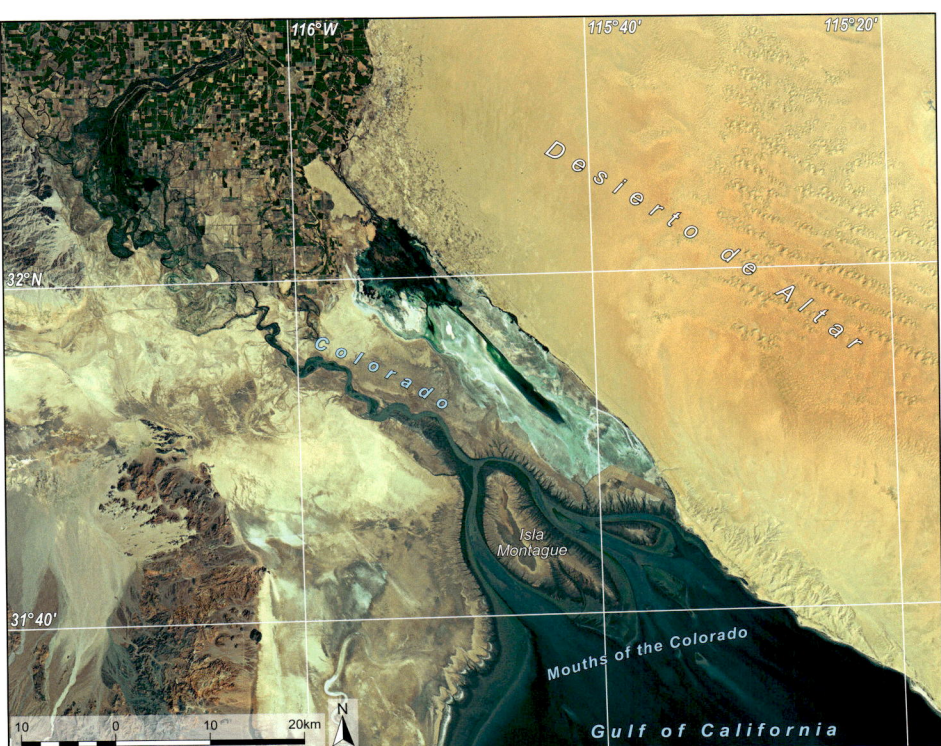

of Hoover Dam, one of altogether 10 major dams built between 1935 and 1966. Completed in 1936, the dam was the first giant step toward controlling the rampaging river. Hoover Dam with adjacent Lake Mead (Figs. 3 a and b) is the main source of water and energy for Las Vegas.

Las Vegas, a city of lights. Though the illumination appears to stretch on forever, the view from above reveals where the light abruptly ends and pitch-black darkness begins. This is because Las Vegas sits in the middle of a desert. To support an exploding population in the middle of the desert, a water source is needed. For Las Vegas, the primary supply (88 per cent) is Lake Mead, a nearly 35-cubic-kilometre holding pen for the Colorado River located 20 kilometres to the east (Figs. 3 a and b).

Waters from the Colorado are diverted and exported to California as well, via the Colorado River Aqueduct and the All-American Canal. The transferred water is consumed in urban agglomerations outside the Colorado River catchment, such as Los Angeles, San Diego and Palm Springs. Vast areas, especially in the Salton Sea District of California, have been developed into farm land since the 1940s. Those areas can be farmed solely due to irrigation. The plots follow the irrigation channels and are therefore highly geometric (Figs. 4 and 5). The water level of Salton Sea is 69 metres below sea level; as a result, Salton Sea has no drainage. Because of that, sewage and all the waters flowing in off the irrigated fields carry fertilisers, pesticides, fungicides, salt, etc. into the Salton Sea basin, causing water quality problems. The border with Mexico can be made out easily, because of the change of the agricultural pattern and the less intense farming. The nearly empty river bed of the Colorado is shown over its last kilometres before it reaches Baja California (Fig. 6).

Water management with satellite data

Remotely sensed imagery, meanwhile, is indispensable for water management in the Colorado River basin. The main applications are monitoring snow cover in order to forecast the runoff to the reservoirs during the melt season. By means of this, the reservoirs can be managed adequately. Furthermore, general land cover and land-use development are monitored for demand forecasting.

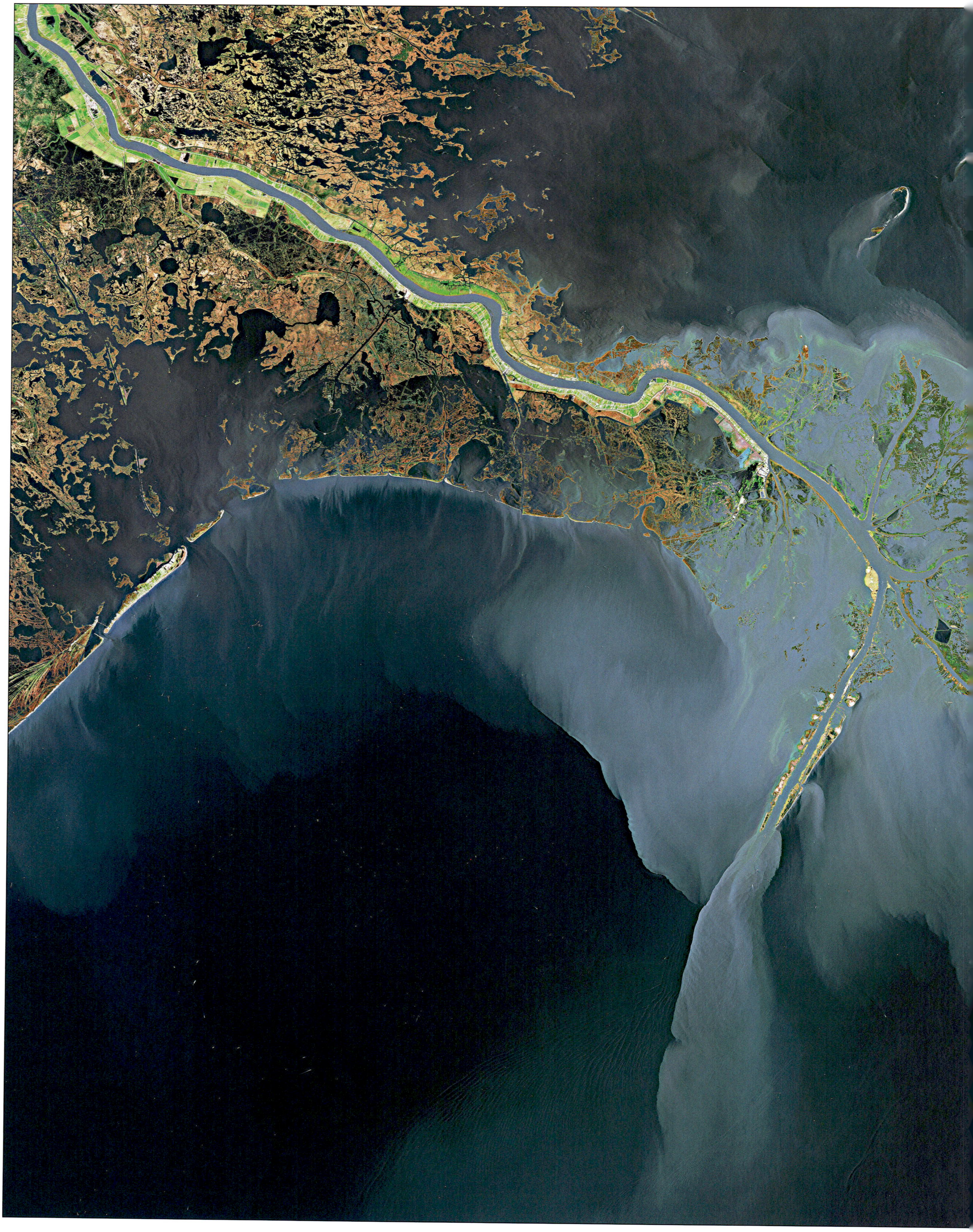

MISSISSIPPI

At 3,780 kilometres in length, the Mississippi is the longest river in North America and rightly known as the "Missi Sepe" by the Indians, or the "Father of all Rivers".

The Mississippi has its source in Lake Itasca in the north of Minnesota and flows south for around 3,780 kilometres to New Orleans, where it empties into the Gulf of Mexico. The river drains the entire region between the Rocky Mountains and the Appalachians, with the exception of the region around the Great Lakes. In its lower reaches, the Mississippi meanders through a broad plain (Fig. 1, p. 94 and Fig. 1, p. 96). It is possible to guess at the earlier path of the river from the countless artificial and natural gaps in the meanders. Meanders at a single level are known as free meanders and arise when a river slows on flatter ground. Depositing its bedload on an inner bend, it begins to build a barrier that then forces the river to turn aside.

The Mississippi flows through one of the largest connected farmland areas in the world. Around half of all the farms in the US are found in its catchment basin. However, the ecological equilibrium of the river has been hugely affected by the input of agricultural fertilisers.

The regions along the Mississippi are also subject to natural processes such as flooding, erosion and embankments of deposits (Fig. 3, p. 95). In addition, humans have also intervened extensively in the river system. In its upper reaches, the Mississippi has been channelled for shipping, its banks secured with gigantic dams and levees, and many reservoirs have been built. As such, humans have deprived many water meadows and wetlands of their natural water source.

Mississippi River Delta

To the south of New Orleans, the Mississippi empties into the Gulf of Mexico in an enormous delta (Fig. 1). The crow's feet of the delta are the result of the river's enormous sediment load, of 550 million tonnes of sediment every year. Within the flat alluvial plains at the mouth of the river lie countless wetlands, marshes and salt marshes.

◁
1 – *The delta of the Mississippi reaches far into the Gulf of Mexico. The mass of sediment that is carried and then deposited enables it to grow.*

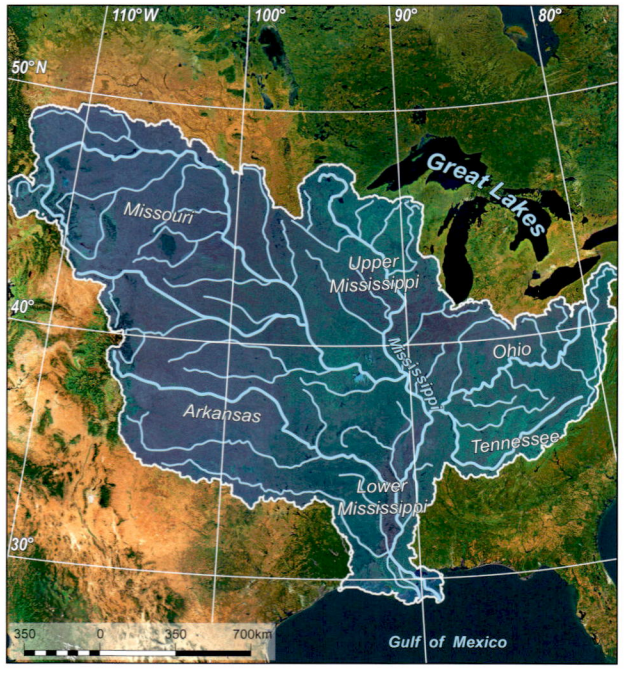

Around every thousand years, the Mississippi changes its lower course, which also changes the shape of the delta. The delta as we know it today has developed over the past 500 years (Figs. 2 and 3, p. 96). Before this time, the river deposited its sediments in a series of deltas roughly where New Orleans is today.

The Southwest Pass, which is around 40 kilometres long, has the largest volume of any channel in the delta. The entire Mississippi drains an average of 18,400 cubic metres of water per second and transports 1.5 million tonnes of sediment into the Gulf of Mexico every single day. Because the sediment is deposited more quickly than the sea can wash it away, the delta grows by around 100 metres a year, extending into the Gulf (Fig. 4, p. 97).

Flooding as a recurring event

Over the years, the Mississippi has burst its banks many times and caused extensive flooding along its course. Particularly in spring, with the onset of snowmelt, the waters swell, often causing the levees to burst. With the intensity of land use also the problems of floods increase.

△
*1 – The Mississippi meanders between the states of Arkansas (to the west) and Tennessee (to the east, map rotated), creating the state border between them.
Huge swathes of farmland extend along its banks and tributaries.
– northern part –*

◁
2 – Map of the Mississippi catchment basin.

▷ 3 – Typical meander in the Mississippi with river-cut cliff and inner bend, breach, and the oxbow lakes caused by the river changing its course.

The catchment basins of the Mississippi and the Missouri, the longest tributary of the Mississippi, cover an area of around 3.24 million square kilometres – one-third of the total area of the USA. The Missouri and lower reaches of the Mississippi have a total length of 6,050 kilometres, making it the fourth-longest river system in the world.

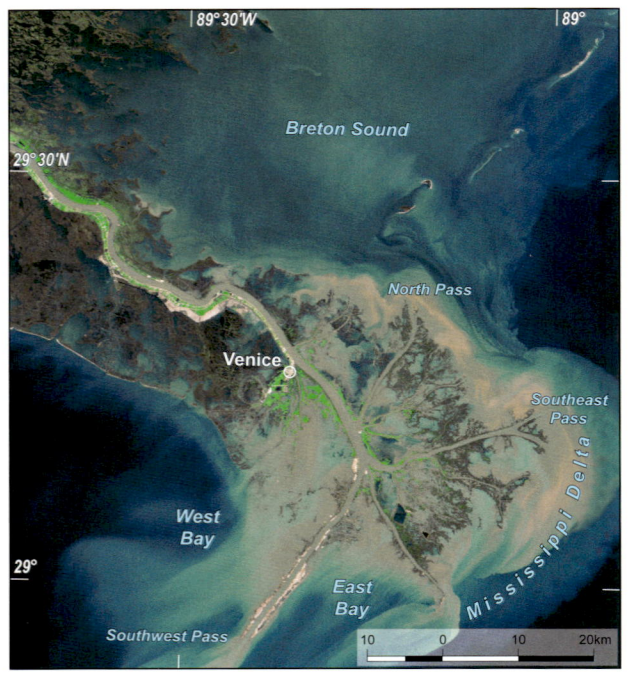

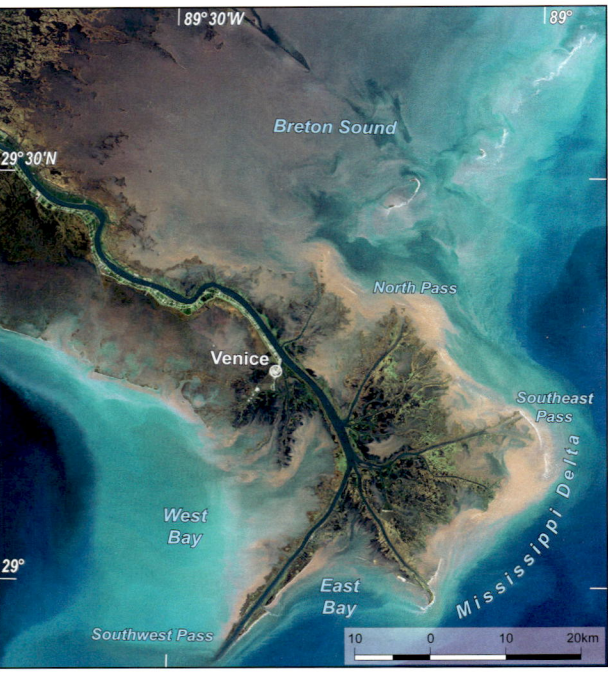

1 – The Mississippi meanders along the border between Arkansas (to the west) and Mississippi (to the east, map rotated).
– southern part –

2 – The satellite image shows the Mississippi River Delta in 1976. The huge, light-coloured sediment deposits can be clearly made out, especially on the Southwest Pass.

3 – The Mississippi River Delta in 2001. The satellite image shows the young, green vegetation of the land irrigated with water from the river.

▷
4 – The Mississippi transports up to two million tonnes of sediment into the Gulf of Mexico every single day. The map shows how deposits and erosion have changed the delta's shape between 1976 and 2001.

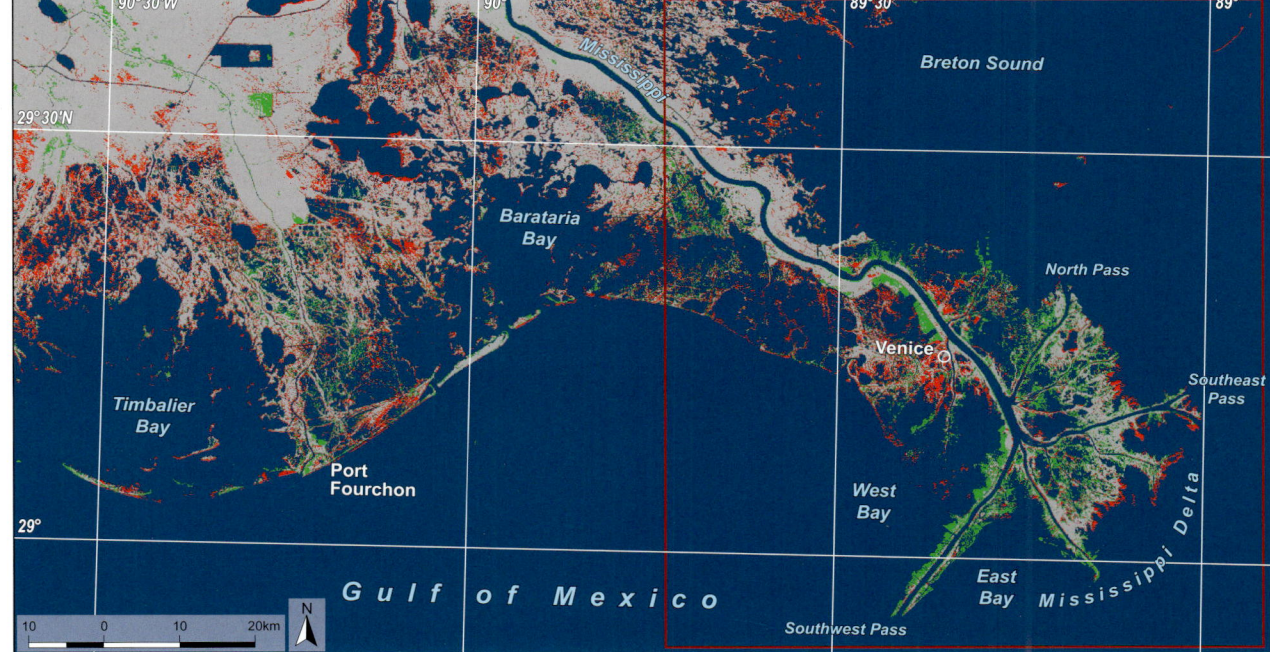

Land shifting on Louisiana's coast line
- Land loss
- Land gain
- Water surface
- no change

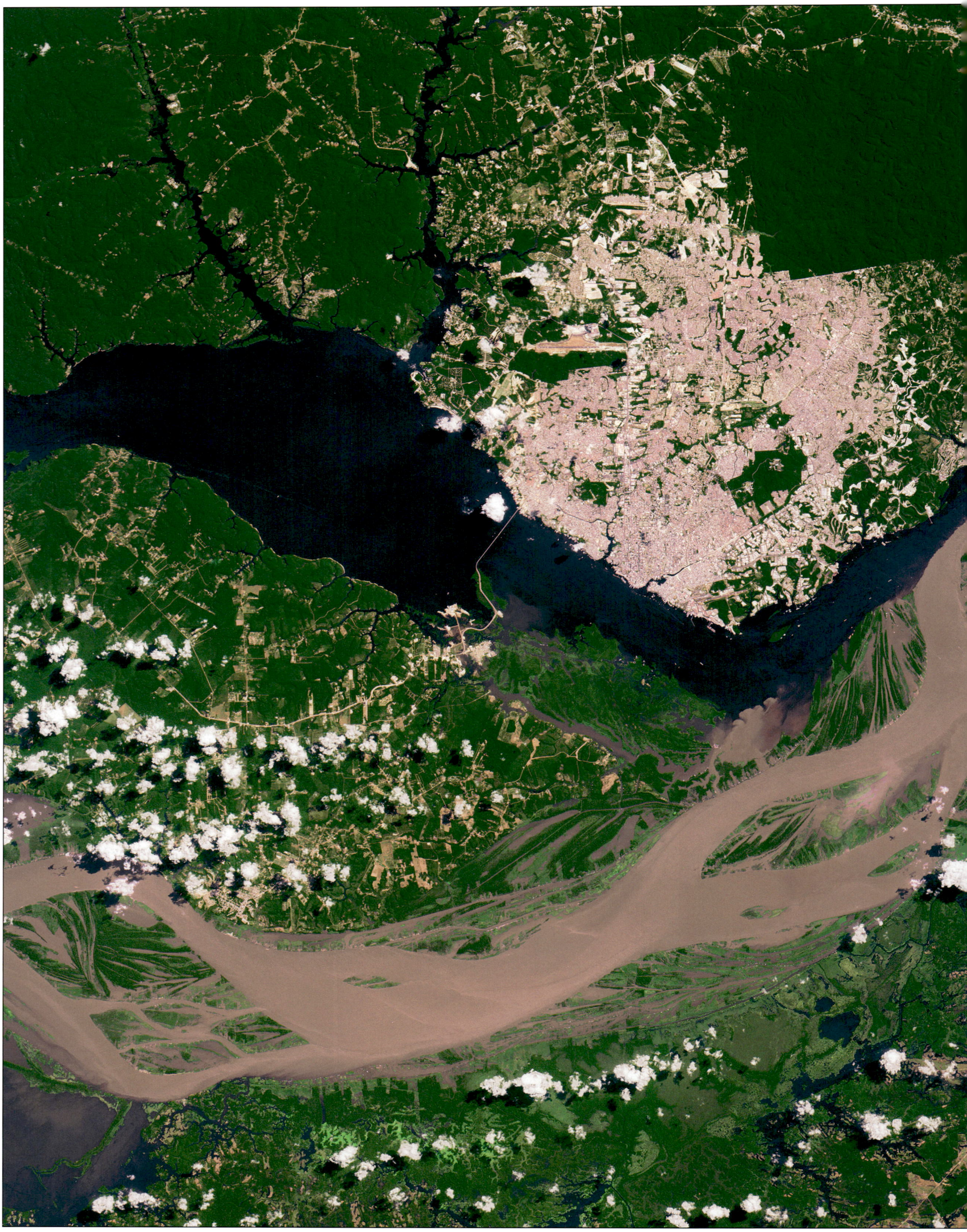

AMAZON

The Amazon is not the longest river in the world, but is by far the largest when it comes to waterflow. It drains the entire Amazon basin from the northern foothills of the Andes to the Atlantic Ocean.

With a length of 6,762 kilometres, the Amazon is one of the longest rivers in the world and also the one with the highest discharge, with an average of 206,000 cubic metres of water per second. It rises in the Peruvian Andes and flows east to the Atlantic Ocean.

The largest headstreams of the Amazon are the Ucayali and the Marañón, both of which flow from the glacial regions of the Andes to the north and join at Nauta to form the Rio Solimões. In the Middle Amazon Basin, to the south of the city of Manaus, the Rio Negro (Black River) joins the Rio Solimões (Fig. 1 and Fig. 1, p. 100). From this point, in the last third of its course, the river becomes known as the Amazon.

The Rio Negro, with its cold, slow-flowing waters, runs towards the north-east. The river's dark waters are the result of the high levels of humic and fulvic acids, which are washed out of the soil in the catchment basin by rainfall. Due to its nutrient deficiency, the Rio Negro cannot support mosquito larvae, which leaves the region along the river practically malaria-free.

The Rio Solimões flows from a westerly direction and has a high sediment load. Due to the low gradient and low flow, the two differently coloured rivers only mix completely a few kilometres after the confluence (Fig. 1, p. 100).

Along the course of the Amazon, large areas are constantly underwater or are flooded regularly, leaving the banks of the river frequently three to 12 metres underwater. The floods can inundate forests up to 100 kilometres away. These areas are known as the 'Várzeas'.

The main channel of the Amazon is deep enough to be navigable for even larger ships as far as Manaus. Smaller boats can travel as far as Iquitos in Peru, around 1,700 kilometres upstream to the west, without any problems.

◁
1 – Manaus in Brazil.
The River Amazon is born after the Rio Solimões (light due to sediment load) and Rio Negro (dark) join.
The contrasting rivers mix only slowly.

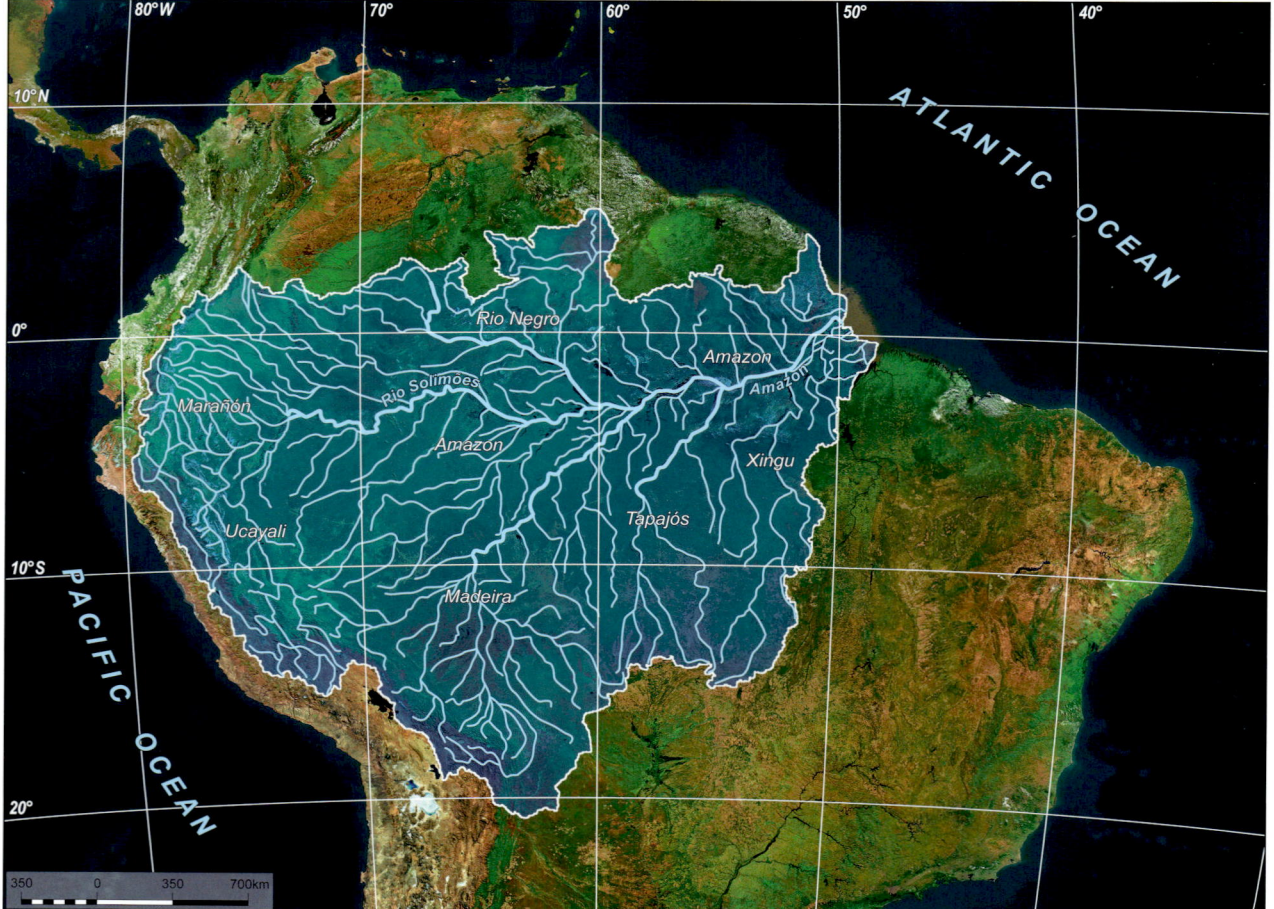

1 – The confluence of the Rio Negro and Rio Solimões near the Brazilian city of Manaus.

2 – The catchment basin of the Amazon River stretches over thousands of kilometres from the Andes in the west to the Atlantic Ocean.

3 – The mouth of the Amazon with the Canal do Norte, Canal do Vieira Grande and Canal do Sul.

The size of the catchment basin of the Amazon Basin currently covers around 6,000,000 square kilometres. The mapping of the tributaries changes constantly as new discoveries are made. Around half of the catchment, which covers nine neighbouring countries, is in Brazil.

The Amazon Basin

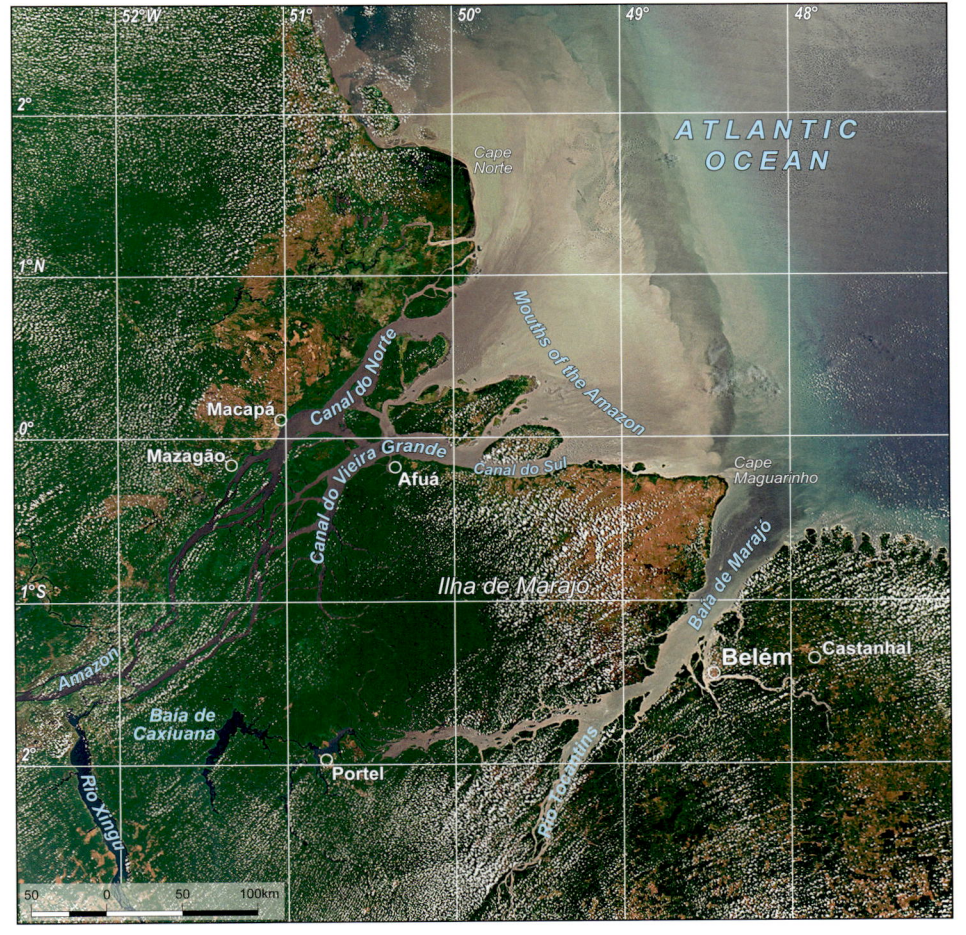

The Amazon Basin is located within the 6,145,186 square kilometres catchment basin of the Amazon River (Fig. 2). With an area of 3.6 million square kilometres, it comprises one-fifth of the total area of the South American continent and is one of the largest single natural landscapes on Earth. It is also home to the largest unfragmented area of tropical rainforest and, with it, the greatest species diversity of flora and fauna on the planet. Many plants and animals can be found only here and are completely dependent on their habitat.

The mouth of the Amazon

Although it is frequently referred to as the 'Amazon Delta', the mouth of the Amazon does not fulfil the criteria of being a delta. In fact, it is much more like an estuary. Despite annual sediment deposits of 900 million tonnes, strong sea currents prevent a delta from forming here. The flat coastline and the influence of the tides lead the river mouth to spread out in a funnel shape (Fig. 3).

Twice a day, the tidal range forces seawater and sediment several hundred kilometres upstream. In spring, a unique natural phenomenon occurs here. With the onset of the tide at low water and spring tide, the "Pororoca", a wave measuring four to five metres high flows up to 800 kilometres upstream. While the native inhabitants of the Amazon region fear the Pororoca due to its destructive force, this wave – the longest-lasting wave on Earth – now draws countless surfers from around the world to enjoy it.

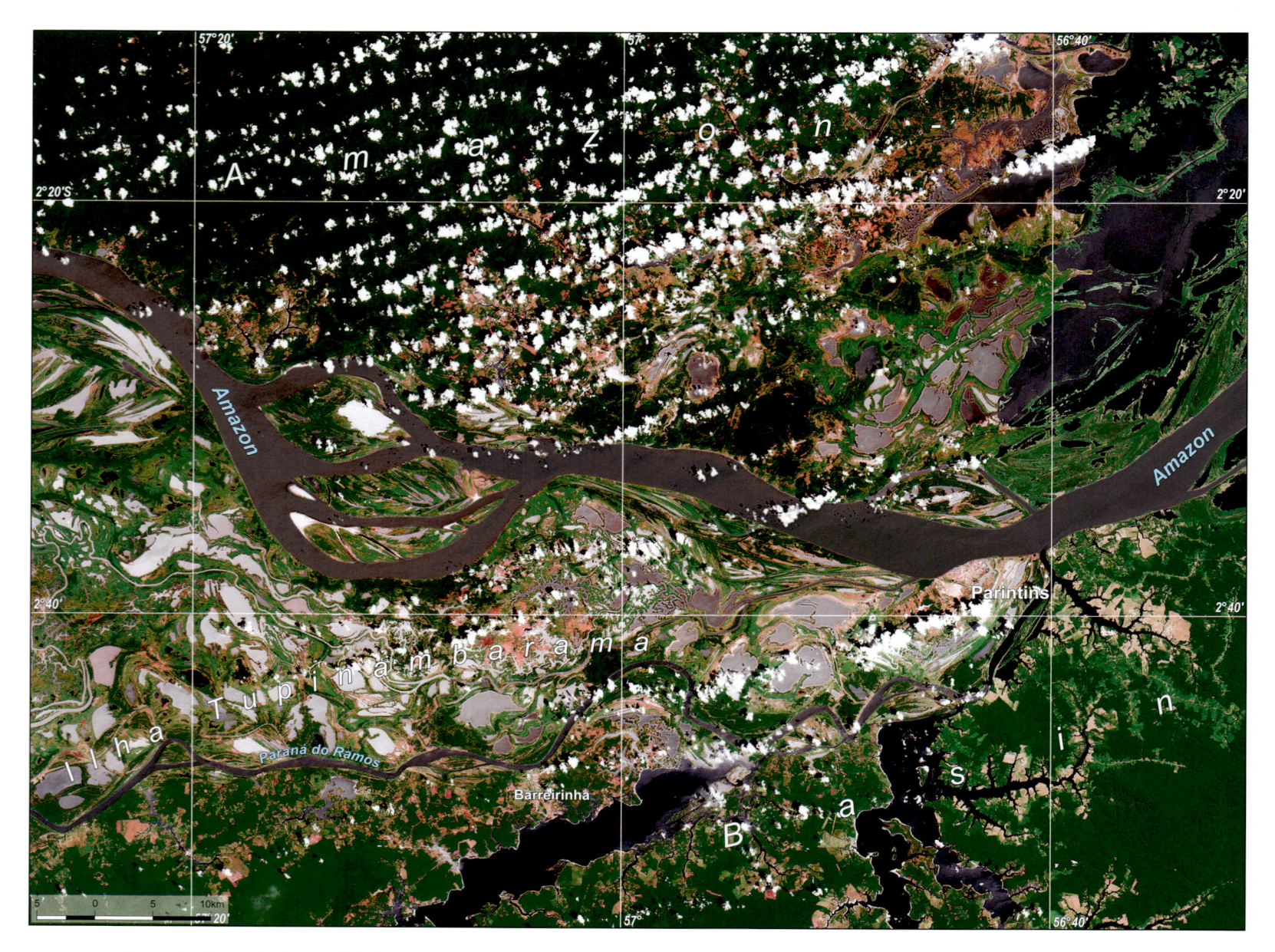

Impact of population and industry in the Amazon Basin

With the exception of the mouth of the river and a few larger cities, the Amazon is generally sparsely populated. Most of the catchment area is not even well-known to science – and in some regions, the native inhabitants still live in the same way they did before the Europeans arrived. The inhabitants of the Amazon Basin generally pursue a simple form of shifting cultivation and fishing.

In recent decades, however, the timber industry, cattle farming and mining have all increased in significance. As such, larger and larger areas of forest have been destroyed through deforestation and slash-and-burn (Fig. 3 and 4 a-c). Other areas have fallen victim to the building of roads and settlements. The soil in the region has very few nutrients and the agricultural land can only be used for a few years. This means that new areas must be slashed and burned every year so that the farmers can continue to make their living.

Forests play an important role in our planet's climate. They store the carbon dioxide that drives the greenhouse effect and release large quantities of oxygen. As a result, the progressive destruction of the green lungs of our planet affects the world's entire climate.

Widespread mining also has devastating consequences for the sensitive ecosystem of the Amazon Basin. Gold deposits are often bound and filtered using mercury, which can lead to the permanent pollution of the soil and the Amazon River.

△
1 – Between the two cities Manaus and Santarém, the city of Parintins lies on the Amazon's largest island of Ilha Tupinambarana.

◁
2 – An oblique aerial image taken by an astronaut on the International Space Station (ISS) shows the Amazon estuary from space.

▷△
3 – This multitemporal ASAR (radar) image, acquired 2 January, 1 February and 3 March 2013, reveals in colour human activities, ever-changing river courses and subtle morphological structures of the terrain not perceivable in optical images.

▷
4 a/b/c – Areas cleared by slash-and-burn in the tropical rainforest in the Amazon catchment basin, documented using optical satellites. These images were taken in July 1992 (left), in August 2001 (middle) and in August 2013 (right) in the state of Rondônia.

67°W
66°45'
Carauari
Rio Juruá
5°S
Rio Juruá
2 0 2 4 6km

63°W
62°50'
11°40'S
Seringueiras
11°50'
12°
12°10'
5 0 5 10km

63°W
62°50'
11°40'S
Seringueiras
11°50'
12°
12°10'
5 0 5 10km

63°W
62°50'
11°40'S
Seringueiras
11°50'
12°
12°10'
5 0 5 10km

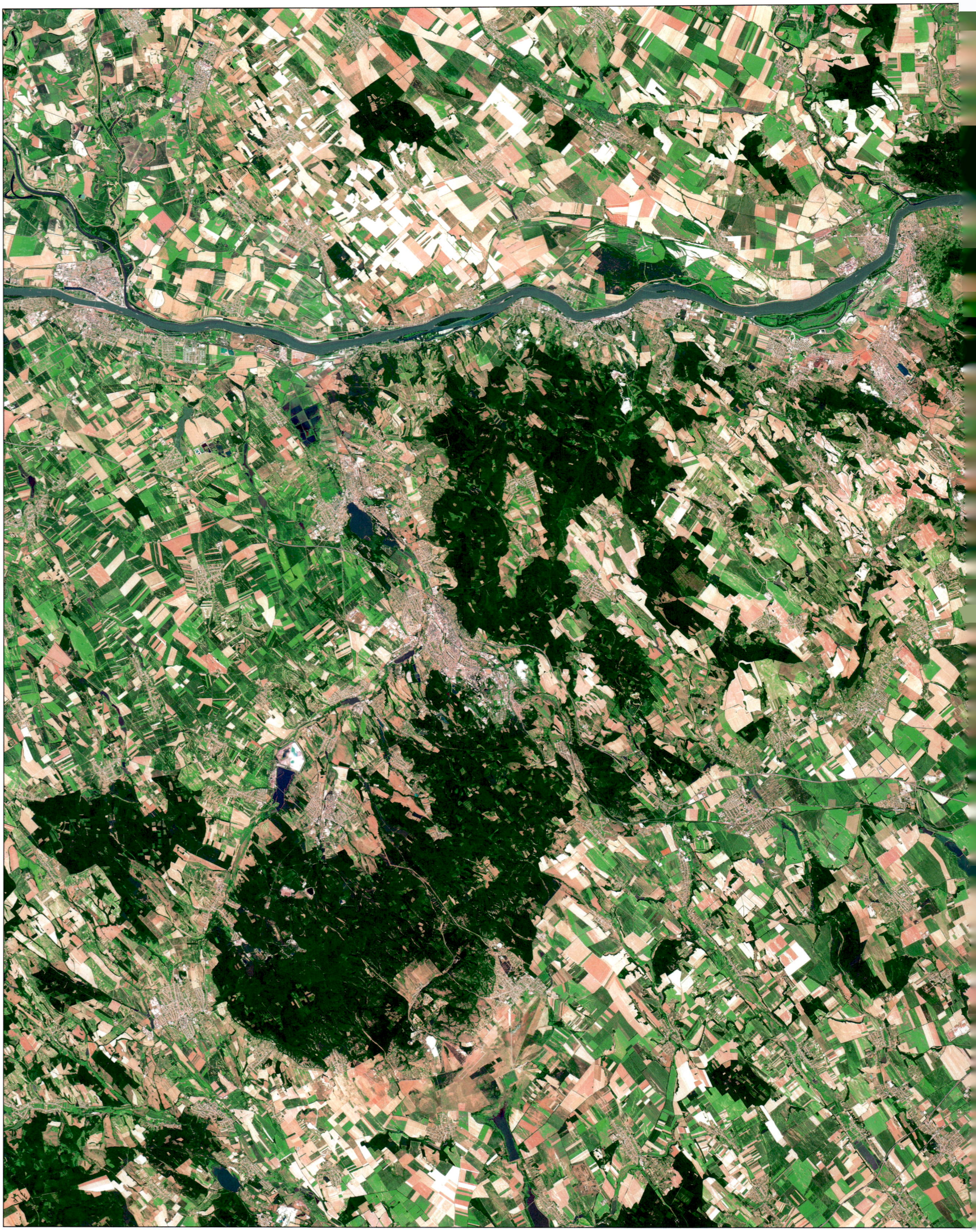

DANUBE

The name of this river flowing through the heart of Europe comes from the Celtic word 'danu', meaning 'river'. With a length of 2,845 kilometres, the Danube is the second-longest river in Europe after the Volga.

The Danube rises in Germany's Black Forest. Following the confluence of its two headwaters, the Brigach and the Breg, the Danube flows east and goes on to form a major delta in southeastern Romania before emptying into the Black Sea (Fig. 1, p. 106/107).

The Danube's catchment basin covers an area of over 795,000 square kilometres. Although the Alps only make up 38 per cent of the catchment area, three-quarters of the Danube's waters originate in the Alps. The Central Alps in particular hold major stores of water in their glaciers, which store precipitation in the form of snow and ice.

As a result of the geology of the bedrock in the catchment basin, the Danube changes course significantly several times. The first change occurs to the north of Budapest (Fig. 1), where it shifts from its eastward course to flow south instead. Another change occurs in Romania east of Bucharest, where the Danube turns north, then starts to flow east once again, just before the delta.

Danube Delta – World Heritage site

Where it flows into the Black Sea, the Danube has created an enormous delta. With an area of over 5,000 square kilometres, it is the largest delta in Europe after the Volga Delta. In this area, the Danube is split into three channels. The Chilia branch in the north forms the border between Romania and Ukraine, while the Sulina branch in the centre of the delta is a major shipping channel. In the south of the delta, the St. George branch empties into the Black Sea. While very few people live in the delta itself, the surrounding region is densely populated and also heavily farmed (Fig. 3 and 4a/b, p. 109).

The Danube Delta forms its own unique ecosystem, which is home to over 300 different species of bird, including pelicans, great egrets, cranes, white-tailed eagles and red-breasted geese, as well as countless freshwater fish, including pike, zander, carp, sturgeon and many more. As a result, the entire area was declared a UNESCO World Natural Heritage Site in 1991.

The exploitation of the Danube

The second-longest river in Europe fulfils many functions for the people living near it. Firstly, the Danube plays an

◁
1 – The Danube divides the Hungarian capital into Buda (the hilly part in the west) and Pest (flatter area in the east).

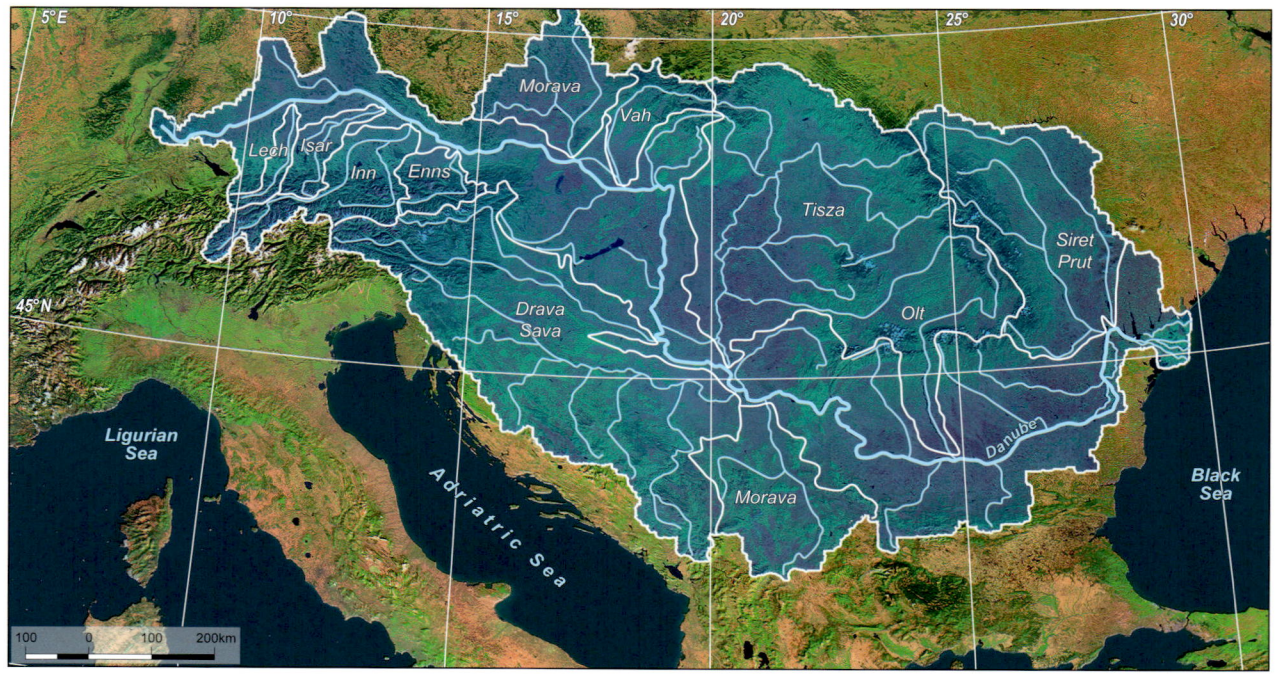

△
1 – The Danube in Europe. On its path towards the Black Sea, the Danube passes through nine countries.

◁
2 – The Danube catchment basin drains an enormous area from the Black Forest to the Black Sea.

The Danube catchment basin covers an area of around 795,000 square kilometres, spread over 18 neighbouring countries.

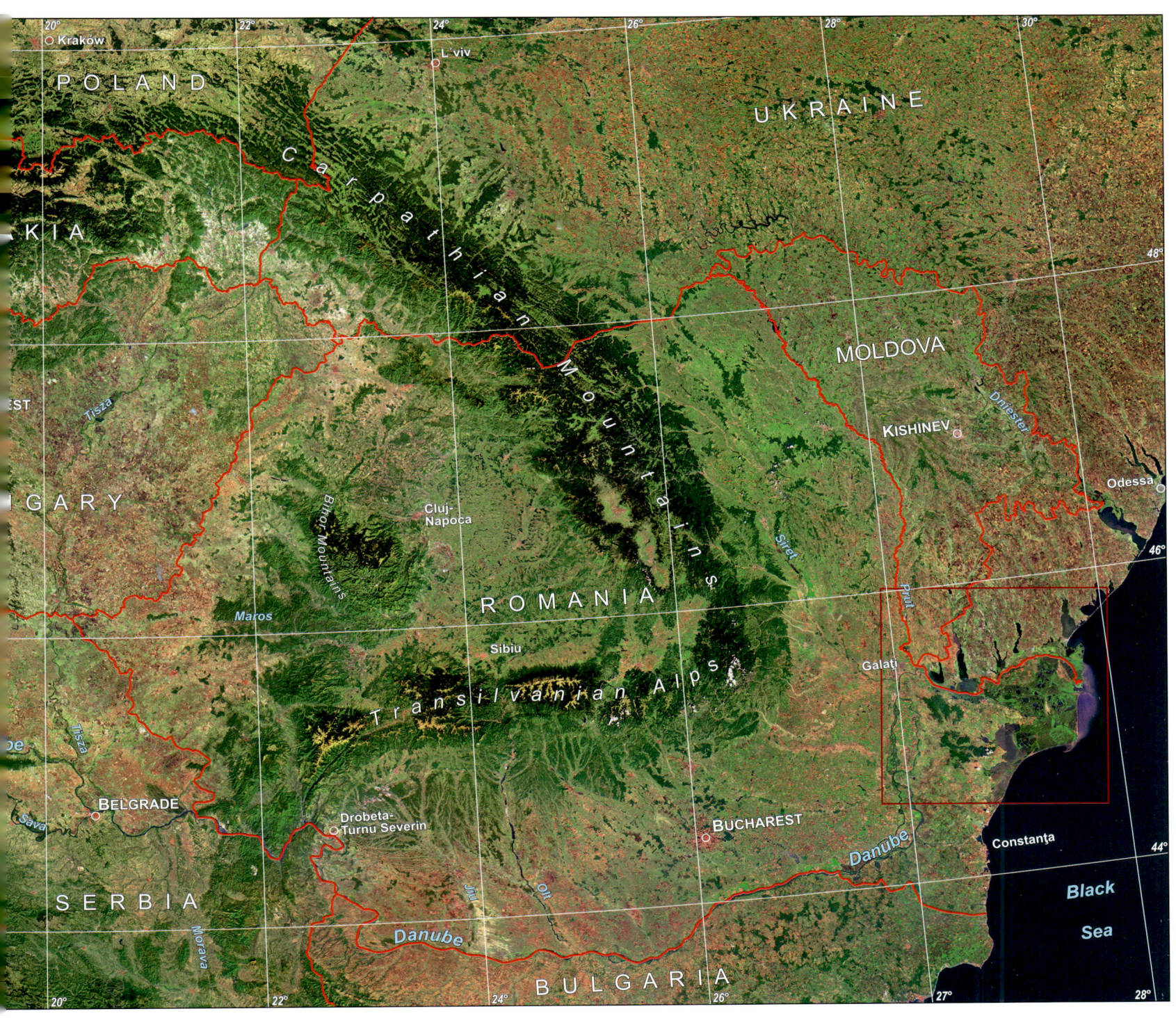

3 – At the Iron Gates the Danube crosses the Carpathians. The dangerous rapids of the river were tamed by the dam of the Iron Gate 1 power station.

important role in inland shipping. Secondly, it is used all along its course for generating energy and irrigating fertile farmland (Fig. 1, p. 108).

The Danube is also an important source of drinking water for ten million people along its banks. German towns and cities in particular are heavily reliant on drinking water from the Danube. As a result of the high levels of pollution in its middle reaches, however, some regions cannot make use of this natural source of freshwater.

The Iron Gate 1 hydroelectricity plant

The largest hydroelectric power plant on the Danube is at the Iron Gates, a narrow river gap between the southern Carpathians and the Serbian Carpathians, 15 kilometres west of Drobeta-Turnu Severin (Figs. 1 and 3), which once was the most dangerous passage in the course of the river. In 1964, construction began on a dam to close the gorge, which resulted in a 150 kilometres reservoir. The power station there has a nominal output of around 2,160 megawatts. The construction of the power station has caused massive incursions on the environment and the lives of the local population. Seventeen thousand people had to be relocated, while archaeological and cultural sites were flooded and the habitats of countless animal and plant species were either changed forever or completely destroyed. However, the power station has been providing essential renewable energy since 1972.

Gabčíkovo hydroelectric power station

As a result of the devastating floods between Györ and Bratislava in the 1950s and 1960s, the countries of Hungary and the former Czechoslovakia signed an agreement to build a series of sluice gates known as the Gabčíkovo–Nagymaros Dams. In addition to the two power stations, the plans also included building embankments along the Danube for 200 kilometres. However, this mammoth project never came to fruition as a result of environmental concerns and protests by environmental campaigners. As such, only the Gabčíkovo power station in modern-day Slovakia was built. It is the largest power station in the country and covers around 11 per cent of the country's annual national electricity requirements.

The Danube as a waterway

The Danube has been used as a waterway for a very long time. Even in early history, ships passed down a large part of the river's course. Goods for trading, such as furs and commodities, were transported on simple rafts.

Today, 2,411 kilometres of the river's course are navigable for modern ships transporting goods such as coal and iron ore. Larger ships can use the watercourse only from Kelheim, Germany, just before Regensburg, where the Rhine-Main-Danube Canal joins the Danube. Since the 171 kilometre-long Main-Danube Canal was opened in 1992, the Rhine-Main-Danube Canal has linked the Black Sea with the North Sea. The total length from the mouth of the Danube into the Black Sea and the mouth of the Rhine into the North Sea is around 3,500 kilometres.

Almost every town or city along the Danube has its own harbour, and these are often some of the biggest freight-transhipment areas in the country. In landlocked Austria, the three harbours on the Danube in Vienna, which at 3.5 square kilometres is the largest freight hub in Austria, exemplify this well (Fig. 2).

△
1 – The Danube between Vienna and Bratislava.

◁
2 – Danube harbour in Vienna.

▷△ ▷ ▷▷
3; 4 a/b – The Danube Delta (3: multitemporal ASAR image, 4a: land use classification, 4b: optical satellite image).

Land cover Danube Delta
- Lagoon
- Sand, dune
- Cultivated land
- Grassland
- Forest
- Inland marshes
- Settlement
- Water surface

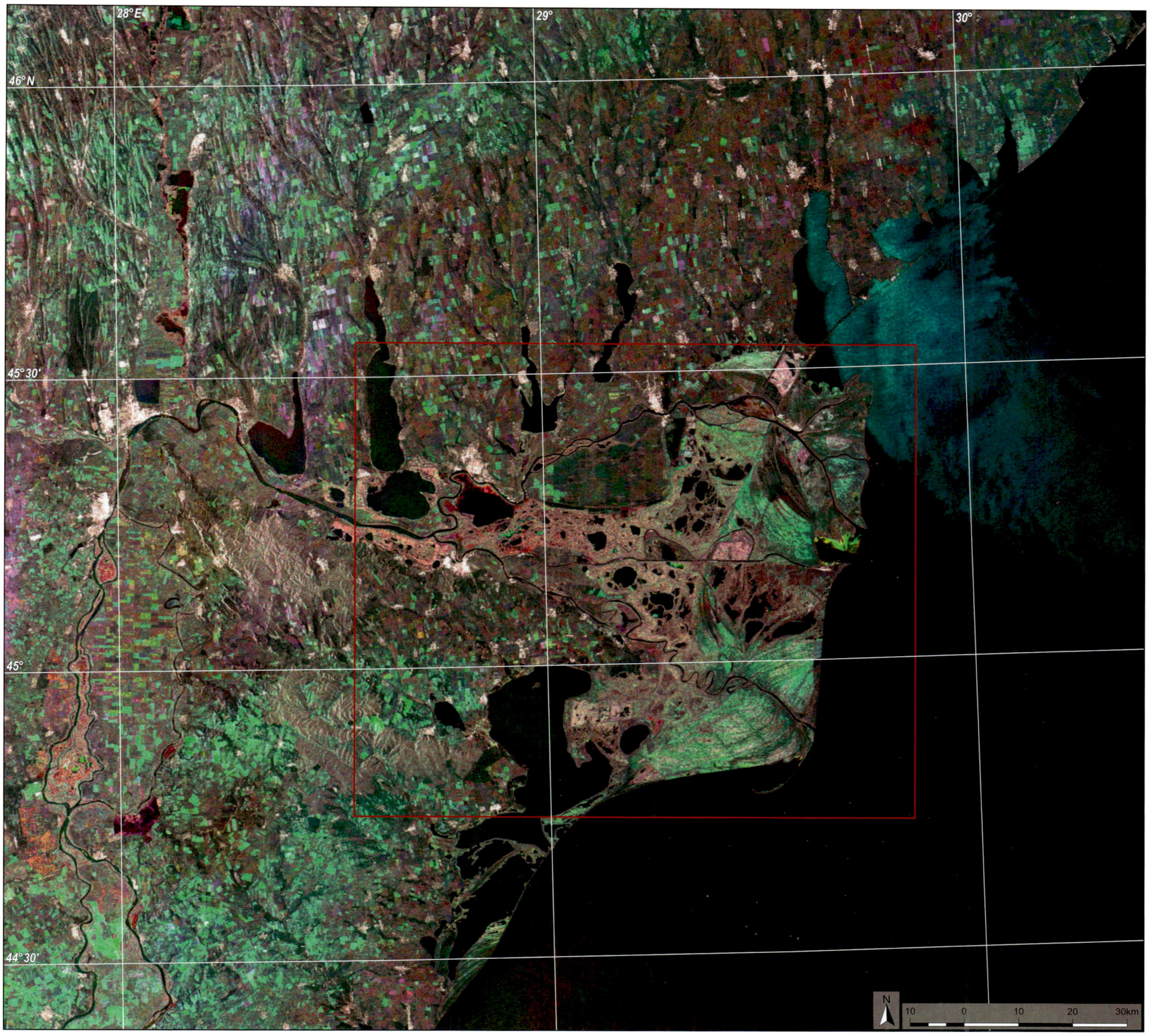
28°E
29°
30°
46°N
45°30'
45°
44°30'
N
10 0 10 20 30km

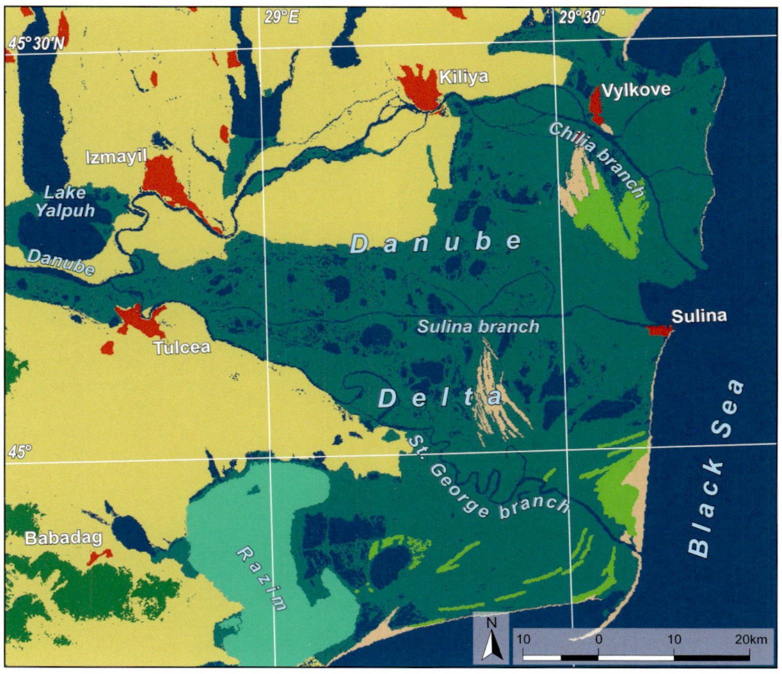
29°E
29°30'
45°30'N
45°
Kiliya
Vylkove
Izmayil
Lake Yalpuh
Chilia branch
Danube
D a n u b e
Sulina
Sulina branch
Tulcea
D e l t a
St. George branch
Black Sea
Babadag
Razim
N
10 0 10 20km

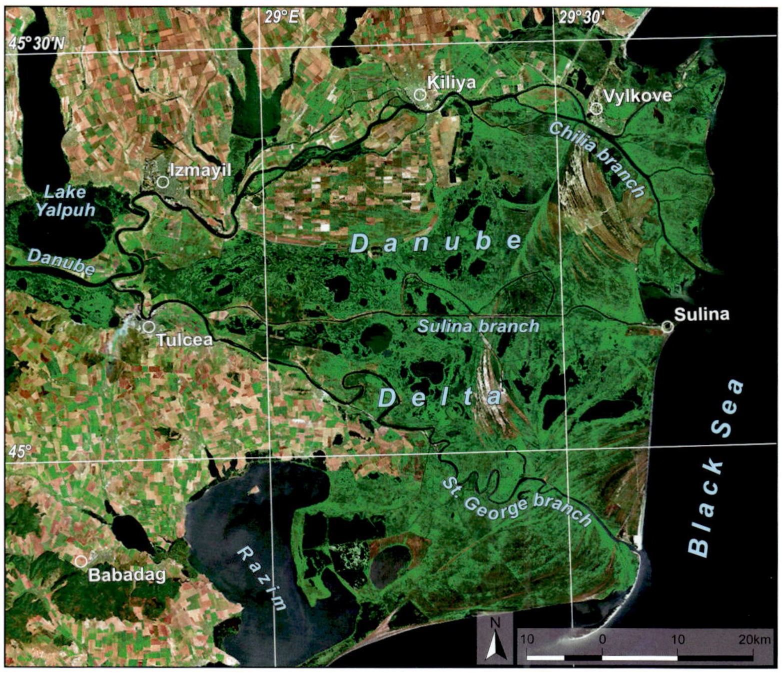
29°E
29°30'
45°30'N
45°
Kiliya
Vylkove
Izmayil
Lake Yalpuh
Chilia branch
Danube
D a n u b e
Sulina
Sulina branch
Tulcea
D e l t a
St. George branch
Black Sea
Babadag
Razim
N
10 0 10 20km

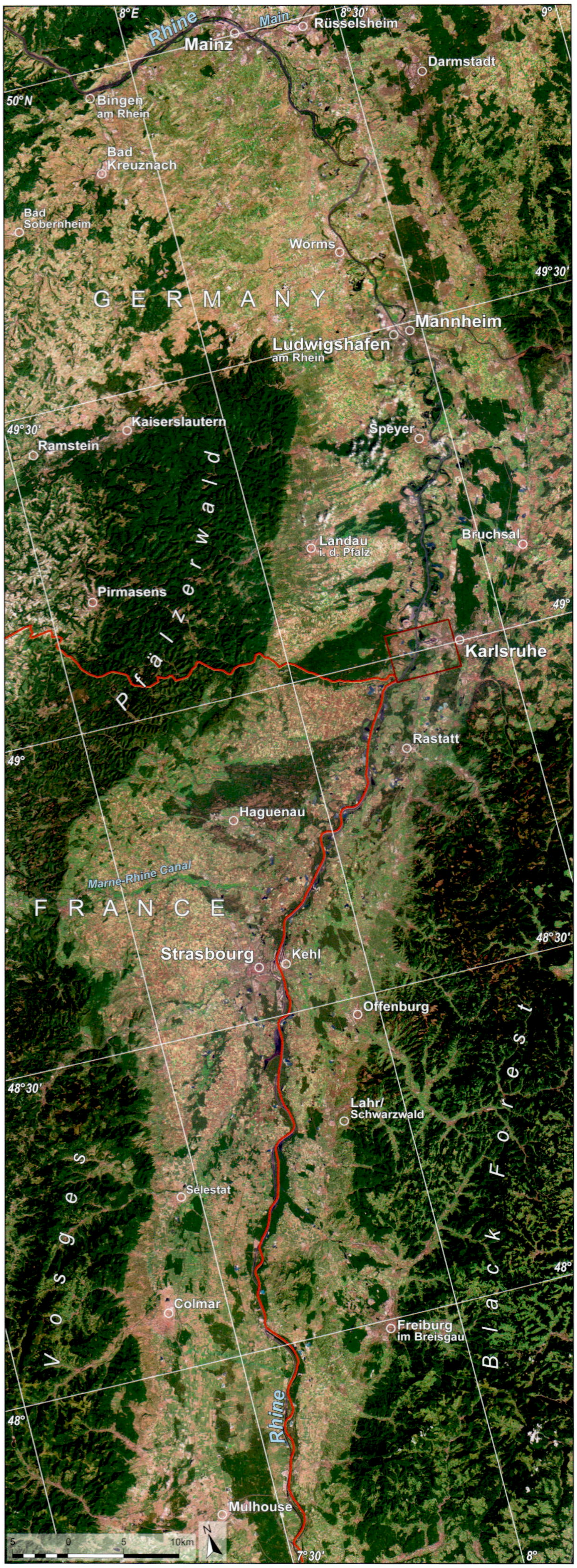

8°E
8°30'
9°
Rhine
Main
Mainz
Rüsselsheim
Darmstadt
50°N
Bingen am Rhein
Bad Kreuznach
Bad Sobernheim
Worms
49°30'
G E R M A N Y
Mannheim
Ludwigshafen am Rhein
49°30'
Kaiserslautern
Ramstein
Speyer
Pfälzerwald
Bruchsal
Landau i. d. Pfalz
Pirmasens
49°
Karlsruhe
Rastatt
49°
Haguenau
Marne-Rhine Canal
F R A N C E
48°30'
Strasbourg
Kehl
Offenburg
48°30'
Lahr/ Schwarzwald
Vosges
Black Forest
Selestat
48°
Colmar
Freiburg im Breisgau
48°
Rhine
Mulhouse
5 0 5 10km
N
7°30'
8°

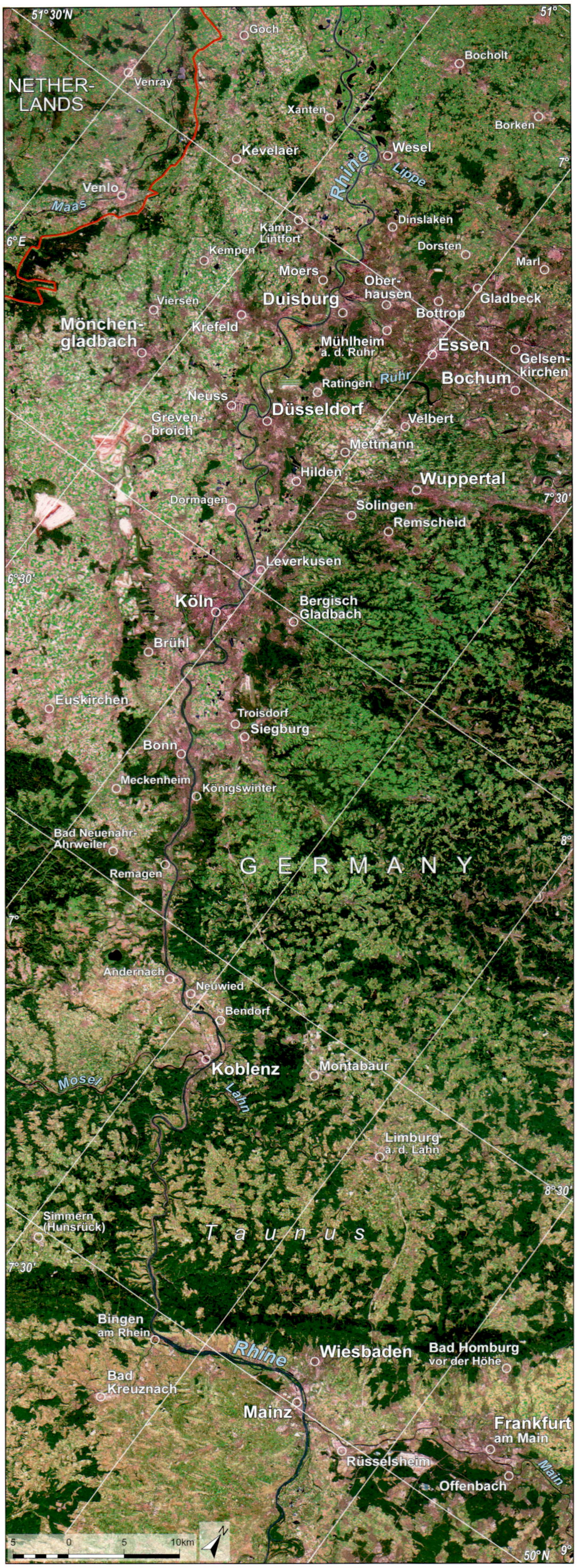

51°30'N
51°
Goch
Bocholt
NETHER-LANDS
Venray
Xanten
Borken
Kevelaer
Wesel
7°
Rhine
Lippe
Venlo
Maas
Dinslaken
6°E
Kamp Lintfort
Kempen
Dorsten
Marl
Moers
Ober-hausen
Viersen
Duisburg
Bottrop
Gladbeck
Mönchen-gladbach
Krefeld
Mühlheim a. d. Ruhr
Essen
Gelsen-kirchen
Ratingen
Ruhr
Bochum
Neuss
Greven-broich
Düsseldorf
Velbert
Mettmann
Hilden
Wuppertal
Dormagen
Solingen
7°30'
Remscheid
6°30'
Leverkusen
Köln
Bergisch Gladbach
Brühl
Euskirchen
Troisdorf
Siegburg
Bonn
Meckenheim
Königswinter
Bad Neuenahr-Ahrweiler
8°
Remagen
G E R M A N Y
7°
Andernach
Neuwied
Bendorf
Koblenz
Montabaur
Mosel
Lahn
Limburg a. d. Lahn
8°30'
Simmern (Hunsrück)
T a u n u s
7°30'
Bingen am Rhein
Rhine
Wiesbaden
Bad Homburg vor der Höhe
Bad Kreuznach
Mainz
Frankfurt am Main
Rüsselsheim
Offenbach
Main
5 0 5 10km
N
50°N
9°

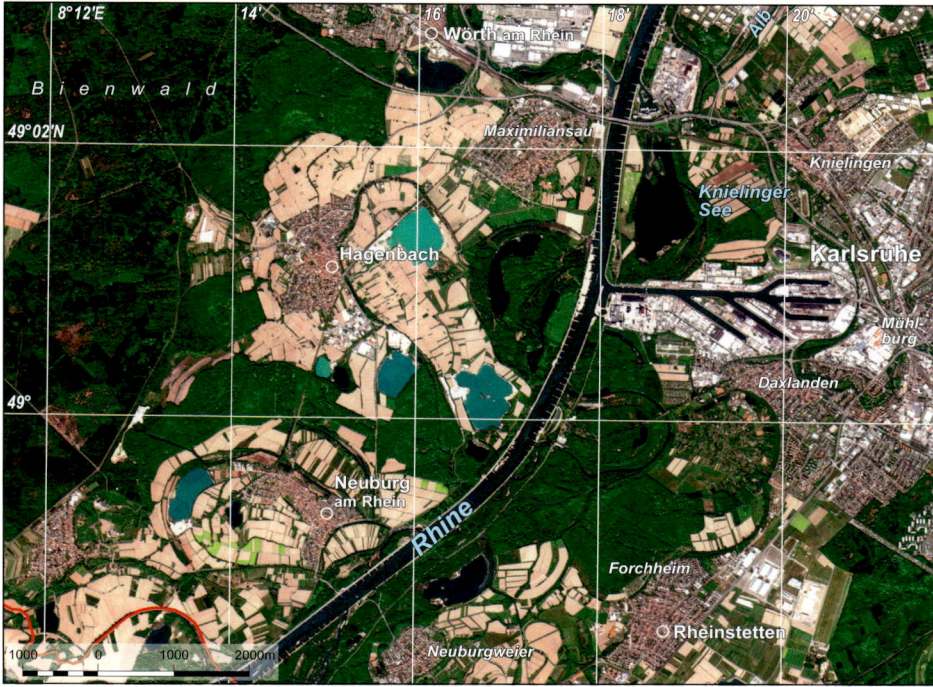

RHINE

The Rhine is a legendary river, whose catchment basin is now home to more than 50 million people. On its 1,233 kilometre-long course, it passes through countless conurbations and industrial areas

The Rhine has its headwaters in the Swiss Alps (Fig. 5). The Vorderrhein and Hinterrhein rise in the canton of Graubünden and join to form the Rhine near Reichenau. The Alpine Rhine empties into Lake Constance to the west of Hard and leaves the lake as the High Rhine near Stein am Rhein. At Schaffhausen, it drops 23 metres at a rate of 700 cubic metres of water per second.

The course of the Rhine, measured officially from Konstanz on Lake Constance, is divided into some more sections on its 1,031 kilometre-long course until it opens into the North Sea: the High Rhine, Upper Rhine, Middle Rhine and Lower Rhine (Figs. 1 and 2). Just after the Germany/Netherlands border, the Rhine opens out into the Rhine Delta, as the river forks into two branches that meet again just before Rotterdam (Fig. 3).

The Rhine as a waterway

Originally, the Rhine, lined by water meadows, snaked through the Upper Rhine Plain in a countless series of meanders (Fig. 1). The Rhine regularly burst its banks well into the 19th century. To make the areas along the banks suitable for farming and settlement, a major project to regulate the river was carried out between 1817 and 1879. Johann Gottfried Tulla headed this project. The landscape architect and his successors constructed cutoffs to force the river into a straight bed with a maximum width of 250 metres. The countless oxbow lakes of the Rhine near Karlsruhe still indicate the river's original course before it was straightened (Fig. 4)

The straightening of the river boosted shipping, which is now restricted only in the event of extremely high or low water levels. The Rhine is now the busiest inland shipping lane in Europe. On the right bank of the middle Lower Rhine in the Ruhrort district of Duisburg lies the largest inland harbour in Europe and a major cargo hub for the entire Ruhr Valley area (Fig. 4).

The Rhine links the major seaports of Rotterdam and Antwerp and via its many canals joins the rivers Ems, Weser and Elbe, thus also linking up the North Sea ports of Emden, Wilhelmshaven, Bremen, Bremerhaven, Hamburg and Cuxhaven and the industrial conurbations of the Rhine-Ruhr and Rhine-Main, as well as Karlsruhe and Basle. The Rhine-Main-Danube Canal also provides a direct link to the Black Sea.

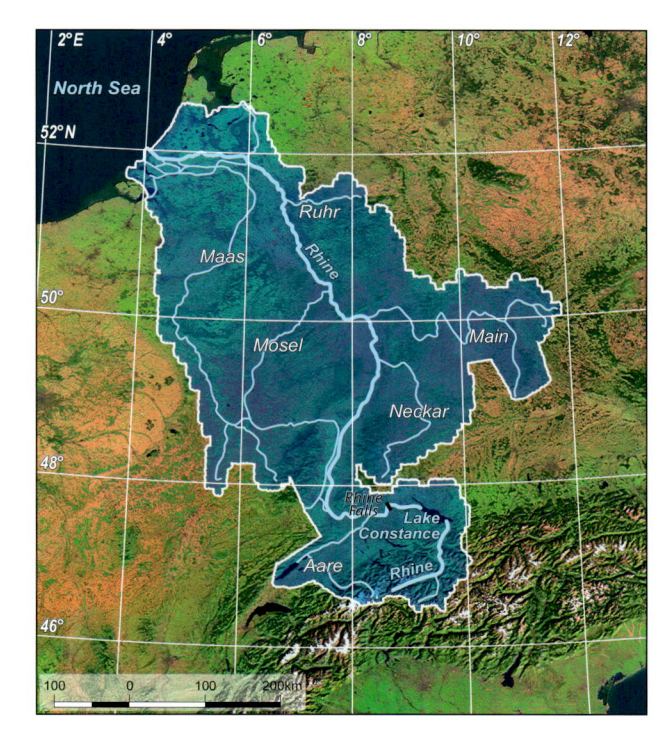

△ 3 – The Rhine-Meuse Delta makes up a large geographical region of the Netherlands.

△ 4 – The finger-shaped basin of the docks of the "Rheinhafen" in Karlsruhe. Water bodies, woods and field structures reveal old river arms

◁ 2 – The course of the Upper Rhine down to Mainz marks parts of the border between Germany and France.

◁ 1 – The course of the Middle and Lower Rhine in Germany.

▷ 5 – Including the Maas Delta, the Rhine catchment area measures about 218,000 sq km².

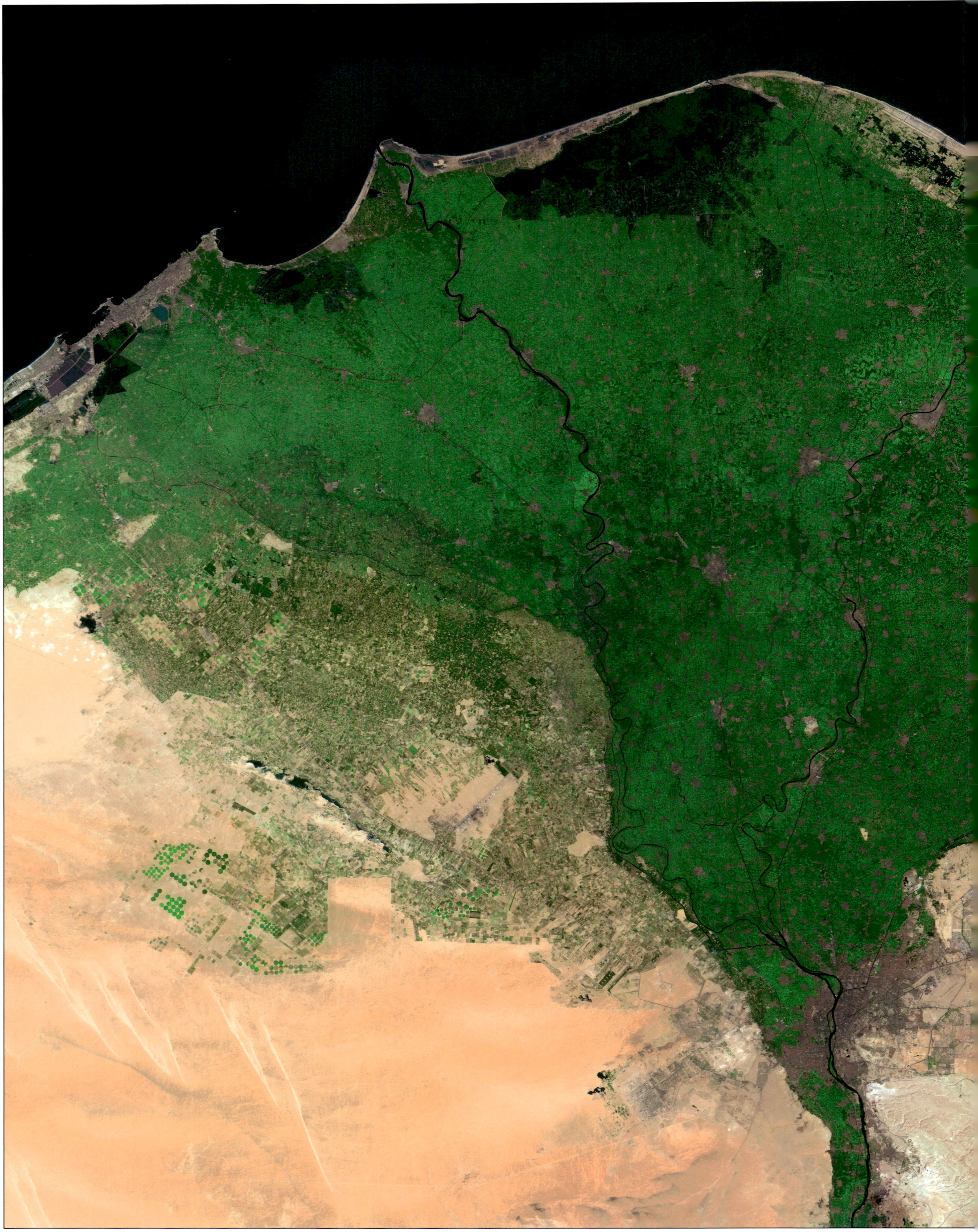

NILE

With a length of 6,695 kilometres from its source at the Equator to its mouth in the Mediterranean Sea, the Nile is the longest river on Earth. Even the Greek historian Herodotus recognised that Egypt was a "Gift of the Nile".

The White Nile rises at an altitude of 1,250 metres in the Equatorial Lakes Plateau (Fig. 3, p. 115). It flows as the Victoria Nile from the northern part of Lake Victoria into Lake Kyoga, and from there into Lake Albert (Mobuto-Sese-Seko Lake). Leaving the lake it is known as the Albert Nile and flows north to the border with South Sudan. It flows into the Sudd as the White Nile (Bahr el-Jebel in Arabic), where more than half of its water evaporates. Joining the Sobat River in the swamps of the Sudd, it flows on towards Khartoum, where it then meets the Blue Nile (Fig. 2, p. 114). The Blue Nile rises in Lake Tana in the Ethiopian Highlands at an altitude of 1,830 metres. The river gets its name from its dark colour, which comes from the sediment washed down from eroding soil. From there until the Mediterranean, the Atbara is the Nile's last tributary. From this point the Nile flows northwards through the desert as an allochthonous river (Fig. 1, p. 114). Allochthonous rivers are rivers that rise in areas of high precipitation but flow through arid zones.

On its path towards the delta, the Nile meanders northwards through six cataracts (powerful waterfalls). These natural granite barriers, which turn the Nile into a storming, unpredictable torrent, are especially dangerous for boats. The first two cataracts have now been submerged beneath Lake Nasser, following the building of the Aswan Dam. The last cataract is north of Khartoum. The distance between the first and last cataract is 1,880 kilometres.

The Nile Delta

The lush Nile Delta stands in stark contrast to the barren desert surrounding it (Fig. 1). Cairo, the capital of Egypt, lies on the southern edge of the Nile Delta. To the north of the teeming capital, the Nile splits into the eastern

◁
1 – The spectacular green Nile delta at the Mediterranean Sea allows arable farming and contrasts greatly with its arid surroundings.

113

30°E
32°
32°N
Mediterranean Sea
Alexandria
Khafr ash Shaykh
Dumyāt
Nile
Al Manşūrah
Port Said
Tanţa
Delta
Zagazig
Al Ismā'īlīyah
30°
Giza
CAIRO
Suez
Sinai
Al Fayyūm
Banī Suwayf
Nile
Gulf of Suez
28°
Al Minyā
Eastern Desert
Western Desert
Asyūţ
Sohâg
EGYPT
26°
Qina
Luxor
24°
Aswān
Sinn al Kadhdhab
Toshka Lakes
Lake Nasser
22°
Lake Nuba
Wadi Halfa
Nile
Nubian Desert
SUDAN
20°
50 0 50 100km

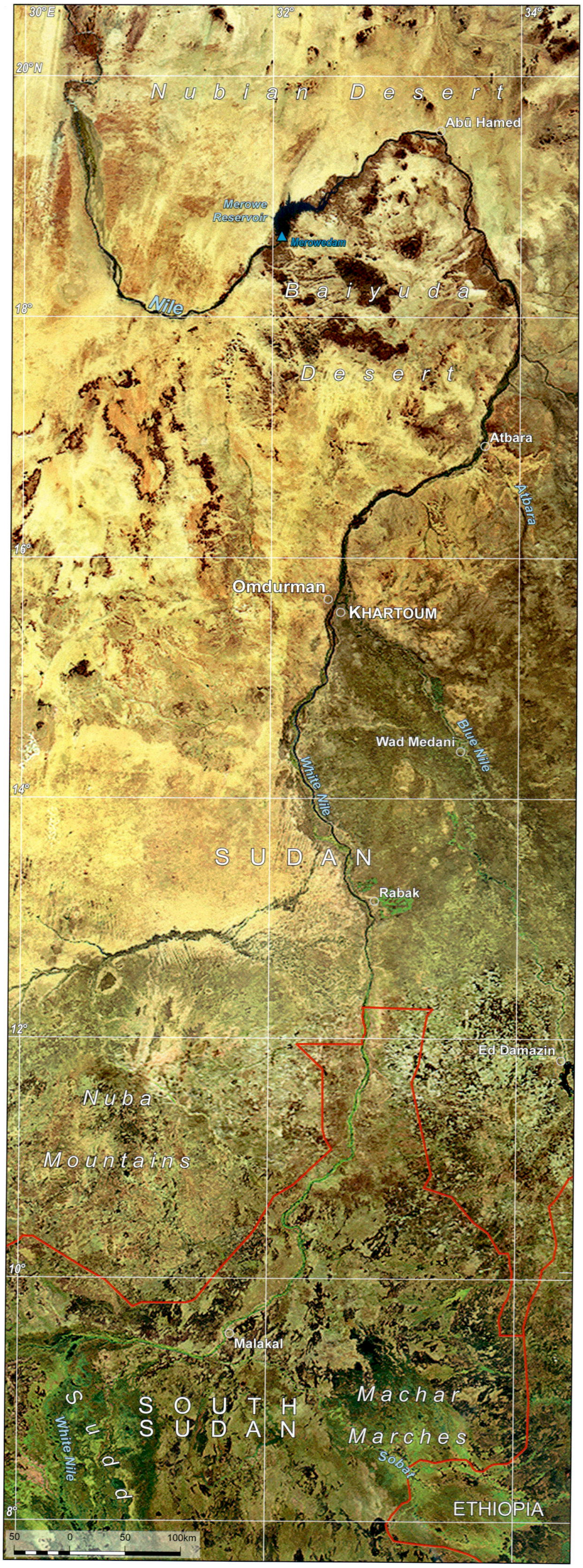
30°E
32°
34°
20°N
Nubian Desert
Abū Hamed
Merowe Reservoir
Merowedam
Baiyuda Desert
Nile
18°
Atbara
Atbara
16°
Omdurman
KHARTOUM
Wad Medani
Blue Nile
White Nile
14°
SUDAN
Rabak
12°
Ed Damazin
Nuba Mountains
10°
Malakal
Sudd
White Nile
SOUTH SUDAN
Machar Marches
Sobat
ETHIOPIA
8°
50 0 50 100km

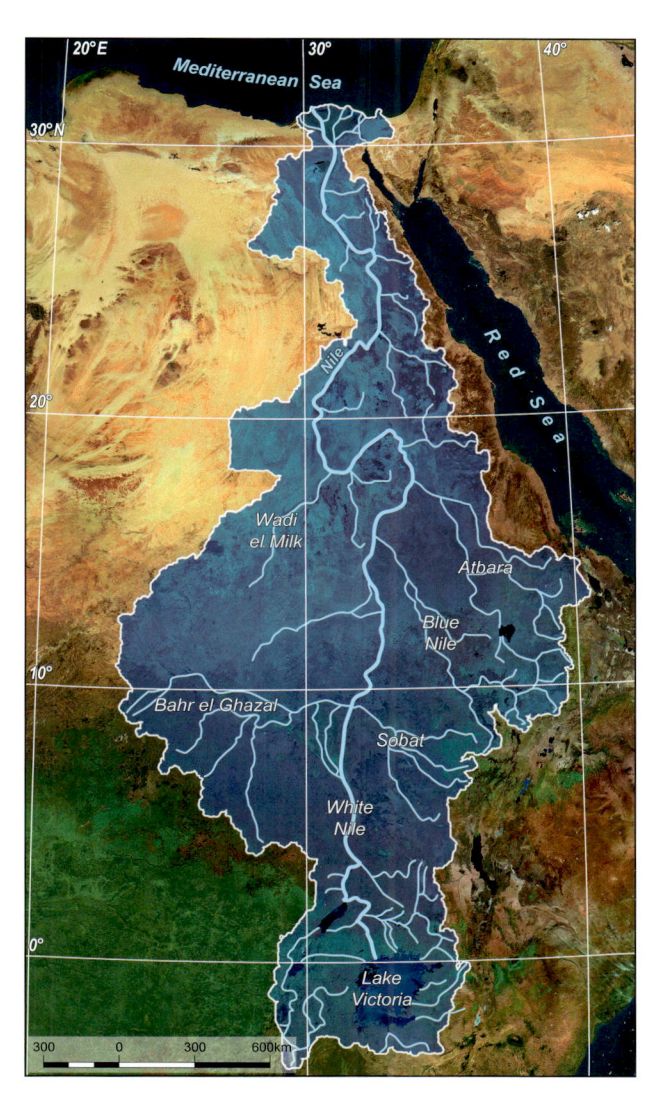

◁
3 - After rising in Rwanda, the world's longest river first flows through Lake Victoria, then Lake Kyogo and finally Lake Albert.

△
4 – The 3.2 million-square-kilometre catchment area of the Nile.

Damietta branch and the western Rosetta branch, both of which empty into the Mediterranean. Most of Egypt's people live in the Nile Delta, and agriculture is the main source of income.

As a result of the fertile soil and irrigated farming, several harvests a year can be brought in. Citrus fruits and cotton are the main crops. The chemicals industry and iron and metalworking also play a major role.

The building of the Aswan Dam severely reduced the sediment load of the Nile. As a result, the delta area is subject to greater erosion from the Mediterranean tides and currents.

The Aswan Dam

In order to control the annual floods on the Nile, to improve inland shipping, generate energy and permanently irrigate agricultural land, the Aswan Dam (Sadd el-Ali) was built with Soviet help between 1960 and 1971. The dam is 13 kilometres south of the city of the same name. Behind the 111 metre-high structure blocking the Nile lies Lake Nasser, which stretches back for 500 kilometres. However, the building of the dam brought with it not just the positive effects that were desired. In addition to putting archaeological sites such as Abu Simbel at risk due to the rise of Lake Nasser and the forced resettlement of countless farmers from the Nile Valley, the construction of the dam also had devastating ecological consequences.

◁◁
1 - The lower course of the Nile from Lake Nasser to the Nile Delta. Green cultivated fields follow the river through the desert.

◁
2 - The central part of the Nile splits Sudan into two parts. Vegetation cover decreases from south to north. Khartoum is where the White and Blue Nile meet. The Merowe dam, built in 2009, is used mainly for producing electric power.

30°30'E
31°
31°30'
32°
23°
23°30'N
Toshka Depression
Toshka
Nasser Reservoir
10 0 10 20 30km
N

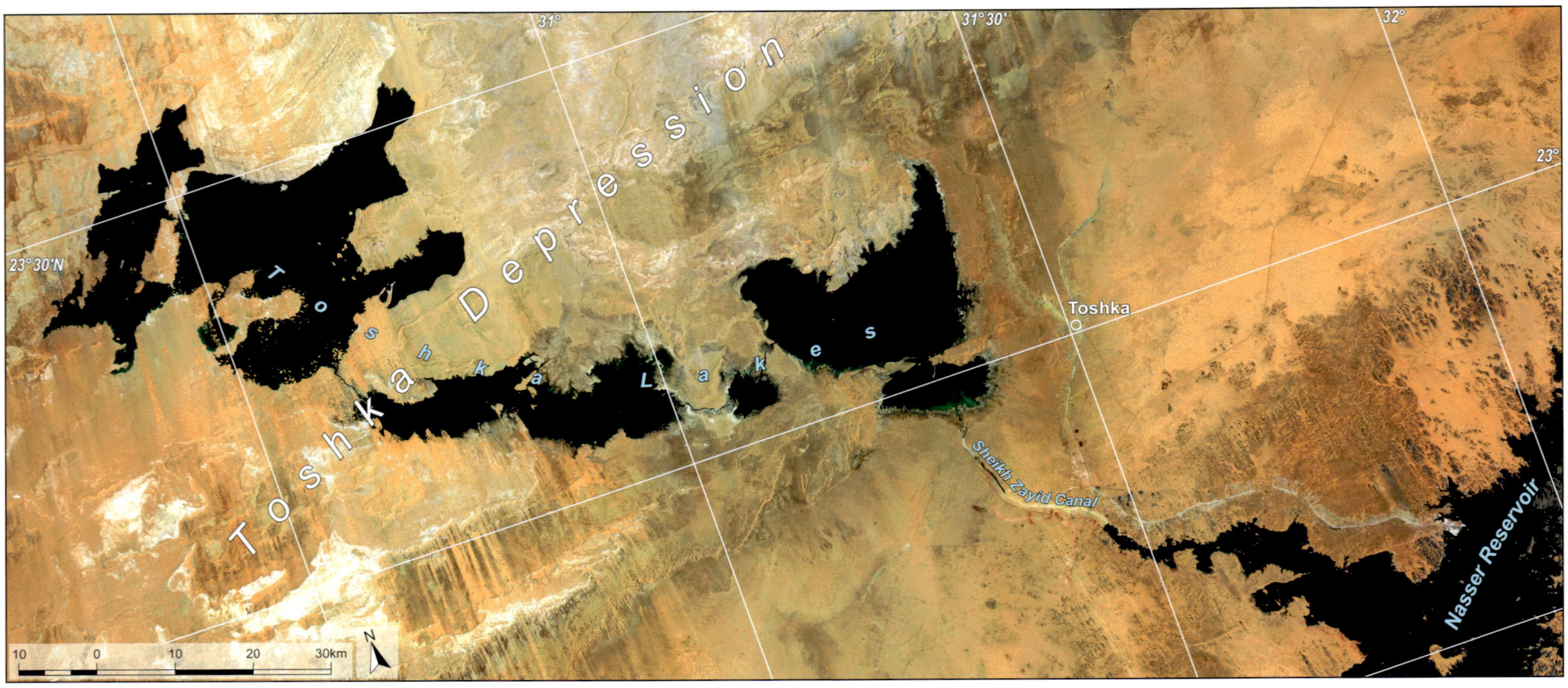
31°
31°30'
32°
23°
23°30'N
Toshka Depression
Toshka Lakes
Toshka
Sheikh Zayid Canal
Nasser Reservoir
10 0 10 20 30km
N

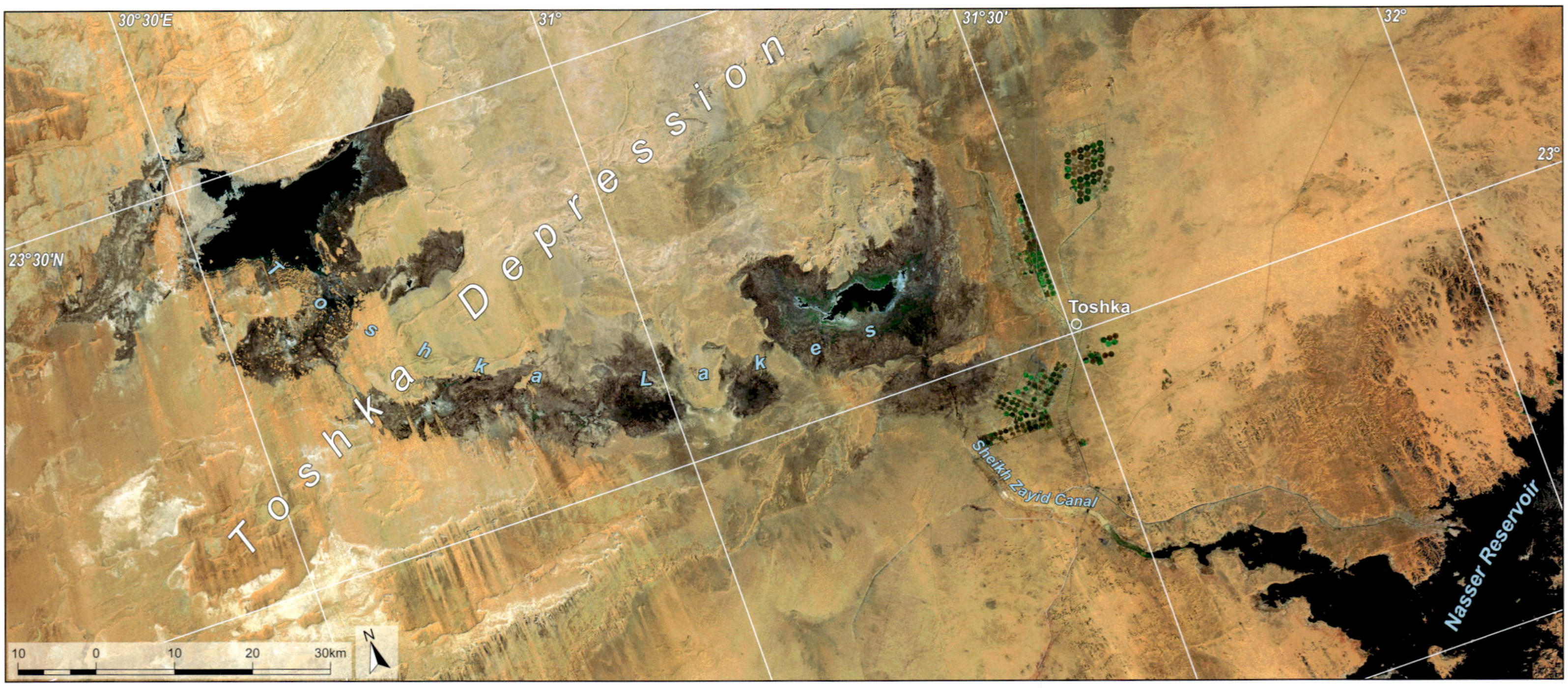
30°30'E
31°
31°30'
32°
23°
23°30'N
Toshka Depression
Toshka Lakes
Toshka
Sheikh Zayid Canal
Nasser Reservoir
10 0 10 20 30km
N

◁
1 – Wadi Toshka before being flooded by waters from Lake Nasser, taken in November 1972.

▷
4 – The way the Egyptians understood the universe is reflected in the distribution of their places of worship. Here in Giza, for example, all the cities of the dead are located on the western side of the Nile, west of the green belt.

◁
2 – The flooded Toshka Depression in March 2002, which has since shrunk. The depression is now known as the 'New Valley'. Since 2005, the Mubarak Pumping Station has been pumping water from Lake Nasser along the new Sheikh Zayed Canal into the new valley, where new towns are to be built.

◁
3 – The Wadi Toshka Depression in December 2013 has now shrunk to just two lakes. As such, only 20 per cent of the lakes' area still exists as compared with 2002. The lakes serve to irrigate new farmland in the desert.

The dam has interrupted the transport of fertile silt along the Nile. As the waters no longer bear nutrients, the farmers have had to resort to artificial fertilisers, and fish stocks in the Nile downstream from Aswan have also dropped precipitously. The lower sediment load has also meant an end to deposition in the Nile Delta, leaving the coastal areas of the delta subject to erosion from the Mediterranean surf.

The lake itself has also experienced negative effects. The Nile sediment held back by the dam is slowly but surely silting up the lake. The high rate of evaporation also expedites the silting-up.

As part of the dam project, a canal (the Sheikh Zayed Canal) was built in 1978 to divert excess water from Lake Nasser to Wadi Toshka, a depression in the dry limestone plateau of the Western Desert. The first lake appeared in 1998, and a further three lakes have sprung up inside the depression. The entire area of the Toshka lakes was 1,540 square kilometres in 2002, but fell to 937 square kilometres in 2006 and 307 square kilometres in 2012 (Figs. 1 - 3).

These lakes are part of the Egyptian government's Toshka project, which aims to use artificial irrigation to create new farmland in the desert.

A precious resource for many countries

Around 437 million people live in the 11 countries through which the Nile travels, 238 million of whom live directly in its catchment area.

Primarily Egypt, Sudan, South Sudan and Eritrea are highly dependent on water from the Nile. Egypt, astride the river's lower reaches, is wholly dependent on the major African river, and this has created strong political tensions among the riparian countries.

Water is the most precious resource in the arid regions of our planet. It often determines wealth or poverty, but always determines the quality of life of the local population. As an allochthonous river, the Nile plays a huge role in Egypt.

Egypt – a gift of the Nile

The Nile has always shaped the lives and cultures of those living along its banks, as well as far beyond its reaches. People have lived from the Nile and alongside it for centuries. For a long time, their survival depended on the annual floods. The nutrient-rich silt maintained the Egyptians' food supply because the fields could be replanted again after the waters had receded. However, there were years when these life-giving floods were mere trickles, or never came at all, which led to failed harvests and periods of famine and drought. To be better prepared for such events, very early on the Egyptians attempted measuring the water levels of the Nile by constructing twenty Nilometers, or shafts with water level markings.

The Nile was the principal transport route in Ancient Egypt and it was possible to travel the entire length of the country from north to south in a boat. It was also used to transport grain, cattle and stone for construction.

The major significance of the Nile to the Egyptians is reflected in their culture and beliefs. Its meaning for them was also reflected in the way the Ancient Egyptians understood the cosmos. The east, where sun rises, was the Kingdom of the Living, while the west was the Kingdom of the Dead. As a result, cities of the dead such as the Valley of the Kings, the pyramids and the funerary temples of the Pharaohs were built on the western bank of the Nile, while houses, temples, schools and such went up on the eastern bank (Fig. 4).

118

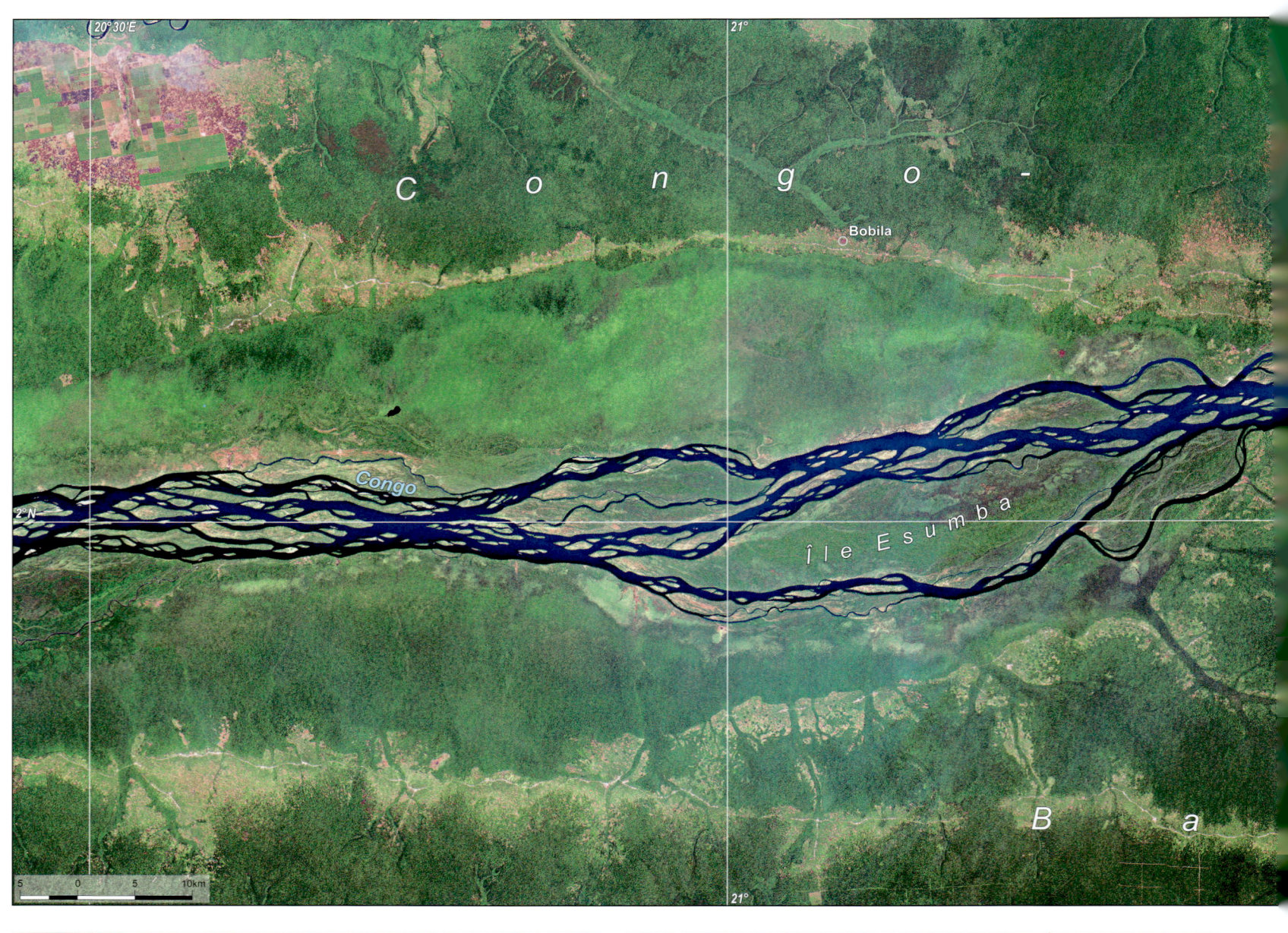

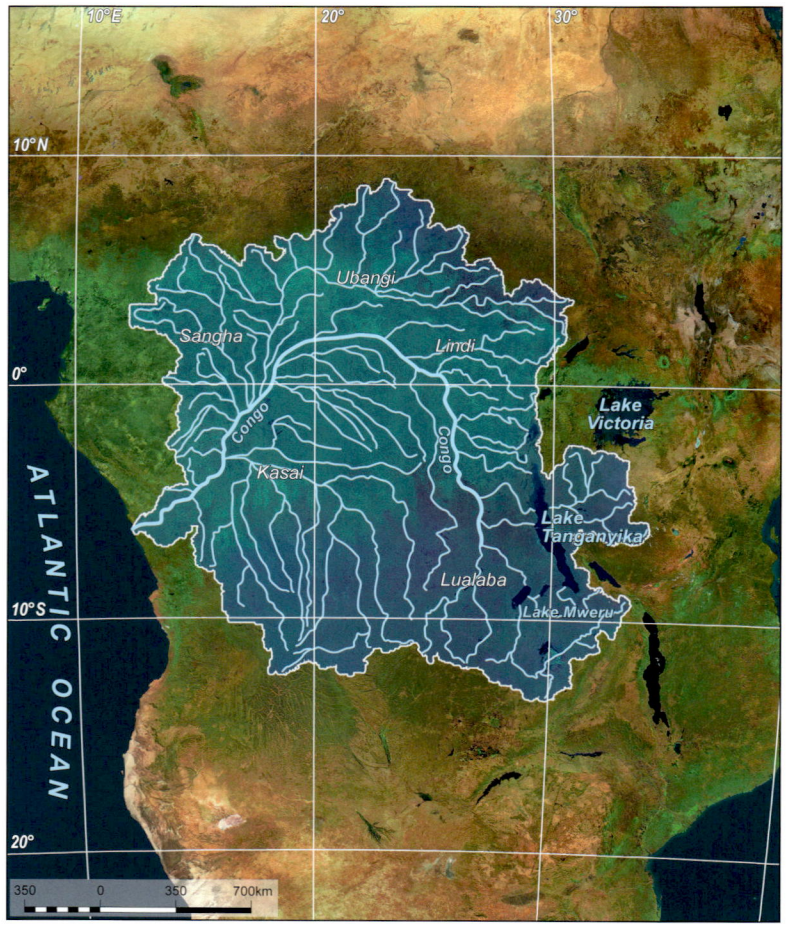

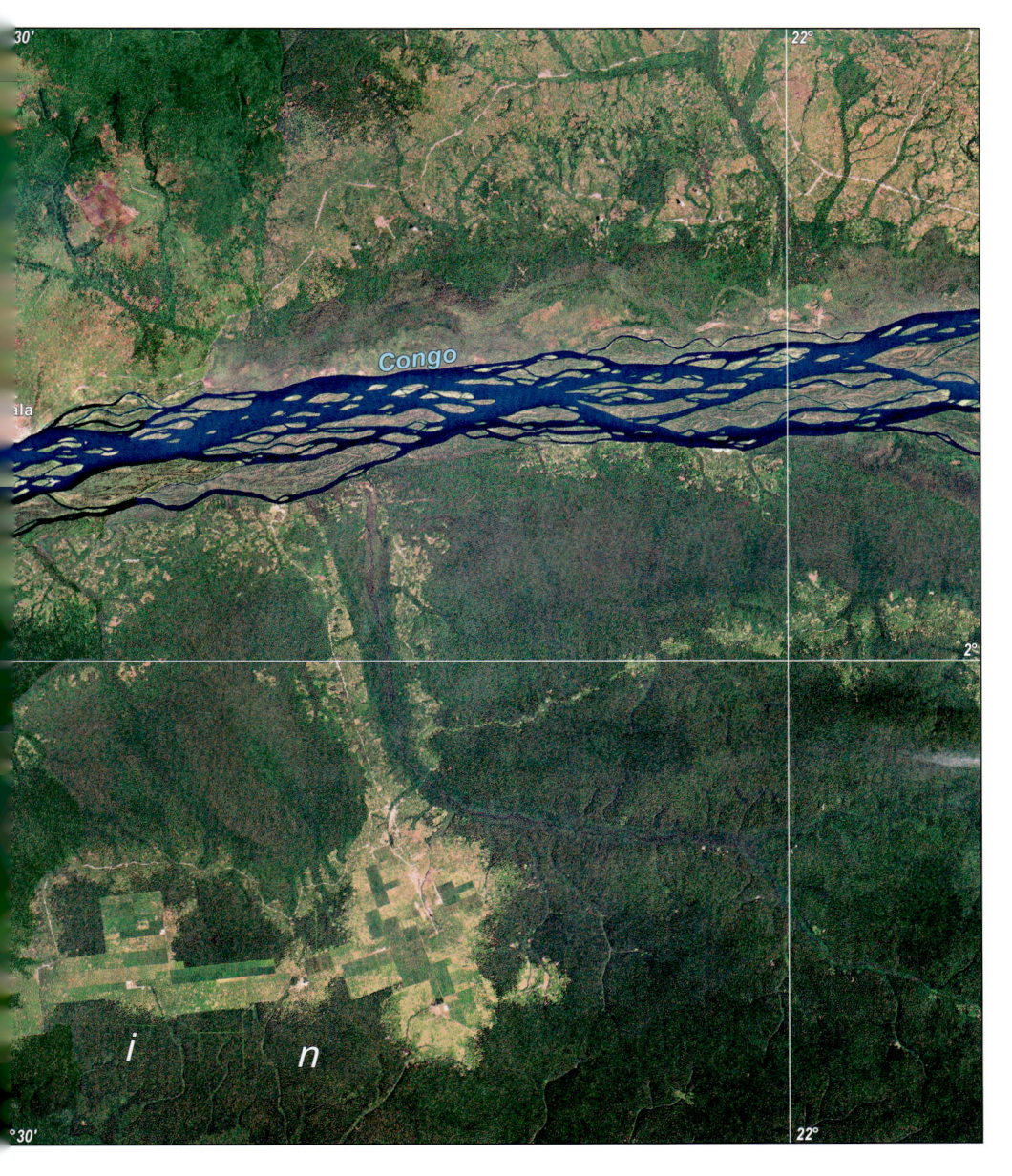

CONGO

The Congo, formerly known as the Zaire River, flows through the Congo Basin, the second-largest unfragmented region of rainforest on Earth and famed for its enormous diversity of flora, fauna and raw materials.

At 4,374 kilometres long, the Congo is the second-longest river in Africa, and its catchment basin of almost 3.8 million square kilometres makes it the second-largest on Earth (Fig. 2). Together with its tributaries, it flows through one of the last remaining great rainforests (Fig. 1). The Congo rises in the foothills of the Mituma Mountains, a region in the East African Rift System. Here Lake Tanganyika and Lake Mweru feed into the Congo's headwater, the Lualaba. Beyond the Boyoma Falls (formerly known as Stanley Falls), theriver is known as the Congo. From Kisangani, right underneath the waterfalls, the Congo flows west before gradually turning slightly to flow south-west. The Ubangi, the Congo's largest tributary, joins the river near Mbandaka. From here on, it forms the border between the Republic of the Congo and the Democratic Republic of Congo. Before reaching the Livingstone Falls on the edge of the Lower Guinea region, the Congo forms a lake known as Malebo Pool, which is dotted with islands (Fig. 3). Further downstream, after leaving the Congo Basin, the river flows for around 350 kilometres in the lengthy rapids of the Livingstone Falls, passing through a river gap with a drop of 274 metres (Fig. 4). Along its course towards the mouth in the Atlantic Ocean, a total of 13 central African countries have access to water from the Congo and its countless tributaries. Most of the catchment basin lies in the Democratic Republic of Congo.

Above the Livingstone Falls, most of the Congo is navigable — a stretch of around 3,000 kilometres. The rapids and waterfalls are circumvented by railway lines. The river is one of the biggest transport routes for trade in central Africa.

The Congo Basin

The Congo Basin, a bowl-shaped landscape in the Congo's catchment basin, is home to around a quarter of the world's tropical rainforests. However, deforestation, slash-and-burn and a steadily growing population are all threats to the rainforest. As a result, several governments and organisations are already pooling their resources in the "Congo Basin Forest Partnership (CBFP)" project in order to protect the biodiversity of the Congo Basin. In addition, the programme aims to combat poverty and strengthen administrative bodies.

△
1 – With its many tributaries, the Congo flows through the tropical rainforest of the Congo Basin (shown here in the north of the Democratic Republic of Congo).

◁
2 – The Congo's catchment basin is one of the largest on Earth and completely fills the Congo Basin.

◁
3 – On the shores of Malebo Pool, Brazzaville, the capital of the Republic of Congo, faces across to Kinshasa, the capital of the Democratic Republic of Congo.

▷
4 – Multitemporal Radar image (R 11.11.2011/G 10.01.2012/B 10.03.2012) of the Congo's lower reaches near Matadi. Here the river crosses the Lower Guinea region, which reach a maximum height of 1,575 metres. Forests and bushland appear in green, agricultural land and grassland in blue and magenta.

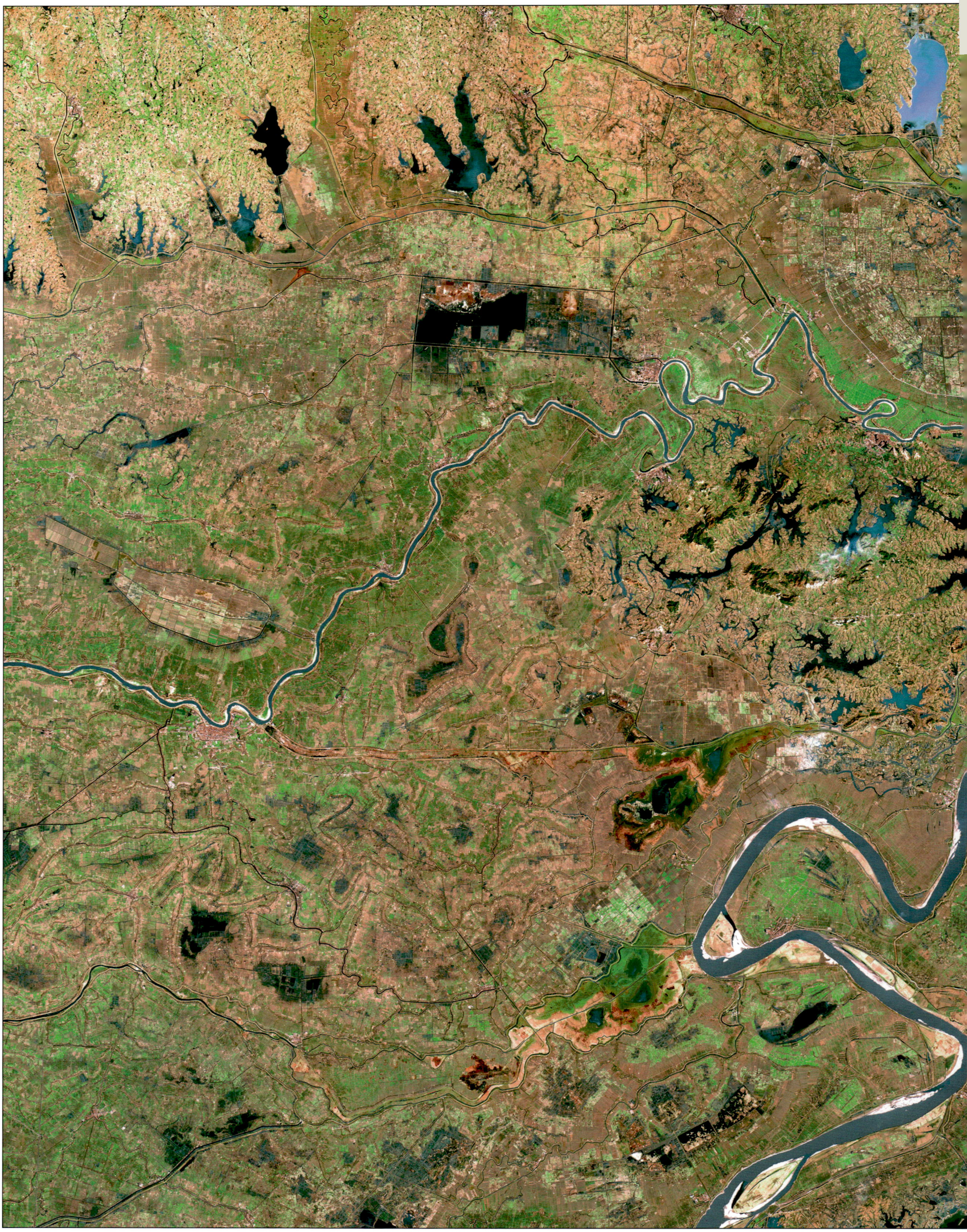

YANGTZE

From its source in the Tibetan Plateau to its mouth in the East China Sea, the third-longest river in the world flows through the bread basket of China. Its depth makes the major waterway navigable for ships deep into China's interior.

At 6,300 kilometres in length, the Yangtzekiang (Yangtze), or the Chang Jiang, is the longest river in Asia. Rising in the Tibetan Plateau, it flows eastwards until it empties into the East China Sea at Shanghai (Fig. 1, p. 122). The areas along the river's path are intensively farmed (Fig. 1). Particularly in the east, large areas are artificially irrigated for rice cultivation. In addition to providing water for irrigation, the Yangtze also has other major economic functions, including shipping, hydroelectricity, and tourism. However, the ecological equilibrium of this great river is being severely jeopardised by the inflow of wastewater from industry and private households, which endangers the drinking water supply for the neighbouring cities. Agricultural fertilisers also lead to a surplus of nutrients in the water and thus to increased algal blooms.

Large stretches of the 1,722,000 square kilometre catchment basin are (Fig. 2, p. 122) threatened by slash-and-burn. The demand for firewood and timber for construction has led to the forests being cut back to just 11 per cent of the original cover. Only at higher altitudes are larger areas of unfragmented woodland still found. The stripping of the protective vegetation and the high rates of precipitation make the entire catchment basin highly susceptible to soil erosion. In addition, the people of the Yangtze valley, who make up around one-third of the population of China, also face the annual threat of flooding.

The Yangtze Delta

The Yangtze Delta is shaped by the tides. Before emptying into the East China Sea, the Yangtze branches into two arms. Between the arms lies an island, built up out of the river's sediment (Fig. 3, p. 123). Every year, an average of 478 million tonnes of sediment are deposited by the Yangtze into the sea.

◁

1 – At Wuhan, the capital of the Chinese province of Hubei, the Han River meets the Yangtze.

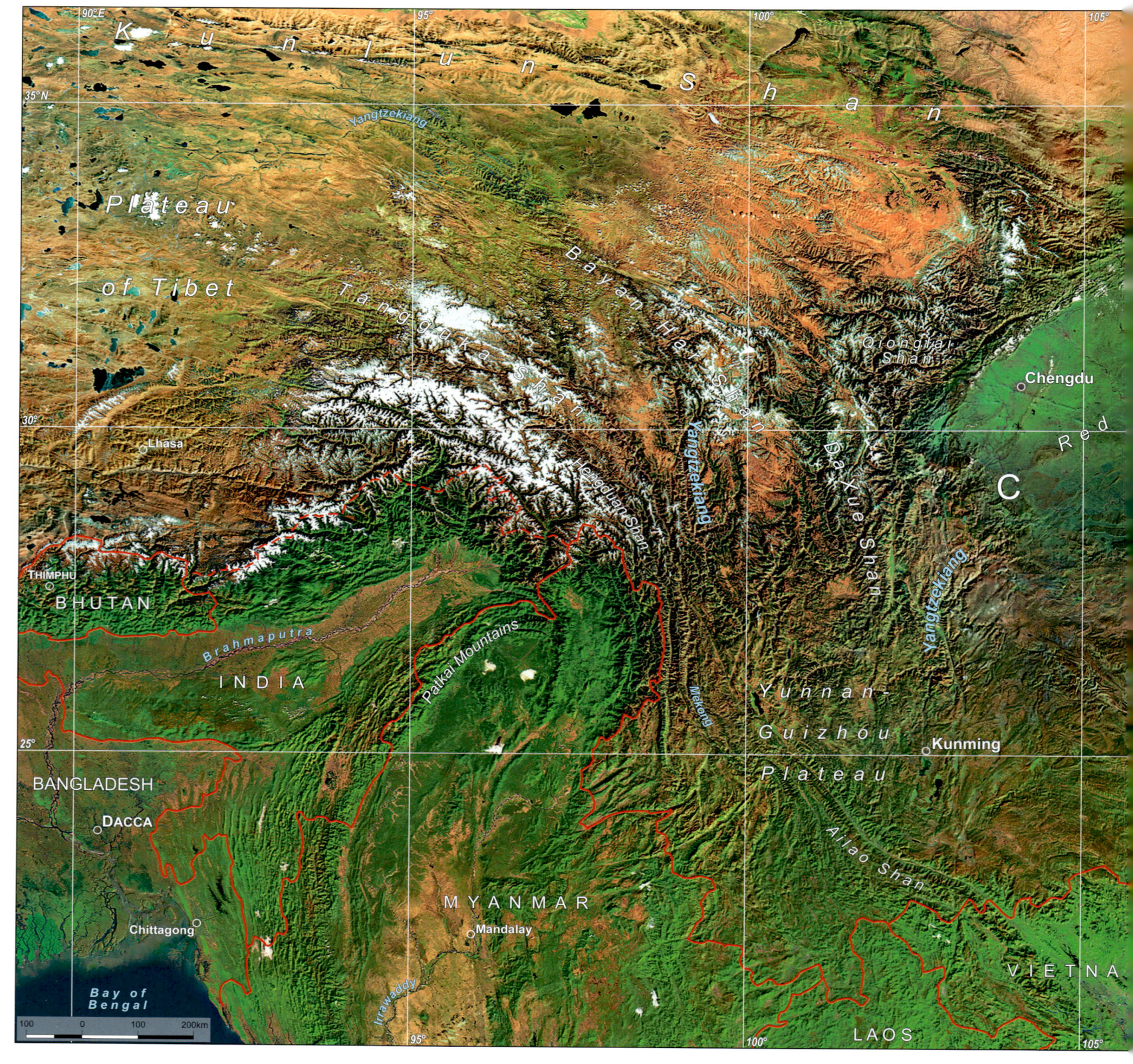

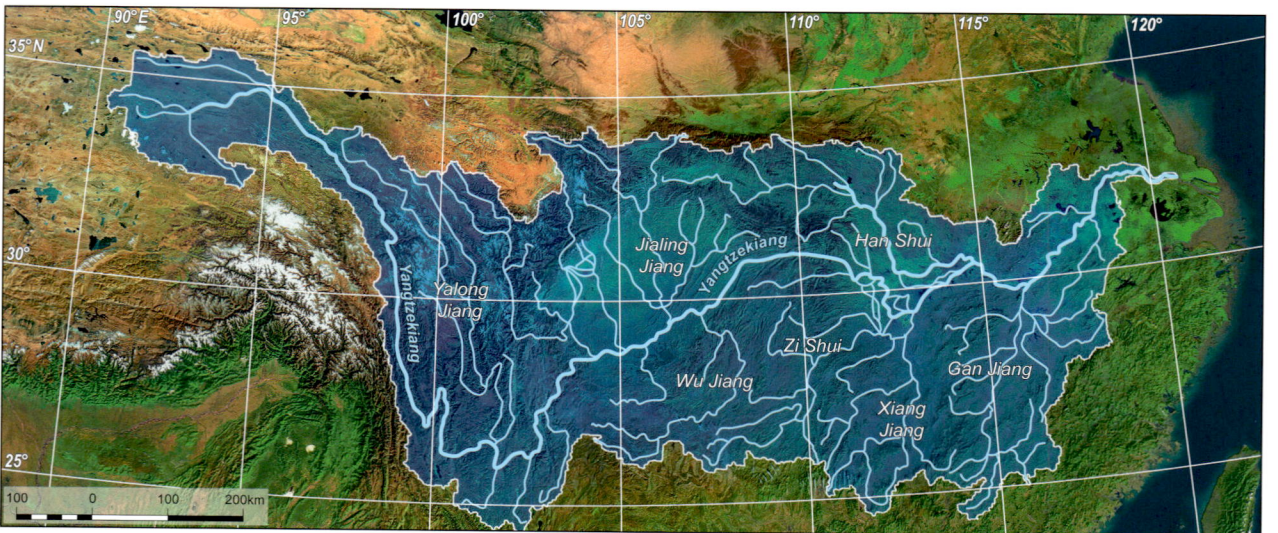

1 – This mosaic of satellite images shows the entire length of the Yangtze, from its source in the Tibetan Plateau to its delta in the East China Sea at Shanghai (red circle east of Red Basin: location of the Three Gorges Dam).

2 – The catchment basin of the Yangtze River drains both large parts of the Tibetan Plateau as well as all of central China.

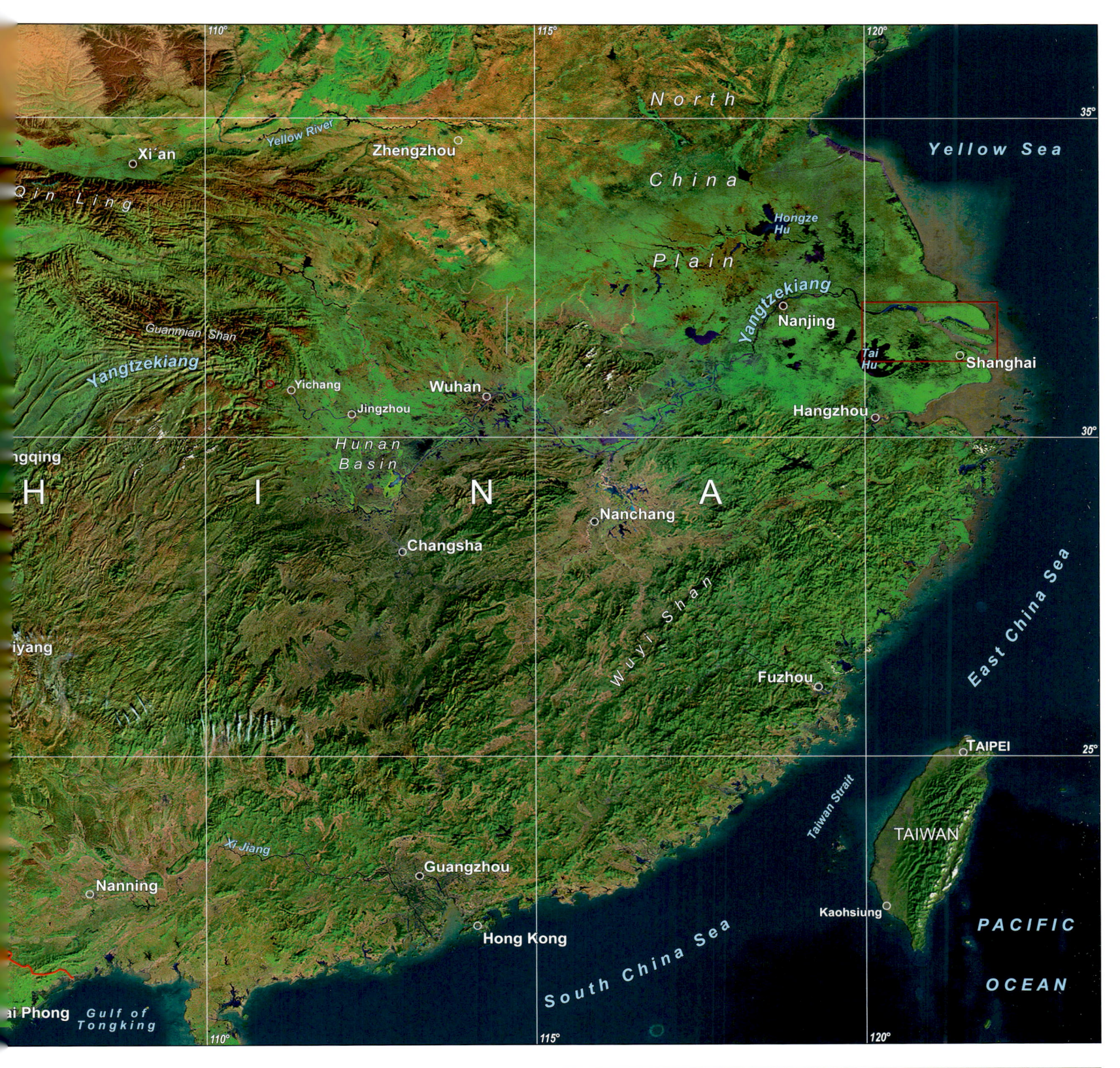

▷
3 – The Yangtze Delta, where the river empties into the East China Sea at Shanghai.
The highly fertile soils have led to this area being intensively farmed.
The delta itself has also been used for aquaculture for decades.

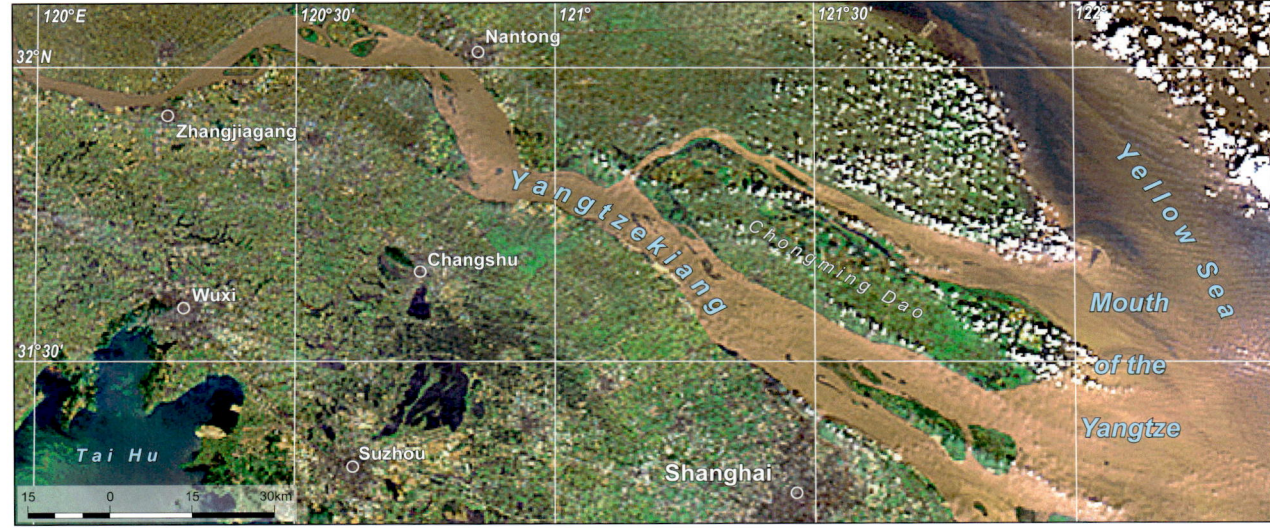

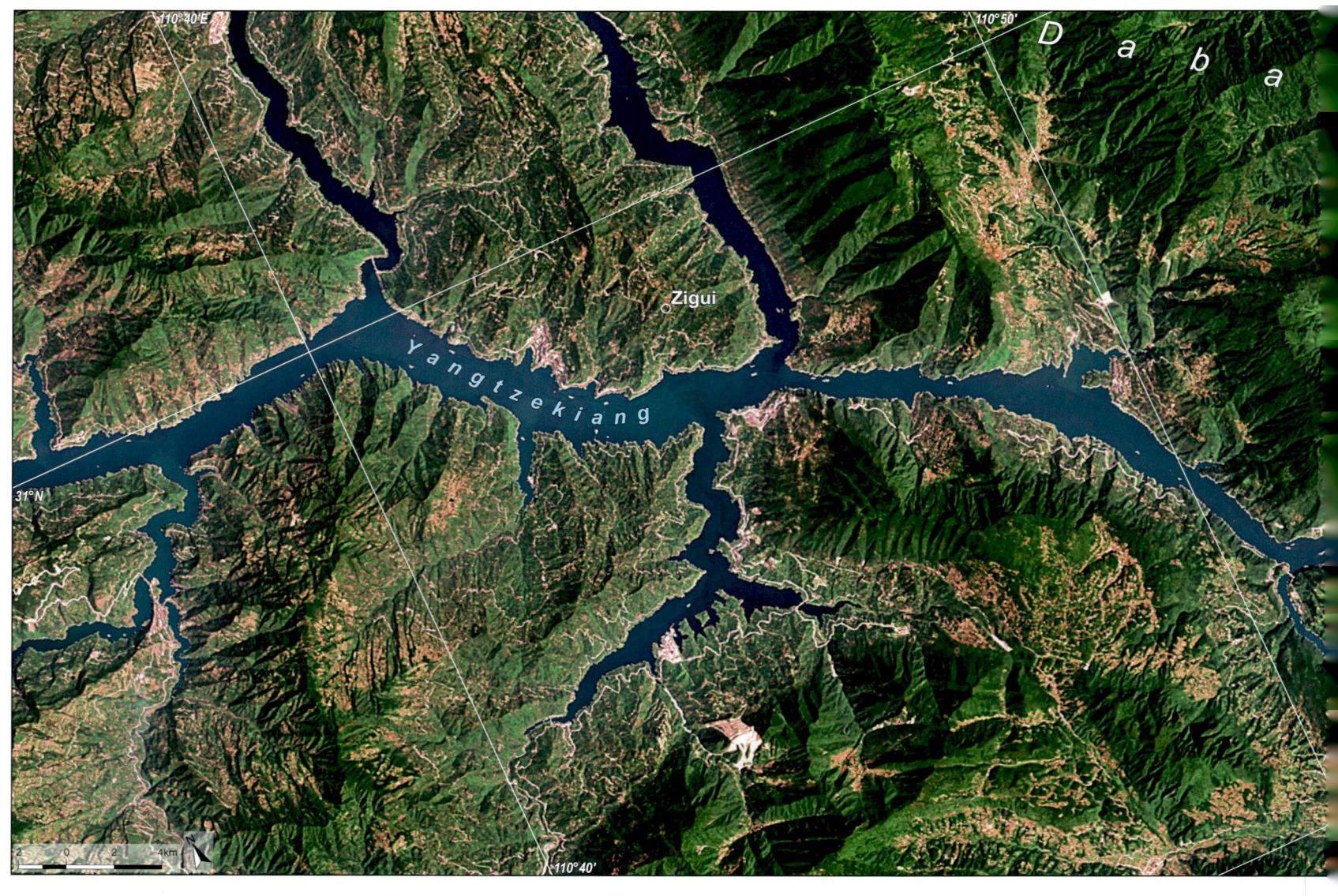

The delta plains, dissected by a large number of canals and dams, consist of dark, fertile alluvial soil, which supports intensive farming. In addition to rice cultivation, various aquacultures also play an important role.

The delta and its surroundings are some of the most densely populated areas on Earth: the greater metropolitan area is home to more than 15 million people. The megacity of Shanghai lies directly in the river's delta (Figs. 1, p. 122, and 3, p. 123), the word 'Shanghai' literally means 'upon the sea'.

The Yangtze Dams

In the past, large stretches of land along the river, primarily in the flat plains of its lower reaches, were subject to devastating flooding and repeated dam collapses affecting huge areas and millions of inhabitants.

After the People's Republic of China was established, a number of major construction projects were initiated along the river. Existing dams and channels were renovated and rebuilt, and new reservoirs were created. According to the latest statistics, there are almost 50,000 reservoirs and 15,000 hydroelectric power stations along the river, including two completed dams and five that are currently under construction. One of the most famous of these is the Three Gorges Dam (Figs. 1 and 4 a/b, Fig. 1, p. 122-123). The dam is 185 metres high, 2,309 metres long and has created a lake 660 kilometres long. Since its completion in 2012, the power station's 34 turbines provide a total capacity of 22.5 gigawatts of electric power. As a result of the high costs of construction, the necessary relocation of over 1.5 million people and the significant effects on the environment, the project has been highly controversial.

△
1 – The river bed of the Yangtze has been dammed by the Three Gorges Dam since 2003 (image taken on 15/9/2013). The water body currently covers an area of over 1,000 square kilometres at normal water levels.

◁
2 – The skyline of Shanghai at night represents a vibrant megacity

◁
3 – Rice cultivation dominates agriculture in China.

4 a/b – Probably one of the biggest and most complex Chinese construction projects since the building of the Great Wall of China – the Three Gorges Dam. The dam is the largest project of its kind on Earth.
Images from the experimental ESA satellite Proba-1 CHRIS show the construction progress in 2003 (top) and 2004 (bottom).

125

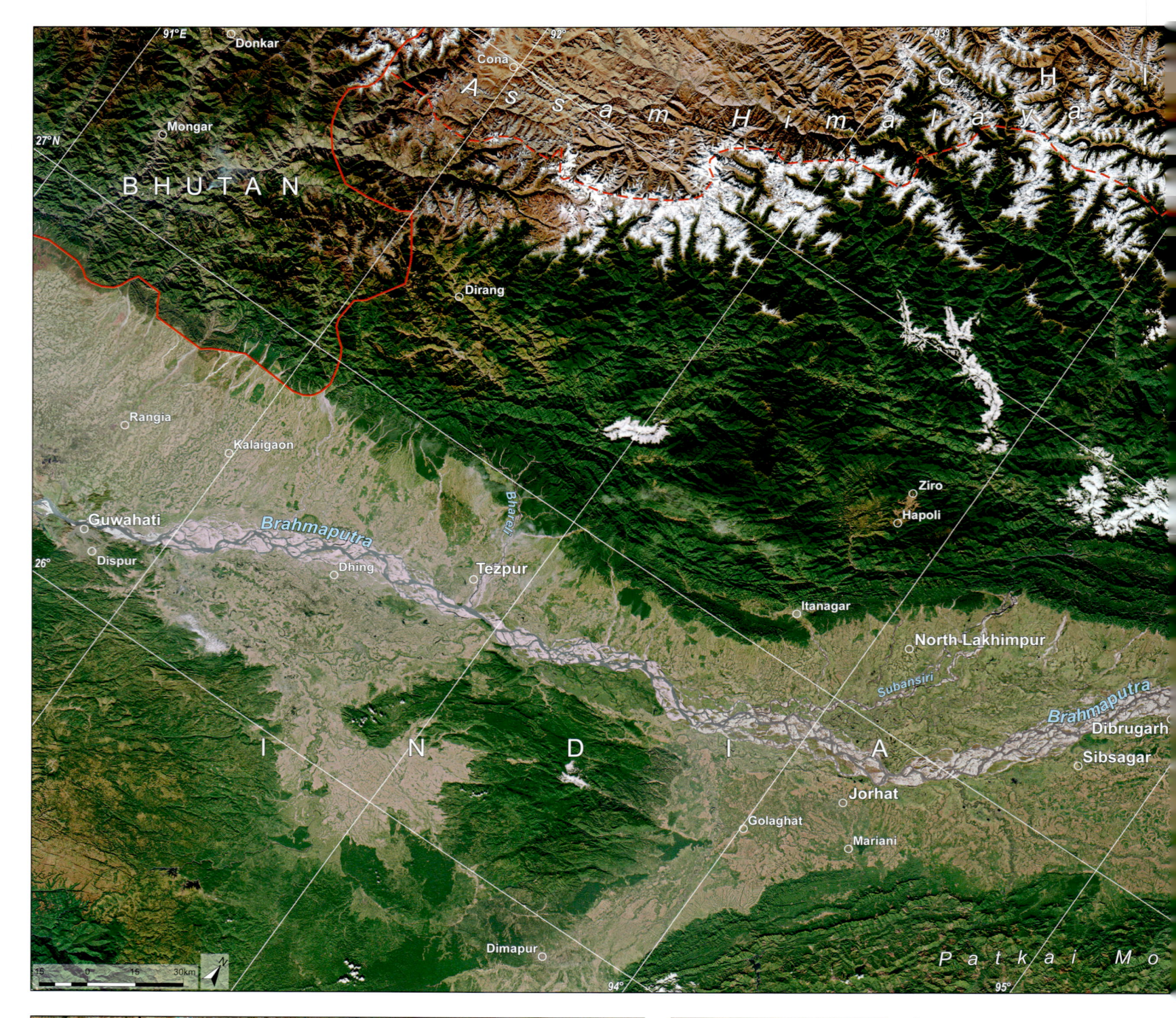

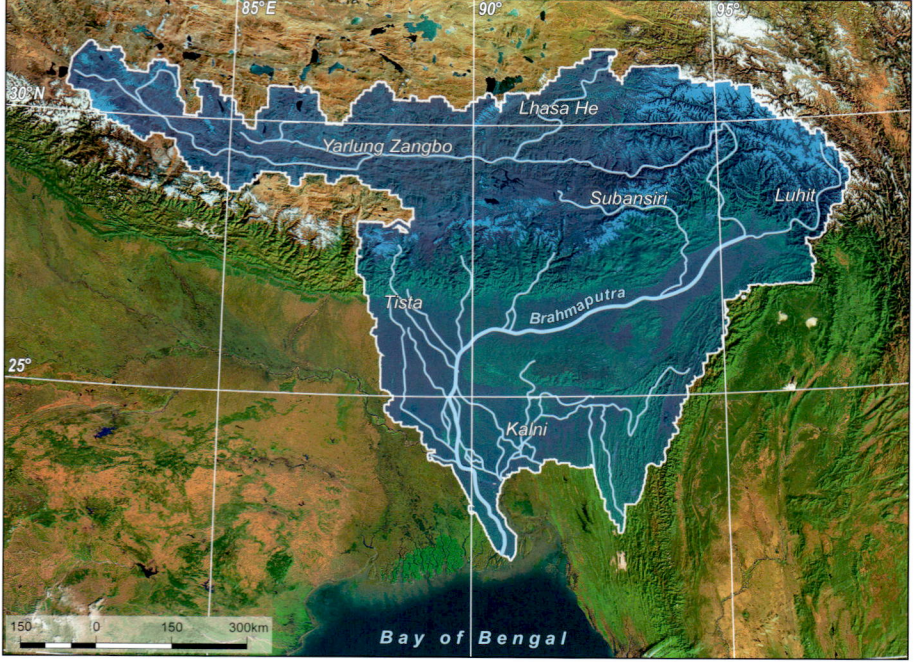

△
1 – Where it rises in the Himalayas the Brahmaputra is known as the Yarlung Zangbo. The confluence of the Yarlung Zangbo and the Luhit just outside Dibrugarh.

◁
2 – The Brahmaputra catchment basin includes most of the Himalayas' northern slopes.

◁△
3 – Mount Kailash towers over the headwaters of the Brahmaputra.

◁
4 – Passengers cross the Meghna in the Ganges Delta.

▷
5 – The multitemporal ASAR image shows the dynamics of the currents in the Ganges Delta.

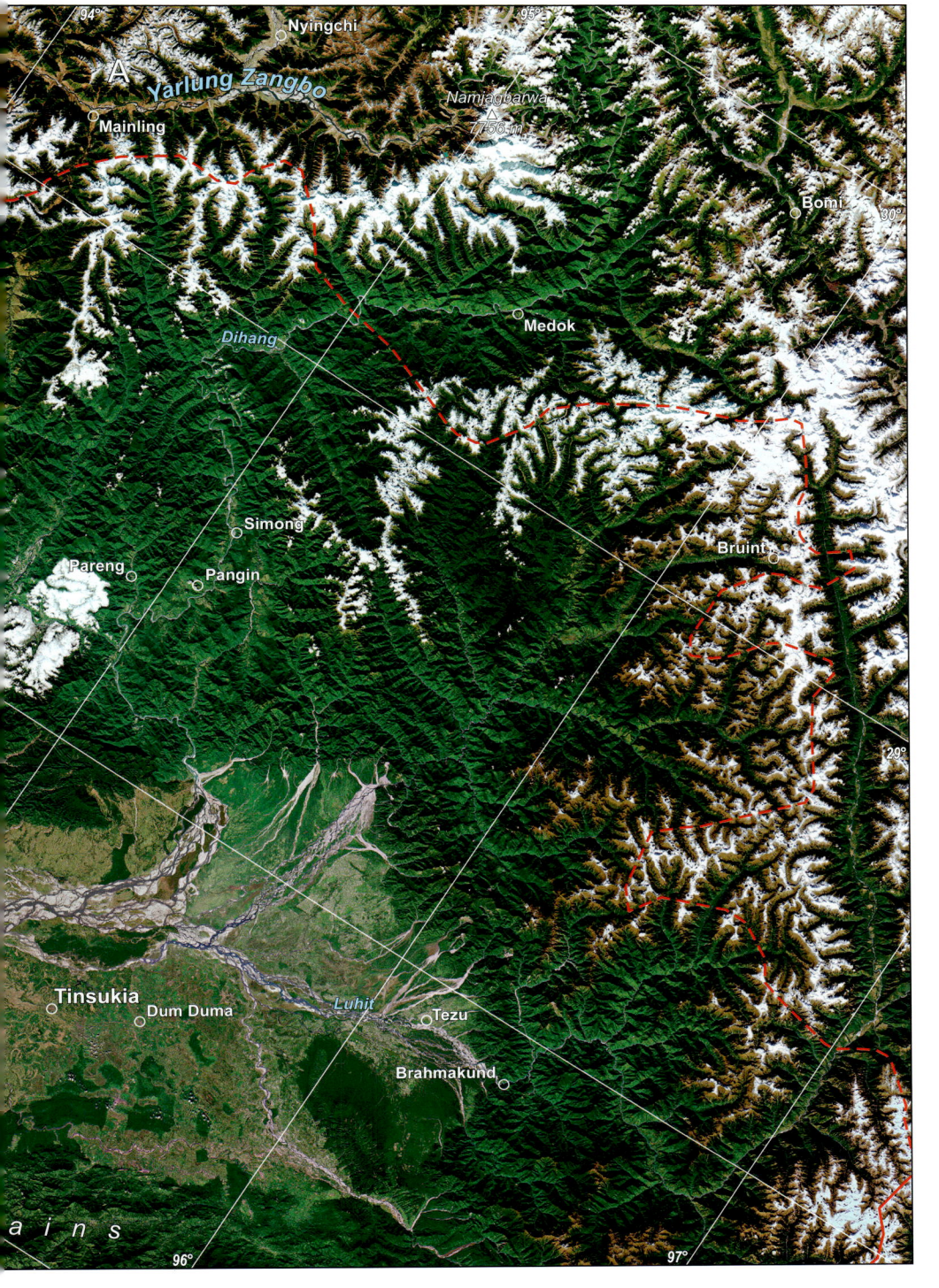

BRAHMAPUTRA

The "Son of Brahma" rises in the 'Roof of the World' and, at 2,900 kilometres in length, is one of the longest and mightiest rivers in South Asia.

The Brahmaputra originates under the Angsi Glacier on the northern face of the Himalayas, near the 'Mountain of the Gods', Kailash. Called Yarlung Tsangpo at this point, it flows 1,500 kilometres through Tibet towards the east. With a dramatic bend through the Yarlung Zangbo Grand Canyon it breaks through the highest mountain range on our planet and streams into the Bengal lowlands. Just a few kilometres to the east of Dibrugarh, India's "Tea Capital", the Yarlung Zangbo and Luhit flow together at an altitude of around 115 metres above sea level to form the Brahmaputra (Fig. 1). From there, the waters flow southwest through Assam for 720 kilometres until they cross the border with Bangladesh near the Garo Hills. The main channel, known as Jamuna, has its confluence with the Ganges near Dhaka. The joined rivers, now called the Padma, flow another 105 kilometres to meet the Meghna River near Chandpur. Together the three rivers form the largest delta on Earth (Fig. 1, p. 20). On its path through China, India and Bangladesh, the Brahmaputra falls through 5,744 metres of elevation.

During the monsoon, the Brahmaputra is characterised by a high flow rate and a high sediment load. The flow rate averages 21,000 cubic metres per second and peaks at about 190,000 cubic metres per second. Depending on the water level, the width of the river can vary from between three and 18 kilometres.

The catchment basin of the Brahmaputra, which takes in over 651,300 square kilometres (Fig. 2), is one of the most thickly populated regions in the world. The highest population density can be found along the river's lower reaches.

The Ganges Delta

At 105,640 square kilometres, the Ganges Delta (Fig. 5) is the largest delta on Earth. It consists of a labyrinth of water channels, swamps and islands of sediment. Although the delta is at a very high risk of flooding due to its flat topography, nearness to the sea and the influence of the monsoon, it is still home to most of Bangladesh's population. The country suffers more from flooding than any other. Major disasters strike almost every two years. In 1988, for example, tens of thousands of people died in the floods and 30 million lost their homes. In 1998, almost three-quarters of the country was hit by the floods. Floods struck again in 2007, affecting every province.

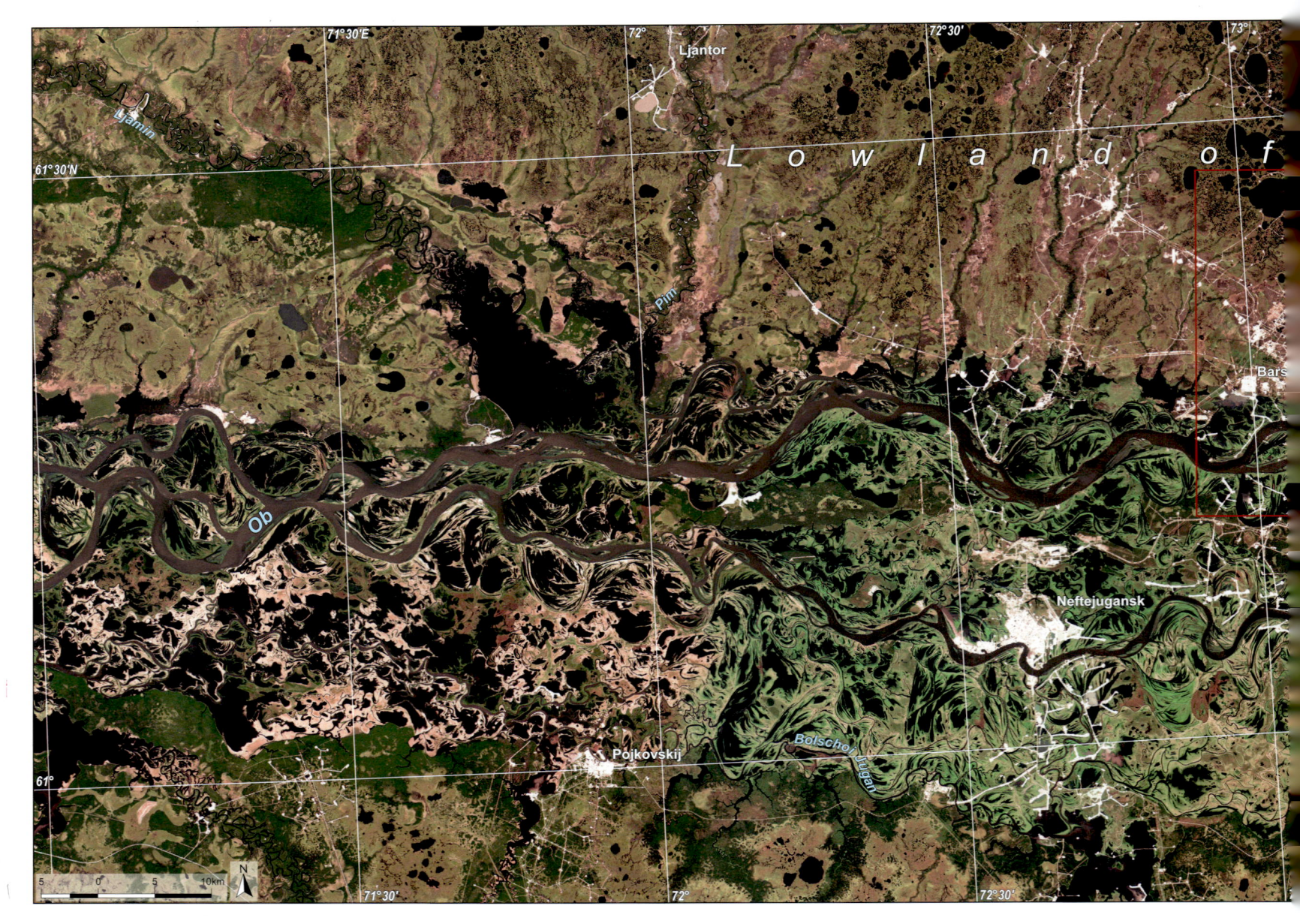

1 – The Ob flows through the autonomous region of the Khanty and Mansi peoples in Siberia – a region rich in oil and natural gas.

2 – The Ob's catchment basin.

3 – Detail of Fig. 1, showing the area around Surgut with its numerous refineries and pipelines on the 06/7/1987.

4 – The area around Surgut in an image from 12/8/2012. Comparison with Fig. 3 shows the development within the industrial area.

128

Ob

The Ob River is characterised by its extreme continental climate with short summers and harsh winters, as well as by human intervention in the natural world.

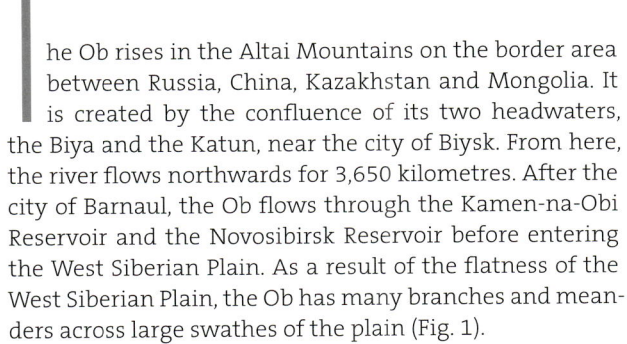

The Ob rises in the Altai Mountains on the border area between Russia, China, Kazakhstan and Mongolia. It is created by the confluence of its two headwaters, the Biya and the Katun, near the city of Biysk. From here, the river flows northwards for 3,650 kilometres. After the city of Barnaul, the Ob flows through the Kamen-na-Obi Reservoir and the Novosibirsk Reservoir before entering the West Siberian Plain. As a result of the flatness of the West Siberian Plain, the Ob has many branches and meanders across large swathes of the plain (Fig. 1).

After the Irtysh River joins it at Khanty-Mansiysk, the Ob makes a sharp bend northwards and eventually empties into the Gulf of Ob (Fig. 2). This gulf, which measures over 800 kilometres long and up to 70 kilometres wide, was shaped into an estuary by Ice Age glaciers and is part of the Kara Sea, which in turn is part of the Arctic Ocean. With its tributary, the Irtysh, the Ob is one of the major rivers in Siberia and, along with the Yenisey and the Lena, also one of northern Siberia's major waterways. The river system's catchment basin takes in nearly three million square kilometres in Russia, Kazakhstan, China and Mongolia.

When the snow melts in spring, drifting ice from the river's warmer southern reaches pile up against an often still very thick layer of ice in its lower, colder, northern reaches. The water is dammed, raising the water level by between six and twelve metres and flooding an area up to 40 kilometres wide. In the five to seven months before the snow melts, the Ob is almost completely frozen.

Industry on the banks of the Ob

From its mouth to the confluence of the Biya and Katun headwaters, the Ob is freely navigable for ships when ice-free and so plays a major role in the transportation of goods for the timber industry of the boreal coniferous forest. A hydroelectric power plant on the Novosibirsk Reservoir provides the region with energy. Another major industry in the Ob catchment basin is the coal mining and oil and gas industry. In the 1950s and 1960s, large oil and gas reserves were discovered in the region around Surgut and have been extracted since then (Figs. 3 and 4). Both these industries and the reservoir represent a major threat to the sensitive ecosystem of the river. Large quantities of oil frequently seep into the soil and water from leaks and ruptures in the pipeline.

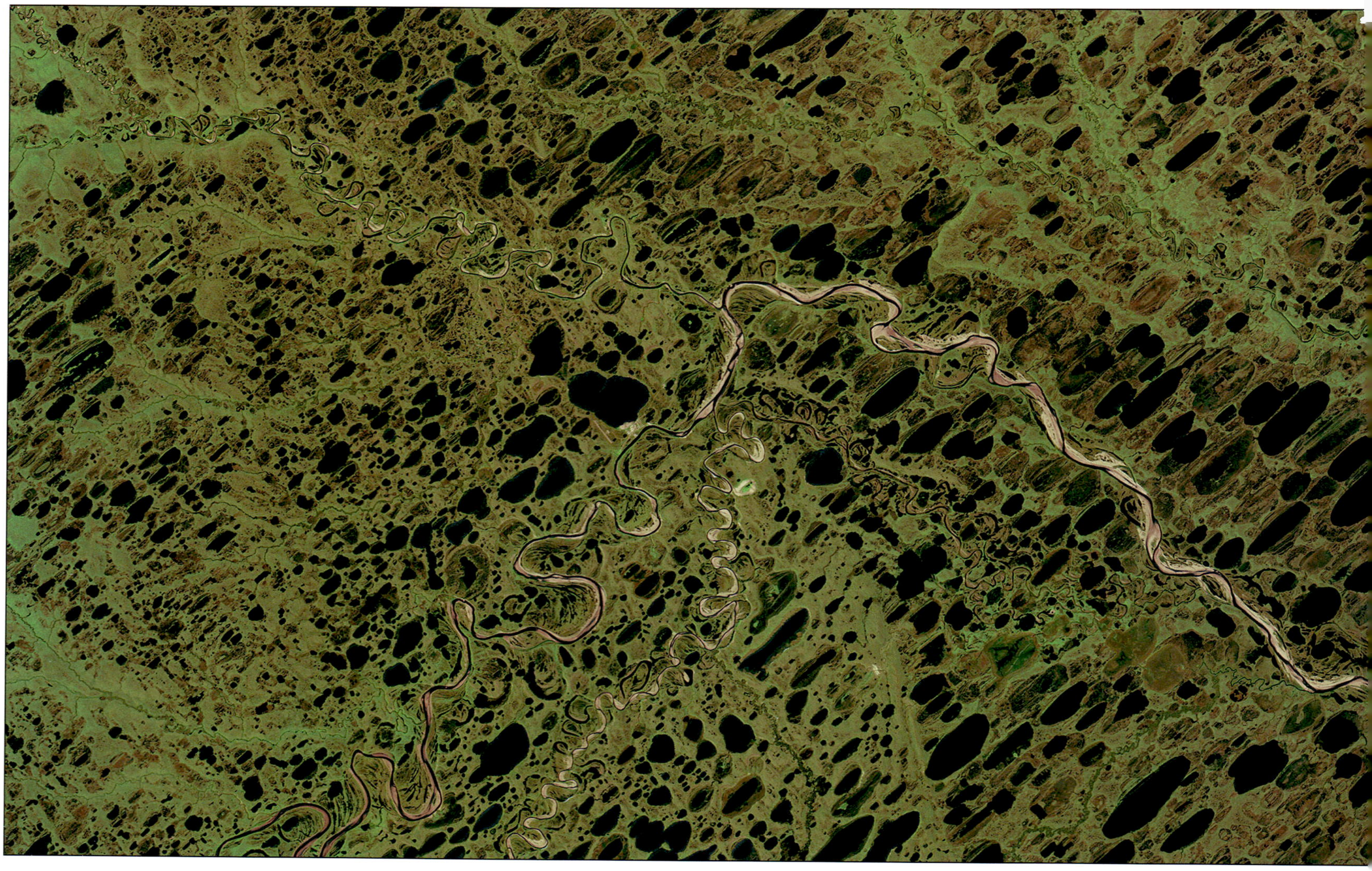

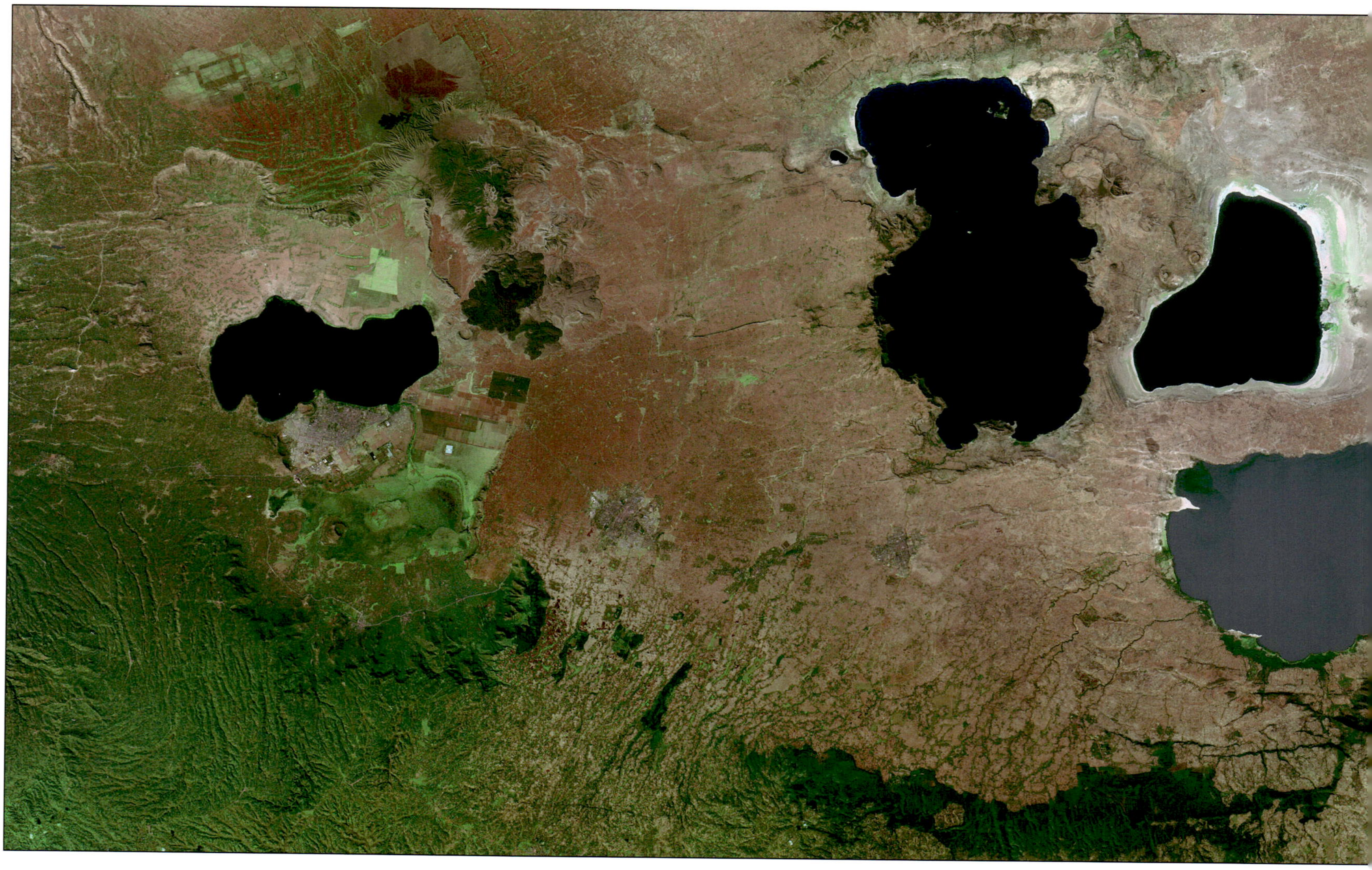

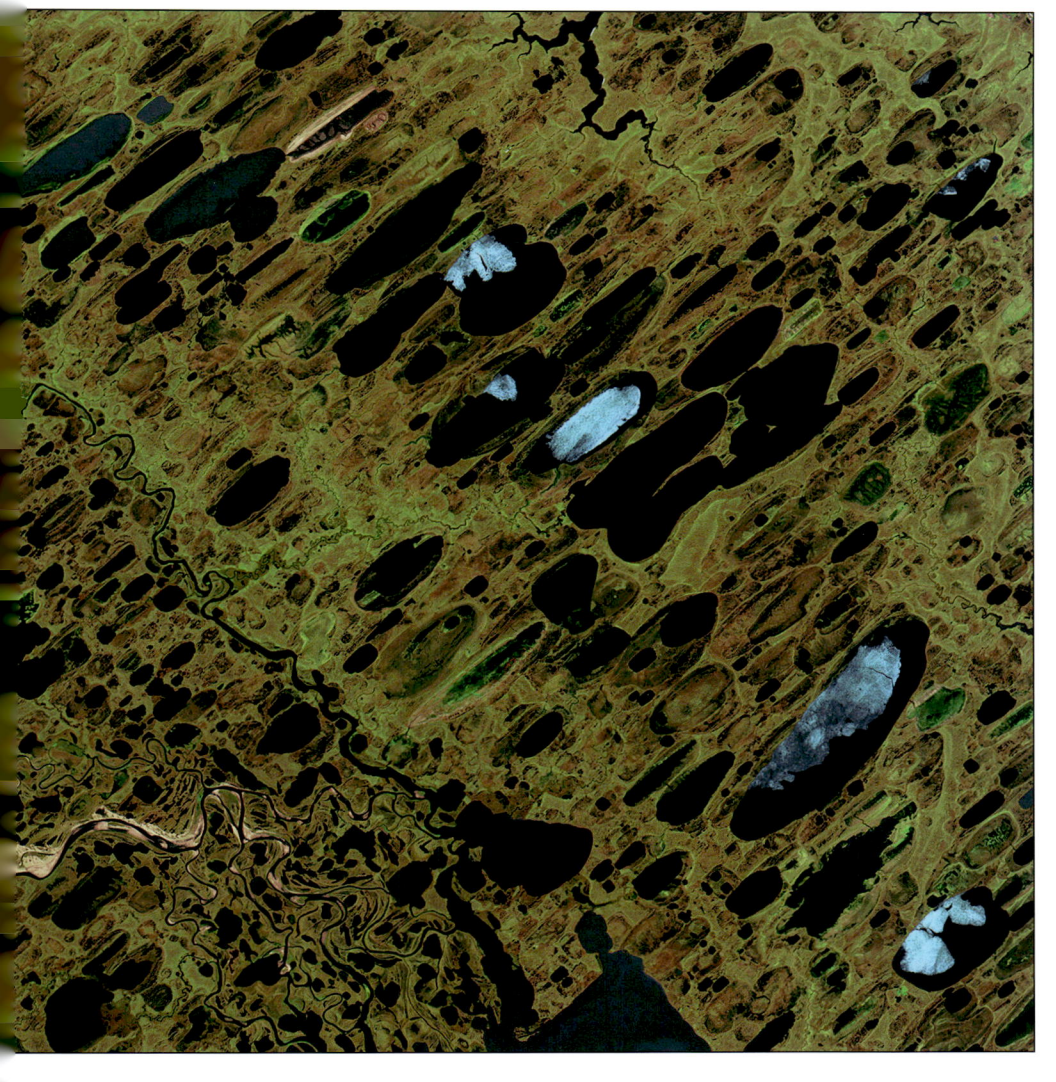

LAKES OF THE EARTH

Most of the inland lakes on our planet are freshwater and thus major reservoirs of drinking water. Beside freshwater lakes, there are also inland seas such as the Caspian Sea and Aral Sea, as well as soda lakes such as Lake Nakuru in Africa and Lake Van in Turkey.

Lakes, depending on their water supply, are defined as permanently, periodically or episodically filled basins that are surrounded by land. If they have no natural outflow and the water leaves the lake only via evaporation, they are known as endorheic lakes.

Across the globe, lakes cover around 2.5 million square kilometres, or around 1.8 per cent of the land. Together with the world's rivers, they contain 225,000 cubic kilometres of freshwater and, as such, are major sources of drinking water. Lake Constance, for instance, provides drinking water for around four million people every day, by extracting around half a million cubic metres a day. Lake Victoria is Africa's largest freshwater lake.

Lakes arise in different ways, and we generally distinguish between natural and artificial lakes. Natural lakes can be classified further according to geomorphological criteria. Most lakes are created as a result of glacial, tectonic or volcanic processes. Glacial lakes, such as the North American Great Lakes or Germany's Chiemsee, can be traced back to the ice ages. Glaciers carved out their basins, where meltwater pooled as the glaciers retreated. This is the most common type of lake globally.

Tectogenic lakes, such as Lake Baikal or Lake Tanganyika, form astride tectonic rifts. As such, they are very deep and usually relatively old. Over time, in the fissures and basins in the fault line, water collects, creating inland lakes. Volcanic lakes, such as Crater Lake and Lake Pinatubo, are found in volcanic craters or explosion craters.

The lake ecosystem is home to countless organisms and serves both humans and animals as a source of food. Lakes are also key features in a landscape, influencing not only the water balance but also, if they are large enough, the regional climate.

◁△
1 – The oriented lakes near the northern coast of Alaska are shaped by the wind and recurring freezing and thawing.

◁
2 – Along the East African Rift System, lakes are filling basins formed by the separating of tectonic plates.

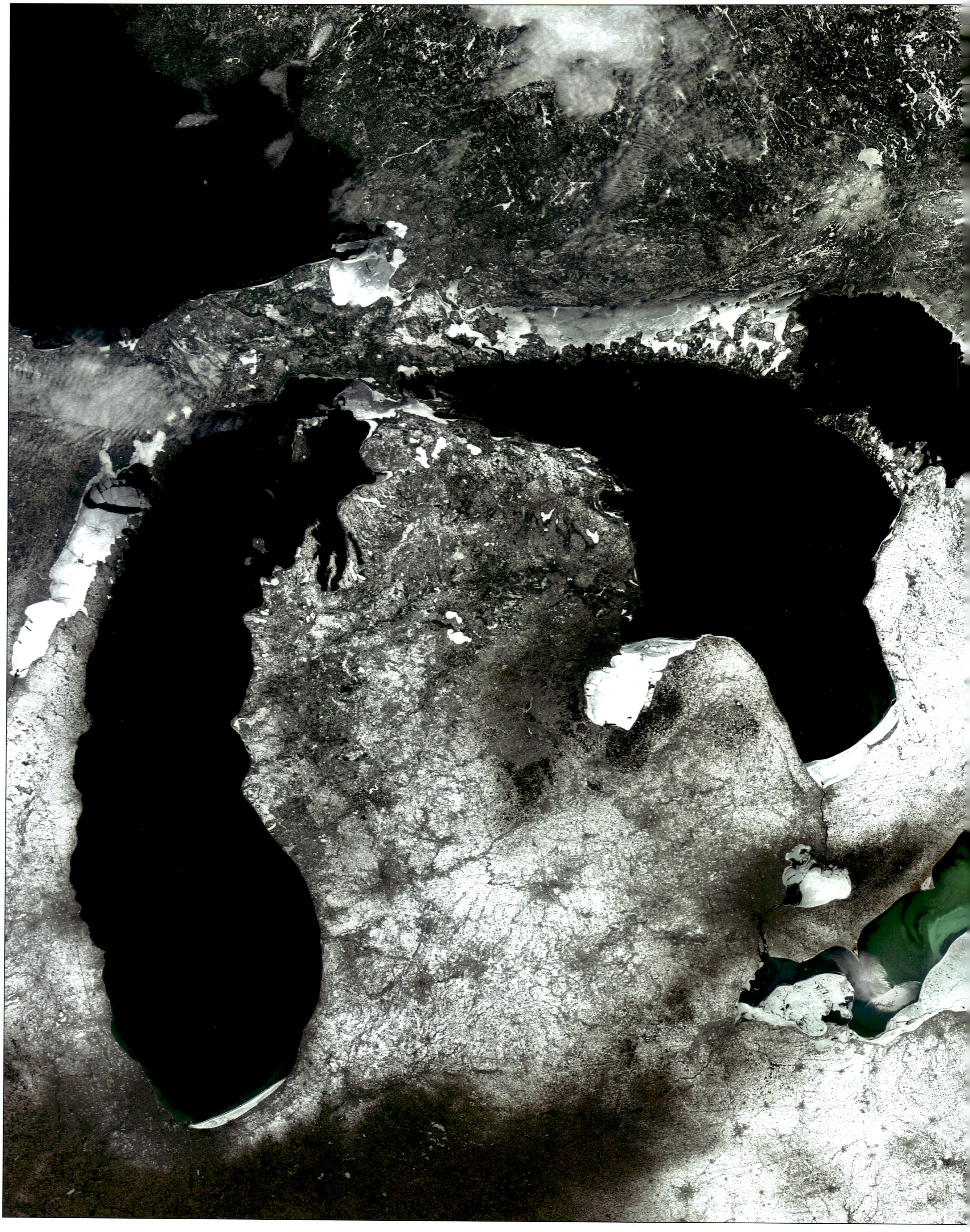

GREAT LAKES

With a total area of 244,000 square kilometres, the Great Lakes constitute the largest area of inland freshwater on Earth. They are a major fresh-water reservoir for the US and Canada.

The Great Lakes on the border between Canada and the USA are a system of five interlinked lakes: Lake Superior, Lake Michigan, Lake Huron, Lake Erie and Lake Ontario (Fig. 1). Lake Superior, at 82,414 square kilometres, is the largest, and also, at 405 metres in depth, the deepest of the five lakes. The catchment basin of the lakes spreads over 767,000 square kilometres. In total, they contain around 23,000 cubic kilometres of water, the largest amount of freshwater held by any inland water bodies in the world after Lake Baikal.

The lakes lie within a tectonic depression. During the last ice age the region was blanketed by thick continental ice sheets. The constant shifting, advancing and retreating of the glaciers during the phases of glaciation carved deep basins into the bedrock. As the most recent ice age came to an end 12,000 years ago, the basins were flooded by glacial meltwater.

As a consequence of their huge areas, the lakes influence the climate of the region. The humid air above the lakes is carried along by the westerly winds, bringing heavy snows to the eastern shores in winter and thunderstorms in summer, which in turn can trigger tornados.

Saint Lawrence Seaway – the link to the North Atlantic

Construction of this 3,700 kilometre-long waterway began in 1945 and was completed in 1959. The system comprises 17 locks, canals and channels and allows ocean-going ships to reach the Great Lakes from the Atlantic between April and mid-December (Fig. 1, p. 134-135). Ships built specifically for the Saint Lawrence Seaway, known as Lakers, have a capacity of 25,000 tonnes. On average, it takes eight to ten days to travel between the port of Duluth on Lake Superior to the Atlantic Ocean. The main cargoes include iron ore, coal, steel, machines, wheat, and the cars manufactured in Detroit. However, the Saint Lawrence Seaway is also open to sailing enthusiasts and cruise ships. Around 250 million visitors relax on its waters and shores every year.

◁
1 – The Great Lakes lie on the border of Canada and the USA. This image taken on 6 March 2010 shows the lakes partially covered by ice. Lake Erie in the south is coloured green by phytoplankton drifting along with the currents in the lake.

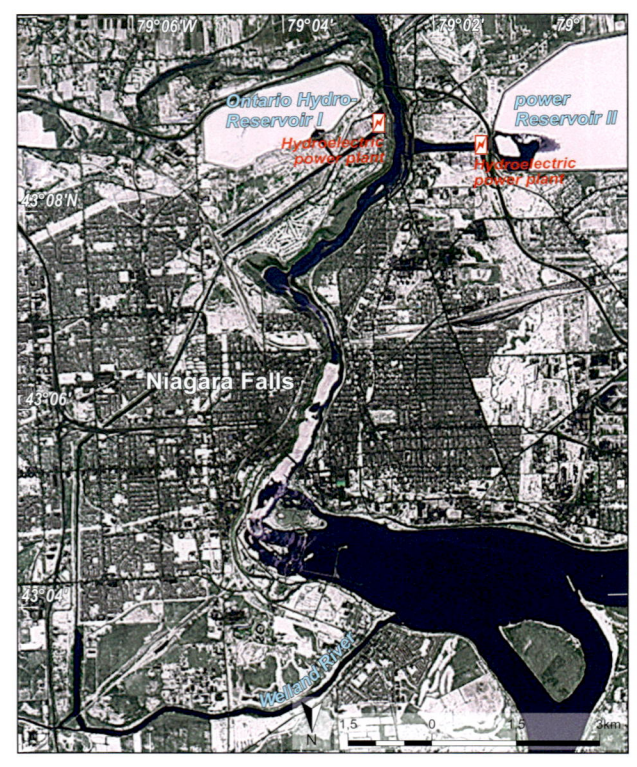

2 – Hydropower is used on both the Canadian (left) and American (right) sides of the Niagara River, including via the Niagara Tunnel since 2013.

3 – The Niagara Falls represent a natural barrier to shipping.

Navigation from the Atlantic Ocean to Lake Superior
- Lock
- Harbour
- International border
- State and Province border
- Navigation route
- Power plant

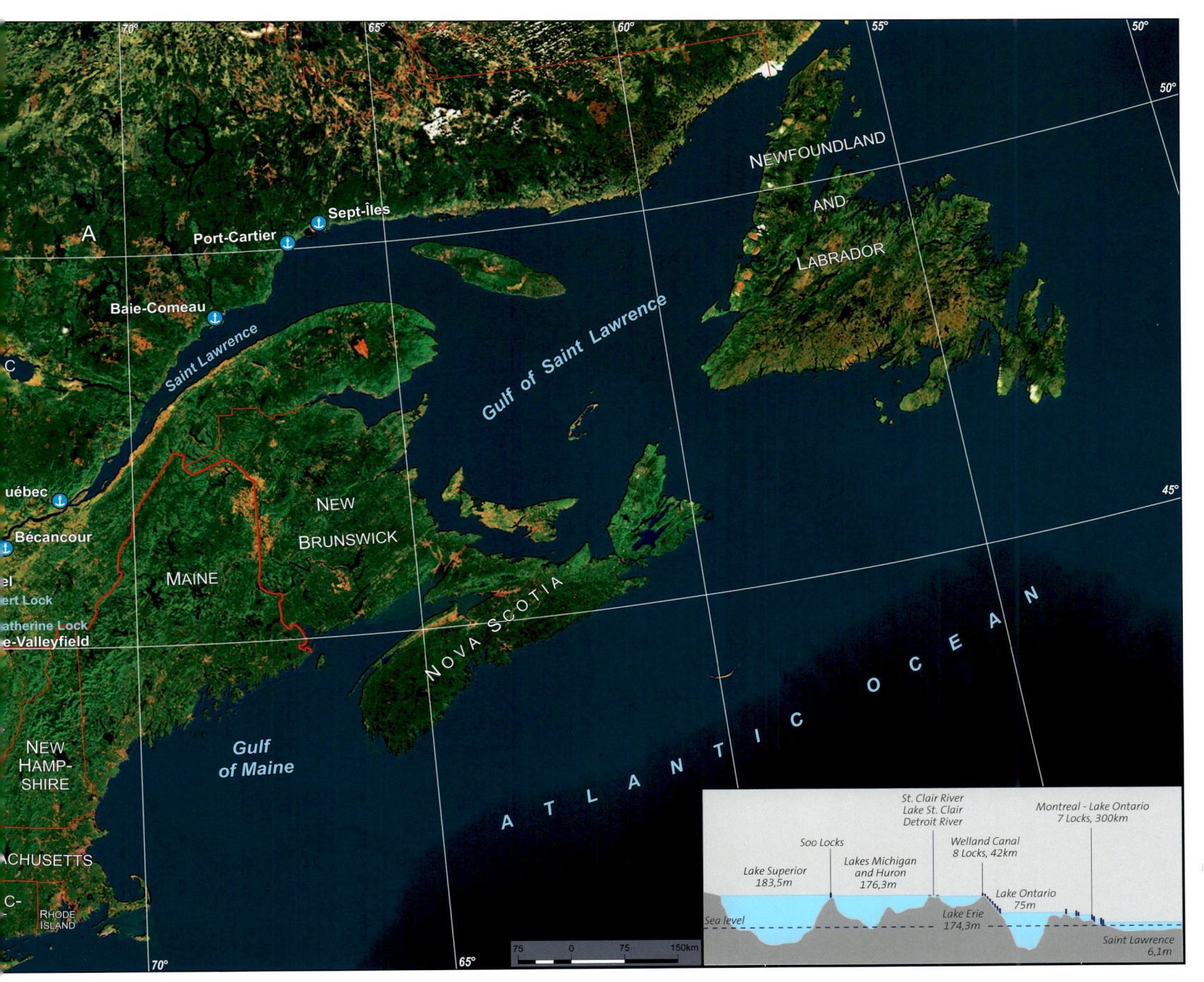

1 – The Saint Lawrence Seaway links the industrial centres of the Great Lakes region with the Atlantic Ocean.

Niagara Falls – natural wonder and energy source

The water from Lake Erie crashes over the Niagara Falls (Fig. 3) to a depth of 60 metres. The Falls are actually three: the 'American Falls' and 'Bridal Veil' on the American side, and 'Horseshoe Falls' on the Canadian side. Around nine times as much water flows over the Canadian falls as over the American falls. The Niagara Falls are one of America's major landmarks and has been visited in 2009 by 28 million tourists.

The Niagara Falls formed around 12,000 years ago, when the meltwater of the last great glaciers overflowed Lake Erie. Those waters created the Niagara River, which flows over the cliffs of the Niagara Escarpment and into Lake Ontario. This geological area consists of hard surface rock underlain by softer rock. The river is eroding the softer layer under the lip of the dolomite cliffs, and once the cliffs can no longer withstand the growing pressure they break off. The erosion has shifted Niagara Falls about 11 kilometres upstream towards Lake Erie since the falls were created, which is an average rate of one metre per year.

The enormous volumes of water going over the falls hold huge potential for generating energy (Fig. 2). The building of several hydroelectric plants has decreased the volume of water flowing over the Niagara Falls by up to 75 per cent since the 1950s. A few kilometres above the falls, underground channels extract up to 4,500 cubic metres of water per second. One side effect of the hydroelectric plants has been to reduce the erosion of the river bed. The cutting away of the cliff edge has thus fallen to less than four centimetres a year in the past few years.

In order to optimize the use of the waters of the Niagara River, a tunnel with a diameter of 14.4 metres has been bored over a length of more than 10 kilometres from the river to the Sir Adam Beck (SAB) power generating station. Set into service in March 2013, the tunnel provides sufficient water to produce additional 150 megawatts of a total of almost 2 gigawatts.

Welland Canal

The Welland Canal is part of the Saint Lawrence Seaway and lets ships bypass the Niagara Falls (Fig. 1). The canal is 42 kilometres long, 80 metres wide and at least 8.2 metres deep. Eight lock gates help to combat a change in elevation of almost 100 metres. The Welland Canal is the most important canal along the Saint Lawrence Seaway because it overcomes the biggest drop, that of the Niagara Escarpment. Over 3,000 cargo ships use the canal every year.

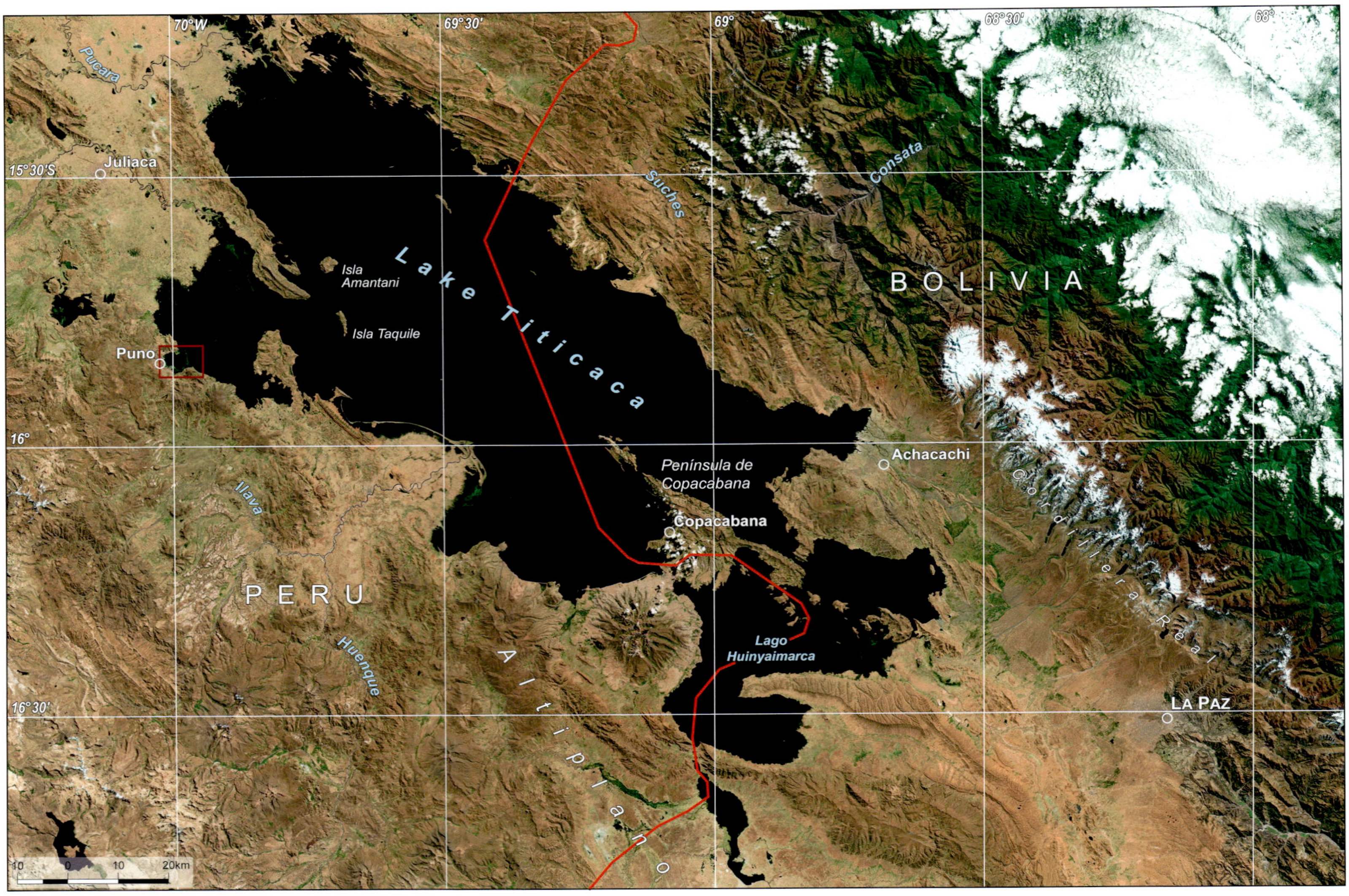
70°W
69°30'
69°
68°30'
68°
Pucara
15°30'S
Juliaca
Suches
Consata
Isla
Amantani
Lake Titicaca
BOLIVIA
Isla Taquile
Puno
16°
Achacachi
Península de
Copacabana
Ilava
Copacabana
Cordillera Real
PERU
Lago
Huinyaimarca
Huenque
Altiplano
16°30'
LA PAZ
10 0 10 20km

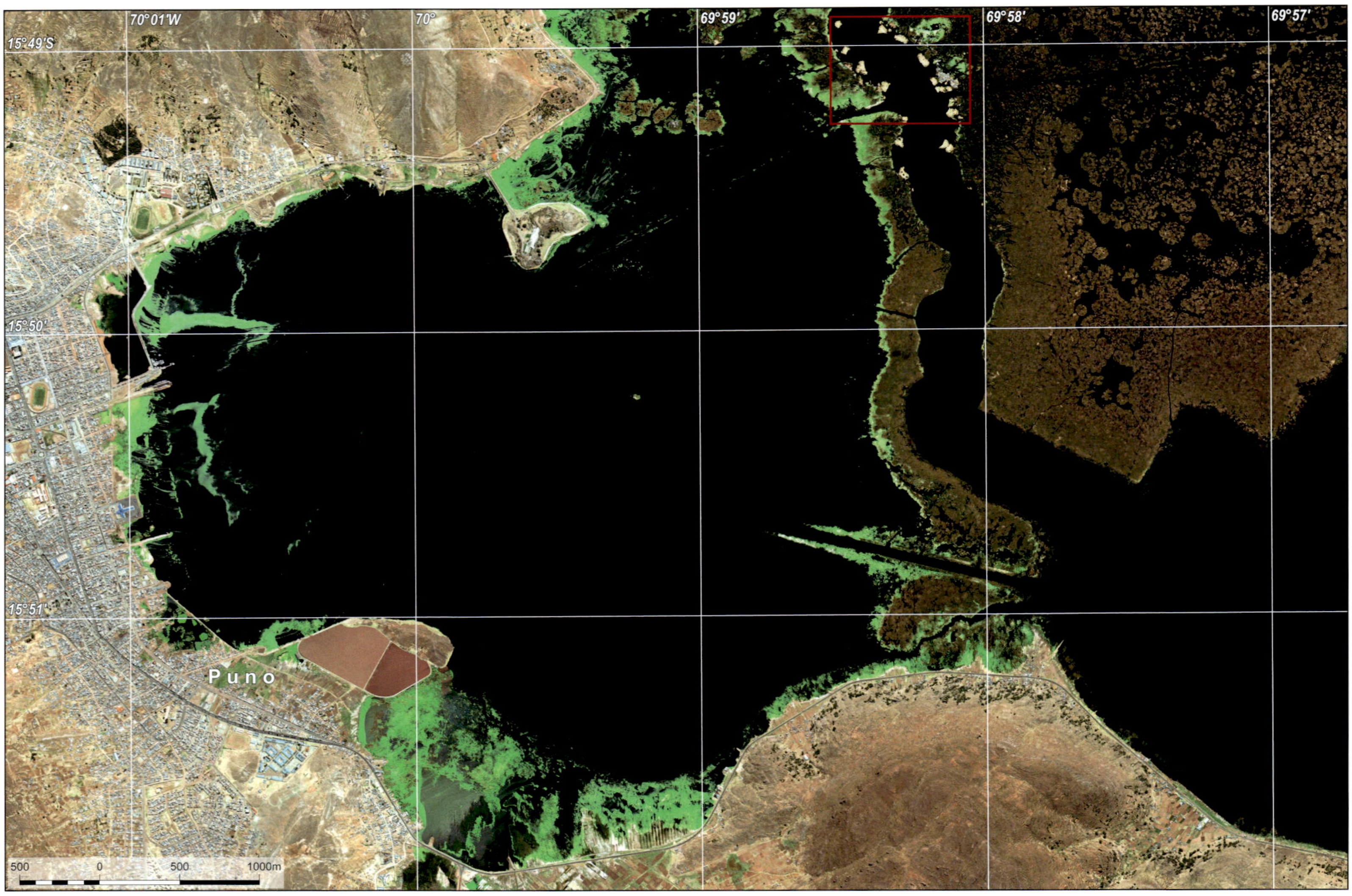
70°01'W
70°
69°59'
69°58'
69°57'
15°49'S
15°50'
15°51'
Puno
500 0 500 1000m

LAKE TITICACA

At almost 4,000 metres above sea level, Lake Titicaca is located in the dry plateau of the Altiplano. Despite the tough conditions here, the Incas and Aymara settled in the region around the lakes many centuries ago. In the Aymara language, Titicaca means 'rock puma'.

◁ 1 – Lake Titicaca lies in the Andes at 3,820 metres a.s.l., between the Cordillera Occidental and the Cordillera Oriental.

▷ 3 – Lake Titicaca is the largest inland lake in South America and also the largest high mountains lake in the world, larger even than Ysyk-Köl in Kyrgyzstan. The satellite image clearly shows why the Altiplano region is very dry – cloudbanks approaching from the east and west are blocked by the Andes.

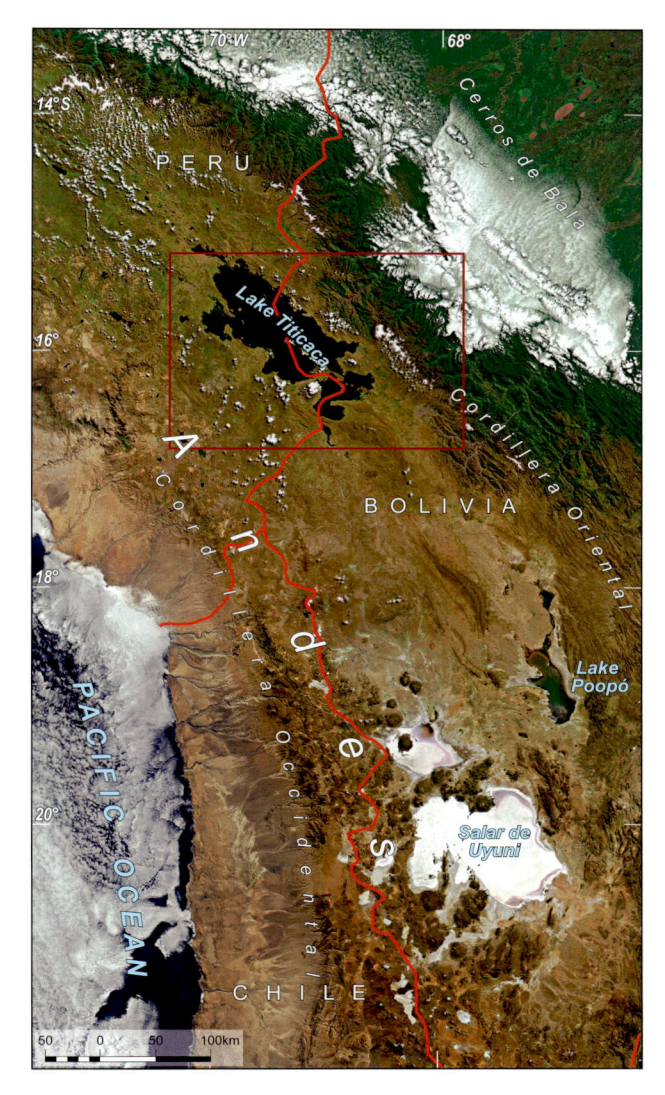

◁ 2 – Large areas of the shores of Lake Titicaca are overrun with algae (green). At Puno, efforts have been made since 2010 to deal with it.

▷ 4 – The high-resolution IKONOS-2 image shows the reed islands of the Uros people.

▽ 5 – One of the 40 or so reed islands of the Uros people that still exist today.

Lake Titicaca lies on the Altiplano plateau of the Andes (Figs. 1 and 3). During the last ice age, the entire plateau was covered by Lake Ballivián. Lake Titicaca, Lake Poopo and numerous other smaller saline lakes are the remnants of this enormous Pleistocene lake. With an area of around 8,300 square kilometres, a length of 180 kilometres and a maximum width of 67 kilometres, Lake Titicaca is the largest inland lake in South America apart from Lake Maracaibo, which is connected to the Caribbean.

A total of 27 tributaries flow into the lake, which is also fed by precipitation. As a result of the high evaporation, low inflow and extraction of its waters for agriculture, the lake's level continues to fall, despite temporary high water periods. Around Lake Titicaca, through which the border between Peru and Bolivia runs, there are numerous settlements and cities that are home to more than 900,000 people. With around 120,000 inhabitants, Puno, on the western shore in Peru, is the largest city on the lake.

The Altiplano and the region around Lake Titicaca have a long agricultural tradition. Llamas and alpacas are pastured on the hillsides around the lake, and their wool is the main source of income for the local population. Wheat, potatoes and maize are also important crops, but because of the arid climate, arable farming is only possible through irrigation. The lake's plentiful fish stocks are another important food source for the locals.

The floating islands of the Uros people

As the influence of the Incas increased and conflicts arose, the original inhabitants of the region around the lake, the Uros people, saw no other choice but to seek shelter out on the lake. They built floating islands made from reeds, which were anchored to the shore and could be cast off in an emergency. Although the region is no longer experiencing conflict, some Uros have retained their traditional way of life. Around 40 of these reed islands still exist today (Figs. 4 and 5).

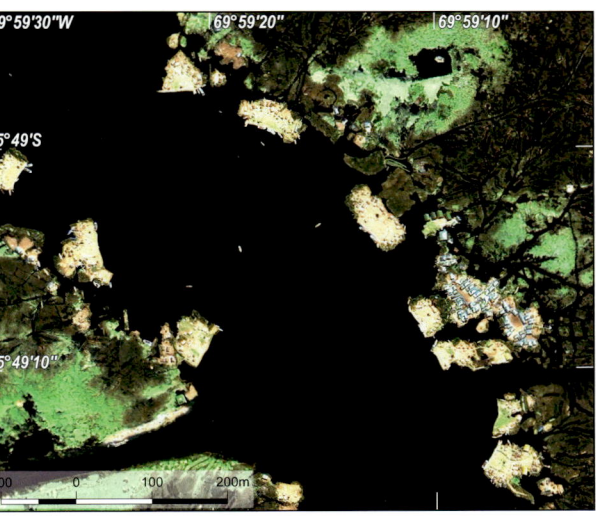

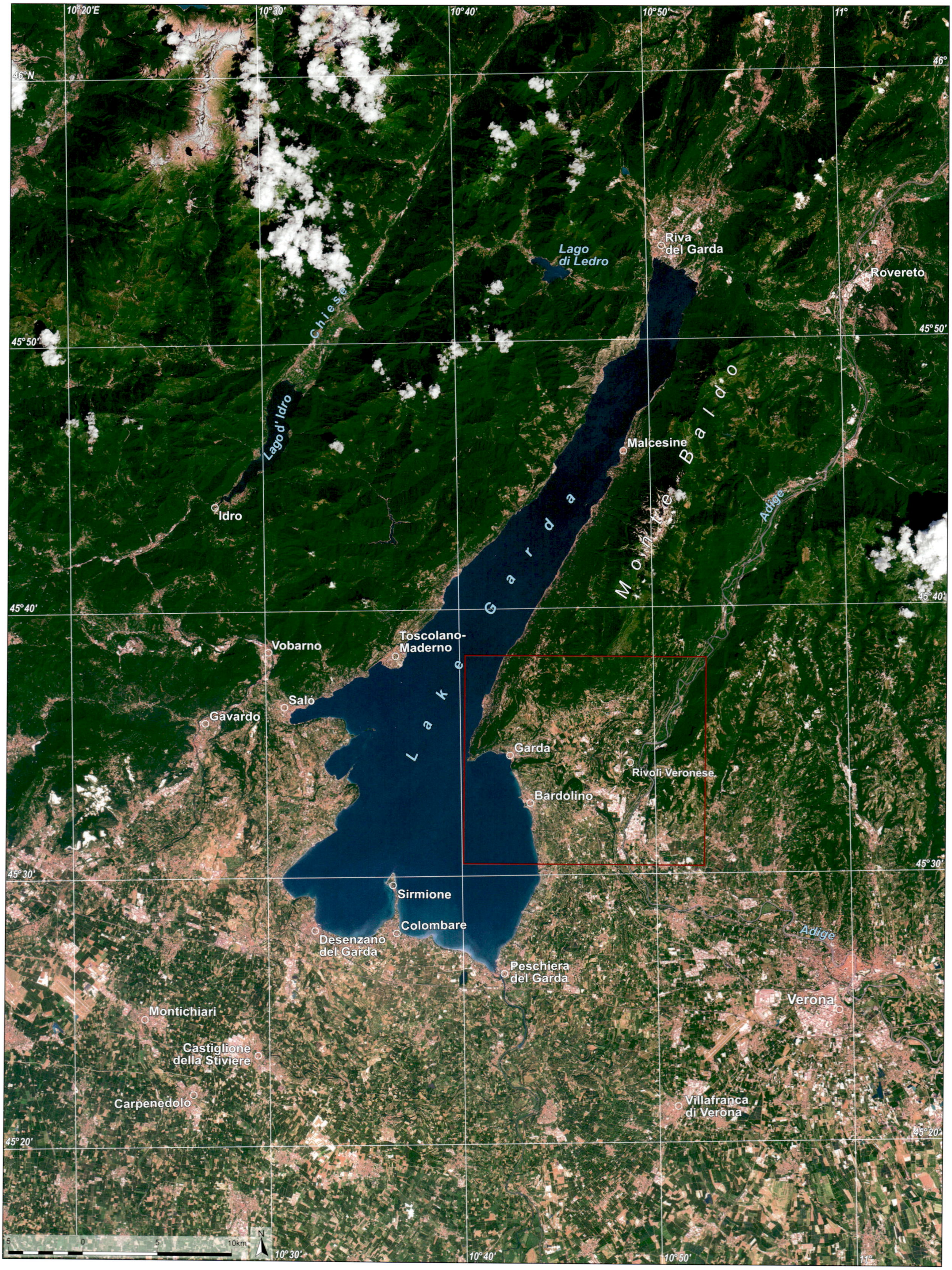

10°20'E
10°30'
10°40'
10°50'
11°
46°N
46°
45°50'
45°40'
45°30'
45°20'
Lago di Ledro
Riva del Garda
Rovereto
Chiese
Lago d'Idro
Malcesine
Monte Baldo
Adige
Idro
Lake Garda
Vobarno
Toscolano-Maderno
Salò
Gavardo
Garda
Rivoli Veronese
Bardolino
Sirmione
Colombare
Desenzano del Garda
Peschiera del Garda
Verona
Montichiari
Castiglione della Stiviere
Carpenedolo
Villafranca di Verona
5
0
5
10km
N

LAKE GARDA

Italy's largest lake is a Pleistocene glacial lake. The mild climate makes the area around Lake Garda good for growing grapes, and it is also a popular tourist destination.

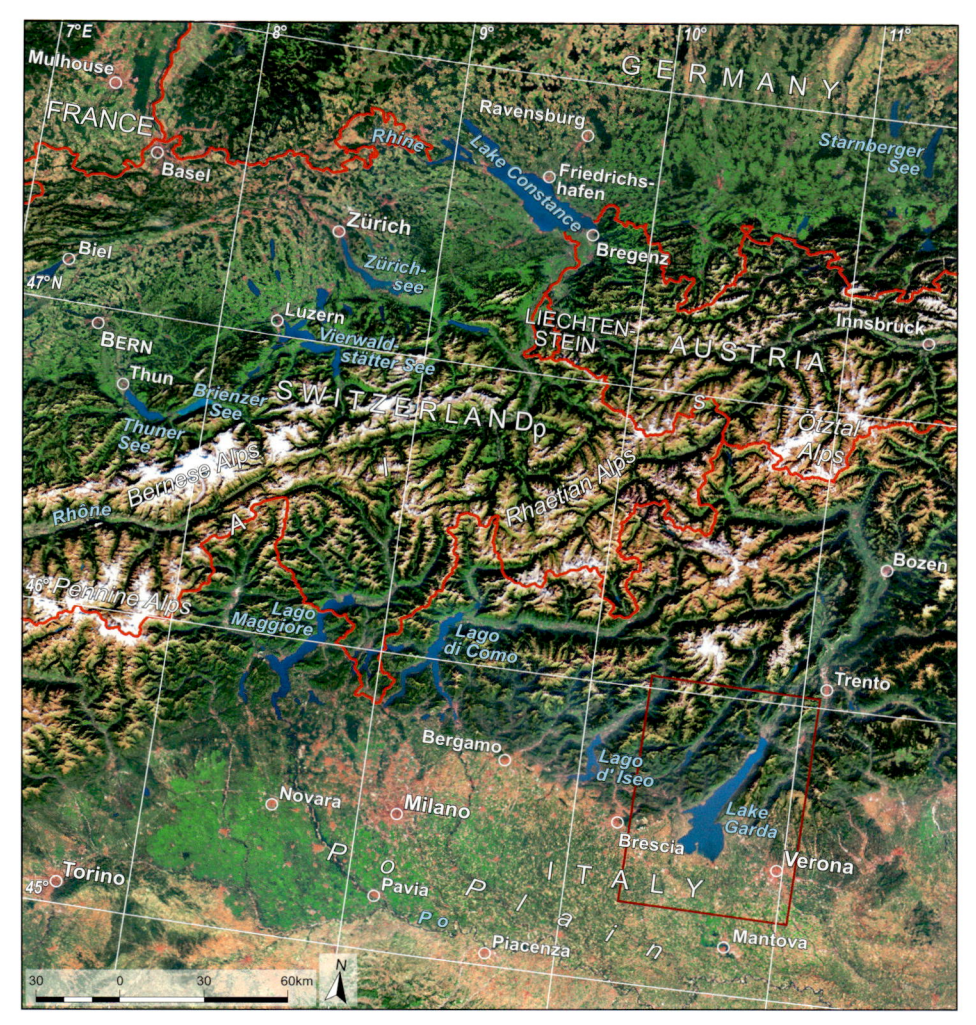

2 – The Alps were transformed during the major ice ages down through Earth's history. The glaciers left behind many lakes and broad valleys.

1 – Lake Garda is Italy's largest lake. The north part is confined by the Southern Limestone Alps around the lake. The flat Po Valley allows the glacial lake to widen out in the south.

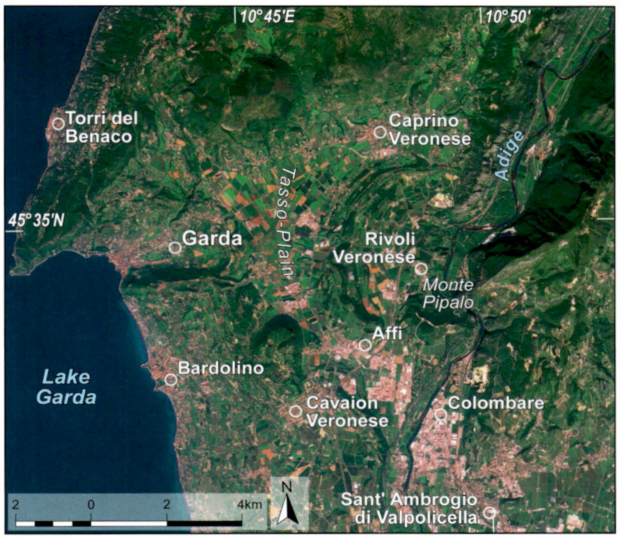

3 – Moraines can be made out in the area between the U-shaped valley, the Adige and the lake, including Monte Pipalo, used by Napoleon as a strategic lookout.

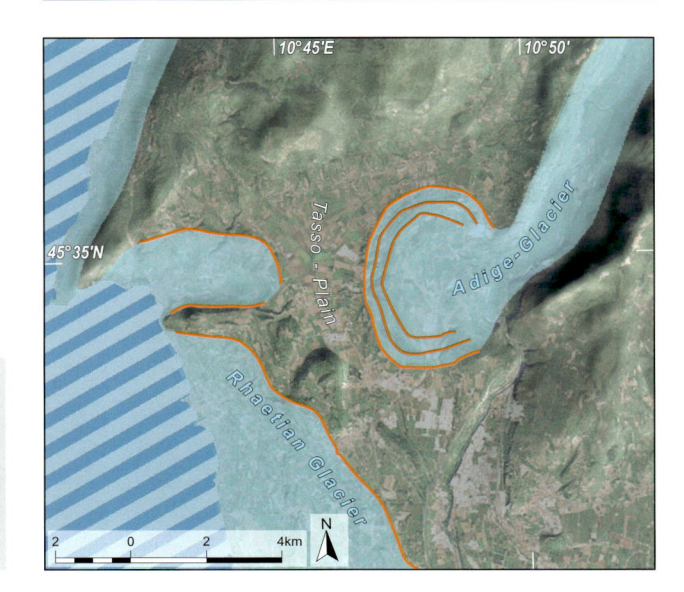

4 – The last major shaping of the landscape was during the Würm glaciation of around 50,000 years ago. Today, the Tasso plain lies between the terminal moraines of the now vanished Adige and Rhaetian glaciers.

Dispersion of glaciers and formation of moraines in the "Würm" ice age some 50,000 years ago
- Dispersion of glaciers
- Glaciers on top of the present Lake Garda
- Moraine

Like many other lakes in the European Alps, Lake Garda (Lago di Garda, Fig. 1) was created by the glaciers of the various ice ages that have scoured Europe (Fig. 2). Lateral moraines near Val dei Molini, around 380,000 years old, are testament to the forces of the ice during the Günz glaciation, when the Adige (Etsch) and Rhaetian (Rhätische) glaciers began to carve out the Garda valley. This process lasted many thousands of years and left scores of terminal moraines around Lake Garda dating back to the Würm glaciation of about 50,000 years ago (Figs. 3 and 4). The glaciers scoured out a basin up to 300 metres deep. After the glaciers retreated, the basin, blocked by lateral and terminal moraines, filled up with meltwater. The bed of the former ice sheets became the largest lake in Italy.

The history of human settlement around the lake region has long been settled, and many great names are associated with it. Virgil, Pliny the Elder, Goethe, D'Annunzio and other well-known figures all spent time near Lake Garda and valued it for the same reasons that still draw tourists to the region today. Once part of the Roman Empire, Northern Italy was elevated to the Roman province of Gallia Cisalpina in 191 BCE. Almost 2,000 years later, Napoleon won one of his greatest victories over the Austrians on January 14, 1797, where he used the landscape shaped by the glaciers to his advantage. From his viewpoint on the highest moraine, Monte Pipalo (Fig. 3), Napoleon was able to observe the troop movements of the Austrians, dressed in bright white, and then cut them off on their march towards nearby Rivoli Veronese. This prevented them from joining forces with the troops of Baron Alvinczy, as they had planned.

Today, Lake Garda is one of Italy's biggest tourist destinations, not just because of the landscape shaped by the glaciers, but because of the sub-Mediterranean climate as well. Mediterranean plants such as date palms, olive trees, cedars and wild oleanders grow all around the lake. Together with the vineyards, the many former orangeries on the western shores of the lake complete the traditional Mediterranean scenery. With craggy mountains over 2,000 metres high, the area around Lake Garda is an Eldorado for hikers, climbers and mountain bikers. Along the northern shore, the reliable "Ora'" thermal winds guarantee exceptional conditions for crowds of windsurfers.

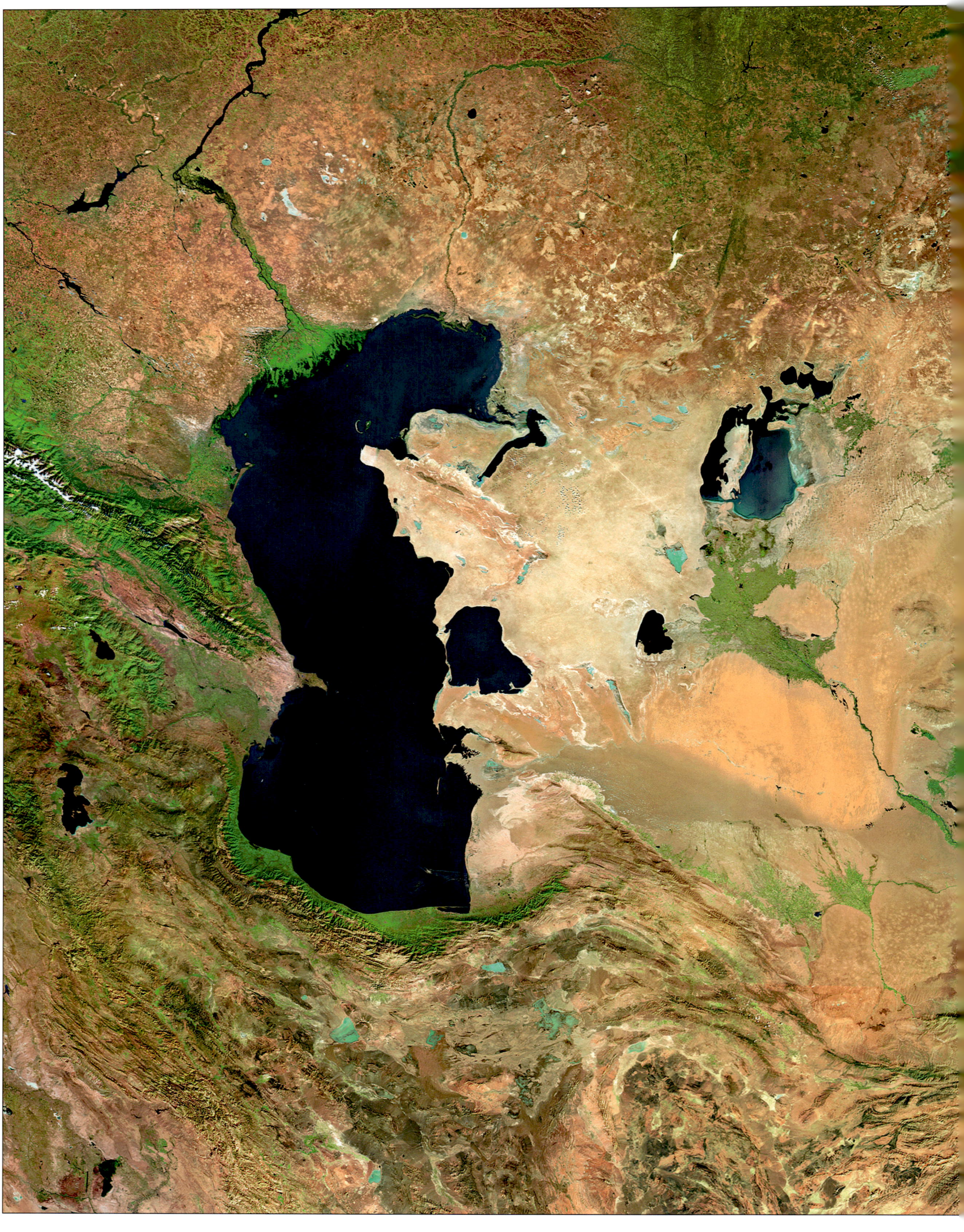

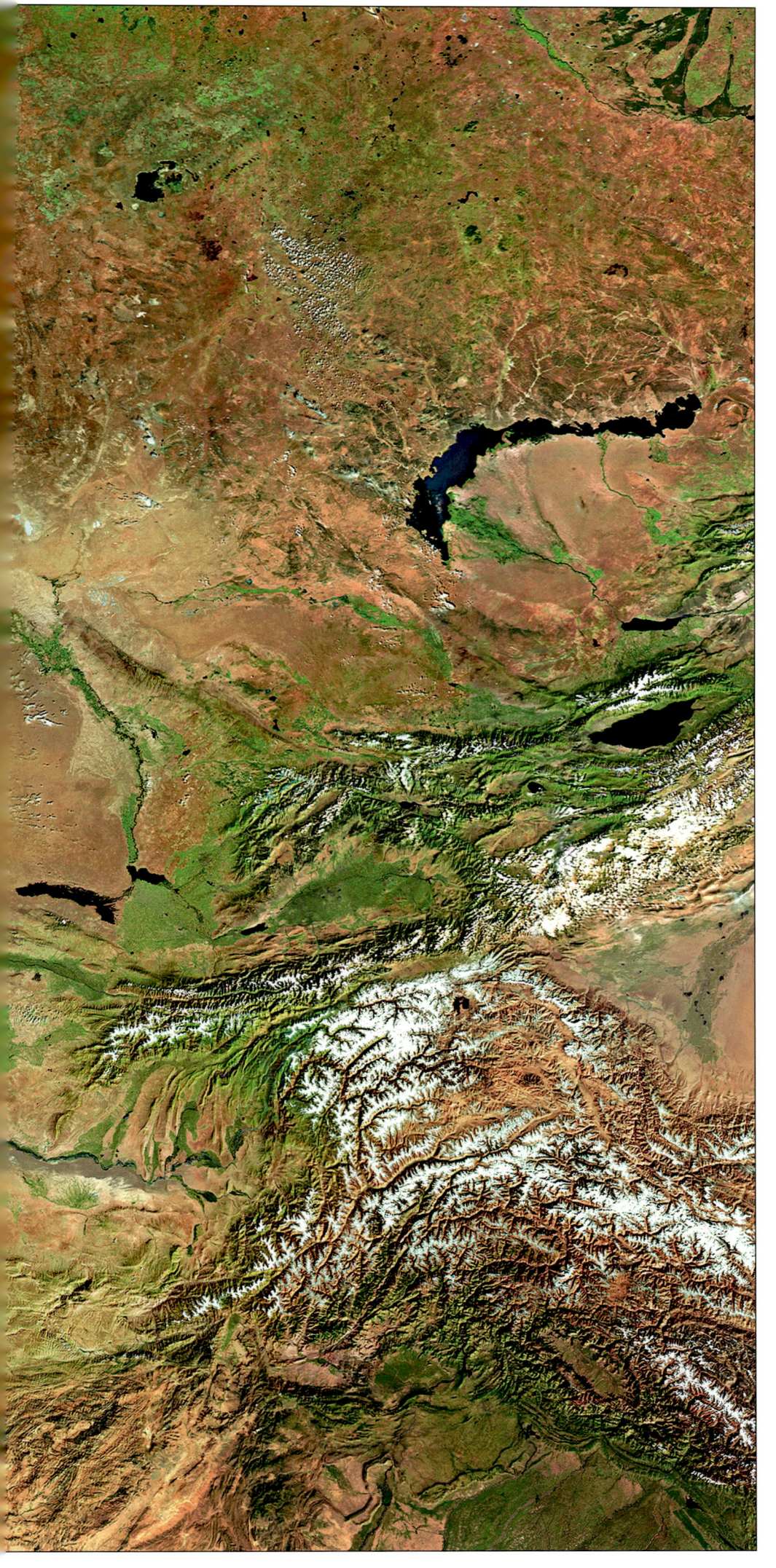

THE ARAL SEA

Where once the water of the Aral Sea lapped against the shore, today nothing but desert spreads. Improper water use along the tributaries feeding it have dried the sea up.

The Aral Sea is a lake in a depression in the Turan Lowland with no natural outlet. Until the 1960s, it was the fourth-largest lake on Earth. Within 50 years, the lake, which once measured 64,000 square kilometres, shrank to around 10 per cent of its original size as a result of uncontrolled water withdrawal. Water was primarily taken from the two autochthonous tributaries, the Amudar'ya and Syrdar'ya, to irrigate vast cotton fields (Fig. 1, p. 142, Fig. 4, p. 143). The 1,415 kilometres Amudar'ya is formed at the confluence of the Vakhsh and Pjandz rivers, which are fed by the glaciers and meltwater of the Pamir Mountains to the west. Most of the water is taken from the Amudar'ya via the Karakum Canal in Turkmenistan. The Karakum is the longest canal in the former Soviet Union (USSR), and the area of southern Turkmenistan that it irrigates is one of the biggest cotton-producing regions on Earth. The lower water levels have also severely limited shipping in the area. The Syrdar'ya has its headwaters in the Tian Shan mountains of Kyrgyzstan, where it is fed with meltwater. It runs 2,212 kilometres from the confluence of the Naryn River and the Kara Darya in Uzbekistan. Its low water levels make it largely impassable for ships, but its water is used to irrigate cotton fields and to generate hydropower. Access to and the use of water as a natural resource also leads to political tensions between the riparian states of this region, a struggle in which nature has a low priority only.

Cotton has been grown in Central Asia for many years. The Soviet Union expanded the amount of arable land and intensified and industrialised agriculture. The irrigation systems were primitively built and are now largely antiquated, with the consequence that almost half of the water transported through their unlined channels is lost (Fig. 4, p. 143). The excessive withdrawal of water from the tributaries has led to continually sinking water levels in the Aral Sea, tripling its salinity and crippling the once-thriving fishing industry. Of the 25 native fish species, most have gone extinct as a result of the receding water line and pesticide pollution.

As water levels in the Aral Sea have fallen, the lake has begun to split up into separate hydrological basins..

◁
1 – The remnants of Central Asia's Aral Sea are situated east of the vast Caspian Sea and downstream a traditional cotton-growing region requiring enormous amounts of water (situation in 2004).

141

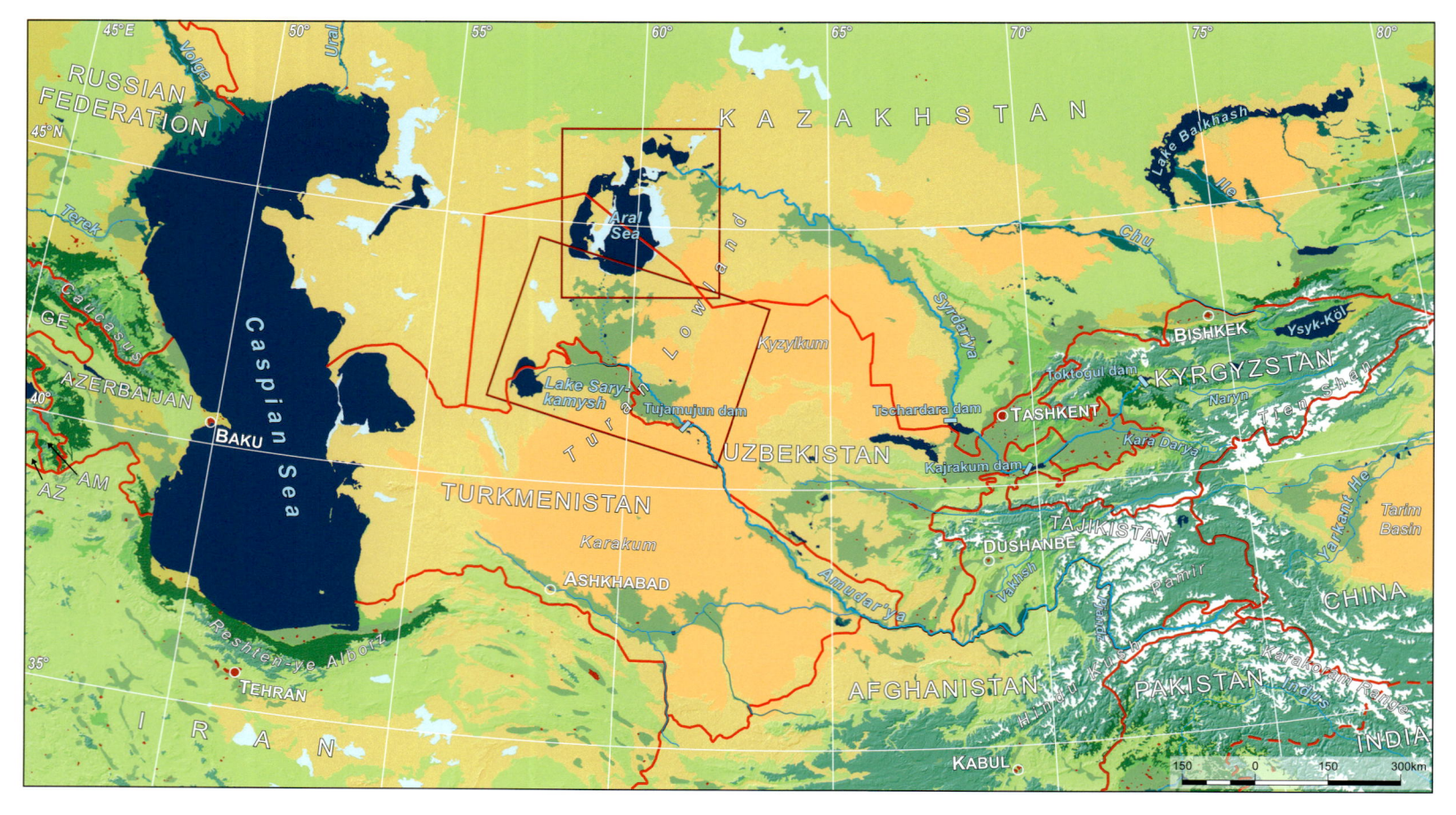

1 – The land cover and land use classification map for Central Asia shows the large irrigated areas in the desert to the south of the Aral Sea (data from the year 2000).

In 1987, the northern part of the lake separated from the southern part, to which it had been joined by a mere rivulet (Fig. 2c). In 2007, the southern part also split into a western and eastern lake (Fig. 2c/d Lake area 2006), which then completely dried up first in 2009. A small strip remains in the south-west, but this too threatens to vanish, since hardly any water enters it now from the Amudar'ya.

The slow poisoning of the Aral Sea and its effects

Apart from the gradual disappearance of the lake, the region is also suffering from decades of pollution by highly toxic agricultural pesticides, herbicides and defoliants. Cold War research into biological weapons on the former island in the north-west of the sea (Fig. 2b) has also left its traces. The wind stirs up the dusty soil with its herbicide and pesticide residues, distributing them far and wide. Up to 150,000 tonnes are carried away by the wind every year. The drinking water supply is contaminated with heavy metals, salts and many other toxic substances, which has led to significant health problems in the local population, such as respiratory disorders and eye irritations. Child mortality and the number of deformities in newborns has increased drastically since the 1960s, with general life expectancy falling to around 50 years. As an environmental consequence, around 140 of the 178 original native animal species and 100 native plant species have died out.

Climate change and the shrinking lake

As the lake has continued to shrink, the local climate has changed, becoming more continental. Short, hot summers are now followed by long, cold winters. Due to the lower evaporation rate and the subsequently lower air humidity, there is less precipitation. Every year, sandstorms churn

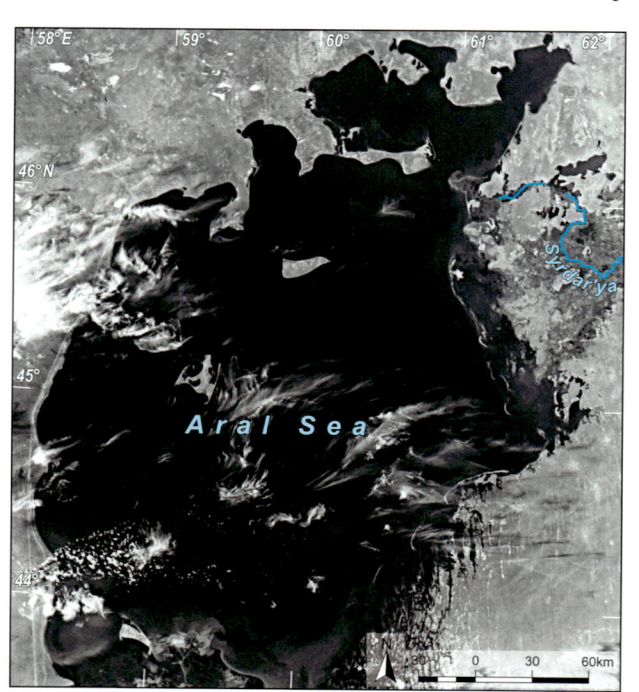

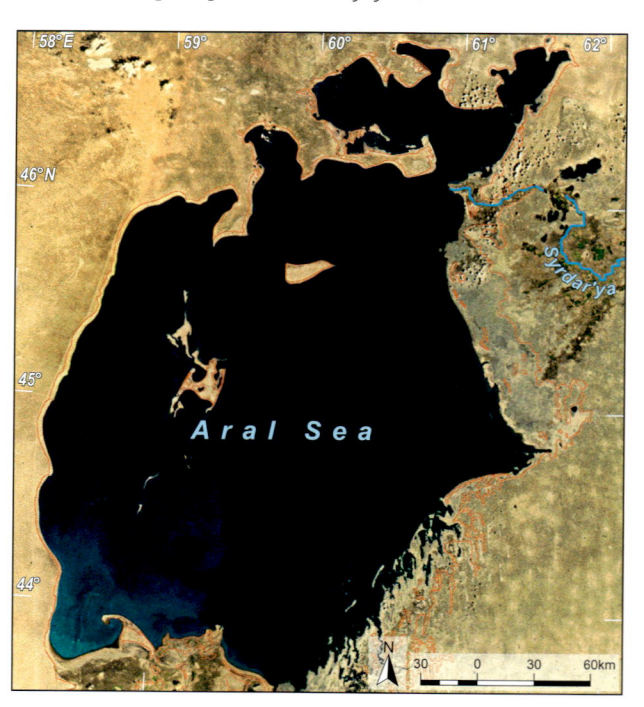

2a – The Aral Sea in 1964.

2b – 1970, when the Aral Sea was still a single body of water.

2c – A natural ridge creates two separate basins in 2000.

3 – Ships grounded on what used to be the bed of the Aral.

▷
4 – South of the Aral Sea, large areas of land are irrigated, predominantly to grow cotton. A part of the waters of the Amudar'ya now feeds Lake Sarykamysh southwest of the Aral Sea (Envisat MERIS image, dated 10/10/2011).

Land cover
- Flood irrigation
- Agriculture
- Extensive pasture farming
- Forest
- High mountain vegetation
- Swamp, riparian forest
- Desert, semi-desert
- Sandy desert
- Steppe
- Snow and ice
- Salt lake
- Water surface
- settlement
- International border
- River
- Dam

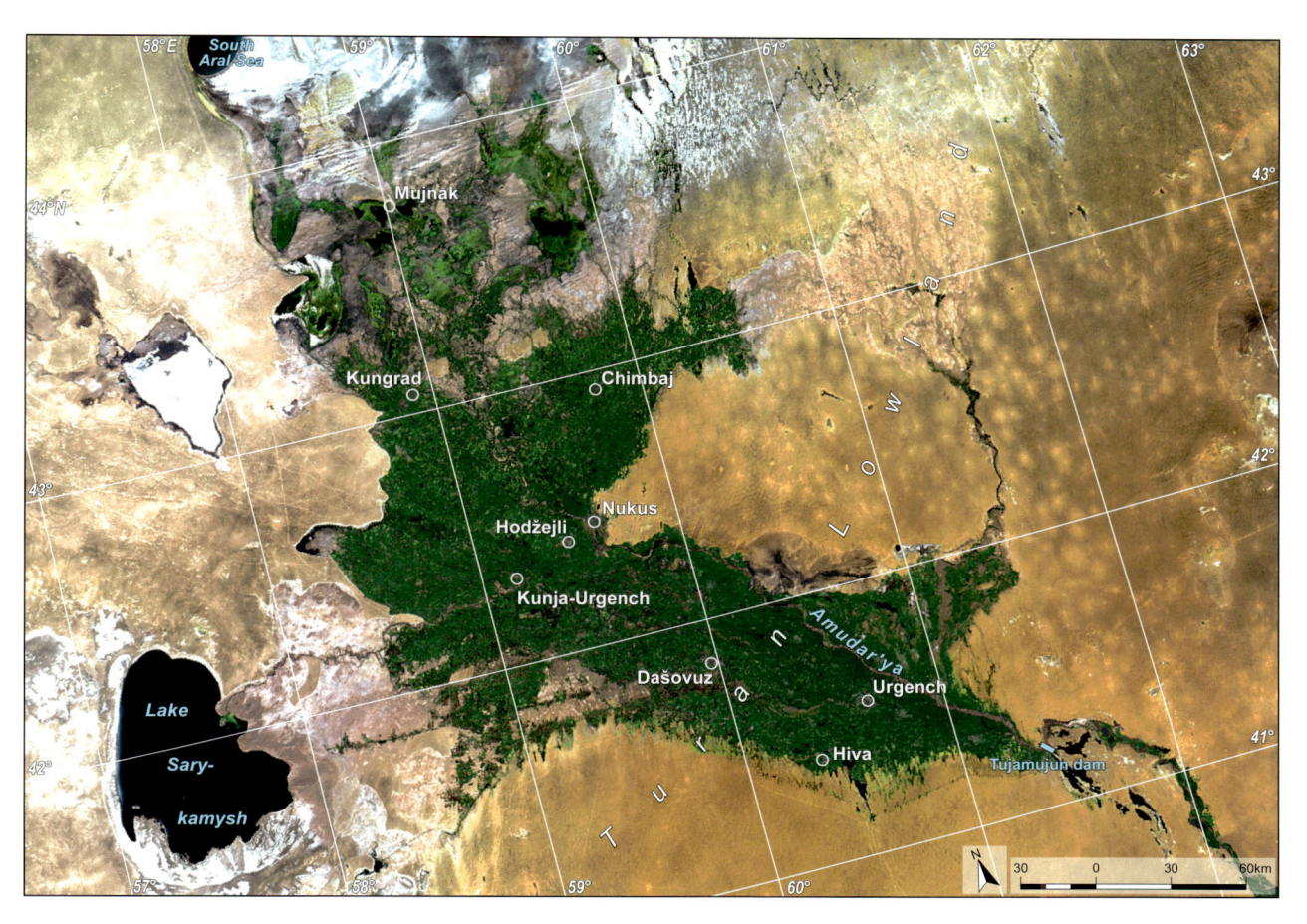

The Amudar'ya starts out as the border between Tajikistan, Uzbekistan, Turkmenistan and Afghanistan, before flowing through the deserts of Central Asia. From the source of the Pjandz River in the Pamir Mountains/Hindu Kush, the Amudar'ya continues for 2,743 kilometres, to where it once flowed into the Aral Sea. The Syrdar'ya, rising from the Naryn headwaters south of Ysyk-Köl lake, has a total length of 3,019 kilometres.

The extensive catchment of the Aral Sea takes in around 1,550,000 square kilometres (FAO).

▷▷
2d – The Aral Sea in Aug. 2011. After completion of the Kokaral Dike along the ridge between the North Aral Sea and the South Aral Sea in 2005, the northern basin began to fill again. The North Aral Sea is now fed with water from the Syrdar'ya, the South Aral – its eastern part dried out in 2009 and 2014 temporarily – by the Amudar'ya and 100 mm rainfall per year. Most of Amudar'ya's polluted water flows into Lake Sarykamysh (Fig. 4), increasing its level of water and pollution. However, people still go fishing.

Decrease of water level
- Lake area in 1964
- Lake area in 1970
- Lake area in 2000
- Lake area in 2006
- Lake area in 2009

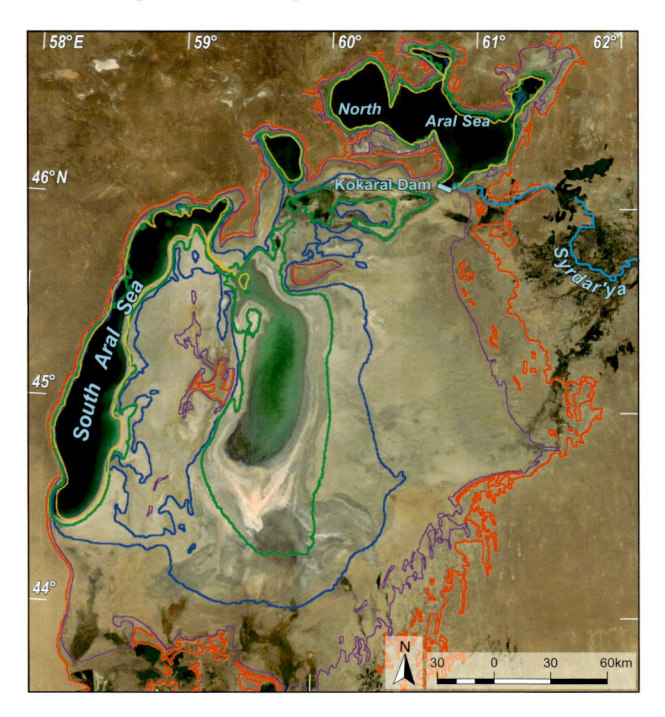

up more than 75 million tonnes of sand and dust and carry it towards the north-west. All of these changes have led to shorter vegetation periods. Crop yields have fallen and the food supply for the local population has worsened. In many regions around the Aral Sea, the situation seems hopeless. The traditional livelihoods, agriculture and fishing, are no longer viable (Fig. 3). With the end of the Soviet era, industry also collapsed on a large scale, leaving many people around the former lake without work. As a result, the few people who have stayed behind are often to be found at the small markets in the towns and villages, trying to sell their last remaining possessions in order to scrape together enough money for essentials.

Possible solutions

Many strategies to save the Aral Sea have been put forward. One is a pipeline from the Pamir Mountains to transport glacier water to the Aral Sea to fill it to a stable minimum level. Another is to divert water from the Volga, Ob and Irtysh rivers into the lake. Water could also be taken from the Caspian Sea and diverted to the Aral Sea via a canal. To date, none of these ideas have been implemented, though, with the exception of the saving of the 'small' North Aral Sea by the building of a dike (Fig. 2d). Since 2006 water levels have risen in the North Aral Sea by the inflow of the Syrdar'ya and salinity levels have dropped, which has created a healthier microclimate and allowed plant and animal life to return. People have recently begun to move back to the shores of the North Aral Sea, where the fishing industry is starting to pick up once again. Saxaul bushes, which store water and stabilise the soil, have also been restored to the area. While this all sounds very positive, the history of the Aral Sea should serve to remind us of how important it is to protect the environment.

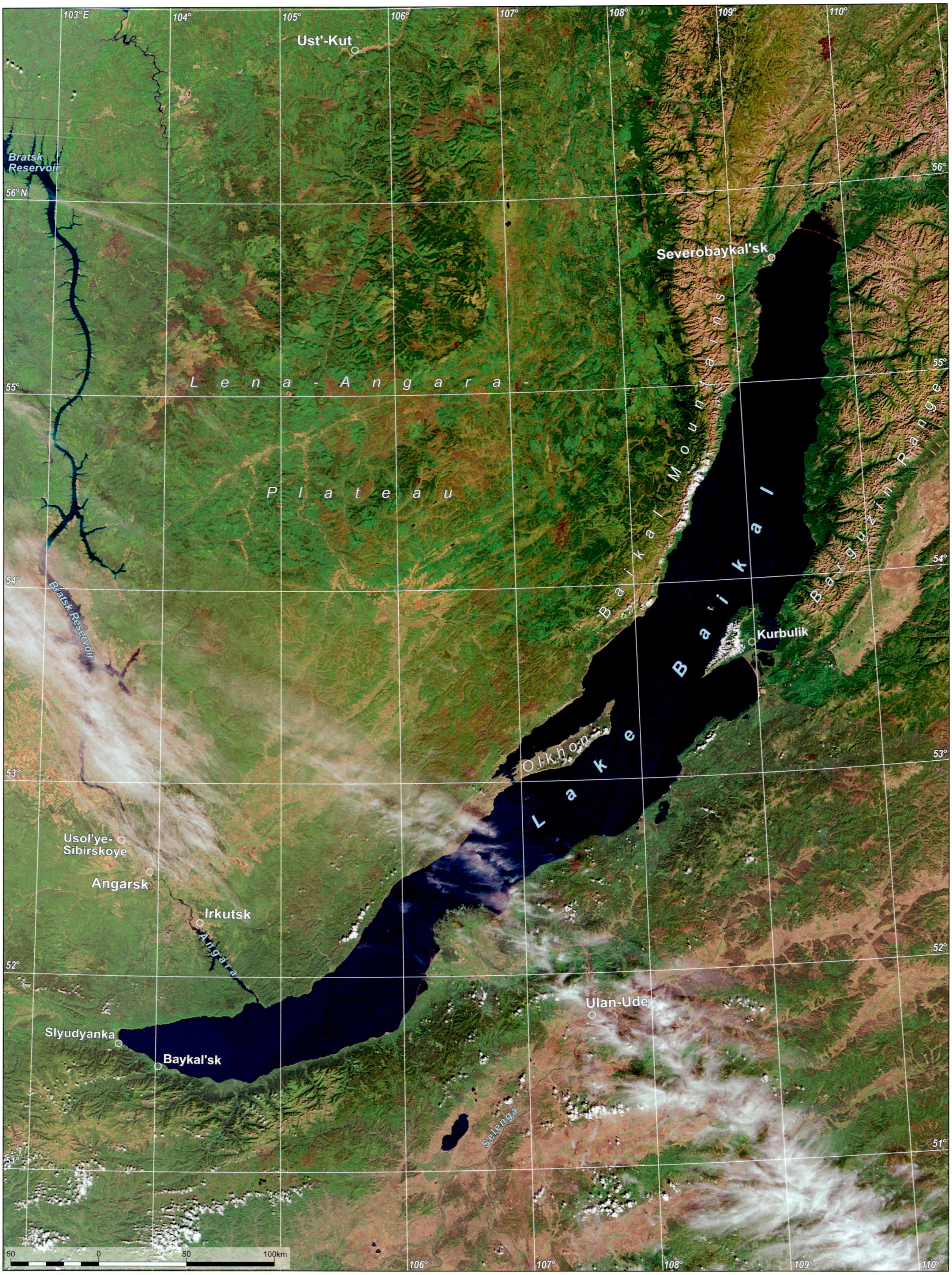
Ust'-Kut
Bratsk Reservoir
Severobaykal'sk
Lena-Angara-
Plateau
Baykal Mountains
Barguzin Range
Lake Baikal
Kurbulik
Olkhon
Bratsk Reservoir
Usol'ye-Sibirskoye
Angarsk
Irkutsk
Angara
Ulan-Ude
Slyudyanka
Baykal'sk
Selenga
50 0 50 100km
103° E
104°
105°
106°
107°
108°
109°
110°
56° N
55°
54°
53°
52°
51°

LAKE BAIKAL

Lake Baikal lies near the Russian/Mongolian border and, at 1,642 metres, is the deepest and oldest lake on Earth. More than 20 per cent of the world's entire drinking water is stored in this lake.

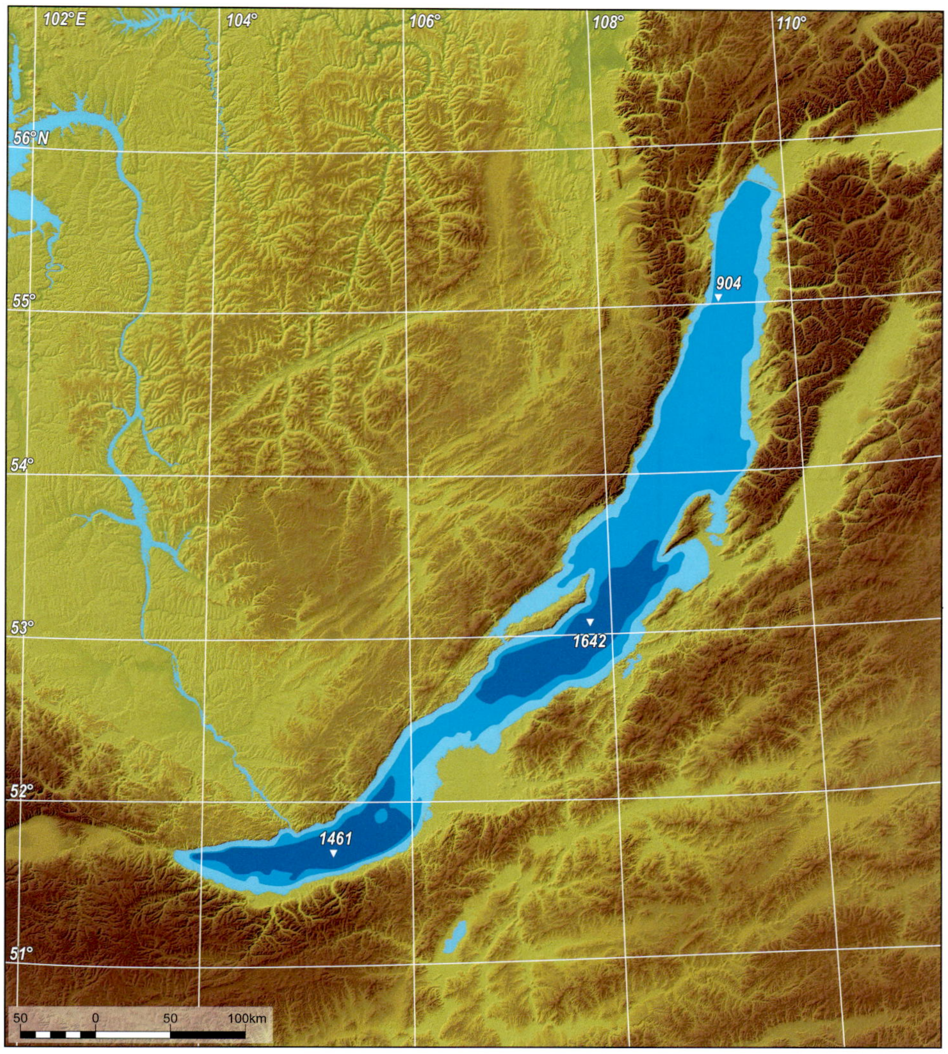

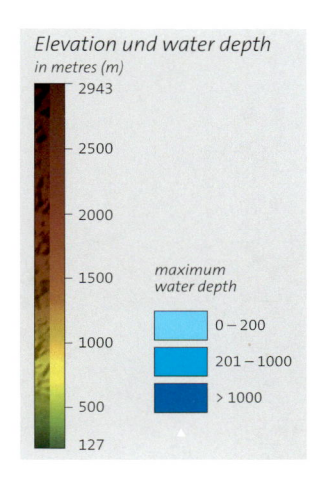

Lake Baikal was created by the slow break-up of the Eurasian continental plate, a process that began around 35 million years ago. As the Eurasian and Amurian plates spread apart, fissures cracked the Earth's crust. Lake Baikal lies in the Baikal Rift Zone, which is the weakest point between the two plates. With a depth of eight to nine kilometres, the rift is one of the deepest active trenches in the world. The rift widens by about two centimetres every year. Researches believe that, many years from now, a new sea will form from Lake Baikal and will split the continent of Asia in two.

Its depth of over 1,600 metres gives Lake Baikal a volume of around 24,000 cubic kilometres. Apart from the polar ice caps, it is the biggest reservoir of freshwater on Earth (Fig. 2). This store, around one fifth of all liquid freshwater on the planet, would be sufficient to provide the entire population of the world with drinking water for over 50 years.

More than 300 rivers and creeks flow into the lake. Almost half of the annual water inflow comes from the Selenga River alone, which rises in Mongolia and empties into the lake at its eastern shore. The sediment it carries has formed a delta 40 kilometres wide, which serves as a hatching and resting place for countless species of waders and migratory birds. Near Irkutsk, just northwest of the lake's southern tip, the Angara River drains Lake Baikal. The Angara is the headwater tributary of the Yenisey, which flows north to Kara Sea.

Lake Baikal is a cold-water lake and freezes over during the winter. Its north-south orientation leaves it partially ice-free from May, but in some places only from June. With an ice sheet over one metre thick, the frozen lake is used as a road that can at times be used by lorries and heavy goods vehicles.

The area around Lake Baikal has its own unique ecosystem, with an enormous diversity of flora and fauna. The lake and its shores are home to around 2,500 species of animals and plants. Most of the animal species are endemic to the region, meaning they live only here and nowhere else. The Baikal seal is of particular zoological interest as it is the only species of seal to live only in freshwater (Fig. 4). The mystery of where the seal came from still puzzles scientists today. The sensitive ecosystem is under threat from unfiltered wastewater from homes and the wood pulp, paper and cement industries.

2 – Lake Baikal, as part of a continental rift valley, is more than 25 million years old.

1 – Lake Baikal and the area around it was declared a UNESCO World Heritage site in 1996.

3 – Shaman Rock on the island of Olchon is the centre of the Buryati faith.

4 – The Baikal seal is the world's only freshwater seal.

145

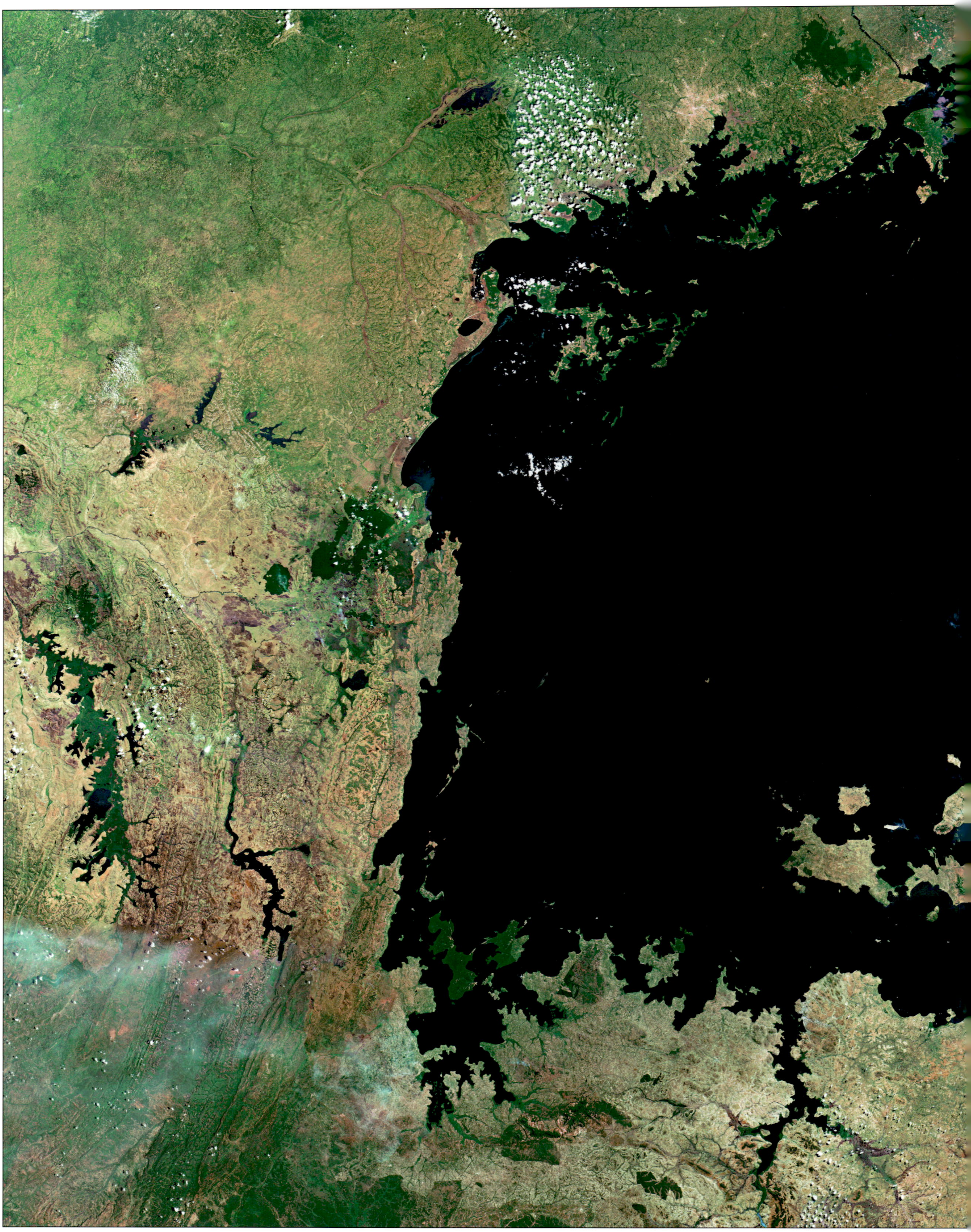

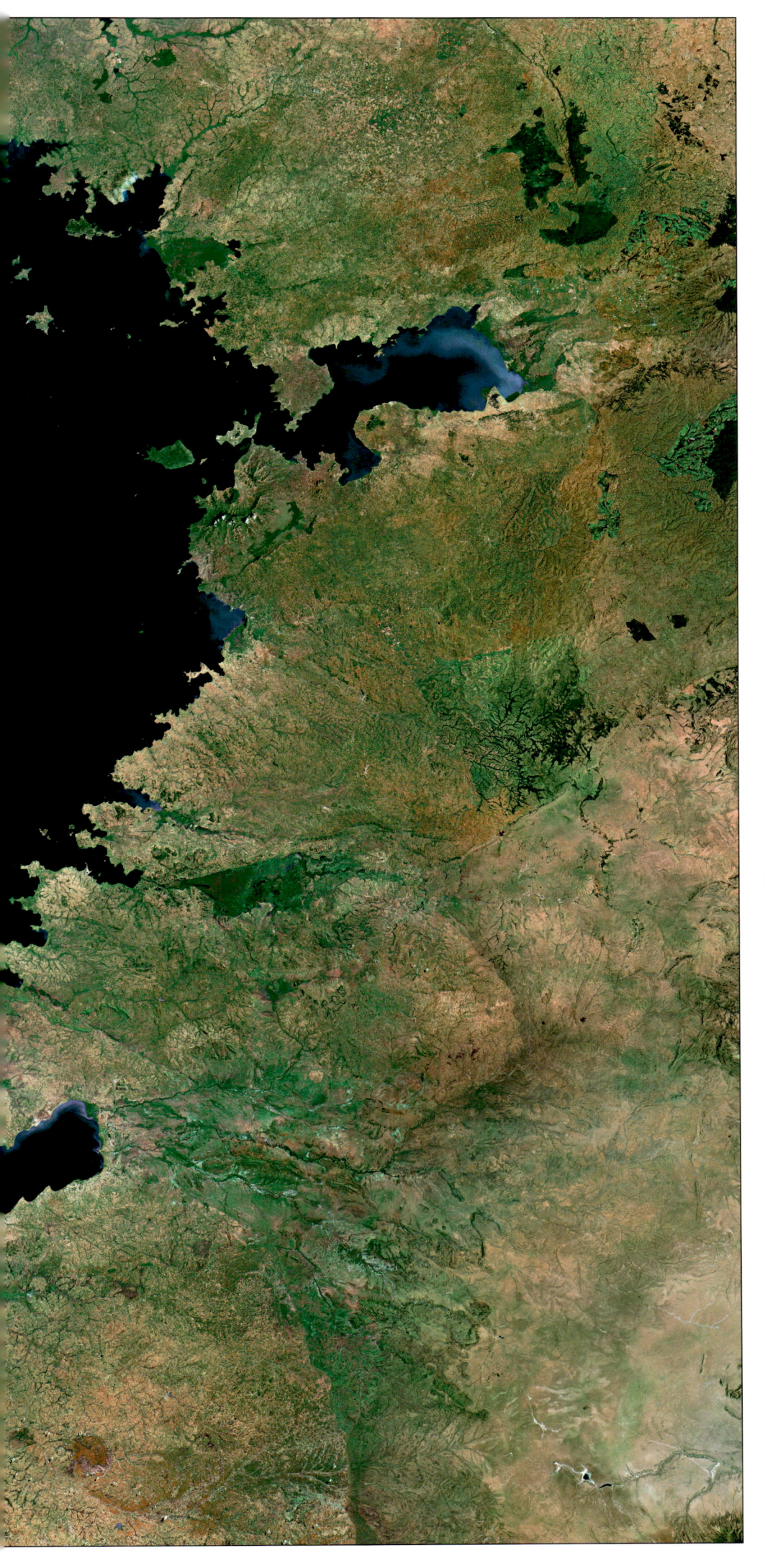

LAKE VICTORIA

Africa's largest lake is beset by a wide range of problems. Input from unfiltered wastewater, the destruction of the vegetation on the shore and the dramatic decline in fish stocks have all upset the ecological equilibrium.

Lake Victoria is in East Africa, on the borders between Uganda, Kenya and Tanzania. The plateau it lies on is near the Equator and is part of the western section of the East African Rift System. The lakes to the west, such as Lake Albert and Lake Edward, are also part of the geological fault line. With an area of 68,800 square kilometres, Lake Victoria is the largest freshwater lake in Africa. At its deepest point, it is 80 metres deep. It is 337 kilometres long, 240 kilometres wide and has a rugged coastline stretching 3,220 kilometres.

As a result of the fertile soils, the favourable climate and the rich fishing in the lake, the coastal areas are densely populated. The population pressure has led to massive environmental problems. In the middle of the 20th century, the Nile perch was introduced to Lake Victoria to boost catches. The rapid increase of the Nile perch population initially led to a boost for the fishing industry, but soon turned into a disaster as the Nile perch, also known as the Victoria perch, drove other fish species extinct. The Victoria perch is the region's main export. Another critical problem is the spread of water hyacinths, which have covered an enormous area and now pose a problem to fishing, the drinking water supply and electricity generation.

◁
1 – *Lake Victoria is Africa's largest lake. Its largest tributary, the Kagera River, is also the source of the Nile and arises in Burundi. The Nile, the world's longest river, leaves Lake Victoria to the north, from here it is known as the Victoria Nile (see also Fig. 4, p. 115).*

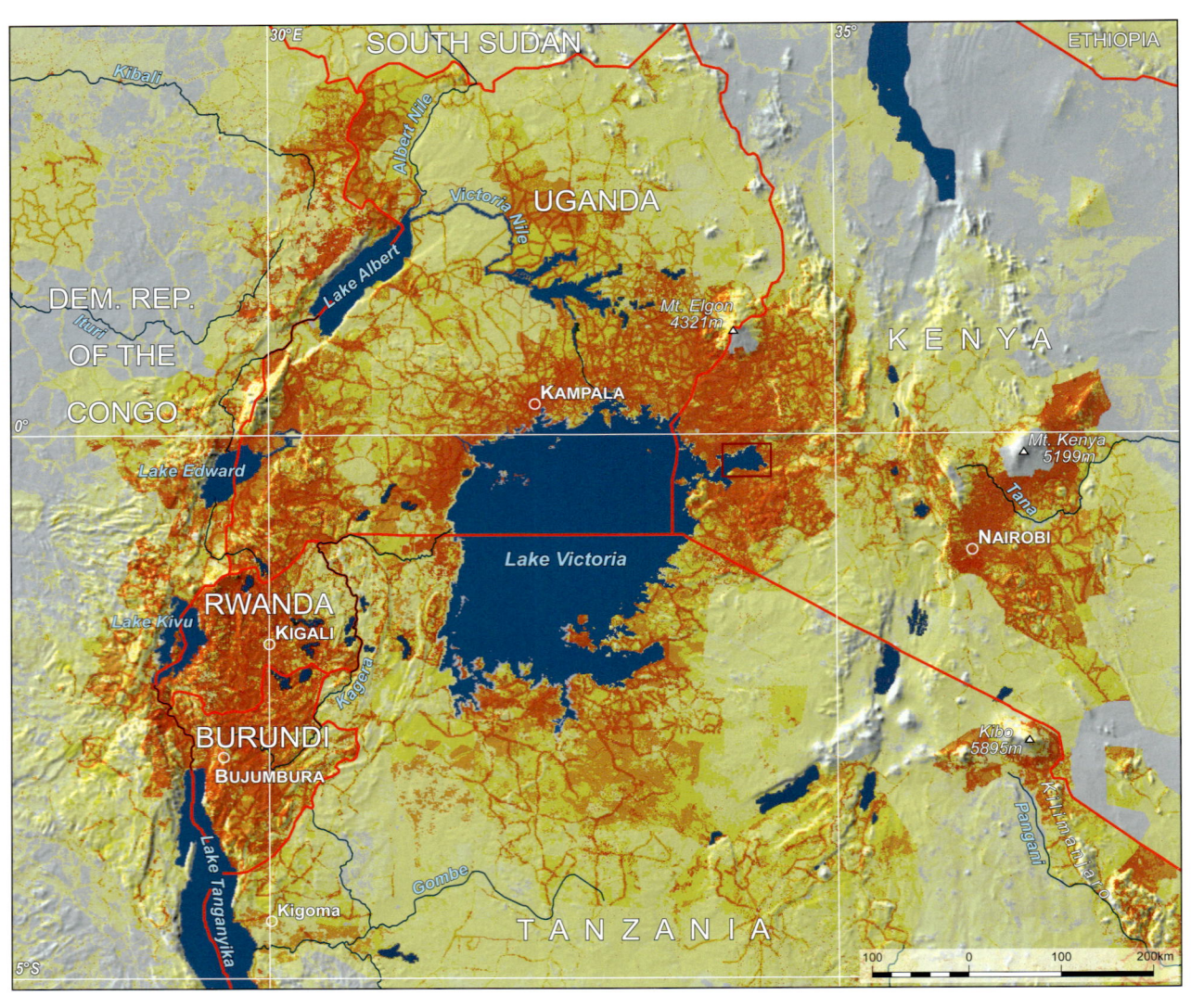

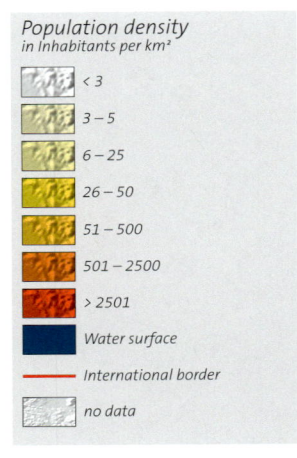

1 – Population density around Lake Victoria and in the northern part of the East African Rift System.

Population density

25 million people live within a radius of 80 kilometres, making the region one of Africa's most densely populated (Fig. 1). Numerous towns and cities have been built on the lake's shores for economic reasons. The fishing industry in Kampala, for example, benefits from the city's location on the lakeshore. In Kisumu, the third-largest city in Kenya, with a population of 250,000, numerous small industries, including fishing and cotton factories, have been established. The fishing villages on Lake Victoria use mostly biomass to generate energy.

The consequence is the deforestation of large stretches of land along the shores and on the inhabited islands on Lake Victoria. The untreated wastewater from industry and households that flows into the lake, worsening the water quality, poses a further threat to the environment.

The invation of water hyacinths

At the end of the 1990s water hyacinths threatened large areas of Lake Victoria (Figs. 2 and 3). The plants spread so quickly within just a few months that it was no longer possible to control them. They not only blocked shipping routes, but were home to mosquitoes and snails that acted as disease vectors. Snakes and crocodiles also hid among the plants, threatening the local population.

For many fishermen, the lake became an impenetrable carpet of the plant. Landing stages became overgrown and the thick plant growth rendered waterways unnavigable. In addition, turbines in hydroelectric plants were threatened with clogging or other damage. The power supply for the local population could thus also no longer be completely guaranteed. In addition, the dense plant growth reduced the speed of the water flow. The spread of the water hyacinths has now been brought under control and reduced. Both mechanical and biological processes had to be deployed. One mechanical aid took the form of boats with a special shredding module attached. This enabled the plant growth to be cut back and disposed of. A biological control method involved the use of weevils, a small beetle. The natural pest uses the stems and leaves of the water hyacinth as a nesting place and food source. The holes the weevils ate in the leaves and the nesting of larvae led to the plant dying off.

In addition, the plants were also used in attempts to manufacture furniture and generate biogas.

The Nile perch – a voracious predator

British scientists released the Nile perch into Lake Victoria in the 1960s. The fish, which can grow up to 70 kilogrammes, is now known as the Victoria perch, and has led to the near extinction of the 400 or so species of cichlids living in the lake. The region is now completely dependent on the fish factories, which processes the perch to western hygienic standards for export. The oily fish cannot be dried in the sun like native species but has to be dried over a fire – a much more intensive process. As such, the vegetation along the shores of the lake are burnt as fuel.

Water pollution

Other serious problems for Lake Victoria include water pollution from agricultural fertilisers and pesticides, untreated wastewater from industry (primarily breweries, sugar cane and soap factories) and the disposal of household wastewater. In the larger cities only a few households are hooked up to the sewage system, while no such sewage system exists in the rural regions. Untreated waste-

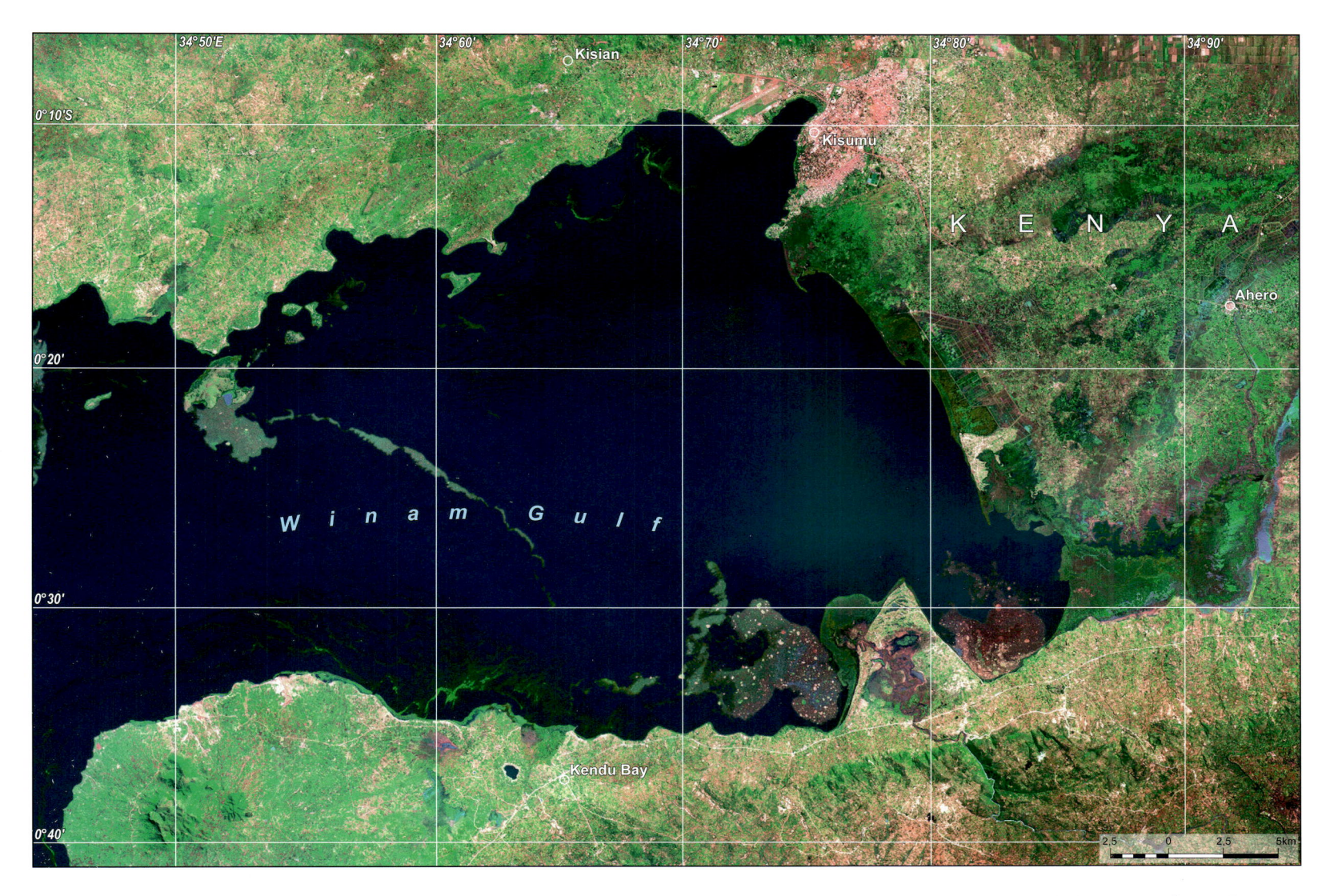

△
2 – The Landsat TM satellite image from Feb. 5, 2001 clearly shows the spread of water hyacinths in the Kenyan Winam Gulf, in the northeast of the lake.

▷
3 – By the end of the 1990s water hyacinths covered a huge area of Lake Victoria.

▽
4 – As the catchment basin of Lake Victoria is relatively small, the water level depends largely on rain falling directly into the lake and thus varies widely.

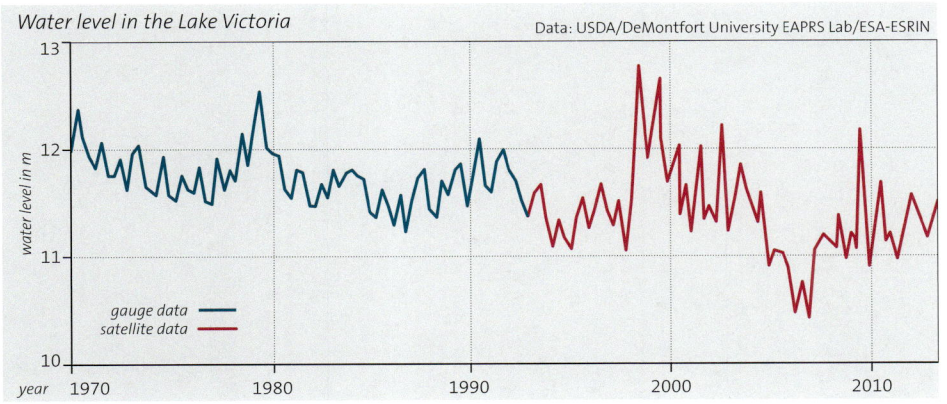

water entering the lake has led to a significant decrease in the water quality, and cholera and typhoid are not unusual in the region. Another threat is from eutrophication, the overuse of nitrogen-based fertilisers (e.g. nitrates) and phosphates in farming.

The eutrophication of lakes is a natural process, but human influence amplifies it. Eutrophic lakes show thick vegetation on the shore and are characterised by brown to greenish water, which results mostly from a high density of phytoplankton near the surface. The upper layer of water contains oxygen from the algae's metabolic processes, while the deeper, cold water layers are oxygen-poor. The increased nutrient levels in the lake facilitate algal bloom as well as the extremely rapid spread of water hyacinths. However, the low levels of oxygen and light are detrimental to fish populations.

Falling water levels

The lake's water level fell by 1.2 metres from 2003 to 2005. The reasons for this loss are both natural and man-made. Because the catchment basin of Lake Victoria is relatively small in comparison to the area of the lake, the water level is largely dependent on the amount of precipitation falling directly into the lake. Around 85 per cent of the water input in the lake is from precipitation, while 15 per cent comes from rivers. As such, the lake's water level varies widely depending on the amount of rainfall (Fig. 4).

Lake Victoria also functions as a water reservoir for the Owen Falls Dam. To provide the growing economy with more electricity, the dam was expanded in 2000 and an extra power station added. The expansion led to more water being let out through the locks, which led in turn to the falling water level.

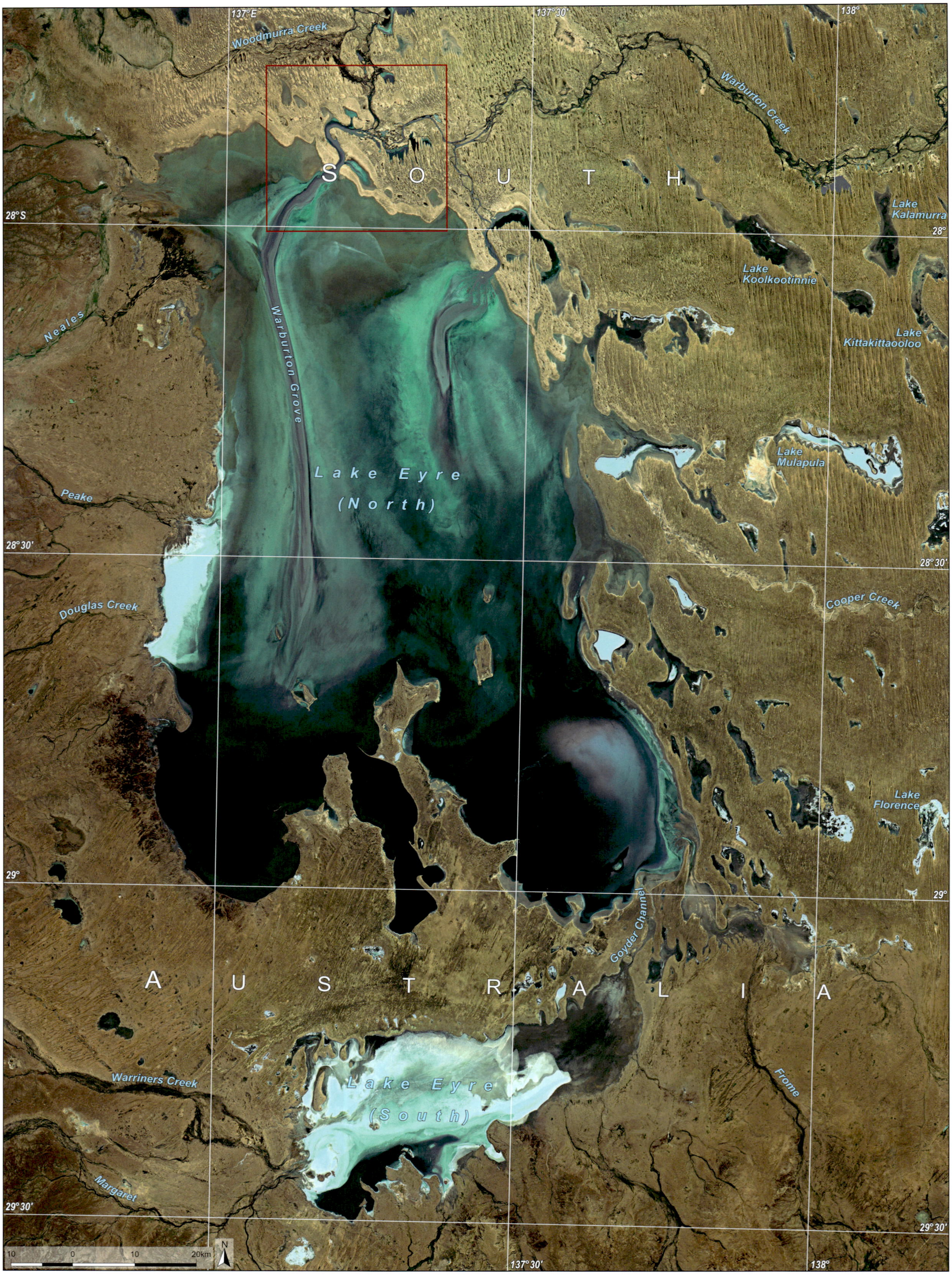
137°E
137°30'
138°
Woodmurra Creek
Warburton Creek
S O U T H
28°S
28°
Lake Kalamurra
Lake Koolkootinnie
Neales
Warburton Groove
Lake Kittakittaooloo
Lake Mulapula
Lake Eyre (North)
Peake
28°30'
Douglas Creek
Cooper Creek
Lake Florence
29°
Goyder Channel
A U S T R A L I A
Warriners Creek
Lake Eyre (South)
Frome
Margaret
29°30'
10 0 10 20km
N

LAKE EYRE

Lake Eyre is possibly the oldest of the ancient lakes in the world. It is estimated to be between 20 and 50 million years old. Lake Eyre's bed is 15 metres below sea level and the lowest point of Australia. Its surface area is 9,400 square kilometres, its volume 30 cubic kilometres, and it has a mean depth of three metres.

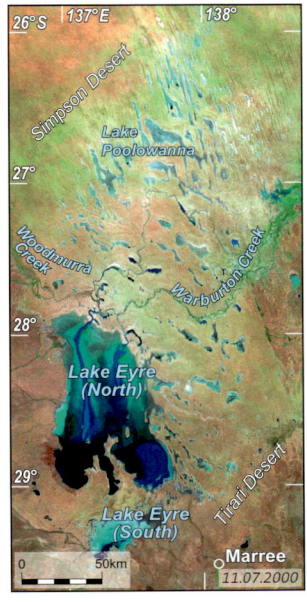

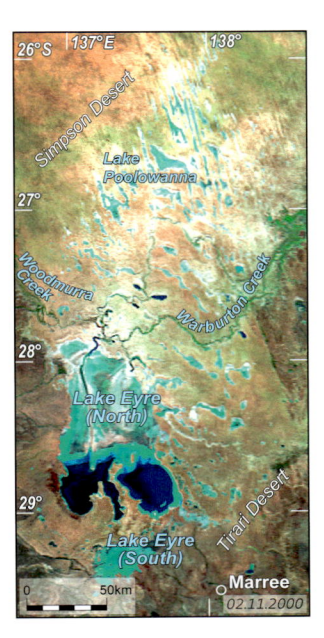

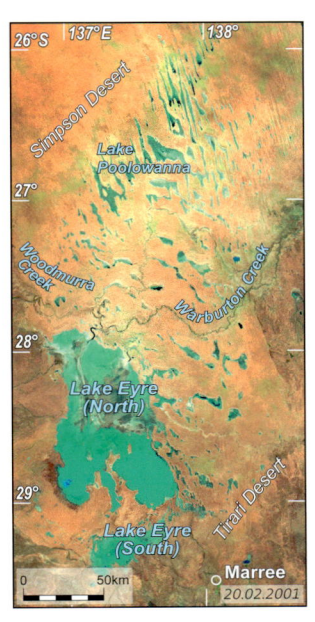

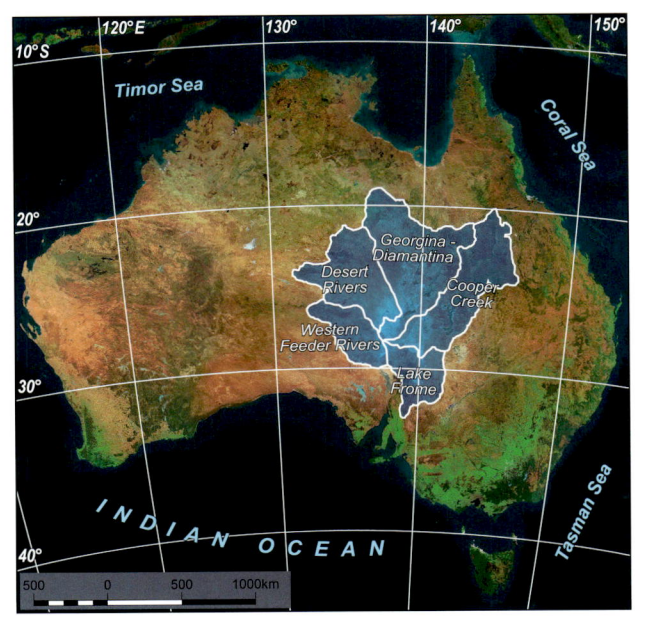

Lake Eyre lies in a depression in the Tirari Desert in the north of the state of South Australia. The lake bed was created in the Tertiary period, when the southeast of Australia subsided. Over millions of years the basin filled in with water and the surrounding area became forested. As Australia drifted northwards and the climate turned drier, the lake began to dry out.

A lake in Australia's outback

As a result of its location in one of the driest areas of Australia and the lack of water there, Lake Eyre is on average only three metres deep. During the rainy season it is fed by rivers from the Outback, including Cooper Creek and Warburton Creek (Fig. 2). Depending on the amount of rainfall, the region can experience large-scale flooding. However, much of the water soon evaporates, leaving white salt crusts over the desert sand (Figs. 3 a–c). The high evaporation rate leaves Lake Eyre's water very salty. In the 20th century the lake was only completely filled three times. In 1974, it reached the highest water level of the century at 5.7 metres deep. Recently, heavy rainfall in 2009, 2010 and 2011 caused severe flooding. From a limnological point of view, the lake is divided into northern and southern basins, linked by the Goyder Channel. The northern part is the larger of the two, measuring 144 kilometres long and 77 kilometres wide.

Episodic floods transform the entire basin into a enormous wetland with a surprising diversity of fish and crustaceans, which in turn feed the flocks of pelicans that come to the water. One species of reptile has become established in the area around the lake and adapted to the conditions there so well that it now bears the name of the lake: the Lake Eyre dragon.

The Lake Eyre Yacht Club might sound strange but it does actually exist – a yacht club that has used the lake during periods of flooding since 2000.

◁
2 – Warburton Creek empties into the north of Lake Eyre (July 2000).
The river is fed by the Diamantina and Georgina Rivers coming from the so-called Channel Country.

△
3 a/b/c – After considerable rainfall the lakebed has been flooded (3a). Thereafter the salt content increases (3b pale blue), the tributaries dry out and vegetation cover decreases (3c).

◁
1 – The South Australian Lake Eyre in July 2000. Here, the endorheic lake (lacking an outlet) is filled with more water than normal after persistent rains, and salinity is lower.

◁
4 – Lake Eyre catchment basin.

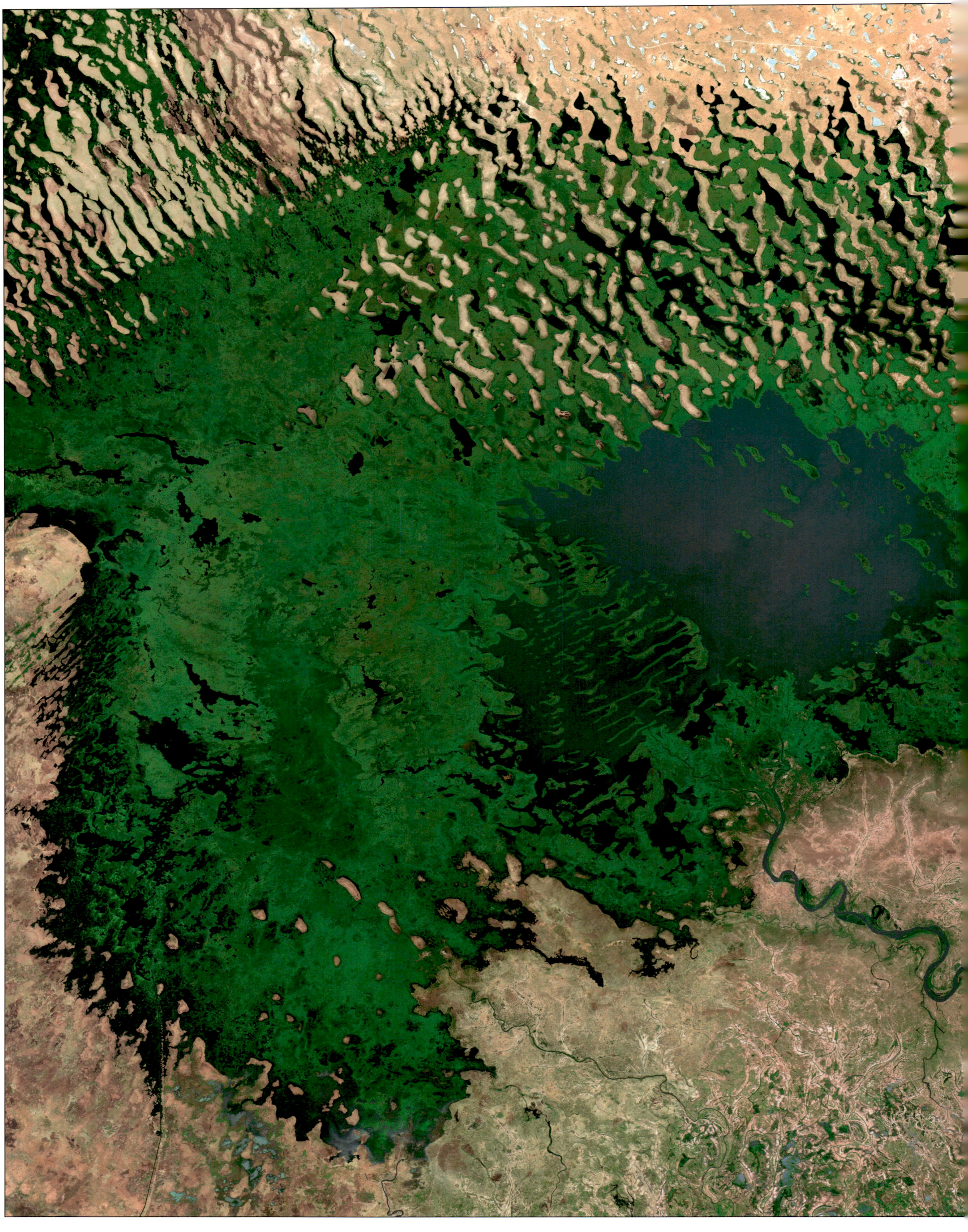

LAKE CHAD

Lake Chad, the only large above-ground freshwater lake in the Sahel, has shrunk dramatically. This large-scale environmental process also has economic and social consequences.

One of the largest lakes in the world, Lake Chad has shrunk markedly since the end of the 1960s. In conjunction with high population pressure, climatic factors and the uncontrolled use of water for irrigation have led to the area of the lake decreasing to down to 10 per cent of its original extent in the past four decades (Fig. 1 a–d, p. 150). Two thousand years ago the lake was the size of Germany and was an important source of drinking water for nomads making their way through the Sahara. Satellite images in particular have highlighted the massive decrease in the water level during the last decade of the 20th century.

Around 90 per cent of the lake's water comes from the Chari and Logone rivers. The Chari rises in the rainy uplands of central Africa and flows from there towards the northwest. The Logone River, which rises in eastern Cameroon, joins the Chari at Kousséri in northern Cameroon. The tributaries' water levels are subject to wide seasonal variations. The water level of Lake Chad is thus largely determined by rainfall in the catchment areas of the Chari and Logone rivers, around 800 kilometres away. With the coming and going of the rainy season, the lake's water level changes, flooding the flat land for kilometres around or retreating. The flood plains, which can extend for up to 8,000 square kilometres, are used by fishermen and for the wet cultivation of rice.

When the amount of water transported by the Chari fell by over 50 per cent during the 1960s, the surface area of Lake Chad also decreased significantly. The drought of

◁
1 – This image from January 2004 shows the depleted lake surface. In 2010 the Ramsar Convention fully recognised Lake Chad as a wetland of international significance, shared by Niger, Chad, Nigeria and Cameroon.

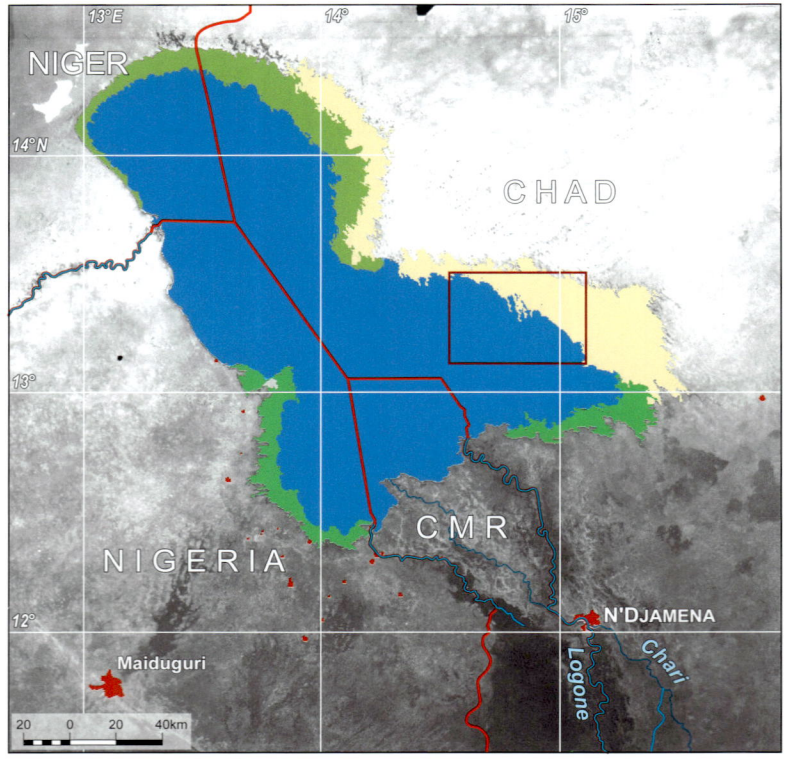

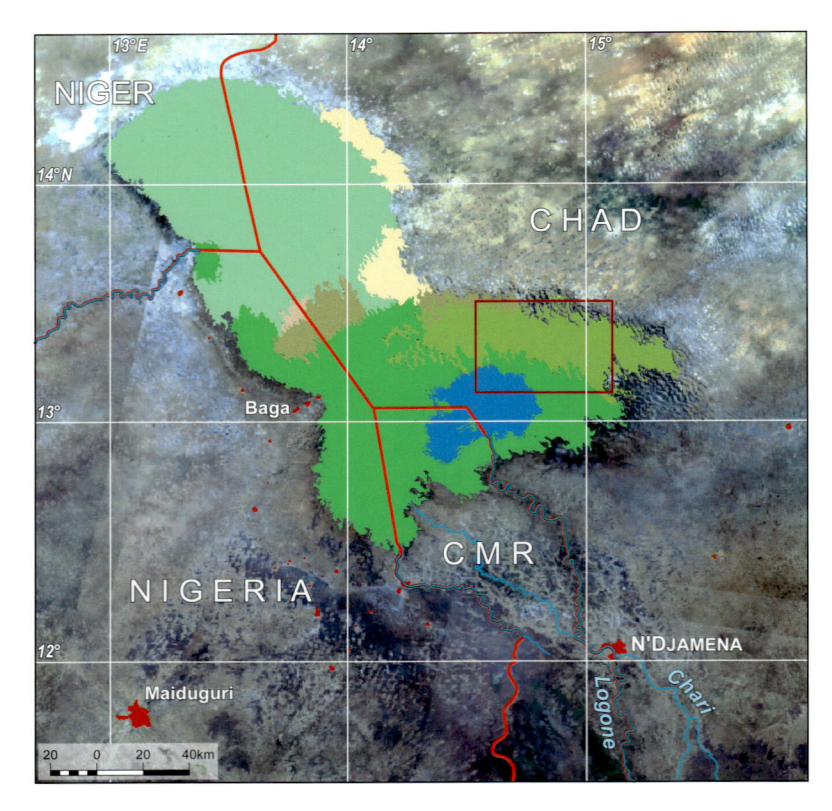

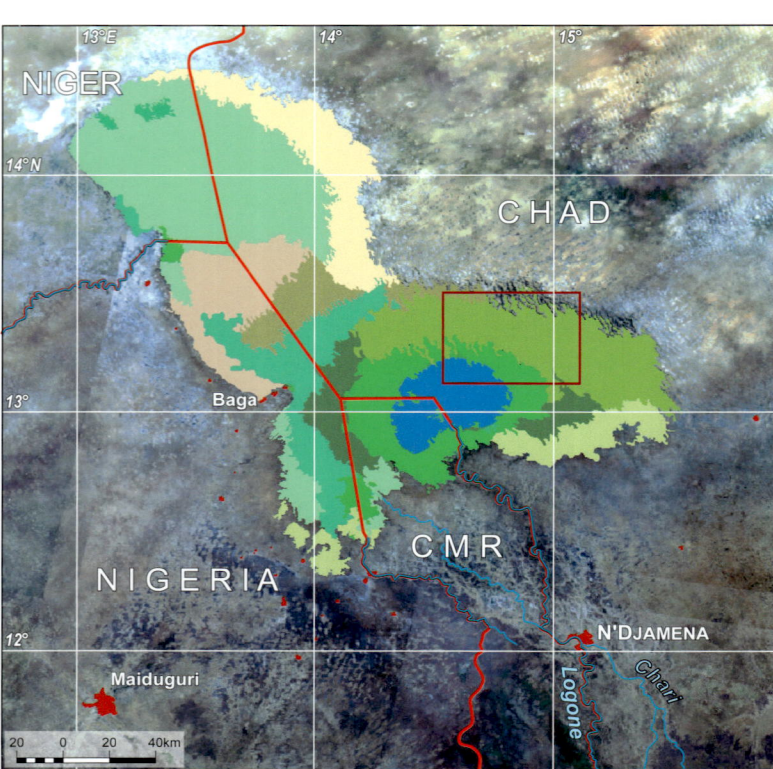

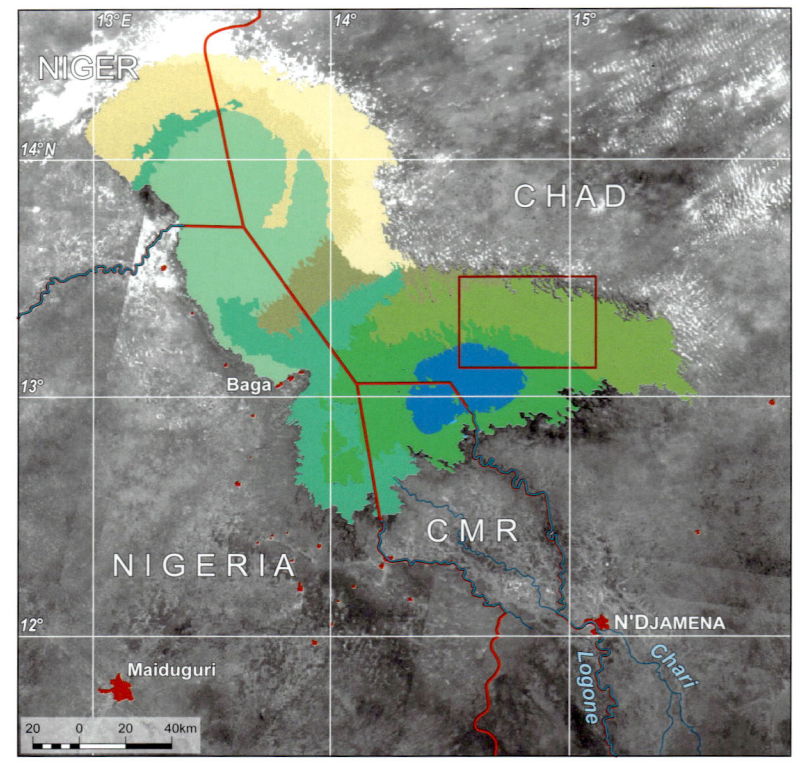

the 1970s had dramatic consequences. The northern basin dried up completely, while only low levels of water remained in the south. Nigeria completely lost its share of the water's surface area (Figs. 1 a–d).

The lake's water level is currently less than 280 metres above sea level and still covers around 1,350 square kilometres (see Fig. 1). The maximum depth varies between four and seven metres throughout the year.

Significance of Lake Chad for the local populations

More than 20 million people in the region depend on the lake directly or indirectly. In addition, the lake and its broad shores are also of exceptional significance for the flora and fauna of the region. It is a habitat for numerous animals, including around 120 species of fish, and is a resting place for millions of birds migrating between southern and central Africa and Europe.

The lake was also an important crossroads for the trade routes crossing west and central Africa. For the people living near the lake, the shrinking lake (Figs. 1 a–d) continued to lose its economic significance. Many fishermen lost their livelihoods. They were not able to create a new life for themselves as farmers, though, because there was not enough water for irrigation. The remaining fishermen found it harder to reach the receding water through the profusion of grass, reeds and papyrus (Figs. 2–4). New villages have also sprung up on the dried-up shores.

Why is Lake Chad shrinking?

Various theories have been put forward to explain the swift decline in the lake's water levels over recent decades. Most of them ascribe great significance to changes in the climate. Higher temperatures lead to higher evaporation rates, which are accompanied by less water flowing into the lake. Another role is apparently played by the

Shrinking of Lake Chad
(1963 / 1978 / 1987 / 2000)

- Settlement
- Dunes
- Sparse Vegetation
- Arable Land
- Riverine Wetland Vegetation
- Seasonally flooded Grassland
- Grassland
- Dense Grassland
- Savannah and Dunes
- Savannah
- Permanent Reed Swamps and Dunes
- Seasonal Herbaceous Swamps
- Permanent Reed Swamps
- Water
- River
- International border

◁
1 a/b/c/d – Satellite images from 1963, 1978, 1987 and 2000 clearly show the decrease in the lake's area by more than 90 per cent. Experts believe that around half of this retreat is due to climate change, while the other half is due to increased water extraction.

▷△
2 – Alongside the coastal area lie islands formed of papyrus and reeds.

▷
3 – The lower water levels mean that many boats can no longer be used for transportation.

▷
4 – With the coming and going of the rainy season, the lake's water level changes, flooding the flat land for miles around or retreating. In the dry season, the lake looks more like a large swamp than a lake. The areas free of reeds and grass are known as 'nki bul' (white water), while the deeper water is known as 'nki tsilim' (black water). When the amount of water transported by the Chari fell during the 1960s, the surface area of the lake decreased significantly and the amount of land available for farming increased.

retreat of vegetation in the savannah regions of the lake's catchment basin, which has led to changes in the regional climate, making it drier. The retreat of vegetation is largely put down to overgrazing. Another factor is the increased usage of the water from the lake and its inflow for drinking water and for irrigating farmland. In Chad, the population has tripled in the past 40 years. From 1983 to 1994 alone, the area of irrigated farmland increased fourfold. At this time, farming was responsible for 50 per cent of the lake drying up.

Lake Chad Basin Commission

The five countries in the lake's catchment basin – Cameroon, Niger, Nigeria, Chad and the Central African Republic – joined forces in May 1964 to create the Lake Chad Basin Commission in order to work towards ensuring the sustainable management of the region's scarce water resources.

Plans have been made for a dam and 97 kilometres of canals to divert water from the Ubangi River in the Congo Basin to the Chari River, which then empties into Lake Chad. The project is highly ambitious and it took years to raise the necessary funds for a feasibility study. Environmental organisations have warned of the consequences of the project due to new species of plants and animals being introduced to the lake, which could change its biodiversity in unforeseen ways. Despite that, plans must be made to ensure the sustainable use of the lake and its tributaries. However, the countries in the catchment basin require international financial aid to implement the enormous undertaking.

Things do not look good for this project, however. The last major project, the South Chad Irrigation Project (SCIP), was initiated 30 years ago. A power station was to generate electricity for pumps to draw water from the lake for irrigation. Before construction had even begun, the lake had started to retreat. Hundreds of kilometres of canals were dug but left unlined, and the water drained away into the sand. The southern part of the lake disappeared, while the canals and the land dried up and turned to desert.

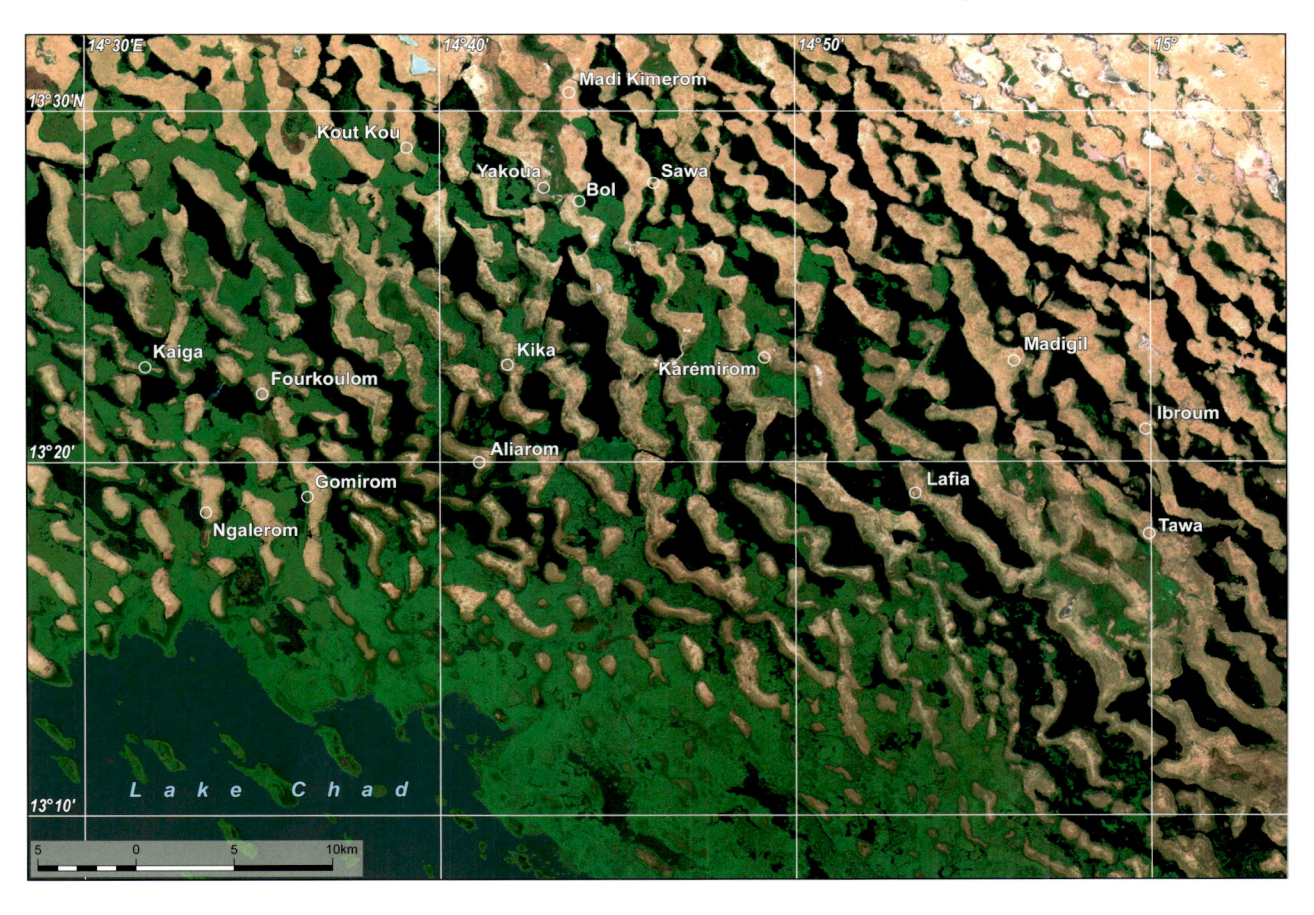

155

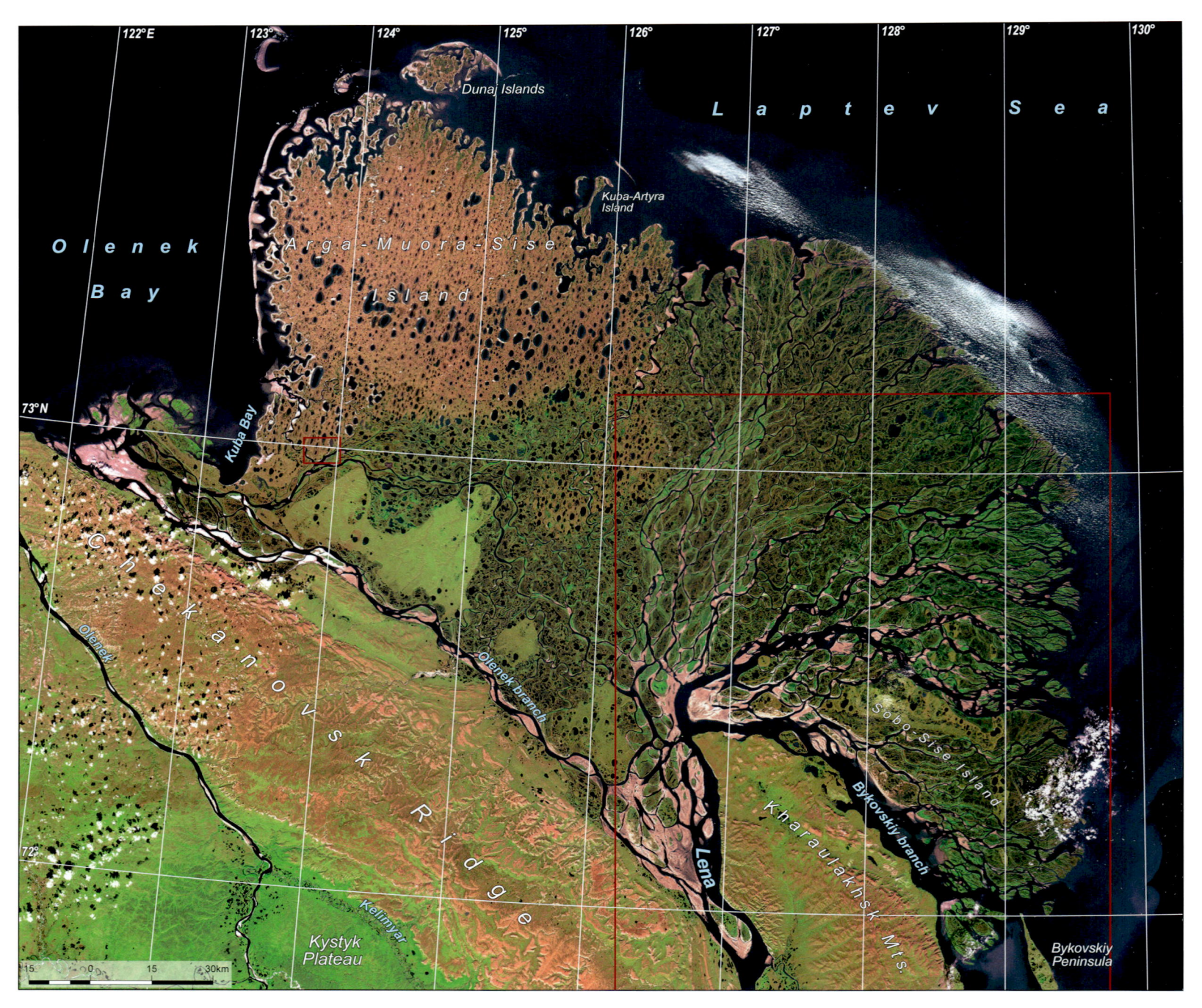

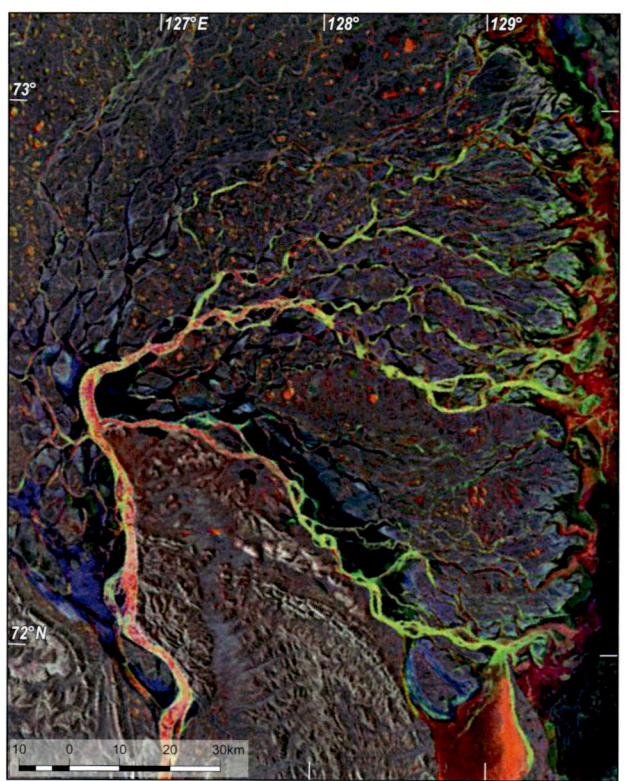

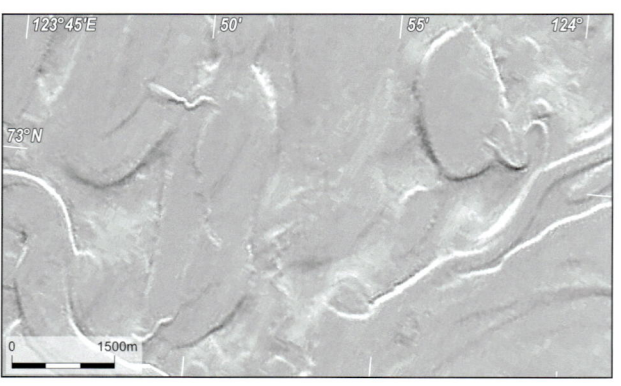

2 – Multitemporal radar satellite images can help monitor the spring thaw in the Lena Delta. Red refers to data acquired on 10/03/2008, green on 22/10/2007 and blue on 13/06/2008. In this colour combination, lakes appearing red were still frozen on 10 March, yellow relates to ice on lakes at least from 22 October to 10 March.

3 a/b – Thermokarst landscapes in the Lena Delta change dramatically in appearance throughout the year. The endless snow plains prevailing during winter (Proba-1 CHRIS image dated 22/04/2006) turns into numerous lakes during the short summer (Proba-1 CHRIS image dated 29/06/2005).

1 – The Lena Delta is home to countless thermokarst lakes. These tundra lakes formed at the end of the last ice age and have continued to exist until this day because of the underlying permafrost soil.

4 – False colour infared image of Tundra lakes in the catchment basin of the Taz River to the north of the Arctic circle in northwest Siberia in 1972. Vegetation appears in red.

Thermokarst lakes are dips in the tundra that are usually left behind as the permafrost melts. The area of the individual lakes increases with repeated cycles of freezing and thawing. When neighbouring lakes join together, they form larger ones that are integrated into the local drainage systems.

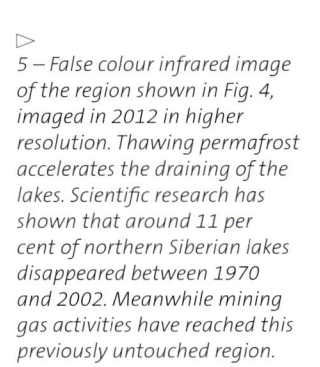

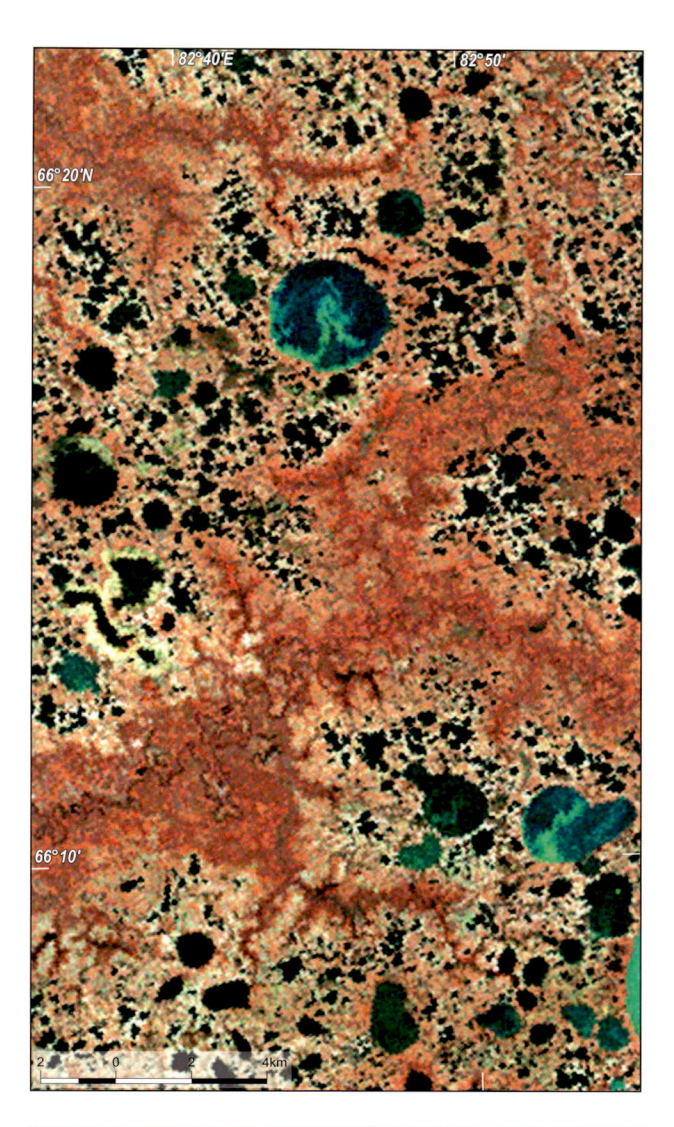

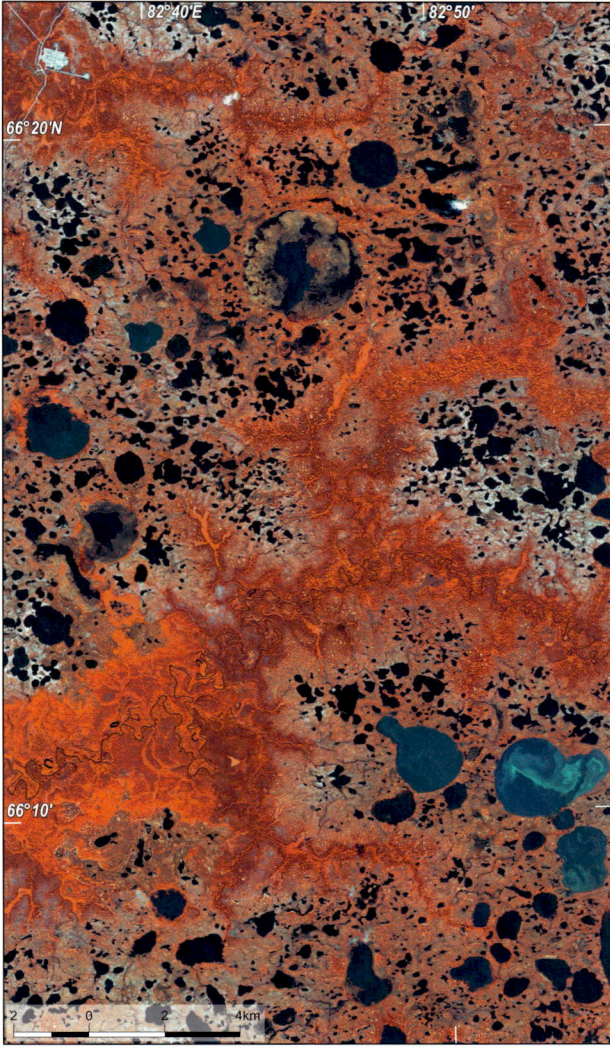

5 – False colour infared image of the region shown in Fig. 4, imaged in 2012 in higher resolution. Thawing permafrost accelerates the draining of the lakes. Scientific research has shown that around 11 per cent of northern Siberian lakes disappeared between 1970 and 2002. Meanwhile mining gas activities have reached this previously untouched region.

TUNDRA LAKES

The tundra, a treeless landscape of permafrost soils, runs between the Arctic polar desert and the boreal forest of the Taiga. Satellite images reveal changes in the water balance of this sensitive system.

Around one quarter of the Earth's surface is underlain with permafrost. The extensive permafrost regions of Siberia, Alaska and Canada have been covered with ice for millennia. The depth of the permafrost depends on the air temperature and soil temperature, as well as the type of soil, and varies from just a few decimetres to over 1,000 metres. Rising temperatures in the short summer months cause the upper active layer of the permafrost to thaw in some places. The resulting changes in volume lead to the creation of ice wedge polygons, whose cores melt when they are exposed, causing the surrounding area to subside. The meltwater gathers in the hollows left behind and forms small lakes that cannot drain through the frozen ground beneath, which functions as an impermeable layer. This phenomenon is known as 'thermokarst'.

Is the tundra drying out?

Thermokarst lakes were created millennia ago and have continued to expand ever since the last ice age and the start of the interglacial period, or Holocene. The joining up of lakes has created larger ones. However, the average annual temperatures on the tundra continue to rise, and even the deeper layers of soil are starting to thaw. As a result, the lakes are losing their impermeable ground layer and the water is beginning to drain away (Figs. 4 and 5). This process is facilitated further by thermal erosion. The protective, but thawing, minerogenic layers of soil are washed away by meltwater and deposited in lakes. The high specific heat of the water in the lakes leads to the further thawing of the surrounding permafrost.

The retreat of the permafrost causes other difficulties. Infrastructure, buildings, oil and gas pipelines and roads can subside and become unstable and deformed. The thawed permafrost also releases plant waste that has been preserved for millennia, and whose decomposition releases large quantities of methane and carbon dioxide into the atmosphere, potentially contributing to global warming.

Life on the tundra

The tundra's frosty soils are primarily home to moose, lichens, grasses and low-growing shrubs. Some small fruit bushes and Arctic creeping willow have also adapted to life on the tundra. Despite this, very few species of plant live in the polar regions. The short summers provide insufficient warmth and light to allow trees to grow. The living conditions on the barren landscape are harsh also for humans. The sparsely populated tundra is home to nomadic tribes who live from reindeer farming and fishing.

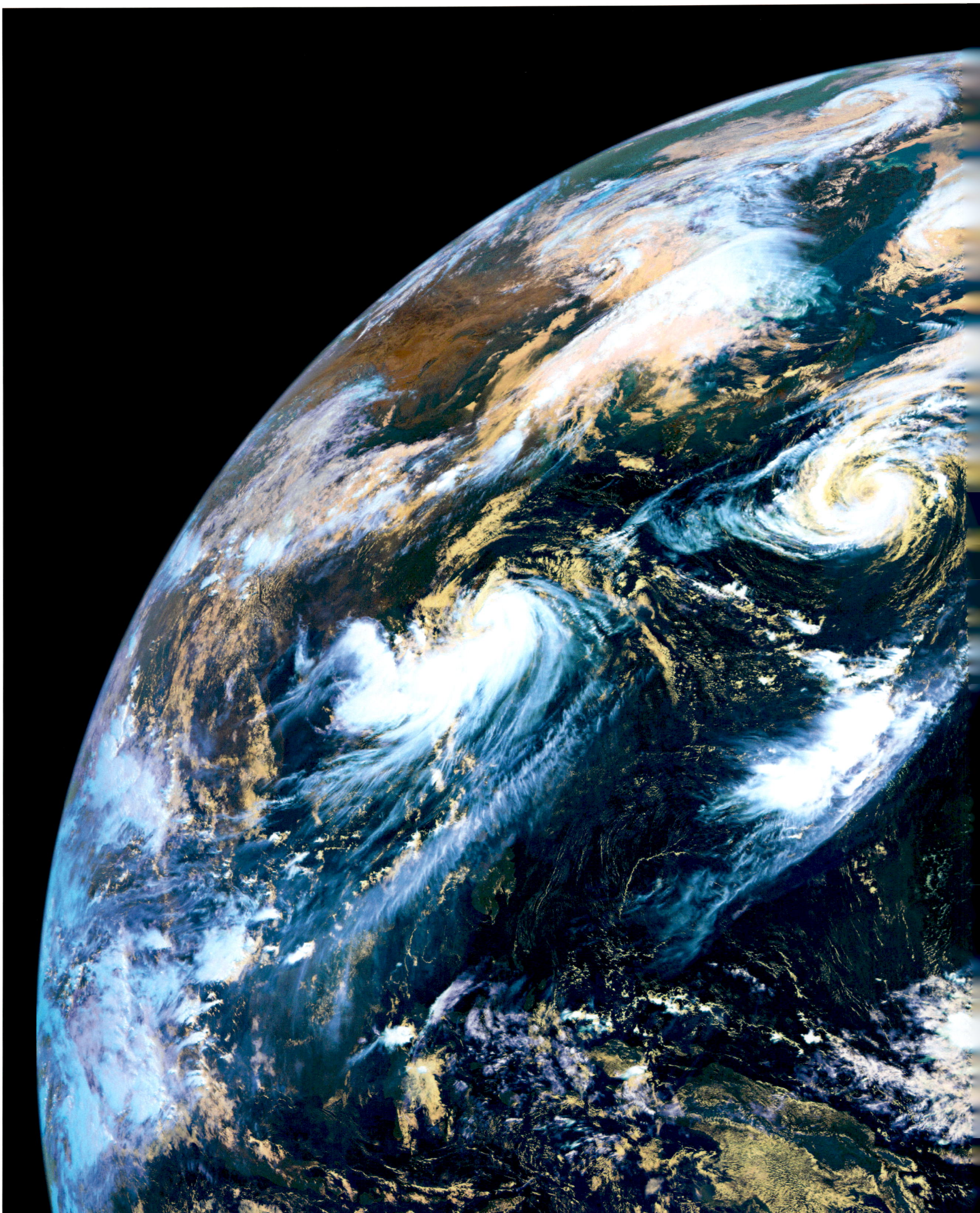

OCEANS

The world's oceans are home to countless organisms – from microscopic life forms to blue whales, the largest mammals on the planet. The three major oceans and marginal seas account for a total of 1,370 million cubic kilometres of water.

The world's oceans cover 71 per cent of its surface and can be roughly divided into three connected basins: the Pacific Ocean, the Atlantic Ocean and the Indian Ocean. With 180 million square kilometres, the Pacific Ocean makes up half of the total area covered by ocean. The water in the world's seas is in a constant cycle of evaporation and inflow. When water evaporates from the surface of the oceans and continents, it travels upwards. As it gains altitude, the water vapour cools, creating clouds and precipitation.

The oceans and seas play a major role in the climate of our planet. As a result of their ability to store heat, the large areas of water maintain a stable temperature over the Earth. The oceans interact with the atmosphere through momentum, heat and freshwater fluxes, aerosol and gas exchanges. Since they can absorb huge amounts of carbon dioxide, they play a major role as a buffer for this greenhouse gas. This process is reversible, and with increasing water temperatures the carbon dioxide dissolved in the water is released back into the atmosphere. In addition to carbon dioxide, the sediment in the oceans also stores methane, a greenhouse gas that is released during the bacterial breakdown of organic substances.

The water in the oceans moves around the Earth like a giant conveyor belt. Water masses are moved from the surface to the depths and then back again. The movement of the water is driven by differences in density that result from variations in temperature and salinity, as well as by the major wind systems (thermohaline and wind-driven circulation).

Despite their enormous significance, the world's oceans and their ecosystems are subject to countless anthropogenic hazards. Industrial fishing with drift nets and floating fish factories, as well as the increase in global fish consumption, are putting a great number of fish species and other sea creatures at risk. In addition, the oceans and seas are subject to enormous amounts of pollution; for example, via unfiltered wastewater from the land, improper waste disposal in the sea, and oil spills.

◁
1 – This GOES 9 satellite image from July 1, 2004 portrays a section of the northern Pacific. The mighty Typhoon Mindulle makes landfall at Taiwan and the Typhoon Tingting blows southeast of Japan.

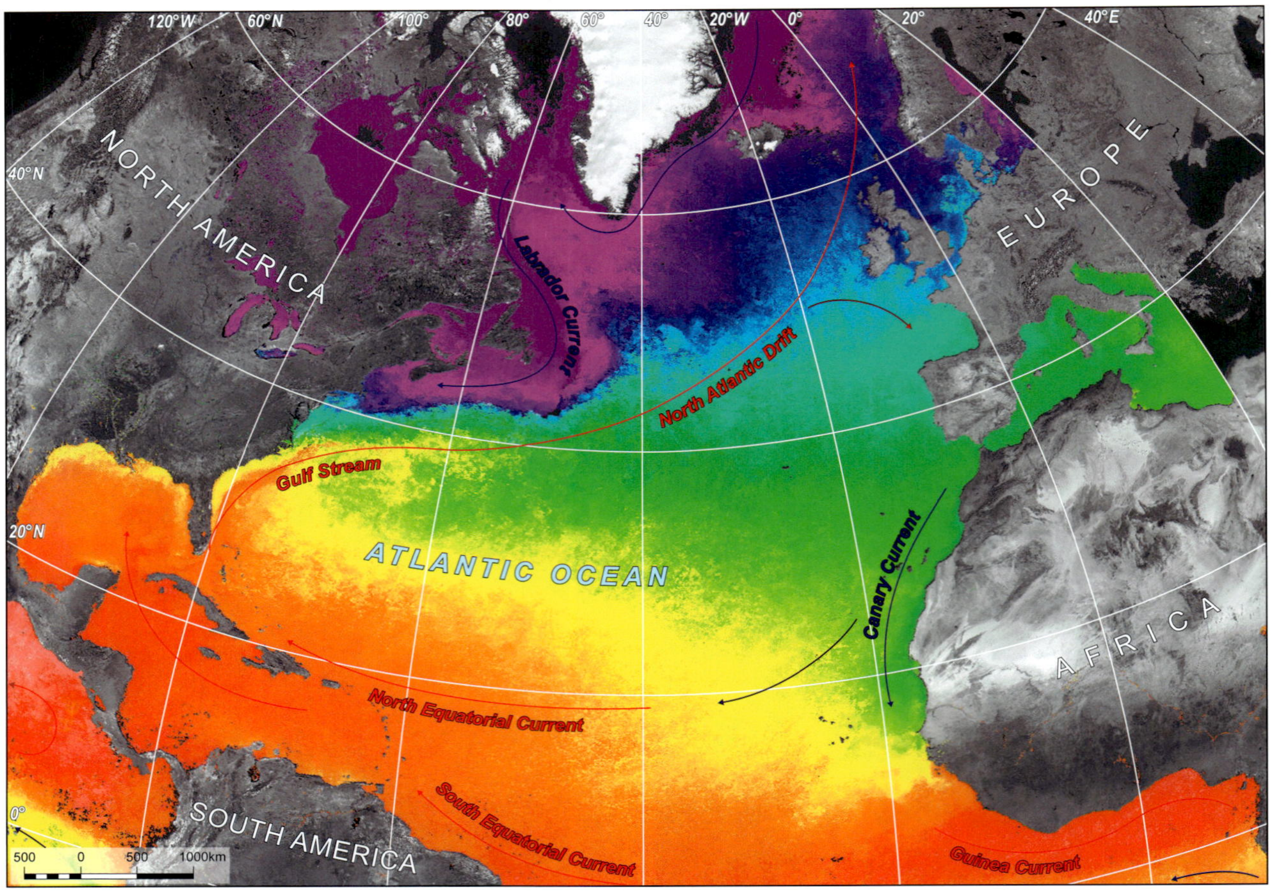

1 – The Gulf Stream originates in the warm water of the Caribbean and flows as the North Atlantic Drift up to the Arctic Ocean.

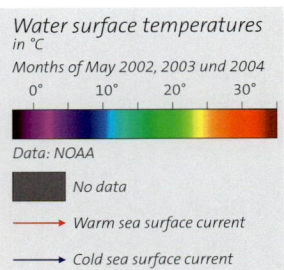

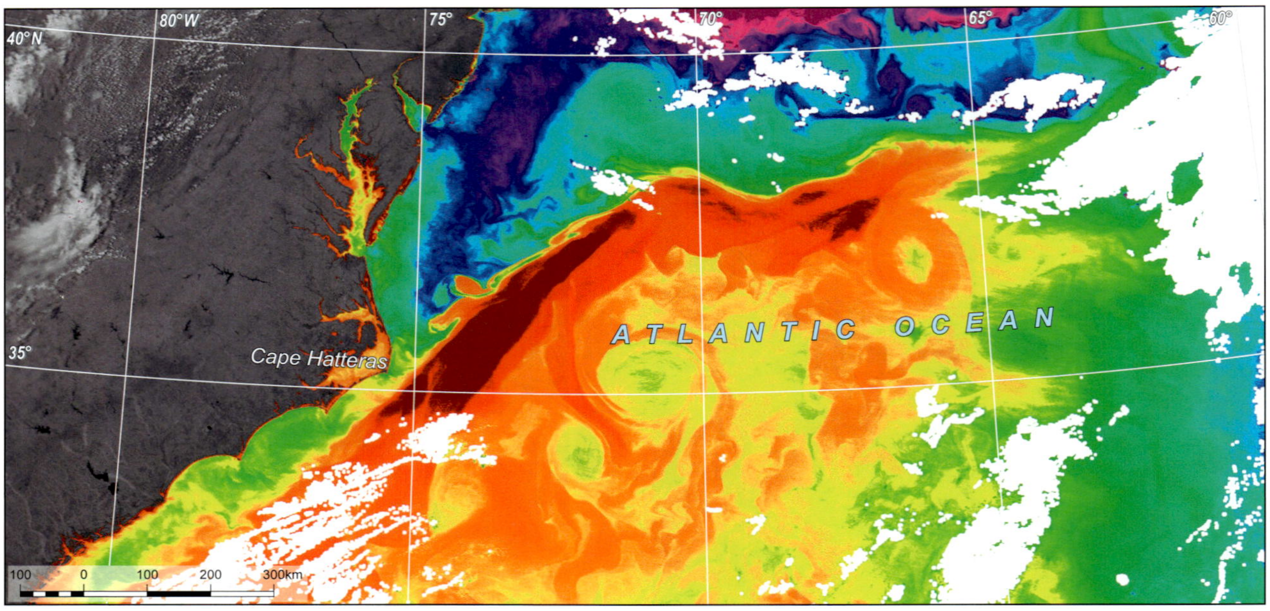

2 – At Cape Hatteras, the cold Labrador Current deflects the Gulf Stream to the northeast and out into the open Atlantic.

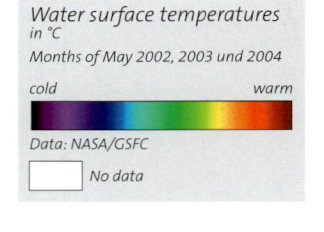

3 a-f – The sea surface temperatures in the Mediterranean vary throughout the year.

Global ocean currents

The oceans play a decisive role in the global climate. Enormous amounts of heat are stored in their water. This energy is distributed by global ocean currents in close interaction with the atmosphere. Ocean currents transport both warm and cold water masses. In addition to exchanging energy, they also transfer mass. As such, solid and solute substances such as icebergs or sediments and pollutants are carried with them. The currents are driven by differences in density as a result of variations in temperature and salinity.

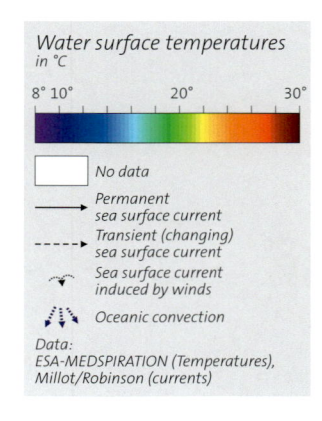

The Gulf Stream and its formation

The Gulf Stream, a warm and fast-flowing ocean current in the Atlantic, is part of the global system of ocean currents. It is formed by the convergence of the Florida and Antilles currents north of the Bahamas (Fig. 1). From here, it flows as a wide band as far as Cape Hatteras and through the North American Basin into the open Atlantic. Here, it meets the cold Labrador Current and flows northeast. Where the warm and cold layers of water meet, extensive areas of turbulence occur (Fig. 2).

The main driver behind the Gulf Stream is in the Arctic Ocean, off the coast of Greenland and Iceland. On its path northwards, the warm water evaporates, which increases the salinity of the water. Cold winds from the polar region then cool the water. As a result of its higher density, the cooler, saltier water sinks into the deep sea. The warmer and lighter water in the Gulf of Mexico creates a slipstream effect between the two regions, which pulls the warm water on the surface northwards and draws the cold water of the ocean depths back south. This effect is also boosted by the Coriolis effect, which causes the Gulf Stream to veer towards northwest Europe. Here the current is known as the North-Atlantic Current, or North Atlantic Drift.

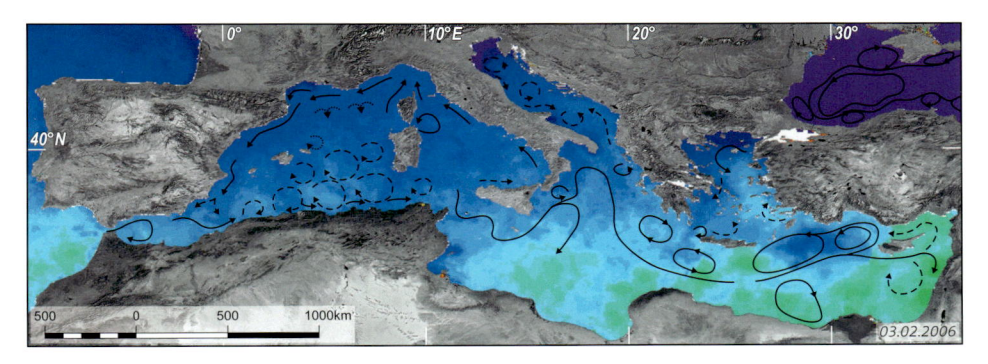

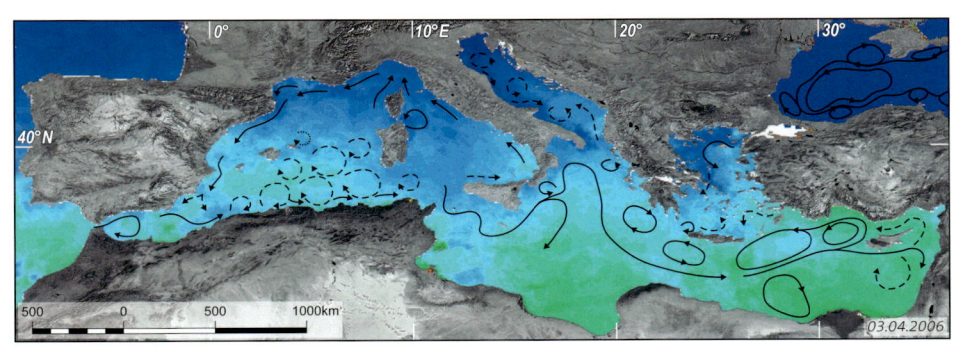

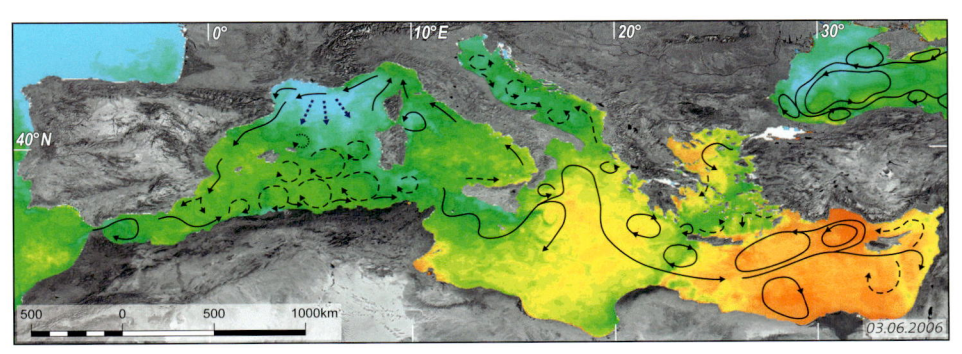

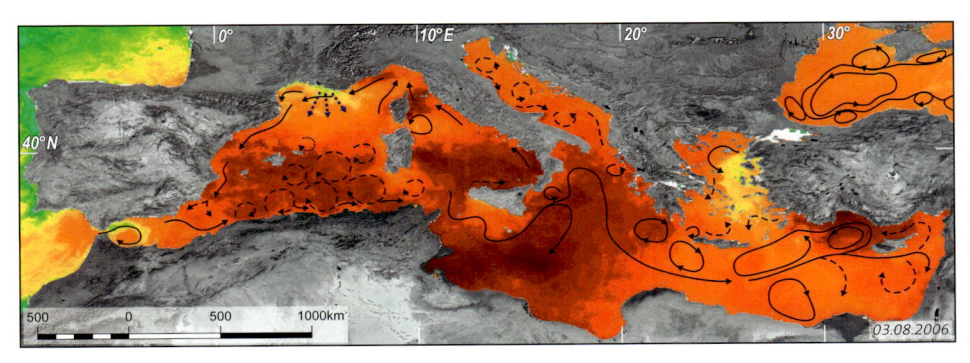

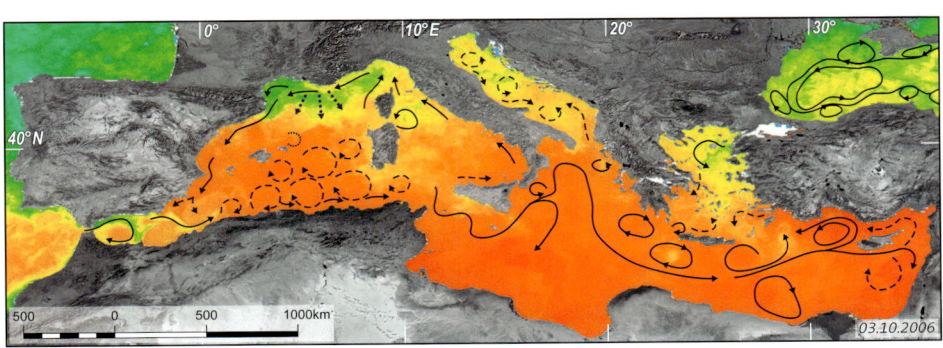

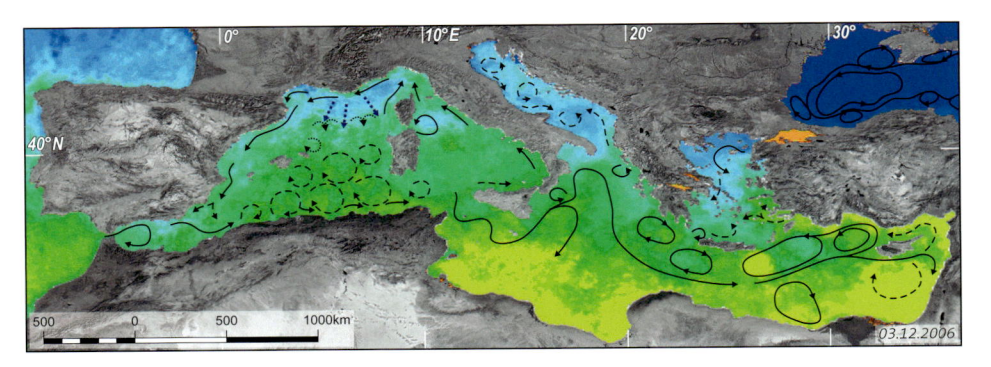

The Gulf Stream and the climate

The warm air heated by the Gulf Stream blows over the European continent in westerly winds and plays a major role in shaping its climate. Most of Europe lies within the temperate latitude zones. As a result of the Gulf Stream's warmth, the climate is milder here than in other areas at the same latitude. At these latitudes, where for example over vast areas in Canada only mosses and lichens grow, farming is possible in Europe. A more extreme example is the partially sub-tropical vegetation in the gardens of southern England. In the mild climate influenced by the Gulf Stream, palms, cedars and pines flourish. Even Lapland, most of which lies to the north of the Arctic Circle, benefits from this 'heat pump'. On the Kola Peninsula, the Barents Sea and the White Sea both remain free of ice as a result of the Gulf Stream, and permafrost does not form on the mainland, in contrast to large parts of Siberia and Canada.

The increasing temperatures as a result of climate change have been linked to localised melting of glaciers. The result is rising sea levels and, due to the increased input of freshwater from the melted ice, decreasing salinity of the seas. This may affect the circulation of ocean currents, as the higher salinity of the water in the Arctic Ocean is partially responsible for the Gulf Stream's existence. Any further decrease in the salinity could cause this system of currents to break down, which would lead to a cooling of the climate in Europe in particular, accompanied by a significant change of the precipitation patterns of the continent.

Currents in the Mediterranean Sea

The Mediterranean Sea extends from east to west for around 3,800 kilometres and measures between 670 and 750 kilometres from north to south. With an area of 2.5 million square kilometres, it is at the same time the largest inland sea and the smallest intercontinental sea in the world. In addition to its natural access to the Atlantic Ocean through the Strait of Gibraltar, the Mediterranean Sea is connected also to the Black Sea via the Bosphorus. Its surface temperatures vary during winter in the northern part between 8 degrees Celsius and 10 degrees Celsius, while in the southern part the temperatures may reach 28 degrees Celsius to 30 degrees Celsius during summer. As part of ESA's MEDSPIRATION project, the surface temperatures of the Mediterranean Sea are monitored continually, exploiting data from various Earth observation satellites (Fig. 3).

Water from the Atlantic Ocean flows through the Strait of Gibraltar and travels in a large vortex south along the North African coast. From here, the water mass moves eastwards, and the counterclockwise currents serve to balance the temperatures in the Mediterranean Sea. The water from the Atlantic Ocean takes about one year to reach the eastern coast of the Mediterranean. The water masses sinking here down to deeper regions of the sea, require up to one hundred years to make their way back to the Atlantic Ocean.

The 14 kilometre-wide Strait of Gibraltar restricts the water exchange with the Atlantic Ocean. The incoming, less salty and colder water of the Atlantic flows along the surface in the Mediterranean. The Mediterranean's saltier water has a higher density and flows back into the Atlantic along the seabed. Without this modest water exchange, the water levels in the Mediterranean would fall by up to one metre a year due to evaporation. This is expected to happen in 1 to 2 million years, when the northwards drifting African continent will close the Strait of Gibraltar.

161

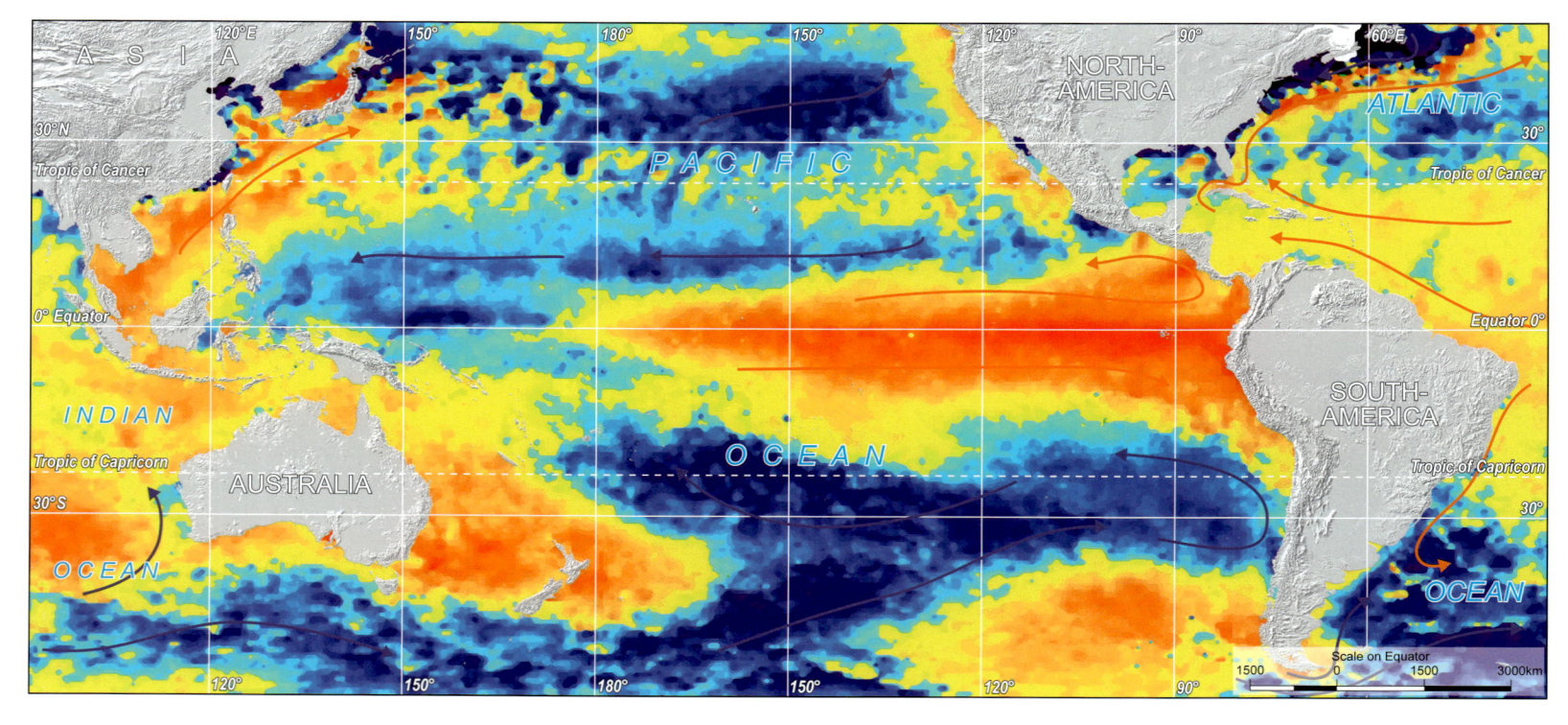

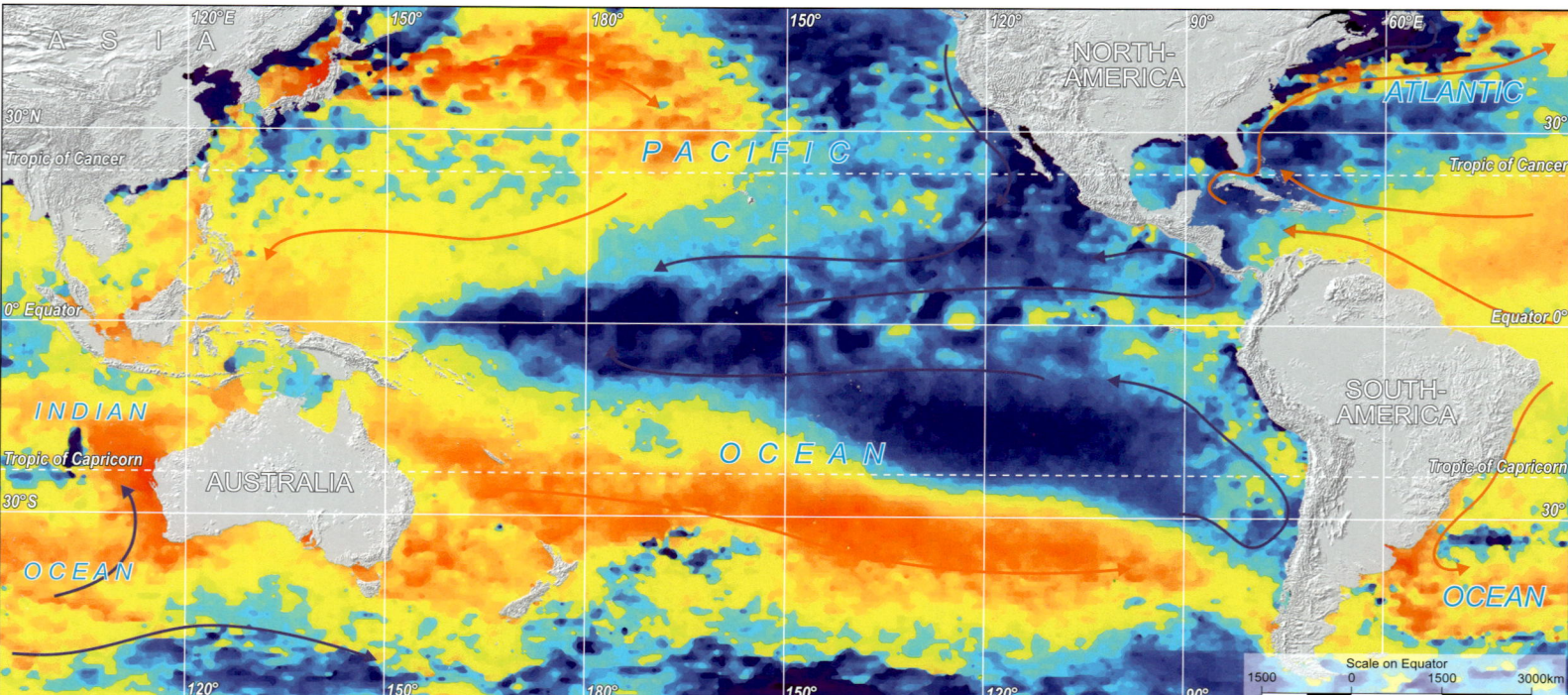

El Niño, La Niña and ENSO

The climatic meteorological phenomenon of El Niño first made headlines in the media all over the world in 1997/1998. Capricious weather situations, such as tropical storms on the Pacific coast of Mexico, droughts in South-East Asia and flooding in Peru, were all traced back to a particularly strong El Niño event that had originated in the Pacific region. The name El Niño, the Spanish expression for 'Christ Child', was given to the phenomenon by the inhabitants of the Pacific coast of South America, who over many years had noticed it showing up mainly around Christmas time. Because the phenomenon is so significant for the economy and the natural world, and for weather forecasts and future climate scenarios as well, El Niño has become the focus of much attention.

El Niño and the related phenomenon, La Niña, are features of what is known as ENSO (El Niño Southern Oscillation), which has existed for centuries as a complex interplay between the atmospheric and oceanic currents in the equatorial region of the Pacific Ocean. When periods of several years duration are considered, ENSO accounts for the strongest known climatic variations on Earth.

Coupling between currents

The ENSO cycles alternate irregularly between normal conditions, El Niño and La Niña. These conditions have different effects on the temperature and currents in and over the tropical Pacific.

Under normal conditions, the surface temperature of the Pacific Ocean increases along the Equator heading west from the coast of South America (page 60, Fig. 1) towards South East Asia and Australia. The reason for this are the eastern trade winds blowing along the Equator, which push the warm surface water westwards and enable cooler water from the depths to replace it in a process called upwelling, resulting in a balancing deep current flowing east. Heavy with moisture, the air rises over the western Pacific and comes back down each day in tropical downpours. Drier and higher, some of the air travels back towards South America, where it sinks and cools.

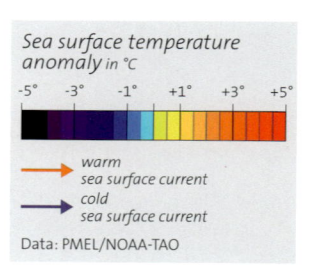

Sea surface temperature anomaly in °C

-5° -3° -1° +1° +3° +5°

→ warm sea surface current
→ cold sea surface current

Data: PMEL/NOAA-TAO

1 – Surface water temperature anomaly in the Pacific on 20/02/1998 (El Niño).

2 – Surface water temperature anomaly in the Pacific on 10/01/2011 (La Niña).

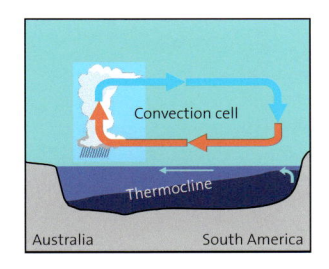

3 – Air and ocean currents as well as water temperatures during a normal situation.

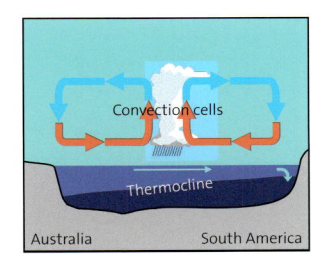

4 – Air and ocean currents as well as water temperatures during an El Niño event.

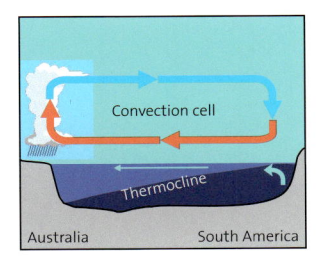

5 – Air and ocean currents as well as water temperatures during a La Niña event.

However, as it has already lost most of its water, it carries only a little precipitation back with it. These air currents travelling along the equator are not deflected by the Coriolis force, and are known as a "Walker circulation", or "Walker cell", and are underlying seasonal changes (Fig. 3).

The El Niño phenomenon occurs when the cold water layer off the coast of South America sinks down to deeper regions of the Pacific Ocean. Then the easterly winds are too weak to shift the warm surface water westwards. The cold water remains in deeper layers, and the water along the Equator becomes much warmer than under normal conditions (Fig. 1). As a result, the currents in the atmosphere and the resulting levels of precipitation in the bordering regions change significantly (Fig. 4).

By contrast, the La Niña phenomenon is an especially strong manifestation of normal conditions. As a result of stronger trade winds, particularly the eastern Pacific Ocean cools down significantly more than usual (Fig. 2), which leads to stronger variations in rainfall patterns between the western Pacific Ocean and the western coast of South America (Fig. 5).

Far-reaching consequences

The consequences of the El Niño and La Niña phases are felt most strongly in the directly neighbouring regions of the equatorial west coast of South America and in the equatorial western Pacific region (Fig. 6).

In South America, Peru is most noticeably affected. The deserts of Peru and Chile, which experience very little to no rainfall, can be hit by extremely heavy rains brought by El Niño. These extreme rainfalls can dump up to four metres of rain in just six months. The reduced upwelling of the cold, nutrient-rich water to the surface near the Pacific coast affects the entire food chain – from plankton and the shoaling fish that are forced to search for food in other areas of the ocean, to marine mammals, which often are not sufficiently mobile to follow their prey. As a result, also the fishing industry is hit hard.

The opposite effects are felt on the other side of the Pacific Ocean. The higher temperatures cause the rains pouring over the Pacific Ocean and leaving the neighbouring state of Indonesia suffering from droughts. These affect yields for rice, maize, coffee and tea, which in turn causes the prices for these products on the global markets to soar. Another consequence is that no monsoon rains arrive to extinguish forest and peat fires. The amount of smoke in the air can then cause serious respiratory problems, such as asthma and bronchitis, for the local population.

The ENSO also affects regions that are further afield in a diverse range of ways, with the effects varying widely from region to region.

As such, in Australia, El Niño can lead to drought and extremely high temperatures. In 1997, for example, extreme temperatures reduced crop and cereal harvests by around 30 per cent and increased the number of forest fires, which destroyed 6,000 square kilometres of forest and bushland. By contrast, in this region, La Niña can cause extended floods, such as those that hit Brisbane in 1974 and in the years 2010/2011.

Africa also goes through more extreme weather events during El Niño – both droughts and floods, which occur mainly in East Africa.

In Asia, El Niño indirectly weakens the summer monsoon, reducing precipitation. On the other hand, it can lead to stronger winter monsoons, which bring more rain to India and Bangladesh. Heavier snowfall in Tibet in 1997/1998 was followed by extensive flooding along the Yangtze River during spring.

In Central and North America, El Niño leads to fewer and La Niña to an increased number of hurricanes over the Caribbean and the Gulf of Mexico. El Niño brings more rainfall to the east coast of the USA, and also to most, but not all, parts of South America, where studies have shown increases in diseases such as malaria as a result of the sanitation problems that come with flooding.

Some researchers have also found interesting links between historical events and El Niño phases. Most of the time, these took the form of local to regional famines caused by crop failures in the course of extreme weather, as well as the social and political consequences such as revolutions and wars they left in their wake. Such examples include the widespread drought in the Mid-West of the USA in 1938 known as the Dust Bowl, and other historical famines.

The future of El Niño

El Niño is of great interest also in the context of climate change, as the probability is high that with increasing temperatures also the global atmospheric and marine current systems will change. According to projected future scenarios, it is likely that, during the 21st century, the eastern Pacific Ocean will become significantly warmer than the rest of the ocean. With a view to the effects of the ENSO, we can therefore predict that El Niño phases and their consequences will become more common and more intense.

6 – Effects of El Niño and La Niña on the weather in remote regions.

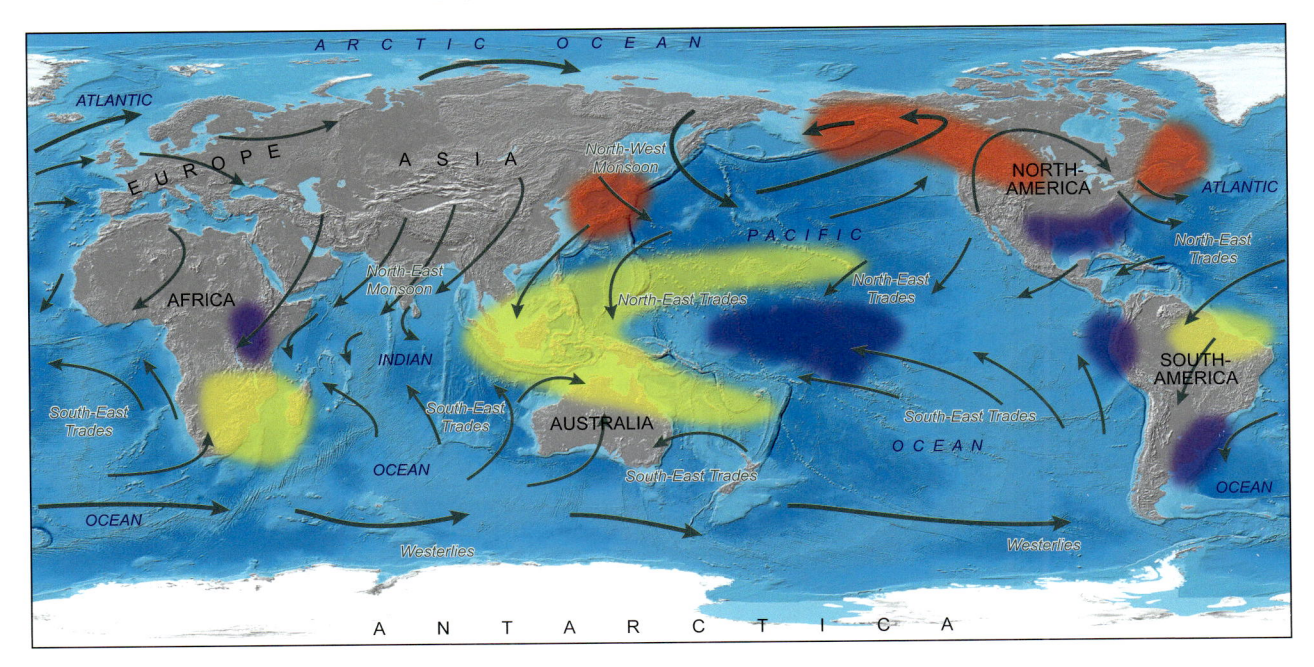

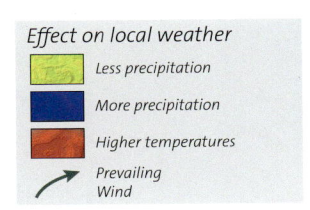

Effect on local weather
- Less precipitation
- More precipitation
- Higher temperatures
- Prevailing Wind

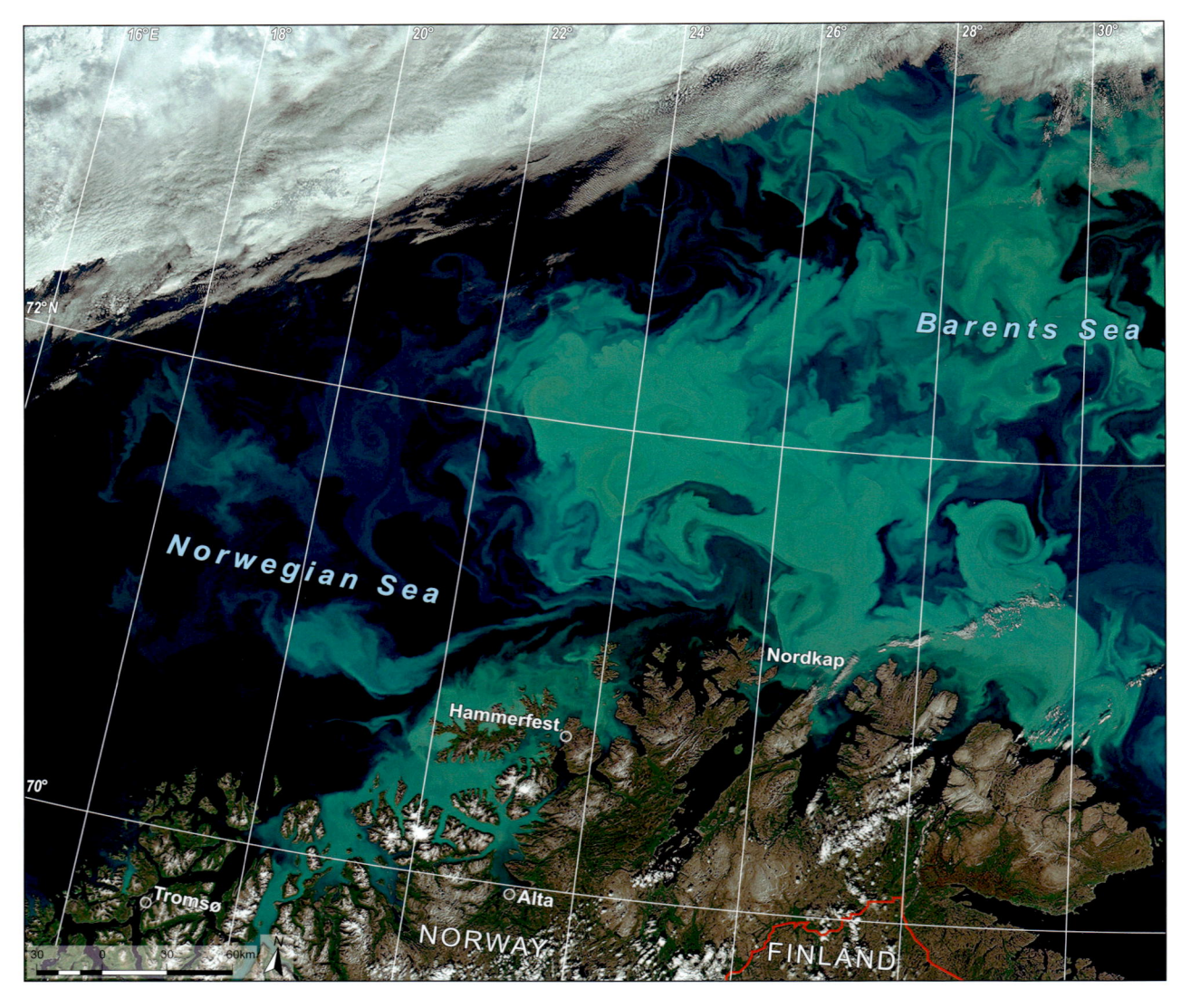

◁
1 – In July 2003, the phytoplankton in the Arctic Ocean is in full bloom. Eddies in the ocean currents swirl the almost complete blanket of plankton.

The phytoplankton requires a naturally available amount of nitrogen and phosphorus compounds in order to develop and form the basis for the food chain. The leaching of fertiliser into the water, also known as eutrophication, causes an explosive increase in algal growth, which in turn leads to an insufficient amount of oxygen, a state known as hypoxia.

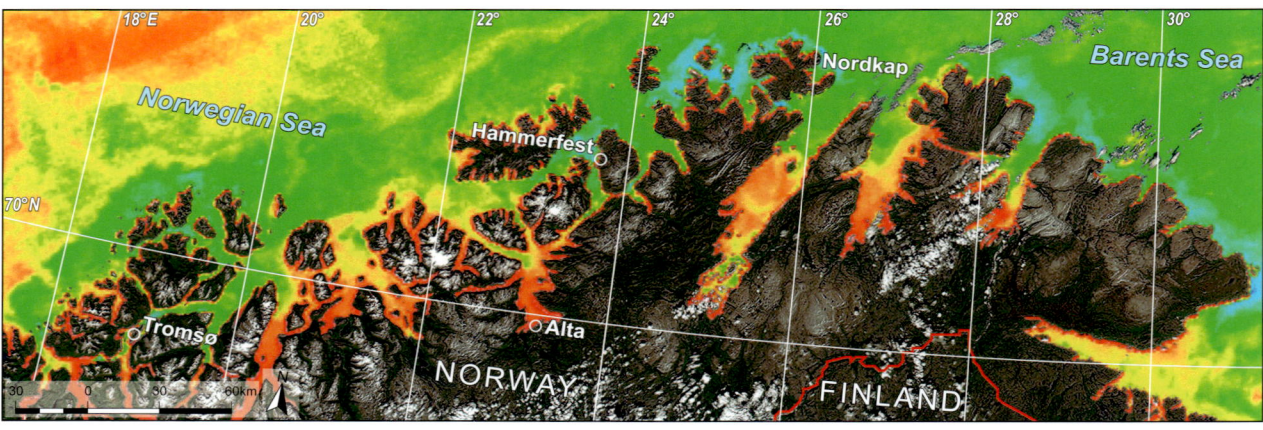

◁
2 – The phytoplankton bloom depends on a large amount of nutrients being available. This is why it only grows in areas with cooler surface water temperatures, where the availability of nutrients is generally high.

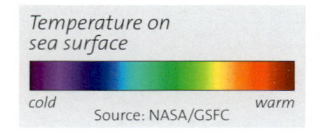

Temperature on sea surface

cold — warm

Source: NASA/GSFC

△
3 – High levels of eutrophication have led to this water being covered by a thick carpet of algae.

Phytoplankton

The umbrella term 'phytoplankton' describes microscopic phytosynthetic algae and is derived from the Greek words 'phyto', meaning plant and 'planktos', meaning drifting. The most common types of phytoplankton algae are diatoms, cyanobacteria, chrysophytes and dinoflagellates. Living in the surface waters of the seas, these single-cell plants (protozoa) are drifting with the currents of the oceans. Some species are, to a limited degree, even able to propel themselves along. Since phytoplankton are plants, they rely on photosynthesis as a source of energy. Using sunlight, carbon dioxide and water, the process of photosynthesis creates organic material. One of the by-products of this process is oxygen. Phytoplankton convert as much carbon dioxide into oxygen as plants on land do. As such, they play a major role in regulating our climate, particularly with regard to absorbing greenhouse gases.

Phytoplankon are also highly significant as primary producers in the carbon cycle of the oceans. The micro-algae are a major food source for zooplankton such as radiolarians, flagellates and jellyfish, which, in turn, are a major food source for various species of fish. This means that regions with phytoplankton blooms may also experience large shoals of fish.

Since phytoplankton forms the basis of the food chain in the world's oceans, water pollution poses a major risk for all marine organisms. Even low concentrations of oil limit their growth and can lead to long-term damages in the food chain.

Algal bloom

The concentration of plankton in water bodies can vary dramatically and depends on a wide range of factors. Some of the most important factors include the availability of nutrients, the amount of sunlight, water salinity and water temperatures. As they are plants, there is a seasonal

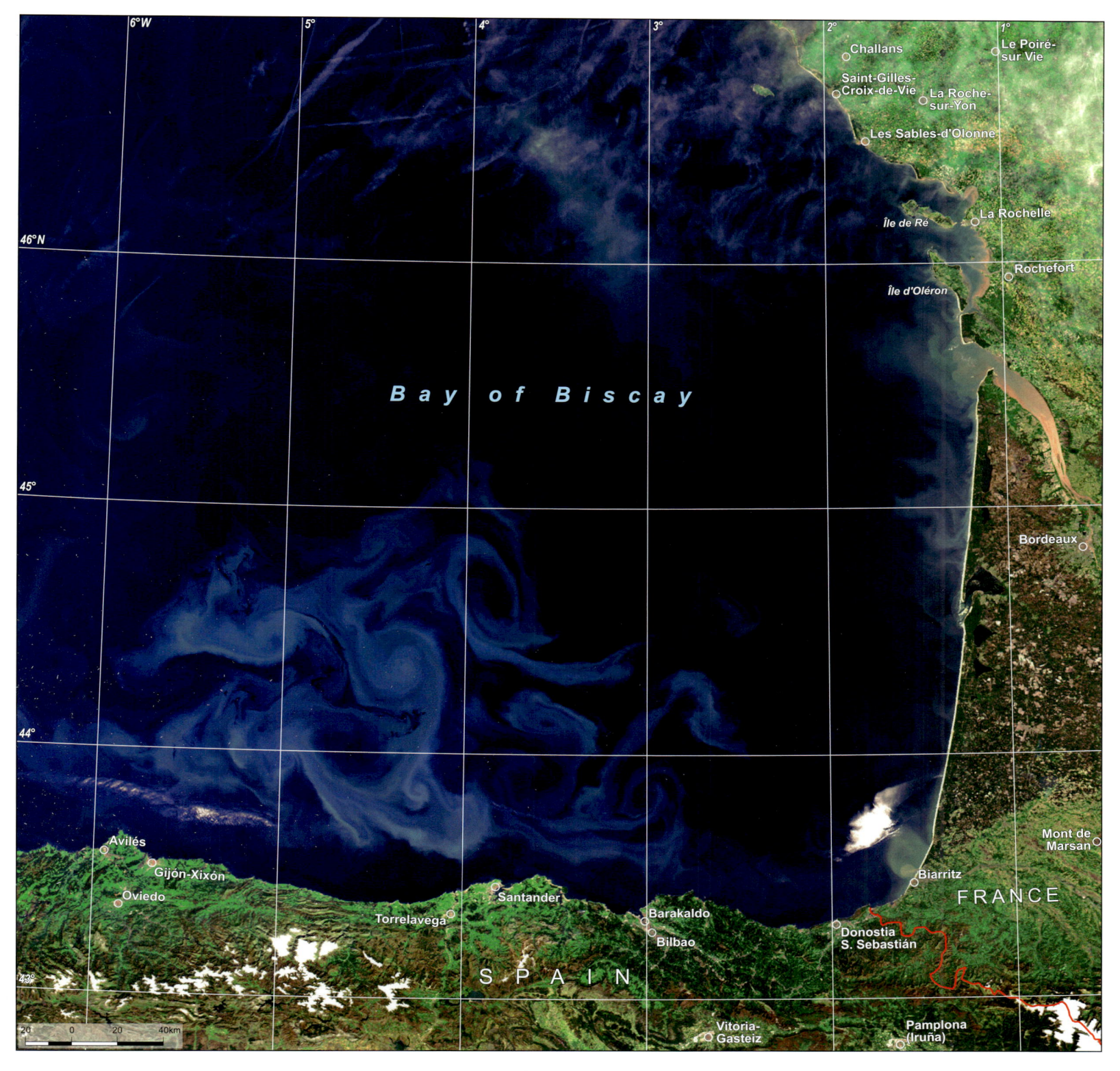

△
4 – The proliferation of plankton is not limited to northern waters but occurs in all seas, including here in the Bay of Biscay in April 2004.

pattern to phytoplankton growth in the temperate and polar regions. This pattern is influenced by physical, biological and chemical processes. Phytoplankton flourishes especially where ideal amounts of sunlight and nutrients are provided. The nutrients that enable the plankton to grow come from the deeper, colder layers of water.

At temperate latitudes, phytoplankton bloom is at its height in spring, when the sun warms the surface and reduces the density of surface water (Figs. 1, 2 and 4). Another bloom occurs in autumn, when the water layers are mixed once again and the nutrient-rich water comes to the surface.

A natural, healthy amount of nitrogen and phosphorus compounds, which enter the seas from rivers or surface run-off, contributes to the biological activity of coastal waters and is absolutely essential to the ecosystem. Areas experiencing surplus levels of nutrients are known as eutrophic. The surplus of nitrates, nitrites, ammonium or phosphates in the water can lead to excessive algal growth, which lowers the water's oxygen levels by respiration and decomposition processes. Hypoxia, or oxygen depletion, results in wide-scale changes in the biodiversity of the areas affected. The toxic species of algae that thrive as a result of the plankton bloom exacerbate the hypoxia. Organisms that are not in a position to leave their habitat are either seriously damaged and may die out or are restricted in their ability to reproduce. Shoals of fish and other mobile species simply leave the affected waters. All this leads to an unnatural disruption to the ecosystem. Usually, the ecological balance is restored through the changes in life conditions within the annual cycle.

During the last two decades, Earth observation satellites have become a valuable tool for monitoring the concentration of phytoplankton, allowing for example to publish warnings to operators of aquaculture farms before an algae bloom reaches a coast.

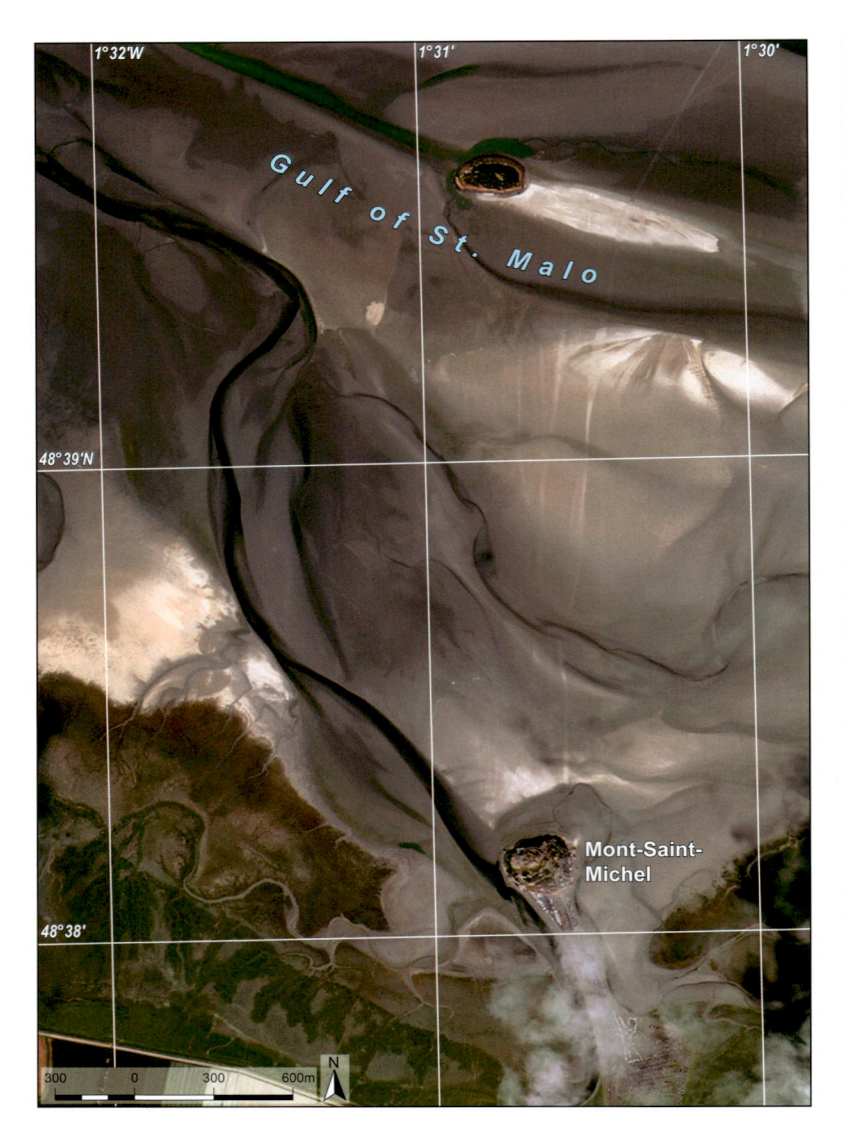

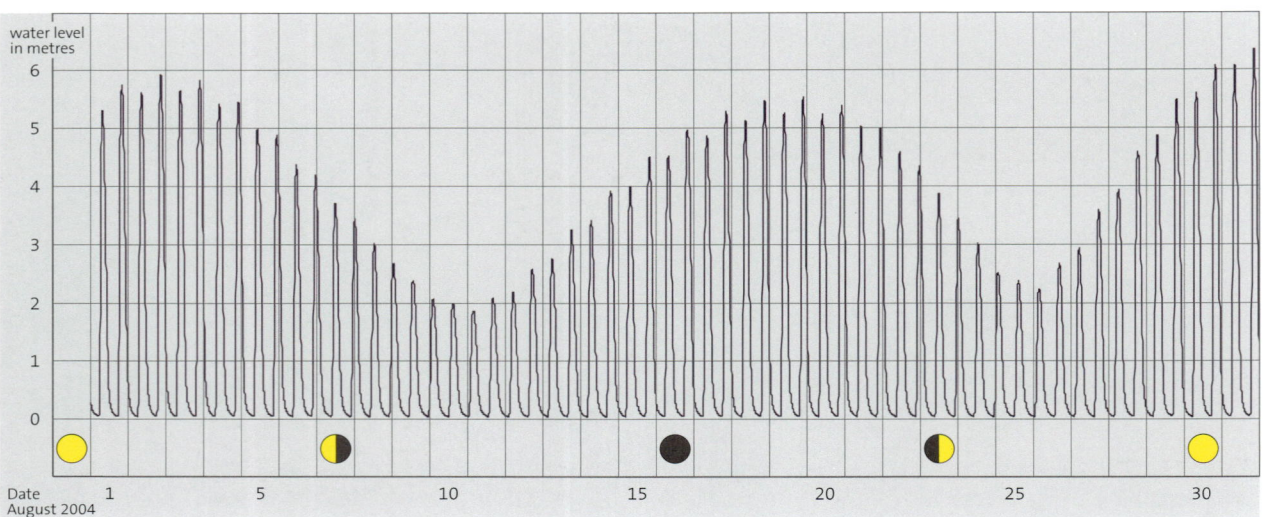

1 a/b – Mont Saint Michel on the French Atlantic coast at low tide (left) and high tide (right).

2 – The tide charts at the Mont Saint Michel survey point show the influences of the moon's phases on the tide.

3 – Mont Saint-Michel attracts large numbers of tourists every year. The surrounding coast is largely shaped by the tides.

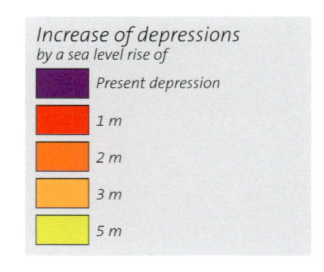

Increase of depressions *by a sea level rise of*
- Present depression
- 1 m
- 2 m
- 3 m
- 5 m

Low and high tides

Large masses of water are tugged into motion by the gravity of the moon and Sun. In the major seas, this causes the tides. Tidal amplitudes are influenced primarily by the type of coastline and the structure of the seabed, but also by wind direction and wind strength, which vary over time. In some regions around the world the tides are strong enough to be used for energy production.

At estuaries, such as the Couesnon estuary near Mont Saint-Michel on the French Atlantic coast near Saint-Malo, tidal ranges, bulked up by accumulating water, can surge up to 14 metres (Fig. 1). Before a bridge was built in the late 19th century, the 80-metre-high granite rock with the Benedictine monastery perched on the top could be reached at low tide only across a natural neck of land.

▷
4 – The sea level showed an exponential increase between 1880 and 2010.
The reconstruction was made possible by monthly tidal range recordings.

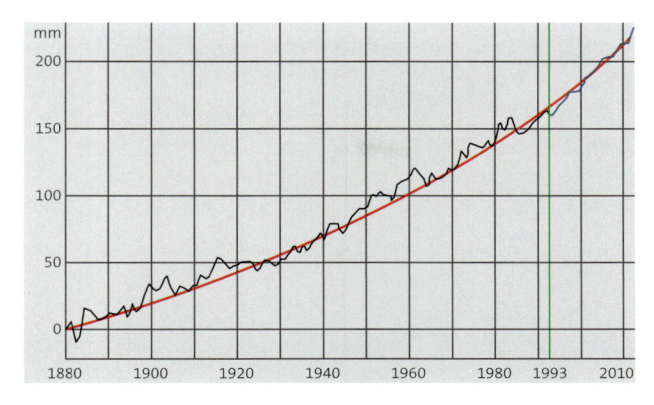

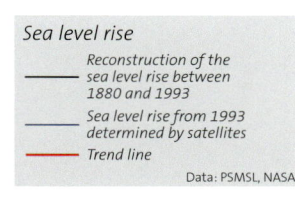

Sea level rise
— Reconstruction of the sea level rise between 1880 and 1993
— Sea level rise from 1993 determined by satellites
— Trend line
Data: PSMSL, NASA

▷
5 – Satellites have been mapping sea level rise since 1993.

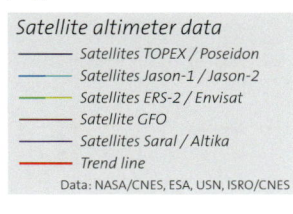

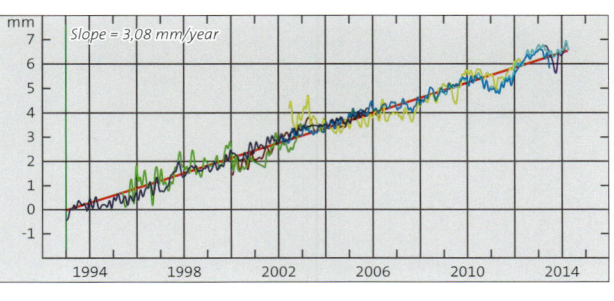

Satellite altimeter data
— Satellites TOPEX / Poseidon
— Satellites Jason-1 / Jason-2
— Satellites ERS-2 / Envisat
— Satellite GFO
— Satellites Saral / Altika
— Trend line
Data: NASA/CNES, ESA, USN, ISRO/CNES

▷
6 – Melting ice around the world would also raise sea levels. The contributions of various types of ice mass would have very different impacts.

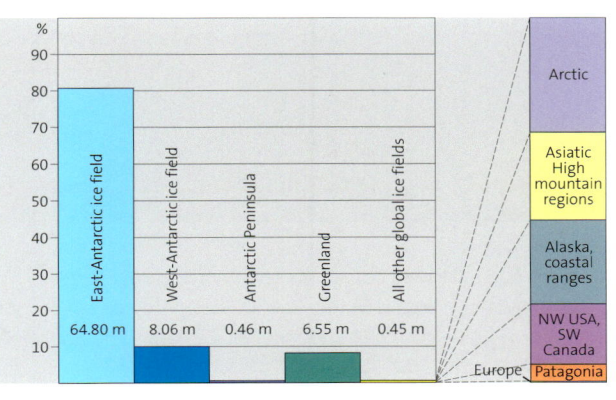

▽
7 – Many coastal regions would be put at risk by a potential rise in sea levels. Land loss can only be prevented by suitable coastal protection measures.

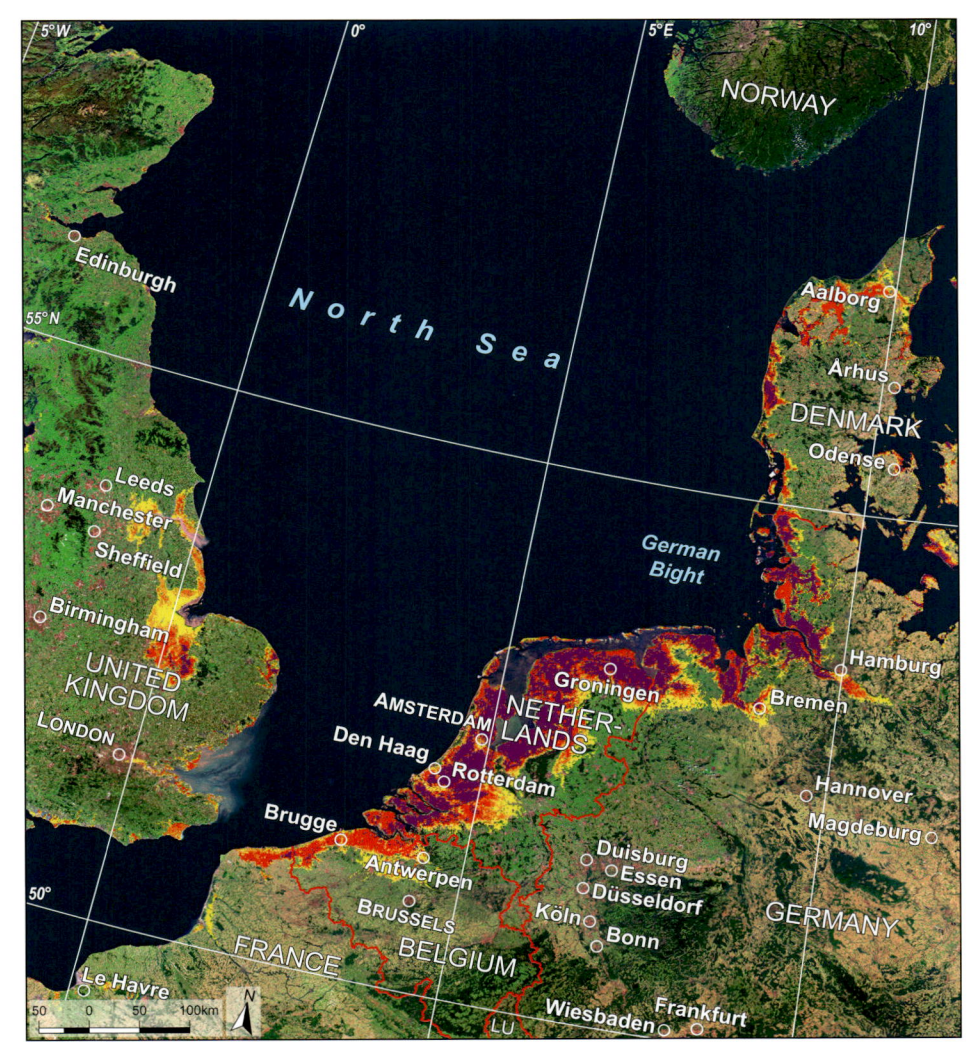

Global rise in sea levels

During the 20th century, the average sea level rose by 10 to 25 centimetres (Fig. 4). The primary cause of this is the thermal expansion of the seawater as a result of the warming upper layer of water. As such, also in the 21st century the rise of the sea levels will be largely determined by the thermal expansion of the water of the oceans. The melting ice from the ice cap in Antarctica, from mountain glaciers and from the Greenland ice sheet plays only a secondary role.

For a long time it has been difficult to determine whether or not global sea levels were rising, because, until the early 1990s, only water gauges could be used. However, they provided only limited information on average changes in sea levels around the world. Since 1992, the TOPEX/Poseidon satellite mission has been providing highly precise data on average sea levels around the world. These measurements have been further improved by the satellites Jason-1, Jason-2, ERS and Envisat, all equipped with altimeters. The data for the period from January 1993 to June 2010 showed an average increase in the global average sea level of 3.2 millimetres per year (Fig. 5).

Effects of sea level rise on coastal regions

The rise in sea levels does not occur everywhere at the same rate, and it affects some regions more severely than others. Flat coastlines and small islands are at the highest risk – especially if they have no effective coastal protection measures in place. This applies in particular to developing countries with densely populated coastlines. Small island nations such as the Maldives or the Seychelles are in danger either because the complete terrain of these countries lies only a few metres above sea level or because almost their entire population is concentrated on a narrow strip along the coast.

In Europe, the rising sea levels are expected to endanger the North Sea coasts of the Netherlands, Belgium, Germany and Denmark, as well as the east coast of England. One-quarter of the area of the Netherlands already lies below sea level. If the Greenland ice sheet melts, which could occur with an annual global temperature increase of over 2 degrees Celsius, the sea level would rise by 6.5 metres (Fig. 6). Many densely populated zones along coasts all around the world would be at risk if this dramatic rise were to occur.

The area around the North Sea has been battered by storm surges for centuries. The region's two biggest storm surge disasters in the last century occurred in 1953 on the Dutch coast and in 1962 in the German Bight. The countries affected reacted by improving their coastal defences, which must soon be strengthened once again for a sea level rise of two metres (Fig. 7).

Coastal protection measures

In order to be able to cope with the consequences of sea level rise, efficient solutions for the protection of coasts will be absolutely essential in the future. In this context also the permanent monitoring of the weather via satellites plays an important role. Storm warning issued early enough, for example, enable floodgates to be closed in time. The Netherlands serve as a model when it comes to existing infrastructure and the quality of coastal protection. In 1958, 'Delta Works' was launched as a consequence of the disastrous 1957 flood. This EUR 5 billion project was set up to protect the southwest coast of the Netherlands with dykes and flood barriers and was completed in 1987.

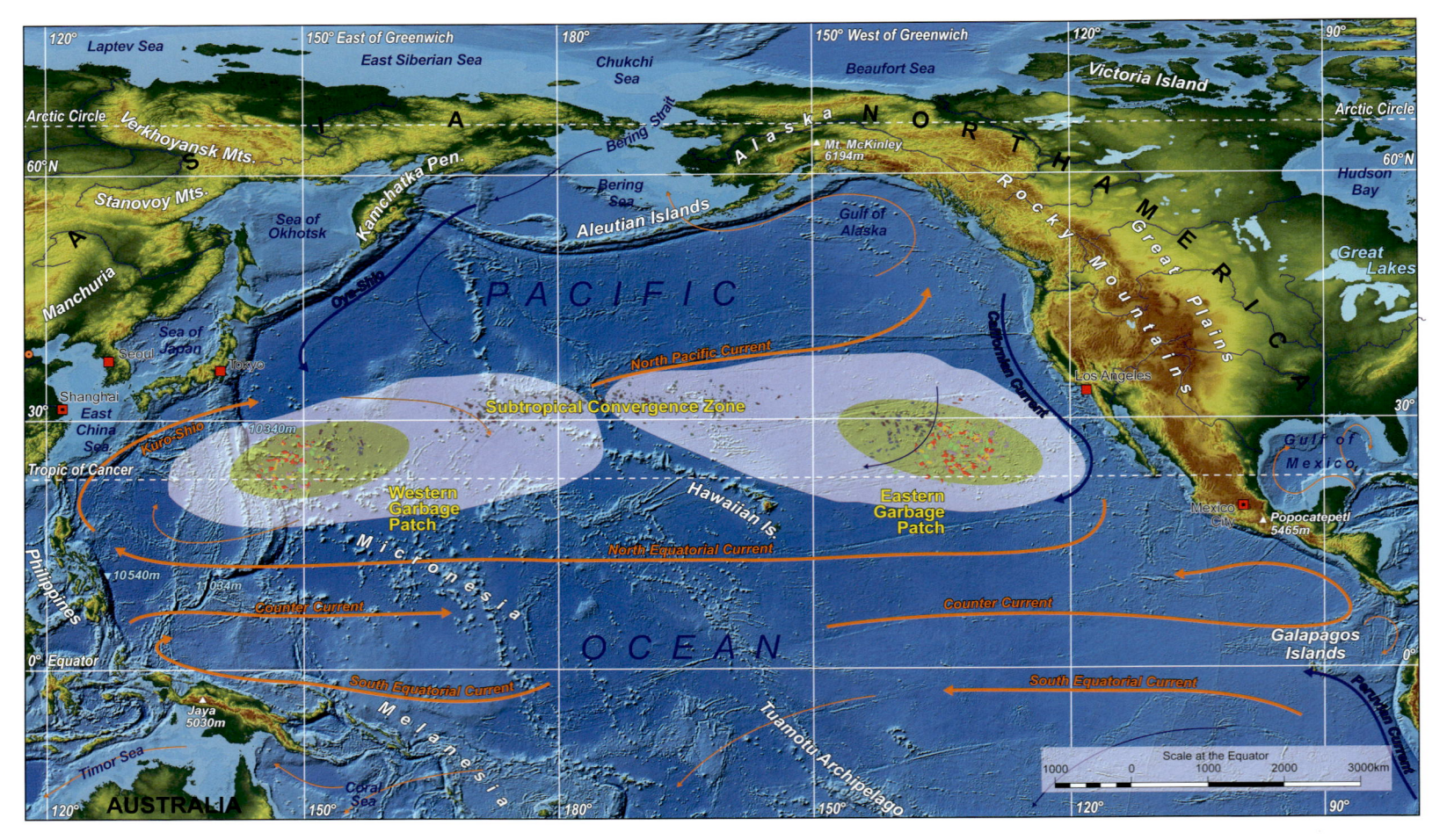

The rubbish dump of developed and developing countries

Huge quantities of plastics have been manufactured industrially since the 1950s. Since then, they have come to dominate almost all areas of our lives. Our world could no longer function without synthetic materials or plastics. The 'Iron Age' was replaced by the 'Plastic Age', which we are now in the middle of. We have been aware of the formation of huge patches of floating rubbish, known as 'garbage patches', since the 1980s. However, this phenomenon only started being communicated to a large public in 1997 when the oceanographer Charles Moore first observed the phenomenon. These patches are collections of litter of varying densities caught in the ocean currents. The best-known of these, and the largest, is the 'Great Pacific Garbage Patch' in the northern Pacific (Fig. 1).

Great Pacific Garbage Patch – a new continent?

The North Pacific is influenced by four major ocean currents: the California Current, the North Equatorial Current, the Kuroshio Current and the North Pacific Current, which together form the North Pacific Gyre. This is where the Great Pacific Garbage Patch (GPGP) is found, the largest known garbage patch, extending over an area of 1.5 to 3 million square kilometres. The GPGP actually consists of two very large patches of rubbish, one between Hawaii and the Pacific coast of North America and another between Hawaii and the coast of Japan, which are linked by a narrow strip of ocean with a relatively low concentration of rubbish. The scale of the GPGP is so large that people now speak of islands of rubbish and of a seventh continent. In reality, the GPGP is not a continent as its average density is five kilograms per square kilometre which is not sufficient to consider it as a land. The patch reaches depths of up to 30 metres, with an average depth of 10 metres, and the highest concentrations are found in the upper three metres. The large distances involved make it hard to detect the litter: here the applicability of satellite images is still under research. The location and size of the largest garbage patch in the world is largely based on estimations (Fig. 2) which is why sceptics believe the problem has been overestimated.

Plastic – a long-term problem for the oceans

Around the world, about 260 million tonnes of plastics are manufactured every year. According to estimates, 10 per cent ends up in the oceans and makes up the largest proportion of marine litter - according to the WWF, around eight million items a day. Most of the rubbish, around 80 per cent, is taken to the sea by rivers. The remaining 20 per cent is directly released in oceans as industrial fishing waste, such as old or lost fishing nets, which are dangerous particularly for marine mammals like whales or seals, or rubbish tossed overboard from ships. In addition, thousands of containers are washed overboard from freighters by storms every year, some of them drifting across the oceans for a long time. Major floods and tsunamis drag additional amounts of debris from the land back into the sea (Figs. 3 and 4). As a result, up to 46,000 items of plastic waste can be found in every square kilometre of ocean.

1 – The extent of the Great Pacific Garbage Patch.

2 – Vortexes of waste within major currents.

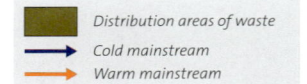

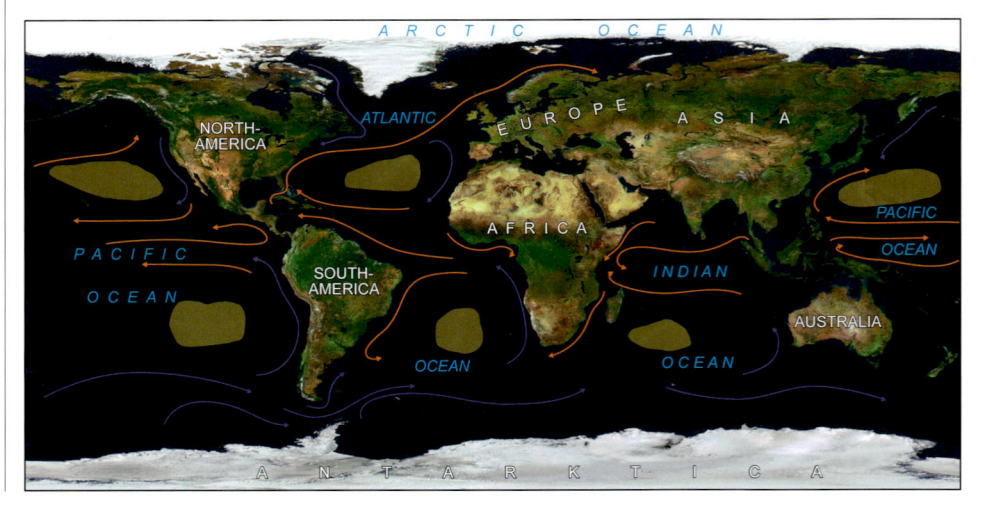

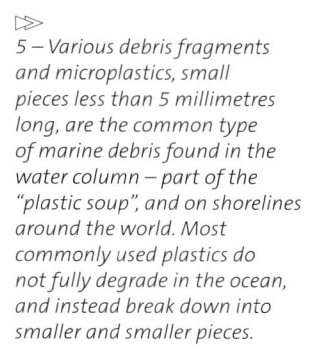

3 – Shells of buildings, fires and wreckage washed from the land into the sea on and in Yamada Bay, three days after the tsunami of 11/03/2011.

4 – Floating debris from the tsunami off the Sendai coast, Japan.

5 – Various debris fragments and microplastics, small pieces less than 5 millimetres long, are the common type of marine debris found in the water column – part of the "plastic soup", and on shorelines around the world. Most commonly used plastics do not fully degrade in the ocean, and instead break down into smaller and smaller pieces.

6 – Decay time of some components of the marine litter.

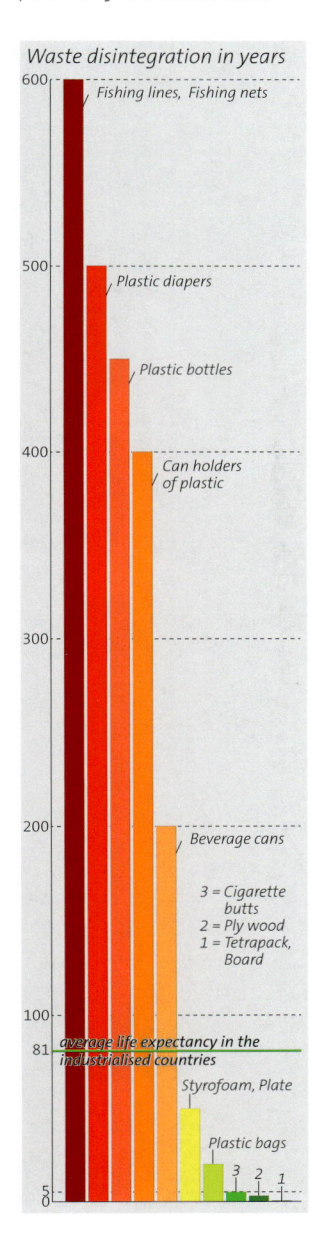

It often takes several hundred years for plastic waste such as bottles, nappies or fishing nets to decay (Fig. 6). Exposed to sunshine, plastic is broken down by photodegradation into smaller and smaller particles - microplastics (Fig. 5), and ends up as what is known as 'plastic soup'. Since only 15 per cent of the rubbish is washed up ashore and almost three-quarters sinks to the sea bed, microscopic particles of plastic and toxic substances released upon their decay pose the biggest threat to marine life. Marine life forms either accidentally eat plastic, mistaking it for food, or absorb toxic substances through their mouths and gills. At the top of the food chain, these toxic substances then end up on our plates. The UN estimates that around one million birds and 100,000 marine mammals are killed every year by plastics in the oceans.

Treat the cause or the effect?

Several ideas and projects have been proposed to fish the rubbish out of the oceans using specially equipped ships and specific technologies. However, this would only address the symptoms, not the cause. Moreover, removing the rubbish out of the ocean would also harm the marine life that would be fished out with it. One example is the 'Fishing for Litter' campaign, directed at fishermen. If they do not throw the litter in their nets back into the sea but bring it back to land for controlled disposal, the fishermen receive money for it.

Dealing with the causes – as is so often the case – starts with the individual consumer. Avoiding waste, especially plastic waste, is an important step, as is avoiding disposing of waste in or near water. To achieve this, sensible, internationally agreed measures are required. Bottle deposits on plastic bottles is just one small but important step, as the example of the city of San Francisco shows. In March 2014 the city decided to become the first major US city to stop selling drinks in plastic bottles at public events and in public buildings. A proposed ban on plastic bags by the EU Commission would also help alleviate the situation.

The Seventh Continent and satellite technology

As many of the individual items of plastic soup in the garbage patch are so small, its structure so dispersed, and because most of the rubbish floats a few metres under the surface, the garbage patches are very hard to detect in satellite images.

The Global Drifter Program of NOAA (National Oceanic and Atmospheric Administration) aims at analysing the waste problem in the oceans using satellite technology. Across the ocean, over 12,000 satellite-monitored buoys transmit data such as position and temperature. This data can be used to simulate the paths of the plastic waste within the major current systems. In this respect, waste floating on the ocean takes about six and a half years to make one circuit of the North Pacific (Fig. 1). This technique could also be used to simulate the route of floating debris from the tsunami along the Japanese coast in March 2011, some of which had reached Hawaii within a year. The coast of Hawaii is particularly badly affected by floating debris. Around five million tonnes of debris and waste from the tsunami are estimated to have been washed into the sea, around 70 per cent of which sank directly off the coast (Figs. 3 and 4).

As part of the educational programme Argonautica of the French space agency (CNES), the project 'Seventh Continent Expedition' was set up to investigate the Great Garbage Patches. In this project, ESA contributes alongside others by assessing the usability of data from Sentinel-1.

Waste in the ocean is an environmental problem but may also affect other domains such the use of satellites for safety applications. For example, during the search for the Malaysian Airlines Boeing 777, initially supposed to have crashed in the South China Sea on 8 March 2014 with 239 people on board, there were significant problems in identifying pieces of wreckage in the estimated region of the crash. This area of the Pacific Ocean has a high density of waste and potential wreckage could not be distinguished from the existing waste of the garbage patch.

169

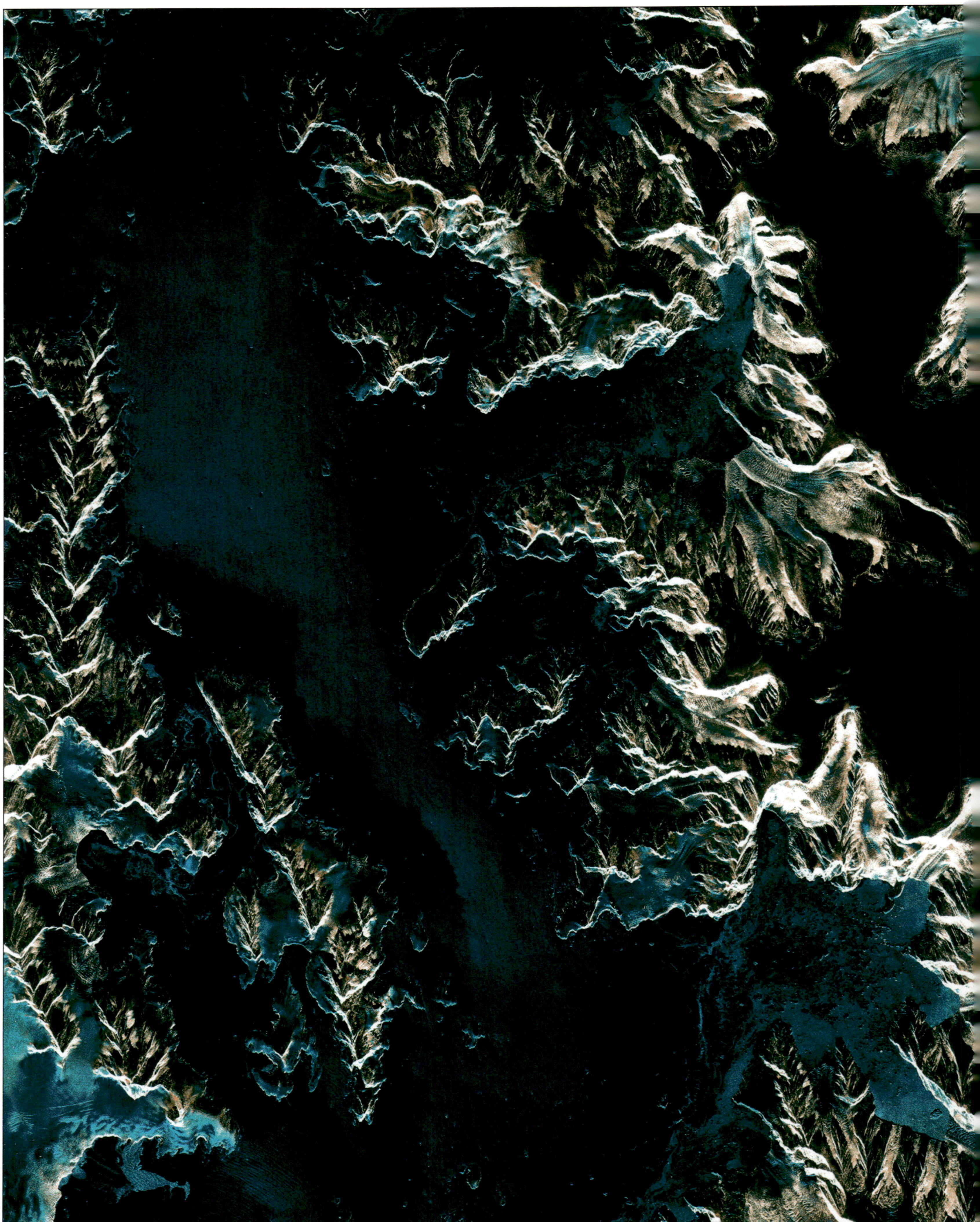

POLAR REGIONS

Vast regions in the polar latitudes are constantly covered by ice. The variations of polar ice extent and thickness, measured by satellites over the last decades, are extremely important since the poles are the Earth's climate alarm bells.

About ten per cent of the Earth's surface is permanently covered by glaciers, ice caps, and ice sheets. Located primarily in the northern hemisphere, seasonal snow covers up to 33 per cent of Earth's land and provides a vital source of fresh water. Permafrost is another component in the water cycle as it consists of permanently frozen soil and stores fresh water. These different forms of ice, mainly found in polar and high-altitude regions, play a critical role in regulating the Earth's climate and sea level. They collectively form the Cryosphere.

Because of the amplified response of the polar regions to global warming, the poles are the climate's alarm bell. They are the first to respond to a change in climate. With the effects of climate change becoming increasingly apparent, the monitoring of the Cryosphere is therefore imperative for the future of our planet.

Floating ice in the oceans and ice on land

An important distinction is to be made between sea ice and land ice (Fig. 1). Sea ice is a relatively thin layer of ice that floats on top of the polar oceans. Sea ice is made of frozen ocean water that forms in winter due to the low atmospheric temperatures at this time of the year. Ground ice, on the other hand, constitutes glaciers, ice caps and ice sheets and is made of compacted snow. This ice sits on land and forms a gigantic reservoir of frozen fresh water.

Differences between the Arctic and Antarctica

The Arctic and Antarctic are polar opposites in many ways, and not only geographically. „Arctos" means bear in Greek. Indeed, bears are found in the Arctic but not in Antarctica. Similarly, penguins live in Antarctica but not in the Arctic.

The Arctic Ocean is covered with sea ice of a few metres thick and with large seasonal variations. It is surrounded a hemisphere of continents. In contrast to the Arctic, the Antarctic is a frozen continent, covered by a 2,000 metres thick ice sheet. It is surrounded by a belt of oceans.

◁
1 – Acquired on 13 April 2014 by Sentinel-1A, this radar image shows a transect of 80 kilometres width over the northern part of the Antarctica Peninsula in HH and VV polarizations. This allows to colour ice and snow qualities differently. The morphology is also much pronounced.

171

Relatively warm ocean waters can reach the Arctic and melt the sea ice and Greenland tidewater glaciers, while Antarctica is relatively protected by circumpolar currents, namely ocean currents that flow all around the Antarctic continent. Atmospheric circulations are also different in both poles due to the contrast between continent and ocean. Sea ice in the Arctic has decreased dramatically, 50 per cent since 1950, while Antarctic sea ice has increased a little in recent years (Fig 2). The reason behind these phenomena is still under investigation.

Because of global warming, Greenland is expected to soon reach a tipping point where snow accumulation gains in the winter will not compensate the summer ice melt losses. At the other end of the planet, most of Antarctica will remain cold – even with an increase of a few degrees in global temperature, because of its very low annual average temperature of around -50 degrees Celsius.

The 30 degrees Celsius difference in temperature between the North Pole and the South Pole is due to several mechanisms. Atmospheric and ocean circumpolar currents isolate the Antarctic from heat exchange. Air is colder at higher elevation and the South Pole is at 3,000 metres, whereas the North Pole lies at sea level. The North Pole also receives heat from the underlying ocean (Fig. 3). Moreover, the albedo effect is more pronounced in Antarctica due to almost permanent, bright fresh snow cover.

Together the Antarctic and the Greenland ice sheets hold 99 per cent of our planet fresh water stock. The Antarctic continent and Greenland are literally covered by a dome of ice more than 2,000 metres thick.

Satellites and ice monitoring

The icy reaches of the polar regions are some of the most inhospitable places on Earth. Routine observations from space provide the most effective and precise means of continuously monitoring these vast environments. Because of the vital role of the polar regions in amplifying Earth's climate variations, observing these areas from space is crucial.

While satellites have been continuously tracking the extent of the sea ice cover for some decades now, measurements of sea ice thickness are needed to work out how the actual volume of the ice is changing. Data from ESA's ice mission, CryoSat-2, allow the analysis of variations in the thickness of Earth's continental ice sheets and sea ice.

ESA and NASA have recently published results showing variations in polar ice extent and thickness, measured from space over the last 35 years. These results show a dramatic decline of Arctic perennial sea ice extent of around 12 per cent per decade during the period 1979-2012 (Fig. 2). This contrasts with the limited increase of the Antarctic sea ice extent of one to two per cent per decade over the same period due to a reduction of open water within the ice pack. Sea ice thickness in the Arctic has decreased by around two metres between 1980 and 2008. Overall the total amount of sea ice is decreasing.

3 – This Envisat image captures the marginal ice zone of the Greenland Sea during the onset of the spring melt season. The bright white swirls at the ice edge are traced out by brash ice. The myriad of swirls show how dynamic the upper ocean is at this time of year because of strong gradients in temperature and salinity.

The geographic North Pole is defined as the most northerly point where the Earth's axis intersects with the Earth's surface. It lies at the geometric intersection of all the lines of longitude and represents 90 degrees North. By contrast, the magnetic North Pole shifts with the Earth's magnetic field. In 2012, it was at 85.9 degrees North and 147.0 degrees West. It is currently shifting north-west by an average of 40 kilometres every year.

1 – Satellite image mosaic of the Arctic Ocean with the bordering continents of Europe, North America, and Asia.

2 – Satellite observations showed that the sea ice extent at the North Pole globally decreased during the last 35 years. The differences are evident especially in September, after the melt season.

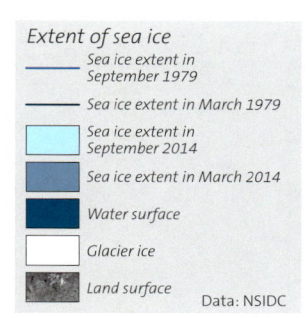

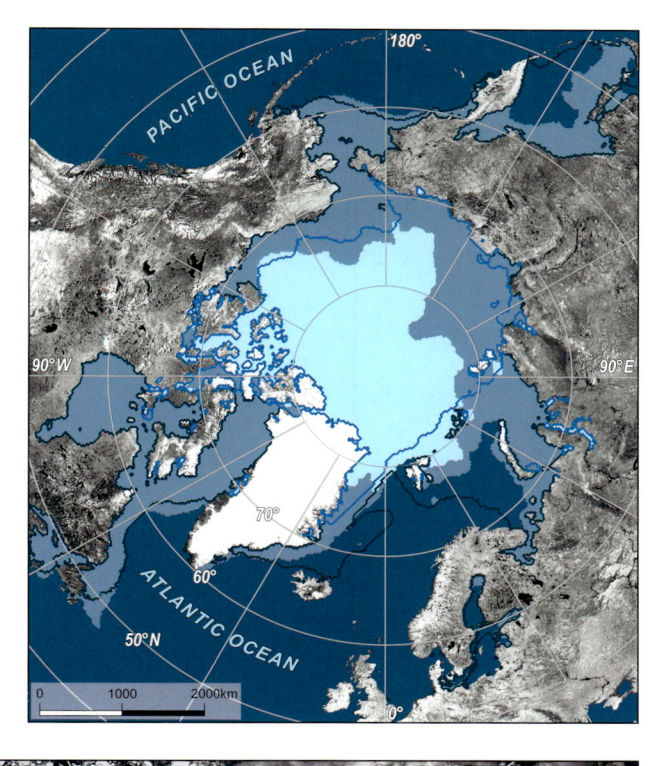

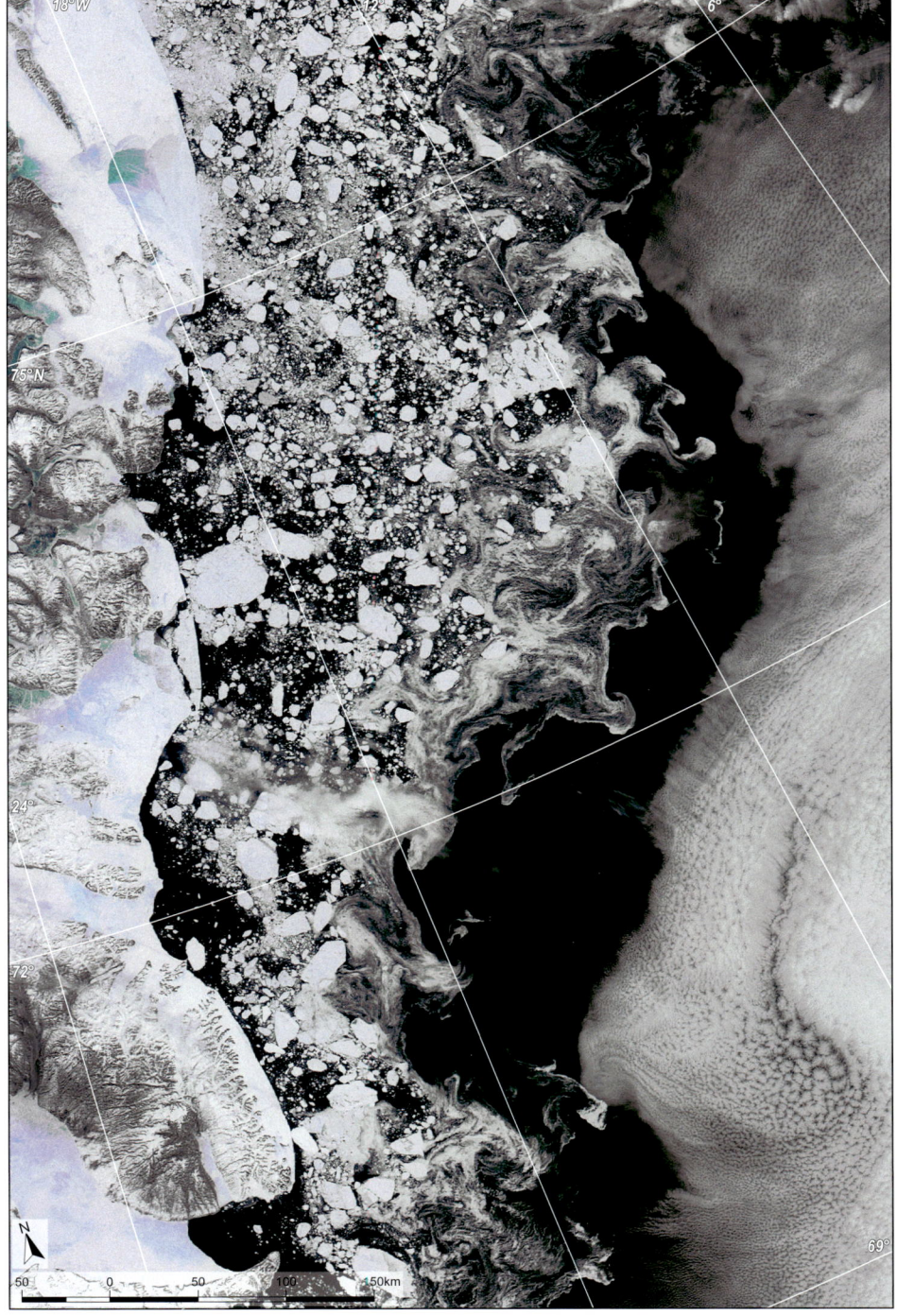

Extent of sea ice
- Sea ice extent in September 1979
- Sea ice extent in March 1979
- Sea ice extent in September 2014
- Sea ice extent in March 2014
- Water surface
- Glacier ice
- Land surface

Data: NSIDC

ARCTIC

The area around the North Pole is known as the Arctic. Over the last 35 years, satellites observing the Arctic have witnessed a reduction in the thickness and extent of sea ice. In September 2014, the ice cover has reached one of its lowest ever summer minima.

The Arctic includes all the sea and land around the North Pole as far south as the boreal tree line. In its centre lies the Arctic Ocean, which is surrounded by the permafrost regions of northern Europe, Russia, Alaska and Canada, a few small island groups, and Greenland (Fig. 1). The total area of the Arctic comprises 26 million square kilometres, of which only eight million are land. The region's climate is harsh: the winters are long and cold, while the summers are short and cool. With average precipitation of 250 millimetres per year, it is very dry. The average air temperature in the winter is -30 degrees Celsius. When the temperature of the Arctic Ocean falls below -1.8 degrees Celsius, the seawater freezes, forming a huge blanket of ice (Fig. 2). Due to the Earth's axial tilt, regions beyond 66°34'N receive up to 24 hours of daylight during summer, a phenomenon known as the midnight sun.

Living conditions in the Arctic

The Arctic is divided into two vegetation zones, each with typical ecosystems: the polar ice desert and the tundra. Extreme living conditions are characteristic of these two regions, and only a very few hardy species such as polar bears, seals, reindeer, Arctic wolves, lemmings and ptarmigans (grouses) can survive in them.

In contrast to Antarctica, which is largely unpopulated, up to four million people live in the Arctic. Climate change is forcing them to adapt to fast changing conditions. The thawing permafrost leads to the destruction of roads and railways and to the collapse of buildings.

Arctic sea ice extent

The extent of sea ice in the Arctic has been regularly monitored by satellites since 1978. Arctic sea ice naturally extends its surface coverage each northern winter and recedes each northern summer, but the rate of overall loss since 1978 has accelerated. Losses in recent years have exceeded predictions made by scientists and within the Intergovernmental Panel on Climate Change (IPCC) reports. As the amount of ice reduces, more heat is absorbed by the ocean in summer, and consequently less ice is formed in winter, accelerating the trend in reducing ice cover. Satellites show that a large dome of fresh water has been building up in the Arctic Ocean over the last 15 years. Since 2002, the sea surface in the studied area has risen by about 15 centimetres, and the volume of fresh water has increased by some 8,000 cubic kilometres – about 10 per cent of all the fresh water in the Arctic Ocean.

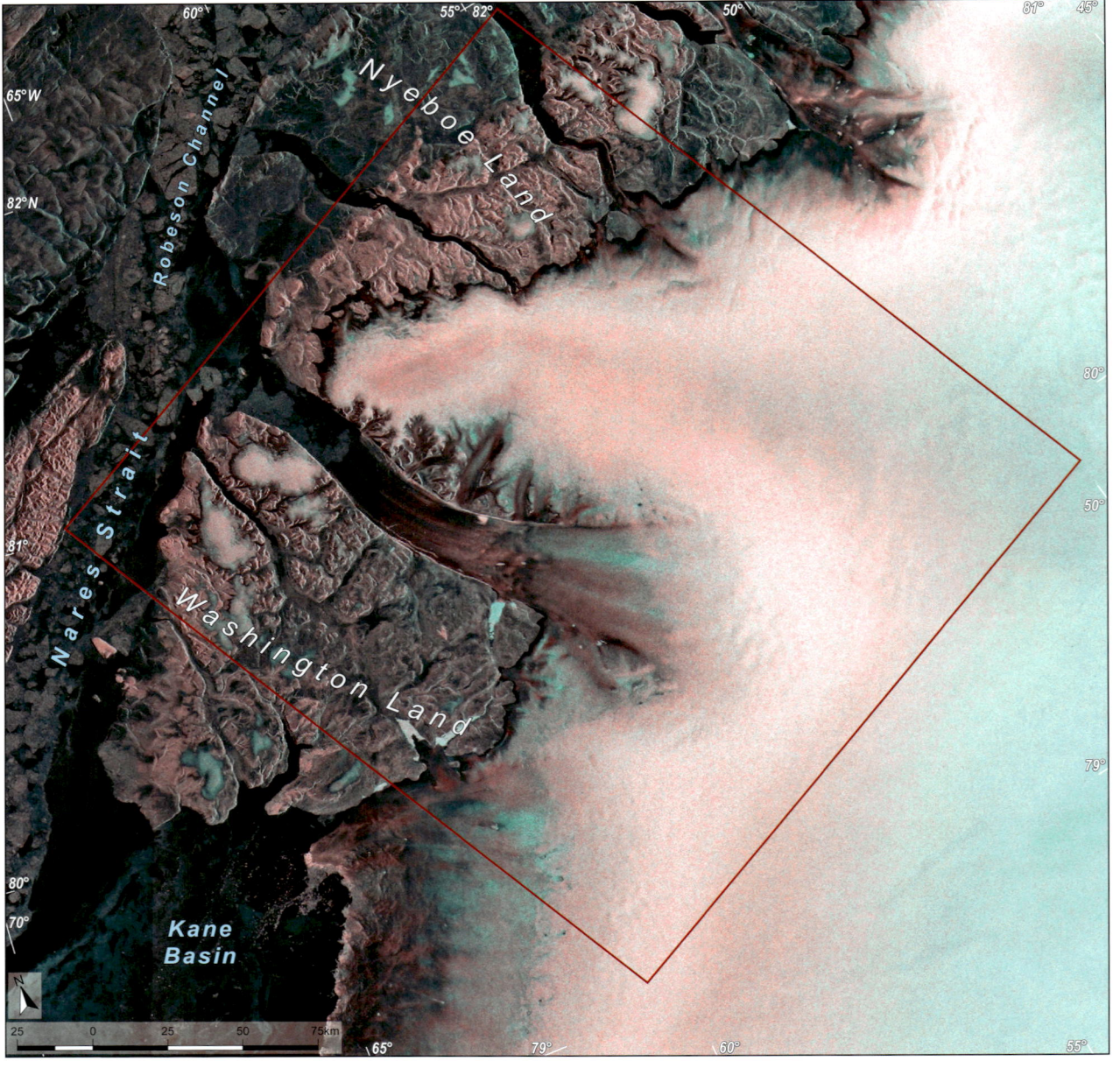

1 – Radar image showing the central part of the northern coast of Greenland with the Petermann Glacier in the centre and the Greenland Ice Sheet to the right. To the left the eastern coast of Ellesmere Island of the Canadian Arctic is visible. In August 2010, a giant iceberg measuring 260 square kilometres broke off from the floating portion of Petermann Glacier, reducing its area by about 25 per cent. The Sentinel-1 image acquired on 6 December 2014 in HH and HV polarisation indicates that the huge iceberg has moved out of the valley while disintegrating.

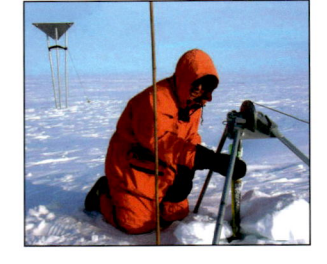

2 a-b – Scientists on the ground are taking in-situ measurements of ice and snow and are placing corner reflectors in view of calibrating and validating the CryoSat-2 data.

Arctic sea ice thickness

The Arctic sea ice extent measurements must be coupled with the information on its thickness in order to understand whether or not the overall volume of ice changes. Sea ice thickness modelling is an activity which demands global and continuous input from satellite images, since other means of observation, such as from aircraft or submarines, can only provide measurements for limited areas. Between 1980 and 2008, satellite observations (including the ESA CryoSat-2, Fig. 2 a-b, 3 a-d) reported an overall decrease in the Arctic sea ice thickness by about two metres. Major changes in the sea ice thickness could redefine the way the atmosphere works at northern latitudes, possibly affecting the global ocean current circulation model.

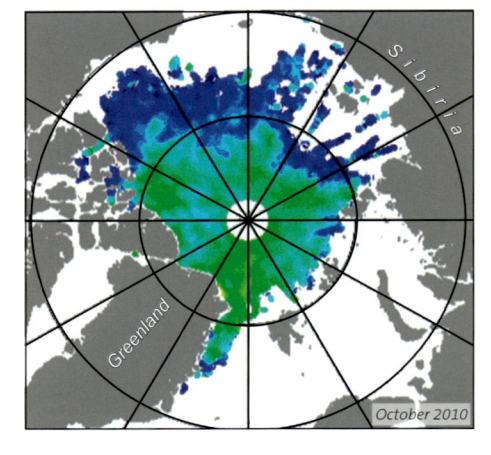

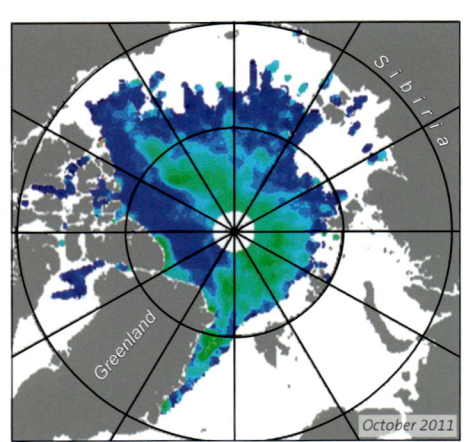

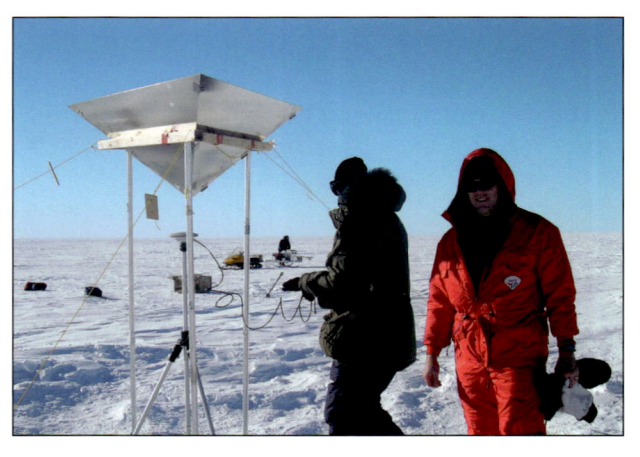

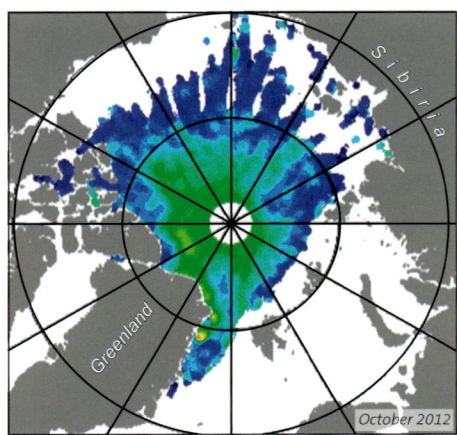

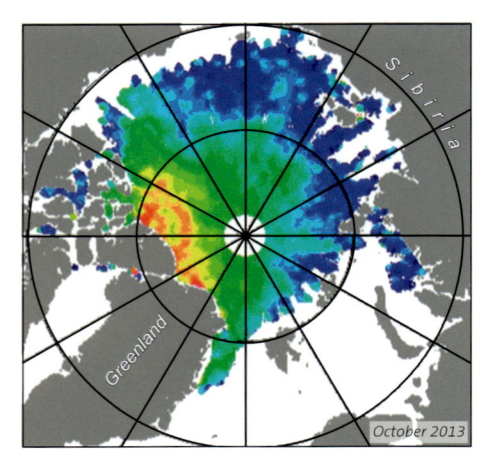

4 – This interferogram shows Petermann Glacier grinding towards the sea along the north-western coast of Greenland. Two RADARSAT-2 TOPS images acquired 24 days apart were used to generate the coloured fringes shown in repeating cycles. The more irregular coloured features to the left of the image represent elevation differences on bare rock of a hilly landscape. The more regular and mostly parallel fringes represent moving glaciated terrain. The narrower the colour cycles are spaced the faster the ice moves downwards towards the sea. The grey zones including also the glacier tongue into the sea (lower left part) do not show any fringes due to terrain steepness, relatively fast movement or freezing/defreezing effects in lower altitudes between the two data acquisition..

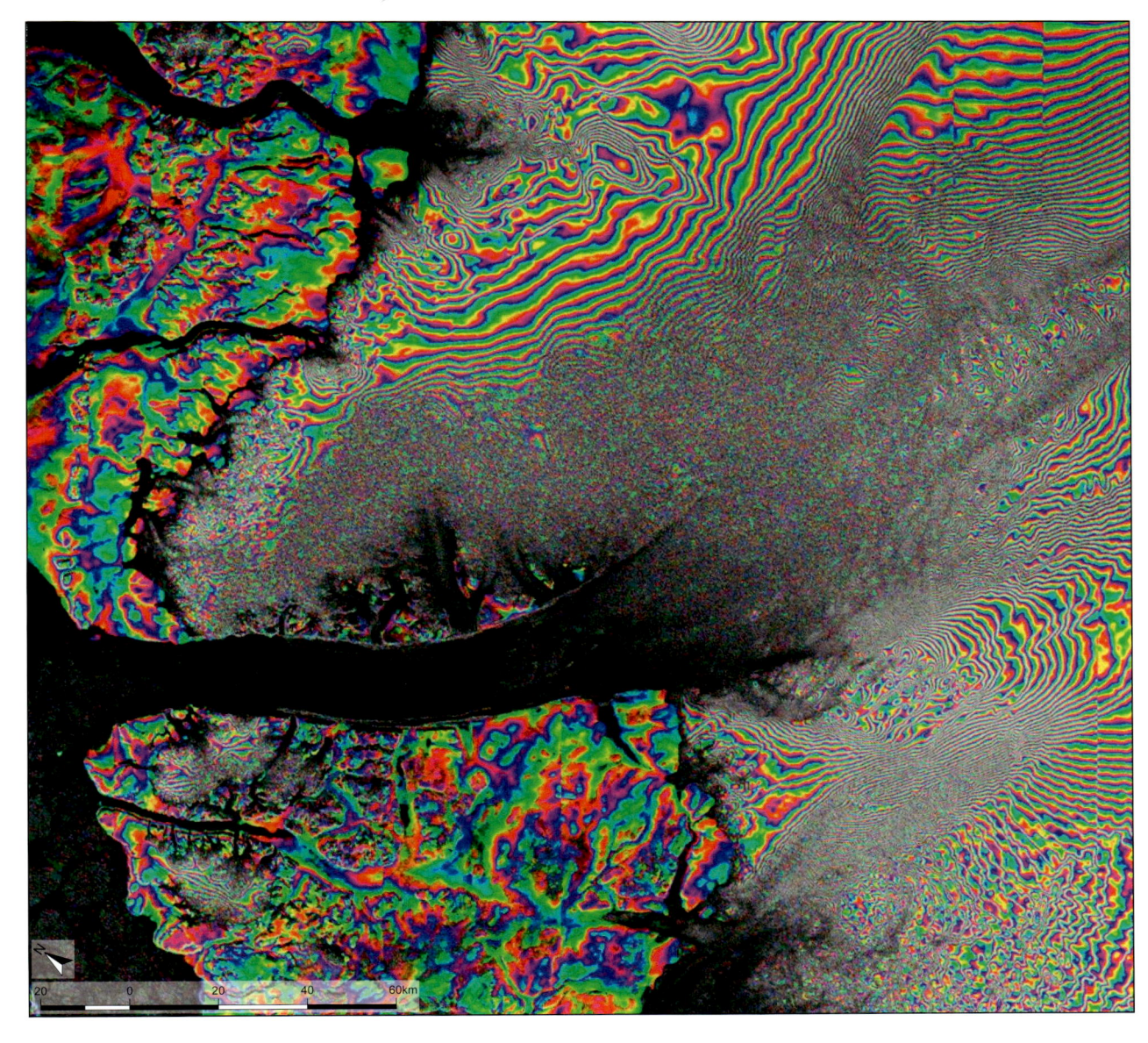

5 – The rate of ice loss in Greenland and Antarctica is increasing. From 1992 to 2012, the two ice sheets contributed a total of 11.1 millimetres to global sea levels. This is about 20 per cent of all sea level rise over that 10-year period.

3 a-d – Maps of the Arctic sea ice thickness between 2010 and 2013 (always October) derived from the ESA CryoSat-2 satellite. In this relatively short time period an increase in sea ice thickness can be observed. This is, however, not the trend in the long run, since observations over the past 35 years show a decrease in arctic ice thickness and ice extent.

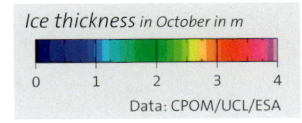

Ice thickness in October in m

0   1   2   3   4
Data: CPOM/UCL/ESA

Permafrost

Like water, soil can freeze if the temperature drops below 0 degree Celsius. When the ground remains frozen for at least two consecutive years it is called permafrost. Vast areas surrounding the Arctic Circle are permanently frozen up to a depth of more than 1,000 metres. Permafrost also appears around the globe in higher mountainous regions. Observing permafrost is of fundamental importance for climate change studies. Permafrost stores large amounts of greenhouse gases such as methane and carbon dioxide, and thawing causes the release of these greenhouse gases into the atmosphere. Acceleration in the loss of permafrost – especially in the polar regions where the ground has been frozen for thousands of years – is expected to have a severe impact on the greenhouse effect.

Greenland and Petermann Glacier

The Greenland Ice Sheet is the largest continental ice sheet after the Antarctic glaciers. These enormous ice masses are particularly vulnerable to changes in the Earth climate system as they are relatively low in latitude. This is why Greenland and its glaciers are kept under strict observation. The melting of tide water glaciers (i.e. glaciers that reach the sea) causes increase in ice discharge into the seas. This melting connected with changes in ocean temperature has a direct impact on sea level rise. Satellites have witnessed huge blocks of ice breaking away from the land, like the one from the Petermann Glacier (Figs. 1 and 4), when an amount of ice three times bigger than Manhattan Island calved from the main glacier and started floating out to sea.

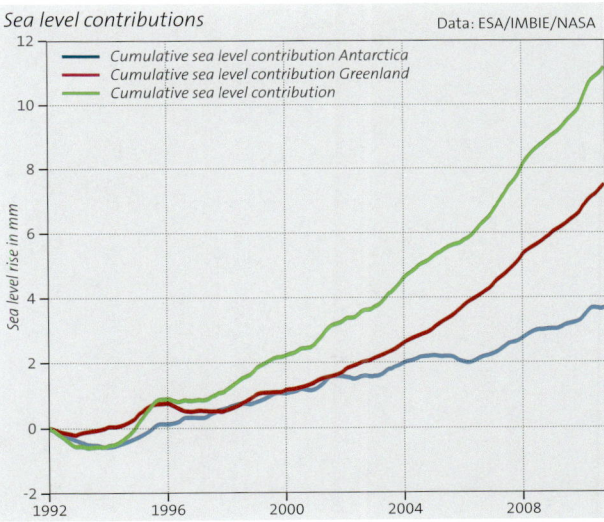

Sea level contributions Data: ESA/IMBIE/NASA

— Cumulative sea level contribution Antarctica
— Cumulative sea level contribution Greenland
— Cumulative sea level contribution

Sea level rise

The melting of icebergs and sea ice does not have an effect on sea level as the principle of buoyancy assures the right balance between the volume of water displaced by the ice and the volume of the ice itself. The melting of ice sheets and glaciers on land, however, adds fresh water into the oceans and has a direct impact on the rise of its level. Given that 70 per cent of human activities and cities are located along the coasts – some of them already affected by sea level rise – it is of extreme importance to have a continuous monitoring system of global sea levels. The complete melting of the Greenland Ice Sheet, for instance, would produce a sea level rise of several metres (Fig. 5).

INDIAN OCEAN
SOUTHERN OCEAN
ATLANTIC OCEAN
PACIFIC OCEAN
ANTARCTICA
SOUTH AMERICA
Kerguelen Is.
Heard I.
Cooperation Sea
Davis Sea
Shackleton Ice Shelf
West Ice Shelf
Vincennes B.
Dumont di Urville Sea
Moscow Univ. Ice Shelf
Wilkes Land
Balleny Islands
Mc Murdo Sound
Cape Boothby
MacKenzie B.
Prydz Bay
Amery Ice Shelf
White I.
Cosmonaut Sea
Lützow-Holm-Bay
Riiser-Larsen-Pen.
Lazarev Sea
Queen Maud Land
Fimbul Ice Shelf
Polar-Plateau
Transantarctic Mountains
Ross Ice Shelf
Ross Sea
Roosevelt I.
Bay of Whales
Riiser Larsen Ice Shelf
Brunt Ice Shelf
Filchner Ice Shelf
Rockefeller Plateau
Sulzberger B.
Ford Range
Berckner I.
Ronne Ice Shelf
Hollick-Kenyon Plateau
80°S
Mt. Sidley 4181m
Vinson Massif 4897m
Weddell Sea
South Sandwich Islands
Getz Ice Shelf
Cape Dart
Amundsen Sea
70°S
Abbot Ice Shelf
Cape Palmer
Bellingshausen Sea
Ronne B.
Larsen Ice Shelf
Antarctic Peninsula
Wilkins Ice Shelf
Alexander I.
South Orkney Is.
Joinville I.
Biscoe Is.
Bransfield Strait
South Shetland Is.
Antarctic Circle
Scotia Sea
Drake Passage
60°S
Falkland Islands
Land of Fire
Strait of Magellan
Argentine Sea
Patagonia
50°S
0°
180°
10°E
20°E
30°E
40°E
50°E
60°E
70°E
80°E
90°E
100°E
110°E
120°E
130°E
140°E
150°E
170°E
10°W
30°W
40°W
50°W
70°W
80°
90°W
100°W
110°W
120°W
130°W
140°W
150°W
170°W
300 0 300 600km

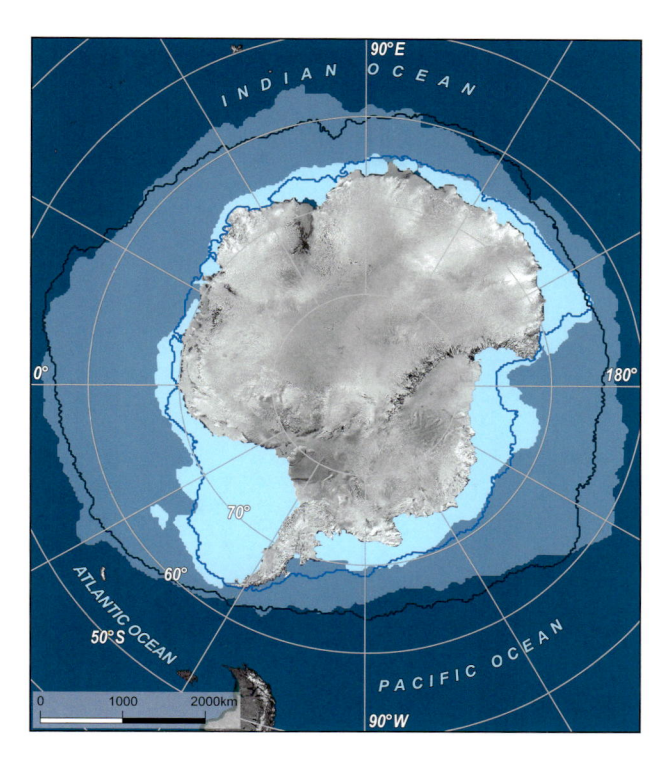

ANTARCTICA

With an area of over 13 million square kilometers, Antarctica is the world's fifth-largest continent. Observations from space have shown that regional changes in the ice sheet are occurring faster than previously thought.

The lands and seas surrounding the South Pole are known as Antarctica. The Antarctic continent contains islands, mountains, and valleys. Most of it is covered by a huge layer of ice called the Antarctic ice sheet (Fig. 1).

Antarctica is not inhabited by humans as such, but scientists do work there for short periods at research stations.

Several species of penguin and seal live along the coasts and edges of the ice shelves. The Southern ocean is teeming with life from enormous swarms of krill and schools of fish to whales in the polar summer.

The Antarctic continent interacts with frosty ocean currents surrrounding the continent. The predominant circulation mechanism of the Southern Ocean around Antarctica is the Antarctic Circumpolar Current (ACC), also called the West Wind Drift (Antarctic Drift), an ocean current flowing clockwise from west to east. This circumpolar circulation is a central part of the global circulation pattern (Fig. 1, p. 62) and is a very distinct feature of Antarctica in the sense that Antarctica is the only continent surrounded in every direction by oceans, thus allowing such a circulation to take place. This circulation provides a thermal insulation for the continent.

In addition to the Antarctic Circumpolar Current, convection occurs in the Antarctic regions. Indeed, because of their high salinity, the water masses produced here by salt rejection from the freezing sea ice sink all the way down to the seabed (Fig. 5). These water masses are called the Antarctic bottom waters (AABW) and flow across the ocean floor halfway around the globe into the Atlantic, the Indian and the Pacific oceans, feeding into the global ocean circulation. This process, like the North Atlantic circulation in the northern hemisphere (Fig. 1, p. 160), redistributes heat and salt to maintain the relatively mild global climate. Ocean currents transport enormous amounts of heat around the world. It is through this mechanism that Antarctica is linked to the global climate. These sinking waters act together with phytoplankton as a carbon (CO_2) pump from the atmosphere to the deep sea.

Despite the cold water, the Southern Ocean is one of the most productive of the world's oceans. As for the formation of Antarctic Deep Waters, it is again sea ice that plays a major role. In this case the sea ice forms a nursery for phytoplankton. Melting sea ice provides macro and micro nutrients which, in combination with light, allow phytoplankton to bloom at the sea ice edge.

◁ 1 – Satellite image mosaic of the Antarctic with its ice shelves.

▷ 2 – Although satellite observations showed that the sea ice extent at the South Pole increased since the last 35 years, this does not contradict the general decrease of ice extent and warming trends on Earth. Differences are shown for March and September.

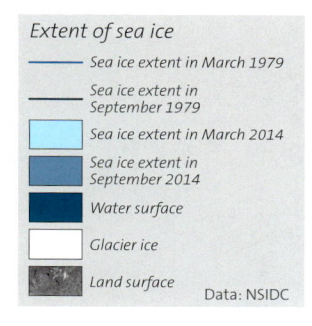

Extent of sea ice
- Sea ice extent in March 1979
- Sea ice extent in September 1979
- Sea ice extent in March 2014
- Sea ice extent in September 2014
- Water surface
- Glacier ice
- Land surface

Data: NSIDC

▷ 3 – A corner cube reflector placed under the flight path of the Alfred Wegener Institute (AWI) Polar-6 aircraft in the Antarctic. The corner cube is used to validate the data from the ASIRAS instrument on Polar-6 and to assess CryoSat's data accuracy.

▷ 4 – Reference station installed in the Antarctica to measure surface height variations and validate Cryosat-2 data. In order to achieve highest accuracies with GPS, the kinematic measurements need to be related to a static reference station. Four reference stations are being used in total, three on bedrock and this one at the field camp.

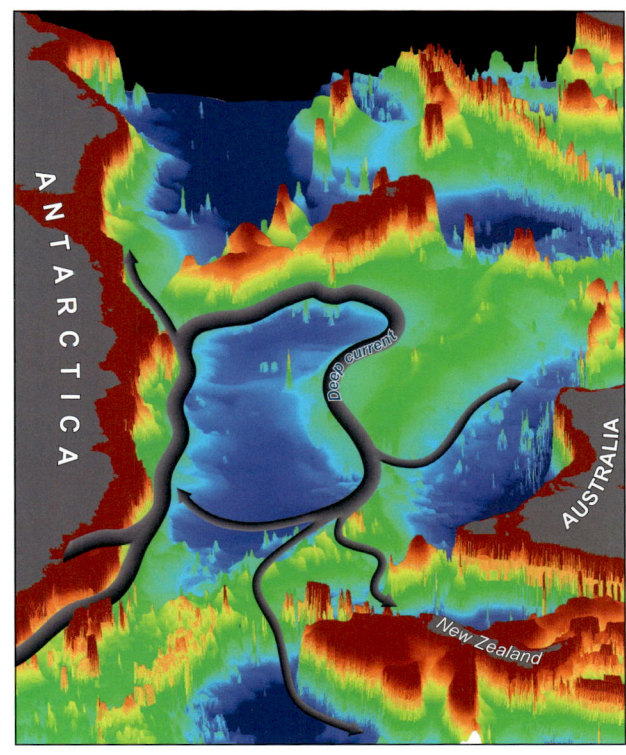

▷ 5 – Bathymetry of the Southern Ocean. The arrows indicate the downwelling of high salinity water from the icy Antarctic coast to the deep sea and as such acting as carbon dioxide regulator.

The ice sheet of Antarctica

The continent is almost completely covered by ice. On average, the Antarctic ice sheet is more than 2,000 metres thick and at its thickest it exceeds 4,500 metres (Fig. 1 and 2). It contains about 30 million cubic kilometres of ice. The inland ice sheet is the largest single ice sheet in the world and stores 90 per cent of the world's fresh water.

The Transantarctic Mountains (TAM) divide the continent into two unequal parts (Fig. 5). Its higher altitudes make the eastern part the colder of the two. The western part, including the Antarctic Peninsula and the Ross and Filchner-Ronne Ice Shelves, is smaller and more unstable.

In East Antarctica, the bedrock on which the ice rests is above sea level, whereas in West Antarctica, the base of the ice sheet can reach as low as 2,500 metres below sea level (Fig. 2).

At the edges of the continent, the ice converges to form fast flowing outlet glaciers that flow into the ocean to become ice shelves, large platforms of floating ice hundreds of metres thick that will eventually break into icebergs and drift in the Southern Ocean (Figs. 3 and 6).

Extremely low temperatures are typical of the continent. The lowest natural temperature on Earth was measured in Antarctica at -89.2 degrees Celsius taken from a ground station and -93.2 degrees Celsius derived from satellite data. Katabatic winds, which blow down from the continent's interior towards the ocean, cause frequent blizzards. Weather fronts only rarely reach the continent's interior, leaving it extremely dry.

Ice thickness in Antarctica

To fully understand how climate change is affecting Antarctica, we need to carefully monitor the changes taking place in this huge mass of ice. In 2011, similarly to the Arctic (see p. 174, 2a), a map of ice thickness was derived using CryoSat-2 which measured the height of the ice sheet over the entire Antarctic continent (Figs. 1 and 2). Such a map will be used to determine how the thickness of the ice is changing over time.

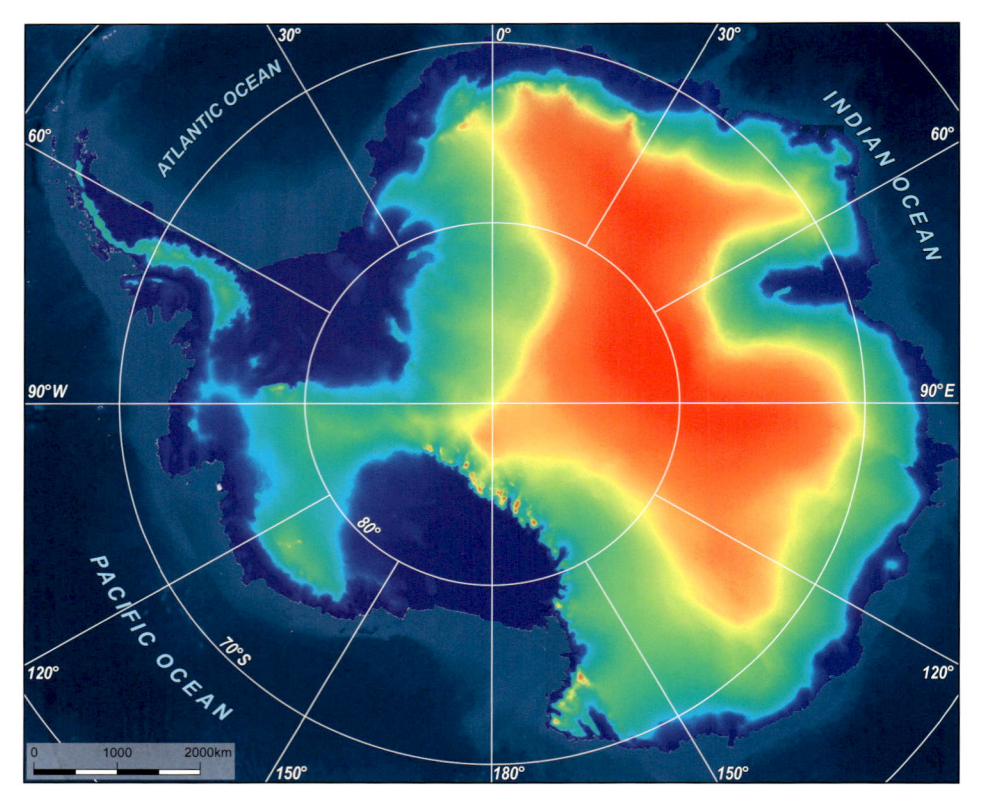

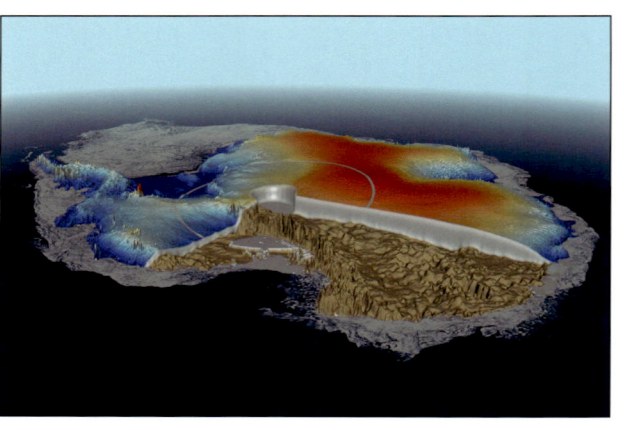

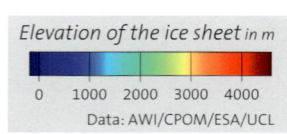

◁
2 – Model exposing the bedrock and revealing the difference between the east (right) and west (left) part of Antarctica.

◁
3 – Acquired on 27 November 2014, this Sentinel-1 image reveals the disintegration of the Thwaites Glacier. The huge iceberg of about 47 kilometres x 77 kilometres or 3620 square kilometres is the largest part of the 5440 square kilometre glacier tongue that broke away from Thwaites Glacier in the 1990ies, but only started to drift as from 2011. This process was observed by the radar sensor Envisat ASAR.

▽
4 – GPS buoys are used to measure sea ice drift. They are deployed through planes or helicopter landing directly on sea ice floes.

◁
1 – This elevation map of Antarctica was derived from ESA's CryoSat-2 satellite data collected throughout 2012. The ice sheet consists of the coloured surface surrounded by the Atlantic, Pacific and Indian oceans. Cryosat-2 revealed that the combined loss of Antarctic and Greenland ice sheets between January 2011 and January 2014 is the highest rate observed since satellite altimetry records began about 20 years ago.

▷
5 – This is the first map of ice velocity over the entire continent of Antarctica. It is derived from ALOS PALSAR, Envisat ASAR, RADARSAT-2, ERS-1 and ERS-2 satellite radar interferometry overlaid on a MODIS mosaic of Antarctica. These new findings are critical for measuring the global impact on sea level rise resulting from ice flowing into the ocean.

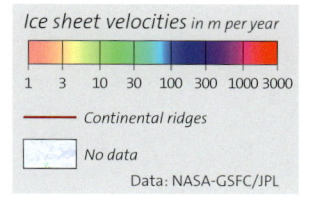

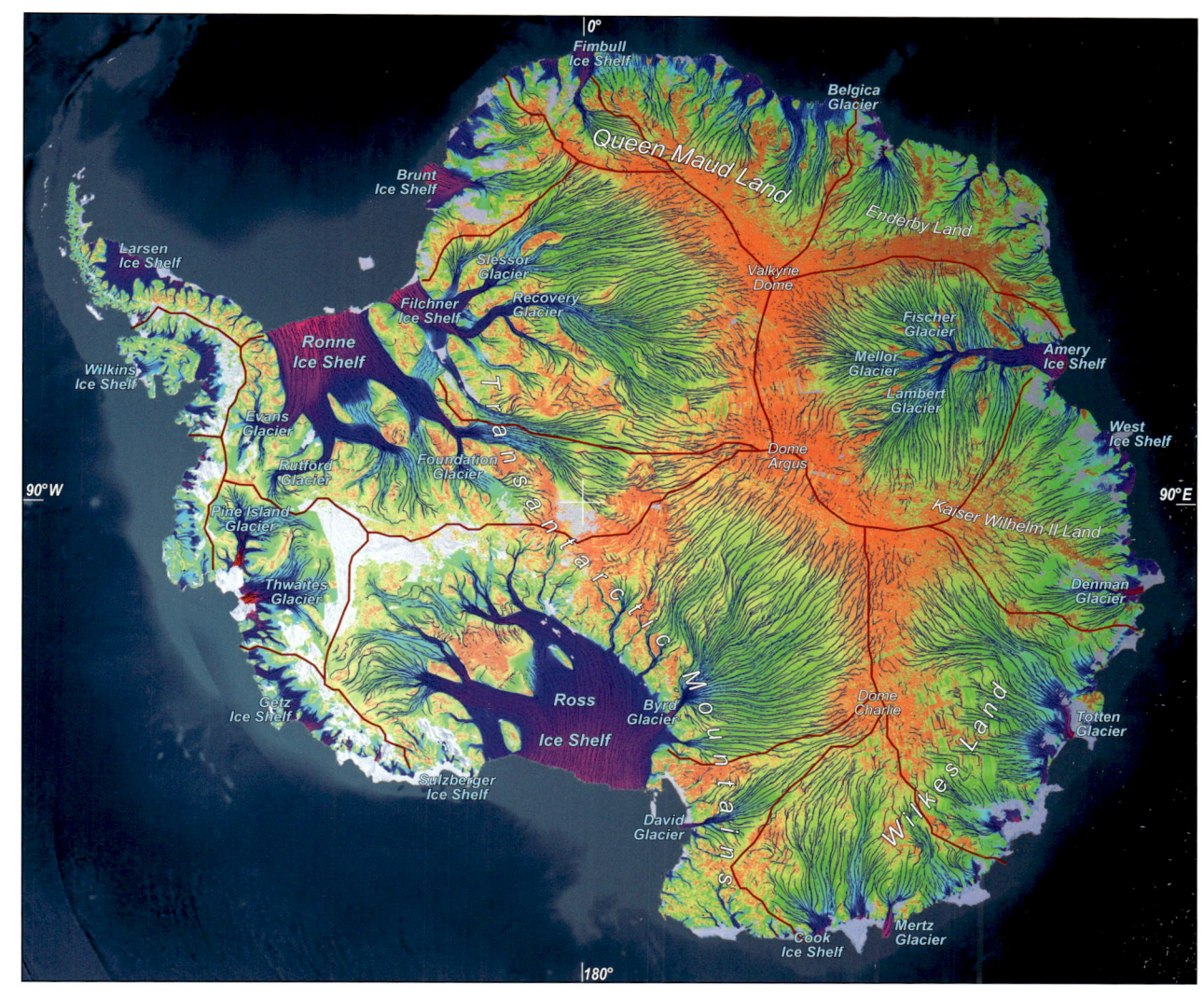

▽
6 – B-15A iceberg is the world's largest recorded iceberg. It broke free of the Ross Ice Shelf in March 2000. The image was acquired by Envisat ASAR in September 2004

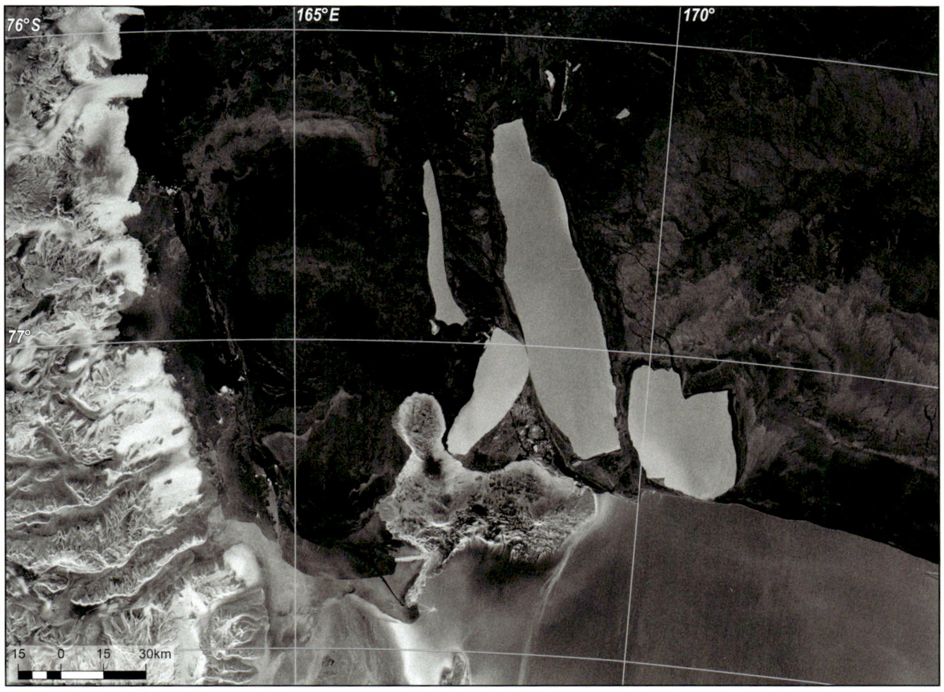

The satellite's sophisticated technology is also improving our understanding of the changes occurring at the more vulnerable edges of the ice sheet and ice shelves.

Antarctic ice streams

Antarctica's glacial ice may seem solid, but gravity and the tremendous pressure created by the mass of the ice causes it to move constantly. The ice sheet is made up of layers of snow that have piled up and compressed over thousands of years. Under its own weight, the ice sheet flows downhill towards the sea.

The amount of snow accumulated on the sheet is balanced by the ice that is released to the ocean. This mechanism was observed by satellites revealing a huge network of glaciers, carrying ice thousands of kilometres across Antarctica. The extent of the sinuous, river-like streams of ice and the speed of discharge from central Antarctica into the ocean is shown on the map of Antarctic ice flow (Fig. 5). The ice velocities vary from orange (near the interior), to green (ice tributaries), blue (ice streams), and red (ice shelves).

Ice sheet movements: the Ross Ice Shelf

Until recently it was thought that the Antarctic ice sheet was relatively stable. However, observations have shown that regional changes are occurring much faster than once thought. It is now known that the ice sheets are melting at their base due to warmer ocean currents. Changes around the edges of the ice sheet can provide a dramatic view of this dynamic environment, such as in the case of the Ross Ice Shelf.

With an area of 500,000 square kilometres, the Ross Ice Shelf (Fig. 1, p. 176) is the largest ice shelf in the world. Ice shelves are the natural extension of grounded ice streams. They are attached to the grounded ice but float on the sea. Because an ice shelf is floating on the ocean, 90 per cent of its volume lies under the sea. The transition point between the grounded and the floating ice is marked by strong tension and fractures, which create fissures in the ice.

At the other end of ice shelves near the open ocean, large icebergs calve off because of fractures in the ice. This happened in March 2000, when a large and long iceberg identified as B-15A calved off and began drifting north-west (Fig. 6).

WATER FOR HUMANITY

Water will play a major role in our future. Many of humanity's problems are either directly or indirectly linked to it. This includes not only access to water but also dealing with water shortages and water surpluses

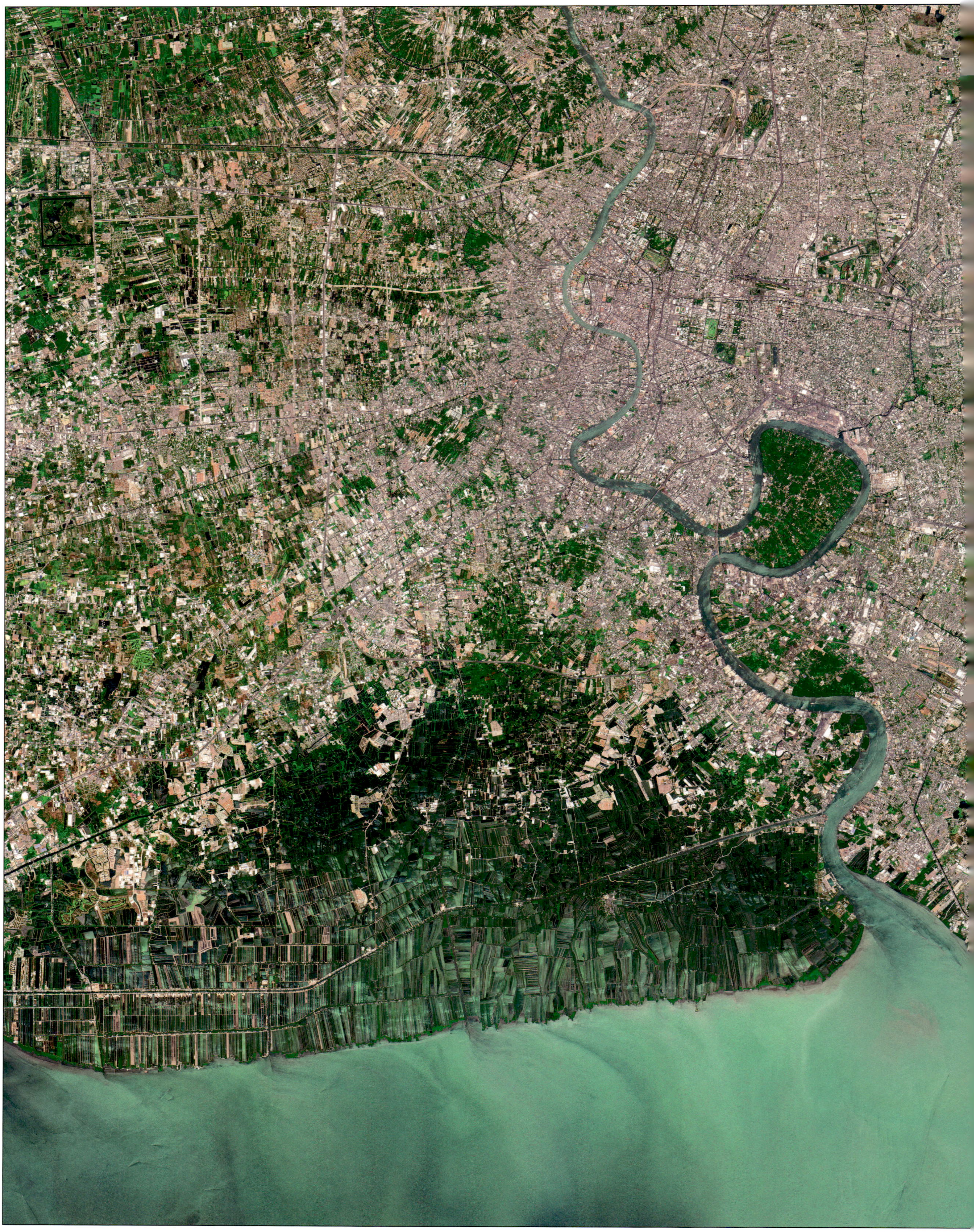

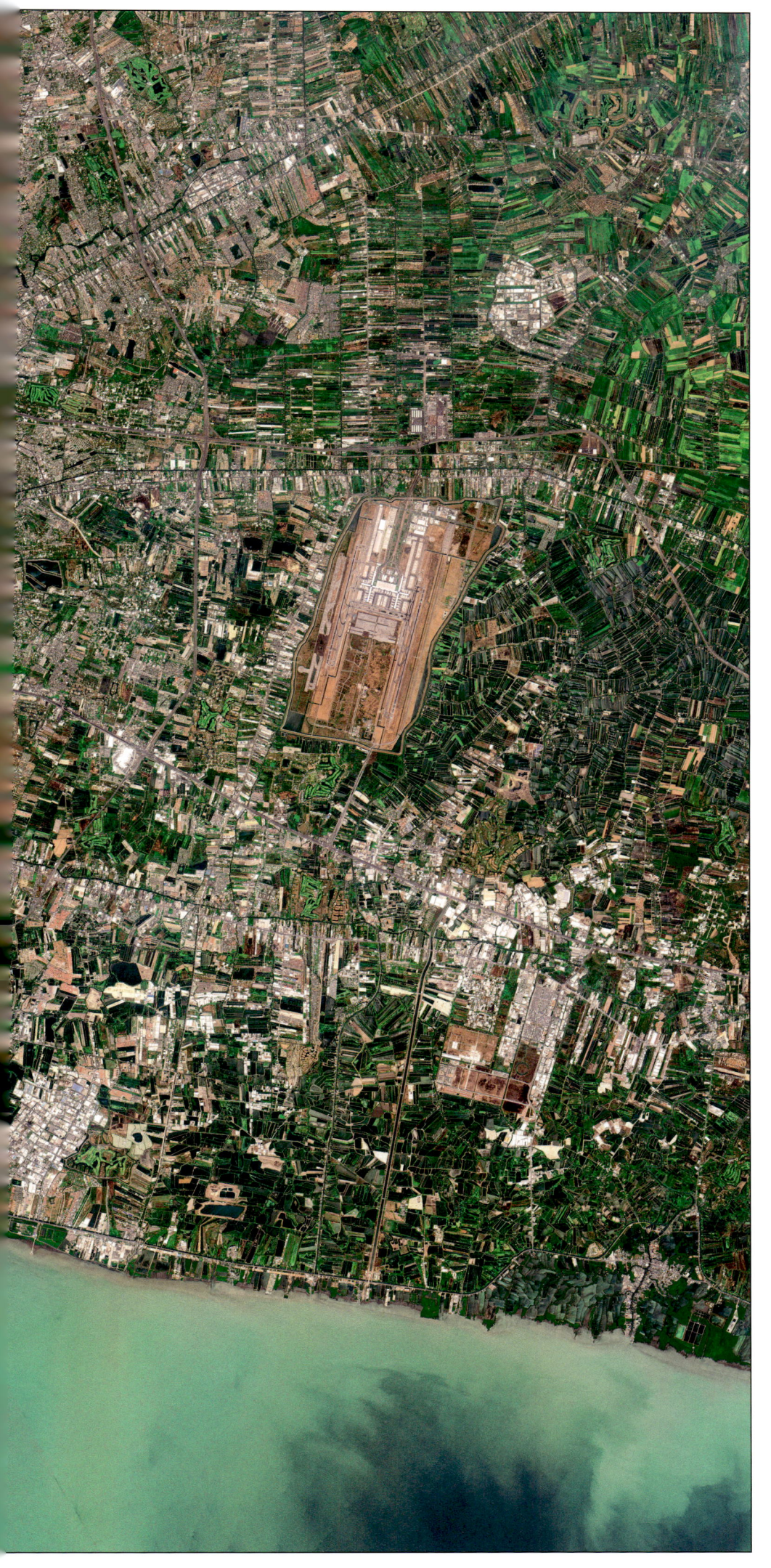

CITIES

According to the latest calculations, by the year 2030 around 60 per cent of the world's population will live in cities. Particularly in developing countries, this trend is associated with major problems with regard to water supply.

As the population increases, urbanisation will also increase. While only around two per cent of the world's population lived in cities in 1800, i.e. one person in every fifty, by 1950 this had risen to 30 per cent, or one in three. By 2000, that figure had risen to 47 per cent and, for the first time in history, in 2008 more people lived in cities than in the countryside. The UN predicts that there will be five billion city dwellers by 2030, with urbanisation increasingly primarily in Asia and Africa. With an increase of one million inhabitants per week, this is where urban populations are growing fastest. The rural exodus, particularly of young people, plays a major role in this development; World Bank estimates show that these make up 25 per cent to 30 per cent of urban growth.

With this rapid growth in urban populations, in addition to many other problems, municipalities are under particular strain to manage water supply and wastewater disposal effectively. After all, two in five people lack access to proper sewage disposal that would meet even minimum standards of hygiene. Around 800 million people have no access to clean drinking water. Wastewater is also a huge problem. In developing countries, 90 per cent of it seeps through the soil unfiltered and then enters rivers or groundwater (Fig. 1). In major conurbations and cities, proper supply and disposal is simply not available. In Africa alone, in the 120 major cities studied, only one in five homes were connected to the sewage system on average.

Since time immemorial, people have preferred to build their cities close to water – either so they could be used as transport routes or to ensure the drinking water or food supply. The risks they posed, such as floods and flash floods, were a constant challenge.

◁
1 – Thailand's capital Bangkok has no centralised water supply network. Up until recently, all wastewater that reached the Chao Phraya river was untreated and then went on to enter the Gulf of Thailand.

1 – Radar image of the coasts of New York, New Jersey and Delaware. The densely populated areas are near the water, and natural harbours form their centres.

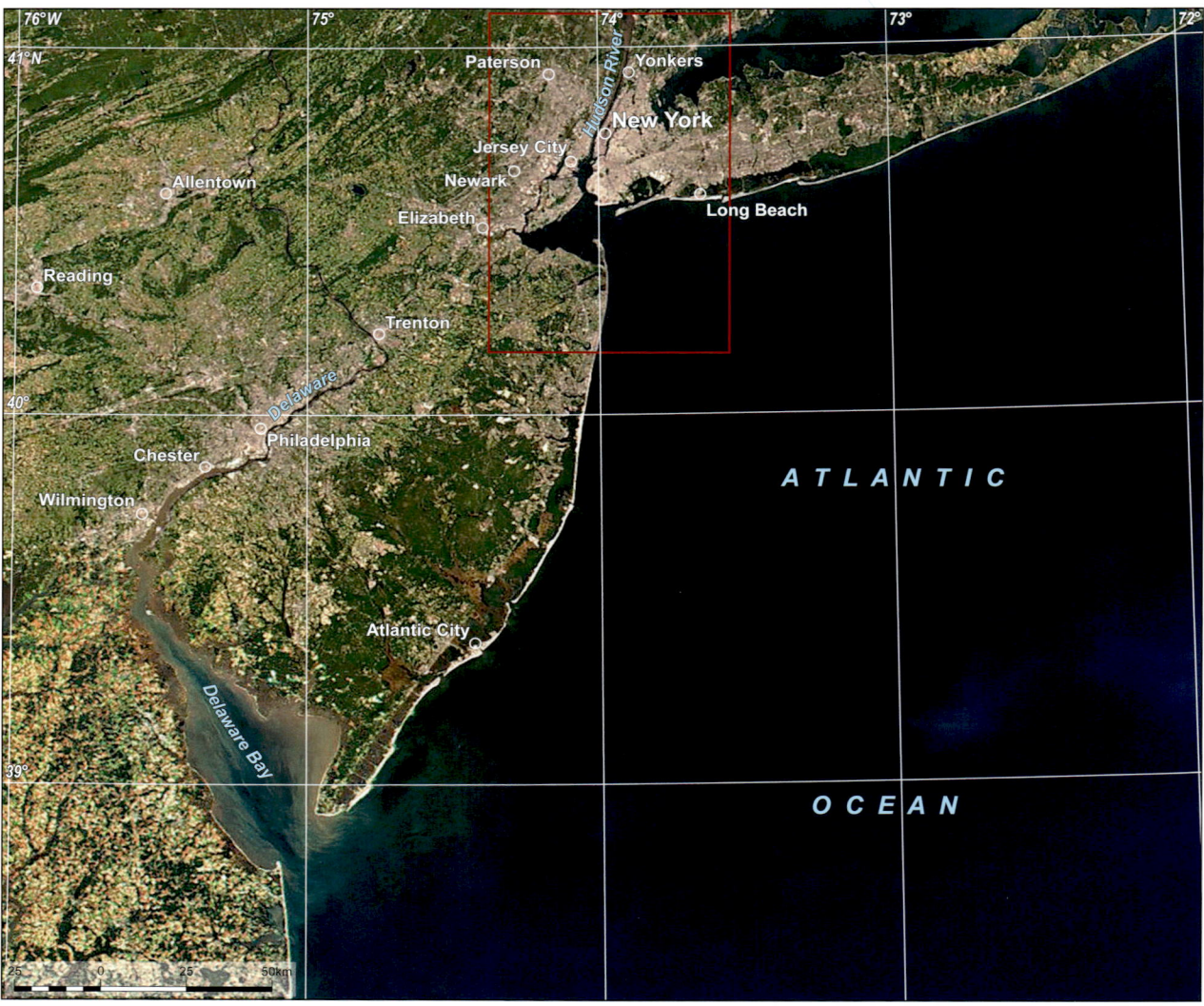

2 – The satellite image in natural colours shows the belt of land use around the settlement and the inland waterways. The settlements developed along the Delaware River in particular.

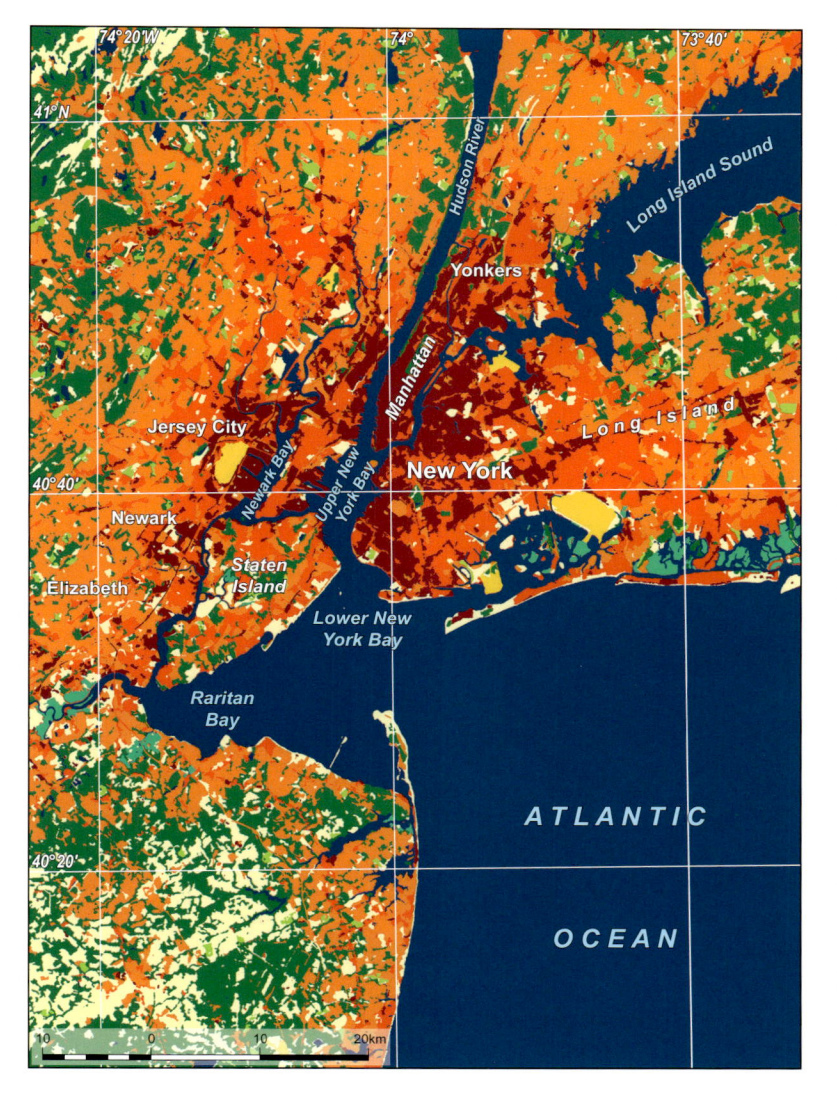

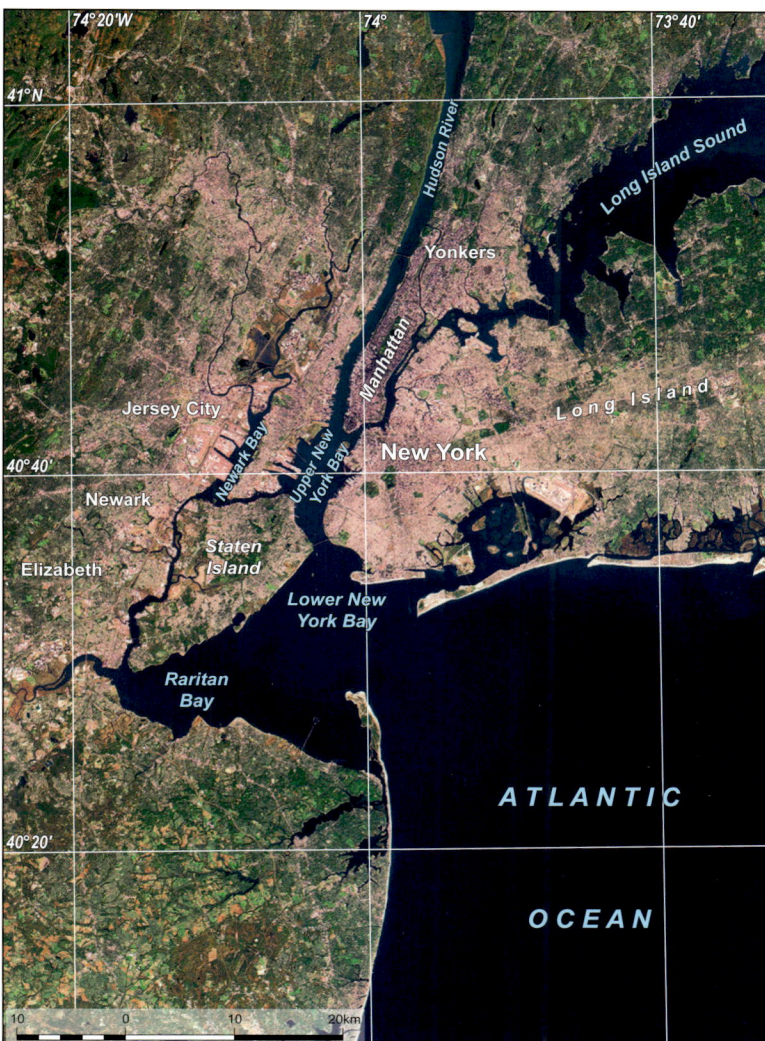

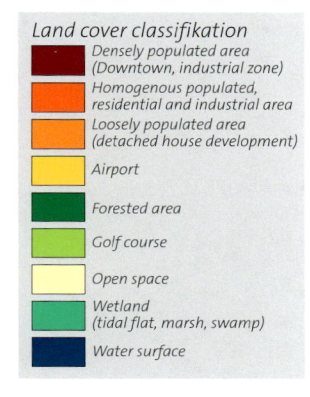

Land cover classifikation
- Densely populated area (Downtown, industrial zone)
- Homogenous populated, residential and industrial area
- Loosely populated area (detached house development)
- Airport
- Forested area
- Golf course
- Open space
- Wetland (tidal flat, marsh, swamp)
- Water surface

△
3a/b – Land use map and satellite image of New York. The port area is the centre of the city, surrounded by areas of lower population density radiating outwards.

Cities built on water

Along many coasts and rivers cities and smaller settlements look strung out like pearls. They appear particularly clearly in night-time images, which show mainly artificial light sources such as road illumination. Often cities can be seen very clearly also in radar images taken by satellites, as the solid surfaces of the buildings are excellently reflecting the radar signals, as for example in the cities along the East Coast of North America, among them New Jersey, New York and Delaware (Figs. 1 and 2).

From a historical point of view, the location by the water provided various advantages, including, with the construction of new ports, good links to shipping routes; guaranteed availability of water for farming, a secure food supply from fishing; but also the possibility for better hygienic conditions by disposing waste in the water, which swept it away. In addition, the higher air humidity and pleasant temperatures of the specific microclimate close to water bodies also provided better air conditions. This more than compensated for the disadvantages.

In the colonisation of far-flung parts of the Earth, it was always the major trading ports on the coasts that explorers reached first that served as bases for the further exploration of the area and as a link with home. The colonised area generally expanded along the coasts and along the rivers leading inland. Nothing changed in this approach to colonisation from the time of the Greeks to the expansion of the British Empire two thousand years later. Another important factor in the siting of a city were possibilities to cross the river via a ford or suitable conditions for building a bridge in order to take a commanding position for the traffic up the river and across it. This strategic location built the foundations for countless political and economic centres of our world.

When deciding on a location, people valued good conditions for defending the settlement, such as building it on a peninsula or in a protected natural harbour. As the historical examples of the Normans and the Vikings show, good accessibility to cities by the water were not in all cases advantageous for the people who lived there. As such, many smaller settlements were divided into a smaller town located by the water and a larger city, which was often fortified, located on a hill (Greek: acropolis), to which the people could retreat in times of danger.

Major cities – the proximity to water

These historical conditions nowadays play a different and often subordinate role as a result of the changes caused by economic, political and technological developments. What has remained is the significance of the growing cities along coastlines and rivers with their ports as important hubs of economic life, around which industry and then service industries, educational institutes and extensive residential areas have been built up. As a result of the positive feedback effect of this accumulation process, many harbour cities that were historically significant have grown in importance until our time. As such, almost all major cities and their conurbations follow this general pattern. Of the largest major cities, most are located near the sea or directly on the coast, as the example of New York shows (Figs. 2 and 3, a/b).

The challenges that water poses to built-up areas are many. They include the need to guarantee efficient and safe transport routes on land and on water, an increased responsibility for protecting the water to keep it usable, and, on the other side, the need for providing reliable protection measures for the population against threats by disastrous floods.

△ △▷
1a/b – Changes in the region around the Lingding Yang delta (Pearl River Delta, China): 1979 (left) and in 2000 (right).

◁◁ ◁
2a/b – The new Chek Lap Kok airport in Hong Kong has made it much easier to fly into the city. The satellite images show the island before and after the building of the airport in 1990 (left) and 2013 (right).

▷△
3 – Land reclamation on the Pearl River Delta (also seen in Fig. 4) primarily serves to create new space for agriculture and aquaculture.
In Kowloon, Hong Kong, however, the ground is used to build new residential areas and industry.

▷▷△
4 – The region around the Pearl River Delta and the megacity of Hong Kong are among the most densely populated areas in South-East Asia. To gain new agricultural land and land for construction, new areas are claimed from the surrounding sea and the delta (see lower legend).

Land reclamation and prosperity

The eastern part of the Pearl River Delta is one of the most affluent areas in China. The driver for prosperity here is the Special Administrative District of Hong Kong, which belonged to the British Empire until 1997. The nearer a city on the Chinese mainland is to Hong Kong, the higher the salaries and land prices. As such, people who live in Shenzhen, which is very near Hong Kong, can expect to earn seven times more per capita than the Chinese average. Shenzhen is one of China's fastest-growing cities (Figs. 1 a and b, 5).

To combat the labour shortage and the constantly rising land prices in the eastern part of the Pearl River Delta, a project was launched in 2009 to build a 50-kilometre long bridge system, which is set to link Hong Kong with the Special Administrative Region of Macau and the Chinese city of Zhuhai once it is completed in 2016. Even before construction began, small and medium-sized businesses had already begun moving to the region. But costs will skyrocket here at the latest by the time the bridge is completed, and maybe before. People are already eyeing new areas to the north of the delta and the provincial capital of Guangzhou (Canton Province) to be able to escape the rising prices for a time.

The area around the eastern part of the Pearl River Delta has been subject to heavy urbanisation since 1979, while the western bank has retained its rural characteristics to this day (Figs. 4, 5). In this time, the aquaculture of seafood and fish has led to a new, forward-looking industry on the shores of the delta. With the decreasing natural fish stocks in the seas and increasingly strict fishing quotas, much more space will be required for aquaculture in the future, boosting the amount of land reclamation used for aquaculture (Fig. 3). To be able to secure the food supply for the growing population, areas of land will be reclaimed from the water to be used for agricultural production. It remains to be seen whether after the Hong Kong-Macau-Zhuhai bridge is built there will be sufficient space left for industry and commerce and building plots for the growing number of workers. Here, too, reclaimed land on the edges of the South China Sea as well as in the Pearl River Delta may be of use. However, the delta region in

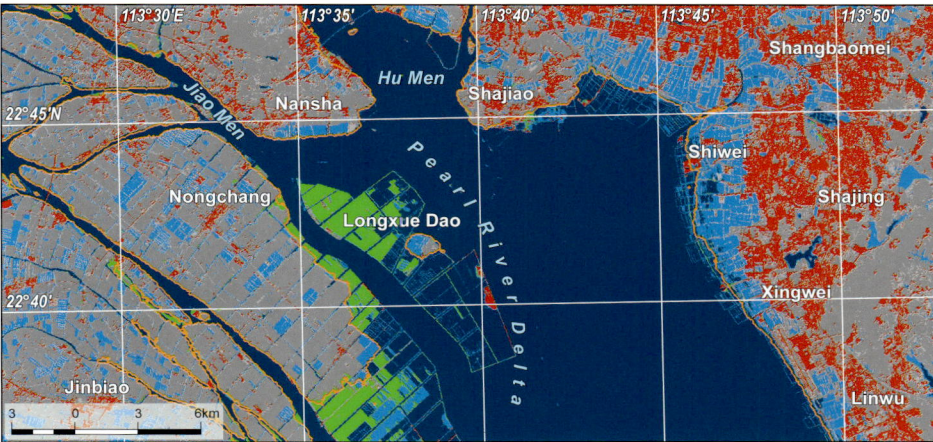

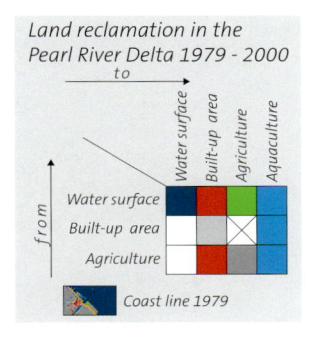

Land reclamation in the Pearl River Delta 1979 - 2000

Land reclamation Hong Kong
- Landfill before 1991
- Landfill after 1991 or already decided
- Planned landfill

▷
5 – The lower reaches of the Pearl River with its delta from Guangzhou to Hong Kong and Macao.

particular is affected by widely ranging water levels and is at high risk of flooding.

In Hong Kong, land reclamation on the coastal areas has a long history. Large parts of Kowloon and Victoria were once coastal waters of the South China Sea. But the space available to the booming population of the megacity continues to be tight, and the area of the city is set to undergo a third expansion (Fig. 4).

One of the most spectacular reclamation projects was probably the construction of Chek Lap Kok airport (Figs. 2a and b). While planes once had to navigate the tips of high-rise buildings in a kind of heart-stopping slalom, they can now approach Hong Kong from across the open sea. The new airport was built on a small island north of Lantau Island. To do this, the island of Chek Lap Kok, which rose to a height of up to 100 metres, was leveled to seven metres above sea level, and 938 hectares of new land were created. In addition to the airport buildings, a completely new city was created for 14,000 inhabitants, and is set to grow further. The transport infrastructure was also completely rebuilt.

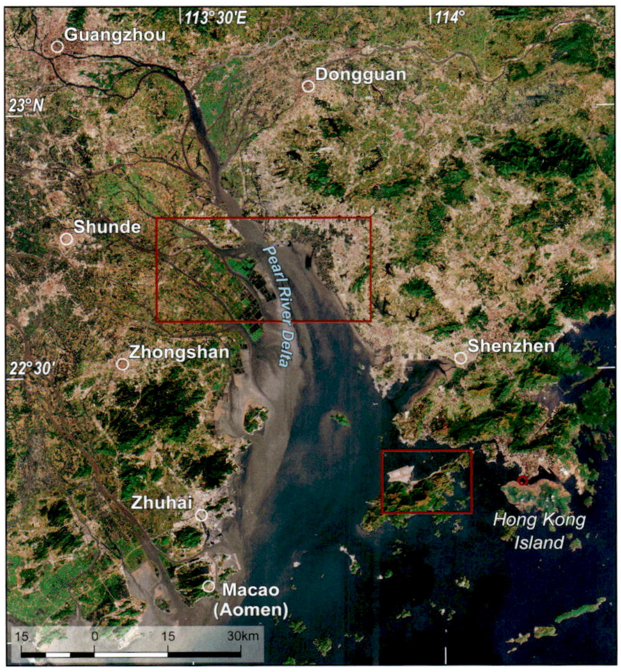

187

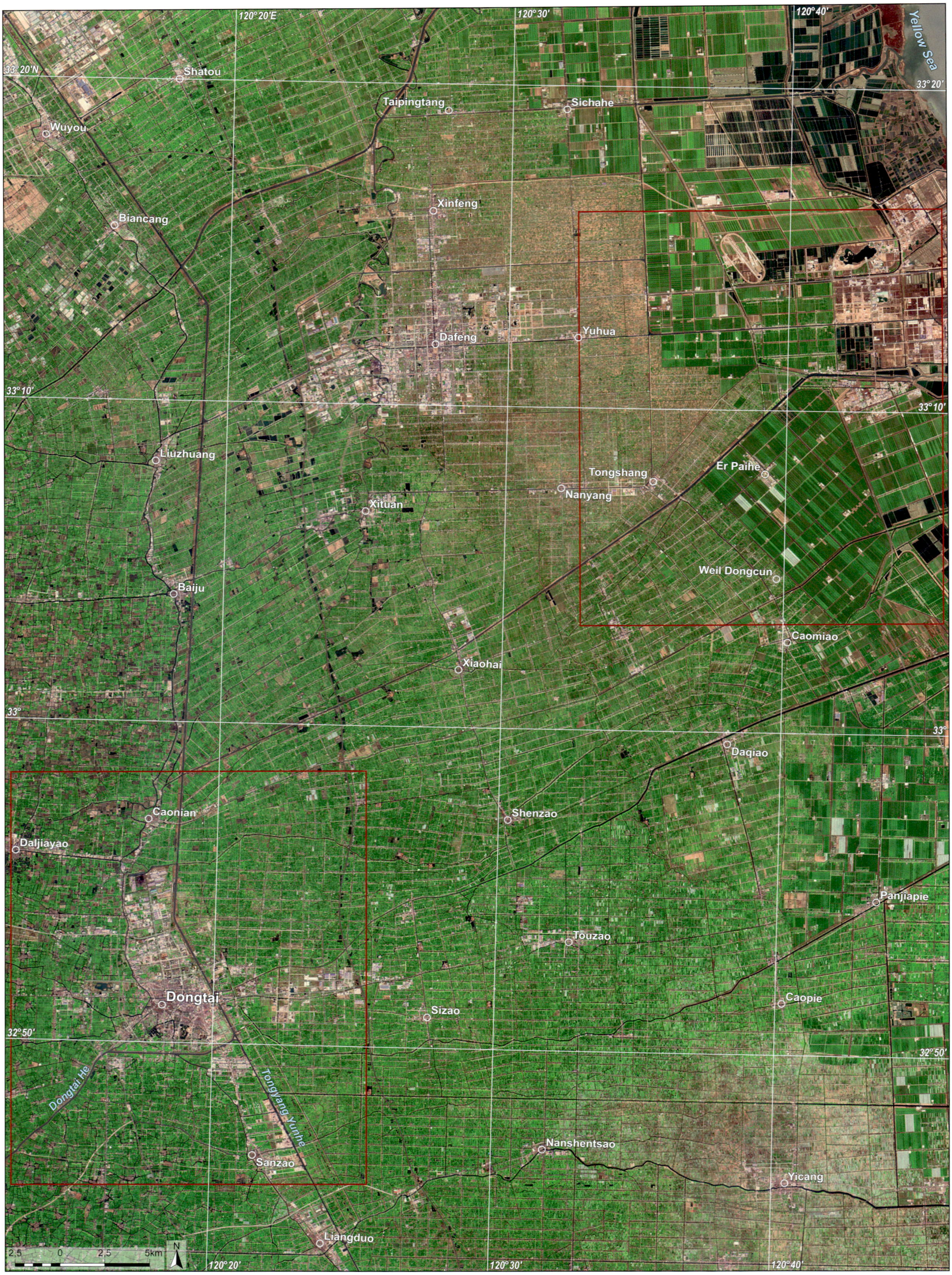

Yellow Sea
120°20'E
120°30'
120°40'
33°20'N
33°20'
33°10'
33°10'
33°
33°
32°50'
32°50'
Shatou
Taipingtang
Sichahe
Wuyou
Xinfeng
Biancang
Dafeng
Yuhua
Liuzhuang
Tongshang
Er Paihe
Nanyang
Xituan
Weil Dongcun
Baiju
Caomiao
Xiaohai
Daqiao
Caonian
Shenzao
Daljiayao
Panjiapie
Touzao
Dongtai
Caopie
Sizao
Dongtai He
Tongyang Yunhe
Nanshentsao
Sanzao
Yicang
Liangduo
2.5 0 2.5 5km
N
120°20'
120°30'
120°40'

1, 2, 3 – Jiangsu Province in the centre of eastern China, with Dongtai as its capital, is criss-crossed by countless canals (image taken in the year 2013). These are used to irrigate the rice and cotton fields (see photo right), and as transport waterways (see photo below). The Grand Canal extends around 80 kilometres to the west of Dongtai (beyond the satellite image).

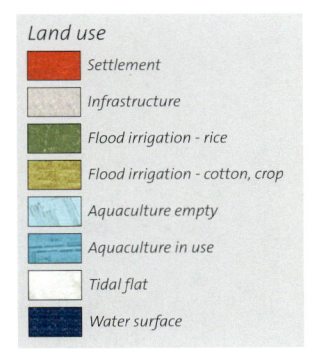

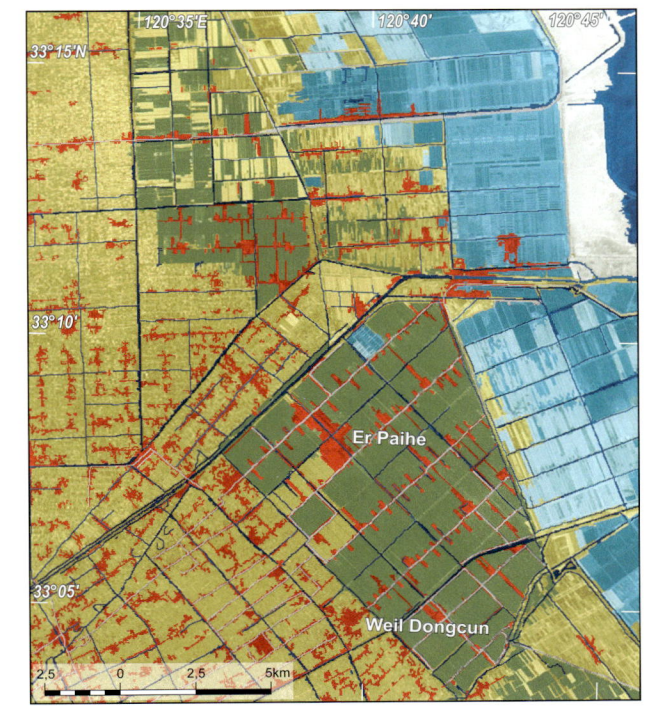

Land use
- Settlement
- Infrastructure
- Flood irrigation - rice
- Flood irrigation - cotton, crop
- Aquaculture empty
- Aquaculture in use
- Tidal flat
- Water surface

4 – Land use map showing a section in the east of Fig. 1 as it looked in the year 2000. For a few years now, it has been not just rice and cotton fields but aquaculture that has come to define the landscape on the coast of Jiangsu.

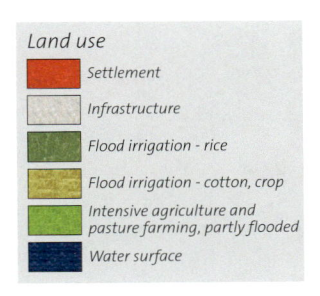

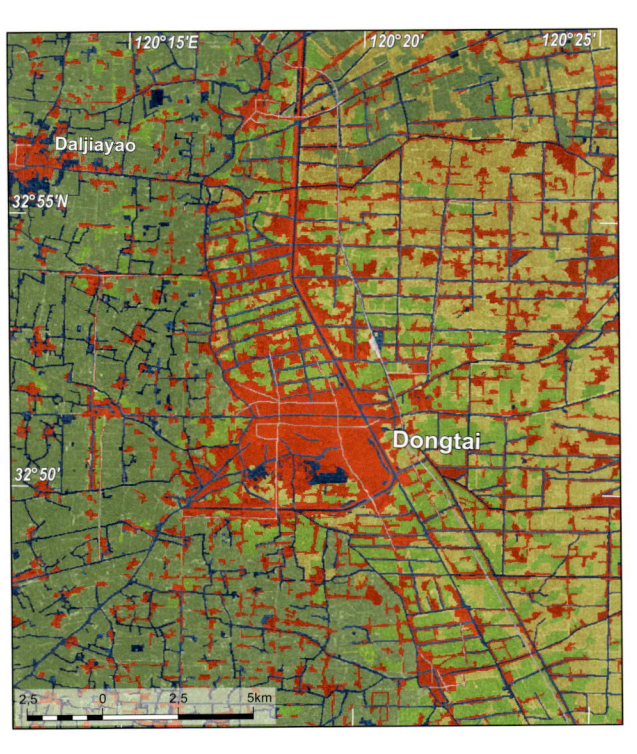

Land use
- Settlement
- Infrastructure
- Flood irrigation - rice
- Flood irrigation - cotton, crop
- Intensive agriculture and pasture farming, partly flooded
- Water surface

5 – The map of the settlement structure around the centre of Dongtai showing the situation of a section in the south-west of the satellite image in Fig. 1 in the year 2000. The settlement structure follows the lines of the irrigation canals.

Spatial patterns of rural settlements in the Jiangsu Province

Jiangsu Province lies in the centre of eastern China, covering both sides of the lower reaches of the Yangtze River. The province's population of 79 million people (2012) makes it, at 770 people per square kilometre, one of the most densely populated provinces in China. At the same time, it is also one of the flattest regions of the country, with an average altitude of only 50 metres above sea level. Of its total area of 102,600 square kilometres, around 17,300 square kilometres are covered by lakes, rivers and canals. In addition to the Yangtze River, which flows for a distance of 400 kilometres through Jiangsu, the province is also home to more than 290 lakes. Two of these, Lake Taihu and Hongze Lake, are among the largest freshwater lakes in China.

The province has an extensive irrigation system which has determined for centuries where the population could live and where land could be farmed. Countless canals, which serve as development axes for the settlements, turn the landscape into a chequerboard. While the rivers from the west flow eastwards into the sea, the main canals flow north–south (Fig. 1).

The canals are used to irrigate the farmland. Due to the excellent availability of water and the mild climate, two harvests a year can be taken. The main crops are rice, wheat and cotton. One promising crop for the future is cotton, grown on new fields along the coast (Fig. 4).

To the west of the city of Dongtai, the network of canals is denser but also less regular than it is in the east (Fig. 5). The clear division between the two zones has been created by a centralised planning system. In accordance with Walter Christaller's theory, the size of regional centres such as Dongtai reflects its central position for the surrounding area.

Owing to its location on the Yangtze River, Jiangsu was the region where the modern industrialisation of China began and is now one of the most developed provinces in the country. However, it too is affected by the exodus of rural populations towards the large cities. As such, the provincial government launched an initiative in the mid-1990s to promote autonomous business locations in order to stem the tide of people moving to the cities. By creating functioning towns, the number of key agricultural workers moving to the towns has now been decreased. In addition to the traditional agriculture, the province's key industries are heavy industry, chemicals and the high-tech sector.

The Grand Canal in China

The Grand Canal, passing around 80 kilometres west of Dongtai, is, at 1,800 kilometres length, even now the longest artificial canal in the world. It links Beijing in the north of China with the Yangtze River delta. Some sections of the canal are up to 2,000 years old and have been maintained to this day. The canal is used for transport and irrigation, and was continually extended throughout countless imperial dynasties. It reached its climax during the Yuan Dynasty (1271–1368), the Ming Dynasty (1368–1644) and the Qing Dynasty (1644–1911), when it was a major waterway used to transport cereals and rice from the fertile south to Beijing. Other canals were built to link up with the Grand Canal from east and west. Roads and an extensive infrastructure for transporting goods were also built in parallel.

The Grand Canal is still in use even today as a regional waterway. However, because of seasonal water shortages in the north of China and the size of modern boats, it is not navigable all year round.

190

MEXICO CITY

Mexico City is the capital of the Latin American country Mexico and one of the biggest cities in the world. The metropolitan area of the city is home to more than 21 million people.

The Metropolitan Area of Valley of Mexico (of which Mexico City is part), spreads over 7,815 square kilometres, of which 1,484 square kilometres are taken up by the capital itself (Fig. 1). At 2,310 metres above sea level, Mexico City is one of the highest capitals on Earth. With more than 21 million inhabitants, the metropolitan area also has the highest population in the country and 20 per cent of Mexico´s entire population. Around 9 million people lived in the city itself in 2013. Mexico City is one of the largest and fastest-growing cities in the world. Between 1990 and 2000, the growth rate for the metropolitan region was 2.9 per cent and 0.4 per cent for Mexico City.

The expanding population, as well as the rapidly increasing industrial, services and commercial activities, have represented a formidable challenge for the institutions responsible for providing the necessary services, including water and sanitation, primarily in terms of management, investments and energy consumption.

Water availability

The water supply in the metropolitan area depends primarily on local groundwater sources and on interbasin transfers. Mexico City, and the most populated 17 municipalities of the State of Mexico, share the same sources of water, as well as the infrastructure for water distribution. In 2002, the volume of water supplied to the metro-

◁
1 – The agglomeration of Mexico City sprawls within the approx. 2,300 m high Valley of Mexico, closed in by mountains. The Popocatépetl and Iztaccíhuatl volcanoes lie southeast of the city.

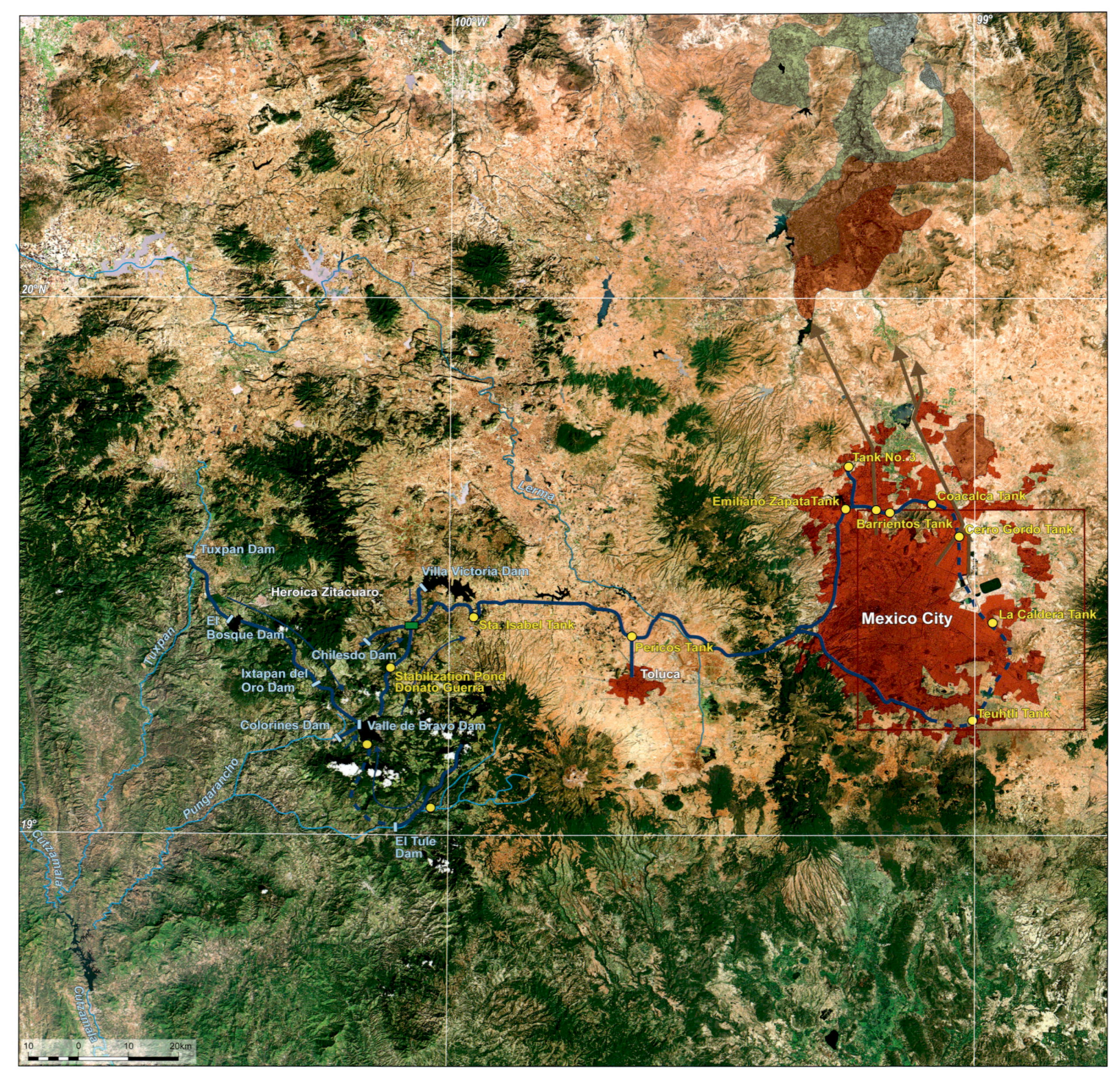

politan area was 2.236 million cubic metres per day. It is estimated that the metropolitan area receives 66 cubic metres per second mainly for domestic supply, with Mexico City receiving about 35 cubic metres per second and 31 cubic metres per second for the State of Mexico. Within Mexico City, the water is distributed to the users through a network of pipelines that stretches for more than 13,000 kilometres. The water supply system comprises 16 dams with a total storage capacity of nearly 2,828 cubic kilometres.

Approximately five per cent of the people living in the metropolitan area and perhaps also beyond, lack access to water (Figs. 1, 2 on p. 194). In these cases, the government provides water through pipes or people buy water from private vendors. Overall, drinking water for much of the population in the metropolitan area comes from 20-litre containers of purified water that are sold commercially. In fact, Mexico is the second largest consumer of bottled water in the world, with consumption at 204.8 litres per person in 2007.

Main sources of water for Mexico City

The metropolitan area is located in the Valley of Mexico basin, which is surrounded by the basins of the Lerma, Cutzamala, Amacuzac and Tecolutla Rivers. The Lerma and the Cutzamala River basins, together with the aquifer of the Valley of Mexico, are the main sources of water for the metropolitan area (Fig. 1). The aquifer of the Valley of Mexico contributes approximately 70 per cent, the Lerma-Balsas River basin nine per cent and the Cutzamala River basins 21 per cent. The very few surface water bodies that still exist in the basin of the Valley of Mexico provide only a small amount of the water supplied.

The average rate of withdrawal from the aquifers is significantly higher than the recharge rate. Between 45 and 54 cubic metres per second are drawn off, but the

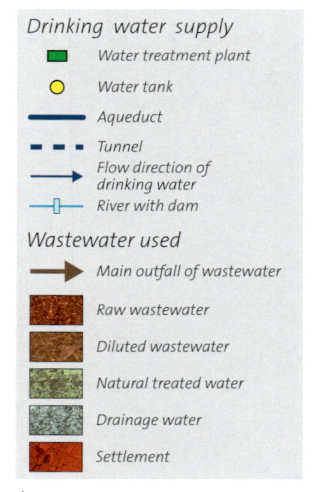

1 – Water supply and disposal for the Mexico City agglomeration.

Subsidence rate *in cm/year*

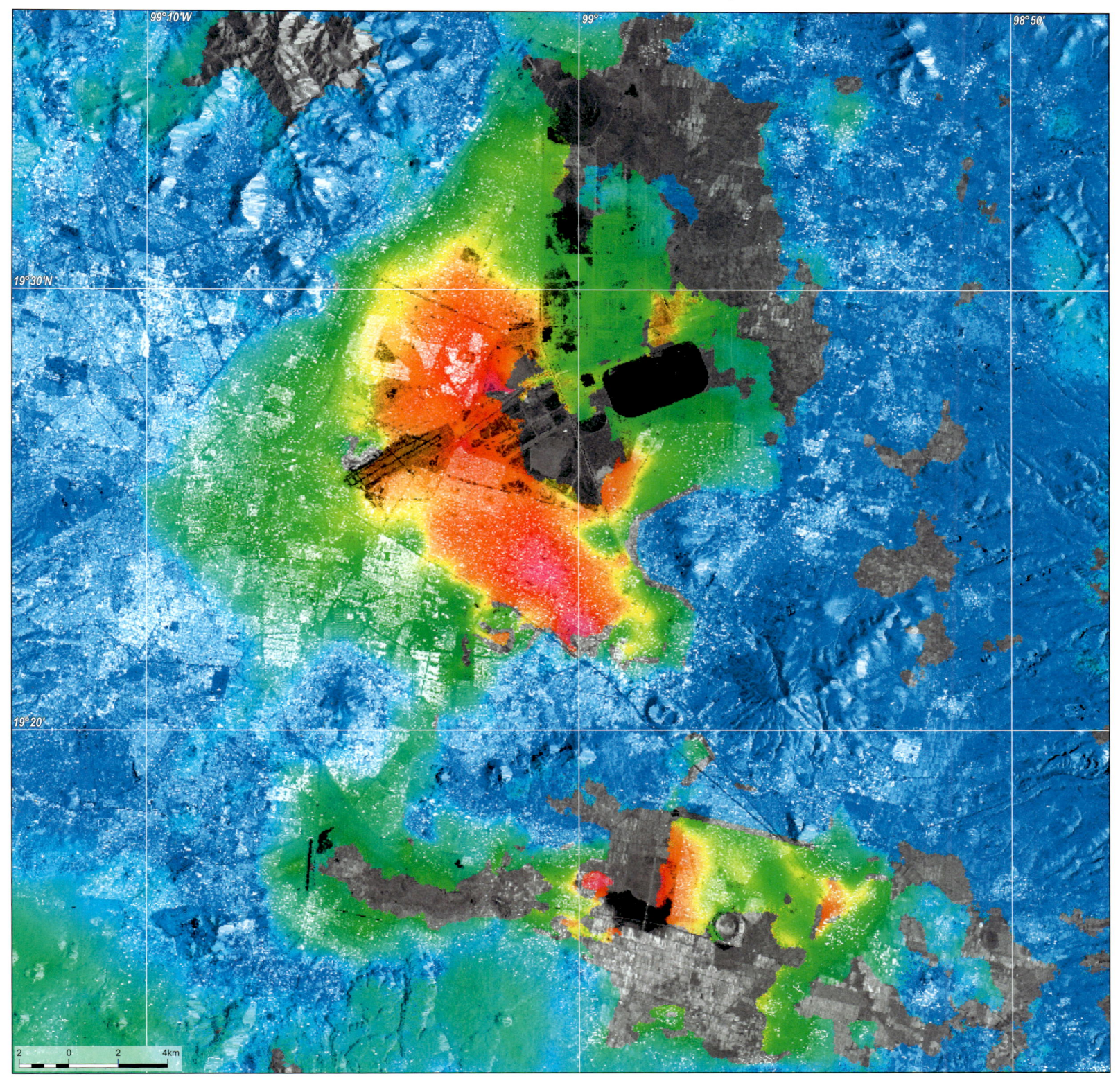

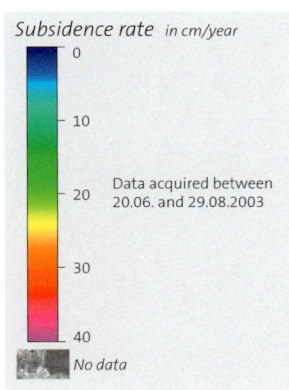

0 — 10 — 20 — 30 — 40

Data acquired between 20.06. and 29.08.2003

No data

2 – Radar interferometry (Envisat ASAR) shows that parts of Mexico City are subsiding by up to 40 cm per year due to the over-extraction of groundwater.

natural recharge rate is only about 20 cubic metres per second. This mismatch has resulted in a significant over-exploitation, which has contributed to the lowering of the groundwater table by about one metre each year. The steady lowering of the groundwater level has increased the land subsidence rate, initially to 10, and later up to 30 to 40 centimetres per year. (Fig. 2).

A high percentage of water in the distribution networks is lost to leakages and illegal connections. Inappropriate overall management, aged pipes, inadequate maintenance over prolonged periods, poor construction practices and continuing land subsidence are all contributing to immeasurable losses of water. Estimates are that more than 40 per cent of the water in the network leaks away, or about 130 litres per person per day. This volume of water would be enough, it is estimated, for four million people.

The programme on drinking water and sanitation of the metropolitan area is considering going ahead with the fourth stage of the Cutzamala project to boost the volume of water brought to the Valley of Mexico from 0.6 (19 cubic metres per second) to 0.76 cubic kilometres per year (24 cubic metres per second). Studies have indicated for years that if the leakages in the distribution system in the metropolitan area were repaired and kept in good condition over time, there would be no need to go ahead with the fourth stage of the project.

In addition to Cutzamala, the other sources of water that the Federal Government has identified for potential contribution to the water supply of the metropolitan area are the Amacuzac, Tecolutla and Atoyac Rivers. For the Amacuzac River project, in addition to the enormous infrastructural development that would be necessary, the annual electric power consumption is estimated to be five per cent of the annual national electric power production, representing 16.5 million barrels of oil per year. It is claimed that this project will make it no longer necessary

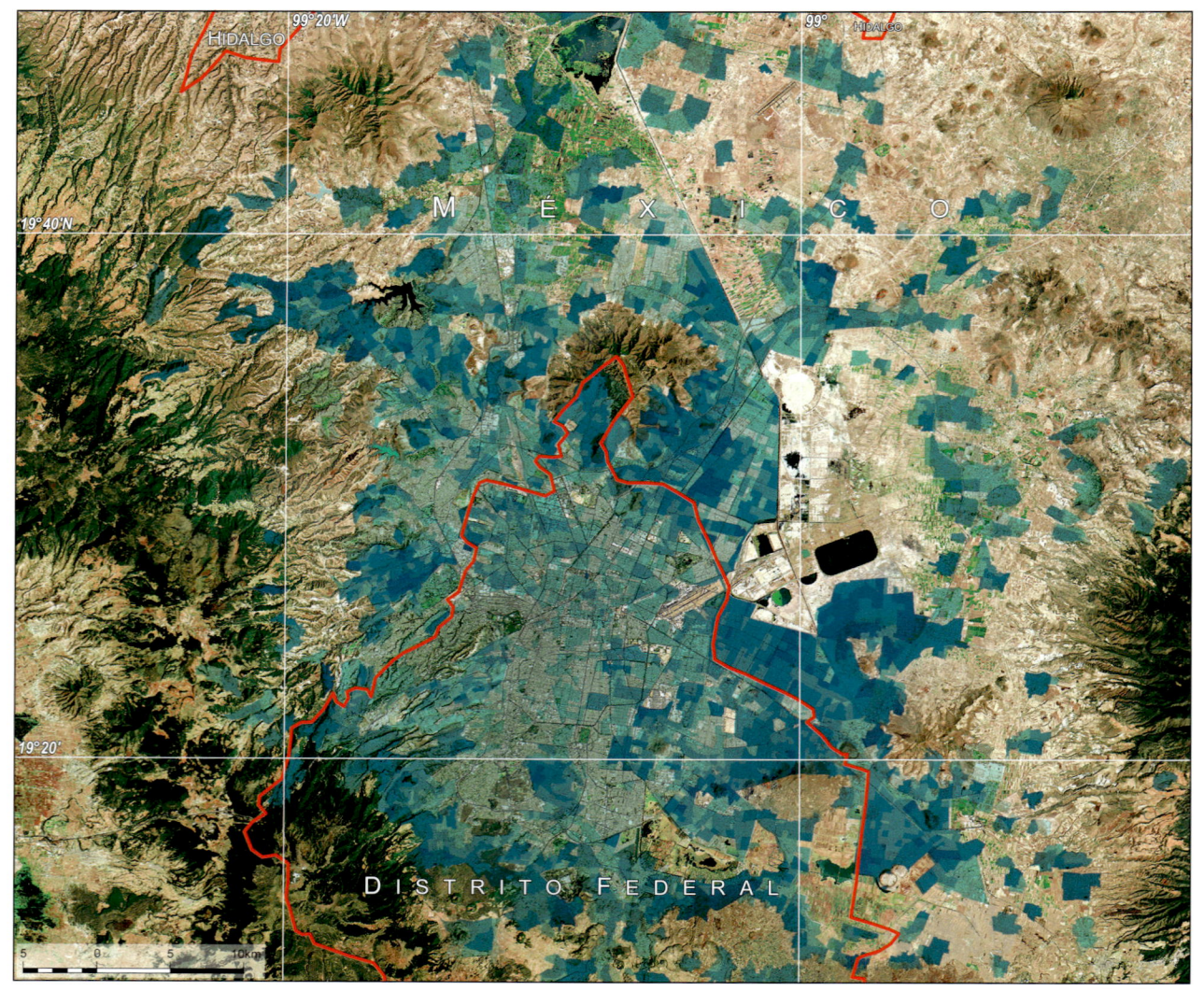

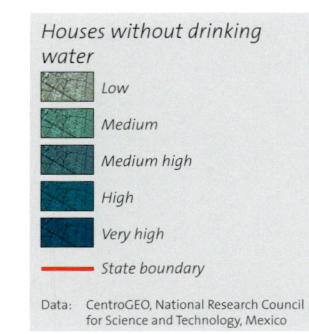

Houses without drinking water
- Low
- Medium
- Medium high
- High
- Very high
- — State boundary

Data: CentroGEO, National Research Council for Science and Technology, Mexico

◁
1 – More than five per cent of Mexico City's inhabitants are not connected to a drinking water supply network. Mexico is the second largest consumer of bottled water in the world.

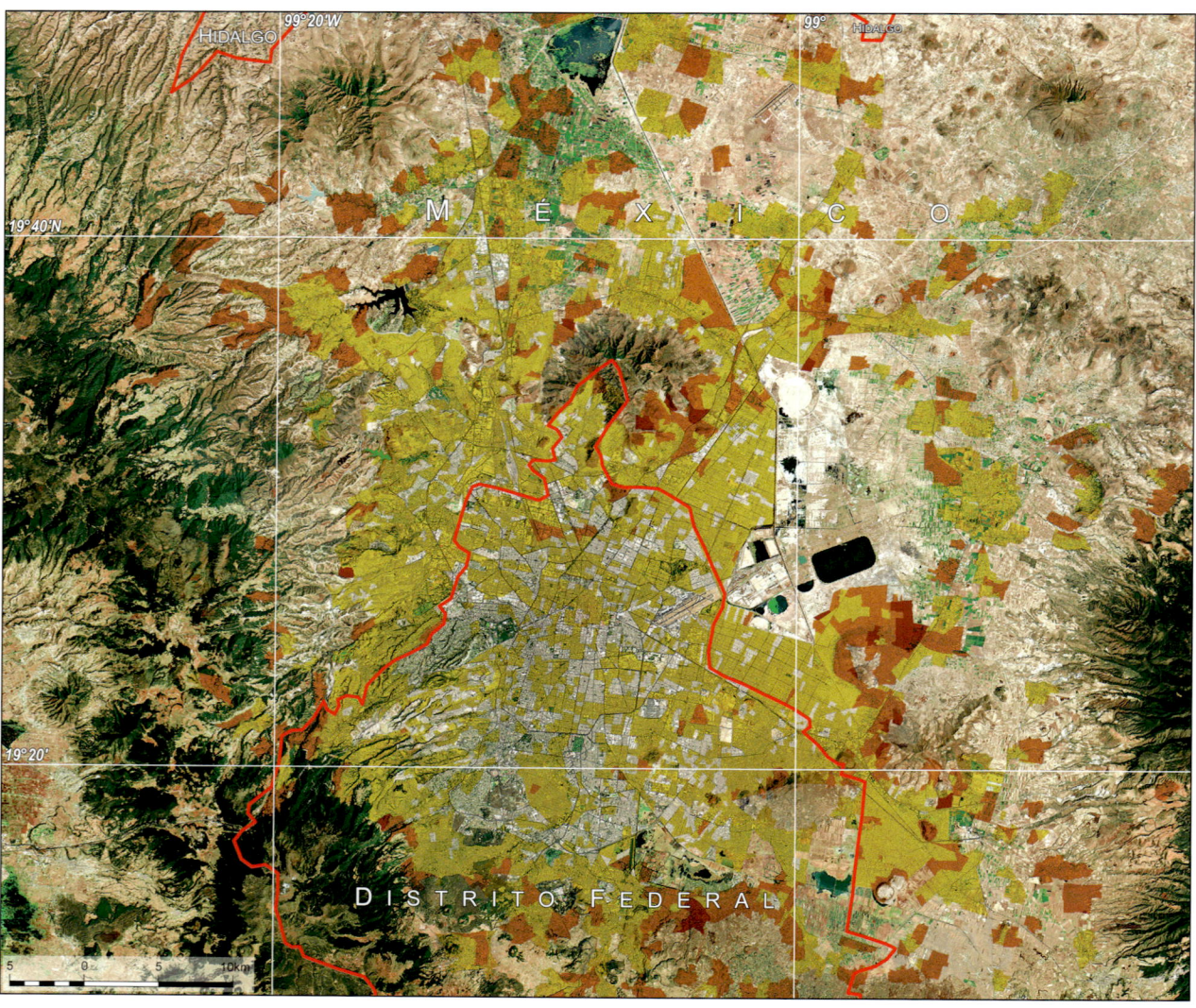

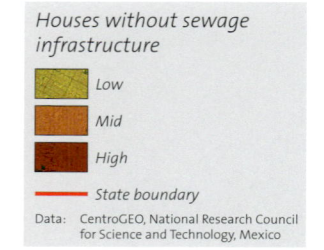

Houses without sewage infrastructure
- Low
- Mid
- High
- — State boundary

Data: CentroGEO, National Research Council for Science and Technology, Mexico

◁
2 – A wastewater disposal network is completely missing in some parts of the city, mainly due to the volcanic ground. Most of the houses use septic tanks, but nevertheless a great amount of untreated wastewater seeps away.

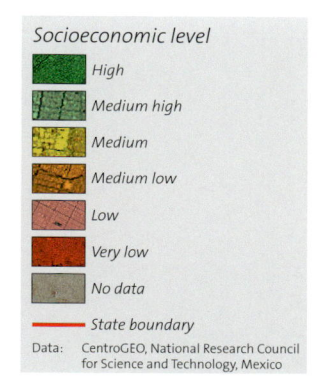

Socioeconomic level
- High
- Medium high
- Medium
- Medium low
- Low
- Very low
- No data
- State boundary

Data: CentroGEO, National Research Council for Science and Technology, Mexico

▷
3 – The access to drinking water supply and to wastewater disposal networks is reflected in the socioeconomic levels of Mexico City.

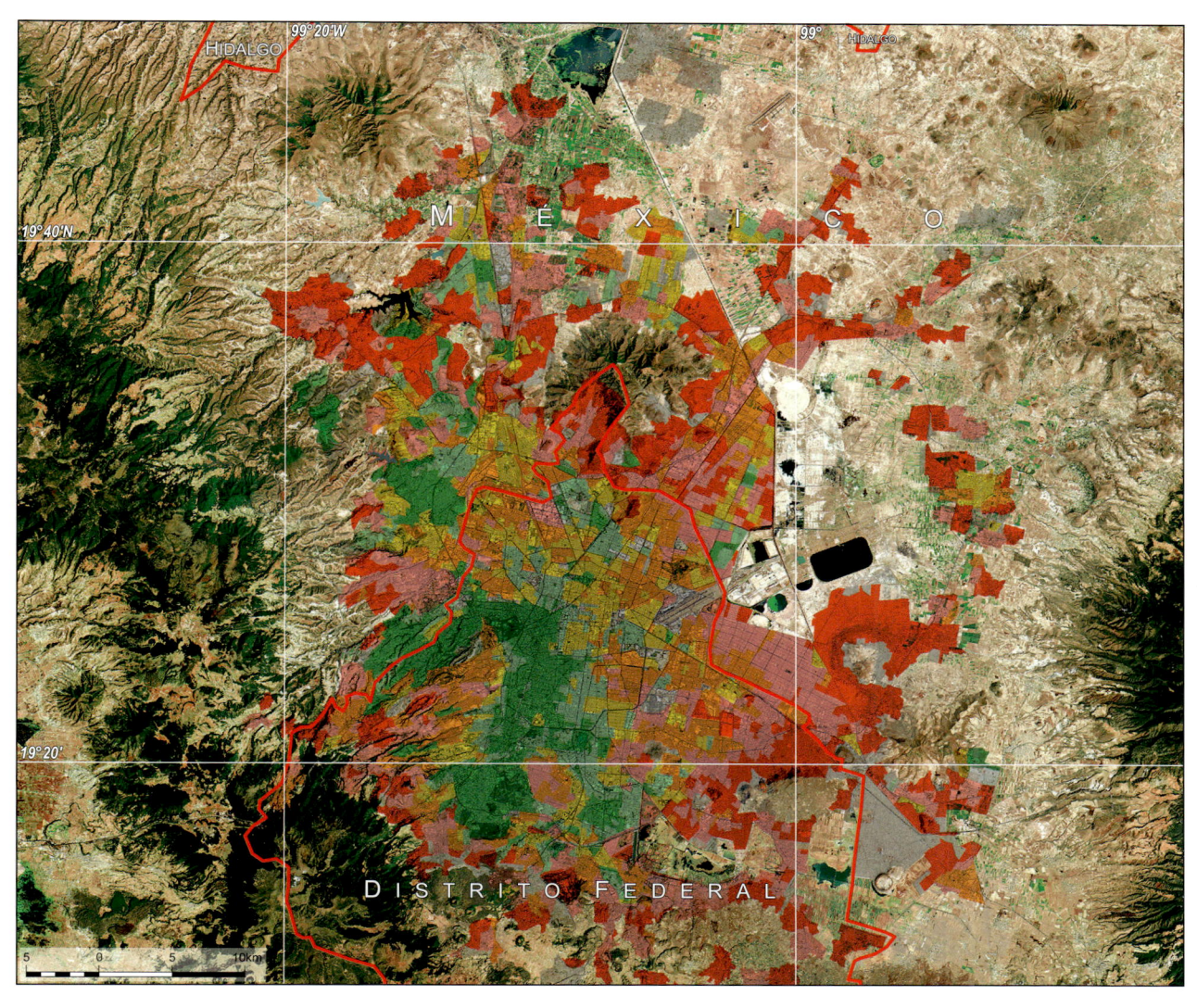

▽
4 – Dating back into the early 18th century, Mexico City's Chapultepec Aqueduct is based on an even older Aztec construction.

to draw off 50 cubic metres per second of groundwater from the Valley of Mexico aquifer. The rational is that the groundwater would be used only during severe droughts, or when the other water distribution systems shut down for maintenance. It has been estimated that, while each cubic metre of water from the Cutzamala River has required an investment of 23 million dollars, this estimate would increase four-fold for the Amacuzac River Project. Alternatives to this infrastructural development could be reduction of losses, water pricing and other water conservation practices.

Wastewater management

The soil of Mexico City is basically clay, and thus susceptible to compaction. Accordingly, the higher the volume of water abstracted, the higher the rate of land subsidence. The sinking of the city has resulted in extensive damages to its infrastructure, including water supply and sewerage systems and degradation of the groundwater quality. It has also required the construction of costly pumping stations to remove wastewater and stormwater from the city. The average volume of waste- and stormwater discharged into the metropolitan area sewerage system is about 2,897 million cubic metres, of which only six per cent is treated.

Since the city is located within a naturally closed hydrologic basin, it is especially vulnerable to floods. Throughout history, artificial channels had to be constructed to bear waste- and stormwater away from the city. The rainy season in the metropolitan area is characterised by storms of high intensity over short duration. The average annual rainfall in the city is 800 millimetres: 500 in the eastern part and around 1000 towards the southern and western parts. The main collector of the Deep Sewerage was designed to carry about 200 cubic metres per second of water over a 45-hour period. However, it has carried up to 340 cubic metres per second. Such sudden fluctuations in the amounts of water create major operational and maintenance problems. The 62-kilometre underground wastewater tunnel Túnel Emisor Oriente was started in 2009 and it is scheduled to be completed in 2014 (Fig. 1, p. 192). This eastern tunnel has been primarily built for flood control. It will provide support for the existing Emisor Central drainage tunnel (Deep Sewerage Tunnel).

The problems of water quantity and quality in the metropolitan area are multidimensional and are directly linked to regional economic development policies and steady increases in population. The government policies have attempted to promote the development of other urban centres to alleviate poverty and to provide improved standards of living as well as quality of life. One constraint stems from the fact that the demand for living spaces from the increasing population has contributed to major changes in land-use practices. Concrete and asphalt now cover areas that are needed for groundwater recharge. The southern area of the city is now heavily urbanised and hence is also one of the main sources of groundwater contamination due of the absence of a sewerage network, which cannot be built at a reasonable cost (Fig. 2).

Lastly, there is no doubt that the potential for improving the existing and proposed water management practices is enormous. In order to be successful, it needs concurrently to consider linkages to policies on urban development (an issue that has been so far ignored), spatial planning and economic and environmental policy.

Text: Cecilia Tortajada

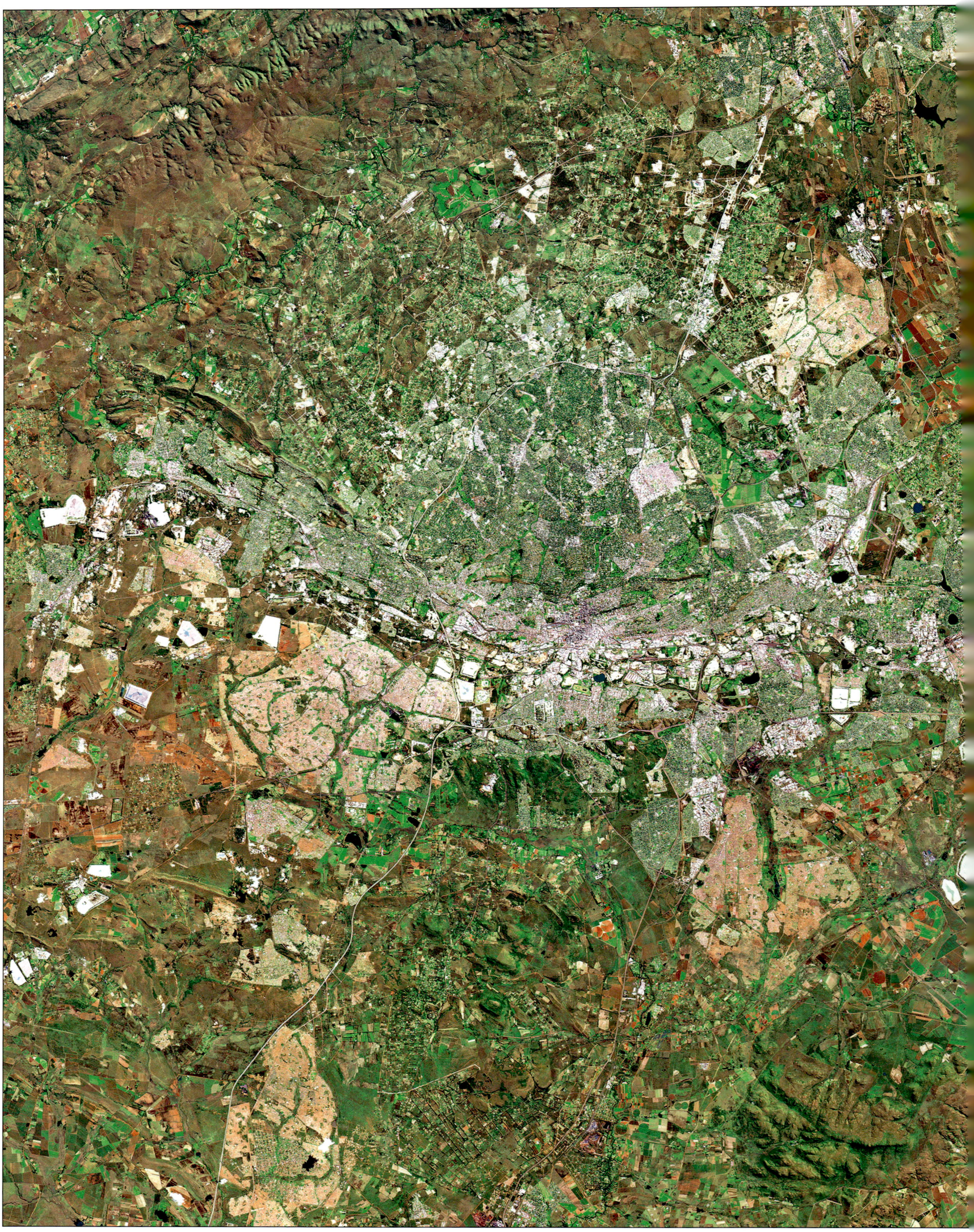

JOHANNESBURG

Johannesburg is one of the few major cities in the world that is not situated directly on a river, lake or sea. Located on the gold-rich Witwatersrand, it is not the capital of South Africa, but it is the country's most populous city.

Johannesburg lies 1,800 metres above sea level on the eastern part of the South African Inland Plateau, also known as the Highveld. The climate enjoys plenty of sunshine and is usually dry. In the summer months of October to April, storms and rain showers are common in the late afternoon. The temperatures in Johannesburg are mild, with a maximum average temperature in summer of 26 degrees Celsius. Most of South Africa is influenced by the south-east trade winds from the Indian Ocean. These air currents transport humid air masses from the warm Indian Ocean towards Africa. The annual rains that fall with the trade winds amount, on average, to 600 to 800 millimetres (Fig. 3, p. 198) and generally fall between October and April.

Urban development

A good hundred years ago, the area where the economic and industrial centre of South Africa now lies was untouched savannah. This changed very quickly when the first gold was found here in 1886. With the start of the gold rush, a small mining settlement developed to house thousands of workers, mainly from the UK, who came to find their fortunes. Within the next ten years, the settlement grew into a city of over 100,000 people. In the decades that followed, the former mining town turned into one of the country's biggest and most powerful financial centres. Today, around one quarter of the entire population of South Africa lives in this region, in Gauteng province. Countless shaft towers and mining pits, which cross the city in a wide band, bear witness to the soil's wealth.

◁
1 – South Africa's largest city is located in the centre of a rich gold mining area.

Water supply

Johannesburg, a city of 4.43 million people (2011), is very interesting from a hydrological point of view. It is one of the few major cities in the world that are not located on a river, lake or sea coast (Fig. 1). Johannesburg lies on a continental watershed, the Witwatersrand, from which rivers flow either eastwards to the Indian Ocean or westwards to the Atlantic (Figs. 2 and 3). The city also lies between the catchment basins of the Orange and Limpopo rivers, two major transboundary water catchment basins.

The water supply of Johannesburg is maintained by the company Rand Water, one of the biggest waterworks companies in the world. With a capacity of six million cubic metres of water per day, it provides water to around 12.3 million people in the metropolitan region.

At the beginning of the 20th century, Rand Water obtained groundwater from the Zuurbekom springs. The water was of high quality and did not need to be pretreated before providing it to the customers. When the spring water was no longer sufficient to meet the demand of the fast-growing city, the Vaal, a river to the south of Johannesburg, was used as an additional reservoir for drinking water. Part of the river was dammed as far back as 1923. Today, two of the most important reservoirs for drinking water are on the Vaal River: the Vaal Dam and the Grootdraai Dam (Fig. 4). The Vaal Dam reservoir is now used to store also water received from the Lesotho Highlands Water Project.

The Lesotho Highlands Water Project

The Lesotho Highlands Water Project (LHWC) is a major damming project set up by the Kingdom of Lesotho and the Republic of South Africa to provide the arid region of Gauteng and the region around Johannesburg with drinking water (Fig. 4). The specific aim of this project is to direct water from the rivers in the Highlands of Lesotho, against the natural direction of flow, to Johannesburg, around 300 kilometres away, by building several dams, transfer tunnels and pumping stations. After all five dams are completed, 50 per cent of the water in Lesotho will be directed to Gauteng Province.

The first construction phase started in 1989 with the building of the Katse Dam. The arch dam, located in the Maluti Mountains, is 180 metres high and 700 metres long (Fig. 5). Finished in 1996, the construction dams the Malibamat'so River. Water from the Katse Dam is drained into the Muela Reservoir via a 45-kilometre-long underground pipeline. From there, it is transported to the Liebenbergs Vlei River, which empties into the Vaal Reservoir via another tunnel system.

A second major dam was completed as part of the project in 2002. The Mohale Dam lies on the Senqunyane River and is linked with the Katse Reservoir via a tunnel (Fig. 7). This means that two of the five dams are now complete. The project also foresees the construction of the Mashai, Tsoelike and Ntoahae dams.

The total cost of the project has been predicted to be around USD 8 billion. The Kingdom of Lesotho will earn income from selling the water and, in addition, the Muela Power Station will generate 72 megawatts of electricity. The project has also had a positive effect on Lesotho's infrastructure because roads had to be built in order to construct the dams.

During the recent years, Lesotho has been hit hard by several long periods of drought, which jeopardised the supply of drinking water. Critics of the project have said that the water is exported at the expense of Lesotho's development and that less water now enters the Or-

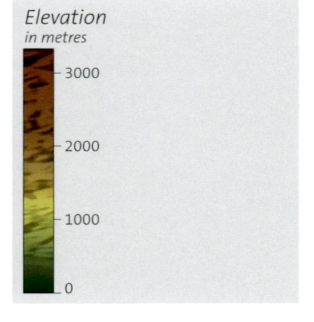

1 – The large, transboundary river catchment basins of southern Africa. The megacities of Pretoria (Tshwane) and Johannesburg are located in a natural savannah landscape (LS Lesotho, MOZ Mozambique, MW Malawi, SZ Swaziland).

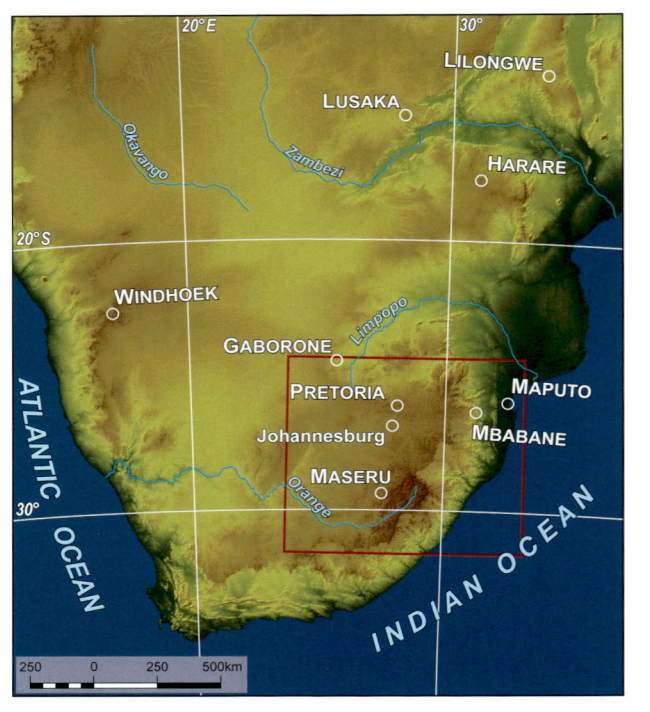

2 – The Highveld, the eastern part of the South African Inland Plateau, is the watershed upon which Pretoria (Tshwane) and Johannesburg are located.

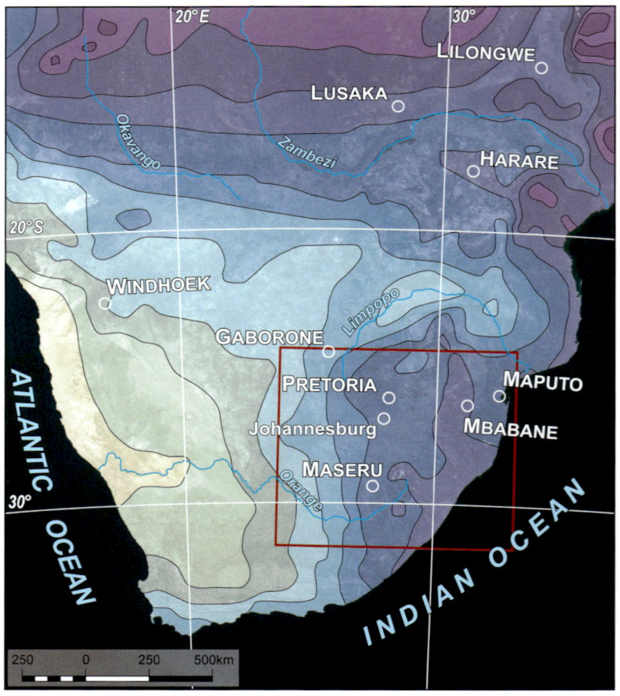

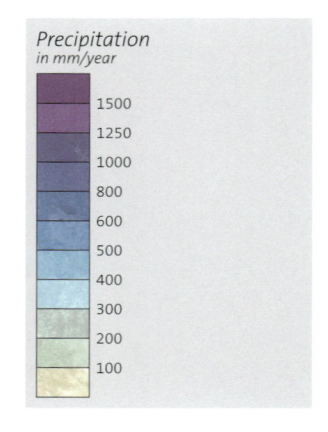

3 – The rainfall map of southern Africa shows the influence of the life-bringing south-east trade winds on the east coast, and the southern offshoots of the Intertropical Convergence Zone in the north.

▷
4 – The Lesotho Highlands Water Project is still in the development stage. Some dams and tunnels are already in place, while others are yet to be built. The project aims to provide water to the central Gauteng province with the city of Johannesburg.

△
5 – The Katse Dam in the Maluti Mountains was the first construction in the Lesotho Highlands Water Project. The dam wall stands 180 metres high.

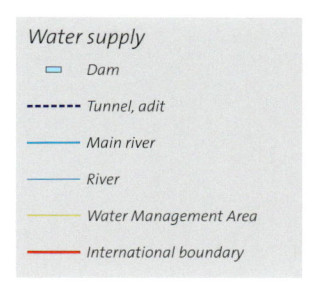

Water supply
- Dam
- Tunnel, adit
- Main river
- River
- Water Management Area
- International boundary

▷
6 – Rainwater is not the only source of freshwater here. Sewage is treated and fed back into the river system, as shown here in Soweto.

△
7 – The Mohale Reservoir is part of the Lesotho Highlands Water Project. It is linked to the Katse Reservoir via a tunnel.

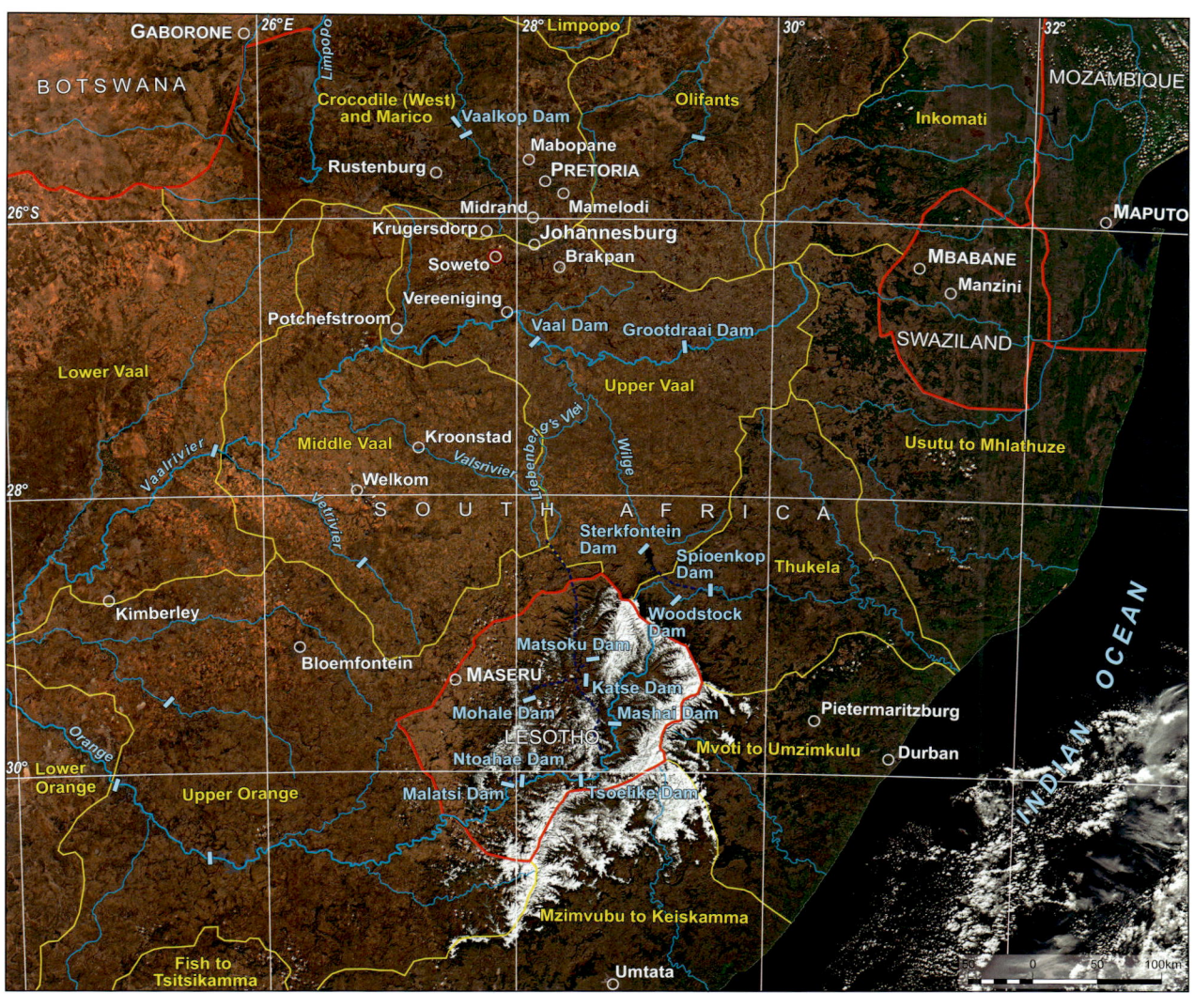

ange River system. In addition, some villages had to be relocated in order to build the dams and large areas of fertile farmland were lost.

The Vaal Dam

The water from the mountains of Lesotho is stored in the reservoir of the Vaal Dam, 56 kilometres south of Johannesburg (Fig. 4). The Vaal Dam is the largest reservoir in South Africa, it has an area of 300 square kilometres and is 47 metres deep at its deepest point. After being treated, the water is pumped to Johannesburg via a system of pipelines. Between the Vaal River and the region around the Highveld, the water has to be transported across a difference in altitude of 380 metres. As a result, huge amounts of energy and money are required to provide the metropolitan region with drinking water.

Wastewater treatment in Johannesburg

Around 800 million litres of wastewater are treated every day in numerous sewage treatment plants in and around Johannesburg (Fig. 6). Around ten per cent of the water treated is used as cooling water in power stations and eight per cent is used to irrigate farmland. The remaining water is returned to the river system and thus can be re-used for drinking water. Currently six wastewater treatment plants are in operation in Johannesburg. Of these, Olifantsvlei Wastewater Treatment Works and Northern Wastewater Treatment Works have the largest capacities, treating 220 million litres and 410 million litres per day respectively. There are already plans to expand these sewage plants.

Text: Anthony Turton

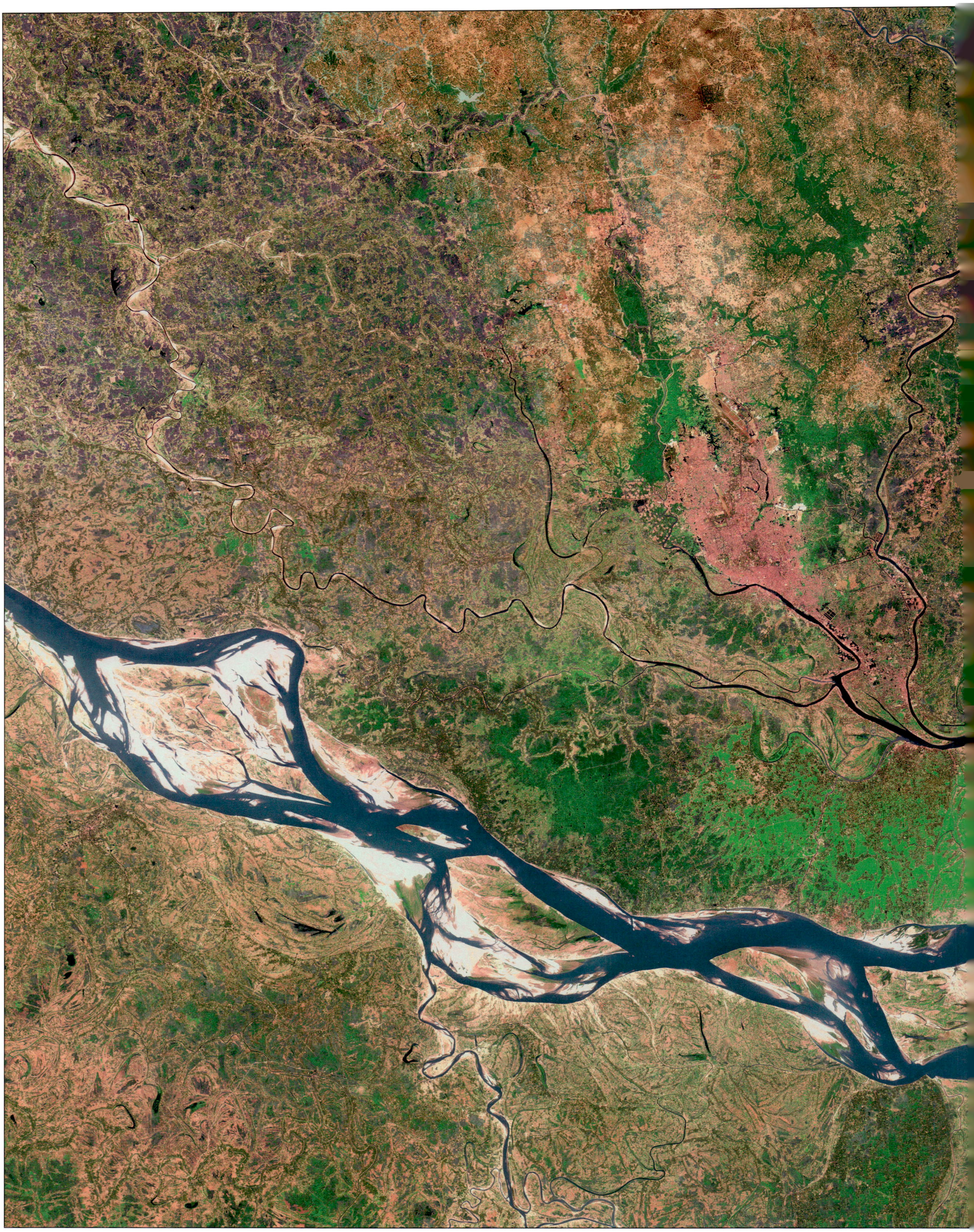

DHAKA

With a population of around 14.4 million, Dhaka is characterised by its high frequency of flooding and by social and political conflicts. Regular floods cause massive damage and worsen the already poor health and hygiene conditions.

Bangladesh is one of the world's most densely populated countries. According to the Bangladesh Bureau of Statistics, more than 149 million people were living on an area of 147,570 square kilometres in 2011, with the population growing by a further 1.6 per cent every year. The growth rate is highest in the capital, Dhaka, at five per cent. The city is situated on the Buriganga, a branch of the Dhaleswari and a tributary of the Meghna. Dhaka is the administrative, industrial and economic centre of the country. Due to its geographical location in the floodplains of the Ganges and Brahmaputra deltas, as well as the high population growth, the city faces numerous problems.

Monsoon floods

The climate in Bangladesh, characterised by very heavy rainfall in the summer and relatively dry and mild winters, is determined by the monsoon (Fig. 4, p. 203). Seventy-five per cent of the country's rainfall arrives in the rainy season from June to September. In the summer months, the warm, humid South-West Monsoon blows in from the Gulf of Bengal, bringing with it drenching downpours. In the winter, the weather is dominated by dry east winds and the cool, dry North-East Monsoon. As such, annual rainfall is less than 1,270 millimetres in the west of the country but can be over 5,000 millimetres in the northeast. Depending on the severity, up to 70 per cent of the country can be hit by flooding. The causes of the monsoon floods are primarily the physical geography of the country, but also, increasingly, anthropogenic factors such as deforestation and badly managed dam projects. In addition to local rainfall in Bangladesh itself, severe flooding is also caused by the combination of heavy rainfall and snowmelt in the catchment basin of the transboundary rivers.

◁
1 – The main branches of the Brahmaputra (Jamuna) and Ganges (Padma) meet in the alluvial plain west of Dhaka (off the image). Coming from the west, the combined river then meanders southeast of the city until it merges with the Meghna (within the image).

◁
1 – Dhaka in the dry season. There is very little land left outside the city that is not built up or farmed. As the water overflows the river banks during the monsoon, there is very little land for it to flow into without causing damage.

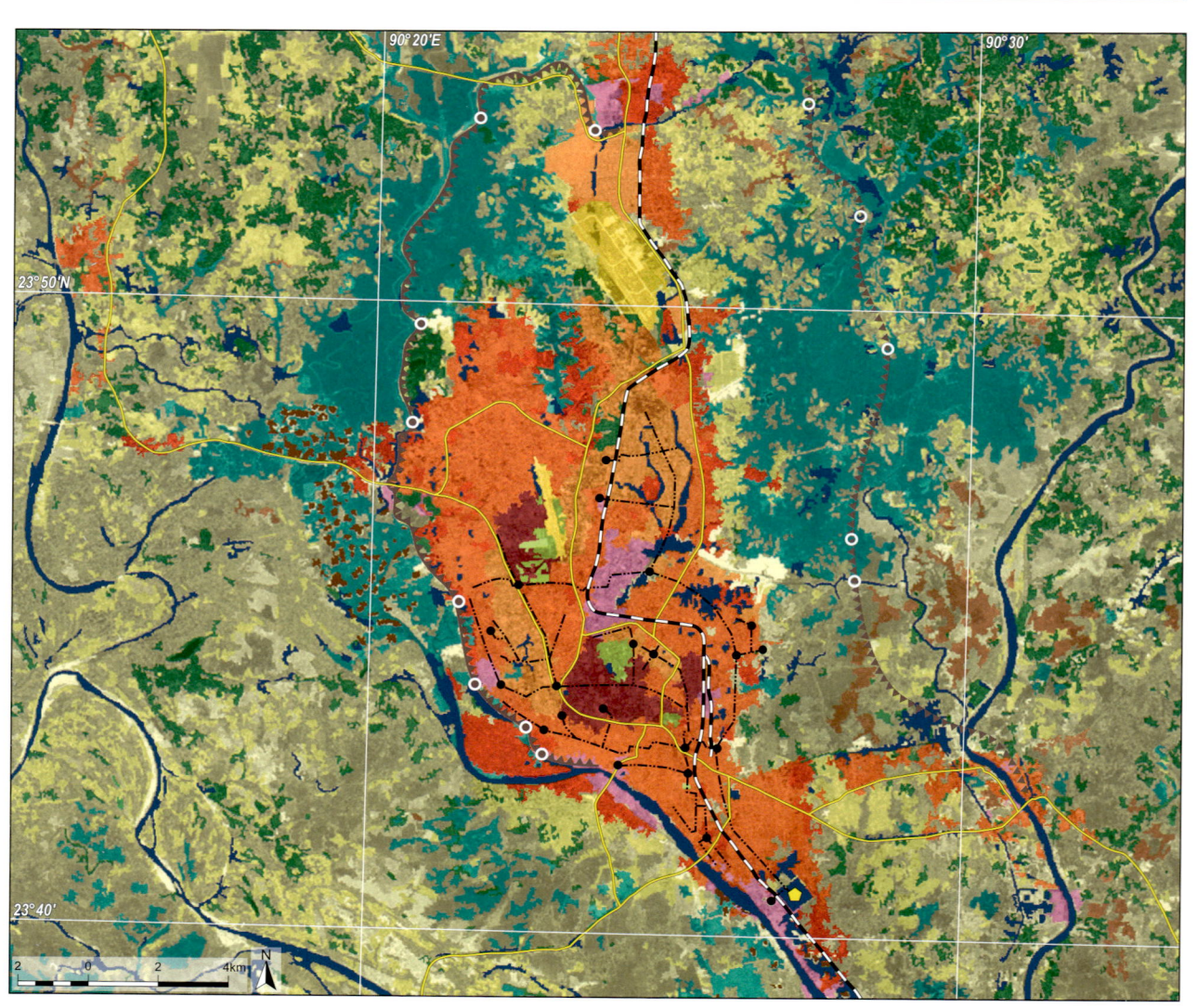

◁▽
2 – The amount of land required for building leads to shrinking retention areas. As a consequence, countless flood protection measures, including dams and lockgates, are essential to the population's survival.

Settlement patterns and land use

- Upper-class quarter
- Middle-class quarter
- Barracks and slums
- Rustic settlement with agriculture
- Administrative utility
- Business and industry
- Airport
- Clay digging and brickyard
- Public park
- Forest
- Shrubs
- Sparse vegetation
- Flood basin
- Swamp
- Water surface
- Main traffic route
- Railway
- Dam for flood portection
- Planded dam for flood protection
- Waste-water disposal line
- Sewer
- Lock gate
- Planed lock gate
- Waste-water treatment plant

3 – Every year in the rainy season, floods threaten the city and its surroundings, often resulting in devastation.

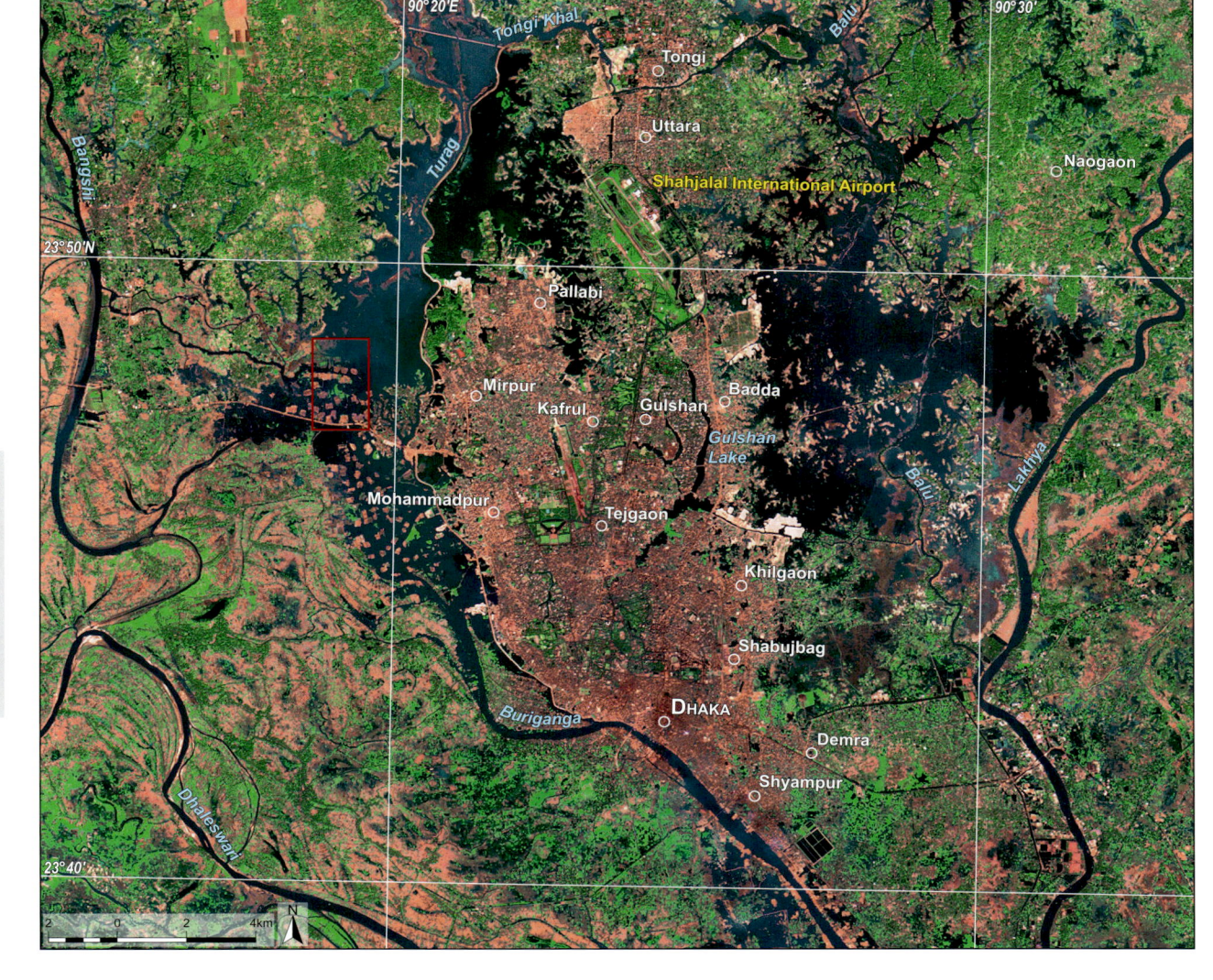

4 – Climate graph for Dhaka. When the South-West Monsoons arrive, rainfall increases dramatically. Many rivers overtop their banks and flood large parts of the country.

5 – In the dry season, clay is removed from the floodplains and baked into bricks in brickworks; this one is located in the west of Dhaka.

6 – Detailed image of the brickworks near Dhaka.

There is the confluence of the Padma (Fig. 1, pp. 200/201) and the Meghna to the south of Dhaka, which overflow their banks during the rainy season (Figs. 1, 3). The monsoon also pushes the water masses from the Gulf of Bengal to the coast, causing a damming effect that obstructs the heightened water flows coming down through the river system. As a result of the increased amount of paved area and the draining of wetlands, less and less land is available to function as natural floodplains (Fig. 4).

Drinking water supply and wastewater disposal

Wastewater disposal networks are highly underdeveloped in Dhaka. Currently, only 30 per cent of homes are connected to the sewage system. According to estimates, a further 30 per cent use 50,000 septic tanks and 15 per cent use latrines. The remaining households drain their sanitary water in open water bodies and on the road. Most of the infrastructure is in bad condition due to poor maintenance. As such, sewage channels regularly overflow during the rainy season, which leads to a lack of hygiene, facilitating the spread of disease.

Eighty-two per cent of the city's drinking water requirements are met with groundwater pumped from more than 390 wells. The remaining 18 per cent comes from the city's three water treatment plants. Before Saidabad, the largest of the water treatment plants, was completed, 97 per cent of drinking water came from boreholes. The city's first modern water supply system went into operation in 1874. Today, in addition to the 390 wells and water treatment plants, the water network comprises 2,400 kilometres of pipes, 216,800 connections and 38 reservoirs.

Text: Khondaker Azharul Haq

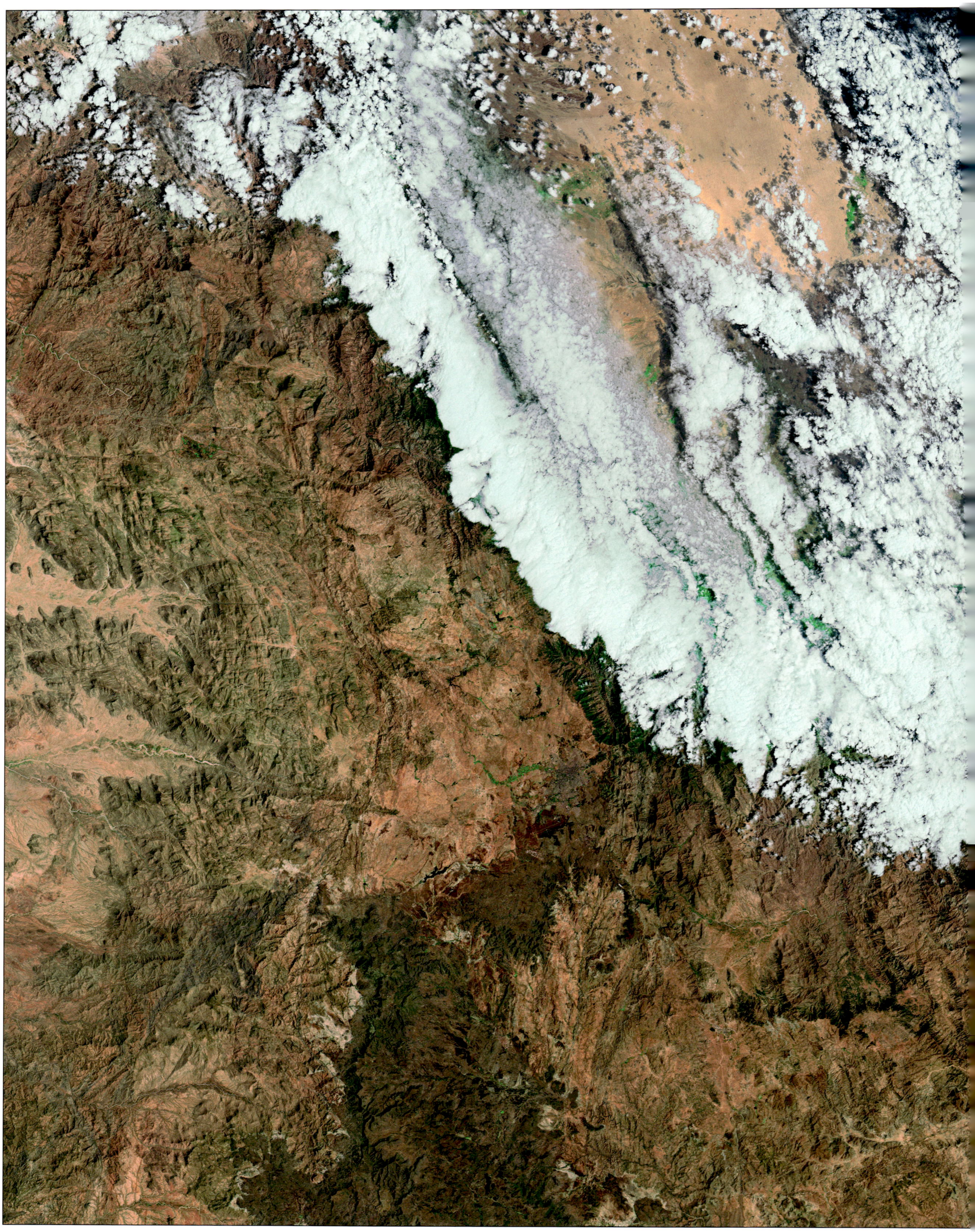

WATER ACCESS

Access to water cannot be taken for granted. Local water projects provide innovative solutions for this challenge and serve as examples to other regions.

Water is a vital resource and an irreplaceable one. While water is plentiful in some regions, water stress is generally increasing in more and more places around the world. According to United Nations (UN) statistics, 11 per cent of the world's population, or almost 768 million people, still lack access to a sufficient supply of drinking water, while almost 2.5 billion have no access to simple sewage and sanitation systems. The statistics are particularly grim in Africa, where 40 per cent of people lack access to a sufficient supply of water. The rural areas of sub-Saharan Africa are particularly badly affected. This is exactly where the population is set to grow significantly in the next few decades, which will exacerbate the situation.

At over 80 per cent, the average supply rate – the percentage of people connected to a water supply system – is much higher in the cities than in rural regions, where it is around 50 per cent. Particularly low supply rates are recorded in the poorer districts on the margins of growing cities in developing countries. In addition, the water price for a household can be up to 100 times higher if the water comes not from the tap but has to be bought in bottles and canisters from street traders. As such, poor people in particular have to spend a larger proportion of their income on covering their essential needs. This situation becomes even more complex in regions that do not have access to water as a result of climatic or geographical conditions. Arid areas are just as hard hit as areas in rugged terrain, or remote mountain areas.

Women and children (especially daughters) are often responsible for obtaining drinking water in poorer countries. According to Helvetas, the Swiss association for international cooperation, people in Africa spend around 40 billion hours every year searching for water. Precious time that could be spent doing more important things, especially for women, and girls could be spending that

◁
1 – In the Eritrean Highlands, drinking water is harvested from fog using nets. The clouds form along the mountains as the humid air rises from the neighbouring Red Sea.

time in school. People often have to walk for hours or even days to find a reasonably clean source of water. Heat and harsh terrain add to the hardships of the journeys of many kilometres to the watering hole, where the women must stand in line, before turning round and heading back home with a few heavy buckets.

The fog-harvesting technique

All over the world, people use different methods to improve their access to water. In addition to major dam projects and technologically complex solutions or expensive desalination plants, there is a whole host of smaller projects. The costs of these are generally manageable, especially compared to the advantages that they offer in partly arid regions. Of all the regions in difficulty, Africa is the one that stands out. Very high population growth is expected in the years to come. In addition to standard methods for improving water availability, new, innovative concepts are also being developed. A very promising technique is known as fog-harvesting technology: large nets are set up in regions where fogs gather (Figs. 1, 5) and strain the mist out of the air through condensation. The nets can 'milk' hundreds of litres of drinking water from the air every day in the foggy season. The technology is extremely simple and solves countless problems.

The projects described below were carried out by foundations located in southern Germany: the WasserStiftung from Ebenhausen near Munich and the Munich Re Foundation (Münchener Rück Stiftung), which is also dedicated to improving water supply in developing countries and emerging economies. The projects are great examples of how intelligent and innovative concepts for improving drinking water access can be implemented in practice. Working with partners in Eritrea and Morocco, the foundations were able to develop exciting and groundbreaking solutions.

Drinking water has been harvested from fog in many countries for about two decades now. The technology is extremely simple: the tiny water droplets settle on hydrophilic threads and, once a certain moisture level has been reached, drip down into a collection channel. Indigenous peoples, such as the San (Kalahari Bushmen) in southern Africa, have been using the technique of 'dew harvesting' since time immemorial. They use the dew, which collects on plants as a result of the cooler night-time temperatures, on a very small scale, of course. On a larger scale, the principle of 'using natural air humidity' or fog was developed and optimised over 20 years ago by the Canadian organisation FogQuest. Fog, which is commonly found in mountain regions outside Africa as well and along the world's coastlines, is collected by special nets that 'harvest' the water droplets.

Eritrea project: the success of fog-harvesting

An interesting fog-harvesting project was initiated in Eritrea in 2007. Here the warm air from the Red Sea rises on reaching the coast and blows inland over the mountainous coastline (Fig. 1, pp. 204/205). As the air rises, fog forms all along the 500 kilometre-long mountain chain, generally from November to March. In the mountains near Asmara, at an altitude of 2,000 to 2,500 metres, the water supply has always been a major problem outside of the rainy season because there are so few watering holes or wells at this altitude. The people have to make a long and difficult journey into the valley in order to get the drinking water they need. Either that, or they have to rely on tankers that come to fill the cisterns. However, the long journey by tanker results in the water being twice as expensive for the mountain residents as it is for inhabitants of the capital of Asmara.

In 2005, test collectors were therefore set up to catch the water droplets from fog. In a preliminary study, the evaluations of a one square kilometres net showed that it was able to harvest almost 30 litres of water from the fog (Fig. 3). In summer 2007, construction was completed for 20 collectors, each with a surface of 36 square metres (Fig. 2), which were able to collect an average of 4,000 litres of water between them every day. A cistern with a capacity of 30,000 litres was built to store the water. To ensure sufficient water is available at all times, the cistern should not drop below half-full. This is enough to provide 1,000 people with three litres of clean drinking water every day for five days. Some of the people to benefit included the people in the upland areas and children at a village school.

In the end, it turned out that the supporting structure and the 36 square metres net were unable to withstand the wind speeds in the region.

As a result, the WasserStiftung foundation teamed up with local partners in Arborobue village in 2008 to improve and stabilise the collector system. The area of the net was also reduced by half. In 2012 it became clear though that even with these improvements the desired results could still not be achieved.

However, the technology had indeed worked. Water from the fog flowed into the cisterns. The case study of Eritrea shows that technology alone is not enough in order to achieve successful, sustainable projects. Stable surround-

1 – Fog rolls off the Red Sea and into the interior of Eritrea.

2 – In summer 2007, the uplands of Eritrea were set up with 20 collectors, each with an area of 36 square metres.

3 – Since 2005, the results from the smaller test collectors have been able to show: the technology works!

5 – Morocco's Anti-Atlas Mountains shrouded in clouds that carry moisture inland from the west coast.

6 – The construction of the new FOG|HARVESTER test collectors at the summit of Mount Boutmezguida (Morocco) in November 2013. Local people help a team from Germany.

7 – Measuring instruments and small test-scale fog collectors of one square metre set up at the start of the project (2007) on the mountainside to get an idea of the water yields the region can expect to see.

4 – Children in Arberobue, Eritrea, enjoying the fresh drinking water from the new well.

ings and ownership, i.e. the assumption of responsibility by the local net owners, are important conditions that must be taken into consideration in the planning stage of a cooperative development project. If the conditions are right, countless villages and schools along the 500-kilometre mountain chain along the Red Sea coast could have their drinking water requirements covered.

Fog-harvesting in Morocco – providing water to villages

In the dry season from June to September, women from the villages of the Anti-Atlas Mountains in Morocco spend over three hours every day going to fetch water from the nearest well for their families. With the support of the Munich Re Foundation, the locally based organisation Dar Si-Hmad has been building fog-harvesting nets to improve the water supply since July 2011 (Fig. 6). As was the case in Eritrea, the aim is to harvest drinking water from fog for several villages and a school in remote mountain regions in the north-west of Africa. The groundbreaking project won a tender put out by the Munich Re Foundation to promote fog and dew-harvesting projects and beat five applications from Tanzania, the Cape Verde islands, India and Morocco.

The potential for producing drinking water in this region of Morocco was investigated in detail in a four-year test phase from 2007 to 2011 using small fog collectors. As a result of the high air humidity of almost 90 per cent from December to June, thick fog forms over the mountains of the arid and semi-arid regions of the Anti-Atlas Mountains (Fig. 5). The amount of water stored in this fog is enormous. Data has shown that one square metre of net here would be able to 'harvest' five to 20 litres of drinking water per day. If water flows from the fog-harvesting nets at the end of the project, the foggy season can expect to produce 3,000 to 4,000 litres of drinking water every day. This would be enough to provide more than 400 people with the water they need and would significantly improve the quality of life of women and children in the villages in particular. In July 2011, Dar Si-Hmad started the construction with 40 square metres of fog nets on Mount Boutmezguida (1,225 metres) to the east of the coastal city of Sidi Ifni. In total, 600 square metres of net were put up (Fig. 6). The water harvested from the nets is collected on the mountainside in cisterns and is then filtered before flowing downhill in a pipe around 7 kilometres in length to the villages of Agni Zekri, Sidi Zekri and Agni Ihya.

The system was completed in spring 2014. Then the project was truly in full flow! But before the water can start to be used in homes, important questions have to be answered: How can adequate fees for water usage be levied? Where should the wastewater go? Together with the University of Colorado, Dar Si-Hmad researched the social aspects. After all, beyond the purely technical issues with regard to net stability, water yield and mineral content, these kinds of projects also bring with them many social implications that must be taken into account.

The future of fog-harvesting

The fog collectors designed by the Canadian organisation FogQuest and built in many countries have provided a very precious service to locals already over the past few decades. However, several regions have found that the 40 square kilometres nets used to date are too large and too unstable. After all, it is not rare for the mountain winds to hit speeds of up to 120 kilometres per hour. The consequence is that the nets tend to tear at certain points under wind stress and become unusable. As such, some of the nets have already been made smaller in several projects in mountainous regions, for instance in Eritrea and Morocco.

A new FOG|HARVESTER has been under development since 2012 with the financial support of the MunichRe Foundation. To improve the stability of the collectors, the net area was reduced to just nine square metres. The fixation points were also improved: rubber expanders and flexible plastic profiles let the nets be hung up with greater elasticity (Fig. 6). The new constructions are resistant to UV radiation and harsh weather, letting them withstand premature aging under the changing influence of the sun and wind.

In autumn 2013, the FOG|HARVESTER was tested for efficiency and stability both in real outdoor conditions and in the laboratory. This development though was just the start. A mountain laboratory for fog-harvesting technology was also set up in the uplands of Morocco.

In addition to the existing fog-harvesting project on Mount Boutmezguida, six FOG|HARVESTER systems were also built. In these systems, six different nets are hung up next to each another to test their suitability. The Technische Universität München [Munich Technical University] assisted in the project. The scientists focused on the yields that could be achieved with the different types of net. The water yields from these new nets using different mesh widths and geometries are currently being compared with the results from standard fog nets. Everyone is looking forward to the initial results when the next foggy season begins.

In addition to the preliminary field tests to determine the suitability of the terrain for fog collectors (Fig. 7), satellite images in particular are a great help in determining potential locations. By collecting and evaluating macro- and microclimatic data for large-scale weather systems and for local weather conditions on the smallest scale, such as a one-kilometre grid, regions with regular relief rainfall can be determined. Measurements of air and soil humidity, collected regularly using radar sensors, offer further reference values for determining the local use and efficiency of fog collectors.

If the project succeeds in developing fog-net technology further, the case study in Morocco will become an international pilot project for drinking water production and serve as a precedent for further projects worldwide. The potential of the project is enormous.

Text: Thomas Loster, Martina Mayerhofer, Dirk Reinhard

1 – The ancient irrigation system of qanats dates back thousands of years and brings water even today to dry regions near mountains (relief rainfall) and without major rivers. This is an example in the north-east of Iran, where a high-resolution satellite image allows the course of underground diversion tunnels to be tracked via the vertical shafts arranged in lines.

A tunnel links the bottoms of the shafts between the mountain and the valley. Draining the water, it 'sucks' the moisture from the ground and also collects condensation from the air, which drips down the sides of the shafts. The tunnels are around 50 to 240 centimetres wide and 90 to 180 centimetre high. Their gradient is very low (almost horizontal to 0.5 per mille), to keep the water from eroding the largely unlined tunnel walls and the suspended load from becoming too high (water quality).
For steeper gradients, steps built into the tunnels can be used to create underground waterfalls to drive water wheels.

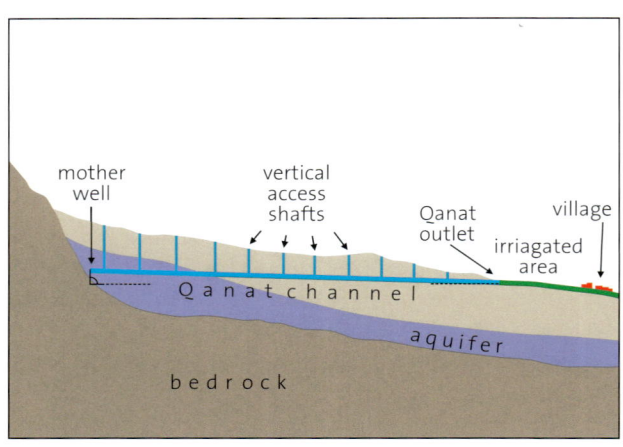

2 – The qanat irrigation system diverts water from the mountains though underground channels to the regions where it is needed, where the aquifers often lie too deep for wells. This means the water avoids the extremely high evaporation rates that affect surface irrigation systems in very dry regions.

3 – The former construction shafts are still used to maintain this Iranian cultural heritage.

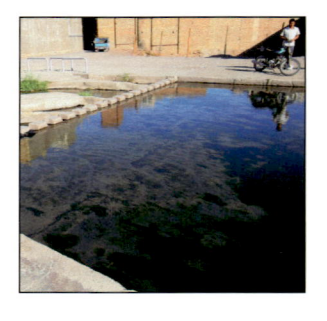

4 – Water from a qanat emerging in the centre of an Iranian village.

Transporting water

Water is very often found in places far from where it is needed. This is usually the case for agricultural irrigation. However, settlements too, because of their location or for reasons of security, may find themselves far from water sources or may find that the originally sufficient water supply can no longer keep up with a growing population. For a very long time the water needed could only be transported in containers carried by people or by beasts of burden and only simple wells and relatively short canals were constructed.

With the rise of the great civilisations, however, engineers started to develop a variety of efficient solutions adapted to the environmental conditions of the respective region. These solutions made use of the natural flow of water and are still used today in countless forms.

Some major examples of water supply systems used even in antiquity include cisterns and pools for storing water, as well as canals, aqueducts (Figs. 5 and 6) and qanats (Figs. 1 to 4 and 7) to transport water to where it will be used. Flow rates began to be regulated very early on by locks, and differences in height were mastered efficiently using scoop wheels.

The principle of the qanat is also nowadays found in regions with arid climates near mountains – from the Spanish and African Mediterranean coasts and the Middle East to the Taklamakan Desert in China. The oldest known examples in Iran date back over 5,000 years. Qanats were built to transport the water that fell as rain in the mountains to where it was needed. An important aspect was to avoid the water from evaporating or becoming polluted in its course. To do this, an initial shaft was dug down to

▷
5 – The Pont du Gard, stretching from Uzès to Nîmes, is probably the best-known Roman aqueduct.

▷
6 – The aqueduct winds its way through the mountains for almost 50 kilometres, or 20 kilometres as the crow flies. With an average gradient of 25 centimetres/kilometres, the Pont du Gard is a masterpiece of Roman engineering.

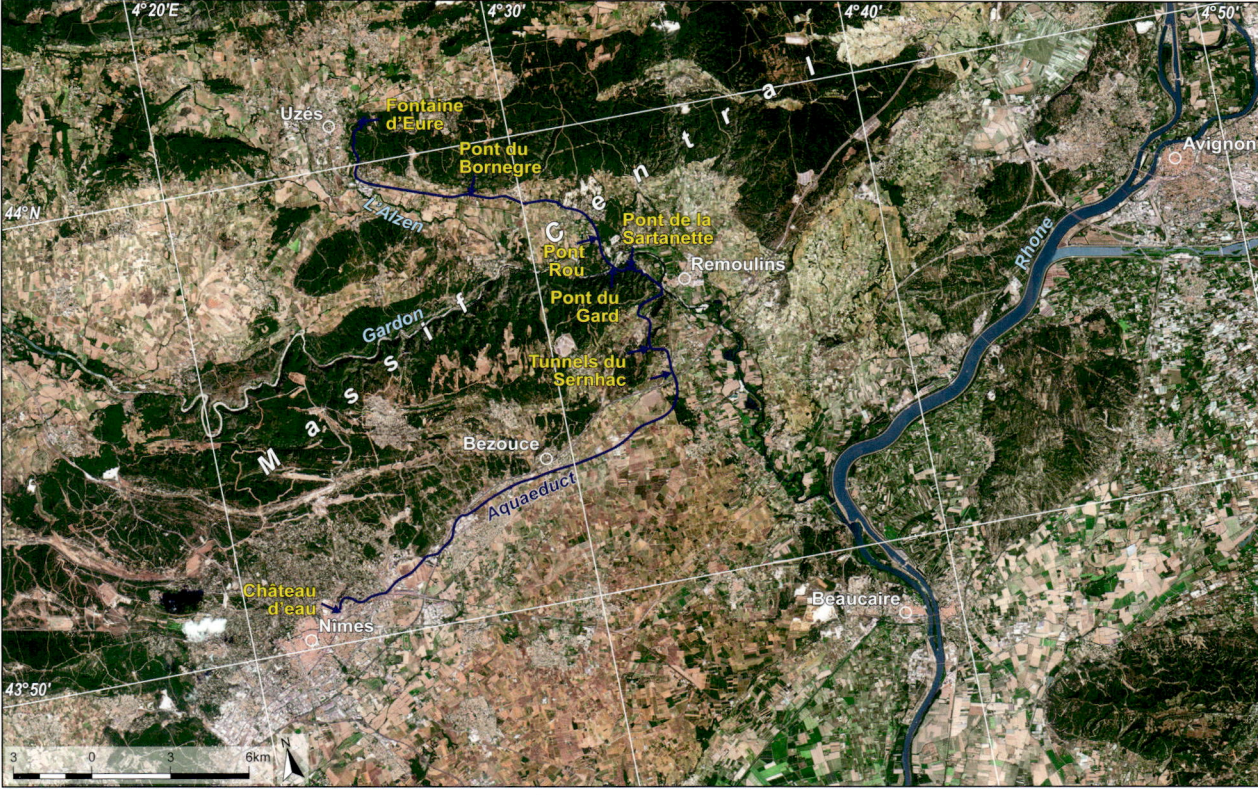

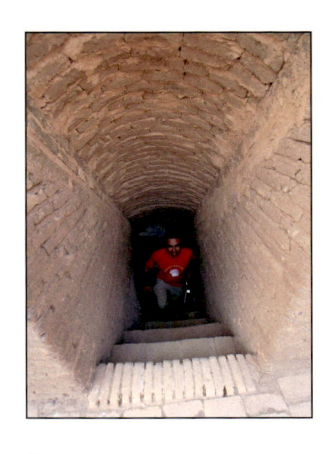

△
7 – Brick-lined maintenance tunnel to a qanat in Iran.

the groundwater table near the mountain foothills. From here, a gently inclined underground channel would transport the water over a distance from just a few to up to 80 kilometres to its destination (Figs. 2 and 4). To let the qanat be built, cleaned and ventilated, vertical shafts spaced 20 to 35 metres apart were dug to depths of 20 to 200 metres (Figs. 3 and 7), leading to the characteristic chains of craters visible in satellite images over distances of many kilometres. In some cases, the shafts hit depths of 450 metres, making the construction of a qanat a long-term project for countless labourers. Not only the construction, but also maintaining the system of tunnels and shafts is highly labour-intensive. Tens of thousands of qanats are still in use to this day in the Middle East, especially in Iran (today as UNESCO World Heritage site), which testifies to the success and sustainability of the technology. This example also shows how important cooperation was even in the early days of human civilisation.

A similar aim was pursued with the building of aqueducts. Here, water had to be transported along a uniform gradient, largely overground, including across uneven terrain and sometimes through tunnels, from its source to a city. The best-known aqueducts were built by the Romans (Figs. 5 and 6). From around 300 BCE Rome was supplied with water via an expanding network of aqueducts, three of which are still in operation today. Even though pressure mains have come to dominate water supply networks, aqueducts have not lost their relevance. For example, the water supply in Vienna is still largely dependent on the two mountain spring pipelines that each carry water 200 kilometres from their sources in the Alps to the city via countless aqueducts.

209

210

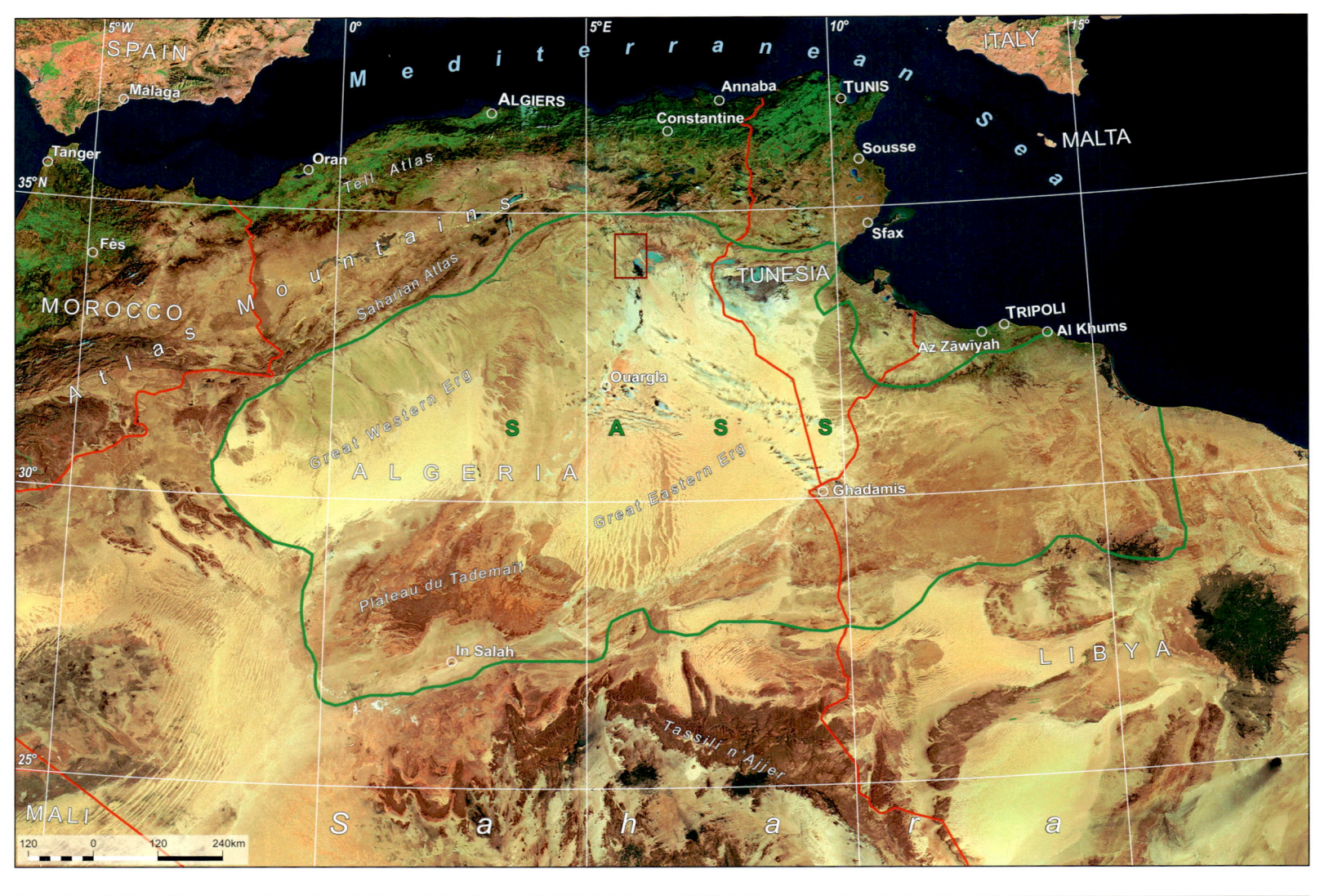

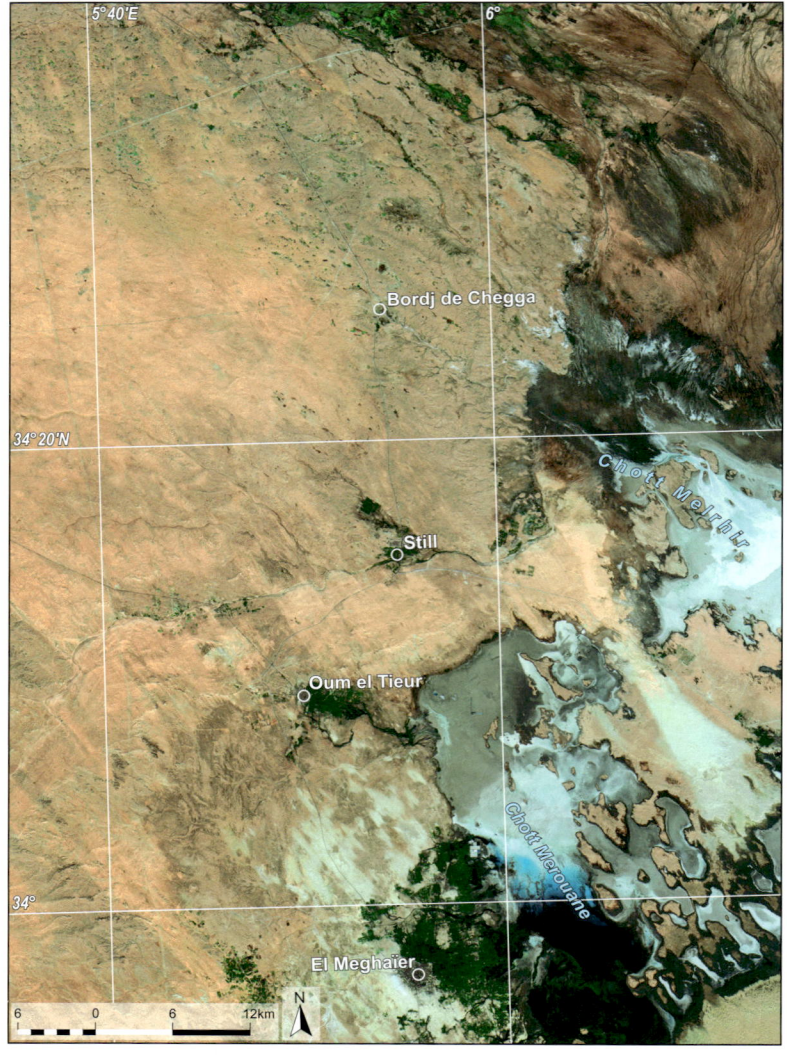

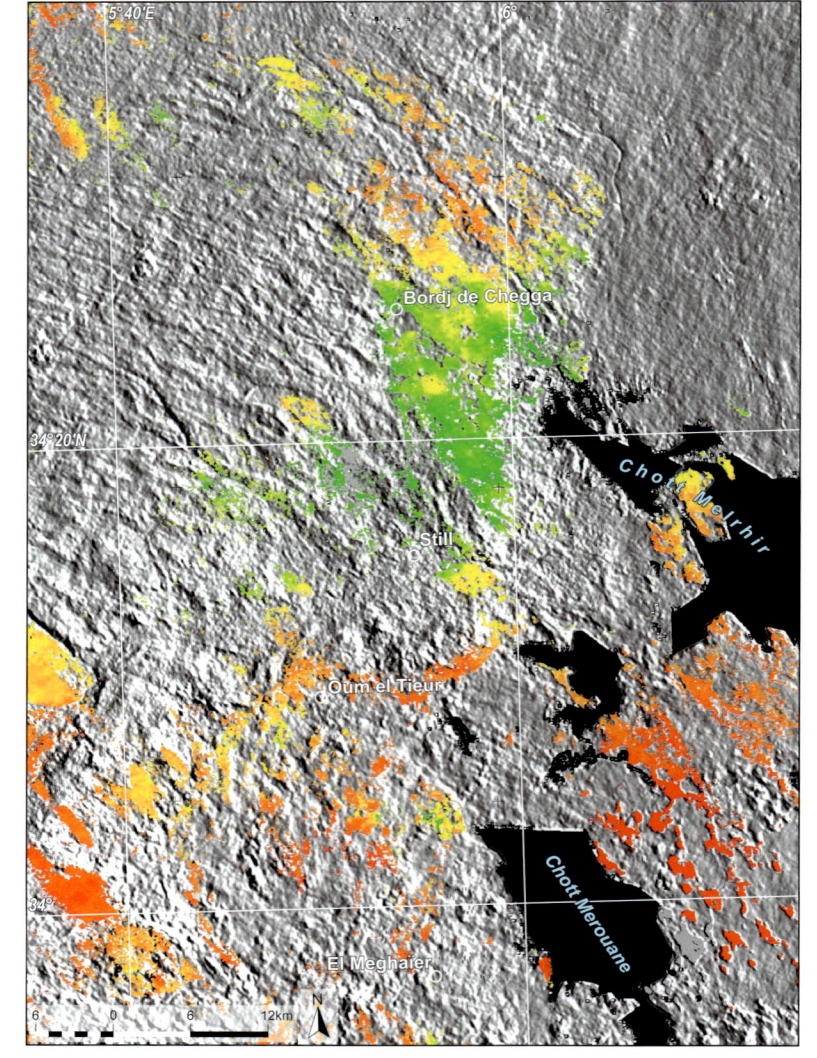

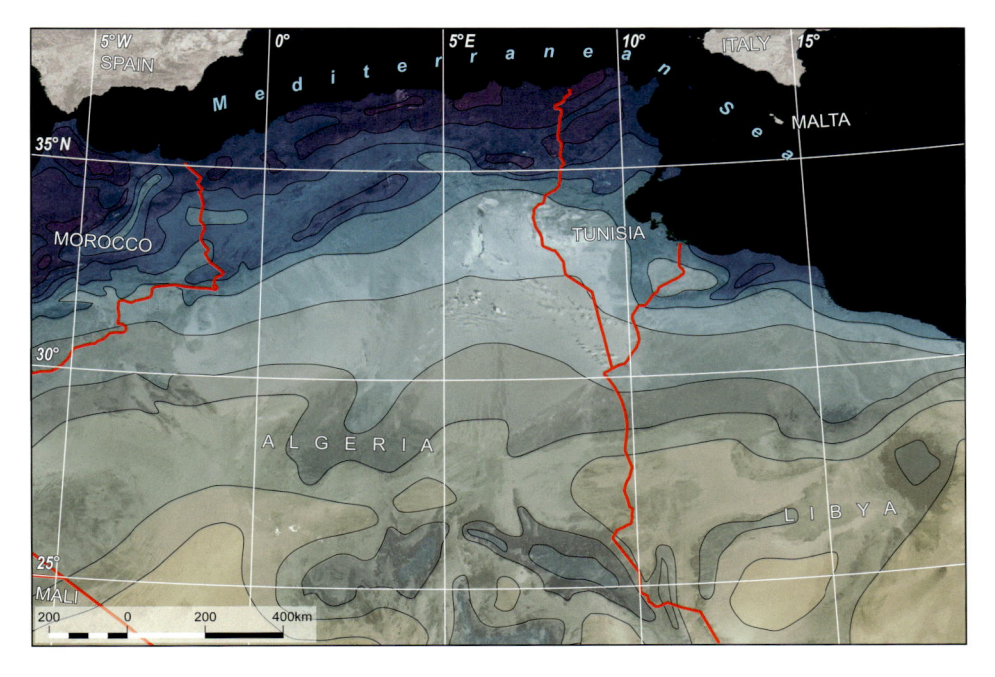

1 – The groundwater of the North-Western Sahara Aquifer contains fossil water and so cannot be recharged naturally.

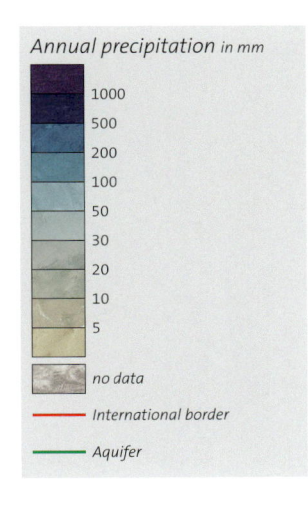

Annual precipitation in mm
- 1000
- 500
- 200
- 100
- 50
- 30
- 20
- 10
- 5
- no data
- International border
- Aquifer

3 – Uneven distribution of precipitation in part of North Africa. The north coast lies in the Mediterranean climatic zone, which has rainy winters.

2a/b – The Chott Merouane is below sea level (left image, 30/11/2013). Radar sensors render visible the subsidence near the aquifer by comparing paired images (right image).

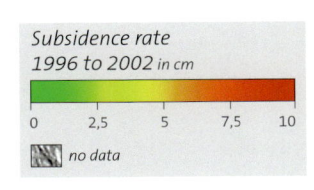

Subsidence rate 1996 to 2002 in cm
- 0 2,5 5 7,5 10
- no data

4/5 – DEM derived from radar data; aerial view (Chott Melrhir).

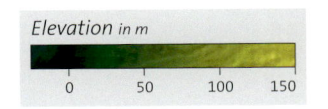

Elevation in m
- 0 50 100 150

Groundwater in the Sahara

The north of Africa is home to the Sahara and the extensive North-Western Sahara Aquifer System (NWSAS), also known as Système Aquifère du Sahara Septentrionale (SASS). This enormous body of groundwater covers a total area of 1 million square kilometres from Algeria through Libya and to Tunisia (Fig. 1). The bulk of the aquifer, or around 700,000 square kilometres, lies in Algeria. Around 250,000 square kilometres are in Libya and about 80,000 square kilometres in Tunisia. With just a few exceptions, the aquifers consist of fossil water dating back to the pluvial era – a period of high rainfall in Mediterranean and tropical regions during the Pleistocene epoch. In Algeria and Tunisia, the groundwater is primarily used for irrigation, which accounts for over 70 per cent of the water usage in the entire SASS basin. Because the body of groundwater is located in an arid zone (Fig. 3), groundwater recharge is severely limited. The water in the lakes of the northern Sahara is largely unusable. The salt content of the water is extremely high because the lakes lie within geographical depressions with no drainage (Fig. 2a). As such, drawing on fossil groundwater is the only option. The high amount of water abstraction leads to lower groundwater levels across the affected regions. As a result, the natural water discharge from artesian wells decreases and the water has to be brought to the surface by powerful pumps, requiring more capital and energy. As the groundwater level falls, the salinity of the water increases. Pumping out the groundwater can also lead to the mobilisation of local salt springs, which leads to further salinisation of the remaining water.

In order to raise socio-economic awareness of the local population and develop solutions for the sustainable use of fossil groundwater in agriculture, Algeria, Tunisia and Libya joined forces in 1999 with the SASS (Système des Aquifers du Sahara Septentrional) project under the auspices of the OSS (Observatoire du Sahara et du Sahel). This project was facilitated by the partnership with the AWF (African Water Facility), the GEF (Global Environment Facility) and the FFEM (French Global Environment Facility). The third phase, or SASS III, completed in 2013, produced a strategic action plan.

AQUIFER project

With its AQUIFER project, a sub-project of the TIGER initiative, the European Space Agency (ESA) has declared its mission to support Algeria, Tunisia and Libya with cutting-edge satellite technology in order to guarantee sustainable water management of the North-Western Sahara Aquifer. This project uses various technologies to gauge the yield of the aquifer, its risk of salinisation and the options available for agriculture. The project is co-financed by the OSS and the AWF.

Monitoring of subsidence using radar satellites

Due to the constantly growing demand for water brought about by the economic and demographic growth of the three neighbouring countries over the past 30 years and the increased water abstraction from the aquifer, the ground in the region has started to subside in places.

Using satellites with synthetic aperture radar sensors (SAR), large-scale changes on the Earth's surface, such as horizontal or vertical ground motion, can be tracked over a long period of time and measured precisely. This SAR interferometry (InSAR) technology can be used to measure subsidence caused by urban construction, mining and all kinds of groundwater abstraction, and it can also be used to evaluate the bodies of groundwater in the AQUIFER project. Additionally, radar interferometry based on at least two radar images from slightly different positions (of at least a few hundred metres apart) is used to create digital elevation models.

The subsidence between 1996 (Fig. 2a) and 2002 (Fig. 2b) around the Chott Merouane in Algeria (Fig. 5) can be seen clearly on the subsidence map (Fig. 2b). A digital elevation model was also derived on this region using radar images to get an idea of the topography (Fig. 4).

211

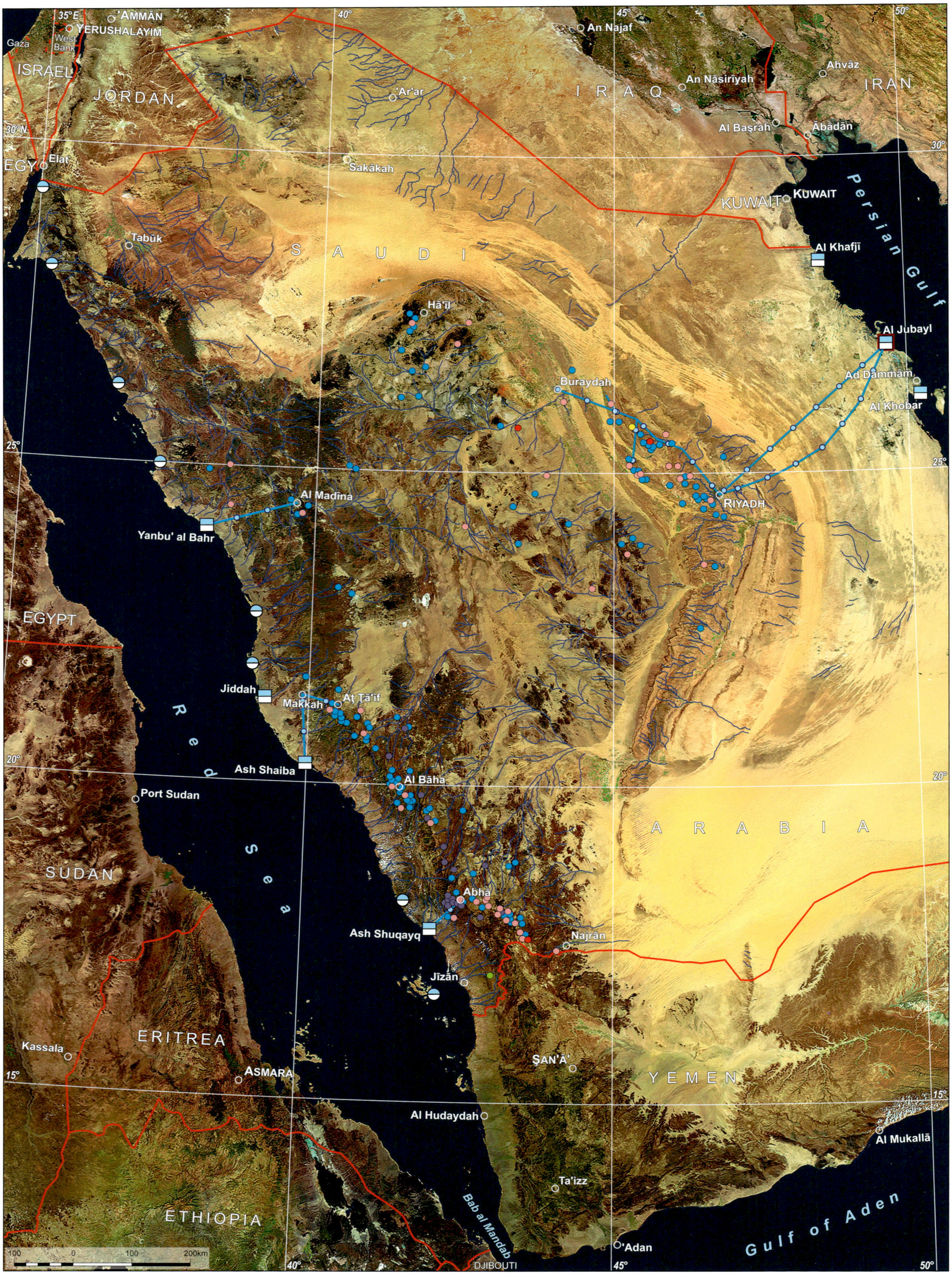

ʿAMMĀN
YERUSHALAYIM
Gaza
West Bank
ISRAEL
JORDAN
EGYPT
Elat
Tabūk
ʿArʿar
Sakakah
S A U D I
I R A Q
An Najaf
An Nāsiriyah
Ahvāz
IRAN
Al Basrah
Ābādān
KUWAIT
KUWAIT
Persian Gulf
Al Khafjī
Al Jubayl
Ad Dammam
Al Khobar
Ḥāʾil
Buraydah
RIYADH
Al Madina
Yanbuʿ al Bahr
EGYPT
Jiddah
Makkah
At Taʾif
Red Sea
Ash Shaiba
Al Bāha
Port Sudan
A R A B I A
SUDAN
Abhā
Ash Shuqayq
Najrān
Jīzān
ERITREA
Kassala
ASMARA
ṢANʿĀʾ
YEMEN
Al Hudaydah
Al Mukallā
Taʿizz
ETHIOPIA
Bab al Mandab
ʿAdan
Gulf of Aden
DJIBOUTI
200km

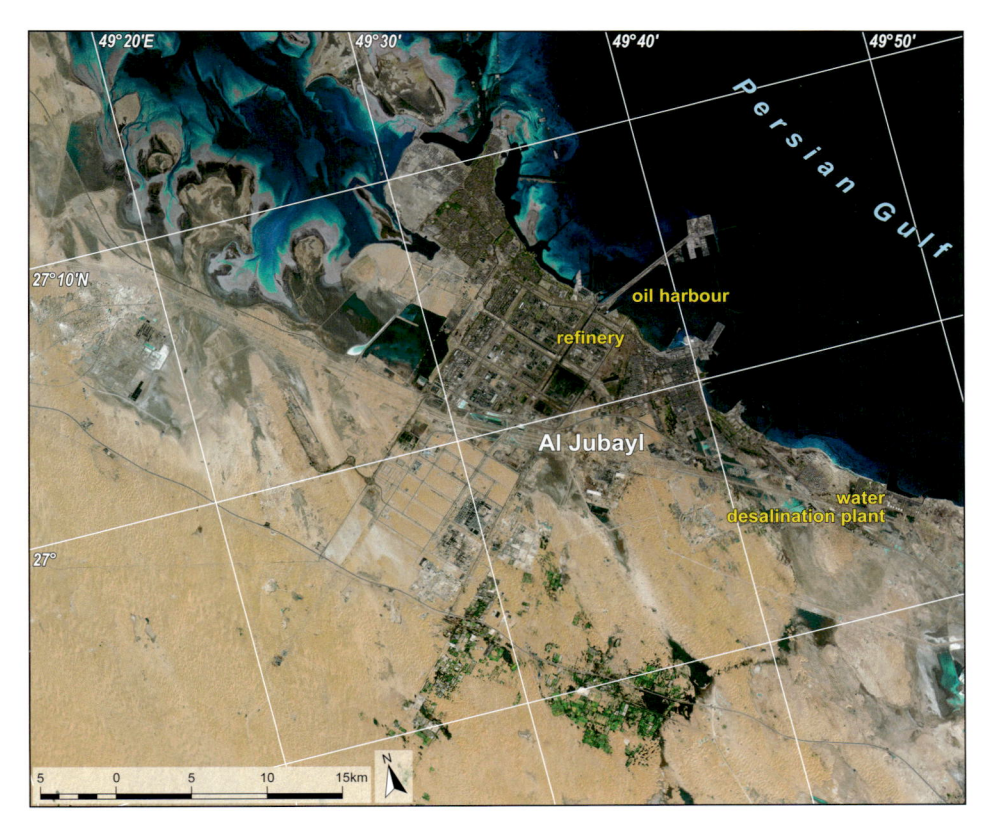

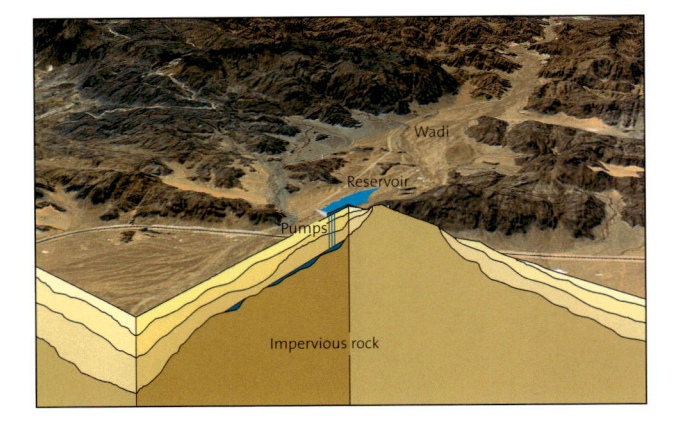

Water supply in Saudi Arabia – a challenge

Most of the Kingdom of Saudi Arabia, which covers an area of 2.25 million square kilometres, lies in an arid zone and is dominated by the Great Arabian Desert. On average, the region receives less than 150 millimetres rain per year. Because rain so rarely falls and the evaporation rate is so high, little water is available from the surface and from groundwater.

In the past two decades Saudi Arabia has experienced an economic boom based on the production and export of crude oil and gas. The impact on population growth and the standard of living, and thus also on the water consumption, has been significant.

Saudi Arabia has four major drinking water resources and water extraction methods: surface water, groundwater, desalinated seawater and reclaimed wastewater (Fig. 1). As a result of the low annual rainfall, surface water is both insufficient and unreliable. The rare rain that does fall is captured in over 200 dams throughout the country (Fig. 4). The largest of these, the King Fahad Dam (Bishah Dam) in Wadi Bishah, can hold around 325 million cubic metres of water.

The groundwater reserves are stored in more than 20 large aquifers from various geological periods. Isotope analysis has shown that some of these aquifers are 10,000 to 32,000 years old. However, most of the aquifers are non-renewable and contain so-called fossil water. This means that the stores are not recharged by rainfall or infiltration or that the replenishing is extremely slow and takes a long time to have any effect on groundwater reserves. As a result, several years ago Saudi Arabia has begun to pump the rainwater in the dams that is not immediately needed by the population for irrigation or drinking water into the groundwater supply (Fig. 5). This also helps to prevent losses through evaporation.

Seawater desalination plants

Because the surface water and groundwater reserves (10 per cent to 40 per cent of drinking water requirements) will not suffice to meet increased water demand in the future, Saudi Arabia has begun investing huge sums into seawater desalination, as due to the geographic conditions there is an abundance of seawater.

Over the past four decades desalinated water has become the most important drinking water source and now accounts for about half of it. Today the country has over 30 desalination plants, most of them located on the coast of the Red Sea. Producing 950,000 cubic metres of drinking water per day, Al Jubayl on the Persian Gulf is home to the second-largest desalination plant in Saudi Arabia (Figs. 2 and 3). Like many desalination plants, it is based on the principle of reverse osmosis involving semi-permeable membranes to separate salt from the water. The Saline Water Conversion Corporation (SWCC) also uses multi-purpose plants. A steam or gas turbine generates electricity and the desalination plant uses the heat given off to distil seawater. To keep costs low and to reduce emission of greenhouse gases, desalination plants will also be powered by solar power in the future, like the plant at Al Khafji, which has been running since 2013.

Currently, 3.4 million cubic metres of drinking water are produced every day in Saudi Arabia, which accounts for around 20 per cent of all desalinated water produced on the planet. Saudi Arabia gets more drinking water from its desalination plants than any other nation. The water is pumped through an expanding network of pipelines and now provides more than 50 cities with drinking water.

△
2 – High-resolution SPOT-5 satellite image of the seawater desalination plant at Al Jubayl on the Persian Gulf.

▷
3 – The largest Saudi Arabian desalination plant at Al Jubayl on the Persian Gulf.

▷
4 – The Najran Dam on the border with Yemen can hold 85 million cubic metres of significant water.

◁
1 – Overview of drinking water supply and flood control systems in Saudi Arabia.

Desalination plants and dams
- Regional desalination plant
- Local desalination plant
- Dam for irrigation
- Dam for the protection of villages
- Dam for water reservoir
- Dam for flood control
- Dam for artificial groundwater recharge
- Water pipelines
- Wadis
- International border

▷
5 – Storing rainwater to recharge aquifers.

213

214

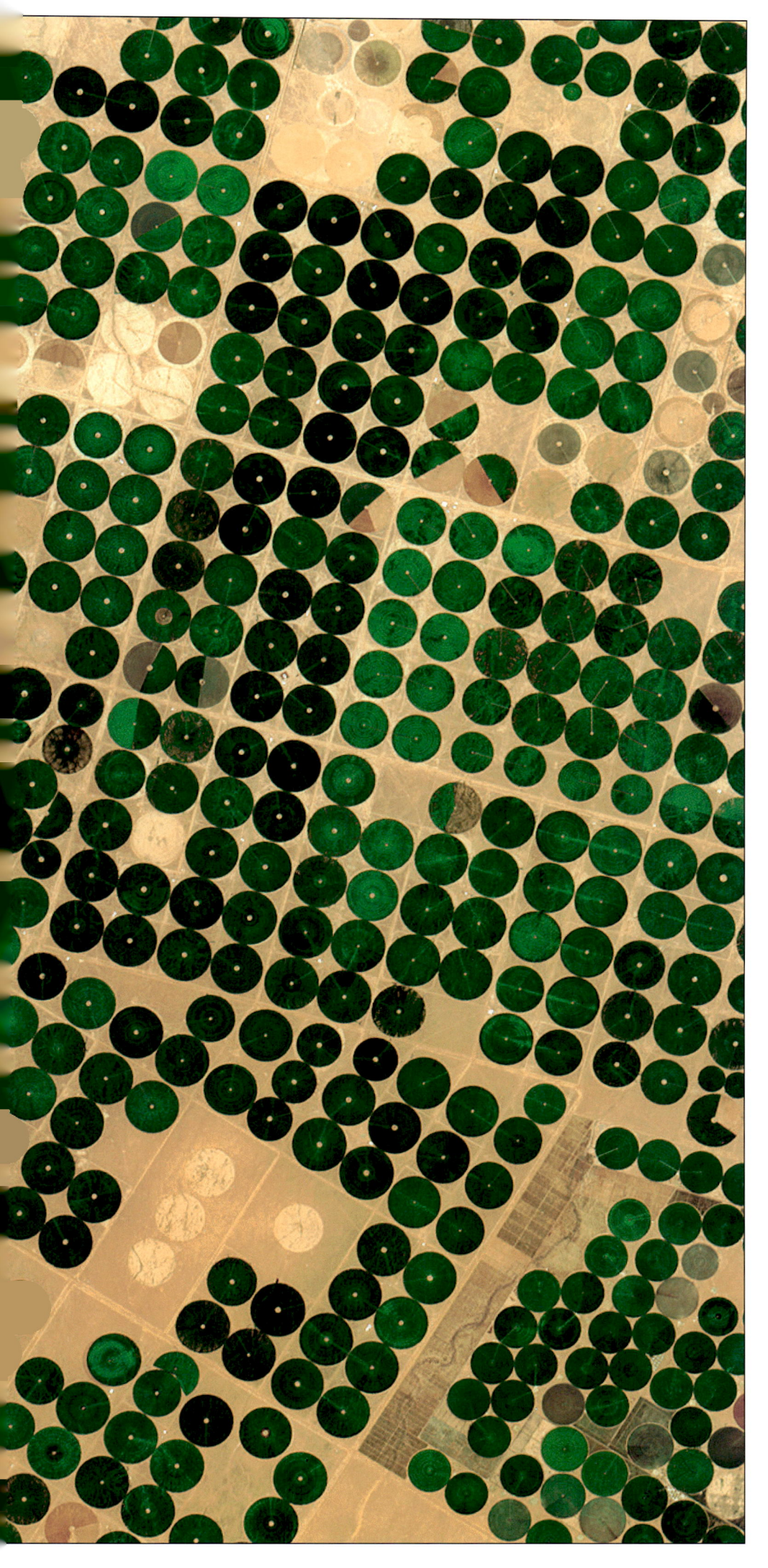

IRRIGATION

Green circles appear in the dry desert as a result of intensive irrigation.

The irrigation of agricultural land dates back over 3,000 years. Even in 1,200 BCE, farmers in Egypt and Syria were increasing their productivity by using scoop wheels to water their fields. Growing rice in paddy fields has an even longer tradition. Using carbon-dating technology, scientists have been able to prove that rice was already being cultivated in the Pengtoushan area of China in around 7,000 BCE.

Today, irrigated farming plays a huge role in agriculture. According to the FAO (the UN's Food and Agriculture Organization), in 2009 an area of around 301 million hectares – 20 per cent of all farmland worldwide – was irrigated. Irrigation accounts for 70 per cent of all the fresh water used by humans worldwide, 40 per cent of which is taken from groundwater. The crop yield from these areas represents around 40 per cent of all food produced on Earth. As a result of its climate and continually increasing demand for food, Asia has the largest proportion of artificially irrigated farmland, or 212 million hectares.

The irrigation techniques are as diverse as the regions in which they are used (Fig. 1, Figs. 1 and 3 pp. 216/217). Surface irrigation, for example, uses various flooding and drip-irrigation techniques, which primarily depend on the terrain of the area to be irrigated. In humid regions, mobile or stationary sprinkler systems are the preferred methods. In areas with low relief, subirrigation is used to reduce the evaporation and drainage losses. The method that is most effective and has the least damaging knock-on effects is drip irrigation, which directs water straight to the roots of the plants via underground pipes. This completely avoids the evaporation or drainage of the water. However, all irrigation systems can suffer from severe side effects. Particularly in arid regions, the land degradation can lead to desertification, which is exacerbated by the sinking groundwater table brought about by irrigation. The main problem with artificial irrigation and flood irrigation is the soil salinisation that results. As a result of high evaporation rates, the minerals that were dissolved in the water are left behind, turning the soil into unusable fallow land. Most of the irrigated areas on Earth are affected by soil salinisation problems.

◁
1 – *The green circles in an otherwise arid landscape depict pivot irrigation systems. This example of extensive farming in Al Busayta, Al Jawf Region of northern Saudi Arabia, is part of a SPOT-4 satellite image.*

1 – A high-resolution QuickBird-2 satellite image (1 metre) shows the fields and settlements involved in rice cultivation on the island of Bali.

2 – The detailed image illustrates the different planting stages involved in growing rice.

3 – The rice terraces are a characteristic feature of the small Indonesian island of Bali – one of around 17,500 islands in the archipelago.

Paddy field farming

Rice is the staple food of more than half of the world's people, representing 20 per cent of the global population's food energy consumption. For over two billion people in Asia, 60 per cent to 70 per cent of their daily energy requirements are covered by rice.

Originating in the area around the mouth of the Yangtze River, rice has been cultivated for millennia. From there, it was introduced to the rest of South-East Asia by nomadic tribes. Rice came later to Europe via Persia and Egypt, then on to the New World following the European discovery of America. Despite having spread widely around the world, most rice is still grown in Asia – over 90 per cent of global production. According to the FAO, around 730 million tonnes of rice were harvested globally in 2012, and that figure increases every year.

In rice-growing, a distinction is made between wet cultivation and dry cultivation. Wet-cultivated rice requires temperatures of 25 degrees Celsius to 30 degrees Celsius and an enormous water supply of up to 5,000 litres of water per kilo of rice. Irrigation takes place by flooding the fields, whose humus-rich and loamy soils are then planted with the rice seedlings. In some regions, such as Bali and in the Philippines, rice fields are carved into the mountainsides in the form of terraces, which are irrigated via a system of channels. The grains of rice are sown out in irrigated seedbeds and then transferred to the paddy fields after one month. After three to six months, the rice can be harvested.

Rice terraces in Bali

Producing 69 million tonnes of rice (2012) on a cultivated area of 13 million hectares, Indonesia is one of the biggest rice producers in the world. Rice grows at various altitudes. Most, or 84 per cent of the rice crop, is grown in irrigated fields.

The Bali rice terraces have a tradition that stretches back over more than 2,000 years (Figs. 1, 2 and 3). The island has a tropical climate, with year-round temperatures of around 27 degrees Celsius. There is plenty of water available for intensive farming thanks to the monsoon rains, and the volcanic soil is very fertile and rich in minerals. As a result of the constant temperatures, rice can be planted at any time, and there can be two to three harvests per year. While rice is being cultivated in one field, the crop in the others can already be harvested. This makes the Balinese rice cultivation system one of the most effective in the world, and little has changed here since the early days of rice cultivation. The steep terraces make it difficult to use machinery, so rice is still planted and harvested by hand. The rice fields consist of a basin of thick soil, the margins of which are reinforced with thickly interwoven grass roots. The fields are flooded and drained through a small opening in the earthen wall, which can be opened or sealed at any time. The water is drained via a widespread system of channels into streams and rivers that reach the sea.

Rice and methane

The link between wet-cultivated rice and the greenhouse effect and greenhouse gases has already been established. Around 10 to 25 per cent of the world's methane emissions result from wet-rice cultivation. The greenhouse gas methane is produced by the micro-organisms involved in the carbon cycle in the flooded rice fields. Methane is a colourless and odourless gas, and its effect on global warming is around 20 times stronger than the huge quantities of carbon dioxide emitted primarily as a result of human activities.

217

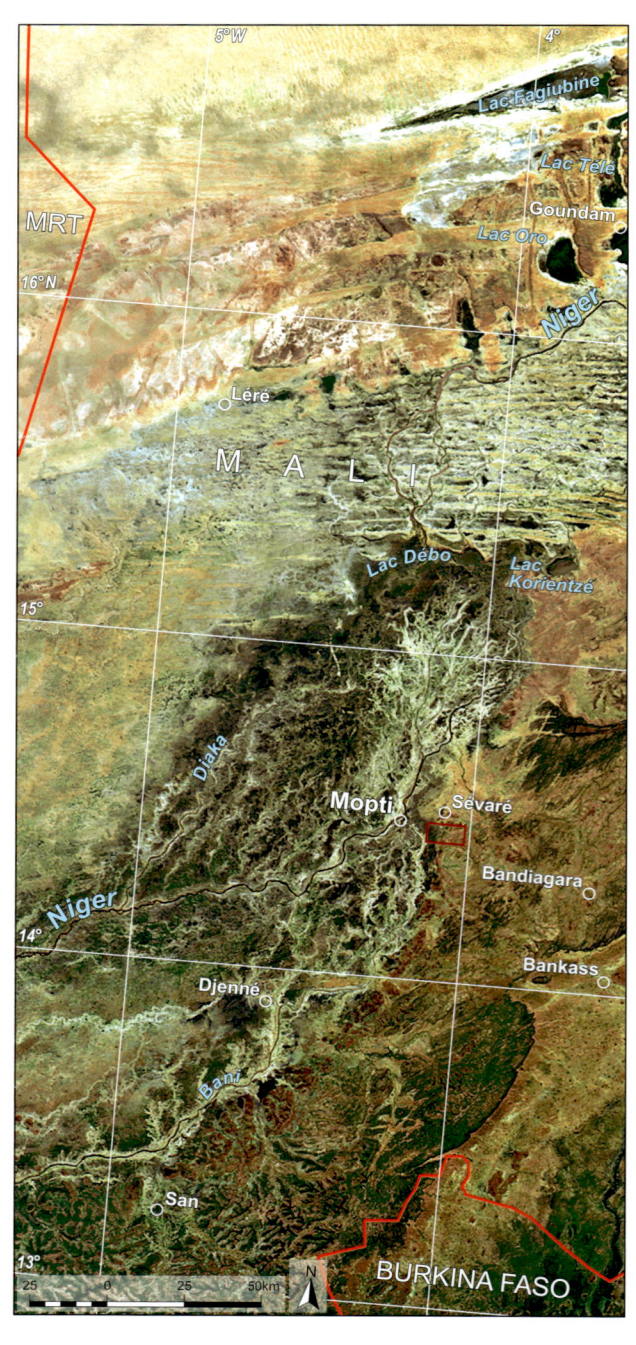

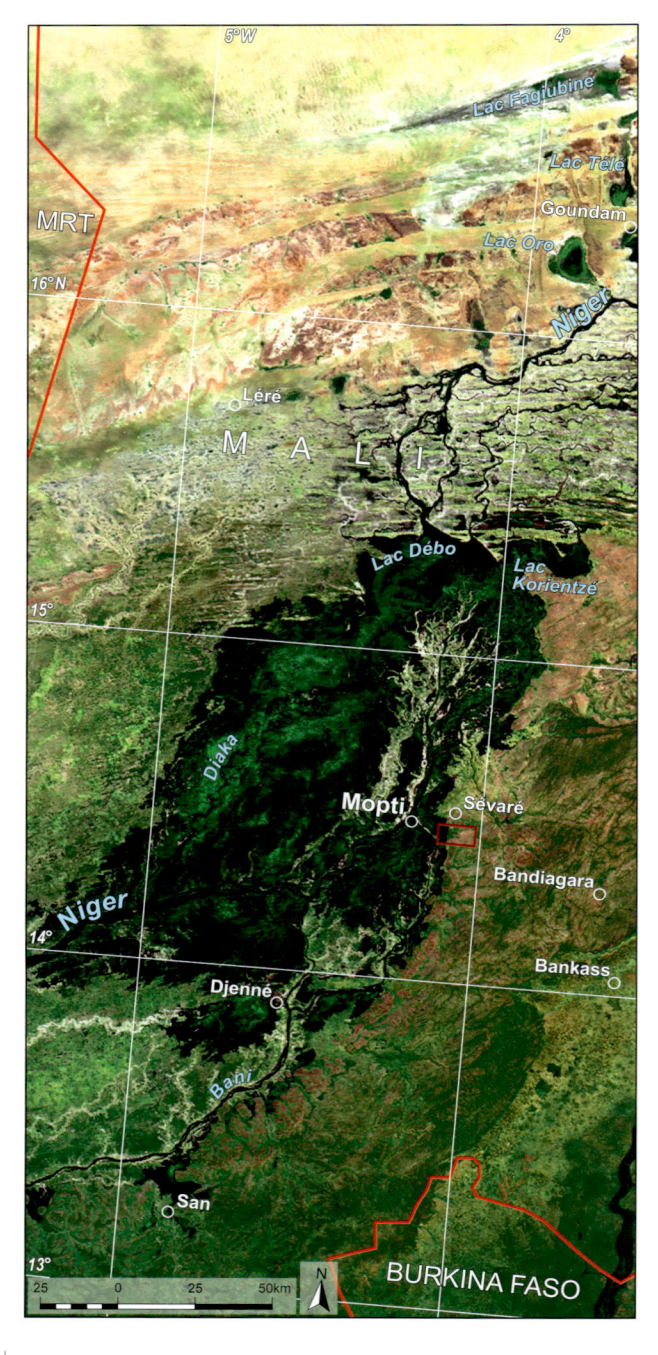

1 – The Inner Niger Delta at the end of the nine-month dry season in June 2003.

2 – The Inner Niger Delta appears in a lush green after heavy rainfall in the south in October 2003.

Inland delta: an inland delta is the delta of a river in the interior of a country or continent. The course either branches off as an endorheic river in a semi-arid to arid basin and drains or evaporates without any outflow (e.g. the Okavango Delta in Botswana) or flows into a lake (Aral Sea), or bifurcates, like the Niger, and flows into a lowland where it forms marshes or a lake. The two arms of the river then join up and flow on towards the sea.

Inner Niger Delta

The Inner Niger Delta in the heart of Mali covers over 60,000 square kilometres, more than 20,000 square kilometres of which are regularly flooded. While the local rainfall plays a minor role, the flooding is mainly caused by the rising water levels of the Niger and the Bani rivers during the rainy season. The rainwater only reaches the delta, after a slight delay, in October (Figs. 1 and 2). With the arrival of the water, the vegetation in the delta also changes, as the dry steppe vegetation transforms into wet savannah and swamps. During this time, the delta changes shape drastically. When the water from the headstreams of the Niger and Bani rivers reaches the inner delta, both the size of the flooded area and its vegetation change (Fig. 3).

With a length of around 4,200 kilometres, the Niger River is the third-longest river in Africa. It rises in the mountains of Guinea, from where it flows north-east towards Mali, where it forms the inner delta. From there, the river draws an arc towards the south-east and runs out in Nigeria into the Gulf of Guinea. On its way to its mouth, the Niger flows through the Sahel and along the southern edge of the Sahara. The river, which rises in an area of plentiful rainfall yet flows through a desert, is essential to the survival of many inhabitants of this desert region.

Agriculture around the Inner Niger Delta

More than one million people live in and around the inland delta (Figs. 1 and 3). The biggest and most important town is Mopti, with around 114,000 inhabitants (2009). As a result of the climactic conditions, the high local demand for staple foodstuffs cannot be met in the region by rainfed agriculture alone. On average, the Inner Niger Delta gets between 200 and 600 millimetres of rain a year. The region's climate is characterised by a nine-month dry season (Fig. 1) and a three-month rainy season, which lasts from July to September (Fig. 2). Irrigation (Fig. 4) offers the opportunity to maximise production with two to three harvests per year.

Rice, wheat and millet are the main crops, with the average household growing 4.4 hectares of rice. In total, 2.3 million tonnes of rice (2000: 743,000 tonnes) were grown on an area of 630,000 hectares in 2010. Rice growing plays an important role for the food security of the local population, and only a small share is exported to neighbouring countries. To be self-sufficient, families also work their own small vegetable gardens, while in most areas a small local market exists for fresh vegetables. A lack of transport infrastructure and consequently the lengthy routes to an outside market make it hard to sell these products further afield.

3 – The appearance of the inland delta alters drastically with the changing seasons. The swamps in particular are subject to enormous change from the dry to the rainy season.

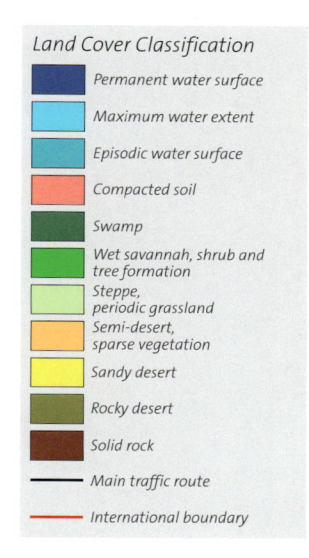

Land Cover Classification
- Permanent water surface
- Maximum water extent
- Episodic water surface
- Compacted soil
- Swamp
- Wet savannah, shrub and tree formation
- Steppe, periodic grassland
- Semi-desert, sparse vegetation
- Sandy desert
- Rocky desert
- Solid rock
- Main traffic route
- International boundary

4 – Large swathes of irrigated farmland near Mopti, the same-titled capital of the Mopti administrative region and the largest town in the Inner Niger Delta. The water comes from the Niger.

"Office du Niger"

This large agribusiness project in the Inner Niger Delta region was set up in 1932 by French industrialists and had various goals. Amongst others, an irrigation system was to create 960,000 hectares of farmland from Ségou in the west and Mopti (Fig. 2) up to the Mauretanian border by 1980 – not even 10 per cent has been achieved to date – and the region was to produce the cotton needed by French spinning mills. The project also aimed to safeguard the food supply in periods of drought and to ease the pressure on densely populated areas by way of relocation.

To achieve these goals, the Markala dam near Ségou was built to provide a constant amount of water for irrigation, regardless of the flood levels (Fig. 3). Mali declared its independence in 1960 and the new republic took over the project. By the 1970s, the intensive cotton cultivation in the region had turned out to be a mistake and was abandoned. The focus was then changed to rice cultivation. In the future, the irrigation system is set to be significantly expanded, upgraded, maintained and improved, funded by a number of NGOs and private investors.

Desertification in the Sahel

As a transition zone between the desert in the north and the semi-arid and sub-humid regions to the south, the Sahel has its very own ecosystem. Global climate change and constant human incursions into the natural world both pose a threat to the Sahel's ecosystem.

Plants grow only very slowly on its sandy soil but, at the same time, the population's needs for firewood and fodder for their livestock are growing. As a result, even the last few, sparse shrubs are disappearing. Without a natural plant barrier to stop it, the desert sand encroaches on more and more land (Fig. 3). Enormous amounts of sand are blowing into the steppe region and affecting plant growth – even when it rains. On top of that, people are moving to the southern steppes in search of usable vegetation. The population is growing extremely quickly and with it the need for wood for fuel and construction, for farmland and animal fodder. Since 1970, the Sahel has lost a belt of land around 100 kilometres wide to the Sahara through proceding desertification.

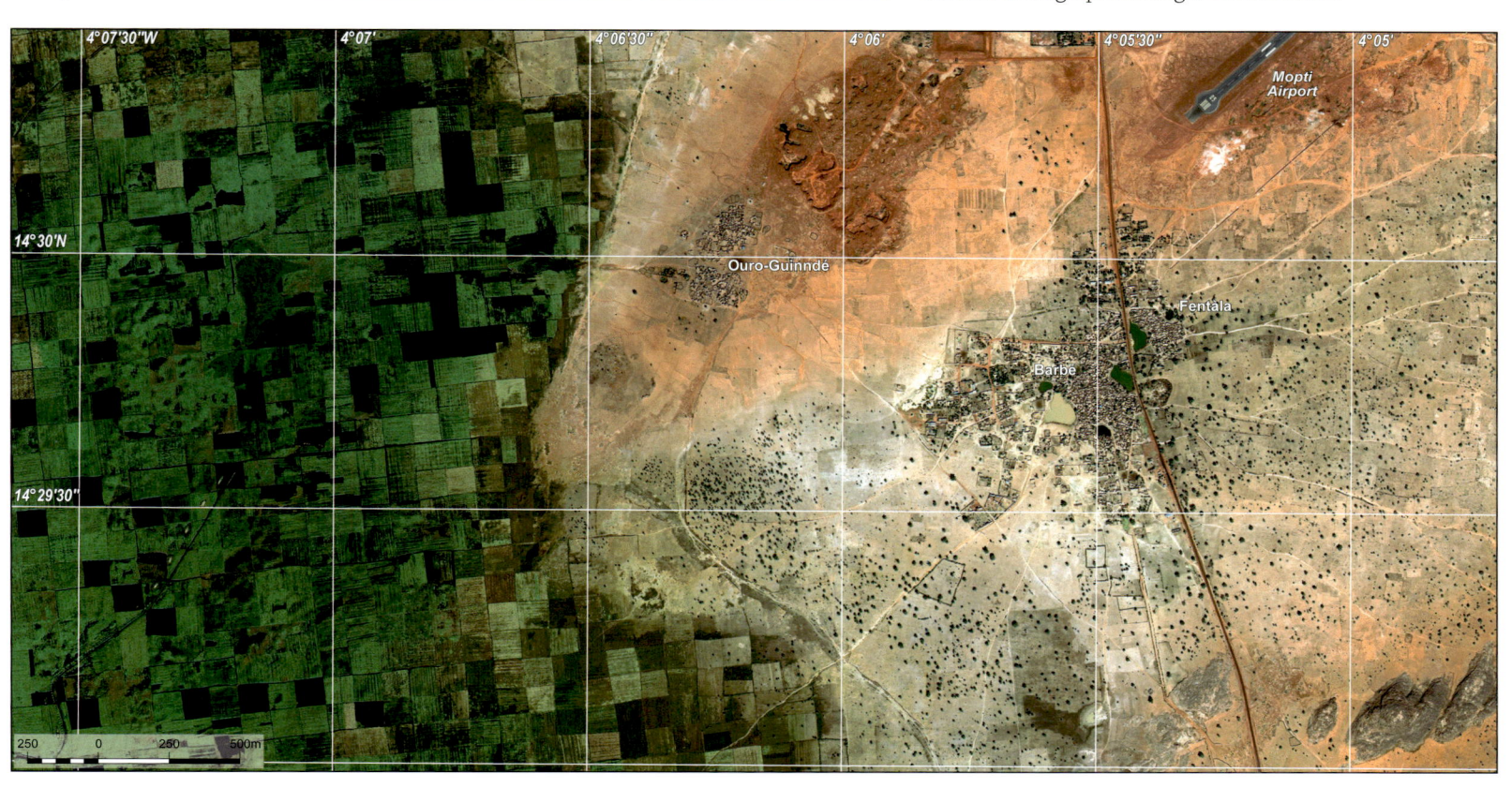

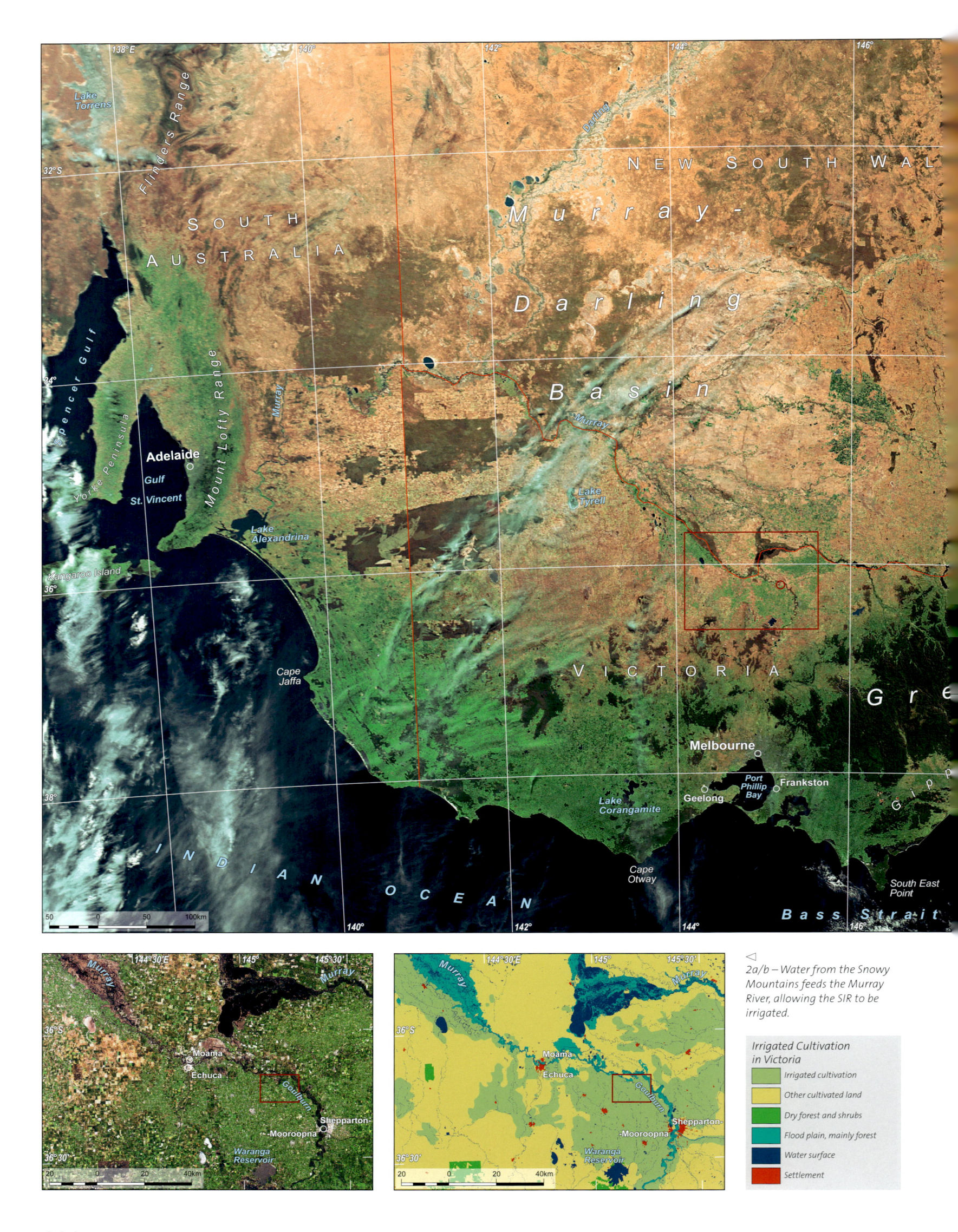

2a/b – Water from the Snowy Mountains feeds the Murray River, allowing the SIR to be irrigated.

Irrigated Cultivation in Victoria
- Irrigated cultivation
- Other cultivated land
- Dry forest and shrubs
- Flood plain, mainly forest
- Water surface
- Settlement

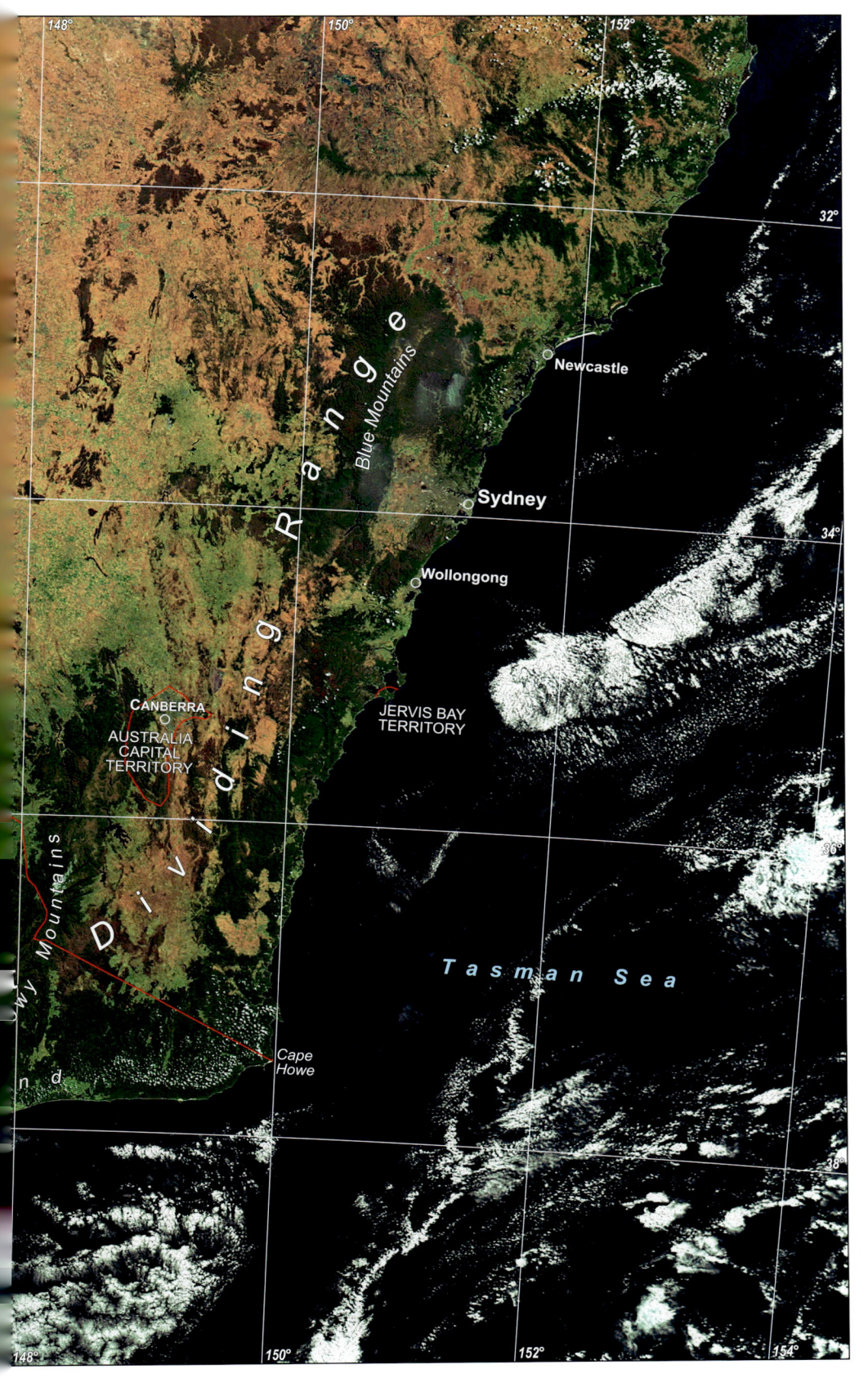

Irrigated farming in the southeast of Australia

After Antarctica, Australia is the driest continent on Earth. All the same, agriculture still plays an enormous role there. Australia provides the world with a large number of export commodities, including coal, bauxite, wool, meat and wheat, and is in fact the world's biggest exporter of some of them. Almost half of the country's area is used for livestock, while 3 per cent is used for arable farming.

The most important crop-growing area is the south-east of Australia (Fig. 1). The maritime subtropical climate is ideal for cultivating wheat, barley, fruit and grape vines, while the mountains, especially the Snowy Mountains, provide the water needed to irrigate the fields. In addition, the two longest rivers in Australia, the Darling and the Murray, also run through this region. The water from the mountains and rivers is diverted to the farmland via countless channels (Fig. 3).

To prevent water wastage and the salinisation of the soil, more and more areas are being equipped with what is known as an "integrated real-time irrigation scheduling system" for drip irrigation. With information provided by soil humidity sensors, the latest weather reports and crop data, the actual amount of water required can be re-calculated every day and this data automatically forwarded to the irrigation control systems.

Shepparton Irrigation Region

Measuring 500,000 hectares, the Shepparton Irrigation Region (SIR) is the largest agricultural region in the state of Victoria (Fig. 2a). Around two-thirds of the area is artificially irrigated (Fig. 2b). This situation made it necessary to construct dam walls along the rivers and streams to store the water so that it could then be distributed via the channels. Every year, around 1.5 billion cubic metres of water are diverted in this way to the fields of Shepparton. Modern irrigation systems aim to reduce water consumption and soil salinisation. The region mostly grows fruit, wheat and alfalfa. Dairy and meat production is also a major industry in the area. One in three people employed in the Goulburn Statistical Division, which includes the SIR, works in agriculture. The average gross annual yield is around AUD 1.5 billion.

Barossa Valley

The biggest wine-growing and internationally known region in Australia, the Barossa Valley, is situated in the state of South Australia in the Mount Lofty Range near the city of Adelaide (Fig. 1). The valley, which is around 30 kilometres long, has a favourable climate with distinct seasons. In the hot and dry summer months, many vineyards have to be irrigated, which is done in a sparing way by using drip irrigation.

In 1838 Germans emigrated to the area in search of religious freedom. The Silesian emigrant Johann Gramp planted the first grape vines in 1847, while Joseph Seppelt laid the foundations for one of the country's biggest wineries in Seppeltsfield. Soon after this, the valley became one of Australia's main wine-growing regions. Wines from the Barossa Valley have been exported to the UK already at the end of the 19th century. The major varieties are Shiraz, Cabernet Sauvignon, Riesling, Semillon and Chardonnay. In terms of area, Shiraz is the most important red variety.

The state of Victoria, to the north and south of the Great Dividing Range, is also home to numerous vineyards. They extend from the border with South Australia to the Murray, which forms the border with New South Wales (Fig. 1).

1 – The southeast of Australia is heavily farmed. The favourable climate here allows crops to thrive and the Snowy Mountains provide water to countless rivers and streams, enabling artificial irrigation.

3 – Water from the Murray and its tributaries is diverted to the artificially irrigated fields via an extensive network of channels.

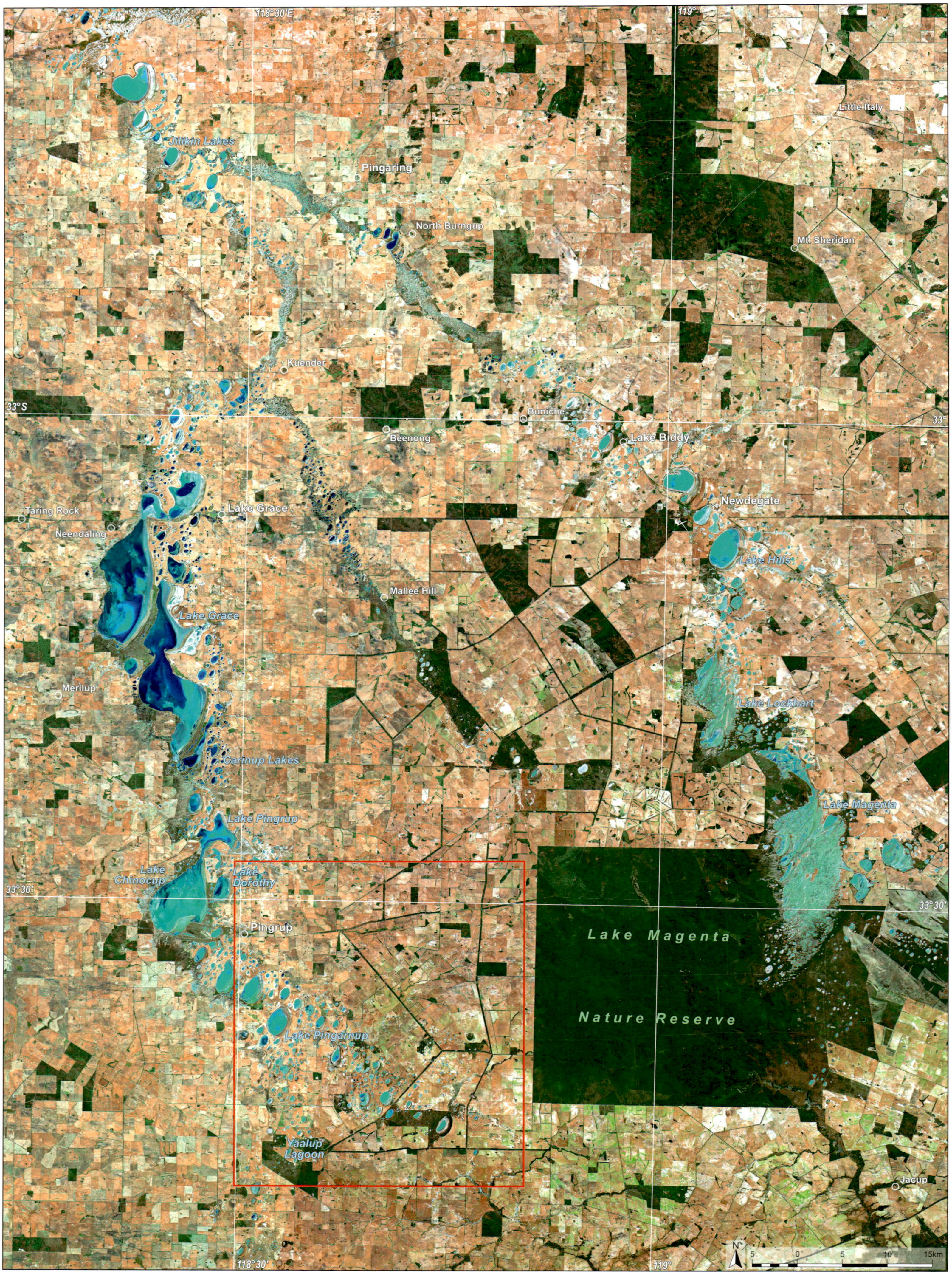
118°30'E
119°
Little Italy
Jilakin Lakes
Pingaring
North Burngup
Mt. Sheridan
Kuender
33°S
Buniche
33°
Beenong
Lake Biddy
Newdegate
Taring Rock
Lake Grace
Neendaling
Lake Hills
Mallee Hill
Lake Grace
Merilup
Lake Lockhart
Carinup Lakes
Lake Magenta
Lake Pingrup
Lake Chinocup
Lake Dorothy
33°30'
33°30'
Pingrup
Lake Magenta
Nature Reserve
Lake Pingarnup
Yaalup Lagoon
Jacup
118°30'
119°
N
5 0 5 10 15km

1 – A summer image of a section of the south-west of Australia shows salt lakes and the remnants of much greener natural vegetation in an extensively cleared, farmed landscape.

2 – Landsat satellite image of a section of the same area in spring (August) at the southern hemisphere. The fields show a higher vegetation density.

5 – This photo highlights the problem of increasing groundwater tables with subsequent salinisation, which leads to the degradation of what was once intact, fertile soil.

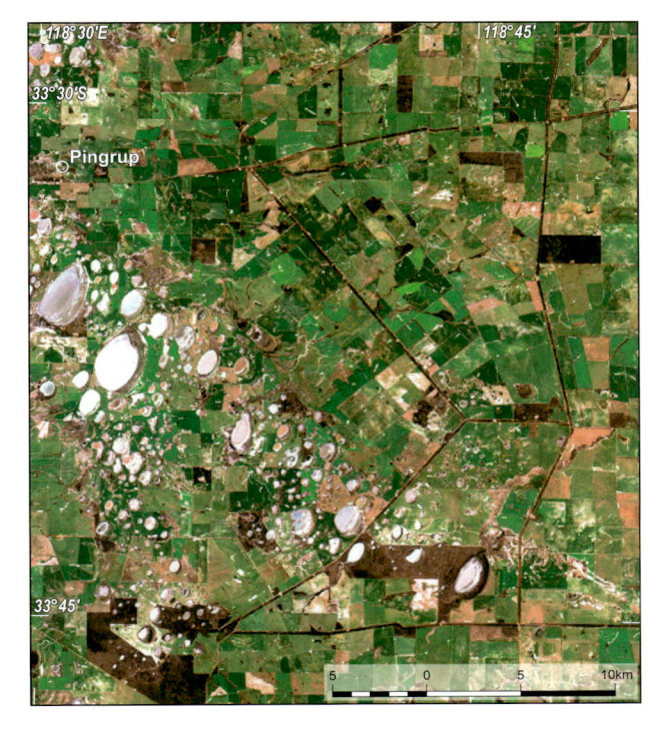

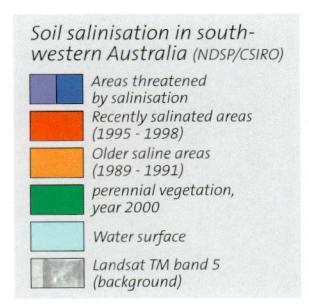

Soil salinisation in south-western Australia (NDSP/CSIRO)
- Areas threatened by salinisation
- Recently salinated areas (1995 - 1998)
- Older saline areas (1989 - 1991)
- perennial vegetation, year 2000
- Water surface
- Landsat TM band 5 (background)

3 – The map shows that large areas are suffering from salinisation, or are at risk of it.

4 – The south-west of Australia enjoys a Mediterranean climate with high rainfall. The native jarrah forest (a type of eucalyptus) appears in dark green, while the bordering yellow shows the farmed land in the drier Avon Wheatbelt region.

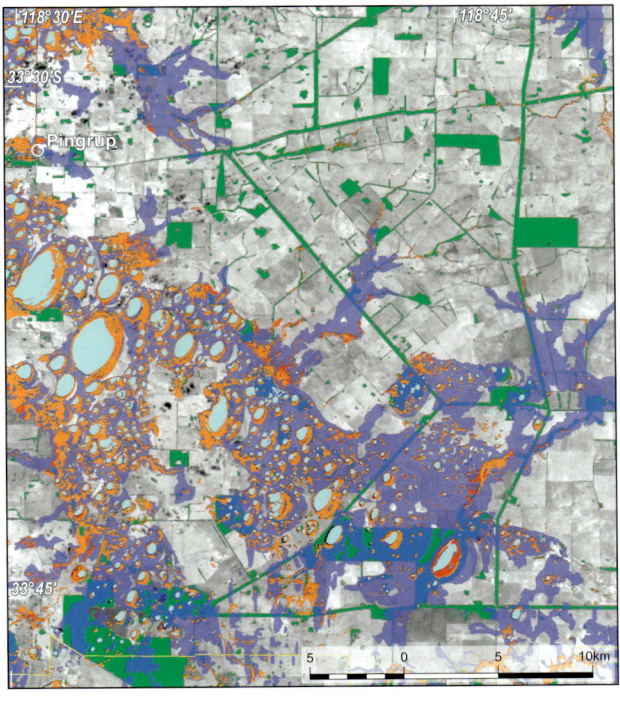

Dryland salinity in the southwest of Australia

Australia's south-western agricultural region covers 24 million hectares. Since European settlement in the 19th century, the native perennial vegetation of eucalyptus and acacia forests has been extensively cleared for agriculture, principally for annual crops and pastures. The deep-rooted, saline-tolerant plants which had adapted to extreme conditions have thus had to make way for cultivated plants (today primarily wheat, barley, rapeseed and lupine).

A combination of climate, geology, widespread land clearing and inefficient irrigation agriculture has resulted in a major dryland salinity problem (Figs. 3 and 5). The soil naturally contains salt as a result of weathering. In addition, maritime salt transported by wind has been accumulating over millions of years in the soils and deep groundwater of the region. In this flat landscape, drainage is poor and the water balance was once maintained by deep-rooted native perennial vegetation. The prevalence of arable crops with short roots results in the water in the soil moving upwards with capillary motion, which transports the salts to the upper layers of soil. Artificial irrigation leads to the additional accumulation of salts in the upper layers of soil and also to salt input into rivers.

Salinisation of land and waterways has been recognised as the highest-priority environmental issue in the region (Figs. 1 and 3). Approximately one million hectares of land are salt-affected and 14,000 more hectares are affected each year. Often, it is highly-productive fields on low-lying land and in valley floors which are lost (Figs. 3 and 5). Almost all streams flowing through the region have increasing salinity levels, with impacts on urban and rural water supplies.

The region is renowned for its high plant diversity. Salinisation is a major threat also to biodiversity values. Former freshwater wetlands have become salt deserts, resulting in the loss of important vegetation and habitat.

In the "Land Monitor" project satellite imagery has been processed and combined with other data to map the extent of salt-affected land. The aim of this project is to monitor changes and to predict the future extent of salinisation (Fig. 3).

Text: Jeremy Wallace

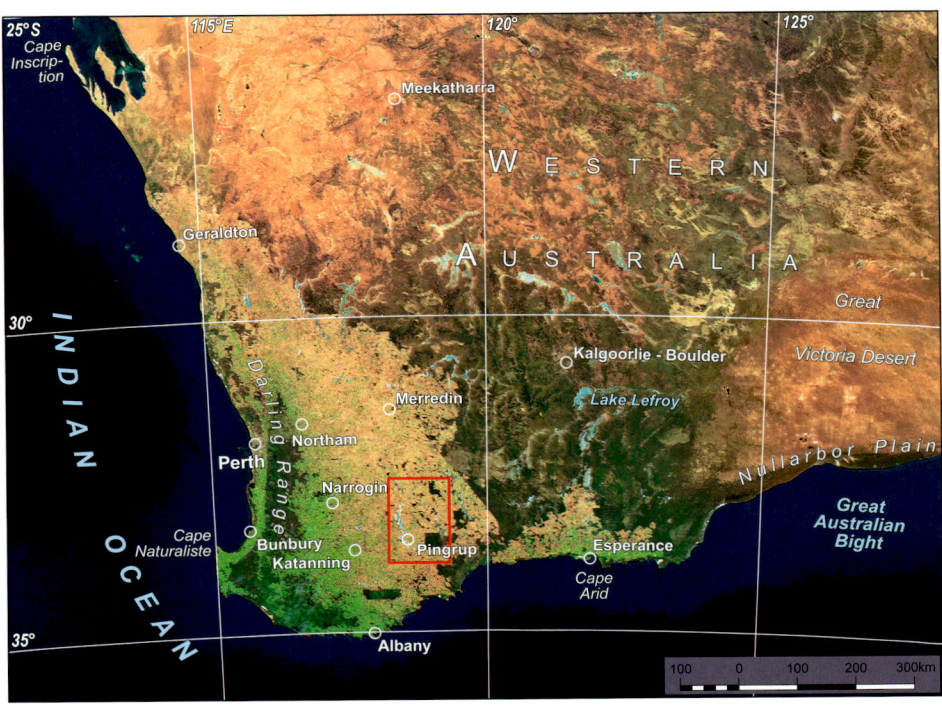

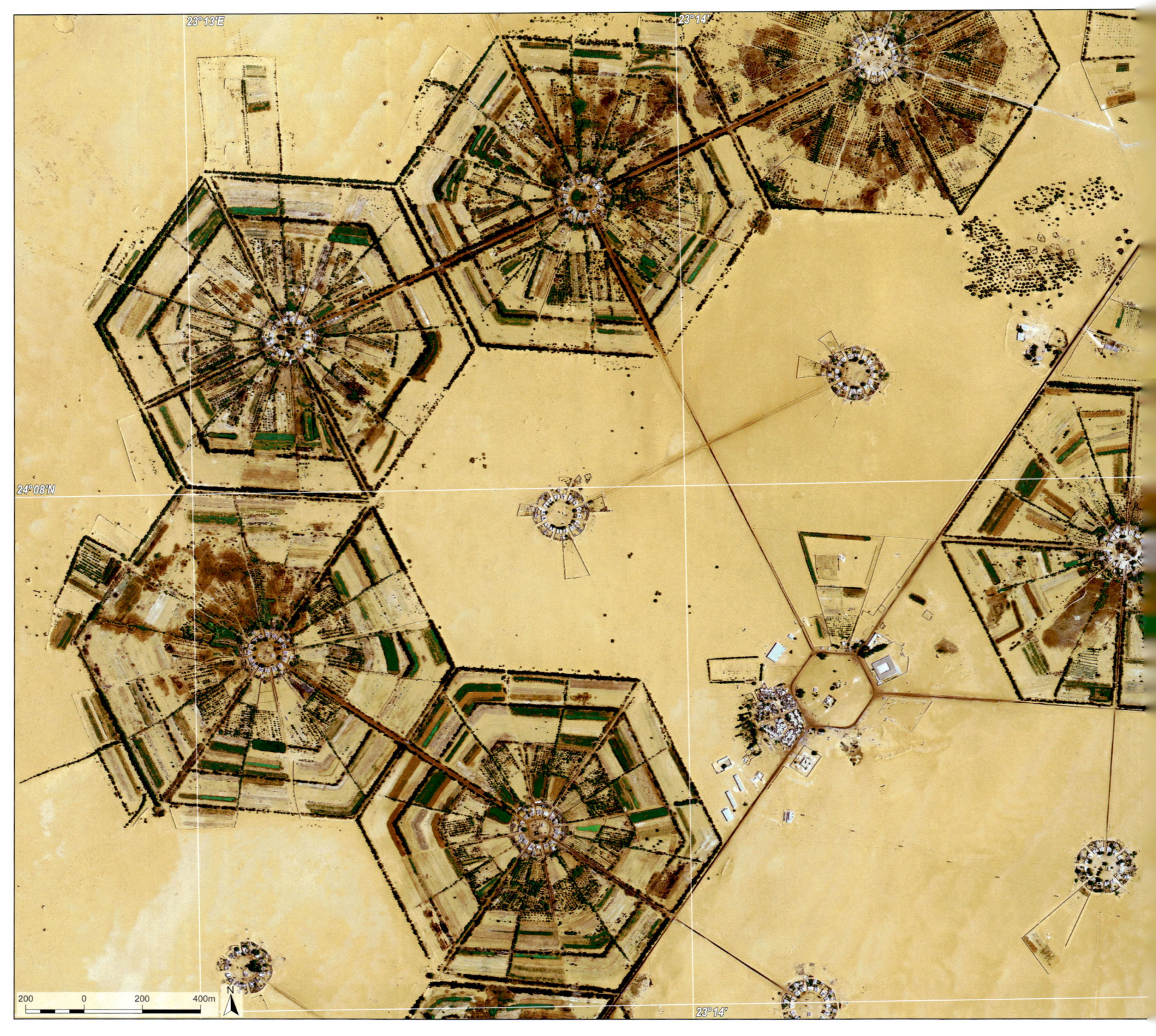

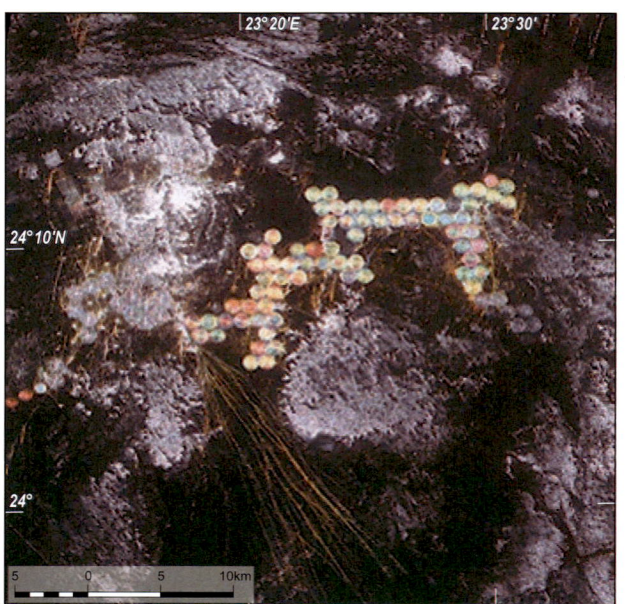

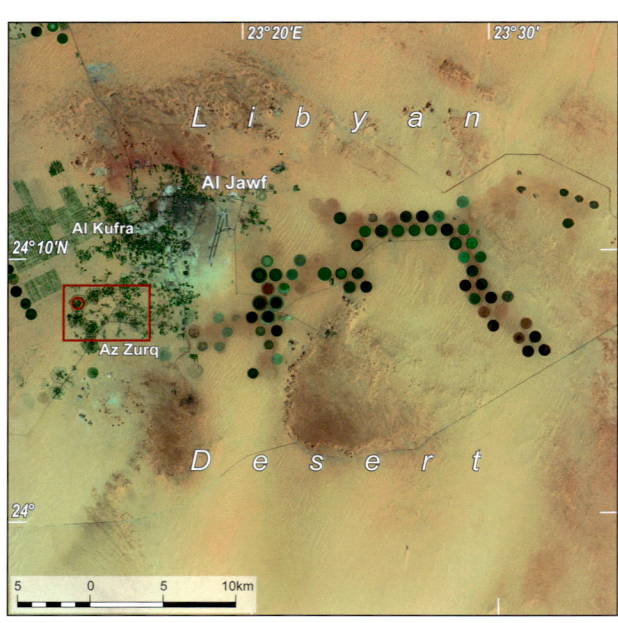

△
1 – The hexagonal shape of the older Libyan irrigation systems are the result of hedges planted to protect against wind erosion and sand accumulation; the western part of Al Kufra is shown here.

◁
2 – This multitemporal radar satellite image from the ASAR sensor (Envisat) illustrates the different geological structures. The coarse rock formations around the oases appear as light grey. As a result of its flatness, the desert sand appears as a much darker shade.
The different vegetation phases of the fields are shown in different colours.

3 – An overview of the Al Kufra oases shows the arrangement and structure of the irrigated areas in the sands of the eastern Sahara. In the west, hexagonal shapes; in the east, centre-pivot irrigation dominates.

4 – In the centre of each hexagon is a well, with farm buildings arranged in a circle around it.

The Al Kufra oases

The province of Al Kufra, with its oasis group of the same name, is located in the south-eastern part of Libya in the central region of the Sahara (Fig. 3). Because of the extremely arid climate, the region receives on average only a few millimetres of rainfall every year. The Sahara covers almost all of the country of Libya. Only six per cent of the country, mostly located near the coast of the Mediterranean Sea, is suitable for natural farming. Without any permanent rivers or lakes, the cultivation of field crops is possible only through artificial irrigation and the pumping up of fossil water. The Kufra aquifer is the source of the groundwater and is one of four major bodies of groundwater in Libya. The Kufra basin has an area of over 350,000 square kilometres and contains an estimated 20,000 cubic kilometres of groundwater.

Using radar images, it is possible to make out the geomorphology of an ancient network of water courses that cannot be seen from the surface. The former river valleys in the eastern Sahara, which are now buried under dunes, primarily originated in the last humid phase in the Sahara (around 9,000 to 5,000 years ago). Some, though, date back even further. Wadi Kufra, with its oasis group, is located within this former river system (Fig. 2). Large-scale irrigation systems were set up here in the 1970s, enabling extensive farming of the area. After 30 years of extraction and the resultant evaporation, the groundwater level had fallen by 60 metres. The reservoir holds only fossil water and is not renewed by natural sources.

The western part of Al Kufra, the original oasis, shows a hexagonal structure of the areas of farmland (Figs. 1 and 3). These areas mark the point when farmers starting using groundwater over 30 years ago. To irrigate the fields, groundwater is pumped into the centre of each hexagon and is distributed from there (Fig. 4) to the peripheral parts of the hexagons. Hedges planted along the edges of each plot shall protect the fields from wind erosion and sand accumulation (Fig. 1).

Most of the irrigated areas in Al Kufra, however, are circular (Fig. 2). As in Saudi Arabia, the more effective and water-conserving centre-pivot irrigation system has begun to be used instead. These fields have a diameter of one kilometre and are irrigated by a network of rotating sprinklers running close over the ground (Figs. 3 and 4). Around 10,000 hectares of land can be farmed in Al Kufra as a result.

However, as is the case in all arid regions where irrigated farming is popular, there is a danger here too of salinisation and the drying out of the fossil water reserves.

The Great Man-Made River project

Test boreholes in the area have shown a rich supply of groundwater, prompting the Libyan government to launch one of the biggest water development projects in the world. The "Great Man-Made River" project (GM-MRP) extracts groundwater from five important bodies of groundwater: the Kufra, Sirt, Murzuk, Hamadah and Jufrah. Through pipelines some of the water is pumped into the drinking water supply network, providing the entire northern coastal region with water. The rest is used by the country's agricultural irrigation systems. Additional boreholes have been drilled nearby in order to observe the groundwater levels.

The question of what will happen to agriculture and the drinking water supply in Libya once the fossil water has run out will be of great importance in the coming years to the population, as well as to hydrologists and other scientists.

226

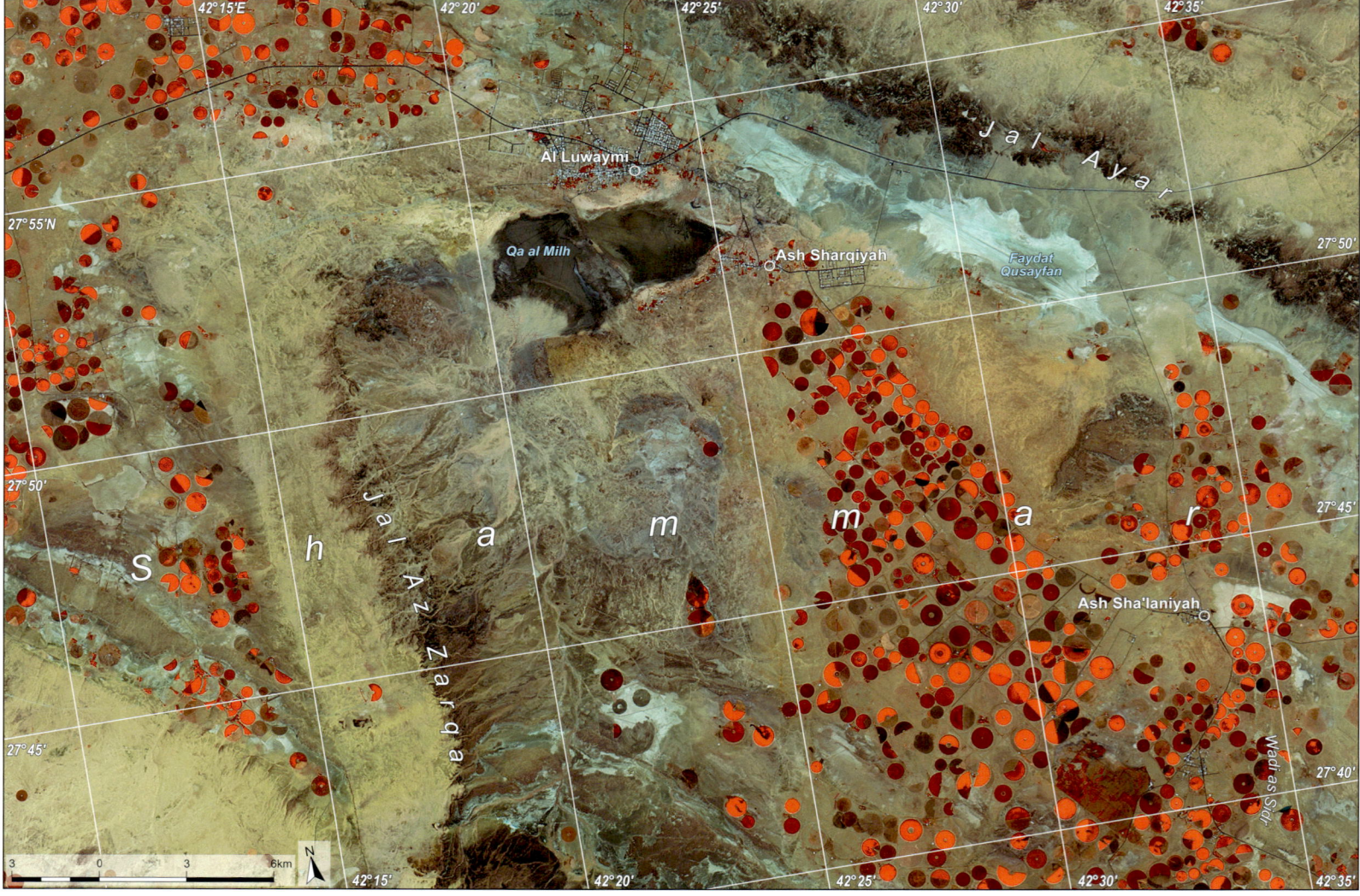

◁ *1 – This Landsat MSS satellite image shows part of the Shammar region to the east of Ha'il in the north of Saudi Arabia.
In 1972, there were no signs of large-scale agricultural cultivation of the desert region through artificial irrigation.*

▷ *3 – The circular fields are characteristic of centre-pivot irrigation, as here in Al Busayta in the Al Jawf region in the north of Saudi Arabia.*

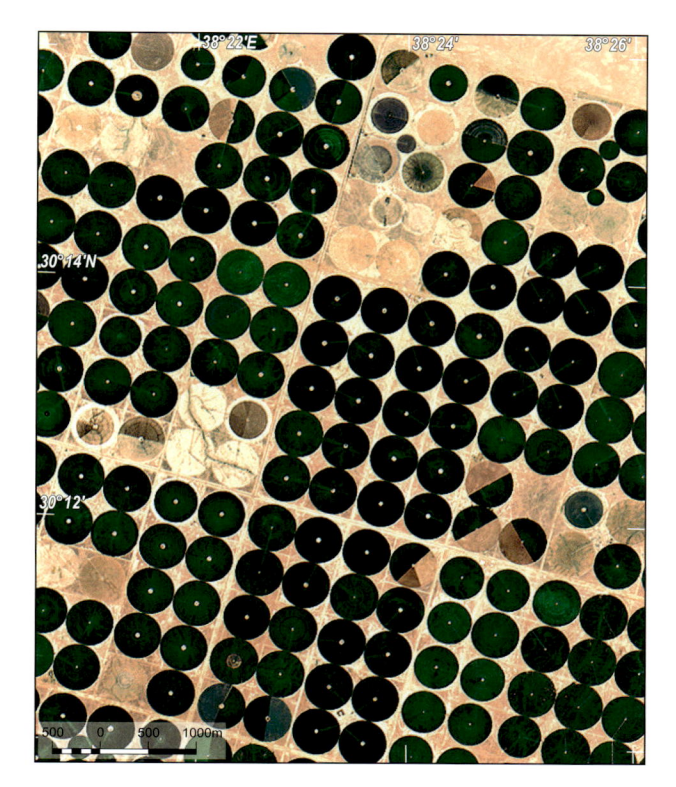

▷ *4 – The angled aerial photo shows a farm irrigated by a centre-pivot irrigation system.*

◁ *2 – The desert region has changed massively over the last 40 years. In the satellite image from 2013, a number of circular fields are visible around Ha'il. The red colour of the irrigated areas results from the infrared false-colour Landsat OLI image.*

▽ *5 – Rotating pivot irrigation system with sprinklers.*

Irrigation in Saudi Arabia

Farming plays an important role here, despite the desert nation's physical geography putting it at a disadvantage. Farms set up in the desert regions of Saudi Arabia have been subsidised by the government since the 1970s (Figs. 1 and 2). To make farming possible here at all major technical and financial efforts are necessary, since without artificial irrigation only a tiny area could be farmed. These areas are primarily oases where date palms are grown. Forage crops, wheat, vegetables and fruit are grown on artificially irrigated land. The breeding and farming of livestock, including cattle, camels, sheep, goats and chickens, also plays a major role.

As a result of the arid climate, farms here require enormous amounts of water. Most of this comes from fossil sources deep underground. These non-renewable bodies of groundwater formed during the ice ages that ended 25,000 years ago. Intensively drawing on the groundwater supply leads to lower groundwater levels and a constant drop in natural water pressure. Therefore the remaining water must be pumped to the surface using powerful pumps, which consume more energy and money.

To fill up the groundwater reserves in Saudi Arabia, many places divert the rainwater that collects in wadis into the ground through a system of pipes. This helps minimise the surface evaporation of the valuable resource, as well as the draw on the now lower levels of regional support available for finite resources. As a result, highly water-intensive wheat farming is to be halted altogether in Saudi Arabia by 2016.

As in almost all arid regions, irrigated farming has serious consequences for the soil in Saudi Arabia too. The high evaporation rate results in the increased salinisation of the farmland (Fig. 2), which is exacerbated by the fact that the sinking groundwater table also increases the salt content of the water pumped up to the irrigation systems. As a consequence, the fertility of the fields is reduced.

The largest farming regions are in the northern plains of Saudi Arabia, where they stretch from Hafr al-Batin in the east to Tabuk in the west. Inside this area lie Ha'il (Figs. 1 and 2) and Al Jawf, two of the largest agricultural regions in the country. The circular fields are typical of the region (Fig. 3).

Centre-pivot irrigation systems

The round fields dominating the satellite images are due to the irrigation method used here, known as the centre-pivot irrigation system (Figs. 2 and 3). The field is irrigated via rotating sprinklers featuring a long, horizontal pipe supported by wheels and driven by a motor (Figs. 4 and 5). The system rotates in a circle around its own axis and is fed by a central water supply in the middle. Because the water falls directly on the plants and is not sprayed into the air first as standard sprinkler systems do, the evaporation rate is lower, which conserves water. In addition, efforts are being made to ensure that the crops best suited to the various regions' soil types and climates are selected. Centre-pivot irrigation is primarily used on flat ground. In contrast, the Asir Mountains in the south-west of Saudi Arabia favour terraced cultivation.

This form of farming requires major financial investments and a high degree of expertise. The Saudi government has supported the cultivation of the desert regions and is now supporting the cultivation of North Africa too, so that it will have access to new farming regions in the future. Today, the country is still largely self-sufficient and even exports agricultural products to neighbouring countries.

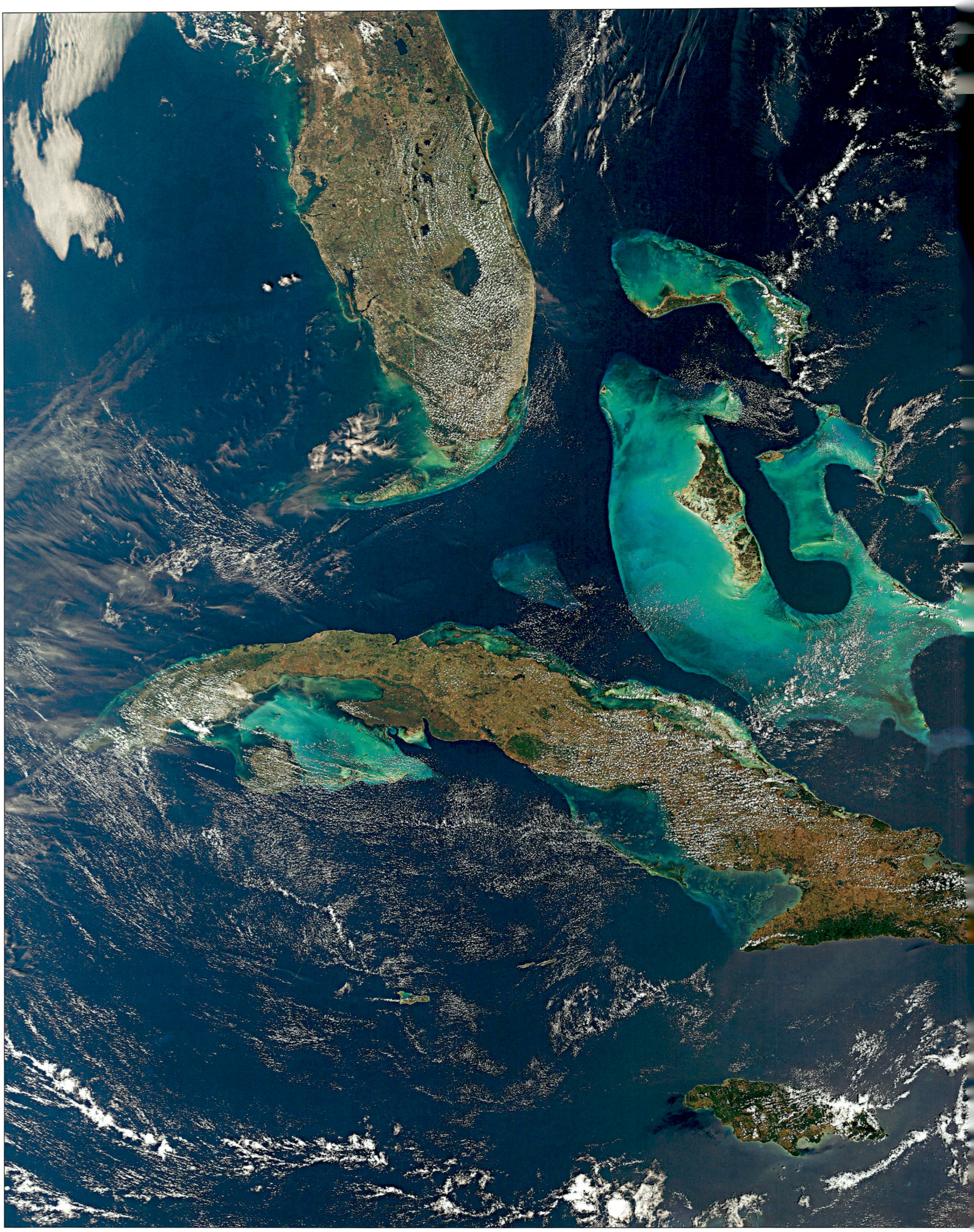

WATER-USE COMPETITION

Various types of usage in one and the same area are often in direct competition with one another.

Since time immemorial, the sea and its coastal regions have offered extraordinary opportunities to the surrounding land. Traditional forms of use are predominantly fishing and shipping, along with the associated industries. Over the course of the last century, however, the demands made on water resources have shot up exponentially. Operators of oil refineries and natural gas plants, wind farms, aquaculture farms and tourist resorts are putting ever more pressure on already stretched coastal ecosystems. All are in direct competition with one another, and all are competing with efforts to protect the environment. In future, the demands on water resources will increase further as a result of population pressure and the limited space available in coastal and marine zones. Even today, we are barely able to deal with the impacts from the overuse of our seas and coastal regions.

Hypoxia in the Gulf of Mexico

Every summer, the northern part of the Gulf of Mexico, just off the coast of Louisiana and along the mouths of the Mississippi and the Atchafalaya, sees incursions of hypoxia. The term hypoxia refers to depleted water oxygen levels that are so low they start to affect aquatic life. Aside from naturally occurring variations in water oxygen levels, hypoxia is primarily triggered by eutrophication – that is, the entry of, predominantly, fertilisers, and also sewage, into the aquatic system. Nutrients such as nitrates and phosphates are important for preserving natural habitats in the water. However, if the nitrate, nitrite, ammonium or phosphate levels in the water are too high, algal growth becomes excessive, which lowers the water's oxygen levels. The resultant phytoplankton blooms block the sunlight from penetrating into the deeper water layers. Shaded by the blooms, the plants growing on the seabed die. Bacteria then break down the dead plants and algae, which further depletes the dissolved oxygen in the water.

Of around 400 dead zones observed worldwide, natural hypoxia occurs on a large scale along the Mississippi River Delta (Fig. 2, pp. 230/231). Less dense, the warmer freshwater forms a layer above the colder saltwater. As the two layers of water fail to mix, the oxygen content of the lower layer declines. Coupled with the anthropo-

◁
1 – Southern Florida, the Bahamas and the Greater Antilles are classed as ecosystem under threat. The waters of the Caribbean are struggling to cope with effects of the increasing number of tourists. Shallow waters show up in light blue/green colours.

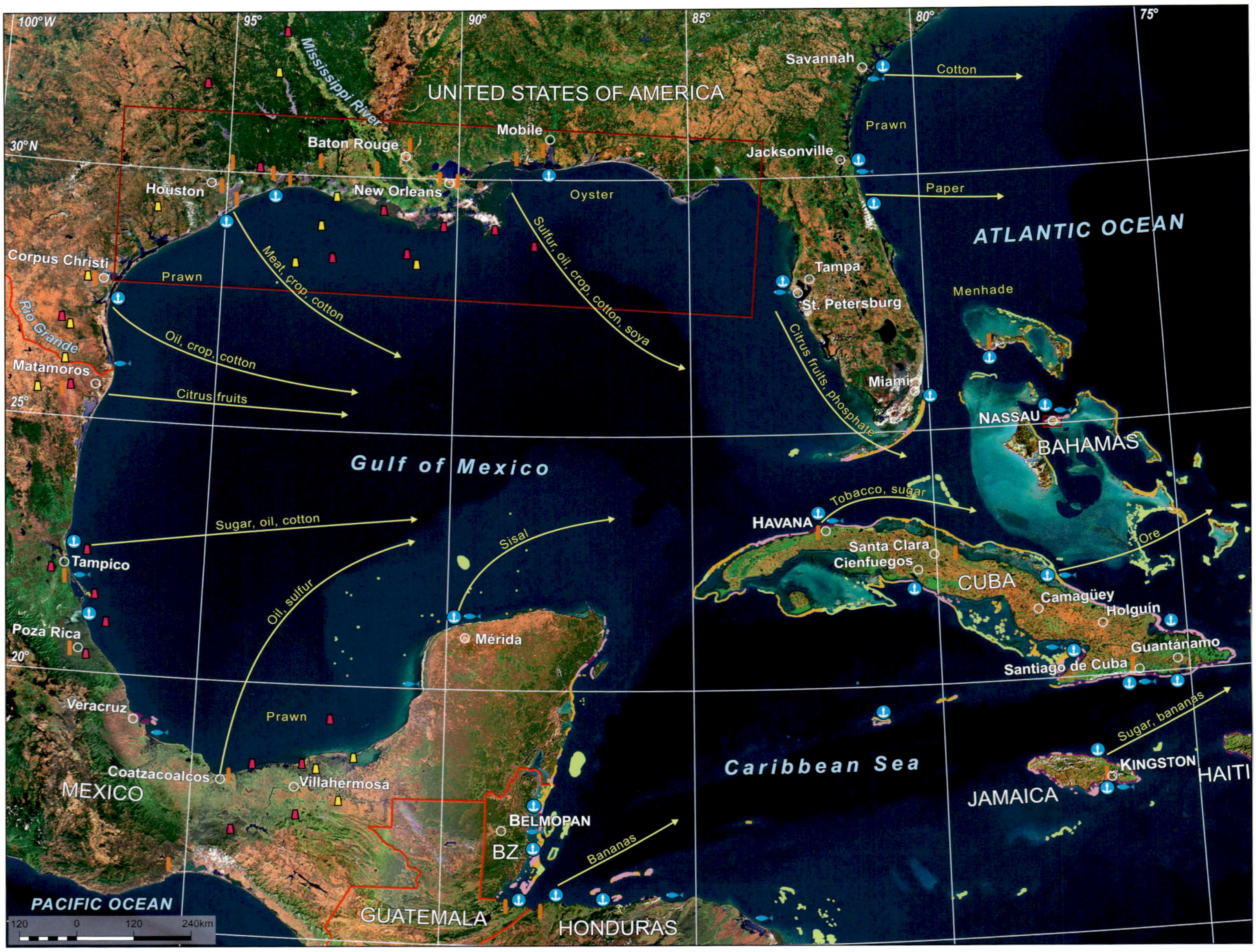
100°W
95°
90°
85°
80°
75°
30°N
25°
20°
UNITED STATES OF AMERICA
Mississippi River
Savannah
Cotton
Prawn
Mobile
Baton Rouge
Jacksonville
Houston
New Orleans
Oyster
Paper
ATLANTIC OCEAN
Corpus Christi
Prawn
Meat, crop, cotton
Sulfur, oil, crop, cotton, soya
Tampa
St. Petersburg
Menhade
Rio Grande
Oil, crop, cotton
Citrus fruits, phosphate
Matamoros
Miami
Citrus fruits
NASSAU
BAHAMAS
Gulf of Mexico
Tobacco, sugar
HAVANA
Sugar, oil, cotton
Sisal
Tampico
Oil, sulfur
Santa Clara
Cienfuegos
CUBA
Ore
Camagüey
Holguín
Mérida
Poza Rica
Guantánamo
Santiago de Cuba
Veracruz
Prawn
Sugar, bananas
Coatzacoalcos
Caribbean Sea
KINGSTON
HAITI
Villahermosa
MEXICO
JAMAICA
BELMOPAN
BZ
Bananas
PACIFIC OCEAN
GUATEMALA
HONDURAS
120
0
120
240km

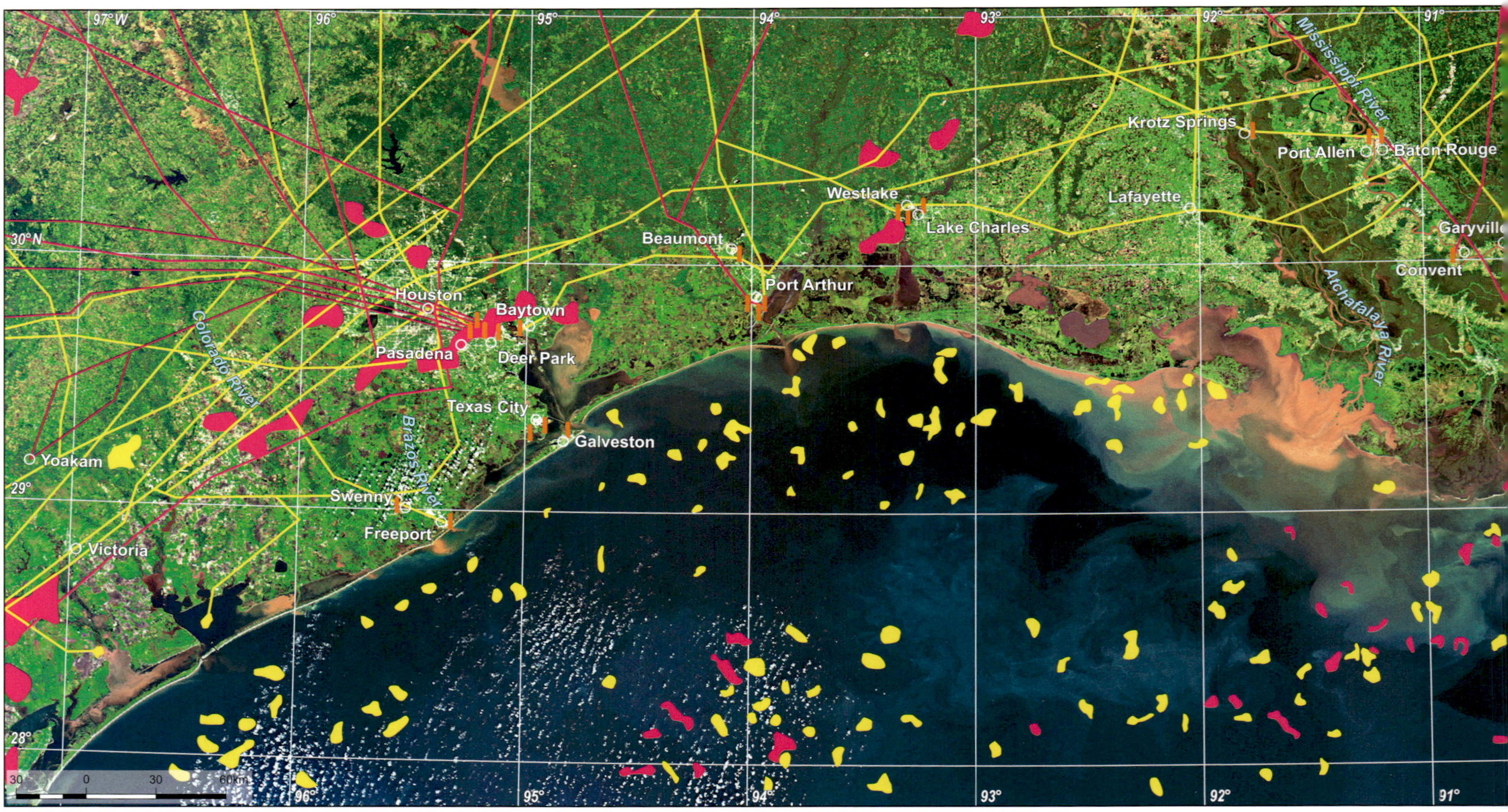
97°W
96°
95°
94°
93°
92°
91°
Mississippi River
Krotz Springs
Port Allen
Baton Rouge
Westlake
Lafayette
Lake Charles
Garyville
30°N
Beaumont
Convent
Houston
Port Arthur
Atchafalaya River
Baytown
Pasadena
Deer Park
Colorado River
Texas City
Brazos River
Galveston
Yoakam
29°
Swenny
Freeport
Victoria
28°
30
0
30
60km
96°
95°
94°
93°
92°
91°

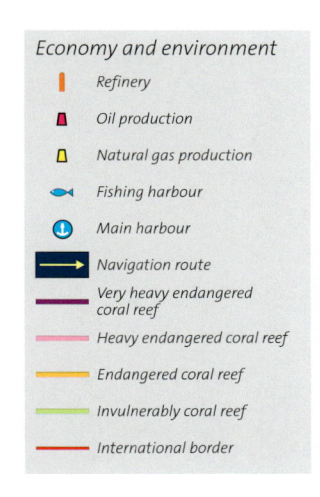

Economy and environment
- Refinery
- Oil production
- Natural gas production
- Fishing harbour
- Main harbour
- Navigation route
- Very heavy endangered coral reef
- Heavy endangered coral reef
- Endangered coral reef
- Invulnerably coral reef
- International border

◁
1 – Both the Gulf of Mexico and the Caribbean are good examples of the differing interests in exploiting the sea.

▷△
3 – New Providence Island, home to the capital of the Bahamas, Nassau, as well as beautiful coral reefs, is one of the biggest tourist destinations in the Caribbean.

▽
2 – There are huge oil and natural gas reserves in the Gulf of Mexico. More and more drill platforms are being built.

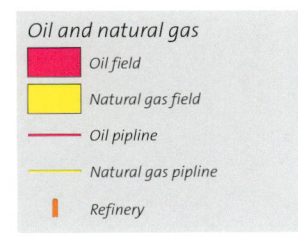

Oil and natural gas
- Oil field
- Natural gas field
- Oil pipeline
- Natural gas pipeline
- Refinery

genic influences, this gives rise to extreme conditions for living organisms. The low oxygen levels pose a threat to commercial fishing as well as to the prawn and shrimp farms along the American coast. Once the oxygen levels decrease beyond a certain point, the schools of fish migrate to other regions, while organisms tied to the area die.

In summer 2002, the hypoxic zone covered 22,000 square kilometres – its largest extent ever recorded (equal in 2007, 2008, 2011). This annually recurring phenomenon continues until the first hurricanes of the year mix the water layers, providing the deeper zones with oxygen. The Gulf of Mexico oil spill following the explosion at the Deepwater Horizon oil drilling platform (Fig. 2) in April 2010 exacerbated the hypoxia and expanded the affected zone.

The Caribbean – a paradise whose days are numbered
Apart from harmful agricultural runoff, pollution in this region is also caused by cruise ships, oil tankers and other ships, and represents an increasing threat to the environment and to the health of the local population. With 50,000 ships passing through it annually, the marginal sea is one of the busiest shipping zones in the world. Cruise ships in particular, carrying 14.5 million tourists per year, mark an extreme trend. The coastlines of many islands along the cruise routes are being strongly impacted by the heavy traffic. This satellite image (Fig. 1) shows how much of the coastline is accompanied by coral reefs. A great many of them are at low to high risk, as far north as the coast off Nassau (Fig. 3). A typical cruise ship with 3,000 passengers on board produces 400 to 1,200 cubic metres of sewage per day, and around one tonne of rubbish. This waste is for the most part disposed of in the sea beyond the three-nautical-mile limit. The ballast water tanks aboard all ships can become home to species that are then transported far from their natural habitats and can sometimes go on to threaten the existence of locally indigenous, and often already at-risk, flora and fauna.

In the Dominican Republic alone, 186 non-native species have been conducted.

In addition to passenger ships, the Caribbean is also crossed by a great many oil tankers (Fig. 1). Oil from the tankers spills into the Caribbean waters as a result of accidents or incorrect tank-cleaning procedures and leaves oily films on the water's surface. Several oil-drilling platforms were also damaged by Hurricane Katrina in August 2005. More than 13 million litres of oil leaked into the sea, forming a slick that covered an area of more than 18,000 square kilometres. Off the coast of Louisiana, around 800 million litres of oil leaked from a borehole under the Deepwater Horizon between April 20 and July 16 of 2010. It was the worst environmental disaster of its kind in history.

Anthropogenic activities on land are also threatening ecosystems in the Caribbean. With ever cheaper air fares and seemingly irresistible all-inclusive holiday packages, the number of holidaymakers heading for the Caribbean is on the rise, and so the number of problems increases. Untreated sewage, toxic substances from overflowing landfill sites and building developments on former mangrove swamps and along the coastlines are all contributing to the destruction of the Caribbean.

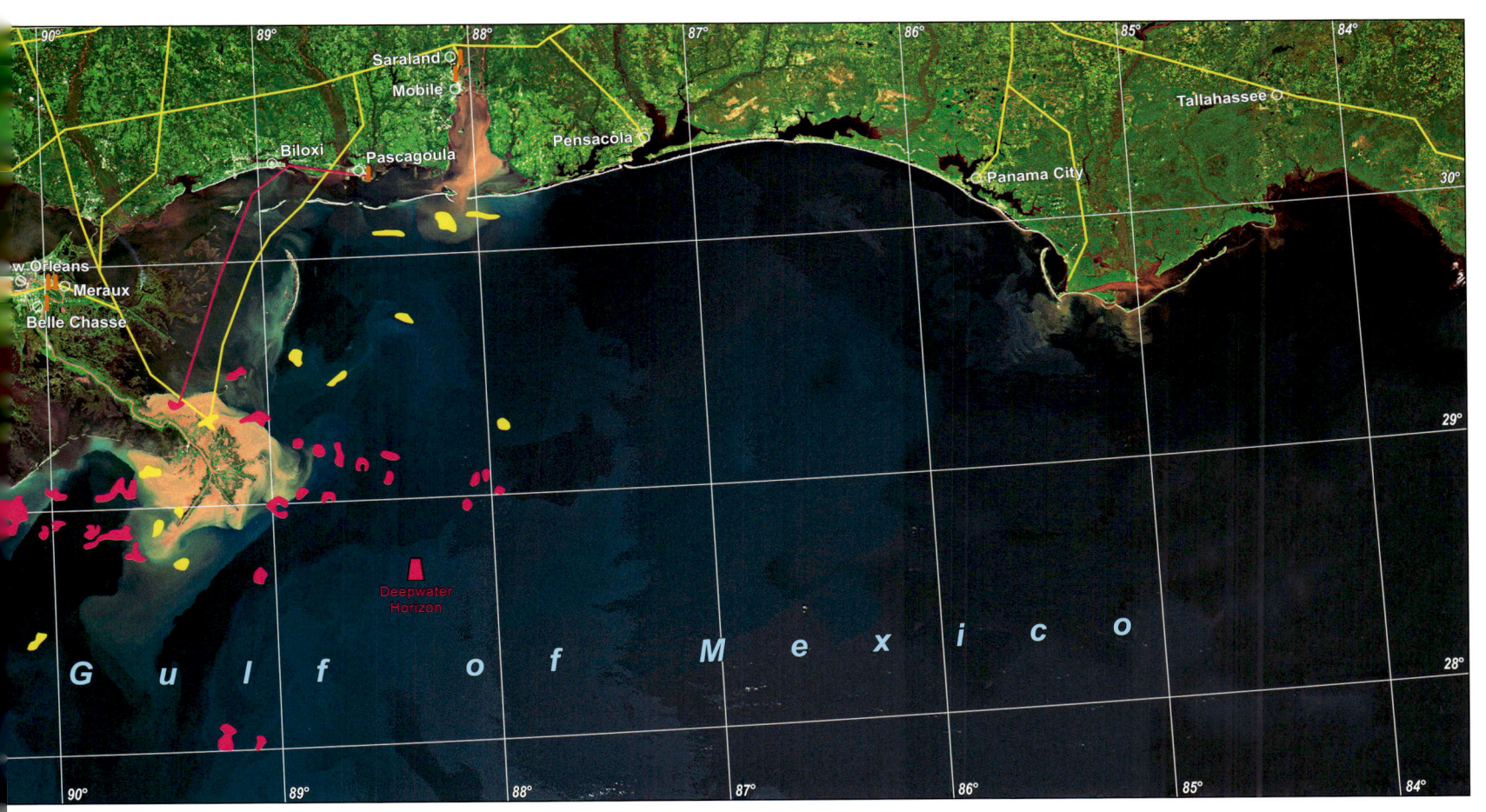

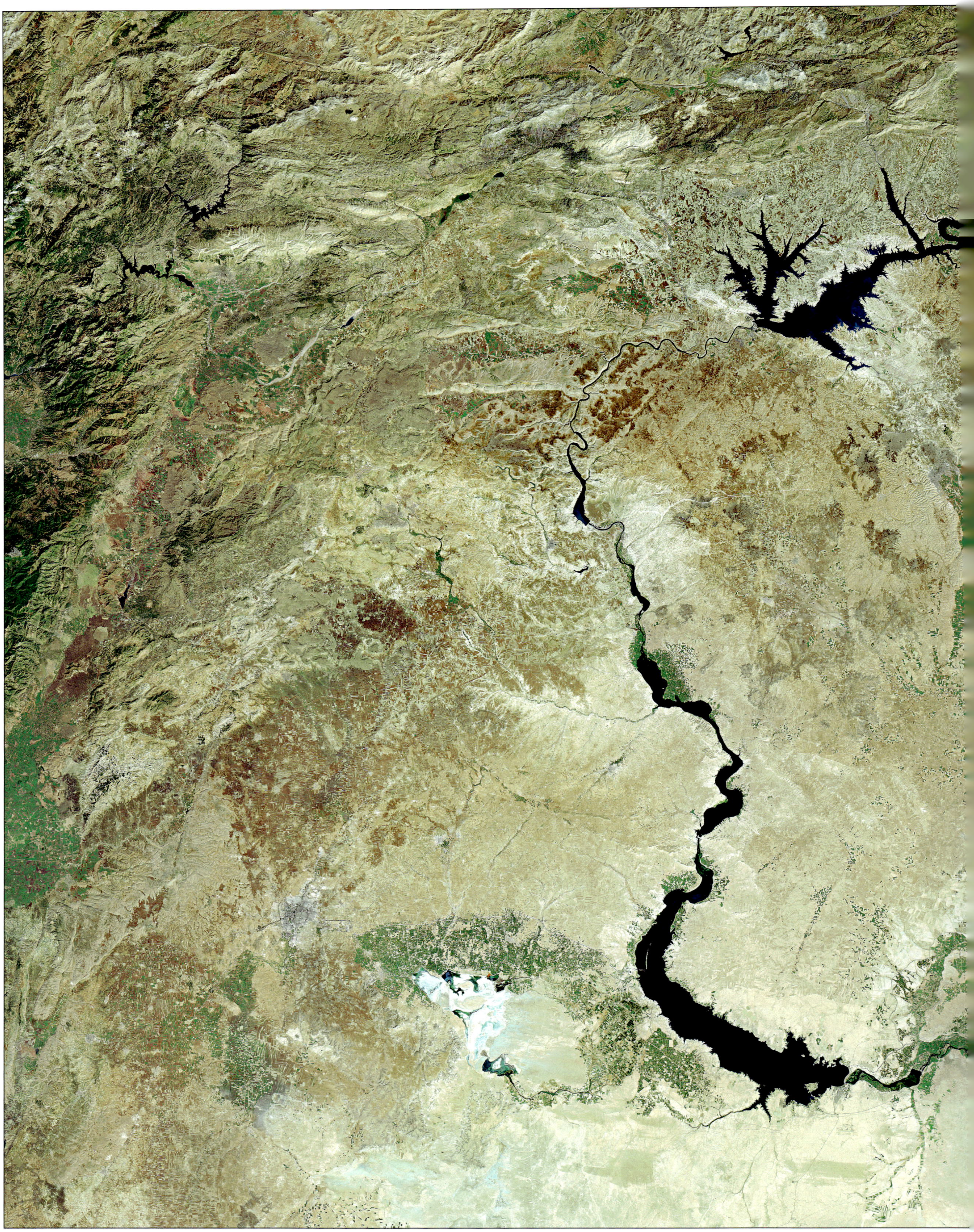

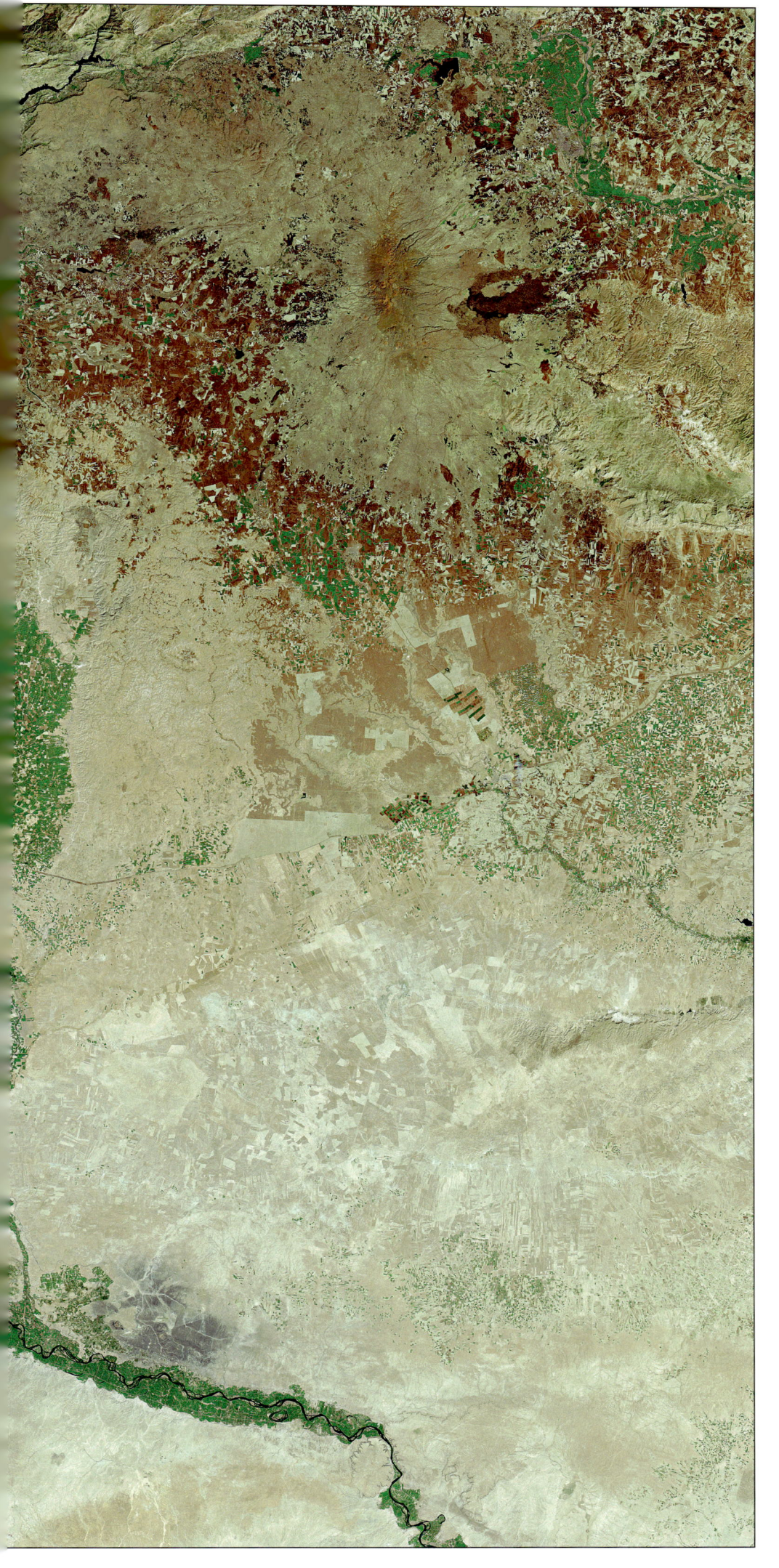

UTILISATION CONFLICTS

Resource scarcity and the unequal distribution of water can lead to conflicts between countries accessing the same water supply system.

Half of the world's population lives next to the 276 trans-boundary river systems that are used by two or more countries. As a natural resource, water is subject to a variety of uses. In addition to its function as a habitat, freshwater is also essential to life. Other important roles are energy generation and the transportation of goods and persons. In addition, water is essential for growing foodstuffs.

Water scarcity can easily lead to conflicts. Arid regions in particular are highly susceptible to tensions between one or more states if one country decides to build a dam or divert a significant amount of water for artificial irrigation, which then reduces the amount of this vital resource available to the countries downstream.

Water usage rights on the Tigris and the Euphrates

The Euphrates and Tigris rivers have been the subject of major conflicts between the riparian states of Turkey, Syria and Iraq (Fig. 1; Fig. 3, p. 235) for many years.

Both rivers rise in Turkey, flow through Syria and join together in the Iraqi lowlands to form the Shatt al 'Arab, which empties into the Persian Gulf. At around 2,800 kilometres, the Euphrates is the longest river in Western Asia. It is formed by the confluence of the Karasu (Western Euphrates) and the Murat (Eastern Euphrates). Most of the river's water comes from Turkey. Only four per cent of its flow is added by tributaries in Syria. The Tigris rises in the Taurus Mountains and, at 1,851 kilometres in length, is the second-longest river in Western Asia.

The debate over water usage rights was sparked in 1977 by the Turkish government's Southeastern Anatolia Project, known as the GAP (Güneydogu Anadolu Projesi) project. It included plans to build 22 dams, 19 power generation plants and countless canals on the Euphra-

◁
1 – The Euphrates crosses the Turkey/Syria border. Syria's Tabqa Dam east of Aleppo created Lake Assad. On the Turkish side, the Atatürk Dam, part of the GAP Southeastern Anatolia Project, has been generating electricity since 1992.

233

Changes in the Euphrates landscape (1976/2000)

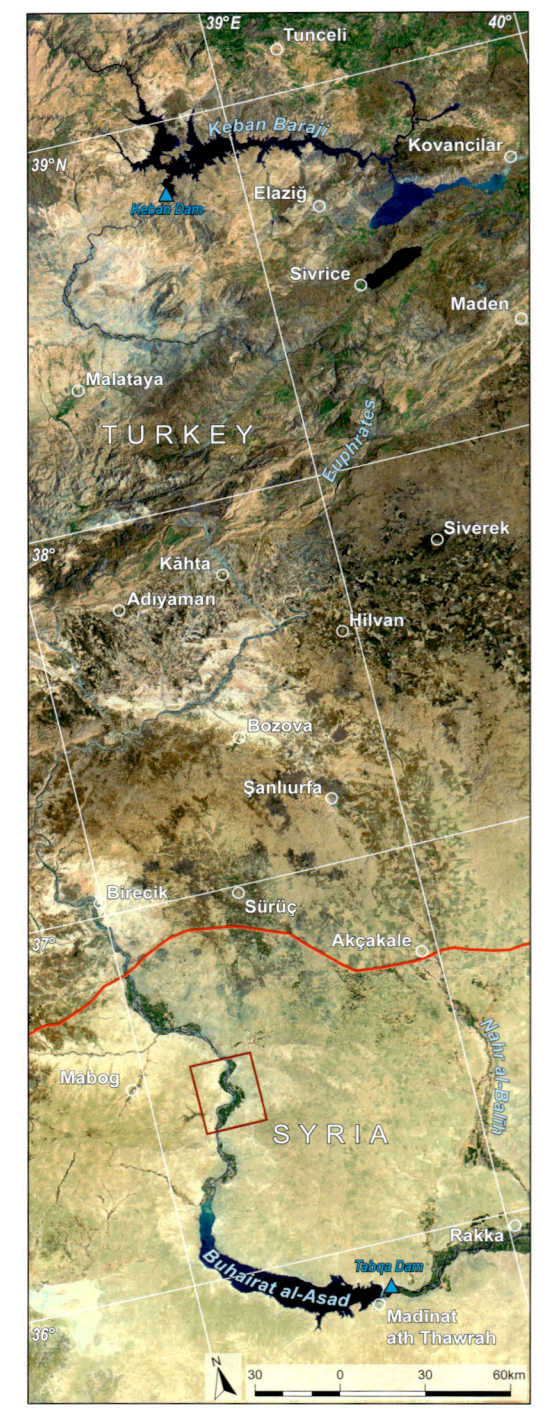

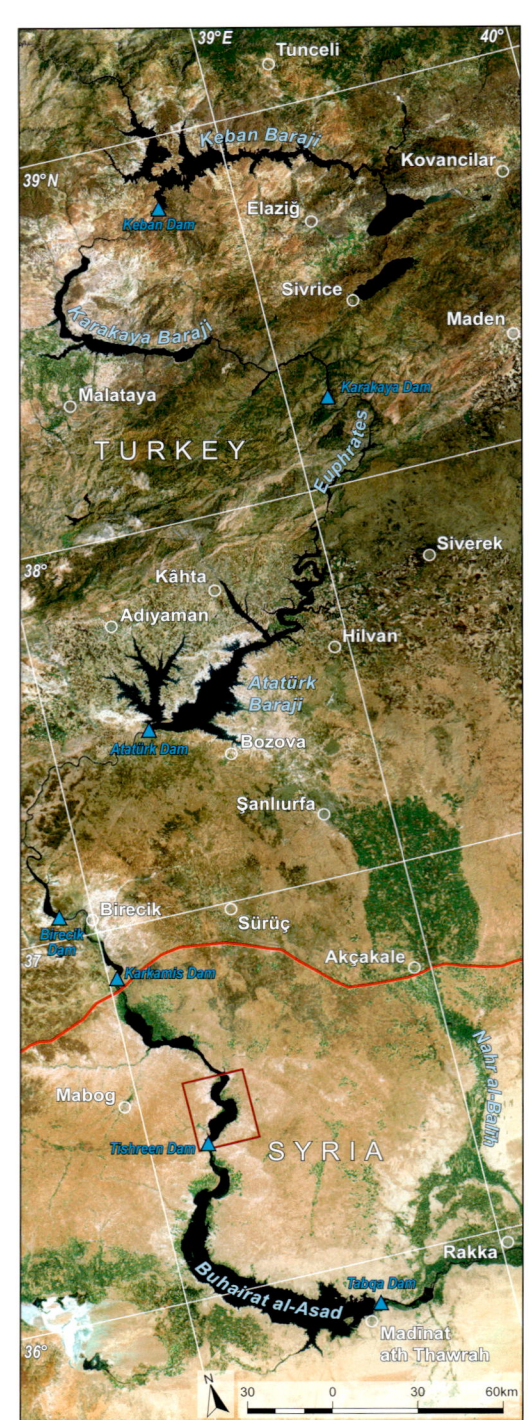

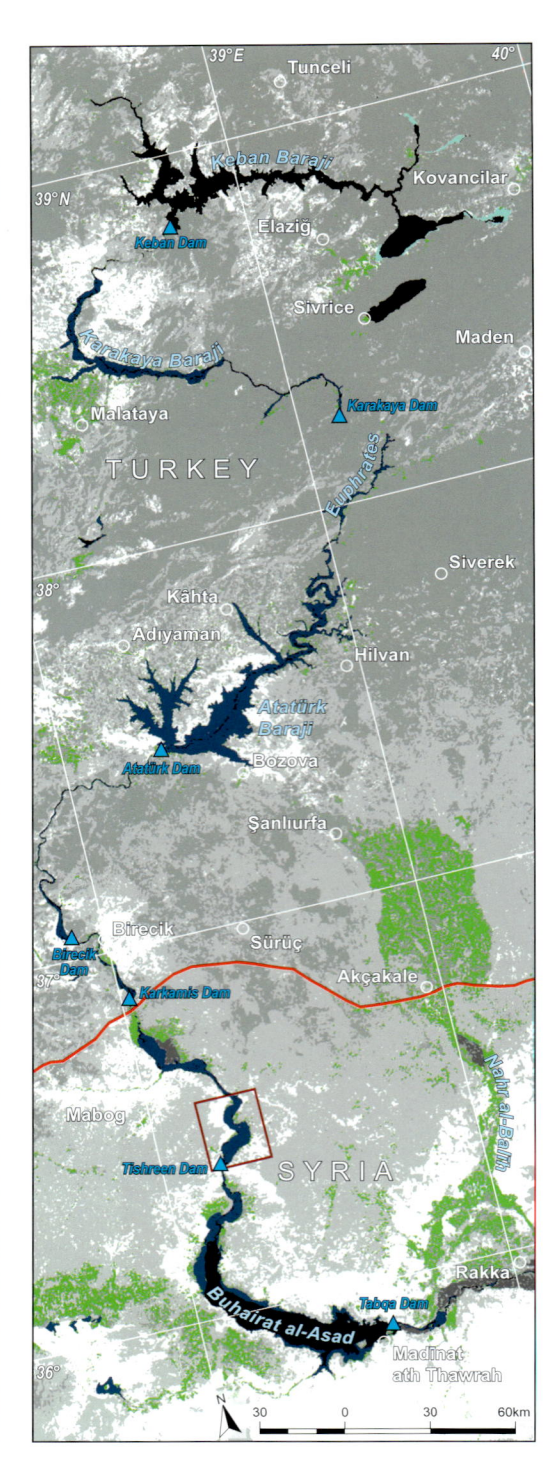

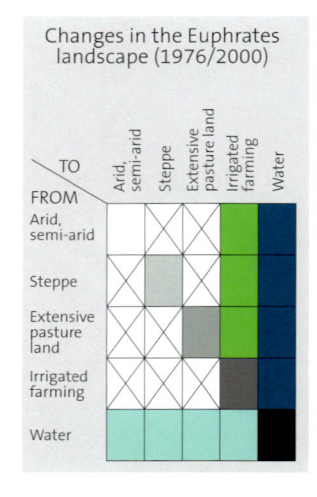

2 a/b – The course of the Euphrates before (1976, left) and after the construction of the Tishreen Dam (2000) in Syria. In 1976, the river's original course, with the irrigated farmland alongside it, can still be seen.

◁
1a/b/c – The landscape along the Euphrates in 1976 (left side), 2000 (centre), and a map charting the changes (right side). Lake Assad filled behind the Tabqa Dam in 1976. Following the construction of the Tishrin Dam, another lake has been present in Syria since 2000. Lake Atatürk Dam can also be seen in Turkey. As such, large bodies of water have formed on both sides of the border (see legend below).

▷
3 – The catchment area of the Euphrates and Tigris, from their sources in Turkey to their mouths in the Persian Gulf.

The area between the rivers' mid- and lower courses is also known as Mesopotamia. The 'land between the rivers' was a major civilisation long before our calendar system began. The Sumerians in Mesopotamia developed cuneiform script there around 3,500 to 2,000 BCE. It is also where the Epic of Gilgamesh was written (3,000 BCE) and home to the Akkadians, Assyrians and Babylonians.

At 2,736 kilometres long, the Euphrates is one of the longest rivers in Western Asia. It is fed by two headwaters. The Karasu has its source in the Eastern Anatolian Mountains, while the Murat rises to the north of Lake Van. Including the Murat, its longest headwater, the Euphrates has a total length of 3,380 kilometres.

The Tigris, at 1,851 kilometres in length, is almost 1,000 kilometres shorter. The Tigris rises in the Eastern Taurus Mountains.

The Shatt al-Arab extends along the Iran/Iraq border for just 193 kilometres.

The entire catchment area of the Euphrates/Tigris river system takes in almost 800,000 square kilometres.

tes and the Tigris, which would generate electricity and provide irrigation water. The aim of the Turkish dam project was to develop economically backwards regions and to improve the quality of life of a population undergoing increasing industrialisation. As a result of its regional politics, social, environmental and economic aspects, the project spurred controversy right from the start. The riparian states downstream, Syria and Iraq, saw the project as a threat to their existence and vehemently demanded that the water use be regulated.

With the filling of the Keban (1966), Karakaya (1986) and Atatürk (1990) reservoirs and the intensive use of the river water for irrigation, the water levels of the Euphrates and Tigris fell significantly (Figs. 1 and 3). After years of protests and legal disputes, work started on the controversial Ilisu Dam on the Tigris in 2010, only to be suspended in 2013. As such, the use of both rivers has been massively restricted for both Syria and Iraq. While the Atatürk reservoir was being filled, the Euphrates occasionally nearly ran dry. Since Turkey controls more than half of the water of the Tigris and almost all of the water of the Euphrates, Syria and Iraq fear that their growing needs for water will no longer be met in the future. The Euphrates is Syria's most important source of water. Syria began to build the Tabqa Dam in 1963, and its reservoir began to fill in 1973 – known as Lake Assad since 1993 (Fig. 1). Thanks to the increased opportunities for irrigation, the region gained significance as a cotton and wheat producer, with countless new settlements established as a result. The power station there has a nominal output of 800 megawatts. To preserve its water supply, Syria needs the Euphrates to maintain a flow rate of 700 cubic metres per second. However, in a 1987 agreement, Turkey assured Syria of an average supply of only 500 cubic metres per second. Despite this, there have been occasions when even this amount has not come downriver, as happened in 2000.

With the aid of satellite images taken over a period of time, it is possible to follow the changes to river beds, dams and the irrigated agricultural areas alongside the rivers (Figs. 1 and 2). We know that there were once large oases along the Euphrates in Syria as it meandered through the country's northern steppes. A new lake was created following the construction of the Tishrin Dam in 1999 (Fig. 2). When the reservoir was filled, countless settlements and significant archaeological sites were flooded. Cultivable land that was once inside the Euphrates valley has now been relegated to the banks of the reservoir. In addition to dwindling freshwater supplies across the whole region, there is also evidence of land degradation as a result of salinisation and erosion.

8°W
6°
4°
2°
44°
44°N
Bay of Biscay
FRANCE
Gijón-Xixón
Santander
Bilbao
Donostia-San Sebastián
A Coruña
Oviedo
Navia
Nalon
Nansa
Altube
Oria
Pamplona (Iruña)
Cantabrian Range
Vitoria-Gasteiz
Ulla
León
Logroño
Burgos
Miño
Ourense
Vigo
42°
Ebro
Zaragoza
Valladolid
Lima
Porto
Douro
Salamanca
Guadalajara
Vouga
MADRID
Móstoles
Getafe
Turia
Mondego
40°
PORTUGAL
Tajo
Júcar
SPAIN
Albacete
Guadiana
Badajoz
LISBON
Segura
Sado
38°
Córdoba
Jaén
Guadalquivir
Almanzora
Tinto
Sevilla
Mira
Granada
Sierra Nevada
Andarax
Huelva
Almería
Gulf of Cádiz
Gulf of Almería
Jerez de la Frontera
Guadalete
Guadalhorce
Málaga
Cádiz
Guadiaro
Fuengirola
Gibraltar (U.K.)
Algeciras
36°
Strait of Gibraltar
Tanger
Ceuta (ES)
Mediterranean Sea
Tétouan
Melilla (ES)
ATLANTIC OCEAN
MOROCCO
30 0 30 60km
8°
6°
4°
2°

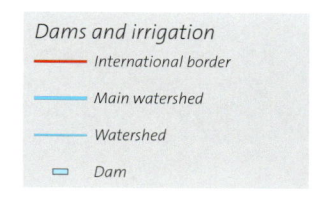

Dams and irrigation
— International border
— Main watershed
— Watershed
▭ Dam

◁
1 – Many of the rivers flowing through Portugal rise in neighbouring Spain, where the main watershed is located.

▷
2 – 2005 was one of the Iberian Peninsula's driest years in decades.

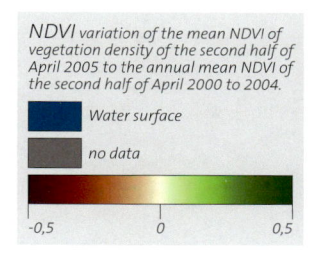

NDVI variation of the mean NDVI of vegetation density of the second half of April 2005 to the annual mean NDVI of the second half of April 2000 to 2004.
■ Water surface
■ no data
-0,5 0 0,5

▷
3a-c: changes in water reservoirs over one year as a result of low autumn (previous year) and winter rainfalls, revealed in a series of satellite images taken over time (Figs. 3a-c).

3a – At the start of the year the reservoirs are, in the worst-case scenario, at only 20 per cent of their capacity. In the best case they are completely full, as was the Rosarito Reservoir south-west of Madrid in May 2013 for example.

▷
3b – Over the year, the reservoir water levels sink as a result of water being taken for irrigation and due to continued lower-than-average rainfall (in some areas up to 80 per cent lower) in winter and spring. After the dry weather in March, April once again brings some rainfall before the dry summer months. The satellite image shows the Rosarito Reservoir in August 2012.

▷
3c – Depending on the weather conditions and dryness of a particular year, water levels in the reservoirs vary enormously. The Rosarito Reservoir in September 2012, as locals impatiently awaited the autumn and winter rains.

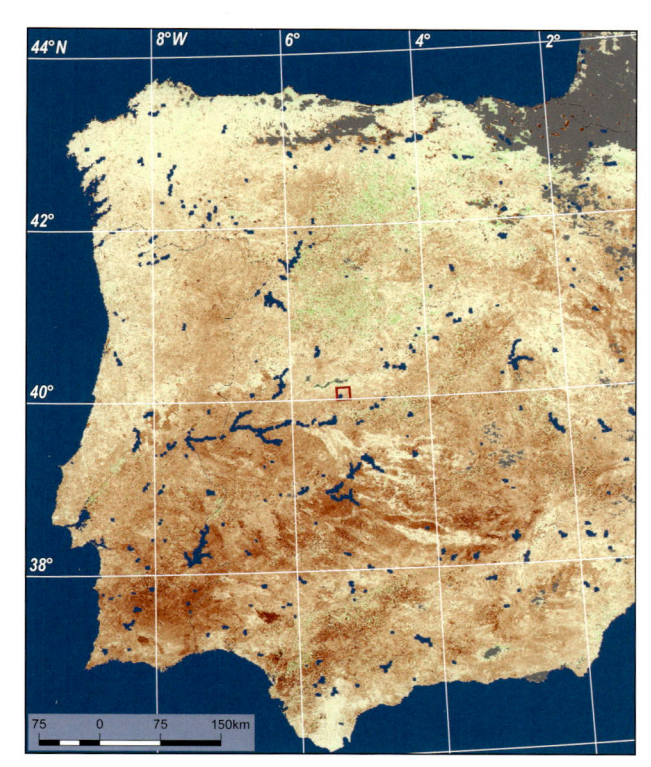

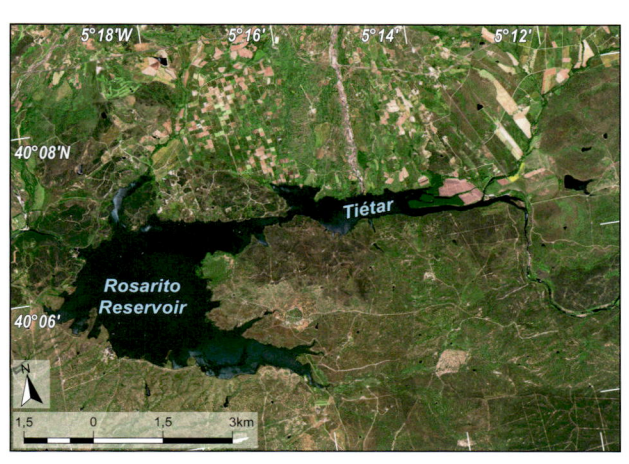

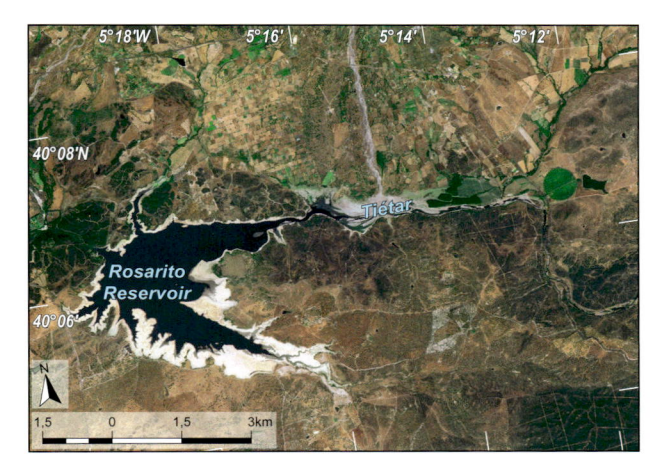

Bilateral water management between Spain and Portugal

Spain and Portugal both share the catchment areas for their five major rivers, the Miño (Minho), the Lima, the Duero (Douro), the Tajo (Tejo) and the Guadiana.

The Duero catchment area is the largest, with 79,000 square kilometres in Spain and 18,600 square kilometres in Portugal (Fig. 1).

The distribution of precipitation on the Iberian Peninsula shows clear north/south and seasonal variations. While some regions of northern Spain have precipitation of 1,600 millimetres (Cantabrian Mountains), the south of the country, with just 300 millimetres, is much drier. Around 900 dams in Spain store around 40 per cent of the water from these transboundary rivers.

Most of Spain's water is used for irrigated farming. Despite the water shortage in the south, intensive agriculture is common in the region. The traditional cultivation of olives and vines has been replaced by the artificially irrigated cultivation of non-native fruits and vegetables. Spain's biggest vegetable-growing area is in Almeria province (Fig. 1). Thousands of polytunnels, or plastic greenhouses, stretch right from the coast across the coast plain to the foothills of the Sierra Nevada, covering an area of around 40,000 hectares.

In addition to agriculture, the other major water user is the tourism industry. Large amounts of water are used to keep golf courses green, for example. To water them, around 10,000 cubic metres water are required per hectare per year.

In contrast to Spain, hydropower plays a major role in Portugal's electricity generation. Around half of Portugal's electricity from hydropower is generated by power stations along the Duero. However, more than half of Portugal's annual water resources have their sources upstream in Spain (Fig. 1). As a result, Portugal is highly dependent on water flow from Spain. In an effort to regulate the intensive use of the transboundary Portuguese/Spanish river catchment areas, the Albufeira Agreement was signed in 1998.

The Albufeira Drought Management Agreement

Contracts and agreements to regulate water usage have a long history in Spain and Portugal, which signed the first such agreement in 1864. A contract from 1968 allowed Spain to divert up to 1,000 cubic hectometres of water per year from the Tejo (Tajo) to other hydrographic basins. Both countries signed the Albufeira Agreement in 1998. This "Cooperation agreement to secure and ensure the sustainable use of water in the Hispano-Portuguese hydrographic basin" was drafted to secure at last a specific annual minimum flow rate for Spanish rivers flowing over the border into Portugal.

In 2005 the Iberian Peninsula experienced one of its worst droughts since the year 1943 (Fig. 2). When winter rains failed to arrive and a long period of high temperatures followed, many rivers, reservoirs and springs temporarily dried up (Fig. 3). As a result of the enormous water shortage, Spain could not maintain the terms of the 1998 agreement. Countless cubic hectometres of water were taken from a number of rivers on the Spanish side, primarily the Tajo, in order to irrigate agricultural land. Since the year 2008 the flow rate has been determined every three months or weekly, to ensure a natural balance. In 2012 the region once again experienced one of its most severe droughts in 70 years, which led to harvest losses of 20 to 40 per cent.

237

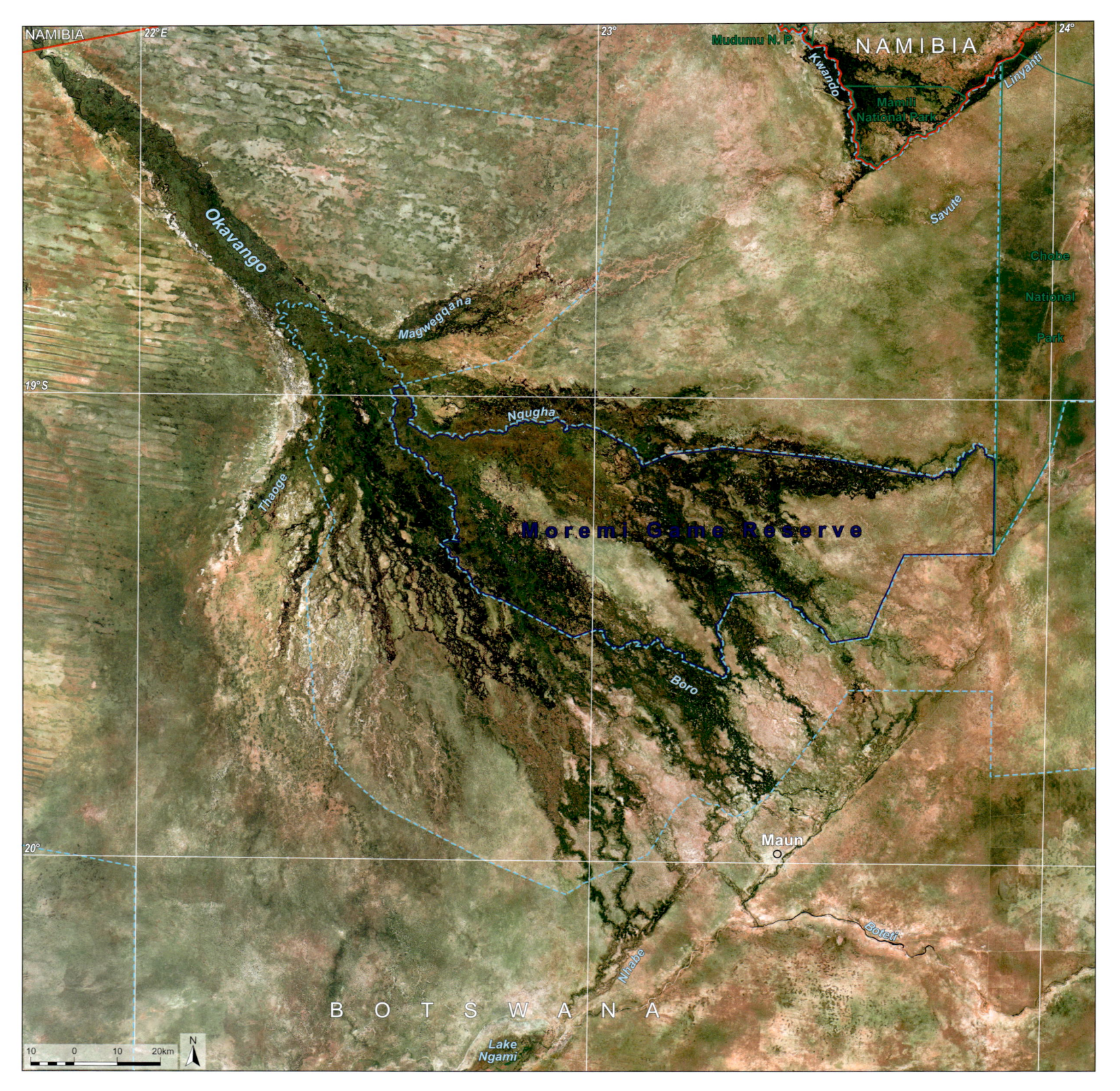

The Okavango Delta

The Okavango covers a distance of 1,700 kilometres and rises in the Bié Plateau of Angola. From there, it crosses Namibia and flows to Botswana, where it spreads out into a large wetland before draining into the Kalahari. With an area of up to 20,000 square kilometres, the Okavango Delta in the north-east of the Kalahari desert is the largest inland delta in the world (Fig. 1).

The Kalahari region lies in a continental arid zone. The long dry periods are broken up by irregular summer rainfall between December and February. The dry climate is the result of its geographical location between 20 and 30 degrees latitude south of the equator. In this region, trade winds force the air masses downwards, warming the air and decreasing the relative humidity, and even the last few clouds that may have formed dissipate. This results in long periods without rain.

The inland delta is subject to an annual vegetation cycle (Figs. 2, 3) depending on annual flood. The flooding is also influenced by major variations in the runoff behaviour of the Okavango River. On average, runoff amounts to 300 cubic metres per second. The highest flow rates, though, measured in March-April, can reach values of up to 1,000 cubic metres per second. As most of the water comes from the Angolan plateau, the annual floodwaters take a few months to reach the inland delta. Water levels vary within the delta itself as well. After entering the delta at what is known as the Panhandle, the water takes another four months to reach Maun at the south-eastern rim of the delta. The highest water levels are measured in July-August, long time after the end of the wet season in the delta region. The vegetation of the Okavango Delta therefore flourishes in what is actually the dry season, which is key to the survival of many wild animals all across southern Africa.

△
1 – The Okavango is the largest inland delta in the world. It is key to the survival of countless animals during the dry season.

▷
4 – The wetlands of the Okavango Delta are criss-crossed by small rivers and streams, ideal habitat for hippos.

▷
2 – The Normalised Difference Vegetation Index (NDVI) shows the presence of vegetation and its density. This highlights, for example, seasonal changes in plant growth (NDVI from May 2005).

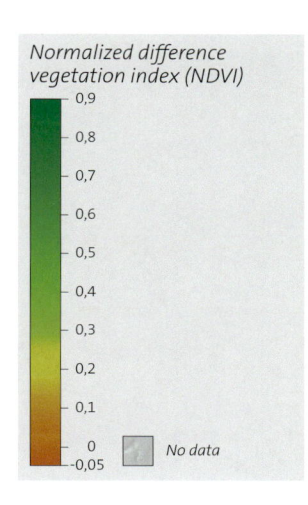

▷
3 – The NDVI from October 2005 reveals the lush green vegetation in the Okavango Delta during the dry season, when the region around the delta appears only scarcely vegetated.

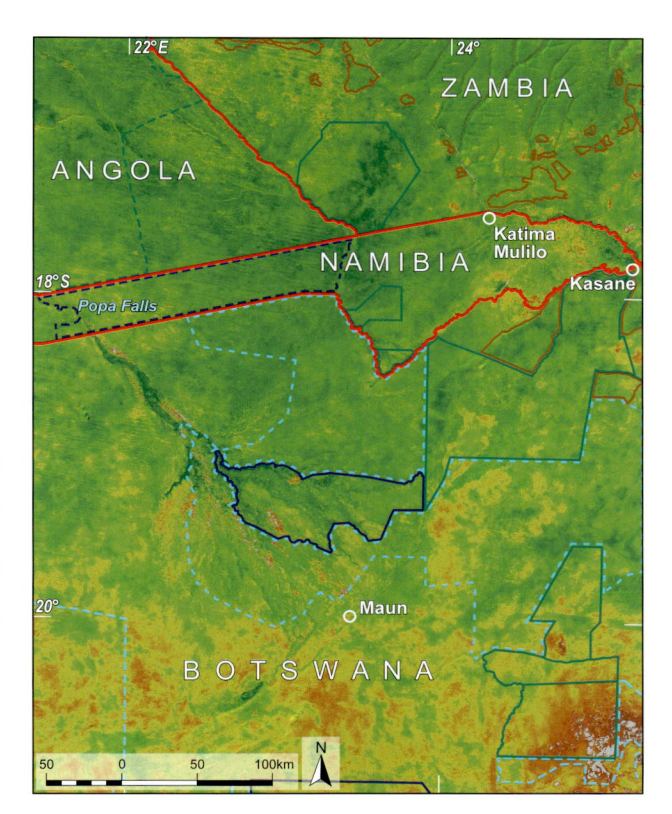

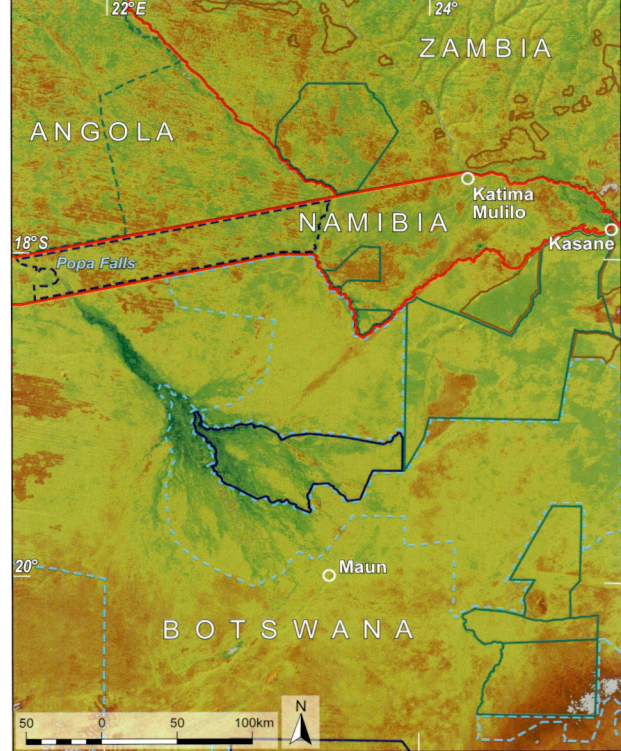

Biodiversity in the Okavango Delta

Apart from water, the Okavango River also carries to the inland delta nutrient-rich deposits that support the unique flora and fauna. The Okavango Delta is home to large populations of elephants, hippos (Fig. 4), giraffes, lions and ospreys, as well as over 2,500 plant species. Depending on the time of year and water levels, the delta is home to vast numbers of all of southern Africa's native animal species.

The Okavango Delta supports an outstanding biodiversity including 150 species of mammals, over 500 species of birds, 90 species of fish and 20 large carnivores, reptiles, invertebrates and amphibians as well as plants. In 2010 it was inscribed in the list of World Heritage, UNESCO declared the delta a World Natural Heritage site. The Moremi Game Reserve is a part of the Okavango Delta system and is unique in that it was founded by the local tribe.

Traditionally, the natural abundance of the Okavango Delta has been used by native hunters and fishermen. The area's low population density has in the past prevented the overuse of resources and so the destruction of the habitat as well. Today, the majority of the 150,000 or so people living in the region still make a living from fishing and hunting for subsistence, but also from subsistence agriculture inside the delta. Wetland farming is common, primarily near the limits of the delta. However, a fast-growing population and booming safari tourism are creating more and more utilisation conflicts in the delta.

Utilisation conflicts in the Okavango Delta

Its geographical location makes Botswana a semi-arid to arid country. As rainfall is low, water must be extracted from the groundwater reserves, which now account for up to 60 per cent of the country's day-to-day water needs. However, low groundwater recharge rates have forced the Botswana government to search for alternatives. Surface water has therefore recently begun to play a bigger role in supplying the population with water, as well as in irrigation.

Along with the Limpopo and the Zambezi/Chobe, the Okavango is one of three rivers in Botswana that flow year-round. All three rivers are transboundary river systems that are used intensively by the inhabitants of the riparian countries. Due to the increasing demand for water in the riparian states, the water supply of the Okavango Delta is reduced and the sensitive ecosystem of the region is expected to suffer lasting damage. The Namibian government is planning to take additional 17 million cubic metres of water every year out of the Okavango at Rundu, which shall be provided to Namibia's population via a 260-kilometre pipeline feeding into the Eastern National Water Carrier system at Grootfontein, located west of Popa Falls. There have also been plans since the 1980ies to use the water from the delta itself. So far, this has been prevented thanks to resistance from international environmental organisations.

Utilisation conflicts in the delta itself are another threat. As a result of the swift population growth, the amount of water required for irrigation is also continuing to rise. It is above all the careless use of the delta's natural resources and uncontrolled population growth that pose the biggest threats to the ecosystem of this lowland area.

As a result, Angola, Botswana and Namibia joined forces in 1994 to form OKACOM (Permanent Okavango River Basin Commission) to coordinate the sustainable use of the catchment area. One of the commission's projects is known as the Okavango Delta Management Plan. The overarching aim of this project is to develop sustainability strategies that will not only protect the inland delta with its fauna and flora, but also benefit the local population.

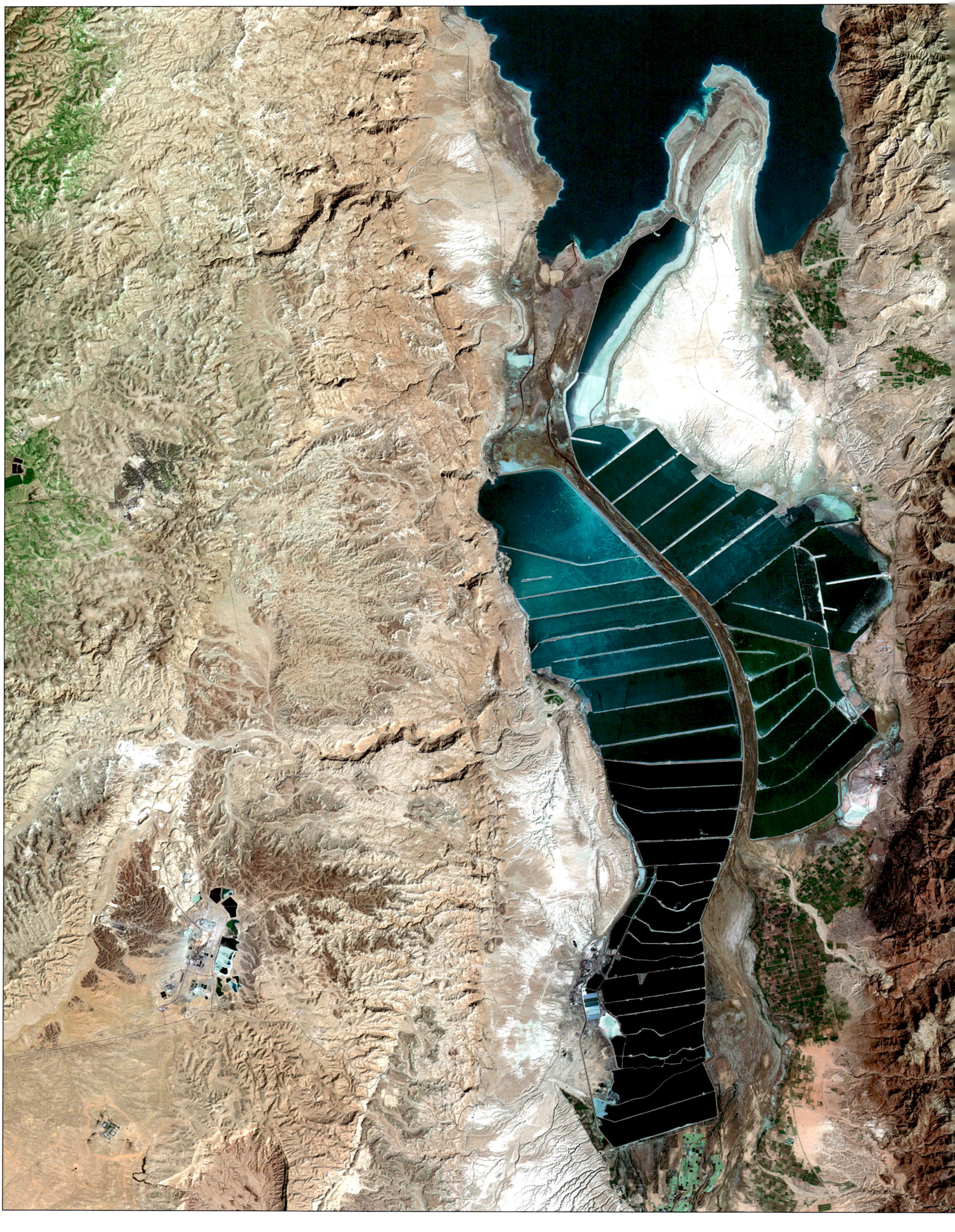

INDUSTRY AND TRANSPORT

In the history of transport of both people and material, water plays just as important a role as it has in industrialisation and energy production

New lands on unknown continents and islands were discovered largely by navigating the sea. Names such as Vasco da Gama, James Cook, Ferdinand Magellan and Christopher Columbus are all major names in the history of human endeavour. Today, countless waterways, with their canals and ports, are used to transport goods. More than 90 per cent of all cross-border goods transportation is via sea routes. Without shipping, commerce as we know it today would not be possible. A large number of different industries such as modern shipyards, high-performance port systems, a large commercial fleet and well-developed infrastructure beyond the port, are all contributing to fulfil the needs of a globalized economy.

The power of flowing water has been used for well over 3,000 years. The first scoop wheels to irrigate farmland were used in Egypt in 1200 BCE. The Romans were also using the mechanical force of water to mill grain at the turn of the eras. With time, water mills sprang up all over Central Europe, and by the 12th century they were already a fixed part of the economy. Sawmills, hammer mills, grinding mills and textile mills soon joined these in exploiting the power of water. At the end of the 19th century, the local water mills were replaced by large water turbines, which were installed to exploit the recent discovery of electricity. The energy could now be transported over longer distances and did not have to be used at the place it was generated. Today, according to the IEA (International Energy Agency), 17 per cent of all the world's electricity is generated from hydropower. As such, this form of energy generation is used significantly more than nuclear power (11 per cent).

Water is not only the source of all life – it is essential for industry, transport and energy generation. However, its use is often linked with serious consequences for the ecosystems affected. River regulation, draining of wetlands, damming of rivers, unfiltered wastewater, overuse of agricultural fertilisers, the lowering of the water table and oil spills are just some of these.

◁
1 – In the south of the Dead Sea, water is channelled into shallow water basins to produce salt on both the Israeli and Jordanian sides. The border runs along a dam and the individual basins are separated by smaller dykes.

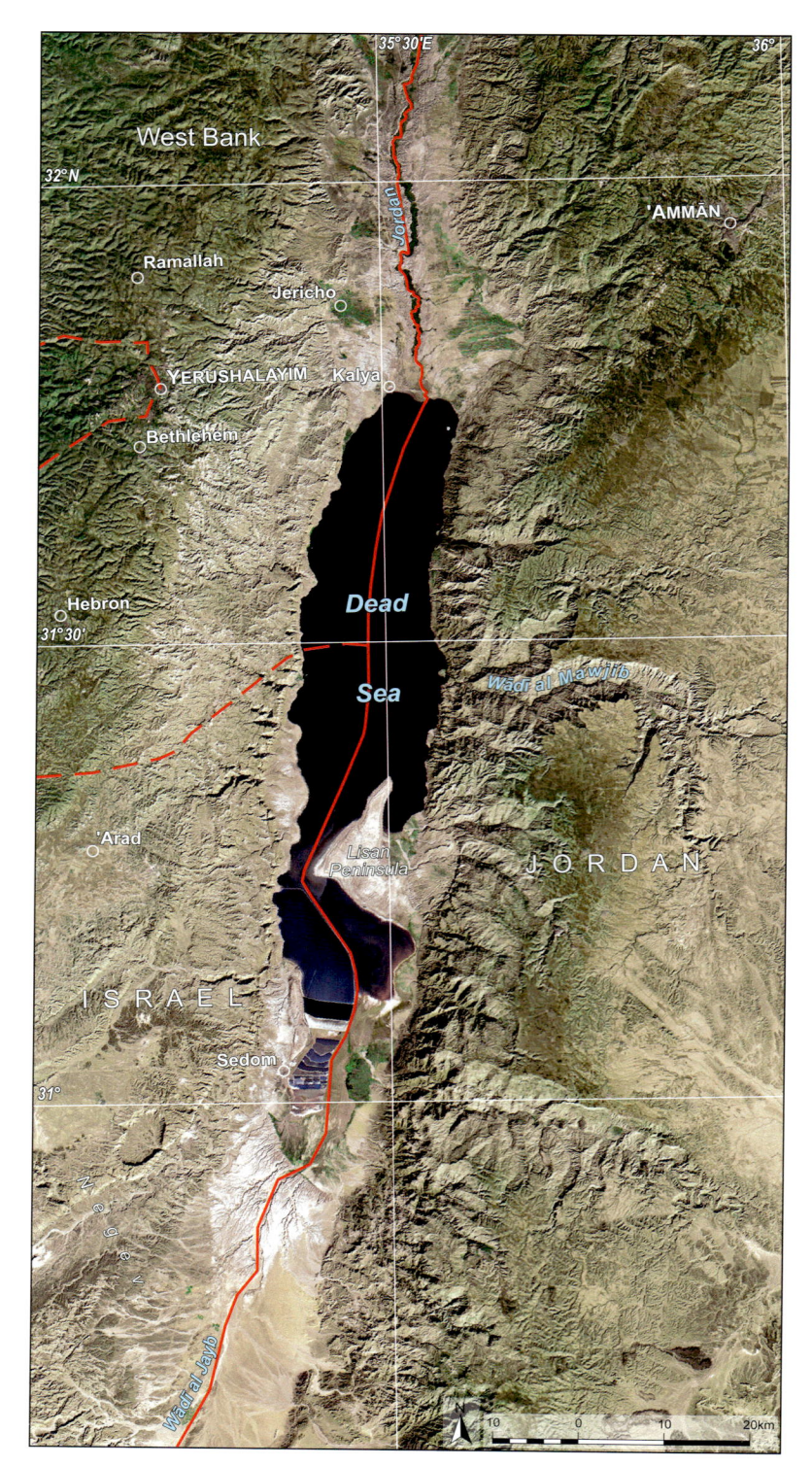

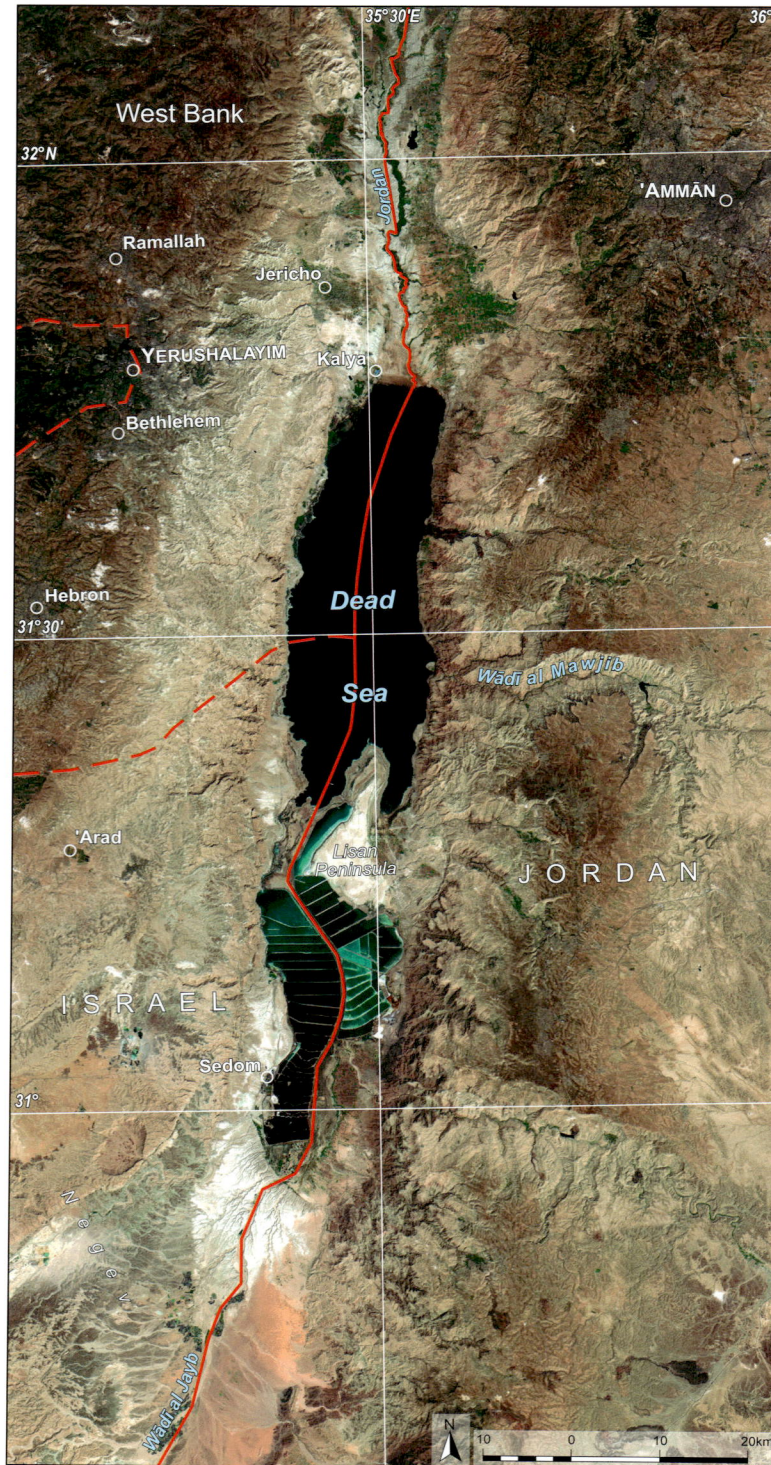

Salt from the Dead Sea

At the start of the 20th century the Dead Sea became the focus of chemists around the world, who identified the water as a major potential source of bromine salts and potassium carbonates (potash). The Palestine Potash Company (PPC) was founded in Kalya on the northern edge of the lake back in 1929. Potassium carbonate was extracted from the brine using evaporation ponds. Soon rising demand led to a second salt factory being built in 1934 in Sedom, southwest of the Dead Sea (both in Figs. 1 a and b). The name of the salt works is based on the Biblical town of Sodom.

To extract the salt, the brine is diverted from the southern part of the Dead Sea into large salt pans, separated from the rest of the Dead Sea by the Lisan Peninsula (Fig. 1 a/b). Heated by the intense sunlight, the water evaporates until the maximum saturation level is reached and the salt precipitates out. The individual ponds are separated by water channels (Fig. 1, pp. 240/241 and Figs. 1 a and b).

The Dead Sea Works Ltd. was set up in 1952 by the Israeli government to extract calcium carbonate from the water. The company's salt works (known as ICL Fertilizers since 2001) produce 1.77 million tonnes of calcium carbonate, 206,000 tonnes of bromide salt, 44,900 tonnes of sodium hydroxide and 25,000 tonnes of magnesium and sodium chloride (table salt) every year. In 1965, Jordan set up the Arab Potash Company, which uses the evaporation ponds to extract two million tonnes of calcium carbonate every year. To extract the salts Both Israel and Jordan employ large salt works, the areas of which have expanded significantly over the past 40 years (Fig. 1 a/b).

Large evaporation basins for salt are found not just near the Dead Sea but are common in other regions of the world too. To extract salt efficiently, the solar radiation must be strong, the shore must be flat and the climate as dry as possible, in order to ensure high evaporation rates. In Europe, salt works are most common on the French Atlantic coast in Brittany.

◁△ △
1a/b – The Landsat satellite images from 1973 (image top left) and 2013 (image top right) and the surface relief (Fig. 2a right-hand side) show the salt works and resulting changes over four decades to the Dead Sea.

▷△ ▷△
2 a/b – The topography of the area around the Dead Sea with the local water industry. A cross-section of the area shows how deep the 12,000-year-old Dead Sea lies.

▷
3 – Swimming in the healing salty water of the Dead Sea. In the foreground crystalline rock salt.

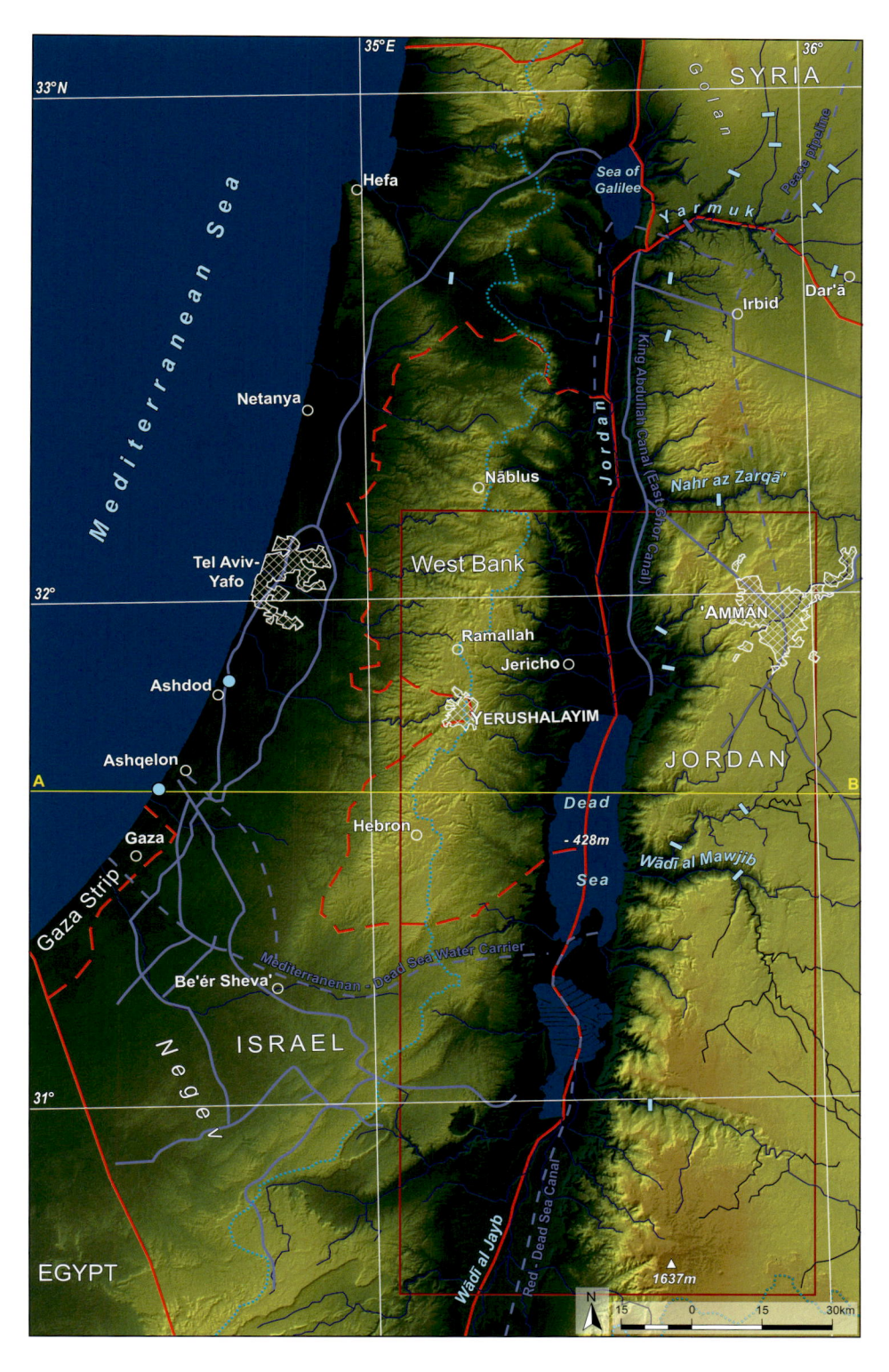

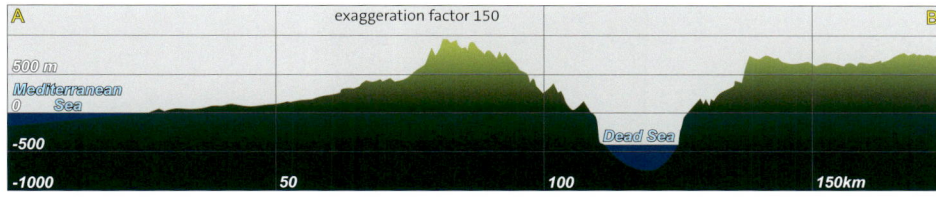

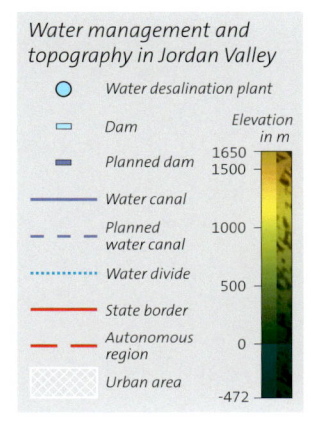

Characteristics of the Dead Sea

A tectonic fault that runs parallel to the coast of the Mediterranean forms the Jordan Valley. As the northern continuation of the East African Rift System together they form the Great Rift Valley. The Jordan Valley is home to the Sea of Galilee and the deepest point on the Earth's surface, the Dead Sea (Fig. 2). The surface of the Dead Sea is more than 420 metres below sea level, and its water, with an average salinity of 28 per cent, is the saltiest of all the seas on earth. Only very few organisms such as halophilic bacteria and algae can survive in this environment. The minerals in the water include primarily magnesium-, calcium-, and sodium salts (rock salt), along with potassium chloride and bromide, which has a curative effect for skin conditions.

As a result of the arid climate and intensive solar radiation, natural evaporation is very high. In addition, only one-tenth of the original amount in the River Jordan and its tributaries and wadis now reaches the lake. Most of the water is drawn off from the river before it reaches the Dead Sea, to be used for industry and irrigation, and by private households. In 1930, around 1,300 million cubic metres of water flowed each year into the Dead Sea; today, just over 260 million cubic metres reach it.

These external influences have led to a rapid fall in the water level. At the start of the 20th century the surface of the Dead Sea lay 389 metres below sea level; by 2014 it had sunk almost another 40 metres, to 428 metres. This has also meant that the sea's area has shrunken from 1,000 square kilometres at the start of the 20th century to around 605 square kilometres today. Since the 1980s alone, the surface of the Dead Sea has shrunk by more than a third. The lake continues to sink by about a metre a year. By 2050 it will probably be at 465 metres below sea level. However, it is expected that the lake will stabilise in 200 years' time at 550 metres below sea level and 450 square kilometres.

As a result of the sinking water level, the lake experiences a drop in pressure and thus slope instability on the shore. Because the groundwater table is also sinking, hollow spaces form in the ground, which sometimes cave in and cause serious damage to buildings, roads and farmland. The drop in water level also changes the stratification of the water in the Dead Sea. Until the 1950s, the Dead Sea had a deeper, salty and low-oxygen layer, which was topped by a slightly less salty layer. In 1979, when the water level fell to 400 metres below sea level, these layers started to mix.

The Red Sea-Dead Sea Conduit – "Two Seas Canal"

To save the Dead Sea, the construction of a 300-kilometre canal has been planned for 2014. The canal would divert water from the Red Sea into the Dead Sea (Fig. 2) to stabilise the water level by 2054 at a level of -416 metres. The drop of over 400 metres should serve to generate electricity, which will power a desalination plant in the Jordanian port city of Aqaba that will desalinate 1,800 million cubic metres of saltwater per year. Half of this will provide Jordan, Israel and the Palestinian zone with drinking water, while the rest will be diverted into the Dead Sea.

This construction project should play a major role in combating the water shortage in the region, provided that industrial water extraction from the Dead Sea does not decrease. A feasibility study conducted by the World Bank in 2012 warned against the effects of an altered water composition in the Dead Sea when mixed with water from the Red Sea and potential consequences for the corals at the tapping point in the Red Sea.

243

1 – European waters are plied by oil tankers every day. Accidents with a huge impact on sensitive ecosystems are caused by technical errors on ships, but by human misbehaviour too.

Oil disasters in European waters
Disasters with an oil entry of 15,000 t or more between 1967 and 2004.
Oil entry in t
- 223000
- 200000
- 100000
- 50000
- 15000

Oil transport and navigation routes in European waters
Oil transports in 2004 in million t
- 210 – 800
- 140 – 210
- 105 – 140
- 70 – 105
- 35 – 70
- < 35
- Petrochemical plant

Data: European Comission JRC, EuroStat, ITOPF, United Nations

Oil pollution in the seas

Oil is lighter than water and therefore floats on the surface. This makes oil pollution the most conspicuous form of pollution in the seas of the world. The oil enters the sea in a variety of ways, including direct discharge by coastal industry, oil refineries, and cities. It comes down rivers and also enters the ocean through dumping or accidents on ships (Fig.3) and drilling platforms. However, there are also natural sources of oil in the oceans, such as leaking oil wells on the seafloor.

The increase in shipping has led to more tanker accidents and the catastrophic effects on the ecosystem that flow from them. Accidents often affect older ships with a single hull. Following a decision by the International Maritime Organisation, tankers of this type are permitted to sail only until 2015. Since 1992, all new tankers have had to be built with a double hull. Once large shipping companies have retrofitted their tankers with double hulls, the severity of the consequences is set to drop rapidly.

Accounting for 22 per cent of pollution, dumping represents the major single source of marine pollution. Dumping is the process of rinsing out tanks on ships and drilling platforms with seawater. This flushes large amounts of highly toxic waste from the tanks into the water. Despite international bans and satellite monitoring, this now-illegal practice is still widespread because the fines can be significantly lower than the costs of disposing of the waste properly at ports.

2 – The high-resolution IKONOS-2 image shows an oil platform and tankers in the North Sea in close-up, demonstrating the potential of this kind of monitoring.

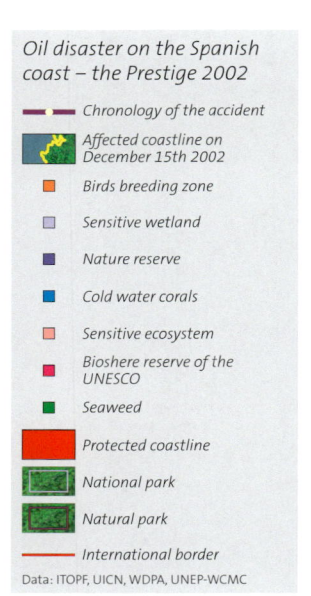

Oil disaster on the Spanish coast – the Prestige 2002
- Chronology of the accident
- Affected coastline on December 15th 2002
- Birds breeding zone
- Sensitive wetland
- Nature reserve
- Cold water corals
- Sensitive ecosystem
- Biosphere reserve of the UNESCO
- Seaweed
- Protected coastline
- National park
- Natural park
- International border

Data: ITOPF, UICN, WDPA, UNEP-WCMC

3 – Oil input into the world's seas by tankers between 1970-2012. Thanks to environmental regulations and modern technology, the number of tanker accidents has been halved in recent decades and the amount of oil input greatly reduced. There has not been another major accident since the 'Prestige' sank, and there were only two events with oil spills of over 700 tonnes per year between 2010-2013, compared red with an average of 7.7 events a year from 1990-1999.

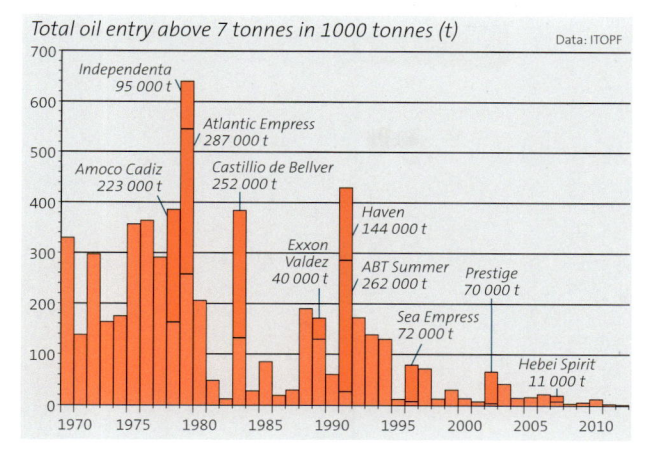

4 – The oil tanker 'Prestige' sinks in the Atlantic Ocean on Nov. 19, 2002.

5 – Traces of the 'Prestige' can be tracked with incredible clarity in the radar image as a result of the traces of oil it left behind.

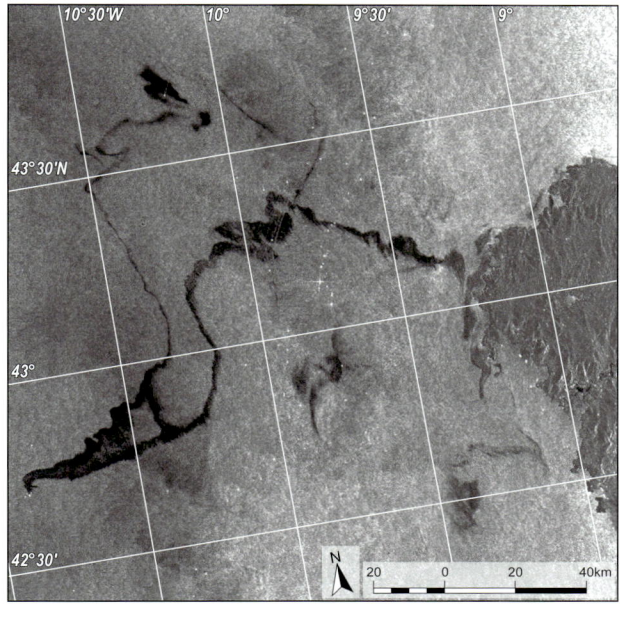

6 – The oil tanker 'Prestige' sank off the coast of Galicia in November 2002.
More than 70,000 tonnes of crude oil entered the sensitive ecosystem along Spain's Atlantic coast.

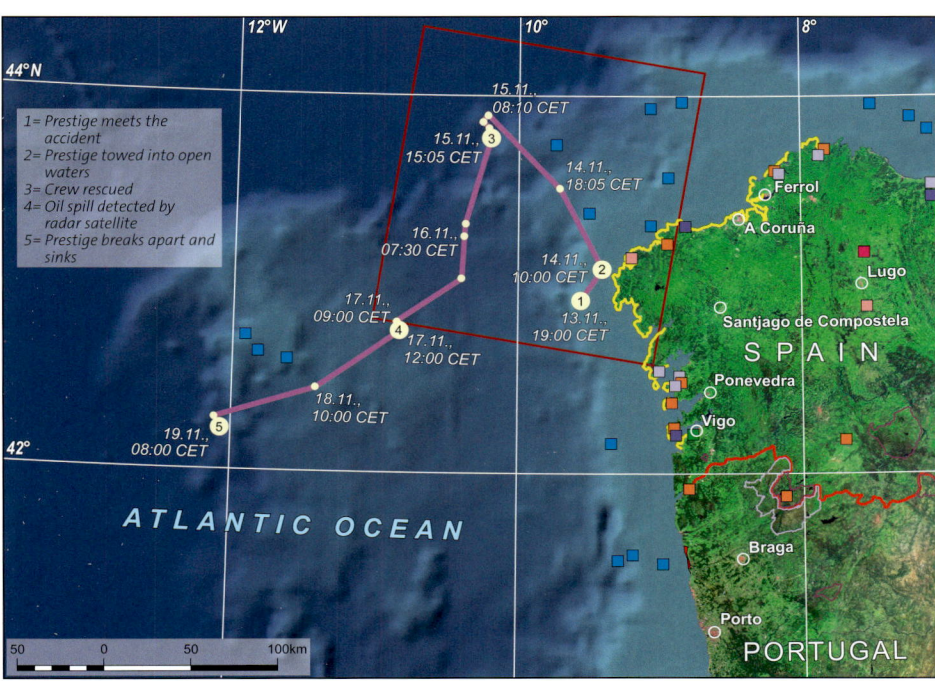

The sinking of the 'Prestige'

In November 2002, a 26-year-old tanker sank in a storm off the coast of Galicia. Unlike more modern tankers, the 'Prestige' was a single-hulled tanker.

The Spanish government ordered the stricken ship (Fig.4) to be dragged out to sea as far from the coast as possible. On November 19 the tanker sank after breaking in two in international waters 233 kilometres off the northern Spanish coast. The wreck of the 'Prestige' now lies on the North Atlantic seabed at a depth of 3,500 metres. From it, 70,000 tonnes of crude oil flowed into the sea, creating an oil slick 3,000 kilometres off the coast of northern Portugal and Galicia and stretching all the way to Brittany. As a result of the disaster, the Spanish authorities banned fishing. Many fishermen and the fish-processing industry faced losing their livelihoods. In France the disaster also affected oyster farming. To say nothing of the extreme damage to the environment, the sinking of the 'Prestige' resulted in financial losses of one billion euros alone.

Oil slicks: impacts and clearance

When a ship experiences a disaster, it doesn't require huge quantities of oil to cause serious environmental damage. Even the smallest amounts are dissolved in seawater and consumed by aquatic organisms. This means the oil enters the food chain and works its way up until it reaches humans consuming fish. Sea birds are the worst-affected by oil spills. When liquid oil covers the plumage of a bird, the feathers lose their ability to repel water. The air held inside the feathers, which serves to give buoyancy and to protect against the cold, is replaced by water and the bird either drowns or freezes to death. As the bird attempts to clean itself, the oil spreads through its entire plumage and also gets into its digestive system.

Oil slicks have often been sprayed with chemicals to accelerate the breakdown of the oil. However, studies have shown that these chemicals or the resulting compounds with the oil can actually be more toxic than the oil itself. Slicks are nowadays therefore surrounded by a system of floats and gathered up with scoops. Only if the coast is in imminent danger are chemicals used. Clearing oil slicks requires a lot of time and money and help often comes too late.

Tracking oil spills from space

Satellites are also used to gather information quickly about the extent and spread of oil spills following tanker accidents. Specifically, radar systems (SAR, synthetic aperture radar) are used because they can operate regardless of light conditions and cloud cover. Traces of oil in a choppy sea can be picked up particularly clearly in radar images because the waves are smoothed by the film of oil on the surface in the area of the slick, which shows up darker than the surrounding area on the radar image (Fig. 5).

SAR-data such as those on board ESA satellite Sentinel-1, Germany's TerraSAR-X, Canada's RADARSAT-2, Japan's JERS-1 and ALOS-2, continue to be used around the world to detect and monitor oil-based pollution of all types such as in the frame of activations of the "International Charter Space and Major Disasters". This is a cooperation mechanism between most space agencies for the provision to civil protections worldwide of maps showing the damage extent produced by large catastrophes, including oil spills.

However, radar satellite data is not only used to detect disasters involving oil. It is also applied to detect oil leaking from natural oil wells at the seafloor as a first step in exploring potential oil fields. In the satellite data they often leave traces very similar to those from tanker accidents. The most important difference is that there is no signature of a ship aligned with the oil slick.

1 – Burning oil on water surface above the Deepwater Horizon drilling and the endeavour to get it under contol.
Use of intensive colour enhancement to highlight the oil and dispersant, 15/06/2010.

4 – From 20–22/04/2010, workers tried to secure the drilling platform (photo: 21 April).

5 – Vessel helping to skim off the floating oil.

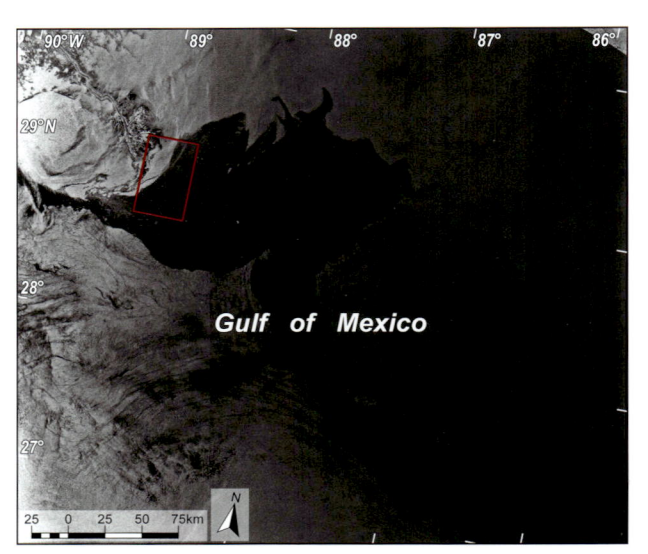

2 – Envisat ASAR image of the oil slick spreading in the Gulf of Mexico, 18/05/2010.

6 – An oiled marsh on Louisiana´s coast seen during an overflight on 20/05/2010.

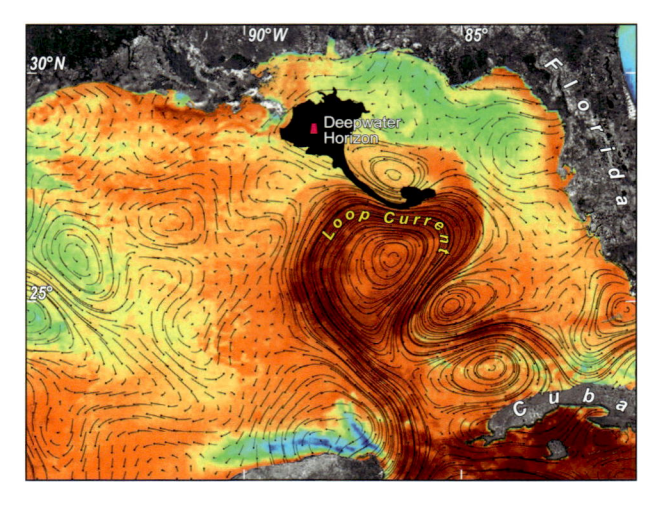

3 – Simulation of the formation of the oil slick (extend on the 17/05/2010, acquired by RADARSAT-2) in the Loop Current (black arrows).

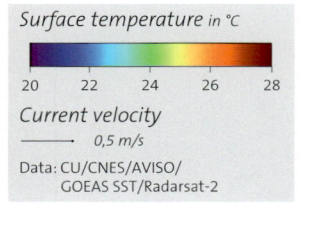

Surface temperature in °C
20 22 24 26 28
Current velocity
— 0,5 m/s
Data: CU/CNES/AVISO/ GOEAS SST/Radarsat-2

Deepwater Horizon – oil spill in the Gulf of Mexico

On 20 April, 2010, the Deepwater Horizon oil exploration rig in the Gulf of Mexico, not 100 kilometres away from the Mississippi River Delta, experienced a 'blowout' – the uncontrolled gushing of oil from a borehole, leading to the biggest environmental disaster of its kind. Over almost three months, over 800 million litres of oil escaped from the borehole 1,500 metres below the surface of the sea. The causes of the catastrophe were just as dramatic as the consequences for humans and the environment (Fig. 6).

The chronology of the disaster

Exploration drilling had been conducted from the platform in the Macondo oil field, south-east of the Louisiana coast, since February 2010. The drilling had reached a depth of 5,500 metres and the project was almost complete, when disaster struck. The team had already started to seal the borehole with special cement. Suddenly, drilling mud, petroleum and natural gas started leaking from the platform. The gas, under immense pressure, ignited, causing explosions and fires that killed eleven of the workers. None of the safety measures, such as a central valve system or emergency shutdown, worked. Several firefighting vessels attempted to control the flames on the platform (Fig. 4), but in vain. Two days later, the platform sank into the sea and enormous quantities of oil continued to gush out from the borehole on the sea floor. The flow of oil was stopped with a temporary cap only on 16 July, 2010. However, large parts of the Mississippi River Delta and the coast of the Gulf of Mexico between Louisiana, Florida and Cuba had already been badly hit by the spill.

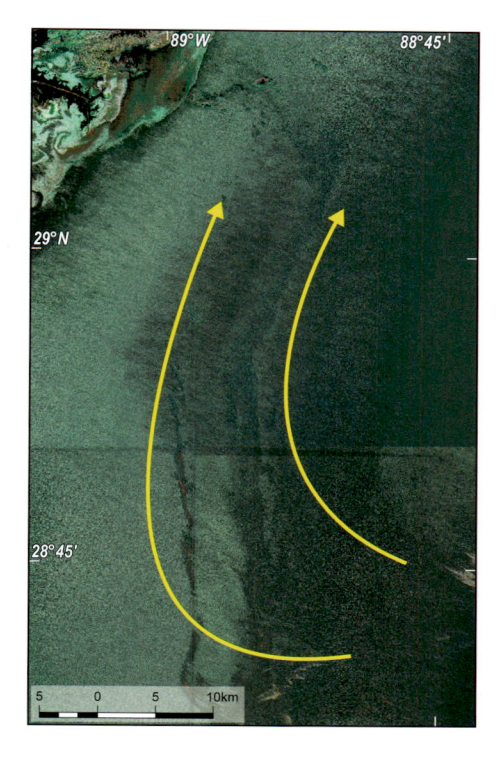

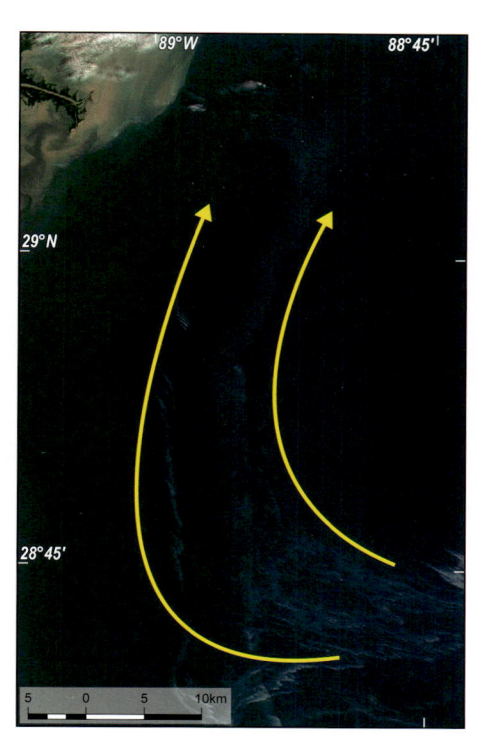

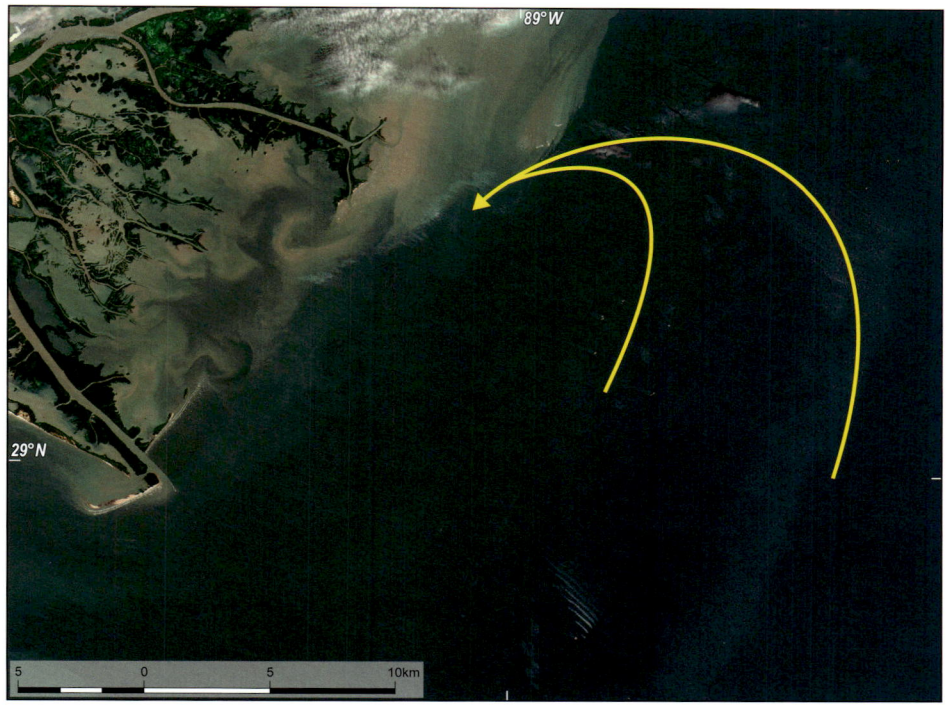

Oil slicks and ocean currents

The jagged topography of the sea bed, the many islands and the curving coastline create a very turbulent system of currents in the Gulf of Mexico, which quickly spread the oil throughout large parts of the Gulf and the neighbouring Atlantic. Around one month after the blowout on the drilling platform, part of the oil slick met the Loop Current (Figs. 2 and 3), an ocean current. The current bore significant amounts of oil towards Florida and, further along the Florida Stream and the Gulf Stream, left lumps of tar washing up along America's east coast. Barely two-and-a-half months after the blowout, lumps of tar also washed up on Texas' west coast.

The oil slick below the sea surface

In addition to the oil on the surface, the enormous quantities of oil underneath the surface, to a depth of several metres, posed a huge problem to those battling the spill. In April 2010, US research company Applied Analysis Inc. (AAI) used two computer programs to develop a method that would estimate the oil under the surface by using satellite data to analyse its extent. Because the reflective properties of oil on the surface, as an emulsion, differ from those of the oil under the surface, the two different spectral ranges can be easily distinguished. Rather like in land use classification, this makes it possible to distinguish clearly between oil above and below the surface on satellite images. Figures 7 b-d illustrate the spread of the oil over the surface off the Louisiana coast. The oil first travelled north, before being diverted south-west towards the Mississippi River Delta by the Louisiana Coastal Current (LCC). Intriguingly, according to the analysis by AAI, the oil under the surface took the same route and was diverted into the coastal current (Fig. 7a, left). As a consequence, the Louisiana coast was polluted by much more oil than could have been guessed by the amount that could be seen floating on the surface alone.

Countermeasures and consequences

The total amount of oil in the leak could not be determined with certainty. Photo and film analyses of the oil gushing from the borehole, however, enabled the extrapolation of a figure of 800 million litres of oil. Many measures to contain the oil spill failed. The controlled burning of the oil slick was just as ineffective as trying to contain it with floating barriers (Fig. 5), which were unable to keep the oil together because of the high waves. In addition, the attempt to burn off the oil slick polluted the atmosphere. Spreading chemicals over the slick also failed to disperse it. This method is very controversial itself, because the chemicals used are very harmful to the environment. The tar lumps washing up on the beaches may be the most toxic consequence of the pollution. Swallowed by marine organisms, they can cause impaired reproduction, stunted growth and abnormalities in development, or lead to death. The precise chemical composition of the tar lumps is, however, elusive, making it very difficult for scientists to predict the long-term toxicology of the residues. Major industries in the region such as fishing and tourism are still battling the fallout from the oil disaster and will do so for many years to come. Court cases against those responsible continue, and damages amounting to several billions are being paid out to those affected, though legal wrangles rage over that very question of who has been affected. As of 2014, British Petroleum has paid out over 26 billion dollars on the clean-up, fines, and compensation.

In the Gulf of Mexico, a further 223 rigs continue to explore for and to pump out oil. To avoid such catastrophes in the future, stricter regulations and catalogues of measures for oil exploration and drilling would be a step in the right direction.

7 a-d – Off the coast of the Mississippi River Delta (see red frame in Fig. 2), the spread of the oil above (7b right) and below the surface (7a left, at a depth of 2.5 m and below) is analysed using RapidEye image data (29/04/2010). The surface current transports some of the oil in the slick towards the coast (7b right). The two northern currents are intercepted by the LCC and diverted to the southwest to the coast (7c middle), where they enter the shelf zone (7d image below).

Oil spill
→ Oil flow direction
Data: AAI/BlackBridge

Cyanide impact of Tisza in January and February 2000

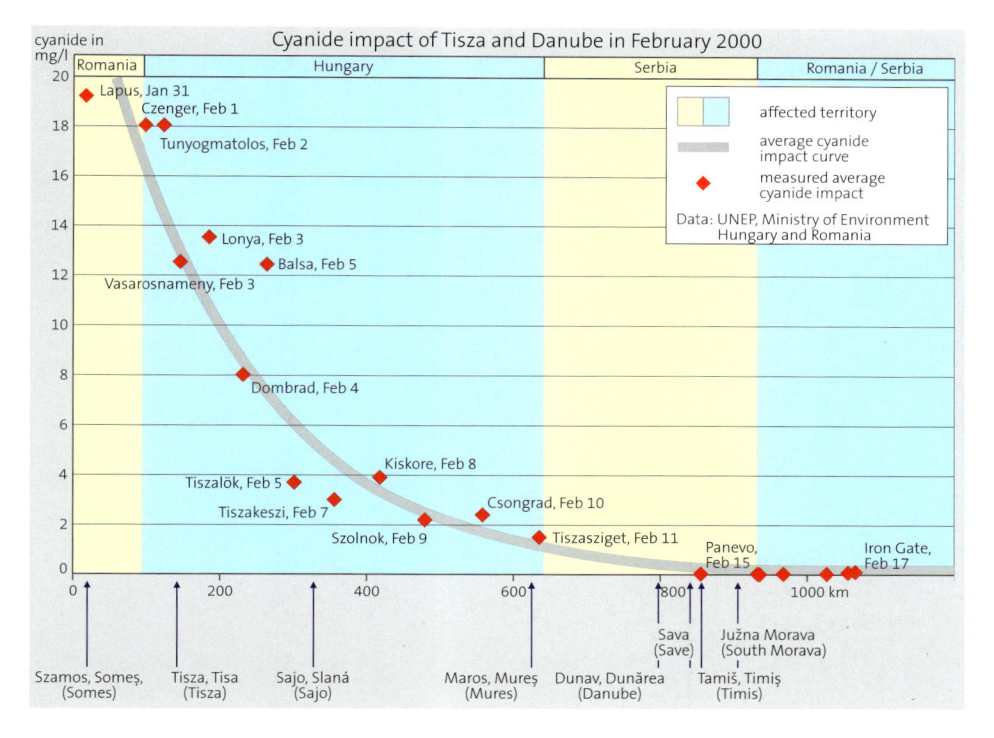

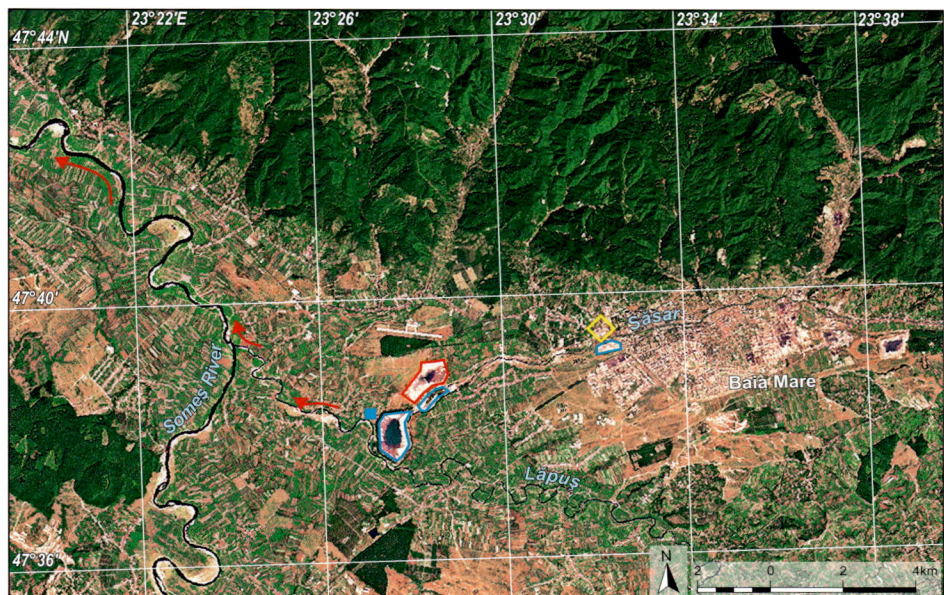

Cyanide and heavy metal mining accident in the Tisza basin

As the longest tributary of the River Danube, the Tisza river rises in the Carpathians in Romania and flows into the Danube southeast of Novi Sad in Serbia (Fig. 1). In 2000, two serious pollution incidents took place in the upper reaches of the river within only a few days. For the Tisza's ecosystem, they had catastrophic consequences.

On 30 January 2000, heavy rainfall burst the dam of a collecting pond at the gold mine in Baia Mare in northern Romania (Figs. 1 and 3). Several hundred thousand cubic metres of cyanide sludge also containing heavy metals poured into the Sasar stream and Lapus and Somes (Szamos), tributaries of the Tisza. On 1 February, the toxic water reached Hungary carrying a cyanide concentration of up to 19 milligrams per litre. After two weeks, the heavily diluted but still cyanide-contaminated water entered the Danube (Fig. 2).

A second serious event happened just a few weeks after the first accident in the mining village of Borsa. Following persistent rainfall also in this case, a dam in the tailings pond at the Baia Borsa lead and zinc mine east of Baia Mare burst on 10 March 2000 (Fig. 1). The pond held large amounts of sludge from ore processing. The dam burst let over 22,000 tonnes of sludge containing heavy metals to enter the Tisza via its tributaries. The ecosystem was once again severely damaged over a stretch of over 400 kilometres. The drinking water supply in the regions nearby was also severely affected. Water could no longer be taken from the poisoned rivers and channels for days.

Cyanide in gold mining

Cyanide is used to leach gold out of ore as it is one of the few chemical substances reacting with gold. Around 95 per cent of all gold mines use this highly toxic compound in their operations, others use even more toxic mercury. The ore is ground down and doused with a cyanide solution. This dissolves the gold, which is filtered out of the solution using chemical filtration. Although most of the cyanide is re-used, the procedure produces large amounts of sludge with toxic concentration of cyanide, which has to be collected in large basins.

Damage from the cyanide disaster in 2000 at Baia Mare

Fish stocks in the Tisza and Szamos were severely harmed by the cyanide in the water. In Hungarian waters, around 1,200 tonnes of fish were killed. By blocking off the affected water from the streams branching off the main channel, however, the toxic substances were kept from spreading further.

In some places along the River Tisza, wells had to be filled in and a replacement drinking water supply set up. The water from the Tisza provides drinking water to around 80,000 people in the Hungarian city of Szolnok (Fig. 1). The drinking water supply was disrupted for several hours while the toxic water flowed past.

Safety procedures at the gold processing plant in Baia Mare have been significantly improved since the accident. A new catch basin has been set up to expand the capacity for sludge (Fig. 3). This basin has been designed to hold back any water overflow from heavy rainfall. In addition, the pipelines and the dam are now checked regularly so that any cracks or leaks can be quickly identified and repaired. The cyanide concentrations in the basins are checked regularly, to allow them to be lowered to more environmentally friendly levels and the cyanide disposed of, if need be.

249

149°E
149°30′
19°30′S
Hook Reef
20°
Coral Sea
20°
Hayman Island
Hook Island
Dumbell Island
Whitsunday Passage
Haslewood Island
Whitsunday Islands
Airlie Beach
20°30′
Lindeman Group
Cape Conway
20°30′
Repulse Bay
Cumberland Islands
Brampton Island
149°
N
5 0 5 10km

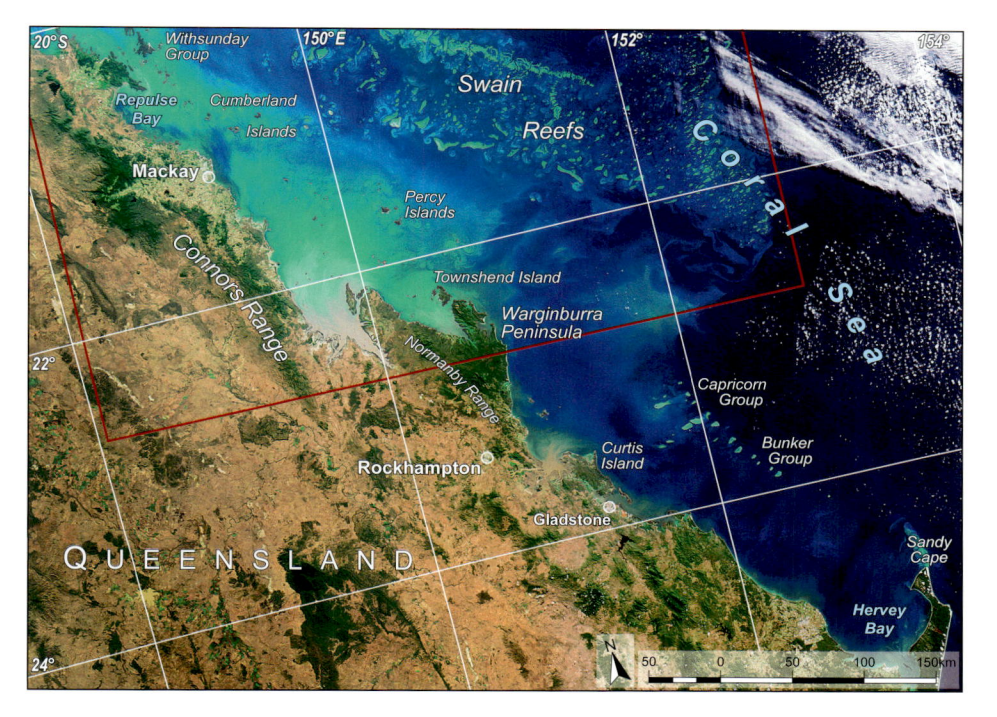

◁
1 – The Great Barrier Reef off the north-east coast of Australia is one of the largest living organisms in the world.

△
2 – Overview of the Great Barrier Reef (Envisat MERIS).

▷
3 – The more than 2,500 coral reefs making up the Great Barrier Reef were declared a UNESCO World Heritage Site.

▽
4 – A third of the Great Barrier Reef has been under the highest level of protection since 2003.

The Great Barrier Reef

The Great Barrier Reef stretches over 2,300 kilometres along the north-eastern coast of Australia (Figs. 1 and 2) and covers an area of 350,000 square kilometres. In 1981 it was inscribed as World Natural Heritage site. It is the world most extensive coral reef ecosystem with some 2,500 individual reefs (Fig. 3) of varying sizes and shapes, and over 900 islands. Collectively these landscapes and seascapes provide some of the most spectacular maritime scenery in the world. The reef grows on average by one or two centimetres per year. The northern part of the reef was created over 18 million years ago, while the southern, much younger part is around two million years old. One third of the reef belongs to the Great Barrier Reef Marine Park, the largest marine park in the world (Fig. 4).

The Great Barrier Reef is home to more than 1,500 species of tropical fish, 400 species of coral and countless shellfish, sea snakes and turtles. Between 1985 and 2012, the coral population halved. Increasing environmental stress in the past has repeatedly led to coral bleaching, which is partly responsible for this decline. Extensive coral bleaching occurred recently in the summers of 1998, 2002 and 2006.

Coral bleaching – a worldwide threat to reefs

Coral bleaching is a global phenomenon, caused by a rise in the sea temperature. Even an increase of one or two degrees Celsius for a period of several weeks can cause coral bleaching. Anomalies of three or four degrees can lead to the catastrophic dying off of coral. In the past, especially in 1998 and 2002, the El Niño weather pattern led to the drastic warming of some tropical waters.

Inside the coral's tissues live microscopic algae called zooxanthellae, which provide the organism with carbohydrates. Warmer water stresses the corals and causes these essential microalgae to die off. Because they are also responsible for the coral's colour, the zooxanthellae turn white when they die, giving rise to the term coral bleaching.

Nature and business on the Great Barrier Reef

Oil shale is mined just 50 kilometres to the south-east of the reef near the city of Gladstone, Queensland (Fig. 2) As part of the Stuart project, oil shale is processed into crude oil and petroleum. Oil shale is the name given to clay-rich or chalky rock that has a high organic carbon content. Oil shale contains not oil but kerogen, a precursor of oil. Oil shale mining releases large quantities of toxic rubble and dust. Blown over the sea and deposited by rainfall, this toxic dust enters the coral reef's ecosystem.

Agriculture along the coastline is another threat to the sensitive ecosystem, due to the high levels of nutrient and sediment input. With the annual monsoon rains, pesticides and fertilisers from the sugar cane and banana plantations also flow into the ecosystem. The heavy use of fertilisers boosts the growth of algae, which then blanket the corals and suffocate them. Starfish are another threat. As their population rockets because of the plentiful nutrients available, they overgraze the coral. In 2013 a plague of crown-of-thorns starfish seriously threatened the reef.

In 1975 the Australian government created the Great Barrier Reef Marine Park Authority environmental protection office. In addition to regulating the fishing industry and tourism, the authority's biggest task is educating people about the threats to the reef. In 2003, a third of the reef was upgraded to the highest protection level. Fishing was prohibited and shipping severely restricted in this area.

12°35'E
12°40'
12°45'
12°50'
47°15'N
47°15'
47°10'
47°05'
Kaprun
Power House Kaprun-Hauptstufe
Pumping Station Maiskogel
Reservoir Klammsee
Dietersbach
Mühlbach
Bypass West
Grubbach
Kapruner Ache
Stub Ache
Imbachhorn 2470m
Fuscher Ache
Fusch a.d. Großglocknerstraße
Hirzbach
Leferetbach
Hirzbach Connection
Power House Oberstufe
Schmiedinger Kees
Kitzsteinhorn 3203m
Reservoir Wasserfallboden
Hoher Tenn 3368m
Wielingerbach Bypass
Ebmattenbach Bypass
Ferleiten
Pumping Station Möll
Reservoir Mooserboden
Gr. Wiesbachhorn 3564m
Tauern-moossee
Möll Connection
National Park Hohe Tauern
Sonnblickkees
Weißsee
Gr. Bärenkopf 3396m
Käferbach Bypass
Käferbach
Karlingerkees
Johannisberg 3453m
Eiskögele 3426m
National Park Hohe Tauern
Pasterze
Großglockner 3798m
Fruschnitzkees
Margaritzen Reservoir
Leiterbach Bypass
Möll
Leiterbach
Heiligenblut
Kaiserbach
Ködnitz
Gössnitz
Großdorf
1 0 1 2km
N

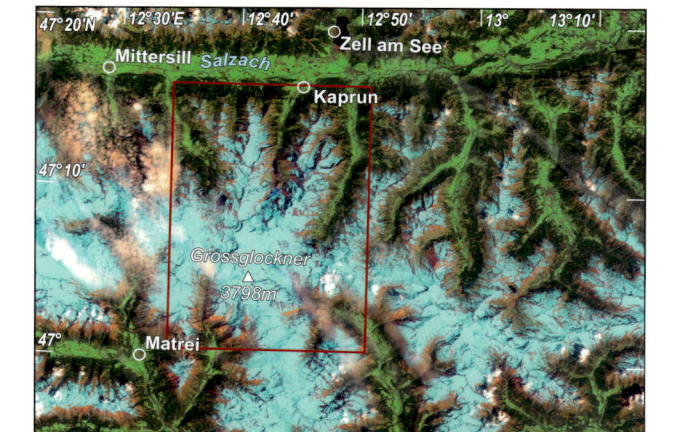

1 – The drainage basin of the Kaprun hydroelectric power station system has been significantly expanded by underground tunnels. Also shown: Austria's highest mountain, the Großglockner (3,798 metres).

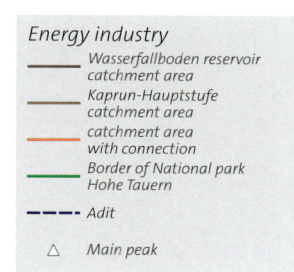

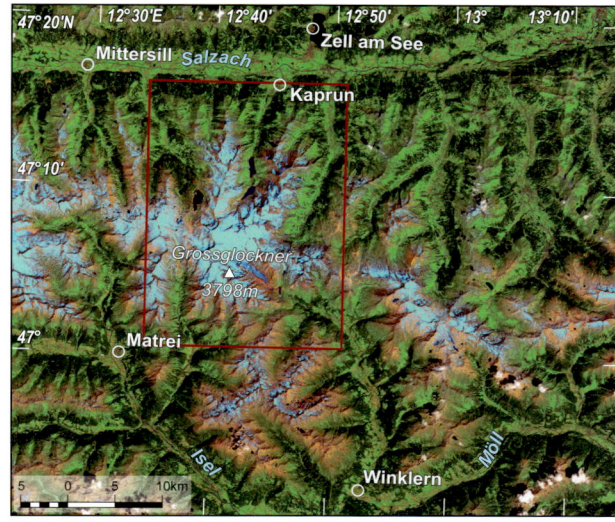

Energy industry
- Wasserfallboden reservoir catchment area
- Kaprun-Hauptstufe catchment area
- catchment area with connection
- Border of National park Hohe Tauern
- Adit
- △ Main peak

2a/b – Differences in the snowline in spring (top) and summer (bottom) in the Hohe Tauern, Glockner Group with the Mooserboden and Wasserfallboden reservoirs.

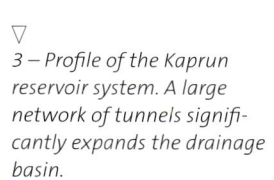

3 – Profile of the Kaprun reservoir system. A large network of tunnels significantly expands the drainage basin.

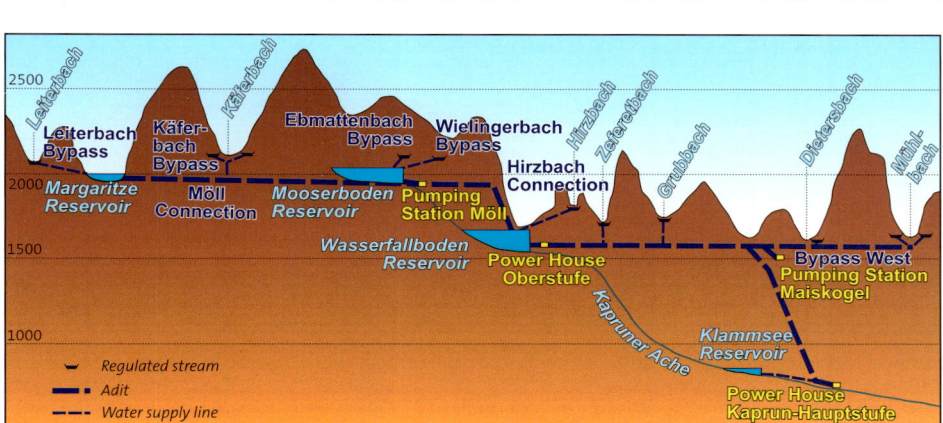

4 – The Mooserboden and Wasserfallboden reservoirs from the northeast.

5 – Discharge hydrograph of the Kapruner Ache at Kaprun before (red) and after construction (blue) of the two reservoirs.

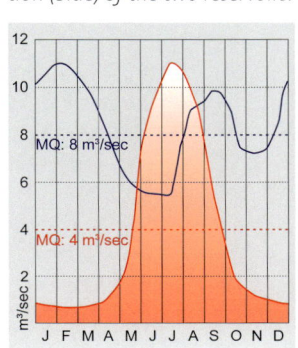

The Kaprun hydroelectric stations

The use of hydroelectric power to generate energy plays a major role in countries where water is abundant. Around 60 per cent of the electricity used in Austria comes from hydroelectric power stations.

The Kaprun hydroelectric stations on the edge of the Hohe Tauern national park (Fig. 1) do not generate electricity continuously like run-of-river power plants. Their turbines are switched on at times of peak consumption and the electricity generated is fed into the grid. The maximum output of the upper and main levels is 833 megawatts, with an additional 130 megawatts for pump operation. This corresponds to 10 per cent of Austria's entire peak electricity requirements. During times of lower demand, water from the Wasserfallboden dam is pumped to the higher Mooserboden reservoir to generate electricity again when required.

The groundbreaking ceremony for the Tauern hydroelectricity station in Kaprun took place in May 1938 and its construction was continued during the war. In the postwar years there was a huge lack of electricity, so the power station was classed as a highly urgent project by the European Recovery Program. Construction of the Kaprun upper level power station began in 1950. By 1955, the Mooser and Drossen dams for the Mooserboden reservoir, both dams for the Margaritze reservoir, the upper level power station and the 12-kilometre Möll diversion tunnels were complete.

The Kaprun hydroelectric power stations comprise the Kaprun main level with the Wasserfallboden reservoir and the Limberg dam; the upper level with the Limberg powerhouse, the Mooserboden reservoir and the Mooser and Drossen dams; and the Möll diversion with the Leiterbach diversion, the Margaritze reservoir and the Möll and Margaritze dams (Fig. 3). The diversions increase the catchment basin for the Wasserfallboden and Mooserboden reservoirs (Fig. 4). From there, the water in the reservoir is diverted via a head race tunnel and a vertical pressure shaft to the powerhouse. From 2011, with the completion of the underground hydroelectric power station Limberg II (2007–2010), the power stations' output was increased by 480 megawatts.

The hydroelectric power stations and the Kapruner Ache

The water used to generate electricity in the power stations is primarily meltwater from the Glockner Group glaciers (Fig. 2 a/b). The Kapruner Ache was originally characterised by a glacial regime. The background behind this seasonal regime is the storage of precipitation in the form of snow and melting glacial ice, which peaks in June and July and hits a period of extremely low water levels during the winter (Fig. 2 a/b). Nonetheless, the entire regime is itself influenced by the operation of the power station. Since the storage power station was completed, the peak discharge is no longer in summer but in January and February. The discharge hydrograph reaches another high in September. Since the hydroelectric power stations were completed, the flow rate in the middle reaches has increased from four cubic metres per second to eight cubic metres per second.

In addition to the change in flow rate, problems have also been experienced within the system of power stations itself. The Margaritze reservoir at the foot of the Pasterze is threatened with silting up. The flushing of glacial striation is having a negative impact on the ecosystem in the rivers and streams. When a reservoir was flushed in 1995, the Möll's entire fish population was killed.

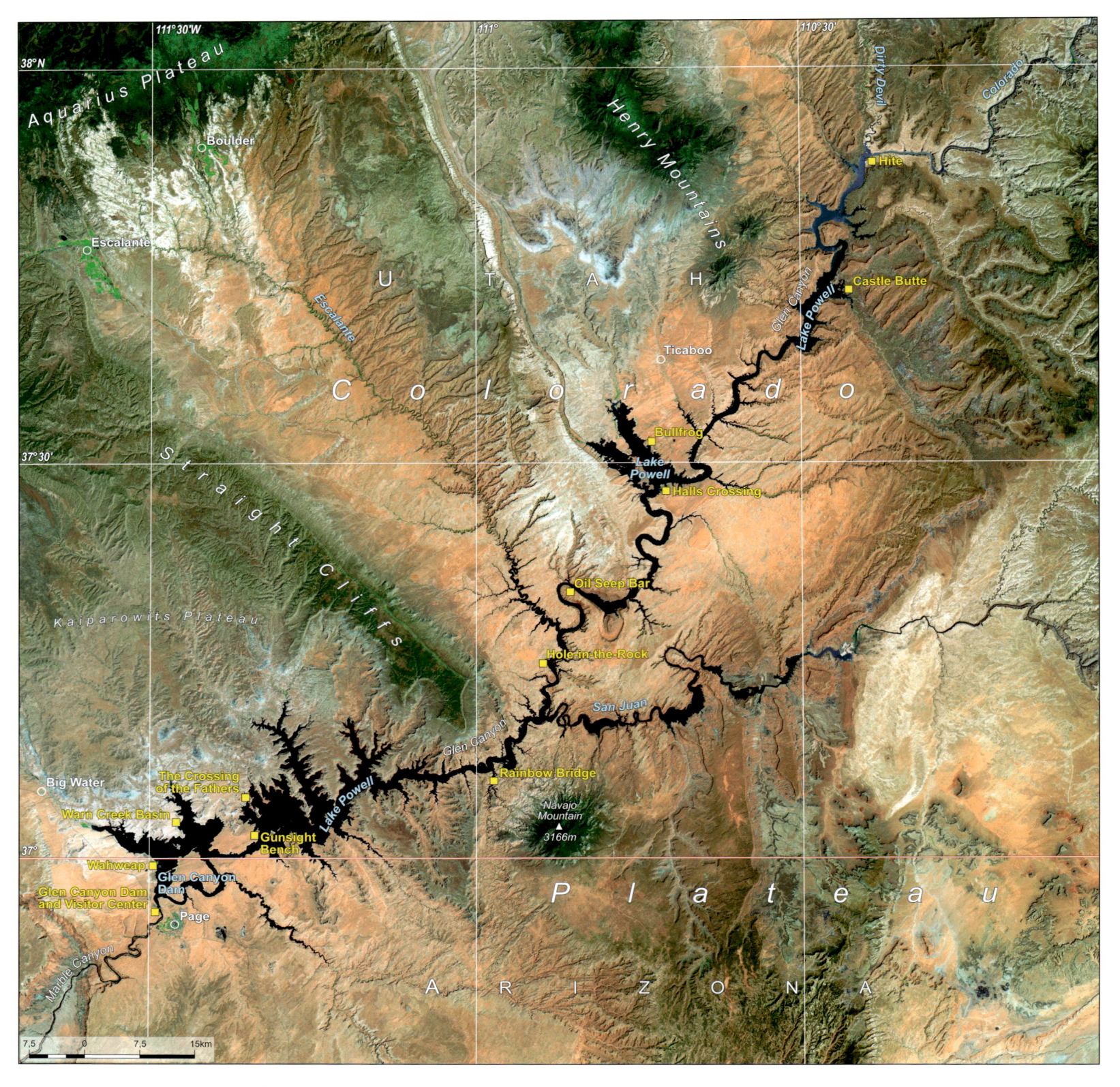

Lake Powell

Three hundred kilometres long and 40 kilometres wide, holding around 33 cubic kilometres of freshwater, Lake Powell is the largest reservoir by area in the United States of America. It is located on the semi-arid Colorado Plateau in the states of Arizona and Utah (Fig. 1). The reservoir to the northeast of the Grand Canyon formed behind the Glen Canyon Dam in 1963. Apart from generating electricity, the reservoir is also a popular leisure destination. In 1972, the US Congress decided to set up the Glen Canyon National Recreation Area.

The enormous water pressure resulting from the construction of the dam altered the geological tensions beneath the surface of the land and led to an increase in seismic activity. In addition, the lower reaches of the river now transport much less debris, which has increased the erosive force of the Colorado and accelerated its deepening into the ground.

Itaipu Reservoir

The Itaipu Reservoir is located on the border between Paraguay and Brazil to the north of Ciudad del Este and Foz do Iguaçu (Fig. 2). The dam, completed in 1982, stores water from the Rio Paraná and is 170 kilometres long. Covering 1,350 square kilometres, the reservoir has a capacity of 29 cubic kilometres. Today, the 20 generators in the hydroelectric power station generate 14,000 megawatts – enough to cover 75 per cent of Paraguay's energy requirements and 17 per cent of Brazil's.

While the construction project has been good for the energy sector, it has nonetheless brought negative social and environmental consequences. Several thousand people had to be resettled, while large areas of farmland and natural virgin rainforest were flooded to fill the reservoir (Figs. 2 and 3). Even more rainforest was then cleared in order to gain new farmland, particularly on the territory of Paraguay.

Glen Canyon National Recreation Area
■ *Tourist attraction*

△
1 – At 653 square kilometres, Lake Powell is the largest reservoir in the United States. It was created by damming the Colorado. Most of the lake is in Utah; only the southernmost arms are in Arizona.

▷
3 – As can be seen on this satellite image from 1973, what is now the bottom of the Itaipu Reservoir was once farmland.

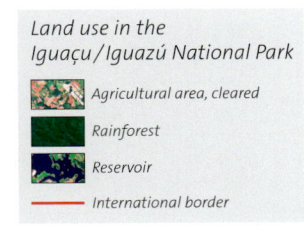

Iguaçu/Iguazú Falls

In addition to the Itaipu Reservoir, the Iguaçu/Iguazú Falls are a popular recreational area and tourist destination. The waterfalls at the borders between Paraguay, Brazil and Argentina are just a few kilometres before the Iguaçu/Iguazú empties into the Rio Paraná. Eighty metres high and 2,700 metres wide, inside a national park with sub-tropical rainforest, the waterfalls rank among the biggest and most spectacular on Earth.

Satellite images show the various types of land use and the way they have changed within the area over time. While large swathes of the rainforest were cleared in Paraguay to create more farmland, in Brazil and Argentina the forest was placed under protection by the creation of the Iguaçu/Iguazú National Park and even reforested in some areas (Fig. 2). As a consequence, a part of the boundary between Paraguay and Argentina is clearly visible in the satellite image (Figs. 2 and 3).

Land use in the Iguaçu/Iguazú National Park
- Agricultural area, cleared
- Rainforest
- Reservoir
- International border

△
2 – The conservation area of the Iguaçu National Park in Brazil and the Iguazú National Park in Argentina can be clearly made out in the lower right-hand corner of this satellite image from 2013. The rainforest in Paraguay, in contrast, has largely been cleared.

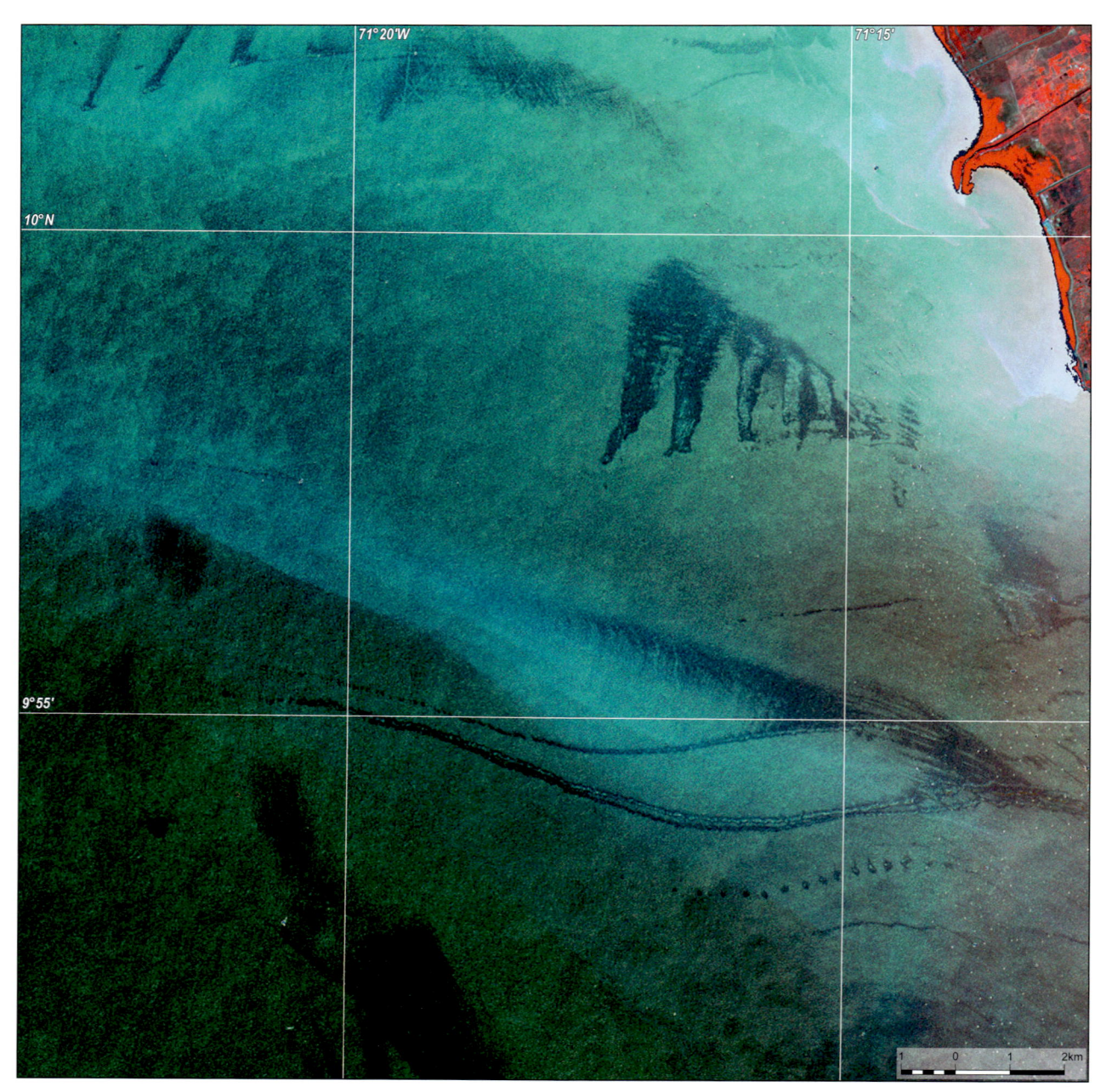

1 – Infrared false-colour image showing the pollution in Lake Maracaibo (Lago de Maracaibo) caused by oil drilling, which reached its highest point from December 2002 to January 2003. Oil flows from every drilling platform into the lake. Leaks from large oil tanks also cause widespread pollution.

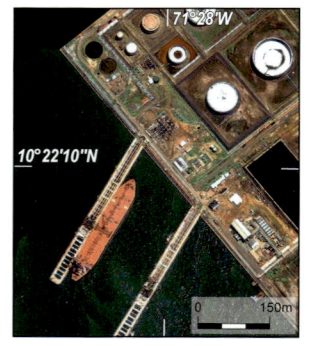

4 – An oil tanker takes on its cargo in the offshore port at Cabimas. Oceangoing vessels can reach the lake via the 8-kilometre wide Canal de San Carlos.

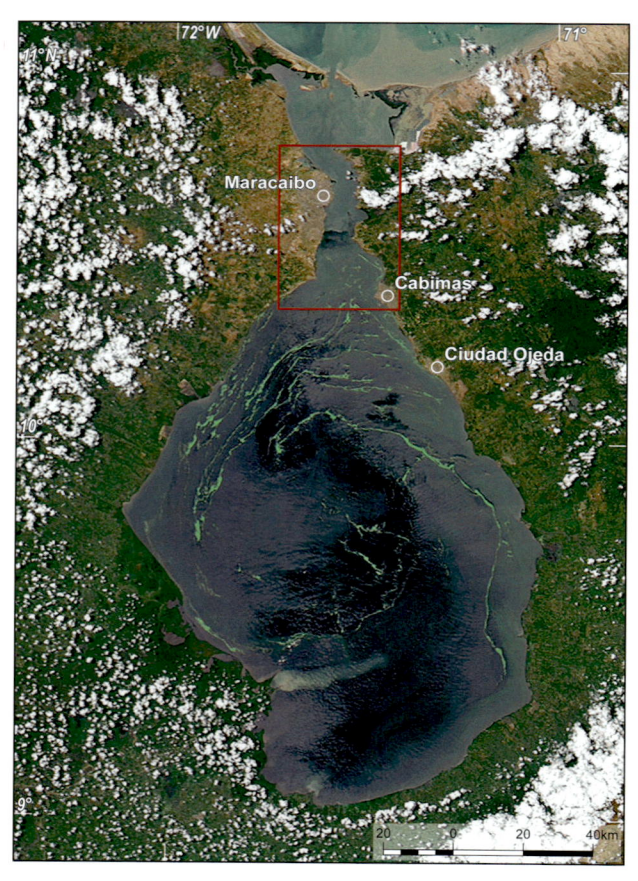

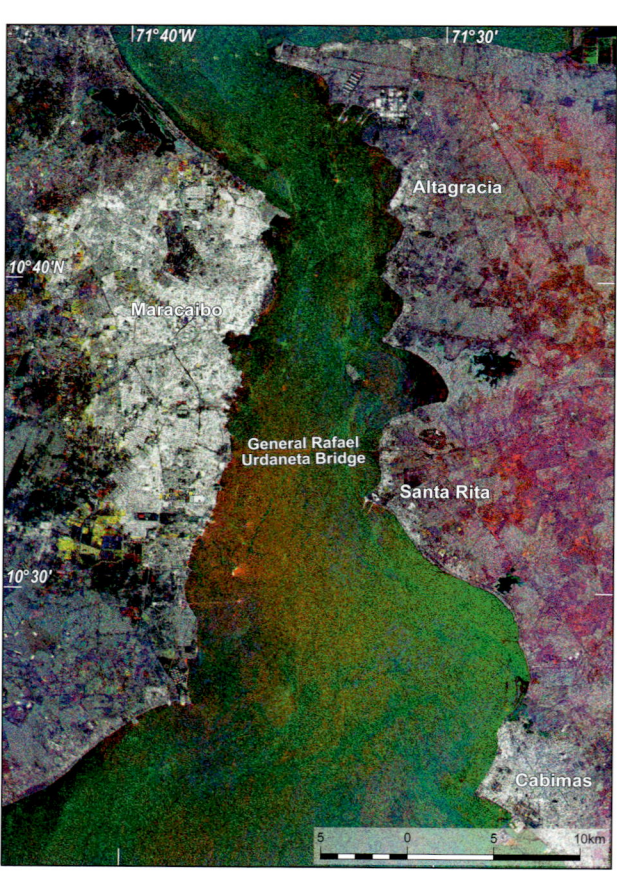

2 – On 26 June 2004, around 18 per cent of the 13,280 square kilometre lake was covered by "Lemna minor", commonly known as duckweed.

3 – The radar image from 08/09/2004 has been coloured red, while the one from 26/02/2004 has been coloured green. The image from 17/06/2004 is shown in blue. The colour combination shows the higher vegetation cover in summer (high proportion of red and blue). The winter image shows the higher wind speeds on the lake (choppier sea, trade winds). The winter image is lighter, i.e. with more green. The populated area is the same in all images and appears to be colourless, i.e. grey to white.

5 – Since Lake Maracaibo's (Lago de Maracaibo) channel to the sea is very narrow, it is classed as the largest inland lake in South America, ahead of Lake Titicaca. Venezuela's largest oil reserves rest underneath the lake bed.

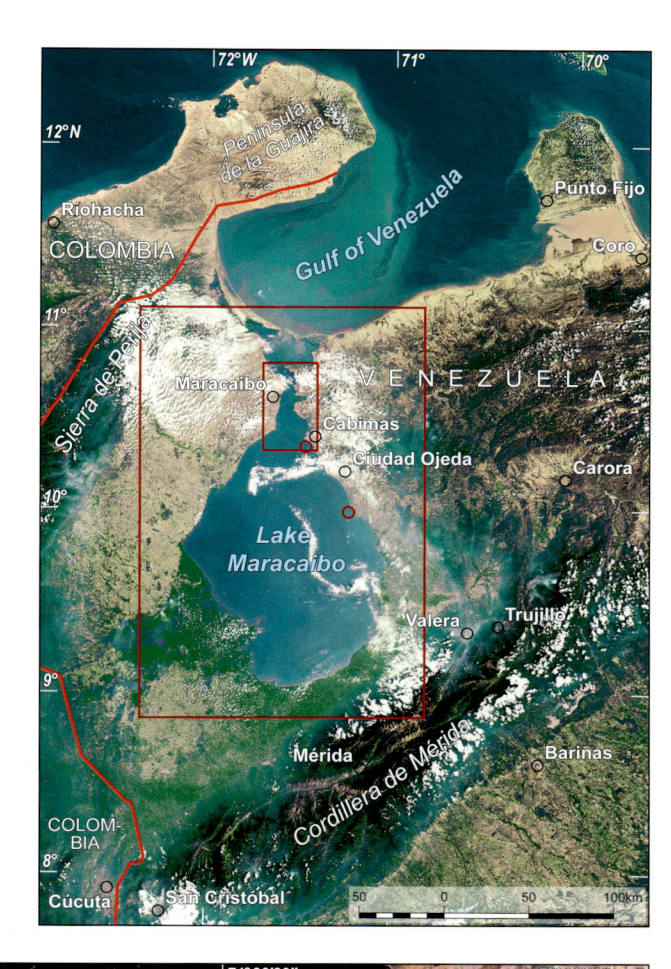

6 – Standing just a few hundred metres apart in the northeast of Lake Maracaibo near Cabimas, oil platforms drill down for the oil buried deep under the lake bed sediments.

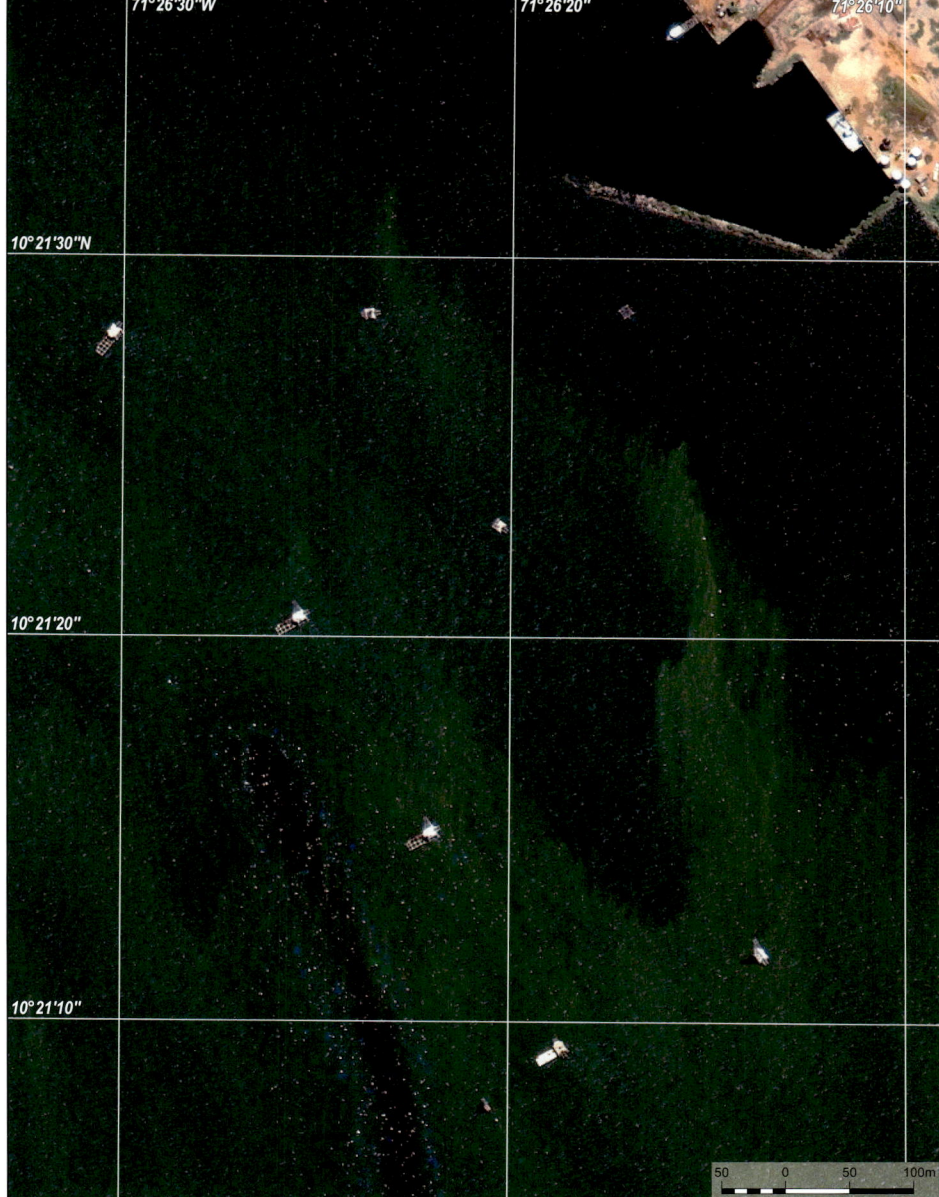

Lake Maracaibo

Lake Maracaibo is the largest inland lake in South America. Although the eight-kilometre wide and 75 kilometre-long Canal de San Carlos links the lake with the Gulf of Venezuela (Golfo de Venezuela) and thus the open sea of the Carribean, the lake is still classed as a freshwater lake (Fig. 5). The heavier saltwater, which enters Lake Maracaibo through the man-made canal, is deposited in a thin layer on the lakebed. The northern part of the lake is therefore primarily brackish, i.e. a mixture of salt- and freshwater. The southern part, however, is entirely freshwater, as the rivers Catatumbo, Santa Ana and Chama all empty into the lake here.

Where once tropical rainforest covered the regions around the shores of the lake, the land has now been cleared for agricultural use. The entire region around Lake Maracaibo is characterised by shifting cultivation (Fig. 3). The main industry on the lake, though, is the production of oil and gas, Venezuela's most important export goods (Fig. 6).

Oil underneath Lake Maracaibo

The oil well Barrosos no. 2 was opened in Lake Maracaibo on 12 December 1922. Success came immediately, and 100,000 barrels of oil a day were tapped from underground reservoirs. By 1929 Venezuela was the biggest oil exporter in the world. Over the years more companies and investors came to build more and more platforms to extract the lucrative natural resource.

To transport the crude oil, a deep sea port was built in the lake in the 1960s (Fig. 4). Both piers are so large that four ships can be moored there at the same time. To let large tankers approach the port, the link to the Gulf of Venezuela had to be artificially widened. This widening allowed more saltwater into the lake and turned the northern part into brackish water. Since then, the shipping channel has had to be repeatedy dredged and freed of silt.

The oil industry has also made its mark on Lake Maracaibo (Fig. 1). For decades now, oil from the drilling platforms has been entering the water – with well-documented effects on the environment. Today, the state-run oil company PDVSA (Petróleos de Venezuela S.A.) implements a series of environmental programmes with a budget in the millions and has meticulously cleaned up the areas affected by oil leaks.

However, environmental experts still fear that the lake will remain contaminated. After all, the pollution is not solely due to the oil industry. According to some scientists, untreated wastewater from households and industry, as well as abattoir waste and, more recently, coal deposits, are also damaging the Lake Maracaibo ecosystem.

Lemna minor

In common parlance, "Lemna minor" is usually known as duckweed. Lake Maracaibo was invaded by this plant in 2004 (Fig. 2). Whether the plants were brought to the lake by visiting ships or is in fact a native species remains unclear. However, the Venezuelan government realised that it had to stop the invasion.

Although duckweed is not poisonous to fish, it competes with the flora and fauna of the lake for key nutrients and oxygen, and it also proved a major hindrance for the 20,000 fishermen navigating on the lake. USD 2 million per month were set aside to combat the duckweed invasion. The duckweed was kept from spreading further only by using mechanical methods on ships carrying special equipment. The causes of the invasion have not yet been clarified.

Global shipping

For centuries now, shipping lanes have been some of the most important traffic and trading routes. Today, they are primarily used for transporting mass goods over long distances. To minimise transport times or avoid obstacles, new routes have always been sought, often under great hardships. Christopher Columbus discovered America, for example, in his search for a shorter passage for trading spices from India.

Over the last two centuries shipping has been revolutionised. Large canals – masterpieces of engineering – have been constructed to shorten some sea routes by several thousand kilometres. Steam ships replaced sailing ships, which depended on the wind, and travelled the world's oceans at hitherto unimaginable speeds. Today there are nuclear-powered icebreakers that open paths for ships through the ice of the Arctic Ocean, GPS navigation and double-hulled tankers.

In this context, ports have always played an important role. As international transport hubs, they are extremely important for the economic development of their cities and hinterlands.

As one of the negative consequences of global shipping (Fig. 1) the likelihood of organisms traveling and surviving in the ballast water of ships has increased. Ballast water is commonly used to stabilise empty or only partially laden ships. Countless non-native species, mainly molluscs, crabs and algae, have already made journeys in this way and settled in areas far off their natural habitats. One example of this phenomenon is an Asian species of crab, which was shipped along in ballast water and is now at home on the French Atlantic coast. The zebra mussel, also transported in ballast water, has now spread throughout the Great Lakes, where it is not threatened by natural predators. Here, the mussels damage water outflow pipes and sewage treatment plants. In addition, the ballast water, especially from oil tankers, is often heavily polluted. Despite strict regulation, the dumping of this water into the sea continues to cause severe marine and coastal pollution.

The Suez Canal

The 163-kilometre long canal links Port Said in the Mediterranean with Suez on the Red Sea (Figs. 2 and 3). Ships with a draught of up to 20 metres and a capacity of up to 240,000 tonnes (TDW) can navigate the canal. Since the canal was built it is no longer necessary to circumnavigate the entire African continent when traveling between

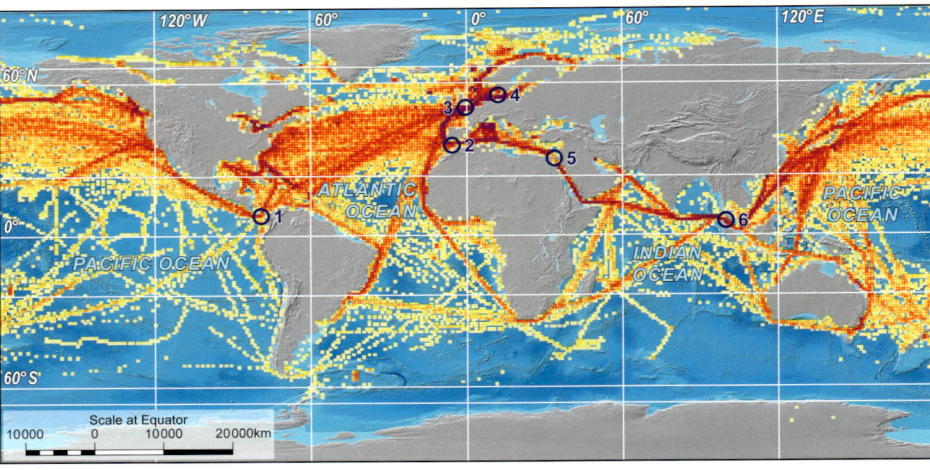

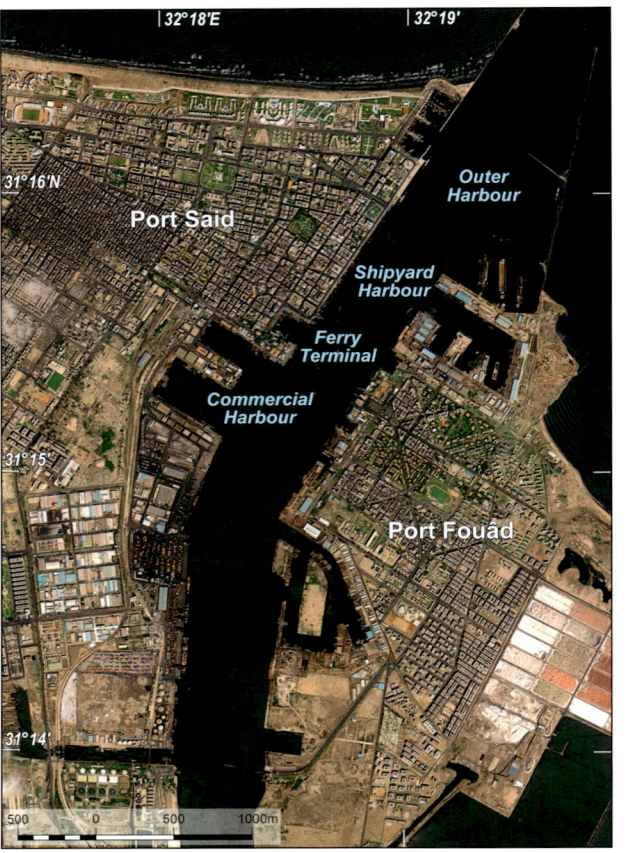

1 – Global shipping routes and their bottlenecks.

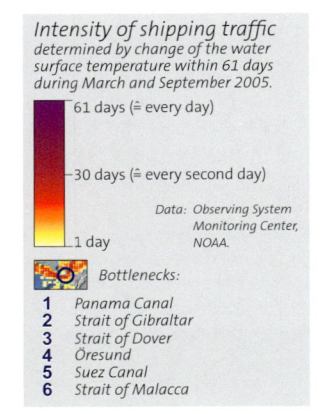

Intensity of shipping traffic determined by change of the water surface temperature within 61 days during March and September 2005.

- 61 days (≙ every day)
- 30 days (≙ every second day)
- 1 day

Data: Observing System Monitoring Center, NOAA.

Bottlenecks:
1. Panama Canal
2. Strait of Gibraltar
3. Strait of Dover
4. Öresund
5. Suez Canal
6. Strait of Malacca

2 – The Suez Canal links the Mediterranean with the Red Sea. It is one of the busiest shipping lanes in the world.

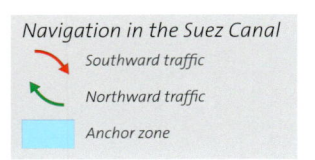

Navigation in the Suez Canal
- Southward traffic
- Northward traffic
- Anchor zone

3 – The northern end of the Suez Canal opens into the Mediterranean near the northeastern Egyptian city of Port Said (with Port Fouâd – East Port Said), the second-largest Egyptian port for goods and cruise ships.

4 – Opened in 2001, the Suez Canal Bridge crosses the canal between Port Said and Ismailija. 70 metres headroom are sufficient also for the largest vessels that are allowed to pass the canal.

5 – The Envisat ASAR image shows ship traffic in the Strait of Dover on 27/07/2004. The ships and their wakes reflect the radar waves differently from the surrounding water, which makes it easier to track the ships' movements.

6 – Close-up showing three ships in the Strait of Dover.

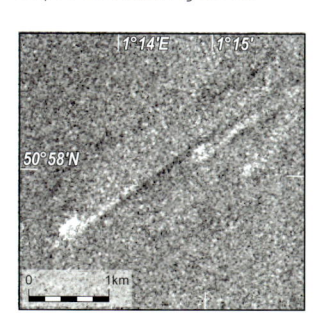

7 – Oil tankers and refineries at the mouth of the River Meuse in the Europoort, part of the Port of Rotterdam.

8 – The Port of Rotterdam is one of the most important major ports in the world for international goods traffic. Covering around 11 square kilometres, it is also the largest port area in the world.

9 – The enormous amount of goods transshipped in large container terminals every day makes it necessary to use highly efficient logistics tools and technologies.

Europe and Asia. More than 17,000 ships pass through the canal every year. The canal was dug at the narrowest point of the isthmus. In the middle, it passes through the Bitter Lakes, a long saltwater lake basin. The flat terrain and the constant water level means that no locks are needed anywhere along the canal. As such, water exchange between the Red Sea and the Mediterranean is unhindered.

Since it opened in 1869 the Suez Canal has played a major role in global trade – and, at the time, in the expansion of the European empires in Africa and Asia. Even now it is playing an important political role.

The English Channel

The English Channel is a natural strait lying between the European mainland and the British Isles (Fig. 5). The narrowest point of the channel – 34 kilometres – is the Strait of Dover. Because most of the shipping routes between the Atlantic and the North Sea pass through the English Channel, the Strait of Dover is one of the world's busiest shipping lanes (Fig. 6). More than 400 ships pass through it every day. In addition, the Strait of Dover is the shortest ferry crossing between England and France, leading to additional traffic interfering with the traffic along the English Channel.

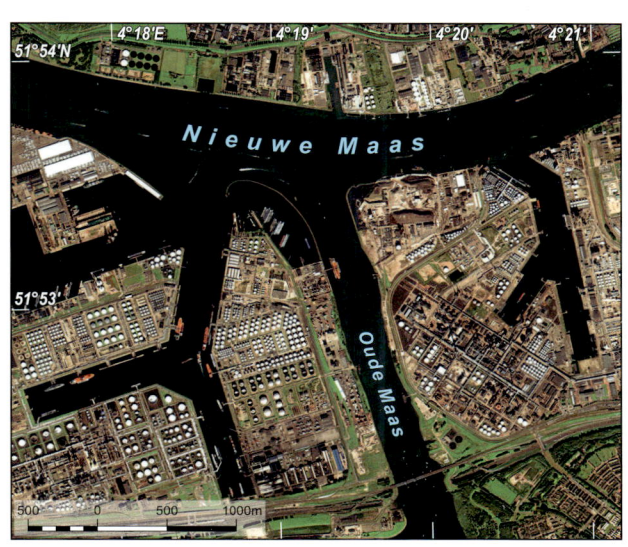

The Port of Rotterdam

The Port of Rotterdam covers an area of 10,500 hectares and extends for 40 kilometres, making it the biggest port in both Europe and the world (Figs. 8 and 9). It is the main transshipment hub for goods coming from and going to the countries in central and western Europe. Several hundred million tonnes of goods are transshipped here every year, primarily from over 30,000 container ships. The goods are carried to their destinations by road, rail or via the rivers Meuse and Rhine. The destinations may even be in eastern Europe, as the Rhine-Main-Danube Canal links the Port of Rotterdam with the Black Sea.

The Nieuwe Waterweg (New Waterway) is a 20-kilometre long, man-made canal linking the North Sea and the Port of Rotterdam (Fig. 7). It enables even large ocean-going vessels with deep draughts to access the port. A barrage protects the canal from storm surges in the North Sea. Docks and terminals line the branches of the channel. The Meuse delta is home to one of the largest industrial zones in the world for the petrochemical industry. In the 3,700-hectare Europoort, oil is transshipped, stored and processed. The big petrochemicals companies also operate refineries in the port itself in order to keep transport cost low.

◁
1 – Map of the main navigation routes in the Arctic region.

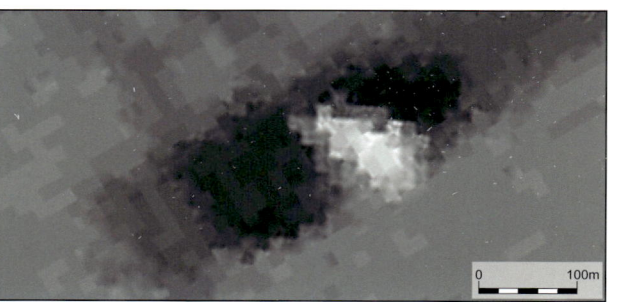

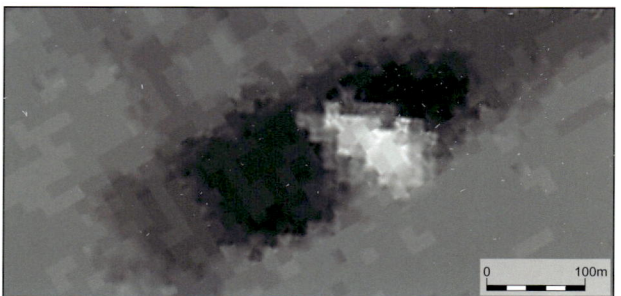

Northeast Passage
- - - «Over-the-Pole»-Route
—— Transit Route
—— Mid Route
—— Coastal Route

Northwest Passage
—— Northwest Passage

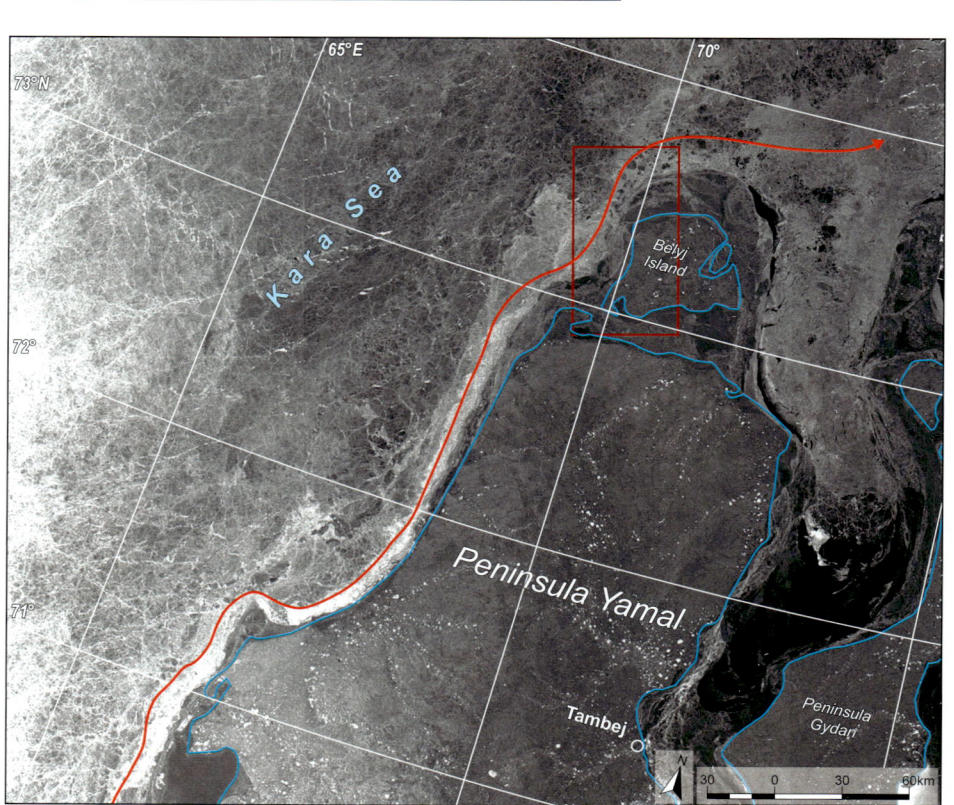

⊙ Main harbour for Arctic navigation

Data: Nansen Environmental and Remote Sensing Center, Arctic Climate Impact Assessment

◁
2 – Some sea ice (icebergs of 100 x 50 m) still drifts along the coast of the Belyi Island (ostrov Belyi) in July 1991.

◁
3 – A subset of a Landsat ETM image zoomed to an iceberg enclosed by sea ice and open water.

Sea ice navigation in the Arctic supported by satellite images

Ice navigation in the Arctic has a long history, especially in the Russian sector, which takes in almost half of the Arctic Ocean. This region shown in the Arctic map is called the Northeast Passage or the Northern Sea Route. It consists of several ice navigation routes between Murmansk in the west to the Bering Strait in the east (Fig. 1), used by nuclear-powered icebreakers to escort cargo vessels to and from Russian harbours (Fig. 6). The use of SAR data to support ice navigation has been developed in the last 15 years, starting with ERS SAR data in 1991. Using satellite SAR data available in near real-time, i.e. two to three hours after the satellite passes overhead, details of the ice cover that are important for navigating through the ice can be mapped (Fig. 5). In particular, ice types such as multiyear ice, first-year ice, young ice and new ice as well as leads, ridges, ice drift and fast ice boundaries, can be identified in SAR images independent of cloud and light conditions.

Envisat ASAR Wide Swath images were used until 2012 to map ice conditions in the Barents and Kara Sea region to support ice navigation and offshore operations (Fig. 4). Each SAR image stripe was about 400 kilometres wide and more than 1000 kilometres long. The SAR data could be downloaded a few hours after the satellite had passed over the area. The image is available from the ESA rolling archive. After geolocation and radiometric correction, the images were sent to the operational headquarters of the Murmansk Shipping Company. Resampled to a pixel size of 400 metres ground resolution, the images gave a reasonable file size for transmission without losing important ice information. In 2014, the new Sentinel-1 will replace Envisat. The sailing routes of the icebreakers are planned based on ice maps and weather forecasts.

An example of a SAR image shows a coastal polynya along the coast of Jamal Peninsula (poluostrov Jamal), identified by a bright signature (Fig. 4). This is a characteristic SAR signature for young ice 10-30 centimetres thick, in contrast to thicker first-year ice, which has a darker signature. The icebreakers can break ice from 1-2 metres thick, but the captain always tries to navigate through the thinnest ice or in open water, as this saves time and fuel. The red line in the SAR image indicates the sailing route for the nuclear icebreaker Sovetsky Soyuz, sailing eastwards to the Enisej Gulf, along usually wind-induced openings in the Arctic sea ice, the polynja.

The danger of icebergs

Icebergs are another hazard for ice navigation. The northern part of the Barents Sea is frequently crossed by icebergs, which are typically 50-100 metres in width, 20-30 metres deep, and extend six to eight metres above the sea surface (Fig. 7). Icebergs break off of calving glaciers and drift with wind and currents into shipping lanes and areas of offshore operations.

Icebergs can be tracked by high-resolution satellite images. The example (subset of Landsat ETM image) shows an iceberg that has a brighter reflection compared to the surrounding open water and the drifting sea ice (Fig. 3). The detection criterion for icebergs is a shadow on their northern flanks, created by the low angle of the sun in the polar regions. Icebergs can also be detected in SAR images with a resolution of 20 metres or better.

Text: Stein Sandven

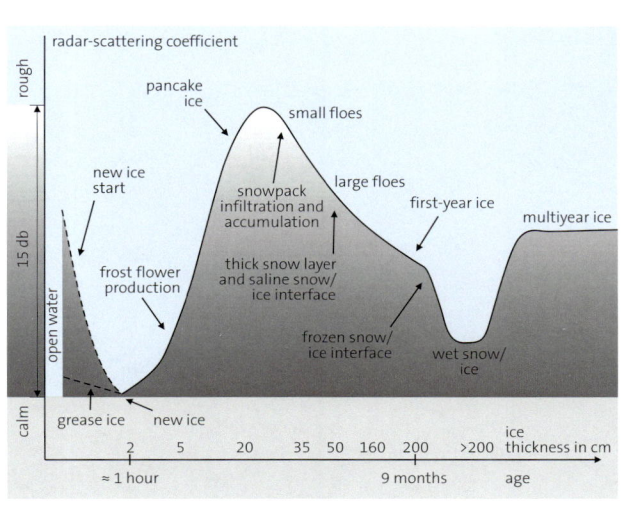

▷
5 – The graphic shows the different radar radiation due to the age, thickness and type of snow and ice surfaces. Using the graphic and including other sources, e.g. weather data, the best navigation routes can be detected.

▷▷
6 – The Russian nuclear icebreaker «Rossia» navigating through Arctic sea ice.

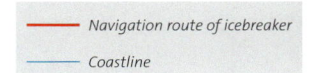

▷
7 – A 30 metre-long iceberg rises five metres out of the sea in the Barents Sea.

◁
4 – A radar image of the shoreline of the Jamal Peninsula (poluostrov Jamal) taken by Envisat ASAR on 16/03/2004. A bright radar signal reflected by ice surfaces indicates thin ice with a thickness of about 10 to 30 centimetres. Navigation through this ice is easy. A nuclear icebreaker can sail at a nominal speed of 14 to 15 knots through such sea ice.

— Navigation route of icebreaker
— Coastline

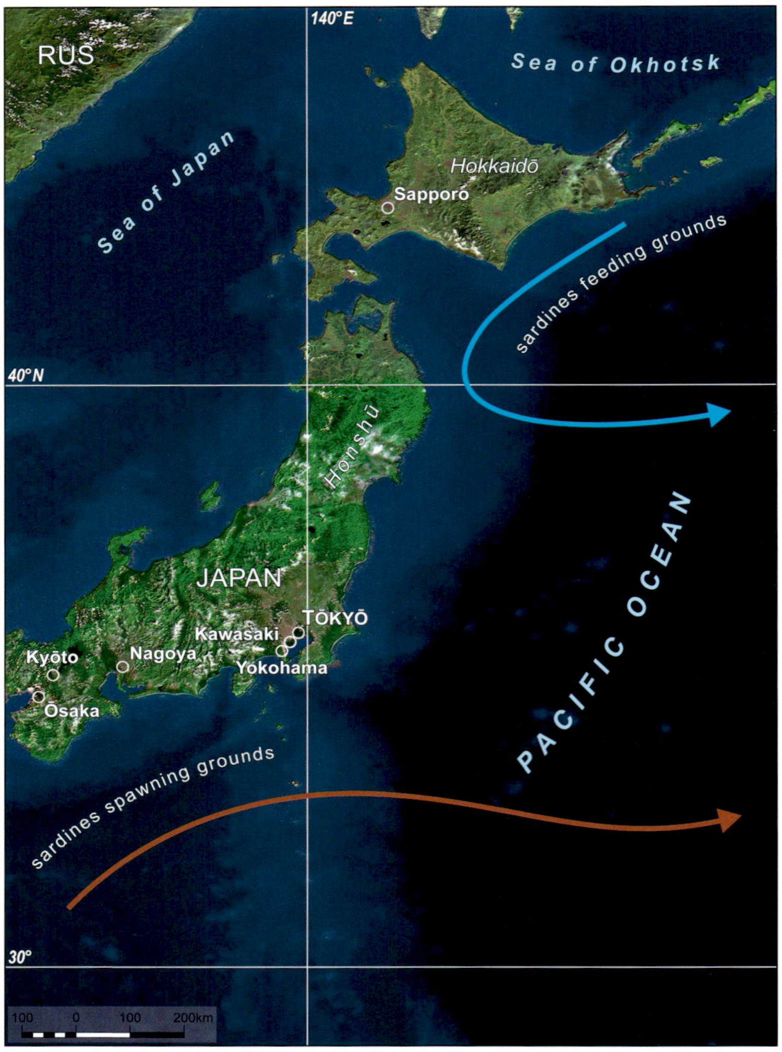
140°E
RUS
Sea of Okhotsk
Sea of Japan
Hokkaidō
Sapporo
sardines feeding grounds
40°N
Honshū
JAPAN
TŌKYŌ
Kawasaki
Kyōto
Nagoya
Yokohama
Ōsaka
PACIFIC OCEAN
sardines spawning grounds
30°
100 0 100 200km

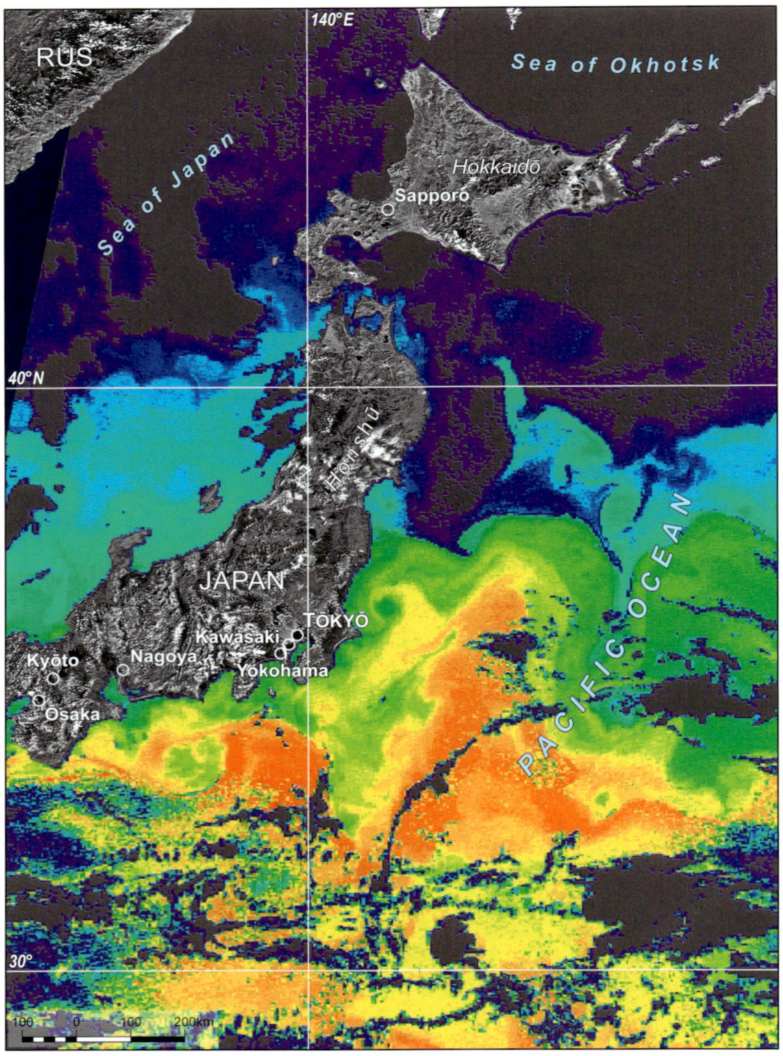
140°E
RUS
Sea of Okhotsk
Sea of Japan
Hokkaidō
Sapporo
40°N
Honshū
JAPAN
TŌKYŌ
Kawasaki
Kyōto
Nagoya
Yokohama
Ōsaka
PACIFIC OCEAN
30°
100 0 100 200km

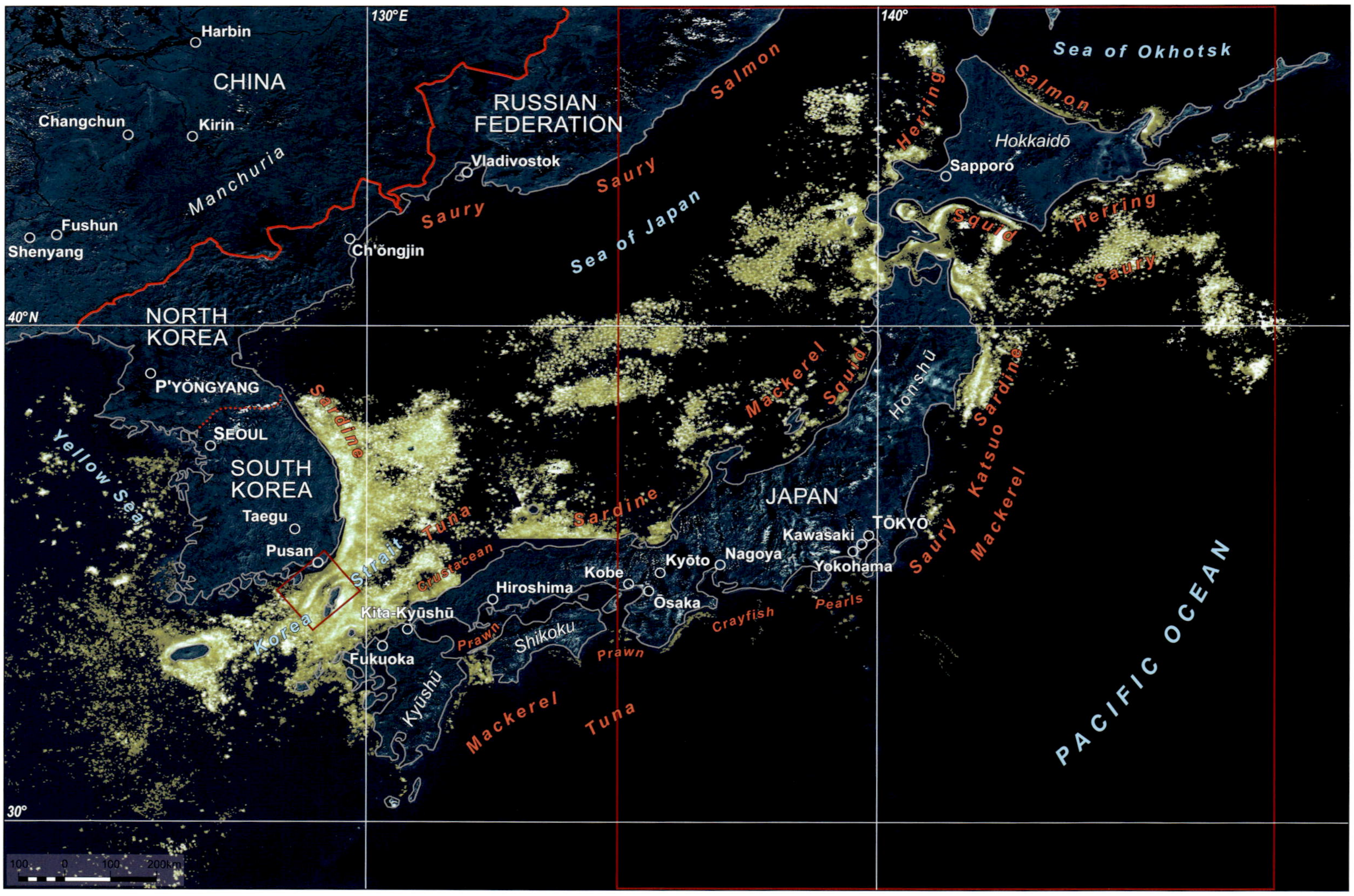
Harbin
130°E
140°
CHINA
Changchun
Kirin
RUSSIAN FEDERATION
Salmon
Sea of Okhotsk
Salmon
Herring
Hokkaidō
Sapporo
Vladivostok
Saury
Manchuria
Saury
Sea of Japan
Fushun
Shenyang
Ch'ŏngjin
Squid
Herring
Saury
40°N
NORTH KOREA
P'YŎNGYANG
Sardine
Mackerel
Squid
Honshū
Sardine
Yellow Sea
SEOUL
SOUTH KOREA
Katsuo
Taegu
Tuna
Sardine
JAPAN
Mackerel
Pusan
Strait
Crustacean
TŌKYŌ
Kawasaki
Saury
Kobe
Kyōto
Nagoya
Yokohama
Hiroshima
Ōsaka
Korea
Kita-Kyūshū
Crayfish
Pearls
Prawn
Shikoku
Fukuoka
Prawn
Kyūshū
Mackerel
Tuna
PACIFIC OCEAN
30°
100 0 100 200km

◁
1 a/b – Spawning and feeding grounds for sardines (shown here in Japan) depend to a large extent on the temperature of the water. The fish prefer warmer waters for spawning and cooler areas for feeding.

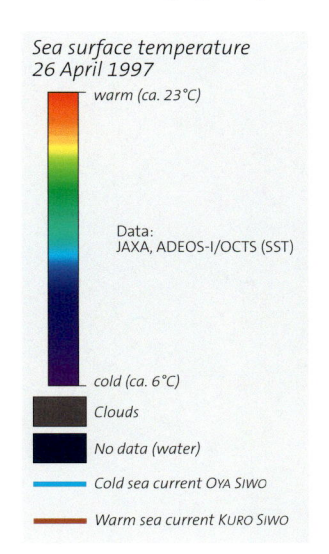

Sea surface temperature
26 April 1997

— warm (ca. 23°C)

Data:
JAXA, ADEOS-I/OCTS (SST)

— cold (ca. 6°C)
■ Clouds
■ No data (water)
— Cold sea current OYA SIWO
— Warm sea current KURO SIWO

▷
3 – Diverse Tuna qualities are prepared for sale at Tokyo's Tsukiji fish market.

▷▽ ▷▽
6, 7 – Squid fishing at night.

▷
5 – Trend of sardine populations off the coast of Japan.

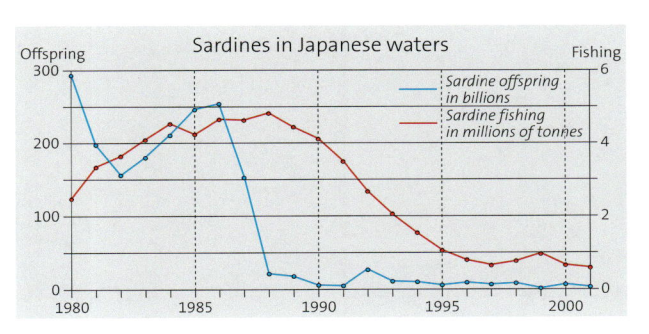

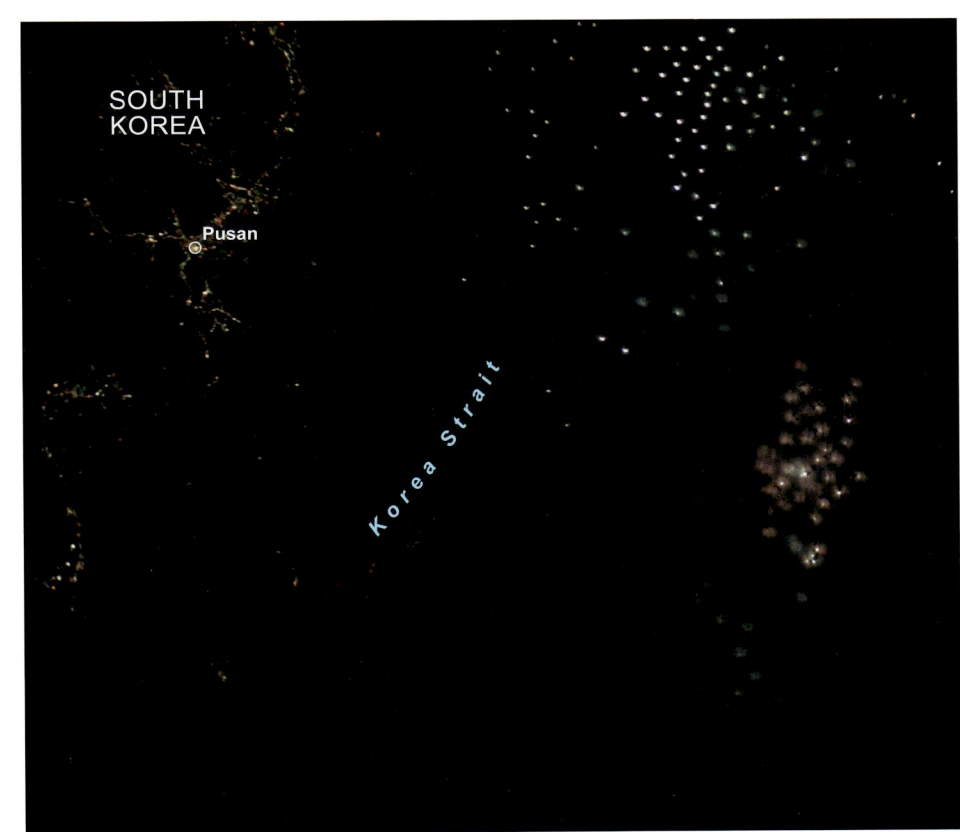

◁ ▽
2/4 – The seas around Japan and South Korea are lit up by countless fishing boats. They can be made out clearly both on the satellite image (ADEOS/ OCTS [SST], Fig. 2 left) and on the ISS oblique space image (Fig. 4).

The fishing industry

Our oceans are populated with over 32,000 species of fish. But sinceindustrial fishing fleets equippedwith highly modern technology have displaced traditional fishing boats, .fish stocks have dwindled.

For a long time, the oceans were considered to have unlimited stocks of fish. Fishing is one of the oldest forms of food-gathering. Traditional fishing was limited to inland waters and coastal waters, but for many years now, deep-sea fishing has taken over to meet the growing demand for fish and seafood. Almost 2,000 tonnes of fish and seafood are sold every day in the largest fish market in the world – the Tsukiji fish market in Tokyo (Fig. 3). According to statistics from the UN's Food and Agriculture Organisation (FAO), 65 million tonnes of fish were caught in the early 1970s. By the early 1990s, the fishing quota had risen to 98 million tonnes and hit 116 million tonnes in 1997. After fishing quotas were brought in, the amount of fish that can be marketed is now pegged at around 90 million tonnes a year. However, added to this are over 30 million tonnes of bycatch: unwanted fish and shellfish, but primarily sharks and sea birds. The FAO estimates that several million sharks and over 50,000 albatrosses are snagged in fishing gear every year. The relationship between the desired catch and bycatch can take on alarming proportions. One Greenpeace study, for example, showed that one tonne of sole can be accompanied by around 11 tonnes of bycatch, while the same amount of shrimp can bring in up to 15 tonnes of bycatch.

The uncontrolled expansion of fishing, with increasingly modern techniques, has led to extensive overfishing of the world's oceans in recent decades. According to FAO, 75 per cent of all the fish species caught for food are either overfished or their stocks have fallen alarmingly. The situation in the north-east Atlantic is particularly critical, where two-thirds of all edible fish species are acutely threatened. Despite the modern navigation and fishing systems of larger fishing fleets, they are bringing in smaller and smaller catches of fish.

Fishing techniques

In the past, fishery yields have increased, mainly as a result of the use of new technologies, in which acoustic methods play a particularly important role. Using sonar, the location and size of a shoal of fish can be determined.

263

In earlier times, fishermen had to rely on the presence of sea birds or dolphins to work out where shoals of fish might be. Today sonars using ultrasound can pinpoint fish to depths of over 1,500 metres. Satellites collect data on ocean currents, sea surface temperature, plankton density and weather conditions that are used to determine the locations and sizes of fish shoals in a region. GPS is also used to facilitate the navigation of fishing fleets.

The long history of fishing has given rise to many different fishing techniques and methods that have been adapted to the depths of the local waters and the local species. However, most of these practices are not sustainable and damage the sensitive maritime ecosystem. Figures 1 a and b on page 233 show just how sensitive this ecosystem is. Shoals of fish require certain conditions of their habitat, including an ideal water temperature.

Trawling uses a dragnet to catch shoaling fish or groundfish. Bottom trawling to catch plaice, sole or lobster is carried out at depths of up to 1,500 metres. However, the trawling movement along the seabed damages it permanently. This type of fishing mainly takes place in the North Atlantic.

Fishing with drift nets has boomed since the invention of nylon lines in the 1950s. Weights on the lower edge of

Aquacultures

- Mariculture
- Freshwater-culture

△
1 – A section of a map showing the south-west of South Korea with the island of Chin-do. Freshwater aquaculture is practised on the mainland, mariculture in the coastal waters.

2 – The south-west of South Korea near Mokpo. Despite heavy reliance on aquaculture, South Korea has designated protected areas and national parks in its waters, where both commercial fishing and the cultivation of fish and other sea creatures are prohibited.

Marine conservation areas
border of marine conservation area

3 – Mariculture farm off the west coast of South Korea near Mokpo. During ebb tide the seaweed beds become visible.

4 – Distribution classes of branch of acquaculture in 2011 worldwide.

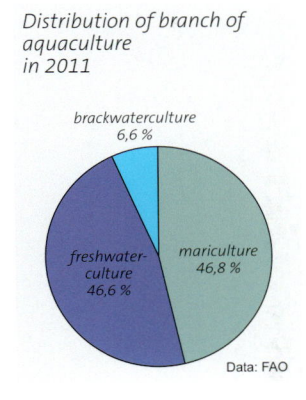

Distribution of branch of aquaculture in 2011

- brackwaterculture 6,6 %
- freshwaterculture 46,6 %
- mariculture 46,8 %

Data: FAO

the net provide the tension to leave the net hanging vertically in the water. The net drifts across the surface, catching shoals of fish by their gills. The costs of this method are relatively low and the yield is high. However, drift nets are not selective – apart from the targeted fish, whales, dolphins, sea turtles and sea birds are also trapped. As a result, the UN passed a resolution in 1991 to ban the use of large drift nets.

Another non-selective method of fishing is dynamite fishing, which is often used by smaller local coastal fisheries. This practice leads to the major disruption or complete destruction of important aquatic habitats. As a result of the heavy impact on the aquatic ecosystem, this type of fishing is prohibited in almost all countries.

Modern commercial fishing uses enormous and highly efficient factory trawlers the size of football pitches. These vessels are equipped with special processing equipment such as filleting machines and industrial freezers. The fish are processed right after being caught and are usually already frozen while still on board. The frozen fish are then packaged ready for sale or processed further once they reach land.

Aquaculture

The term aquaculture describes the controlled cultivation of aquatic organisms such as fish, molluscs, crustaceans and plants comparable to farming practices. Simple forms of aquaculture can be traced back in Asia as far back as 2500 BCE in China – probably even back as 6000 BCE in Australia, and over the recent decades it has developed substantially and become much more widespread. Traditional pond aquaculture has by far been surpassed by industrial aquaculture. In the past few decades, yields from aquaculture have rocketed. While just under one million tonnes of fish were raised in this way in the early 1950s, by 2011 this figure had already surpassed 62 million tonnes (Fig. 4, p. 267). As a result of the growing demand for fish products and seafood on the global markets and of the increasing problems connected with catching wild fish, aquaculture may one day completely replace traditional fishing.

◁
1 – Aquaculture was already being practised in the Bohai Bay off the coast of the northern Chinese province of Hebei back in 1979, albeit on a small scale.

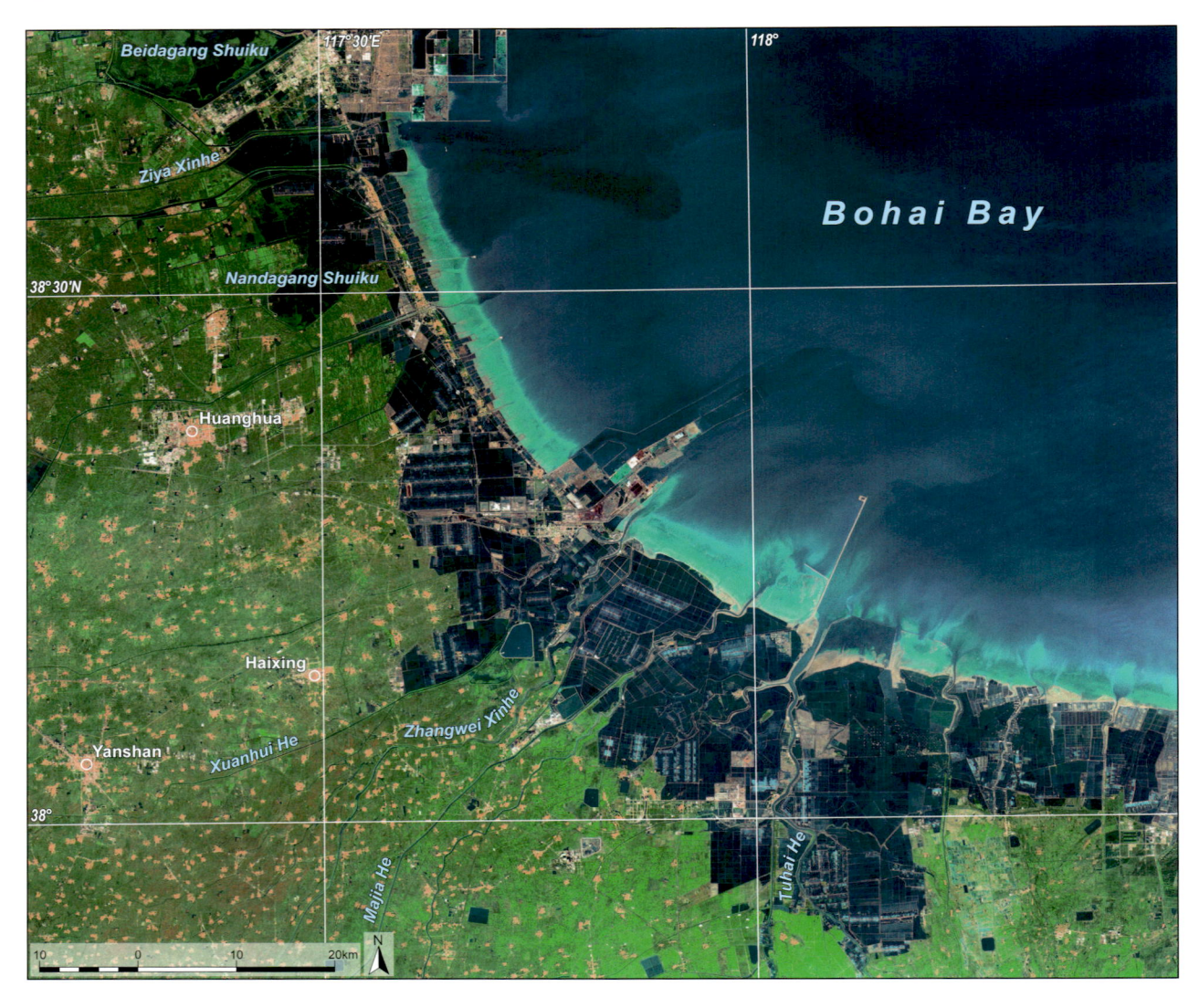

◁
2 – Between 1979 and 2013, individually operated aquacultures developed into a major industry. Whole sections of coast are now dedicated to aquaculture operations.

With the ecological impact of fishing in mind, many consumers are not sure whether it is acceptable to eat fish or not, be it wild fish or fish from aquaculture. Generally the consumption of fish is problematic considering the conflict between overfishing and the protection of oceans and coasts. The negative impact can be minimized by checking Greenpeace's Fish Guide prior to selecting the fish to be purchased. The Fish Guide lists protected fish, but also all fish species, whose consumption is acceptable with respect to their ecological status..

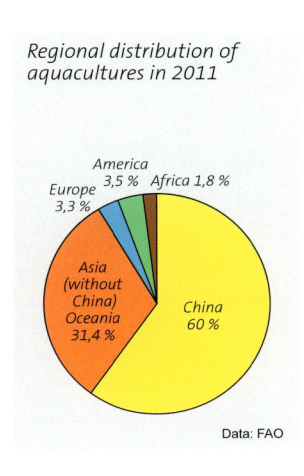

Regional distribution of aquacultures in 2011

America 3,5 % Africa 1,8 %
Europe 3,3 %
Asia (without China) Oceania 31,4 %
China 60 %
Data: FAO

△
3 – Most of the world's aquacultures are found in Asia, primarily in China. China alone produces more than half (2011: 60%) of the world's farmed fish and seafood. The image on the bottom right shows a typical landscape in China holding ponds for farming fish.

▷
4 – Between 1950 and 2005, the aquaculture industry has become a major business worldwide (data provided by the FAO).

▷▷
5 – Aquacultures in Guangzhou, south-eastern China.

According to recent data from the Food and Agriculture Organisation of the United Nations (FAO), more than a third of fish products already come from aquaculture. By 2030, this will have risen to just under two-thirds. Most of this increase is accounted for by Asian aquaculture, in which China is the market leader. Figures 1 to 5 clearly illustrate this development.

The products of the different regions vary widely. While carp are primarily farmed in South Asia, China and South-East Asia, fish farmers in Eastern Asia prefer to farm high-value saltwater fish. When it comes to salmon sales, more than half hail from western European aquaculture businesses (Fig. 3).

The term aquaculture covers both pond aquaculture (freshwater aquaculture) and mariculture (Fig. 1, p. 264). Most aquaculture is in freshwater. Fish, primarily carp, are bred in ponds. In mariculture, nets or floats are anchored to the seabed in the open sea (Fig 3, p. 265). This production method has only been possible since stable materials that can withstand the tough weather conditions have become available. One advantage of mariculture is that the fish are constantly provided with fresh water thanks to the natural sea currents, which reduces the negative impact on the environment and at the same time enables denser stocking levels.

Prawns are cultivated in brackish water. As such, ponds that have both a saltwater and freshwater supply are dug out along the coast. This method is most popular in Thailand, Indonesia and Ecuador. One of the threats of fish farms are algal blooms, which can be observed from space, as explained in the section "OCEANS" of the chapter "THE WATERS OF THE EARTH"..

Finally, environmental conditions such as temperature and water currents determine which species of fish can be bred in what quantities.

Aquaculture – a blessing or a curse?

As a result of the booming aquaculture industry, many problems have arisen and need solving. For example, the amount of space available for aquaculture is declining. This means increased pressure for existing aquaculture businesses to operate more efficiently. However, the large-scale destruction of tropical coastal landscapes remains the major problem. The deforestation of tropical mangroves for new shrimp farms has a devastating impact on the ecosystem and on coastal protection. It is estimated that 70 per cent of Ecuador's mangrove forests have been destroyed in order to farm shrimp. In Thailand, even areas located far from the coast, once used for rice cultivation, are now being used as large shrimp farms. The saltwater required is transported from the sea in tankers. This puts large areas of land at risk of salinisation, making it impossible for the land to be used again for agriculture in the future.

Another problem connected with aquaculture relates to how the fish are fed. For example, in order to produce one kilogram of salmon on a Norwegian fish farm, as much as four kilos of wild fish have to be caught from the sea and processed into fish meal and fish oil, which are then used to feed the salmon. According to data from Action for World Solidarity, this ratio increases to 1:15 for shrimp farming.

Humans are also directly affected by the problems faced by aquaculture. The high stocking density and low water quality encourage pathogens, which have to be treated with chemicals and antibiotics. As a result, nutritional scientists are starting to categorise farmed fish and especially prawns as potential health hazards. This has already led to an import ban on Indian prawns in the EU.

Between 2002 and 2007, aquaculture saw an average annual growth in production of 6.5 per cent. Currently, many places are rethinking their strategies in order to ensure environmental sustainability (Fig. 2, p. 265). There are now countless organic aquaculture operations around the world that have lower stocking densities, use organic feed and minimise the use of chemicals.

Squid fishing at night

Using satellite images from the Defense Meteorological Satellite Program (DMSP), a US Armed Forces weather satellite programme, it is possible to observe spatial and temporal variations in light sources. In the Sea of Japan in particular, night-time images show the high density of fishing boats (Figs. 2 and 4 pp. 262/263), which use bright lights to attract squid and catch them (Figs. 6 and 7, p. 263).

As a result of the wide availability and diversity of squid, squid fishing is highly lucrative. People fish for squid in almost all coastal regions, and the seafood is highly prized. In 1986, 1.8 million tonnes of squid and cuttlefish were caught worldwide, a figure that rose to 4.4 million tonnes by 2007. Japan is the biggest buyer. Squid stocks are not currently under threat, partly as a result of the declining numbers of the whales that eat them.

Do we have to stop eating fish?

Considering the effects on the ecosystem, many consumers are concerned about whether it is environmentally responsible to eat fish that has either been caught in the sea or raised in aquaculture. Generally speaking, eating fish is not really ethical for those concerned with protecting the seas and coastal habitats and their inhabitants. If one wants to be on the safe side when selecting which species of fish to eat, a good place to start is the Greenpeace Seafood Red List, which lists endangered fish that the organisation deems not acceptable to eat.

Growth of aquaculture production since 1950 (Mil. t)
- China
- Asia (excluding China)/Pacific
- All other

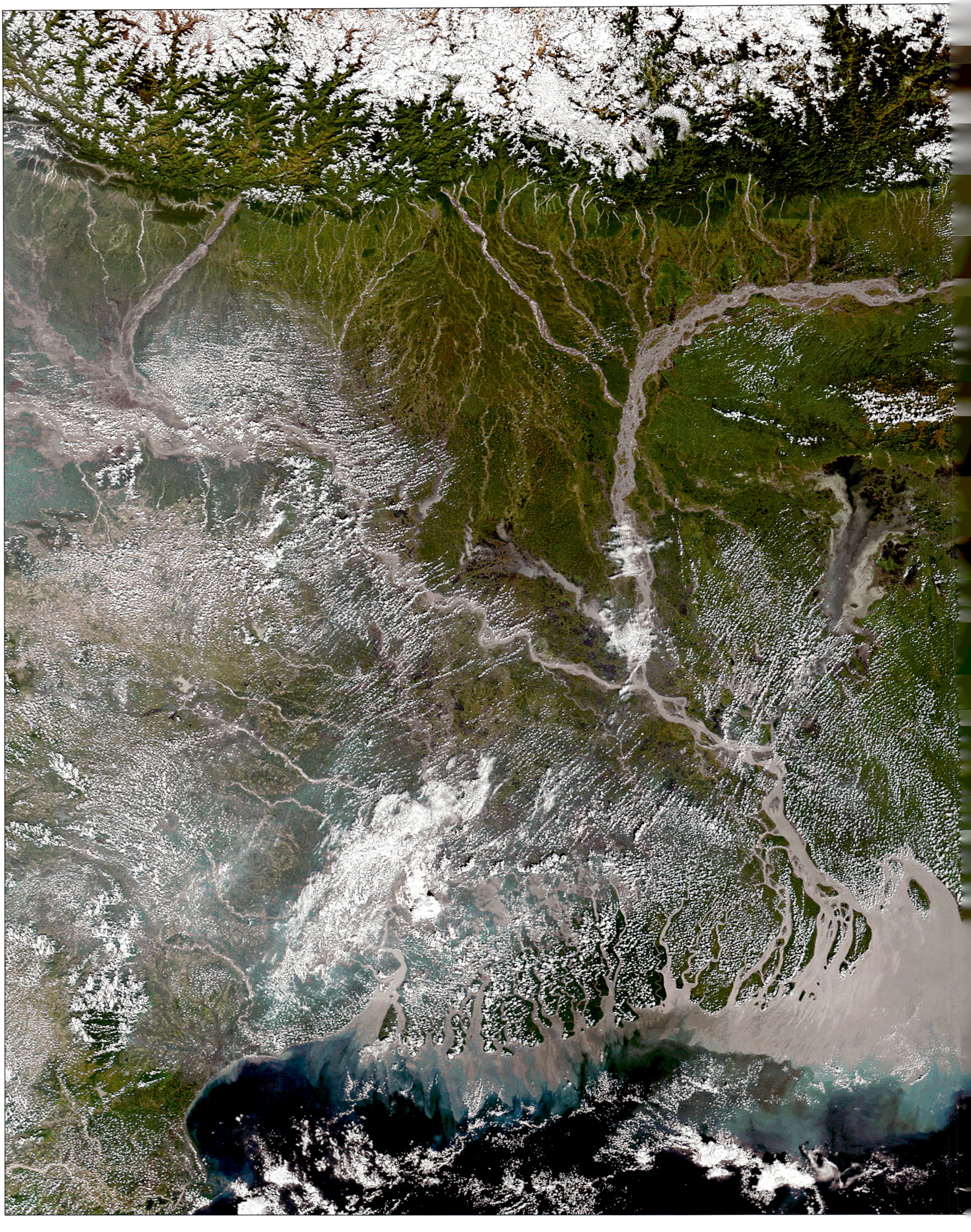

NATURAL HAZARDS

Water is the source of life, the main constituent of all living creatures, and – after the air we breathe – the substance we need most to stay alive. But water not only sustains life, it also threatens life. Since too much water is as dangerous as too little. Droughts and floods claim more lives than all other natural catastrophes.

Water-related events are more frequent and much more deadly in some regions than in others. This difference is expressed in the term 'hazard'. But even if the hazard is the same, the effects of an extreme event are quite different. Take the Netherlands and Bangladesh (Fig. 1), for example. Although the storm surge hazard is comparable in these two countries, there is a vast difference in the way it is reflected in the casualty statistics. Why? Because the hazard is tackled in different ways. Which takes us to the aspect of risk.

For all practical purposes, risk is the product of the size of a hazard and the probability of that hazard occurring at a specific location and the potential effects of such an occurrence. A natural catastrophe can only occur at a certain location if two conditions are met: firstly, an extreme natural hazard event must occur and, secondly, vulnerable values (human beings and/or assets) must be present. A large earthquake in an empty desert is simply a natural event, whereas a smaller quake in an inadequately protected city can trigger a natural catastrophe. In other words, the risk is small when the hazard or the vulnerability is small. The latter can be influenced by prevention measures.

Natural catastrophes have killed around 1.7 million people since 1980, and about half of these deaths (48 per cent) were due to catastrophes related to weather (Fig. 5, p. 271). While most of the victims of climate-related deaths died from extreme heat or cold, many of

◁
1 – The lower course of the Ganges and Brahmaputra (India/Bangladesh) on 06/10/2002 at the end of the monsoon. The rivers are coloured brown by the mud swept away, and their courses are accompanied by extended flooded areas.

269

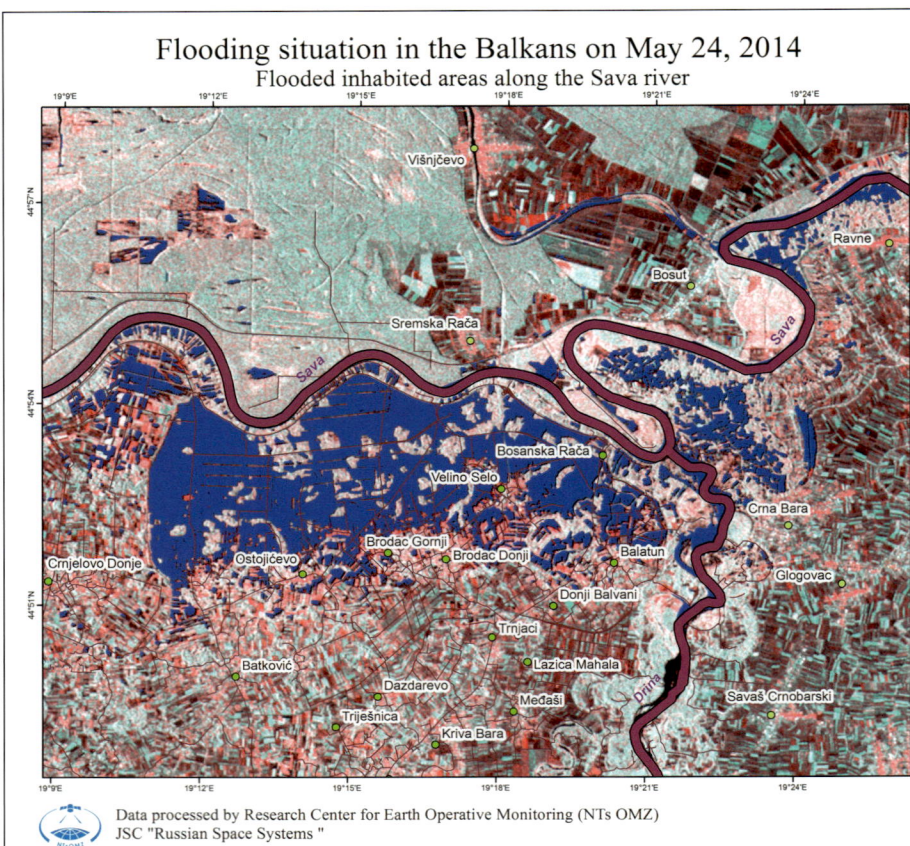

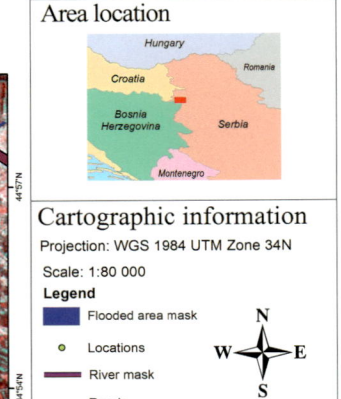

Flooding situation in the Balkans on May 24, 2014
Flooded inhabited areas along the Sava river

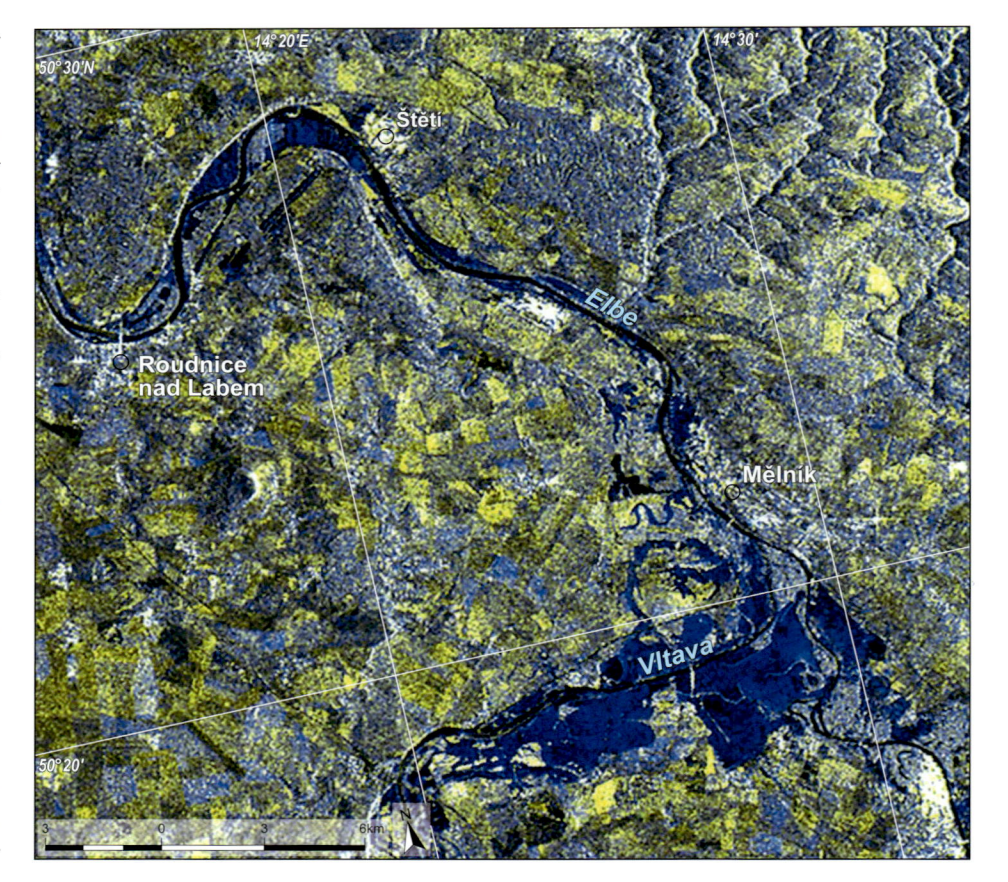

◁
1 – Flooding map of inhabited areas along the Sava River (Serbia, Bosnia and Herzegovina) after heavy rainfalls during the days from 14/05 to 16/05/2014. The map was published on www.disasterscharter.org

▽
2 – Flood along the Elbe and Vltava, August 2002, Czech Republic (multitemporal radar image 13/08/1998 and 16/08/2002).
Flooded areas at the confluence of the two rivers near Mělník appear in blue.

◁▽ ▽
3, 4 – Hasle, Switzerland 1987, before and during a flash flood.

them were killed by meteorological events involving water (storm surge) (Fig 7). Almost 40 per cent of all damage resulting from natural disasters can be traced to various kinds of storms and their consequences, such as storm surges. Flooding alone accounts for around another quarter. Of the insured losses, storms account for over 70 per cent of the total damage. Damage from natural disasters has increased in the past few decades (Fig. 6), and this also applies to purely flood-related disasters. In particular, a series of individual events have caused damages of an extent which has been seen never before (Fig. 8); as such, total annual claims vary widely.

Causes of floods

There are few cultures on this earth that do not have a Great Flood in their mythology. After all, floods represent a threat throughout the world. Regions where they are a regular occurrence (e.g. Bangladesh; Fig. 1, p. 268/269) will at some time or another be affected by very extreme floods ("thousand-year floods") and these will become entrenched in oral tradition. And in regions that have no floods for several generations, a solitary flood can become the stuff of legend.

When we talk of floods, it is important to realise that they may be due to quite different causes. Besides the three main types – storm surges, river floods, and flash floods – there are a number of special cases such as tsunamis, dam-break floods, glacial lake outburst floods, debris flow, and water-level rises in seas and lakes (like the seasonal rise of the Poyang Hu in China; Fig. 2, p. 272), backwater floods, high groundwater table, and so on.

Storm surges

Storm surges can occur on the sea coast and along the banks of large lakes. They have the largest loss potential and, prior to the tsunami in the Indian Ocean in December 2004, were the deadliest of all flood events. The Bangladesh storm surges with death tolls of 300,000 (1970) and 139,000 (1991) are the best-known of recent years but not

270

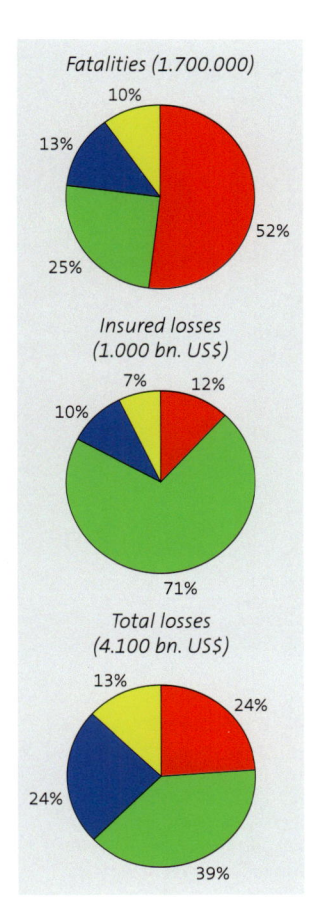

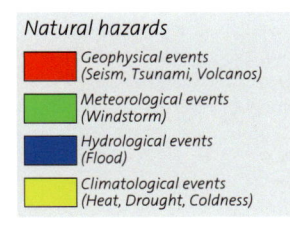

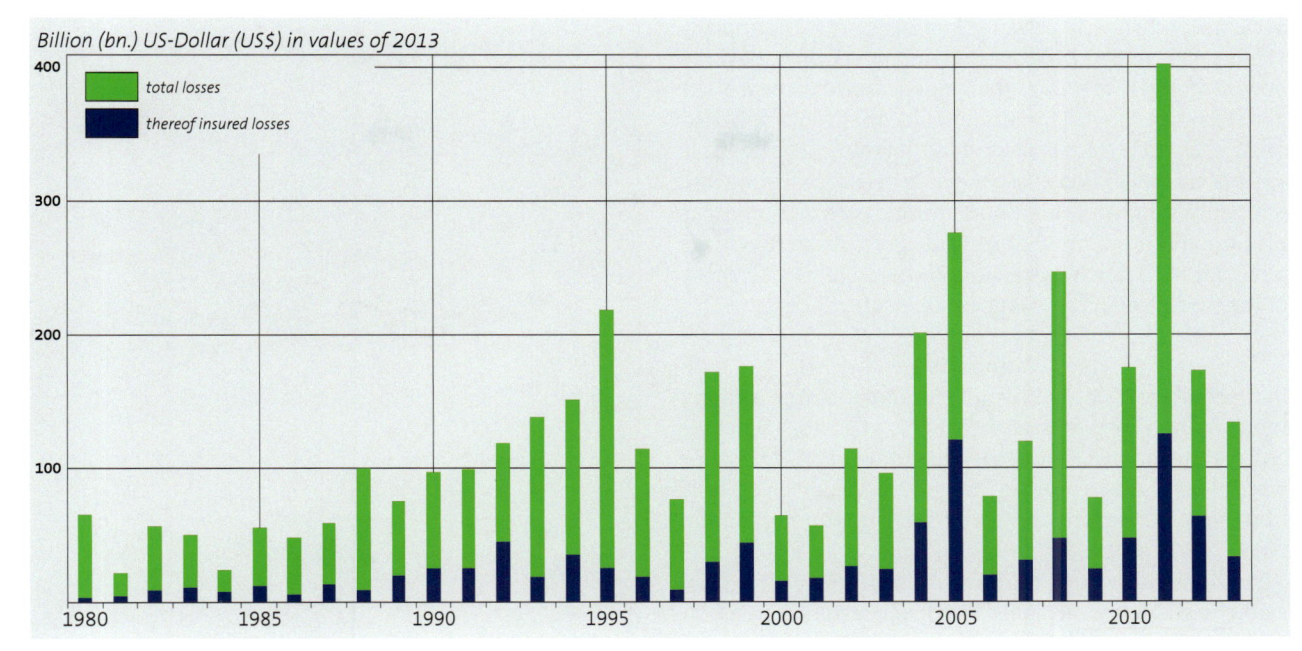

the only ones. Even in Europe, thousands of people died in storm-surge events during the second half of last century (e.g. in the North Sea in 1953 which left 2,150 dead). However, great storm-surge catastrophes have become less common in recent years thanks to major improvements in sea defences and, in particular, the enhancement of forecasting and early-warning facilities. Nevertheless, storm surges still represent an immense loss potential in what is a relatively narrow strip of land on the coast.

This was demonstrated with extreme clarity by Hurricane Katrina at the end of August 2005. Still ranking as a Category 5 hurricane shortly before landfall, Katrina caused overall losses of some USD 125 billion (including insured losses of USD 62 billion). It generated a storm surge that caused widespread devastation along a 200-kilometre strip of coast in Louisiana, Mississippi and Alabama, and that swamped New Orleans. The accelerating rise in sea levels that is certainly to be expected will aggravate the risk of storm surge and coastal erosion all around the globe – and will be one of the most detrimental effects of global warming.

River floods

River floods are the result of copious rainfall usually falling for a period of days over a large area. The ground becomes saturated and can absorb no more water, and the rain flows directly into lakes and rivers. Frozen ground has the same effect, since it prevents the water from seeping away. River floods do not occur abruptly but build up gradually – although occasionally in a very short time. As a rule, they last from a few days to several weeks. The affected area may be very extensive if the river valley is flat and broad and the river carries a large volume of water (Fig. 1, p. 272). In narrow valleys, the flooded area is restricted to a relatively thin strip along the river, but the water may be quite deep and flow at high speeds.

Flash floods

Flash floods can occur almost anywhere and so threaten nearly everyone. Sometimes they mark the beginning of a major river flood, but usually they are separate, individual events of only local significance, scattered randomly in space and time. Flash floods are caused by what are usually short periods of intense rain often occurring over a very small area and typically in conjunction with thunderstorms. The soil is not usually saturated; but as the rainfall intensity exceeds the infiltration rate, the water runs off on the surface and soon gathers in the receiving waters. This results in a rapidly growing flood wave which can gush downstream and in next to no time forge into areas where it may not even have rained at all. This phenomenon has given rise to the well-known paradox that 'more people drown in the desert than die of thirst'. The high rates of flow lead to erosion, causing buildings to

5 – Number of fatalities, general losses and insured losses due to various natural hazards from 1980 until 2013, inflation-adjusted in values from 2013 (Source: Munich Re).

6 – Damage from major natural catastrophes since 1980. (Losses in USD billion, inflation-adjusted in values from 2013, as of 1 February 2014), Source: Munich Re).

7 – In terms of the number of casualties, the worst floods since 1970 (Source: Munich Re, January 2014).

8 – The most expensive floods worldwide since 1990 (original values not adjusted for inflation, source: Munich Re, January 2014).

Rank	Year	Area(s) mainly affected	Fatalities
1	1970	Bangladesh (storm surge)	300,000
2	2004	Indian Ocean, esp. Indonesia (tsunami)	220,000
3	2008	Myanmar (storm surge, Cyclone Nargis)	140,000
4	1991	Bangladesh (storm surge)	139,000
5	1985	Colombia (mudslides following eruption of Nevado del Ruiz)	25,000
6	2011	Japan (tsunami)*	15,880
7	1977	Bangladesh (storm surge)	14,200
8	1985	Bangladesh (storm surge)	11,000
9	1998	Bangladesh (storm surge)	10,000
10	1998	Central America, esp. Honduras (Hurricane Mitch)	10,000

* 2011 / Japan (tsunami) / USD 210 billion total damage / USD 40 billion insured losses:
Figures assigning the damage to earthquake damage and tsunami damage, respectively, are not available. The tsunami, however, must have accounted for much more than a quarter of the overall damage.

** These figures take into account damages caused by wind and water. Exact figures for the individual contributions of wind and water are not available, but an equal distribution can be considered realistic.

Rank	Year	Area(s) mainly affected	Losses in USD millions	
			Overall	Insured
1	2005	USA (Gulf Coast, Hurricane Katrina)**	125,000	62,200
2	2012	North America, Caribbean (Hurricane Sandy)	68,500	29,500
3	2011	Thailand	43,000	16,000
4	1998	China (Yangtze, Songhua)	30,700	1,000
5	1996	China (Yangtze, Yellow River, Huai)	24,000	445
6	2002	Southern, central and eastern Europe (Elbe, Danube)	21,200	3,400
7	1993	USA (Mississippi)	21,000	1,270
8	2013	Western and Eastern Europe	15,200	3,100
9	1995	North Korea	15,000	0
10	1991	China (Huai, Lake Taihu)	13,600	410
11	1993	China	11,000	0
12	2013	Philippines, Vietnam, China (Typhoon Haiyan)	10,500	700
13	2004	12 countries on the Indian Ocean (tsunami)	10,000	1,000
14	2008	USA (Midwest)	10,000	500
15	2010	Pakistan	9,500	<100
16	1994	Italy (southern Alps)	9,300	65

271

collapse and thus increasing loss amounts enormously. The term 'flash flood' is also used in connection with cloud bursts on even terrain, when floods occur because the water cannot flow off fast enough due to the lack of a sufficient gradient (Figs. 3 and 4, p. 270). It is almost impossible to forecast flash floods because they give no warning and happen within minutes. Short-term loss reduction measures are therefore more or less ruled out. Flash floods are also over with much more quickly than river floods. Most of the water will have disappeared in a few hours.

Tsunamis

In December 2004, the word tsunami became synonymous with the power of water when some 220,000 people around the Indian Ocean were killed. The inability of even highly developed countries to protect themselves fully from such waves was shown by the tsunami in Japan in 2011.

Tsunamis are waves that are caused when a mass of water is suddenly displaced. This can result from a continental plate shift in conjunction with an earthquake, as in 2004 in the Indian Ocean (see Fig. 5, p. 281), a volcanic eruption, a landslide, or a meteorite crashing into the ocean. The waves spread out in all directions at high speed – relative to the water depth – with hardly any attenuation, such that the waves may wash up along coasts thousands of kilometres away. As in the open sea the tsunami's wave length, defined as the distance between two wave peaks, may be several hundred kilometres while the wave height usually is only a few decimetres, tsunamis are hardly noticeable before they reach a coast.

If a tsunami wave hits a coast, however, its kinetic energy is converted into potential energy. Consequently, the once gentle ocean wave turns into a monster wave up to 30 metres high that smashes onto the shore. Its devastating force destroys everything in its path – but only on a narrow strip stretching perhaps 500 metres to 1000 metres inland, which is decisive for the people that live in coastal areas (Figs. 3 and 4).

An approaching tsunami is usually announced by the sea first retreating from the shore in an unusual manner. If the people know how to interpret this signal properly and are not enticed towards the exposed seafloor but flee inland, they are usually able to reach safety. Those who stay are in danger of being overrun by the incoming wave or being dragged out to sea by the receding water. A land-use policy that prohibited construction in the immediate beach area would be an effective precaution too. Early-warning systems, on the other hand, can only help if the affected population can be contacted and know how to react to the warning properly.

A tsunami is the classical case of a water catastrophe that is generated by a different natural event, e.g. by an earthquake. There are other cases, however, in which water can trigger a catastrophe without having any direct effect itself. Many landslides are caused by seepage water acting as a lubricant between two soil layers, causing the upper layer to slide over the lower. In mountainous permafrost areas the ground is held together to a large part because it is frozen. A thaw will reduce the stability of the ground and lead to rockfalls and landslides. Water also plays a central role in many volcanic events. Entire mountains can explode if magma comes into contact with water. And even earthquakes can be triggered by water, as happened in 1967 after the building of a reservoir dam in India. The increase in weight caused by the dam lake and the water penetrating the lower soil layers were held to be responsible for the earthquake in Koyna.

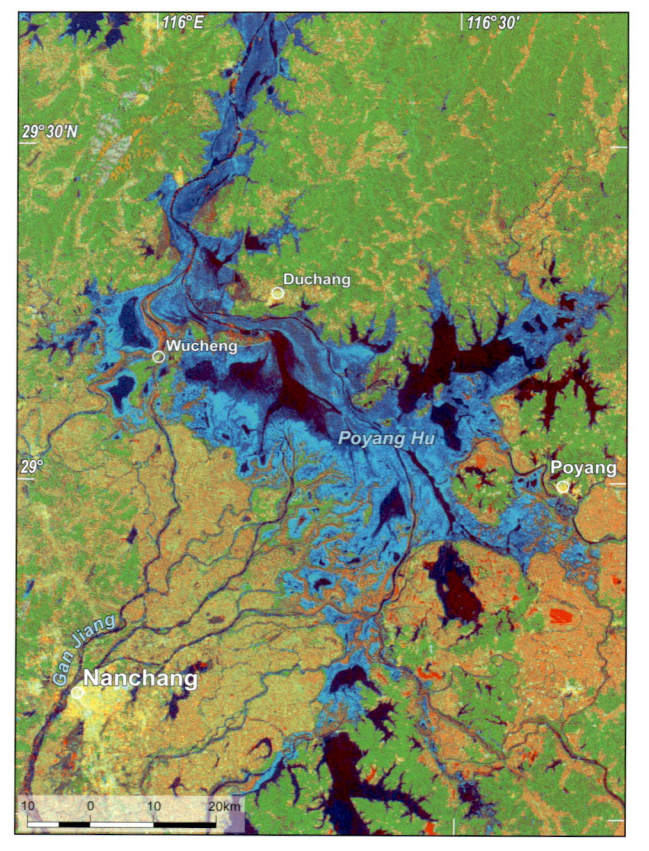

1 – The flooded Li River in southern China.

2 – High water level at Poyang Hu, China (light blue: maximum area of water surface). During the monsoon rains in summer, the lake is the largest freshwater lake in the country. The multitemporal image (29.01.–21.08.2005) shows its extent in winter in dark blue.

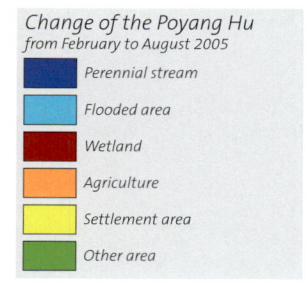

Change of the Poyang Hu
from February to August 2005
- Perennial stream
- Flooded area
- Wetland
- Agriculture
- Settlement area
- Other area

3 – Destruction in Khao Lak, Thailand after the 2004 Boxing Day Tsunami.

▷
4 – This 60 cm QuickBird-2 satellite image featuring the Kalutara Beach along the village Wadduwa in the south-west of Sri Lanka was taken at 10:20 a.m. local time, slightly less than four hours after the 6:28 a.m. earthquake and shortly after the moment of tsunami impact on 26 December 2006

The formula for calculating the velocity of propagation v of tsunami waves is:
$v = (g \cdot D)^{1/2}$
with
g = gravitational constant,
D = water depth.
At a water depth of 4,000 m, for example, the velocity of propagation is thus about 200 m/s or 720 km/h. If the wave length is 480 km, the water surface would rise by a few decimetres over a period of ten minutes.

Increasing impact of worldwide floods

There is at first a direct correlation between the increase in losses and the number of people that live in areas at risk. Whilst the population pressure often leaves the people in poor countries with no other choice than to settle in exposed areas, the motivation in industrial countries comes from other factors.

Flood valleys are usually cheap as building land, attractive, and, as flat flood plains, easy to develop. They offer good conditions for establishing the necessary infrastructure. The proximity of a river is particularly advantageous for commercial and industrial facilities that need large amounts of space and sometimes process or cooling water. Larger rivers and the sea also offer the possibility of transporting freight by ship.

Towns and cities have an interest in their own growth and prosperity. They have to make land available for housing or for commercial and industrial facilities. Many owners are either not aware that there is a danger of flooding because they do not come from the region and assume that if land is released for development it will be safe, or they ignore the danger. Others consciously accept the danger emanating from a nearby river, but often forget it if nothing untoward happens. It is only when a dangerous situation arises or a loss occurs that those affected are shaken awake again.

Moreover, many people still believe that flood events can be controlled effectively as long as appropriate technological precautions are taken. The positive effect of flood control is that frequent losses and discomfort are prevented. This effect is counterbalanced, however, by the fact that the feeling of security it creates leads people to expose more and more objects of increasing value to the risk of flood. This feeling of security is transmitted not only by dykes and embankments, early-warning systems, and the availability of disaster relief organisations, but also by the intentional or unintentional transmission of false information and by local authorities or groups with a vested interest (e.g. the tourist trade) playing down the risk. If an unexpected event occurs which existing safeguards cannot cope with, an immense loss potential may suddenly be revealed.

Never before people have had so many valuable but at the same time vulnerable possessions. Houses that used to have cellars to stock coal and wood, rooms to store jams and preserves, potatoes and apples, and areas to keep junk, now have party rooms with wall-to-wall carpeting, three-piece suites, and stereos, playrooms and home offices with computers, hobby rooms with expensive DIY equipment, and places for washing machines and refrigeration units. The greatest problem, however, is presented by electronically controlled central heating equipment and oil tanks, the rule of thumb being that the original water damage is roughly doubled by escaping oil. The basements of relatively large housing complexes or commercial buildings often accommodate underground car parks, the central control systems of lifts and air-conditioning facilities, storage rooms, and sometimes even computer centres. Underground car parks may become a deadly trap.

Prevention strategies against floods

Not every flood necessarily leads to flooding. And even if flooding does occur, the losses can still be kept within reasonable bounds and do not always have to be major losses. This presupposes a suitable prevention strategy which embraces all aspects of floods, from their genesis to the avoidance of loss potentials.

Floods are a part of the natural water cycle; but mankind has ways of intervening in this cycle. They include influencing the climate (resulting in more frequent and more intense precipitation), changing the infiltration capacity of the soil (due to paving and to soil being compacted by agricultural activities), discharging water into rivers and lakes (drainage ditches, sewers), and directing it towards the sea (e.g. river regulation, removal of flood retention areas). Retaining water must have top priority whenever possible. One thing must be noted, however: extreme floods in large catchments are only marginally attributable to surfaces that have been made impervious by human activity. Likewise, the masses of water flowing down large rivers during floods are sometimes so huge that decentralised flood retention, river restoration, and dyke relocation can only reduce the extreme flood peaks to a limited degree.

Flooding occurs when the soil, a lake, or a river is unable to take up any more water. The water then stands or flows in areas that are usually dry. Flooding can be influenced by technological measures such as retaining the water at specially designated places such as flood detention areas, polders, and reservoirs (Fig. 1), or by directing the flood waters via dykes within a predetermined area, possibly by means of flood channels (Fig. 2). All these measures are based on what is called a design flood, i.e. a relatively high flood value used as the basis for designing protection measures.

The most effective way of preventing damage is to keep people and their belongings away from flood-prone areas, i.e. to institute an appropriate land-use policy that does not permit building development near bodies of water. Where this has not been done, much can still be achieved by taking permanent and temporary structural measures, adjusting the management of values, and responding to danger in the correct manner, e.g. by evacuating threatened parts of buildings. But even if these measures help to reduce the risk of loss significantly, a residual risk will still remain.

Only if the risk of flood is shared among several carriers is effective disaster reduction possible. Three partners – the state, the people affected, and the insurance industry – must cooperate in a fine-tuned relationship in the spirit of a risk partnership. Reducing the underlying risk for society as a whole is primarily the job of the state. It sets up observation and early-warning systems, controls flood discharge, and, by enacting statutory provisions, determines the framework for the use of exposed areas. Those affected are obliged to make their own contribution to loss prevention by building in an appropriate manner, being prepared for emergencies (e.g. writing a checklist of what to do when there is a flood), and being ready to take action as soon as disaster strikes. Finally, insurance companies should be on hand, their main task being to compensate financial losses that would have a substantial impact on insured people or even ruin them. This means that although insurers are not social institutions (in the sense of charities), they are indispensable institutions within the social system. They distribute the burden borne by individuals among the entire community of insured people, which is ideally composed in such a way that they all have a chance of being affected – albeit with different degrees of probability.

The identification of hazard zones and areas affected by natural hazards and their visualisation on hazard and damage maps furnish an important basis not only for water resources management and land-use planning but also for disaster management, emergency aid and the insurance industry. On the basis of such maps, which are being produced in more and more countries, the flood hazard can be determined for any given address.

Numerous satellite missions and the data they collect are extremely useful today for the long-term observation, recording, prediction and damage analysis of natural

△
1 – Check dams attempt to combat the destructive force of water, as shown here along the river Lech in Austria, originating in the Alps.

▷△
2 – In order to manage the effects of flooding, it may be necessary to disable flood barriers, as shown here by the blowing up of a dyke near Vehlgast on the Havel River in Germany during the major floods of August 2002.

▷
*3 – Enlarged section of grading map of the damaged docklands of Tacloban City, Philippines, after the Typhoon Haiyan on 08.11.2013. The map is scaled-down from the original size and depict a width of a approximately real extend of 750 metres.
Map published on the 15.11.2013 at the Copernicus Emergency Management Service of the EU Commision (www.emergency.copernicus.eu)*

catastrophes. This includes the significant role played by ESA's global partnership projects, including the Copernicus European Earth Observation Programme and the International Charter "Space and Major Disasters", which offers specific information services to make data quickly available in the event of a disaster.

Anti-selection plays an important role in the insurance of flood losses. The only people who show real interest in buying insurance are those that live near rivers or on the coast and are often affected by floods. Owners of property located away from large bodies of water, on the other hand, feel safe from floods, and therefore reject insurance protection. Consequently, the insured community is relatively small and, what is more, its members are exposed to a large risk.

One of insurance's important functions besides preventing personal disasters is to promote its clients' willingness to take their own precautions. As a rule, insurance companies react very quickly when settling claims. The purely material support and the psychological effect of speedy assistance are both very important to those affected since they are given the feeling that they are not being left alone in an extremely difficult situation. This is a problem that plays a significant role in the often sluggish provision of financial assistance by the state.

The potential risks for the future

There is little doubt that the climate change we are currently witnessing is most probably due to human activity. Although there still seem to be a few sceptics and deniers, this is now accepted as fact by the overwhelming majority of scientists.

A warmer climate means that precipitation will increase in many areas, whereas other areas will experience longer dry periods. Above all, however, extreme weather conditions will increase, and that is another decisive factor with regard to disasters. Isolated extreme events are nothing new, but in the future we will have to reckon with more frequent and more catastrophic events, which generally will cause greater losses and more serious consequences. There is sufficient evidence available that this development has already begun and that it is continuing at increasing speed.

Even if our own human activity is partly responsible for many catastrophes, we must appreciate that the errors we make are not to blame for all of them. We will simply have to get accustomed to living with extreme – and even catastrophic – natural events, as mankind always had to do. It is important that we come to terms with the fact and refrain from placing our hopes on – or our trust in – these kinds of events being controllable by technological or other means.

There will always be a residual risk. The crucial factor is to respond appropriately to this residual risk. Therefore, if we take the correct action in time, we can make an existing risk bearable even if we cannot make it controllable. Catastrophes are not only products of chance but also the outcome of interaction between political, financial, social, technical, and natural circumstances. Effective safeguards are both achievable and indispensable, but they will never provide complete protection. The decisive point is to be always aware of the fact that nature can and will always come up with events against which no human means can prevail.

As Aristotle (384–322 BCE) said,
'It is probable that the improbable will happen.'

Text: Wolfgang Kron

275

Central European floods in 2002

In August 2002, major flooding caused Central Europe to hold its breath while a Genoa low, or V-track cyclone, slowly moved north-east with two consecutive periods of heavy rainfall. As a result of a very hot summer in 2002, the air masses above the Mediterranean were able to absorb much more water vapour than usual. The resultant heavy rainfall in the Czech Republic, Germany and Austria led to catastrophic flooding across Central Europe (Fig. 1). Two major trans-boundary rivers were involved – the Elbe and the Danube.

The Elbe floods in Saxony and Czech Republic

The Elbe rises in the Krkonoše Mountains of the Czech Republic, where it emerges as the Labe River and flows over 1,090 kilometres to its mouth in the North Sea at Cuxhaven near the old seaport of Hamburg. A stretch of 727 kilometres runs through the Federal Republic of Germany. The river's catchment basin covers an area of almost 150,000 square kilometres (Fig. 1). In the Czech Republic, the Elbe's course is primarily regulated by dams, while dykes are more common in Germany.

The floods of summer 2002 started along the Elbe and its tributaries in Saxony and also in the Czech Republic, with the biggest floods ever recorded in these regions. Record water levels were broken at almost all points. In Dresden, water levels reached a historic level of 9.40 metres on 17 August (Fig. 2). The capital of Saxony was affected particularly badly by flooding along the Elbe and its tributary, the Weißeritz. The main train station and parts of the old town with Dresden's landmarks, the Semperoper opera house and the Zwinger palace, were all flooded.

Flood damage along the Elbe and Danube

The catastrophic Central European floods along the Elbe and Danube in summer 2002 resulted in damage valued at EUR 17 billion. Intense downpours in the catchment basins caused devastating flash floods. Buildings and transport infrastructure such as roads and bridges were severely damaged by flotsam and undercutting. Due to a long period of intensive rain, the saturated soil was no longer capable of absorbing the additional rainfall (Figs. 4 and 5). River embankments were washed away and homes were carried off by the floodwater. Even after the water had retreated, many buildings were still affected by the mud left behind.

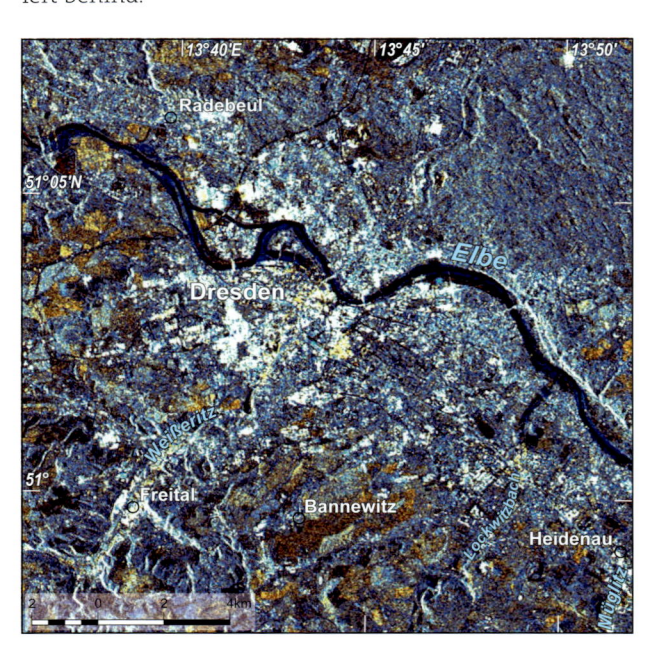

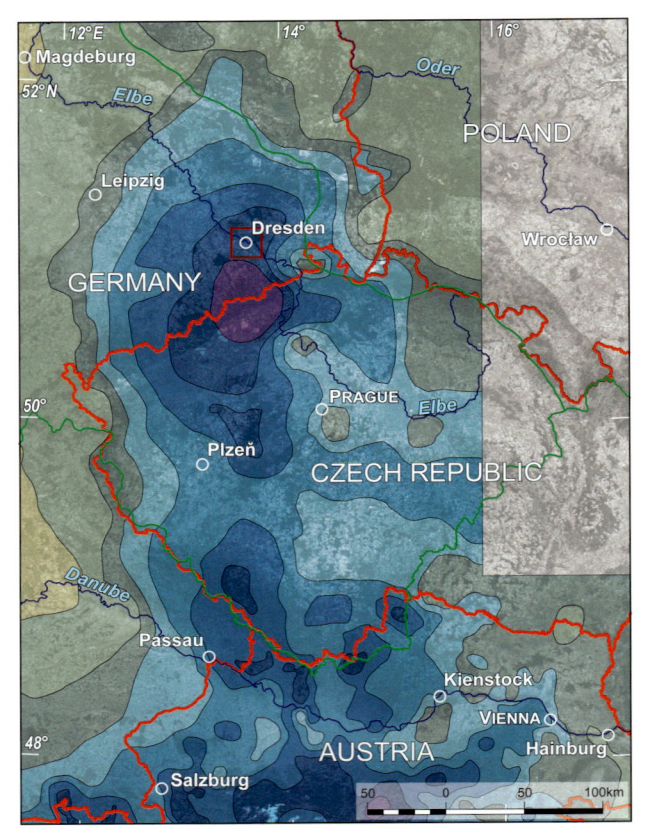

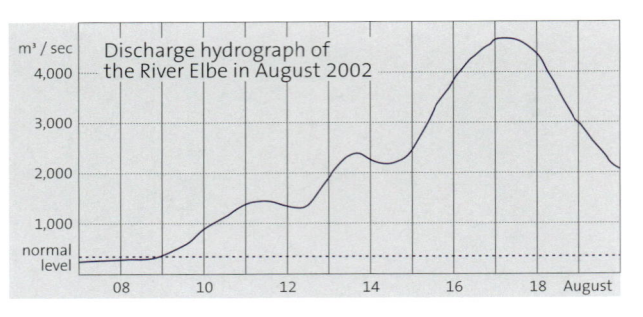

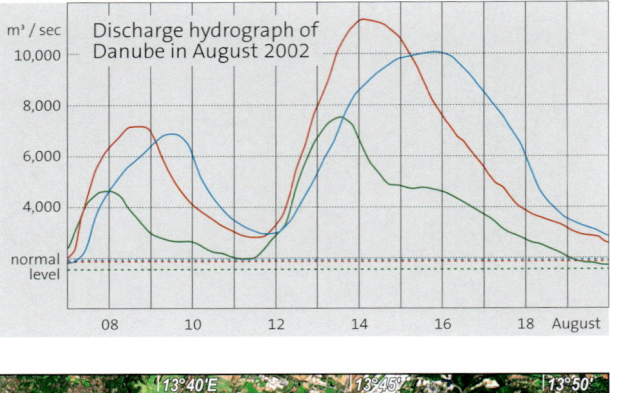

7 – Water surfaces can be easily distinguished as a result of their low reflectance in infrared false colour plots.

1 – Heavy rain in Central Europe in August 2002 led to record rainfall and extensive flooding.

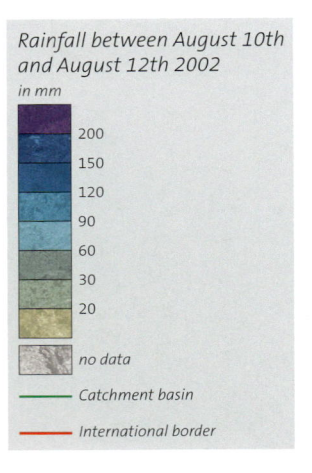

2 – On 17/08/2002, the Elbe floods led to a record water level in Dresden of 9.40 metres at 7:40 am.

3 – Extremely high water levels were also recorded at measuring points along the Danube, which overflowed its banks at many places.

4 – Multitemporal radar data provide information about the extent of the flooding in all weather conditions. The ERS-2 images taken on 13/08/2002 (red) and 09/07/2002 (green) show the usual extent of the bodies of water (black) and the areas flooded on 09/07/2002 (very dark blue).

5 – Flood extent in Dresden as derived from satellite data (SPOT-4, 17/08/2002) on a near-real colour satellite map (Landsat ETM, 28/07/2002).

6 – Air photo of Grafenwörth following the 2 periods of heavy rain between 7–12/08/2002.

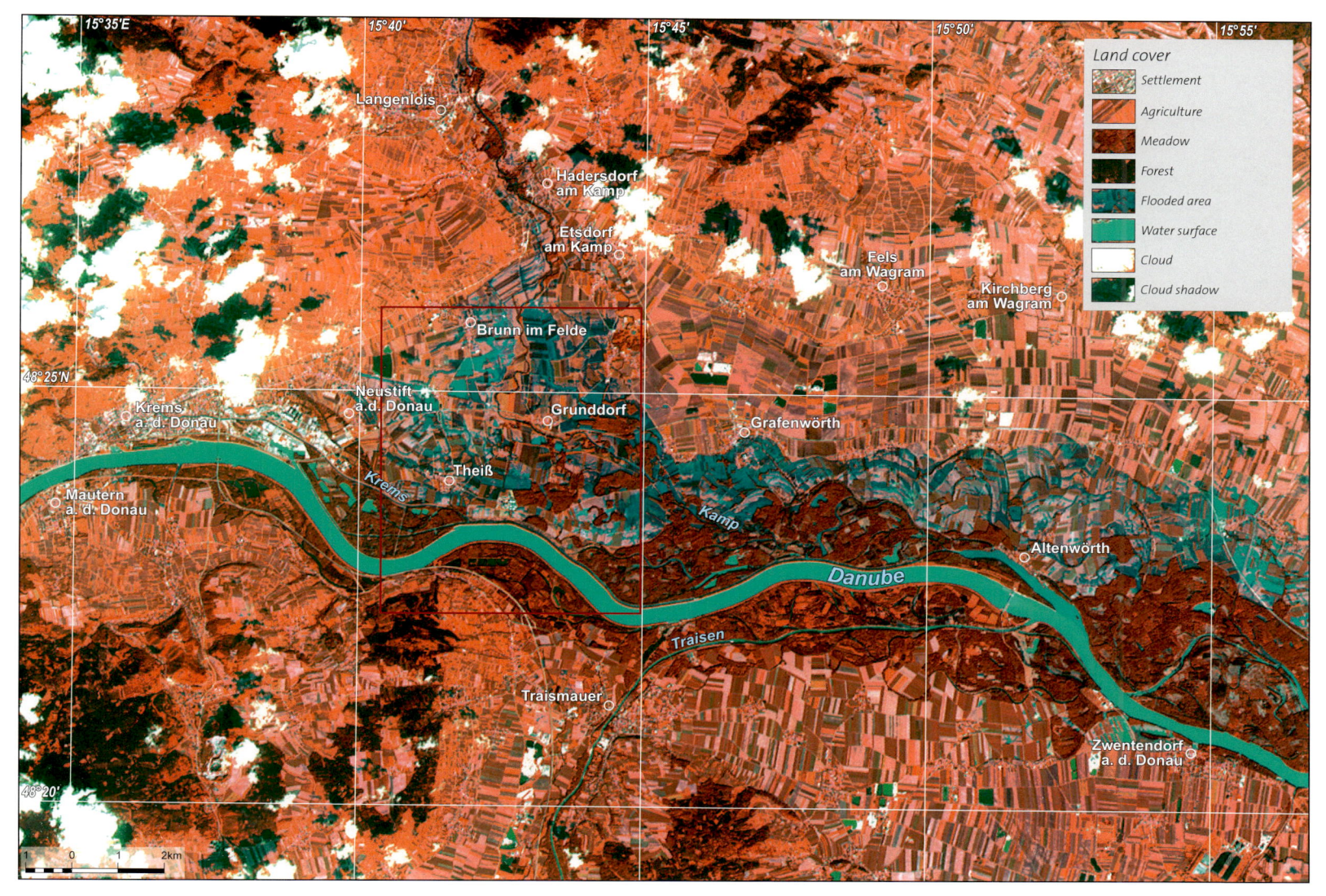

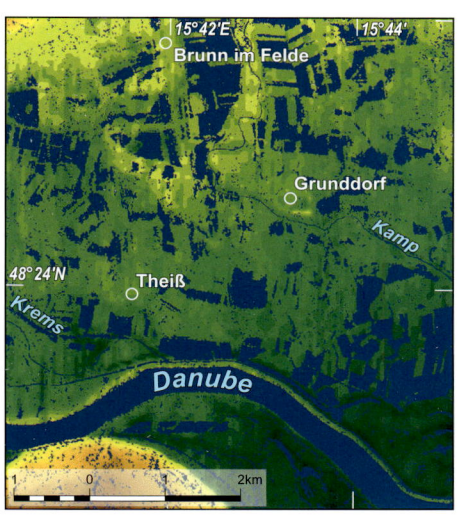

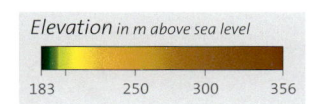

8 – Surface relief maps are also a useful aid for emergency response teams, which are then overlaid with flood data.

9 – To assess the flooding more accurately, emergency response teams use basic topographical maps, which are then supplemented with flood data.

The Danube floods in Austria

In August 2002, Austria was hit by two periods of heavy rain, each lasting two to three days. Within five days, two flood waves travelled through the region eastwards from Salzburg to Lower Austria and Vienna as well as through Styria. They were in the top ten of the worst floods since records began in 1821. In many places, the persistent bad weather led to new records in terms of rainfall and water levels along the rivers (Fig. 3). Orographic precipitation affected the northern edge of the Alps and the Mühlviertel and Waldviertel region. The extremely high flow rates of the rivers in the Kamp Valley and along the Danube River had the most severe effects (Figs. 6, 7 and 8). At the confluence of the Kamp with the Danube, dams prevented water masses from flowing into the Danube. As a result of the backlog of water, the villages of Gedersdorf and Brunn im Felde were largely flooded.

Flood mapping using radar

The best results for observing flooding are achieved using data from radar satellites. They enable permanent data recording, regardless of weather and light conditions. During the Danube floods in August 2002, the International Charter Space and Major Disasters was activated, and ERS-2 as well as RADARSAT were able to provide the data required for the region within just a few hours after being requested. The data was recorded on 14 August at 4.27 a.m. (UTC) and was available to emergency response teams at 3.53 p.m. (UTC). The flooded areas were extrapolated from the radar images and overlaid with topographic maps, elevation models and digital cadastral maps (Figs. 8 and 9). The data thus provided the basis for disaster management of the areas affected.

Trajectory and intensity

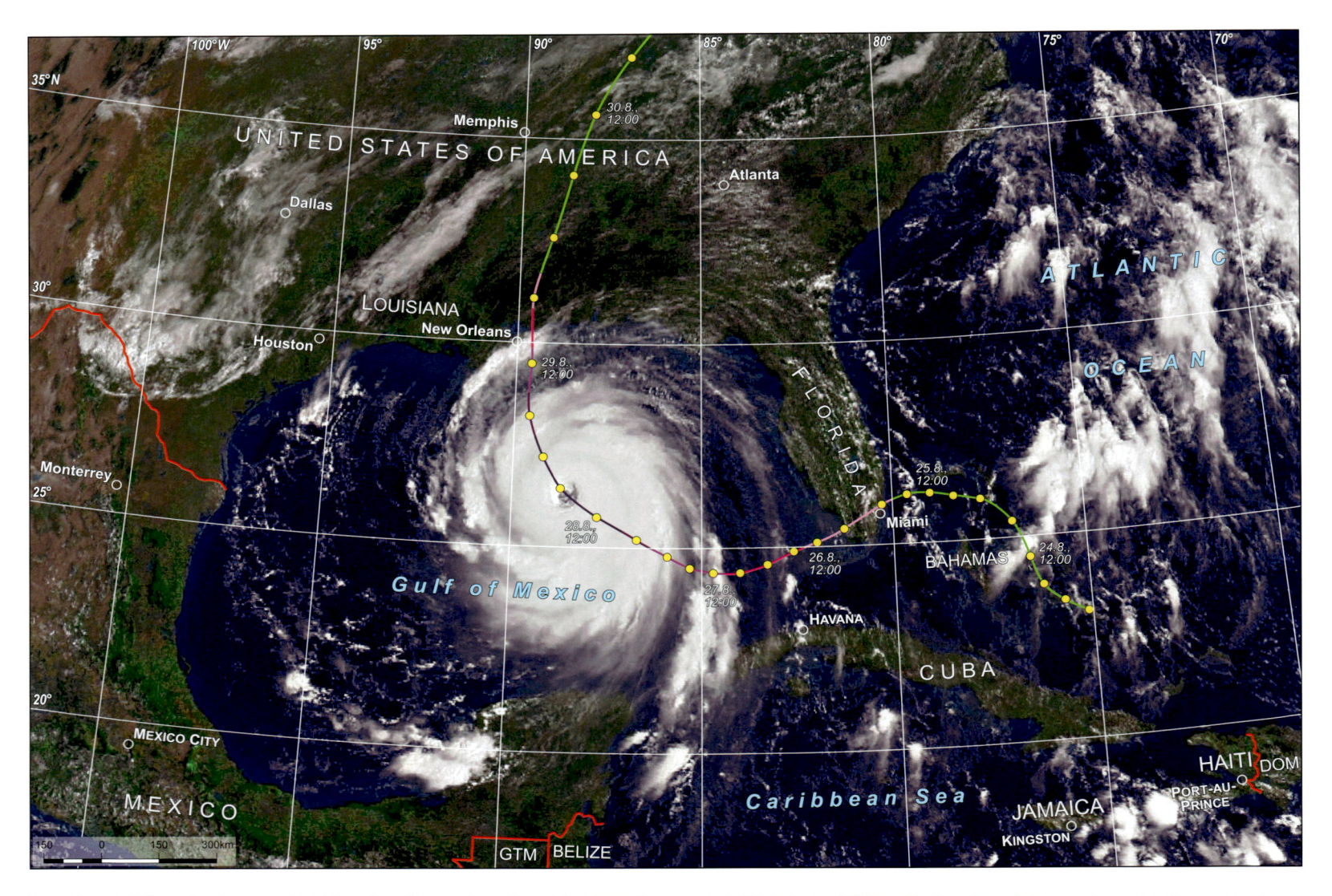

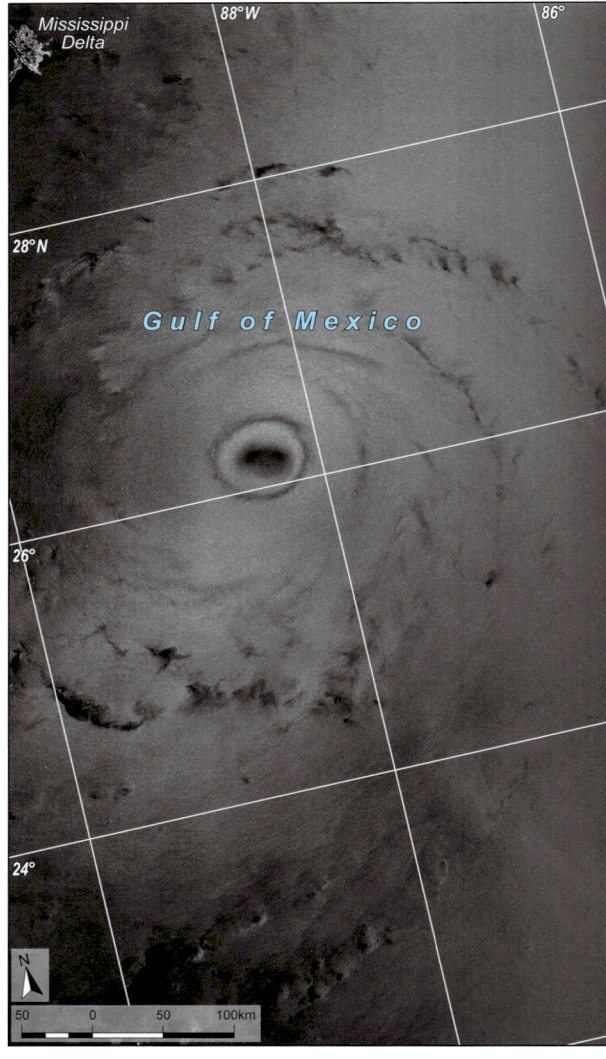

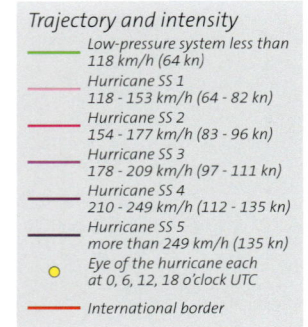

- Low-pressure system less than 118 km/h (64 kn)
- Hurricane SS 1 118 - 153 km/h (64 - 82 kn)
- Hurricane SS 2 154 - 177 km/h (83 - 96 kn)
- Hurricane SS 3 178 - 209 km/h (97 - 111 kn)
- Hurricane SS 4 210 - 249 km/h (112 - 135 kn)
- Hurricane SS 5 more than 249 km/h (135 kn)
- ○ Eye of the hurricane each at 0, 6, 12, 18 o'clock UTC
- International border

△
1 – On its path across Florida and the Gulf of Mexico, Hurricane Katrina continued to gain strength until weakening slightly before making landfall on the coast of Louisiana.
The satellite image was taken on 28/08/2005 at 3.45 p.m. (UTC).

◁
2 – Crossing the Gulf of Mexico, Katrina reached category 5 on the Saffir-Simpson scale (optical satellite image dated 28/08/2005).

◁
3 – In the radar image dated 28/08/2005, it is possible to make out the stormy seas below the cloud cover. The lighter the area, the higher the wind speed.

4 – The radar image (Envisat) dated 28/08/2005 of New Orleans with Lake Pontchartrain shows the water-saturated ground in light blue. The black and very dark areas show those zones that were completely flooded.

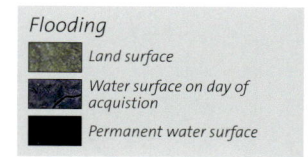

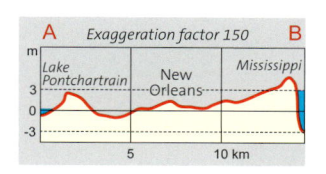

Flooding
- Land surface
- Water surface on day of acquistion
- Permanent water surface

5 – A profile of New Orleans illustrates the dangers of flooding if one of the Mississippi dams breaks.

The twelve-level Beaufort Scale of wind strength is insufficient to describe the strength of hurricanes. A new classification system must therefore be created.
The five-category Saffir-Simpson hurricane scale:
- 1 – Weak
- 2 – Moderate
- 3 – Strong
- 4 – Very strong
- 5 – Devastating

The scale is named after the engineers who developed it, Herbert Saffir and Bob Simpson.

6 – The floods in New Orleans peaked on 30/08/2005. The flooded areas are shown in dark colours on the infrared image as a result of the high level of absorption.

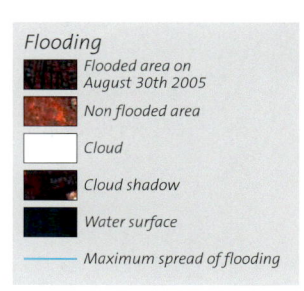

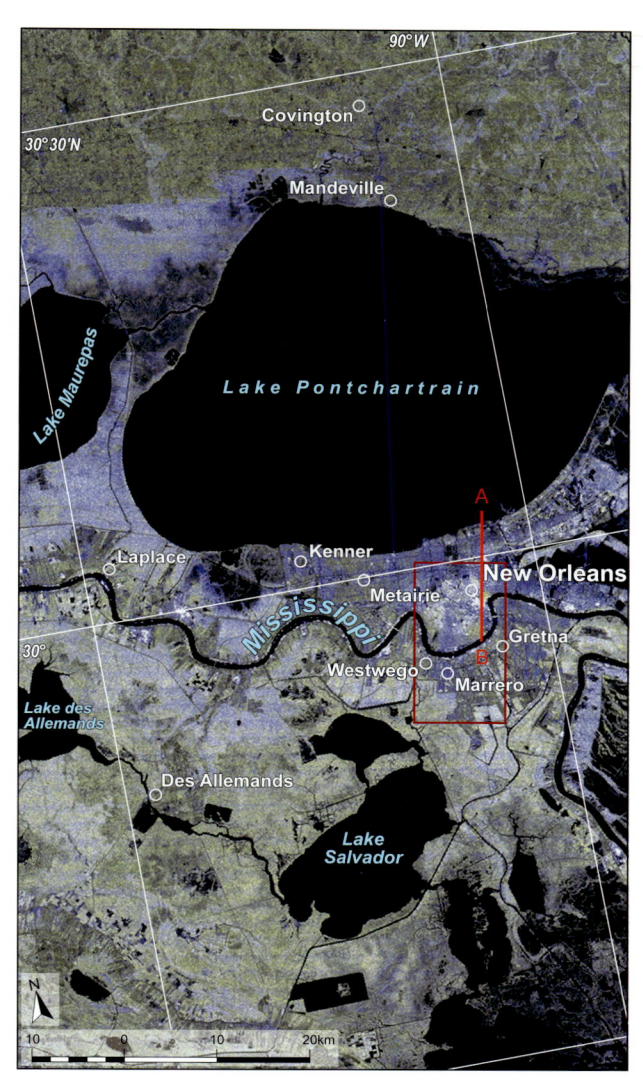

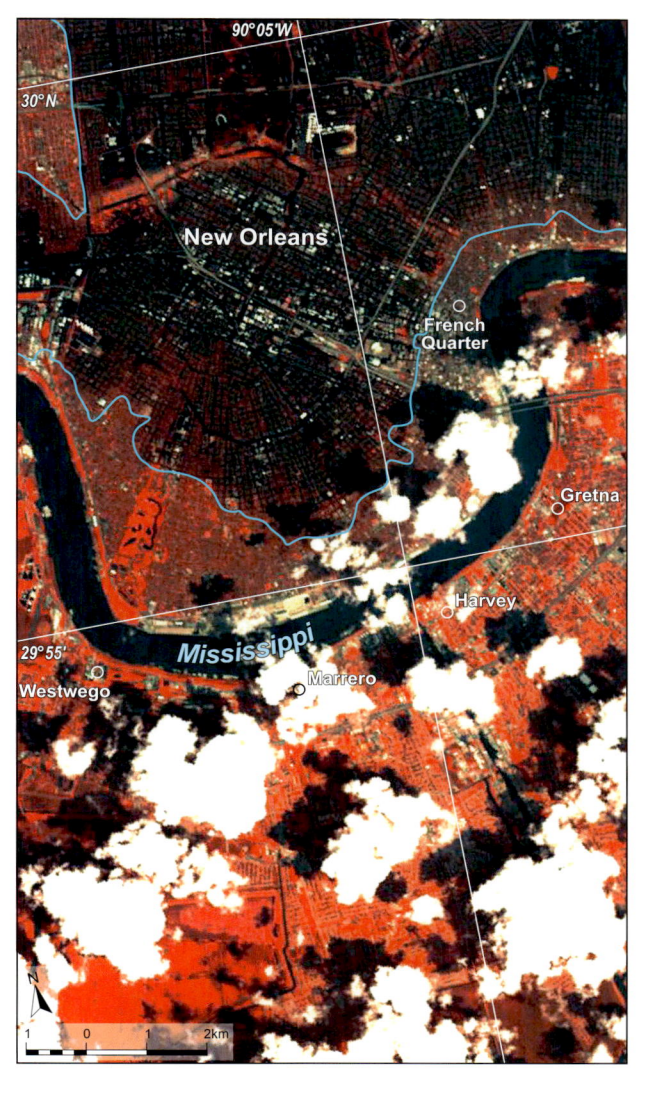

Flooding
- Flooded area on August 30th 2005
- Non flooded area
- Cloud
- Cloud shadow
- Water surface
- Maximum spread of flooding

Hurricane Katrina

On 23 August 2005, a large system of low pressure over the Bahamas in the Atlantic Ocean turned into Hurricane Katrina (Figs. 1–3). Like all areas of low pressure in the northern hemisphere, the air was moving anticlockwise, following the Coriolis force. If a tropical storm is to form, the water temperature of the sea surface must be at least 27 degrees Celsius. As a result of the Sun's radiation, water evaporates, which rises as humid air and forms clouds. The Coriolis effect results in a cyclone, which draws the air upwards in a large spiral movement. The inner, cloud-free zone of this cyclone is known as the 'eye' of the hurricane. In the eye, the winds are weak or change quickly and the air pressure is extremely low. Humid air from the sea streams into the eye and continues to rise, taking cooler air with it, which it then warms. This forms a stable system in which extremely high wind speeds can occur.

The Atlantic hurricane season lasts from 1 June until 30 November, when the sea surface temperatures are high enough to form hurricanes. Hurricanes are extremely hazardous for the population and the infrastructure because, in addition to extremely high wind speeds, they can also bring heavy rainfall and flooding.

Katrina's course

On 25 August 2005, Katrina made landfall on the densely populated state of Florida with gusts of 130 kilometres per hour, causing widespread damage. Heavy rainfall caused severe flooding. The hurricane then moved across the Gulf of Mexico, gathering strength over the warm water and reaching category 5 on the Saffir-Simpson scale. On 29 August, Katrina made landfall on the south coast of the U.S.A., where it destroyed large parts of the infrastructure along about 160 kilometres of coast. By the time it hit New Orleans, Katrina already had decreased to category 3. Travelling across the land, the hurricane quickly lost its force and petered out on 31 August 2005 on its journey towards the north-east (Fig. 1).

Katrina´s damages in New Orleans

New Orleans lies on the Mississippi River, which empties into the Gulf of Mexico as an enormous delta near the city. To the north of the city is Lake Pontchartrain, a brackish lake covering an area of around 1,800 square kilometres (Figs. 4 and 5). Large parts of the city lie below sea level, which is why it is at particular risk of flooding. Only the oldest part of the town, the French Quarter, is located on a small incline and was thus spared from the catastrophic flooding in August 2005 (Fig. 6). In addition to the city's location, the extent of the flooding that followed in Katrina's wake was also largely due to the loss of swamp forests and marshes during the last decades. These wetlands originally created a natural buffer zone to protect the Louisiana coast from the effects of hurricanes.

Hurricanes have hit New Orleans repeatedly over the city's 300-year history, but the city had never been hit by a hurricane of this force. Although the major levees along the Mississippi River held, two smaller ones were breached along the channels over a length of 150 metres. All attempts to close these gaps were in vain and the brackish water from Lake Pontchartrain spilled into the low-lying city. As a result of the power outages which were caused by the hurricane, it was not possible to pump the water out for a long time. Many people gathered in elevated places within the city, such as the Superdome and the Convention Centre, from where they were evacuated by buses and helicopters. The official death toll of Katrina in New Orleans was more than 1460 people.

280

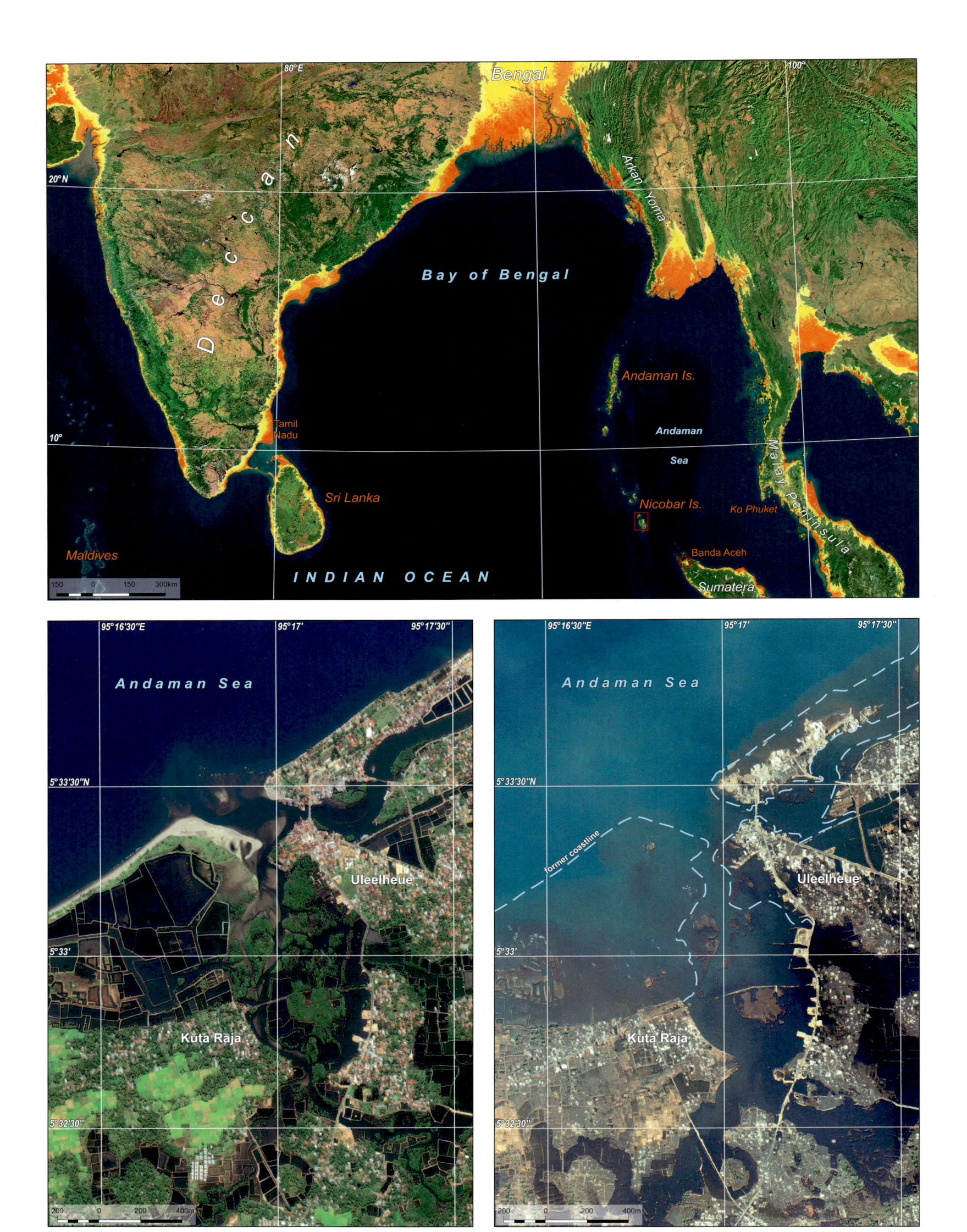

1 – Areas at risk of tsunamis in the Indian Ocean as a result of their low-lying location.

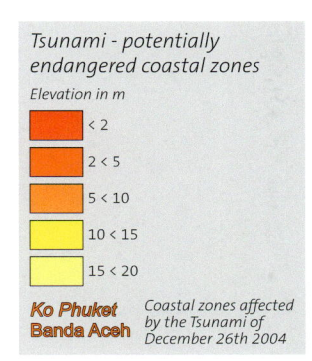

Tsunami - potentially endangered coastal zones
Elevation in m
- < 2
- 2 < 5
- 5 < 10
- 10 < 15
- 15 < 20

Ko Phuket
Banda Aceh *Coastal zones affected by the Tsunami of December 26th 2004*

4 – The relief map of the Nicobar Islands, India, illustrates which areas of the land are at sea level or just above sea level.

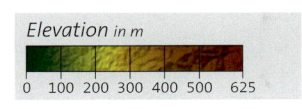

Elevation in m
0 100 200 300 400 500 625

5 – Multitemporal radar images of the Nicobar Islands, India (27/01/1992, 12/01/2005). Flooded coastal areas are shown in red.

2 – Banda Aceh, Indonesia, on 10/01/2003, before the Boxing Day Tsunami in 2004.

3 – Banda Aceh, Indonesia, on 29/12/2004, after the Boxing Day Tsunami on 26/12/2004.

6 – Simulated propagation of the tsunami in the Indian Ocean.

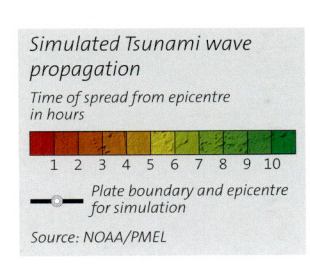

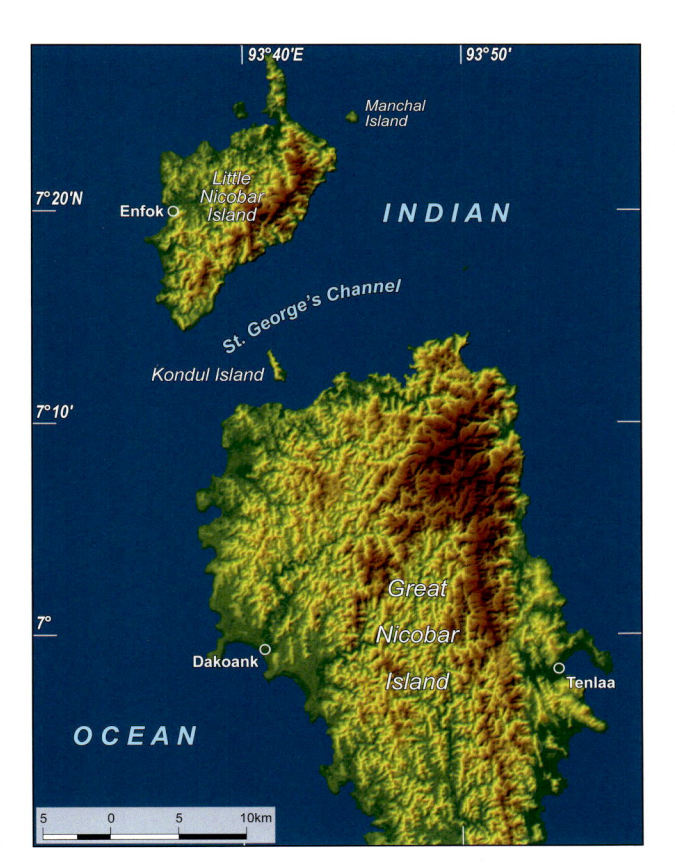

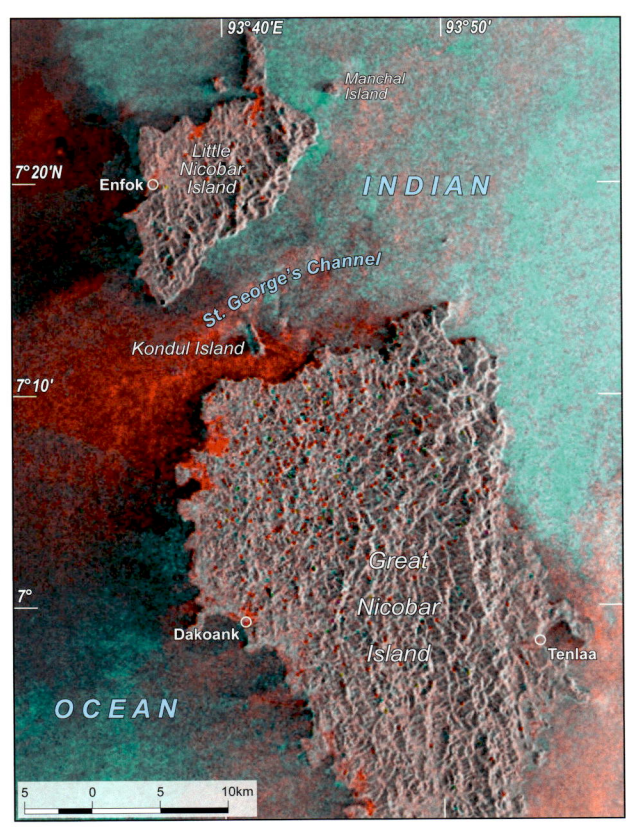

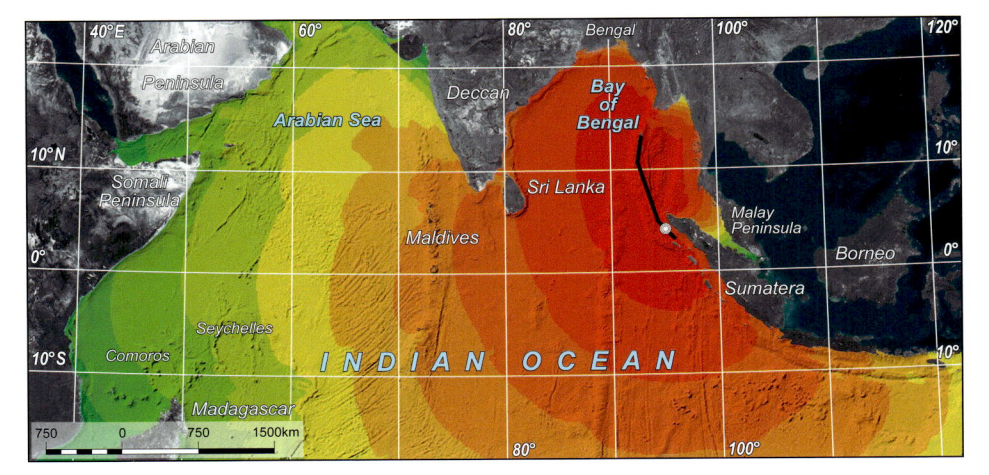

Simulated Tsunami wave propagation
Time of spread from epicentre in hours
1 2 3 4 5 6 7 8 9 10
Plate boundary and epicentre for simulation
Source: NOAA/PMEL

The Sumatra-Andaman earthquake

The example of the devastating tsunami resulting from the Sumatra-Andaman earthquake illustrates how this type of natural phenomenon occurs, as well as its effects.

On 26 December 2004, a deep-sea earthquake in the Indian Ocean measuring 9.2 on the Richter scale triggered one of the biggest tsunamis ever recorded. The epicentre of the quake, which was caused by tension between subducted continental plates, was to the north of the Simeulue island, west of Sumatra. The tsunami killed 220,000 people, primarily in the coastal regions of Indonesia, Sri Lanka and Thailand.

Banda Aceh, the most northerly province in Indonesia, was hit particularly hard by the tsunami as a result of its proximity to the epicentre of the undersea quake. It was not just coastal regions that fell victim to the waves: the tsunami hurtled several kilometres inland, leading to widespread devastation.

Propagation speed of the tsunami

Using simulation data for tsunamis, it is possible to estimate when an at-risk region (Figs. 1 and 4) might be hit by a tsunami following the triggering event (Fig. 6).

In the case illustrated, the tsunami struck the island of Sumatra straight after the quake (Fig. 3, p. 272 and Fig. 4, p. 273). The wave reached the Indian coast two hours later and the African coast around eight hours later. As a result of its proximity to the epicentre of the earthquake Sumatra was hit by waves measuring up to ten metres high in December 2004. Further from the epicentre, such as Sri Lanka and Thailand, the wave still reached heights of up to four metres, influenced by the shape of the coastline and the shape of the seabed.

Mapping tsunami damages using satellite images

Satellite images provided useful information that could help quickly and effectively in the areas affected. Detailed maps were delivered to emergency response teams, giving an overview of the extent of the catastrophe (Figs. 3 and 6). In addition, they also enabled swift access to the areas affected in order to initiate the clear-up mission in a fast, targeted way.

GITEWS – The German-Indonesian Tsunami Early-Warning System

Satellite technology also plays a major role in tsunami early-warning systems like those now used in the Indian Ocean. The 2004 catastrophe was the catalyst for the creation of the German-Indonesian Tsunami Early-Warning System (GITEWS), which aims to warn the population before such a wave hits. Existing systems, such as the Pacific early-warning system, could not be used as a result of the specific local geology. In addition to their role in providing telecommunications and GPS, satellites will also fulfil other functions in future within the GITEWS project. Among other things, earthquakes and tsunamis cause changes in the ocean's surface. Short-term rises in sea levels can be detected by radar sensors.

On 25 October 2010, another tsunami was detected as a result of an undersea earthquake off the coast of the Pagai Islands off Sumatra. Although the early-warning system worked, the three-metre waves still caused devastation and claimed 500 lives primarily on the Mentawai Islands as a result of the nearness to the epicentre. This shows that early-warning systems cannot offer complete protection. However, the further the distance from the epicentre, the longer the warning time.

Soil moisture anomaly
from 21. to 31.03.2007 in %

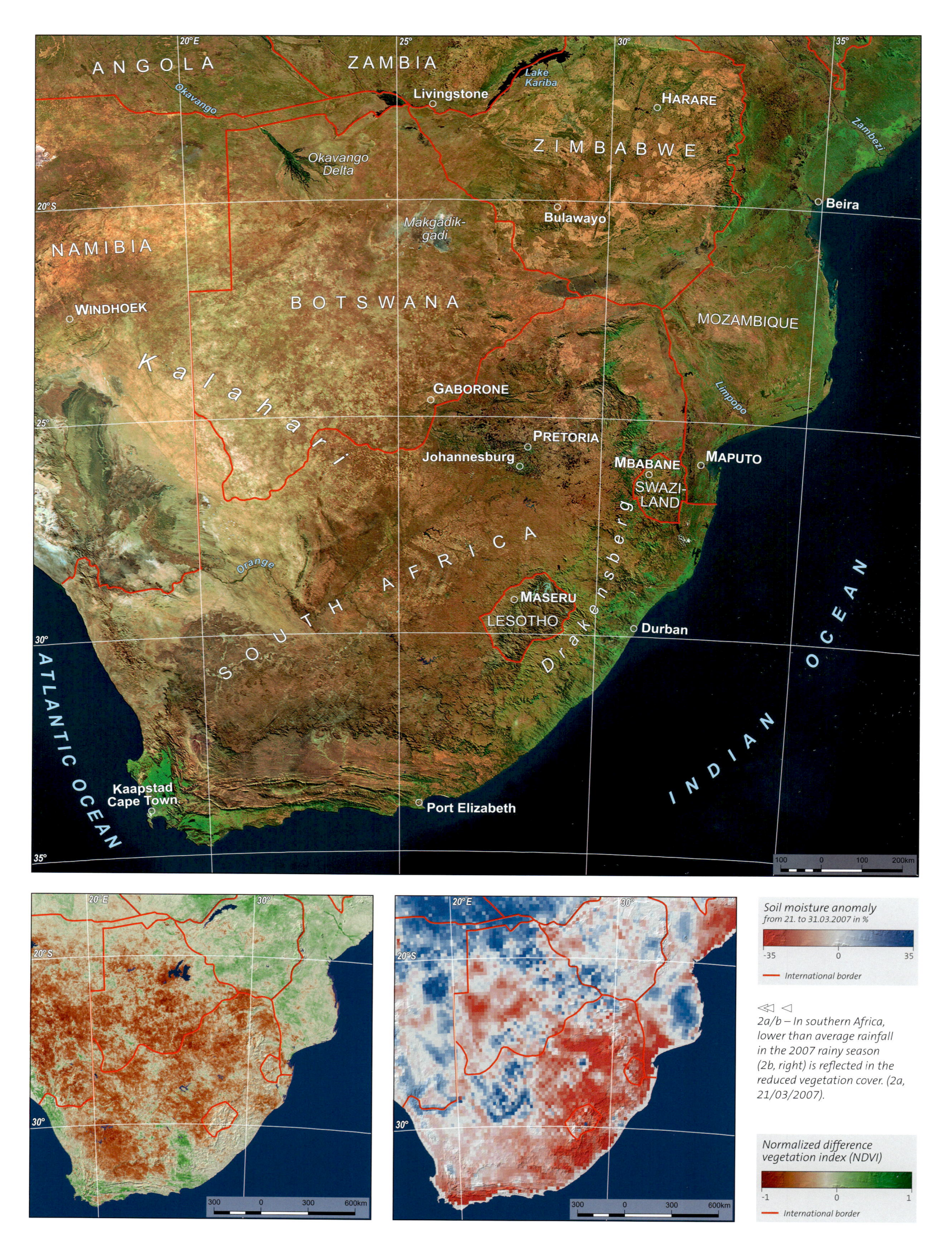

−35　　0　　35

— International border

◁◁ ◁
2a/b – In southern Africa, lower than average rainfall in the 2007 rainy season (2b, right) is reflected in the reduced vegetation cover. (2a, 21/03/2007).

Normalized difference vegetation index (NDVI)

−1　　0　　1

— International border

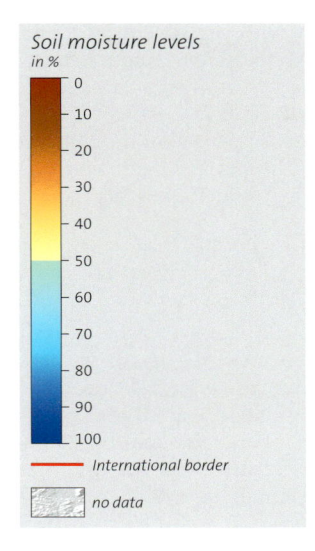

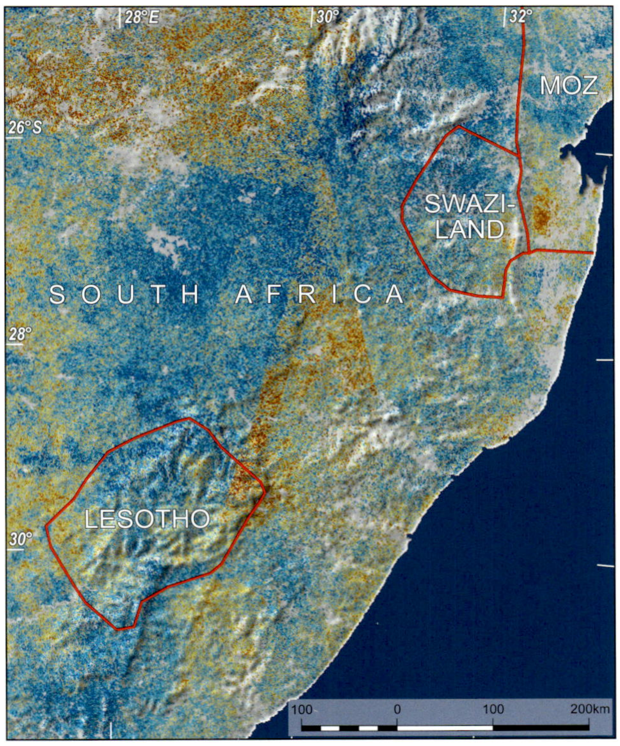

Droughts and soil moisture monitoring

During droughts, the lack of water goes hand in hand with significantly lower soil moisture in the affected region. Soil moisture is the water held in the soil within the reach of plant roots that can be used by vegetation. All in all, only 0.005 per cent of the world's water resources is stored in the soil. Although the amount of water stored in the soil is small, it plays a prominent role in the development of vegetation, but also in the interactions between the hydrosphere, biosphere and atmosphere. The productivity of agricultural land depends on soil moisture, but also on their capacity to store precipitated water. As a consequence, soil moisture plays an important part in many natural resource applications such as crop growth modelling (Fig. 2a), runoff monitoring and modelling, flood forecasting.

Similar to numerous other applications in hydrology, data from radar satellites are ideal for use in the analysis of soil moisture. An algorithm for the estimation of soil moisture from the Advanced Scatterometer (ASCAT sensor on board the MetOp-A satellite), was developed at the Vienna University of Technology. First experimental data with a ground resolution of 25 kilometres shows the water saturation in the upper soil layer down to two centimetres on a regional scale (Fig. 2 b). These data have been collected continuously since 2008.

The rainy season in southern Africa

In the Southern African Development Community (SADC) region, which has comprised most African states south of the equator since 1992, the rainy season roughly lasts from November until February and brings with it most of the region's annual rainfall. Farmers therefore greatly depend on the amount of precipitation that falls during this time of year and on the resulting soil moisture conditions. The example maps represent the varying soil moisture conditions during the wet months of January 2005, 2006 and 2007, which in turn resulted in varying crop yields (Figs. 3 and 4). The maps represent monthly means computed from all data available for the particular month.

While the northern part of the SADC region performed very well in January 2005 with respect to the soil moisture level, the central and southern parts of the SADC region evidently lacked moisture in 2007. The prolonged dry spell was reported for the 2005 rainy season in northern South Africa, southern Mozambique, Tanzania, southern Zambia, and Zimbabwe, and resulted in serious drought in these countries (Fig. 2a). In the 2005–2006 rainy season, the SADC experienced heavy precipitation that resulted in floods within most SADC countries. January 2006 is an example of a wet month with above-average soil moisture across most of the study area (Fig. 3). Similar conditions to those in the 2005 rainy season were reported in 2007. While the northern part of the SADC region experienced high relative soil moisture levels, central and southern SADC lacked moisture in soil, with negative impacts on the crop performance in the subsequent months.

Provided there is a reference database covering a sufficiently long period of time, deviations from the average soil moisture can be identified. These can be used to reveal areas at higher risk of droughts or floods. Conventional methods to measure soil moisture are labour-intensive, costly, non-uniform, and can be applied only on a local scale. The evaluation of radar satellite data constitutes an innovative and efficient way to monitor spatial and temporal patterns of soil moisture – from 2009 also by the ESA Earth Explorer SMOS satellite, allowing high-level administrative bodies and organisations to react to negative developments in good time and to prepare for any support measures required in the affected regions.

Text: Marcela Doubková, Wolfgang Wagner

▷ 3 – Heavy rainfall in the 2005/2006 rainy season led to flooding in large parts of the SADC.

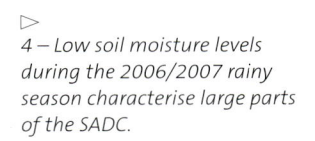

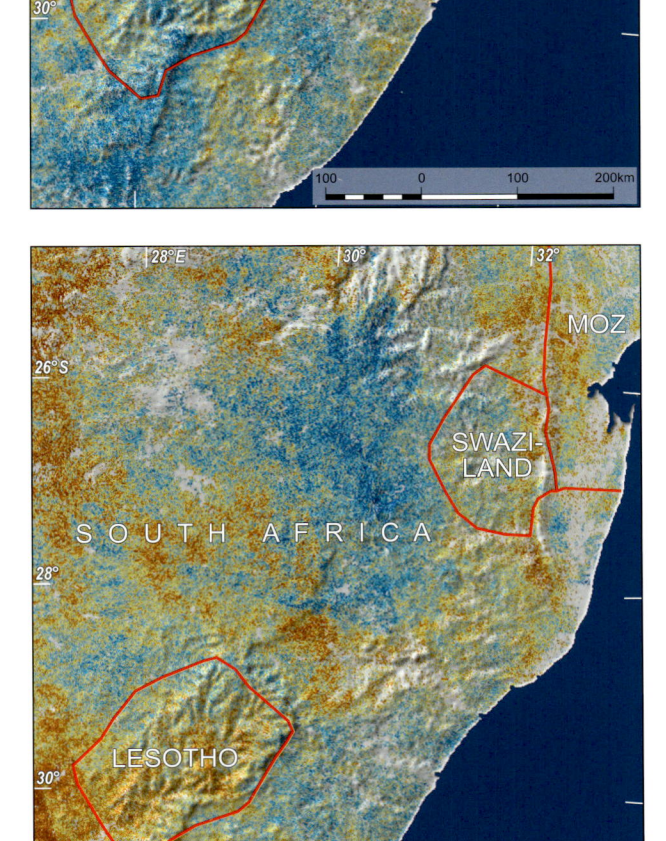

▷ 4 – Low soil moisture levels during the 2006/2007 rainy season characterise large parts of the SADC.

◁ 1 – Deserts and wetlands are characteristic of southern Africa.

▷ 5 – The long, hot dry season led to crop failure in March 2007 (maize field near Bothaville, South Africa) and economic shortages. The hardest-hit areas were dependent on food aid. Swaziland experienced its worst drought since 1992, while Lesotho experienced its worst in 30 years. According to recent studies, southern Africa looks set to experience more and more droughts over the long term as a result of climate change. Extreme values were recorded also in 2009.

EXTERNAL AUTHORS

Marcela Doubková works as a Project Assistant at the Vienna University of Technology. Her research interests encompass microwave remote sensing of water in vegetation and soil and the error understanding of the derived products. She received her MA in geography, specializing in cartography, remote sensing, and GIS from the University of Nebraska-Lincoln (UNL) in 2006 and her PhD in natural science from the Vienna University of Technology in 2012.

Khondaker Azharul Haq obtained a PhD degree in engineering, a master's in agricultural engineering and a BSc in agricultural engineering from the University of California in Davis in 1981. He has over 40 years of experience from all across the world in the water sector: in water resource development and management, management of irrigation systems, agricultural and rural development, impact assessment and management of large public sector utilities dealing with water supply and sanitation, both in Bangladesh and some other countries in Asia and Africa. For his contribution to helping the urban poor of Dhaka access water supply and sanitation, he was recognized as a "water champion" by the Asian Development Bank in 2005. He has 15 publications to his name.

Wolfgang Kron studied civil and hydraulic engineering at the University of Karlsruhe (today's Karlsruhe Institute of Technology) and at the University of California in Davis. From 1983 to 1994 he performed research and taught at Karlsruhe and gained his doctorate with a study on the application of reliability theory to sediment transport processes. In 1990 he was appointed Secretary to the Scientific Advisory Board of the German Committee for the UN International Decade for Natural Disaster Reduction (IDNDR). In this position, he transferred to the German Research Centre for Geosciences in Potsdam in 1994. He joined the Geo Risks Research Department at Munich Re in 1996, where to this day he has been responsible for "everything to do with water" as head of the section dealing with hydrological risks. He continues to play an active role in national and international committees addressing aspects of disaster reduction, water management, and science.

Walther Lichem started his career at the UN Centre for Natural Resources, Energy and Transport in New York where he launched the UN programme on international water systems. He served as adviser to the National Water Council of the Government of Ethiopia, the Senegal River Development Organisation, and established the Institute for Water Resources Economics, Law and Administration in Argentina. As Austrian diplomat he was Ambassador in Chile and in Canada, in the Ministry i.a. with responsibilities for international organizations and for outer space.

Heinz Löffler (1927-2006) was born in Vienna. After studies in Biology and Chemistry he worked in the field of saline and high mountain lakes. After his thesis he was invited as a visiting professor to universities in the United States and to collaborations in international research projects, among others in the framework of UNESCO, the International Biological Program (IBP) and World Bank projects. In 1967 H. Löffler became director of the Biological Station Lunz (Austria), in 1979 professor at the University of Vienna, and in 1982 founded the first limnological institute in Austria, the Institute of Limnology of the Austrian Academy of Sciences located at the Mondsee. Far reaching consequences included the creation of a limnological postgraduate course for graduates from developing countries, which was started in 1974. Already in the early 1980s, Mr. Löffler alerted to the disastrous development the Lake Aral was taking.

Thomas Loster has been CEO of the Munich Re Foundation since 2004, after having been a member of the Geo Risk Research team of the reinsurance company Munich Re for 16 years. In 2004 Mr. Loster was appointed CEO of the Munich Re Foundation. This foundation deals with global challenges, such as defeating poverty, environment and climate change, water as a resource and as a risk, population dynamics and disaster preparedness, and supports people in a situation of risk. Mr. Loster is member of the German National Committee of the UN decade "Education for Sustainable Development" and was member of the German Council for Sustainable Development from 2006 to 2010. He is also member of the World Bank/IFC Advisory Panel on Business and Sustainability. As member of the executive board of the Munich Climate Insurance Initiative (MCII) he searches for insurance solutions concerning weather disasters in developing and newly industrialised countries.

Martina Mayerhofer studied political science with a major in economics. Her areas of research included sustainable development and sustainable economics. Before her university studies, she was trained as a bank officer and worked for various employers including Deutsche Bank, Munich. Martina Mayerhofer has been working as a project manager for the Munich Re Foundation since October 2007. She manages projects relating to water as a resource, climate education and sustainability, and student projects.

Dirk Reinhard has more than ten years experience in the field of sustainability and finance industry. From 2001 to 2004 he worked in the environment department of the reinsurance company Munich Re, where he was responsible for sustainable investment. Before joining Munich Re, he worked from 1995 to 2000 as sustainability analyst for oekom research AG. In 2004 Mr. Reinhard was appointed Vice Chair of the Munich Re Foundation. He is responsible for the capital investments of the foundation and for the project field microinsurance. Mr. Reinhard has been a member of the Board of Directors of the Microinsurance Network since 2008. Ever since the first International Microinsurance Conference in 2005, Mr. Reinhard has been head of the Conference Steering Committee. This conference is the largest event worldwide dealing with microinsurance.

Stein Sandven is director at Nansen Environmental and Remote Sensing Center and Professor II at University Centre in Svalbard (UNIS). He has more than 30 years experience in marine and polar remote sensing, polar oceanography, sea ice research with emphasis on satellite remote sensing. He has been coordinator of many Arctic research projects funded by EU, ESA, Norwegian Space center, Norwegian Research Council and industry. He has published more than 50 papers in international refereed journals and books.

Cecilia Tortajada is the president of the Third World Centre for Water Management, Mexico. Her work is on the future of the world´s water beyond 2020, especially in terms of water, food, energy and environmental securities through coordinated policies. She has been an advisor to major international institutions like FAO, UNDP, JICA, ADB, OECD and GIZ, and has worked in countries in Africa, Asia, North and South America and Europe on water and natural resources and environment-related policies. She is a member of the OECD Initiative in Water Governance and has collaborated actively on the UNDP Post-2015 Development Agenda. She is also engaged in independent studies on Corporate Social Responsibility of major multinational corporations. Ms. Tortajada is past President of the International Water Resources Association (2007-2009), an Honorary member of the IWRA and Editor-in-Chief of the International Journal of Water Resources Development.

Anthony Turton holds a professorship in the Centre for Environmental Management at the University of Free State. His current work is in the mining sector where he specializes in acid mine drainage (AMD) and the development of strategies and technologies to mitigate the risk arising from the uranium contamination of Johannesburg. As a Trustee of the Water Stewardship Council of Southern Africa he encourages behavioural change through positive inducement. He is co-founder of the South African Water and Energy Forum (SAWEF) that introduced the notion of the Water-Energy-Food Nexus to the public domain. He is the past Vice President of the International Water Resource Association (IWRA) and a past Deputy Governor of the World Water Council. He currently serves as Editor of the international journal "Water Policy" and sits on the editorial boards of various technical journals including "Water International", "Water Alternatives", the "International Journal of Water Governance" and the Springer Verlag textbook series on water resource management. He has been appointed to the American Society of Mechanical Engineers as a Contributing Member to the Water and Energy Group Subcommittee on Innovative Water Conservation, Reuse and Recovery Technologies for a term ending in June 2019.

Wolfgang Wagner is professor for remote sensing at the Vienna University of Technology (TU Wien), Austria, head of the Department of Geodesy and Geoinformation of TU Wien, and co-founder and head of science of the Earth Observation Data Centre for Water Resources Monitoring (EODC). His main research interests lie in geophysical parameter retrieval techniques from remote sensing data and application development. He focuses on active remote sensing techniques, in particular scatterometry, SAR, and full-waveform airborne laser scanning. Before joining TU Wien, he received fellowships to carry out research at the University of Bern, Atmospheric Environment Service Canada, NASA Goddard Space Flight Centre, European Space Agency, and the Joint Research Centre of the European Commission. From 1999 to 2001 he was with the German Aerospace Agency (DLR).

Jeremy Wallace is a remote sensing scientist with Australia's national research agency CSIRO. He works in a group which specialises in monitoring systems for land and vegetation.

INDEX OF GEOGRAPHICAL NAMES

A

A Coruña 236, 244, 245
Aalborg 167
Aare 111
Ābādān 212
Abbot Ice Shelf 176
Abhā 212
Abu Simbel 115
Acaray 255
Achacachi 136
Aconcagua 56, 58
'Adan 212
Ad Dammām 212
Adelaide 220, 221
Adige 138, 139
Adige Glacier 139
Adıyaman 234
Adriatic Sea 106
Affi 139
Afghanistan 36, 142, 143
Africa 31, 36, 37, 39, 54, 55, 56-57, 58-59, 73, 74, 117, 119, 131, 147, 160, 161, 163, 168, 197, 205, 206, 207, 218, 239, 258, 259, 267, 282, 283
Afuá 101
Agassiz Glacier 82
Aggteleki 248
Agni Ihya 207
Agni Zekri 207
Agulhas Basin 57
Agulhas Ridge 57
Ahero 149
Ahvāz 212
Ailao Shan 122
Airlie Beach 250
Akçakale 234
Al Bāha 212
Al Başrah 212
Al Busayta 215, 227
Al Fayyūm 114
Al Hudaydah 212
Al Ismā'īlīyah 114, 258
Al Jawf 215, 227
Al Jubayl 49, 212
Al Khafjī 212, 213
Al Khobar 212
Al Khums 210
Al Kufra 224
Al Kufra (province) 225
Al Kufra oases 224, 225
Al Luwaymi 226
Al Mādina 212
Al Manşūrah 114
Al Minyā 114
Al Mukalla 212
Alabama 271
Alaska 54, 56, 62, 82, 131, 157, 167, 168, 172, 173, 260
Alb (river) 111
Albacete 236
Albany 223
Albert Nile 113, 115, 148
Aleppo 233
Aletschhorn 83
Aleutian Islands 56-57, 168
Aleutian Trench 56
Alexander Island 176
Alexandria 114
Algeciras 44, 236
Algeria 36, 58, 210, 211
Algiers 210, 244
Aliarom 155
All-American Canal 91
Allentown 184
Almanzora 236
Almelo 111
Almere 111
Almería (city) 236
Almeria (province) 237
Alps 11, 54, 57, 63, 83, 105, 106, 139, 209, 271, 274, 277
Alta 164
Altagracia 256
Altai 57
Altai Mountains 129
Altenwörth 2777
Altiplano 136, 137
Altube 236
Amacuzac 192, 193, 195
Amazon 16, 44, 56, 58, 72, 74, 85, 99, 100, 101, 102, 103
Amazon Basin 53, 99, 100-101, 102
Amazonas Delta 101
America 39, 258, 267
American Falls 135
Amery Ice Shelf 57, 176, 179
'Ammān 212, 242, 243
Amsterdam 111, 167
Amudar'ya 54, 141, 142, 143
Amundsen Sea 56, 176
Amur 57, 59, 260
Amurian Plate 145
An Najaf 212
An Nāsirīyah 212
Andaman Island 280
Andaman Sea 280
Andarax 236
Andernach 110
Andes 56, 62, 63, 99, 137
Angara 144, 145
Angarsk 144
Angola 198, 238, 239, 282
Angola Basin 57
Angsi Glacier 117
Annaba 210
Antalya 77
Antarctic Peninsula 56, 62, 171, 172, 178
Antarctic/Antarctica 31, 47, 53, 54, 81, 163, 167, 168, 171, 172, 173, 175, 176, 177, 178, 179, 221
Anti-Atlas Mountains 207
Antwerpen 111, 167, 244
Aomen (Macau) 187
Apeldorn 111
Apennines 106
Appalachian Mountains 56, 62, 93
Apuseni 248
Aqaba 243
Aquarius Plateau 254
Arabian Basin 57
Arabian Peninsula 53, 57, 281
Arabian Sea 57, 281
'Arad 242, 248
'Ar'ar 212
Arberobue 206, 207
Arcaray Reservoir 255
Arctic Mid-Ocean Ridge 57
Arctic Ocean 31, 56-57, 62, 129, 157, 160, 161, 163, 164, 167, 168, 171, 172, 173, 174, 175, 258, 260, 261
Arga-Muora-Sise Island 16
Argentina 255
Argentine Basin 56
Argentine Sea 56, 176
Århus 167
Arizona 89, 90, 254
Arkabutla Lake 95
Arkan Yoma 280
Arkansas (federal state) 94, 96
Arkansas (river) 96
Arkhangelsk 260
Armenia 142, 235
Arnhem 111
Arzew 244
Ash Shaiba 212
Ash Sha'laniyah 226
Ash Sharqiyah 226
Ash Shuqayq 212
Ashdod 243
Ashkhabad 142
Ashqelon 243
Asia 31, 54, 57, 59, 74, 145, 162, 163, 167, 168, 172, 173, 183, 215, 259, 267
Asir Mountains 227
Asmara 206, 212
Assam 127
Assam Himalaya 126
Astrakhan 86
Aswān 114, 117
Aswan Dam 39, 113, 115
Asyūt 114
Aţ Ţā'if 212
Atacama Desert 58
Atacama Trench 56
Atatürk Baraji 234, 235
Atatürk Dam 233, 234
Atbara (city) 114
Atbara (river) 113, 114, 115
Atchafalaya 229, 230
Athens 244
Atlanta 278
Atlantic City 184
Atlantic Ocean 31, 36, 39, 53, 54, 56-57, 62-63, 99, 119, 133, 134, 159, 160, 161, 162, 163, 168, 172, 176, 177, 178, 179, 184, 198, 230, 231, 236, 245, 247, 258, 259, 260, 263, 278, 279, 282
Atlantic-Indian Antarctic Basin 56-57
Atlas Mountains 56, 210
Atoyac 193
Augusta 244
Australia 31, 39, 53, 54, 57, 59, 150, 151, 162, 163, 168, 177, 220, 221, 222, 223, 251, 265
Australia Capital Territory 221
Austria 47, 49, 58, 106, 108, 139, 253, 274, 276, 277
Avignon 209
Avilés 165
Az Zāwiyah 210
Azerbaijan 142, 235
Azores 56

B

Bab al Mandab 212
Babadag 109
Bad Homburg vor der Höhe 110
Bad Kreuznach 110
Bad Neuenahr-Ahrweiler 110
Bad Sobernheim 110
Badajoz 236
Badda 202, 203
Baffin Bay 56, 172, 260
Baffin Island 56, 172, 260
Baghdad 57, 68,
Bahamas 160, 229, 230, 231, 278, 279
Bahr el Ghazal 115
Baia Borsa 249
Baia de Caxiuana 101
Baia de Marajó 101
Baia Mare 248, 249
Baie-Comeau 135
Baiju 188
Baikal Mountains 144
Baikal Rift Zone 145
Baiyuda Desert 114
Baja California 89, 90
Baku 142
Balaton 106
Bali 11, 216, 217
Balleny Islands 176
Balsa 248, 249
Baltic Sea 260
Balu 202, 203
Banda Aceh 280, 281
Bandiagara 218, 219
Bangkok 57, 68, 183,
Bangladesh 122, 127, 163, 201, 203, 269, 270, 271
Bangshi 202, 203
Bani 218, 219
Banī Suwayf 114
Banja Luka 106
Bankass 218, 219
Banks Island 172
Bannewitz 276
Barakaldo 165
Barataria Bay 97
Barbate de Franco 44
Barbé 219
Barcelona 244
Bardolino 138, 139
Barents Sea 57, 128, 161, 164, 172, 260, 261
Barguzin Range 144
Barinas 257
Barnaul 129
Barossa Valley 221
Barreirinha 102
Barren Grounds 56, 62, 172
Barsovo 128, 129
Basel 106, 111, 139
Bass Strait 220
Baton Rouge 230
Bay of Bengal 57, 87, 122, 126, 201, 203, 280, 281
Bay of Tina 258
Bay of Whales 176
Bayan Har Shan 122
Baykal'sk 144
Baytown 230
Bear Peninsula 178
Beaucaire 209
Beaufort Sea 56, 168, 172, 260
Beauharnois Lock 134
Beaumont 230
Bécancour 135
Beenong 222
Be'ér Sheva 243
Beidagang Shuiku 266
Beijing 57, 68, 189
Beira 282
Belém 101
Belgica Glacier 179
Belgium 28, 111, 167
Belgrade 107, 248
Belize 230, 278
Belle Chasse 231
Bellinghausen Sea 56, 176
Belmopan 230
Belyj Island 260
Belyj Jar 128, 129
Bendorf 110
Bengal 280
Bengal Lowlands 127
Benin 36
Berckner Island 176
Bergamo 139
Bergen 77
Bergisch Gladbach 110
Bering Sea 56, 168, 260
Bering Strait 56, 168, 260, 261
Berlin 57, 68
Bern 139
Bernese Alps 139
Bethlehem 242
Bezouce 209
Bhareli 126
Bhutan 122, 126
Biancang 188
Biarritz 165
Bié Plateau 238
Biel 139
Bienwald 111
Big Water 254
Bihor Mountains 107
Bilbao 165, 236
Biloxi 231
Bingen am Rhein 110
Birecik 234
Birecik Dam 234
Birmingham 167
Bishkek 142
Biscoe Islands 176
Biserta 244
Bitter Lakes 259
Biya 129
Biysk 129
Black Forest 105, 106, 110, 139
Black Sea 57, 105, 106, 107, 108, 111, 161, 259, 260
Bloemfontein 199
Blue Mountains (Australia) 221
Blue Nile 113, 114, 115
Blythenville 94
Bobila 118
Bocholt 110
Bochum 110
Bogotá 56, 68
Bohai Bay 266
Bol 155
Bolivia 136, 137
Bolschoi Jugan 128
Bomi 126
Bonin Trench 57
Bonn 77, 110, 111, 167
Bordeaux 165
Bordj de Chegga 210, 211
Borken 110
Borneo 48, 281
Boro 238
Borsa 248, 249
Bosnia and Herzegovina 106-107, 270
Bosphorus 161
Boteti 238
Bothaville 283
Botswana 36, 37, 86, 198, 199, 218, 238, 239, 282
Bottrop 110
Boulder 254
Boulogne-sur-Mer 259
Boyoma Falls (Stanley Falls) 119
Bozen 106, 139
Bozova 234
Braga 245
Brahmakund 127
Brahmaputra 20, 73, 122, 126-127, 201, 269
Brakpan 199
Brampton Island 250
Bransfield Strait 176
Bratislava 106, 108
Bratsk Reservoir 144
Brawley 91
Brazil 44, 99, 100, 254, 255
Brazil Basin 56
Brazilian Highlands 56, 62
Brazos River 230
Brazzaville 118, 119
Breda 111
Breg 105
Bregenz 139
Bremen 111, 167
Bremerhaven 111
Brescia 139
Breton Sound 96
Bridal Veil 135
Brienzer See 139
Brig 83
Brigach 105
Brisbane 163
Bristol Bay 260
British Isles 56, 259, 260
Brittany 242, 245
Brno 106
Bruchsal 110
Brugge 111, 167
Brühl 110
Bruint 127
Brunn im Felde 277
Brunt Ice Shelf 176, 179
Brussels 111, 167
Bucharest 105, 107
Budapest 105, 106
Buenos Aires 56, 68, 87
Buffalo 134
Buhayrat al Manzilah 258
Bujumbura 148
Bükki 248
Bulawayo 282
Bulgaria 107, 248
Bunbury 223
Buniche 222
Bunker Group 251
Buraydah 212
Burgos 236
Buriganga 201, 201, 203
Burkina Faso 36, 218, 219
Burundi 36, 76, 115, 147, 148
Bykovskiy branch 156
Bykovskiy Peninsula 156
Byrd Glacier 179

C

Cabimas 256, 257
Cabo da Roca 11
Cádiz 236
Cagliari 244
Cairo 56, 68, 77, 113, 114
Calcutta 57, 68
California 89, 90, 91
California City 77
Calimani 248
Camagüey 230
Cambodia 76, 77
Cambrai 111
Cameroon 36, 153, 154, 155
Campbell Island 58
Canada 29, 54, 75, 133, 134-135, 157, 161, 167, 173
Canada Basin 56
Canadian Arctic 174
Canal da San Carlos 256
Canal do Norte 100, 101
Canal do Sul 100, 101
Canal do Vieira Grande 100, 101
Canary Islands 56
Canberrra 221
Cândido Rondon 255
Cantabrian Range 236, 237
Caomiao 188
Caonian 188
Caopie 188
Cape Arid 223

Cape Basin ... 57
Cape Boothby ... 176
Cape Brewster ... 172
Cape Conway ... 250
Cape Dart ... 176
Cape Hatteras ... 160
Cape Howe ... 221
Cape Inscription ... 223
Cape Jaffa ... 220
Cape Maguarinho ... 101
Cape Naturaliste ... 223
Cape Norte ... 101
Cape Otway ... 220
Cape Palmer ... 176
Cape Town (Kaapstad) ... 59, 282
Cape Verde ... 56, 207
Capricorn Group ... 251
Caprino Veronese ... 139
Carauari ... 103
Cardiff ... 77
Caribbean ... 137, 160, 163, 231, 271
Caribbean Sea ... 56, 230, 278
Carinup Lakes ... 222
Carora ... 257
Carpathian Mountains ... 107
Carpathians ... 249
Carpenedolo ... 138
Caspian Depression ... 57, 86
Caspian Sea ... 36, 57, 86, 131, 141, 142, 143, 235, 260
Castanhal ... 101
Castiglione della Stiviere ... 138
Catatumbo ... 257
Caucasus ... 54, 57, 63, 142
Cavaion Veronese ... 139
Central Africa ... 153, 154
Central African Republic ... 36, 155
Central Alps ... 105
Central America ... 9, 163, 271
Central Asia ... 73, 141, 142, 143
Central China ... 122
Central Europe ... 55, 276
Central Europe ... 55, 241
Central Pacific Basin ... 56
Central Siberian Plateau ... 57, 63
Cerros de Bala ... 137
Ceuta ... 44
Chad ... 36, 59,
Challans ... 165
Chama ... 257
Chandpur ... 127
Changchun ... 262
Changsha ... 123
Changshu ... 123
Channel Country ... 151
Chao Phraya ... 183
Chapultepec Aqueduct ... 195
Chari ... 153, 154, 155
Charleroi ... 111
Cheile Nerei-Beusnita ... 248
Chek Lap Kok ... 186, 187
Chekanovsk Ridge ... 156
Chengdu ... 122
Cherrapunji ... 58
Chester ... 184
Chicago ... 56, 68, 134
Chiemsee ... 131
Chiese ... 138
Chile ... 58, 137, 163
Chile Basin ... 56
Chile Rise ... 56
Chilesdo Dam ... 192
Chilia branch ... 105
Chilia Channel ... 109
Chimborazo ... 56, 58
China ... 9, 121, 122-123, 124, 126-127, 129, 142, 186, 208, 215, 262, 265, 266, 267, 270, 271, 272
Chindo ... 264, 265
Chin-Do ... 264, 265
Chittagong ... 122
Chobe ... 239
Ch'ŏngjin ... 262
Chongming Dao ... 123
Chongqing ... 123
Chott Melrhir ... 210, 211
Chott Merouane ... 210, 211
Chu ... 142
Chukchi Sea ... 56, 168, 172, 260
Cienfuegos ... 230
Ciudad del Este ... 254, 255
Ciudad Ojeda ... 256, 257
Clarion Fracture Zone ... 56
Clarksdale ... 96
Cleveland ... 96, 134
Clipperton Fracture Zone ... 56
Cluj-Napoca ... 107, 248
Coast Mountains ... 56
Coatzacoalcos ... 230
Colmar ... 110
Cologne ... 28, 110, 111, 167
Colombare ... 138, 139
Colombia ... 257, 271
Colorado (federal state) ... 90
Colorado (river) ... 55, 58, 72, 74, 76, 89, 90, 91, 230, 254
Colorado Plateau ... 89, 254
Colorado River Aqueduct ... 91
Colorines Dam ... 192
Colubac ... 248, 249
Comoros ... 36, 281
Cona ... 126
Congo ... 57, 59, 72, 118, 119
Congo Basin ... 57, 63, 118-119, 155
Conneaut/Ashtabula ... 134
Connecticut ... 134-135
Connors Range ... 251
Consata ... 136
Constanța ... 107
Constantine ... 210
Convent ... 230
Cook Ice Shelf ... 176, 179
Cooper Creek ... 151, 151
Cooperation Sea ... 176
Copacabana ... 136
Copenhagen ... 77
Coral Sea ... 57, 151, 168, 250, 251
Cordillera de Médrida ... 257
Cordillera Occidental ... 137
Cordillera Oriental ... 137
Córdoba ... 236
Coro ... 257
Corpus Christi ... 230
Cosmonaut Sea ... 176
Côte d'Ivoire ... 36
Côte Ste. Catherine Lock ... 134
Couesnon estuary ... 166
Covington ... 279
Cozia ... 248
Craiova ... 248
Crater Lake ... 131
Croatia ... 106
Csenger ... 248, 249
Csongrad ... 248, 249
Cuba ... 230, 246, 278
Cúcuta ... 257
Cumberland Islands ... 250, 251
Curtis Island ... 251
Cutzamala ... 192, 193, 195
Cuxhaven ... 87, 111, 276
Cyprus ... 36
Czech Republic ... 106, 270, 276
Czechoslovakia ... 55, 107

D

Da Xue Shan ... 122
Daba Shan ... 124-125
Dacca ... 122, 127, 201, 202, 203
Dafeng ... 188
Dakoank ... 281
Daljiayao ... 188, 189
Dallas ... 278
Damietta branch ... 115
Danube ... 57, 59, 72, 74, 76, 105, 106, 107, 108, 109, 248, 249, 270, 277
Danube Delta ... 105, 108, 109
Daqiao ... 188
Dar'ā ... 243
Darling ... 220, 221
Darling Range ... 223
Darmstadt ... 28, 110
David Glacier ... 179
Davis Sea ... 176
Davis Strait ... 56, 172, 260
Daxlanden ... 111
Dead Sea ... 241, 242, 243
Debrecen ... 248
Deccan ... 57, 280
Deer Park ... 230
Delaware (federal state) ... 184, 185
Delaware (river) ... 184
Delaware Bay ... 184
Delft ... 111, 259
Delhi ... 57, 68, 77
Democratic Republic of Congo ... 36, 59, 76, 115, 118, 119, 148
Demra ... 202, 203
Denman Glacier ... 179
Denmark ... 167
Denmark Strait ... 56, 172
Denpasar ... 11
Des Allemands ... 279
Desenzano del Garda ... 138
Desierto de Altar ... 91
Detroit ... 133, 134
Detroit River ... 135
Deventer ... 111
Dhaleswari ... 201, 202, 203
Dhing ... 126
Diaka ... 218, 219
Diamantina ... 151
Dibrugarh ... 126, 127
Dietersbach ... 252, 253
Dihang ... 127
Dikson ... 260
Dimapur ... 126
Dinaric Alps ... 106
Dinslaken ... 110
Dirang ... 126
Dirty Devil ... 254
Discovery Bay ... 186
Dispur ... 126
Distrito Federal ... 194, 195
Djama ... 76
Djenné ... 218, 219
Djerdap ... 248
Djibouti ... 36, 212
Dnieper ... 59
Dniester ... 107
Dombrad ... 248, 249
Dome Angus ... 179
Dome Charlie ... 179
Dominican Republic ... 231, 278
Domogled-Valea Carnei ... 248
Don ... 59
Dongguan ... 186, 187
Dongkar ... 126
Dongtai ... 188, 189
Dongtai He ... 188
Donostia S. Sebastián ... 165, 236
Dordrecht ... 111
Dormagen ... 110
Dorsten ... 110
Douai ... 111
Douglas Creek ... 150
Douro/Duero ... 72, 236, 237
Dover ... 259
Drake Passage ... 56, 176
Drakensberg ... 57, 282
Drava ... 106
Dresden ... 276
Drina ... 106-107
Drobeta-Turnu Severin ... 107, 248
Drocea ... 248
Drossen Dam ... 253
Drygalski Ice Tongue ... 82
Dublin ... 75, 77
Duchang ... 272
Dudinka ... 260
Duisburg ... 110, 111, 167
Duluth ... 134
Dum Duma ... 127
Dumbell Island ... 250
Dumont dí Urville Sea ... 176
Dumyât ... 114, 258
Dunaj Islands ... 156
Durban ... 199, 282
Dushanbe ... 142
Düsseldorf ... 110, 111, 167
Dyersburg ... 94

E

East African Rift System ... 119, 131, 147, 243
East Bay ... 96, 97
East China Sea ... 57, 121, 123, 168
East Pacific Rise ... 56
East Siberian Sea ... 57, 168, 172, 260
Eastern Anatolian Mountains ... 235
Eastern Desert ... 114, 258
Ebenhausen ... 203
Ebro ... 236
Echuca ... 220
Ecuador ... 267
Ed Damazin ... 114
Edinburgh ... 167
Egypt ... 9, 36, 54, 74, 76, 113, 114, 115, 116, 117, 212, 215, 217, 241, 243, 258
Eindhoven ... 111
Eisenhower Lock ... 134
Eiskögele ... 252
El Bosque Dam ... 192
El Centro ... 91
El Meghaïer ... 210, 211
El Tule Dam ... 192
Elat ... 212
Elaziğ ... 234
Elbe ... 72, 87, 111, 270, 271, 276
Elizabeth ... 184, 185
Ellesmere Island ... 172, 174, 260
Ellswoth Land ... 56
Emden ... 111
Emperor Seamountain Chain ... 57
Ems ... 111
Enderby Land ... 57, 179
Enfok ... 281
England ... 259
English Channel ... 259
Enisej Gulf ... 261
Enns ... 106
Entre Rios do Oeste ... 255
Equatorial Guinea ... 36
Er Paihe ... 188, 189
Erie ... 134
Eritrea ... 36, 76, 117, 206, 207, 212
Eritrean Highlands ... 205
Escalante (city) ... 254
Escalante (river) ... 254
Esperance ... 223
Essen ... 110, 111, 167
Ethiopia ... 36, 76, 114, 115, 148, 212
Ethiopian Highlands ... 57, 63, 74, 113
Etsdorf am Kamp ... 277
Euphrates ... 9, 59, 73, 233, 234, 235
Eurasian Plate ... 145
Europe ... 27, 29, 34, 35, 37, 39, 44-45, 55, 56-57, 58-59, 71, 74, 154, 160, 161, 163, 167, 168, 172, 173, 217, 242, 258, 259, 267, 270, 271
Euskirchen ... 110
Evans Glacier ... 179
Ewigschneefeld ... 83

F

Falkland Island ... 56, 176
Faydat Qusayfan ... 226
Fels am Wagram ... 277
Fentàla ... 219
Ferleiten ... 252
Ferrol ... 245
Fès ... 210
Fiescherglacier ... 83
Filcher Ice Shelf ... 176, 178, 179
Fimbul Ice Shelf ... 176, 179
Finland ... 164
Fischer Glacier ... 179
Flinders Range ... 220
Florida ... 229, 246, 247, 278, 279
Folkestone ... 259
Forchheim ... 111
Ford Range ... 176
Foshan ... 186, 187
Fos-sur-Mer ... 244
Foundation Glacier ... 179
Fourkoulom ... 155
Foxe Basin ... 172
Foz do Iguaçu ... 254, 255
France ... 106, 110, 111, 139, 165, 166, 167, 236, 245, 259
Frankfurt am Main ... 110, 167
Frankston ... 220
Franz Josef Land ... 57
Frascati ... 28
Fredericia ... 244
Freeport ... 230
Freiburg im Breisgau ... 110
Freital ... 276
French Quarter ... 279
French Guiana ... 26, 28, 30
Friedrichshafen ... 139
Frome ... 150
Fruschnitzkees ... 252
Fuengirola ... 236
Fukuoka ... 262
Fusch a.d. Großglocknerstraße ... 252
Fuscher Ache ... 252
Fushun ... 262
Fuzhou ... 123

G

Gabčíkovo-Nagymoros ... 107
Gabon ... 36
Gaborone ... 198, 199, 282
Galapagos Islands ... 56, 168
Galați ... 107
Galicia ... 245
Gallia Cisalpina ... 139
Galveston ... 230
Gambia ... 36
Gan Jiang ... 122, 272
Ganges ... 20, 57, 59, 73, 74, 127, 201, 269
Ganges Delta ... 87, 126, 127
Garda ... 138, 139
Gardon ... 209
Garo Hills ... 127
Garonne ... 72
Garyville ... 230
Gauteng ... 197, 198, 199
Gavardo ... 138
Gaza ... 243
Gaza Strip ... 243
Gdańsk ... 244
Gedersdorf ... 277
Geelong ... 220
Gela ... 244
Gelsenkirchen ... 110
Gendersdorf ... 277
Geneva ... 77
Genova ... 106, 244
Gent ... 111
George V Land ... 48
Georgia ... 142
Georgian Bay ... 134
Georgina ... 151
Geraldton ... 223
German Bright ... 167
Germany (Federal Republic of) ... 13, 28, 58, 66, 105, 106, 108, 110, 111, 139, 153, 206, 274, 276
Getafe ... 236
Getz Ice Shelf ... 176, 179
Ghadamis ... 210
Ghana ... 36
Gibraltar ... 44, 236, 244
Gijón-Xixón ... 165, 236
Gila River ... 89
Gippsland ... 220-221
Gisr el-Mudir ... 117
Giza ... 114, 117
Gladbeck ... 110
Gladstone ... 251
Glen Canyon ... 90, 254
Glen Canyon Dam ... 254
Gobi ... 57, 63
Goch ... 110
Golaghat ... 126
Golan ... 243
Golubinje ... 248, 249
Gombe ... 148
Gomirom ... 155
Gössnitz ... 252
Göteborg ... 244
Goulburn ... 220, 221
Goundam ... 218, 219
Goyder Channel ... 150, 151
Grafenwörth ... 276, 277
Gran Chaco ... 56, 62
Granada ... 236
Grand Canal ... 189
Grand Canyon ... 89, 90, 254
Graubünden (canton) ... 111
Graz ... 106
Great Aletschfirn ... 83
Great Aletschglacier ... 83
Great Arabian Desert ... 213
Great Artesian Basin ... 57
Great Australian Bight ... 57, 223
Great Barrier Reef ... 57, 251
Great Basin ... 56
Great Bitter Lake ... 258

Great Dividing Range ... 57, 220-221
Great Eastern Erg ... 210
Great Lakes ... 56, 93, 131, 133, 134, 135, 168, 258
Great Plains ... 56, 62, 168
Great Pyramid of Cheops ... 117
Great Pyramid of Chephren ... 117
Great Rift Valley ... 243
Great Sandy Desert ... 57, 63
Great Victoria Desert ... 57, 63, 223
Great Western Erg ... 210
Greater Antilles ... 56, 229
Greater Sunda Islands ... 57
Greece ... 29, 36
Green Bay ... 134
Green River ... 89, 90
Greenland ... 14, 31, 54, 56, 62, 81, 160, 167, 172, 173, 174, 175, 179, 260
Greenland Sea ... 172, 260
Greenville ... 95
Gretna ... 279
Grevenbroich ... 110
Grimsby-Immingham ... 244
Groningen ... 167
Grootdraai Dam ... 198, 199
Großdorf ... 252
Großer Bärenkopf ... 252
Großes Wiesbachhorn ... 252
Großglockner ... 11, 47, 252, 253
Großvenediger ... 47
Grubbach ... 252, 253
Grunddorf ... 277
Grüneggfirn ... 83
Guadalajara ... 236

Guadalete 236
Guadalhorce 236
Guadalquivir 236
Guadiana 236
Guadiaro 236
Guangzhou 123, 186, 187, 267
Guanmian Shan 123
Guantánamo 230
Guatemala 230, 278
Guayana Highlands 56, 62
Guiana Basin 56
Guinea 36, 218
Guinea Basin 56-57
Guinea-Bissau 36
Guiyang 123
Gulf of Aden 36, 212
Gulf of Alaska 56, 168
Gulf of Almería 236
Gulf of Biscaya 165, 236
Gulf of Cádiz 236
Gulf of California 55, 89, 91
Gulf of Guinea 57, 218
Gulf of Maine 135
Gulf of Mexico 56, 85, 86, 93, 94, 160, 163, 168, 229, 230, 231, 246, 247, 278, 279
Gulf of Ob 129
Gulf of Oman 36
Gulf of Saint Lawrence 135
Gulf of St. Malo 166
Gulf of Suez 114, 258
Gulf of Thailand 57, 183
Gulf of Tongking 123
Gulf of Venezuela 257
Gulf of Venice 106
Gulf St. Vincent 220
Gulshan 202, 203
Gulshan Lake 202, 203
Guwahati 126
Gyeongju 77
Györ 106

H

Ha'il 227
Hadersdorf am Kamp 277
Haenam 264, 265
Hafr al-Batin 227
Hagenbach 111
Haguenau 110
Hai Phong 123
Hāil 212
Hainburg 276
Haiti 230, 278
Haixing 266
Hajo-Do 265
Halula 234
Hamburg 58, 111, 167, 276
Hamburg Wassen Sea 87
Hamilton 134
Hammerfest 164
Han River 121, 122
Hangzhou 123
Hannover 167
Hanoi 122
Hapoli 126
Harare 198, 282
Harbin 262
Haringvliet 259
Harvey 279
Harwell 28
Hasle 270
Haslewood Island 250
Hatchie 94
Havanna 230, 278
Havel 274
Hawaii 168, 169
Hawaiian Island 56, 168
Hawaiian Ridge 56
Hayman Island 250
Heard Island 176
Hebei (province) 266
Hebron 242, 243
Hefa 243
Hei Ling Chau 186
Heidenau 276
Heiligenblut 252
Helena 95
Hengduan Shan 122
Henry Mountains 254
Heroica Zitácuaro 192
Hervey Bay 251
Hidalgo 194, 195
High Rhine 111
Highlands of Lesotho 198
Highveld 197, 198, 199
Hilden 110
Hilvan 234
Himalaya 57, 63, 126
Hindu Kush 57, 142, 143
Hinterrhein 111
Hiroshima 262
Hirzbach 252, 253
Hoggar 57
Hohe Tauern 252, 253
Hoher Tenn 252
Hokkaidō 262
Holguín 230
Hollik-Kenyon-Plateau 176
Honduras 230, 271
Hong Kong 57, 68, 123, 186, 187
Hong Kong Island 187
Hong Kong-Macau-Zhuhai bridge 186
Hongze-Hu 123
Honshū 262
Hook Island 250
Hook Reef 250, 251
Hoover Dam 89, 91
Horseshoe Falls 135
Hortobágy 248
Houston 230, 278
Hu Men 187
Huai 271
Huanghua 266
Huangpu 186, 187
Hubei 121
Hudson Bay 56, 168
Hudson River 134, 184, 185
Hudson Strait 172
Huelva 236, 244
Huenque 136
Hunan Basin 123
Hunedoara 248
Hungary 106-107, 248, 249

I

Iberian Peninsula 237
Ibroum 155
Iceland 56, 160, 260
Idro 138
Igarka 260
Iguaçu/Iguazú (river) 255
Iguaçu/Iguazú-Falls 255
Ilava 136
Ile 142
Île de Ré 165
Île d'Oléron 165
Île Esumba 118
Île M'Bamou 118
Îles de Kabongo 118
Ilha da Trinidade 101
Ilha de Marajo 101
Ilha Tupinambarana 102
Ilısu Dam 235
Illinois (federal state) 134
Illinois (river) 134
Ilse of Man 30
Imbachhorn 252
In Salah 58, 210
India 58, 75, 122, 126, 142, 163, 207, 258, 269, 272, 281
Indian Ocean 31, 36, 55, 57, 151, 159, 162, 163, 168, 176, 177, 178, 179, 197, 198, 220, 258, 270, 271, 272, 280, 281, 282
Indiana (federal state) 134
Indian-Antarctic Basin 57
Indonesia 267, 271, 281
Indus 59, 73, 75, 142
Inga 119
Inn 106
Inner Niger Delta 218, 219
Innsbruck 58, 106, 139
Iowa 134
Iran 36, 142, 208, 209, 212, 235
Iraq 36, 212, 233, 235
Irbid 243
Irish Sea 30
Irkutsk 144, 145
Iron Gate I 107, 248, 249
Iroquois Lock 134
Irrawaddy 122
Irtysh 128, 129, 143
Isar 106
Ishim 128
Isla Amantani 136
Isla Montague 91
Isla Taquile 136
Israel 75, 212, 241, 242, 243
Istanbul 57, 68, 77, 244
Istria 106
Itacoatiara 101
Itaipu Reservoir 254, 255
Itaipulândia 255
Italy 11, 28, 36, 58, 106, 139, 210, 211, 271
Itanagar 126
Itaquyry 255
Ituri 148
Ixtapan del Oro Dam 192
Izmayil 109
Izmir 244
Iztaccíhuatl 191

J

Jacksonville 230
Jacup 222
Jaén 236
Jakarta 57, 68
Jal Ayar 226
Jal Az Zarqa 226
Jamaica 230, 278
James Bay 134
Jamuna 127
Japan 159, 168, 169, 262, 263, 267, 271, 272
Japan Trench 57
Jaya 57, 59, 168
Jerez de la Frontera 236
Jerf El Ahmar 234
Jericho 242, 243
Jersey City 184, 185
Jervis Bay Territory 221
Jialing Jiang 122
Jiangmen 186, 187
Jiangsu Province 189
Jiao Men 187
Jiddah 212
Jilikin Lakes 222
Jinbiao 187
Jingzhou 123
Jiu 107
Jiujiang 85
Jiulong (Kowloon) 187
Jīzān 212
Johannesburg 54, 57, 68, 75, 77, 197, 198, 199, 282
Johannisberg 252
Joinville Island 176
Jordan (country) 36, 75, 212, 235, 241, 242, 243
Jordan (river) 242, 243
Jordan Valley 243
Jorhat 126
Juba 114
Júcar 236
Juganskaja Ob 129
Juliaca 136
Jungfraufirn 83
Jungfraufirn 83

K

Kabul 142
Käferbach 252, 253
Kafrul 202, 203
Kagera 75, 147, 148
Kâhta 234
Kaiga 155
Kaiparowits Plateau 254
Kaiser Wilhelm II Land 179
Kaiserslautern 110
Kajrakum Dam 142
Kalahari 57, 63, 86, 238, 282
Kalaigaon 126
Kalgoorlie-Boulder 223
Kalni 126
Kalserbach 252
Kalundborg 244
Kalutara 273
Kalya 242
Kamchatka Peninsula 57, 168, 260
Kamen-na-Obi Reservoir 129
Kamp 277
Kamp Lintfort 110
Kamp Valley 277
Kampala 115, 148
Kane Basin 174
Kangaru Island 220
Kaohsiung 123
Kaprun 252, 253
Kapruner Ache 252, 253
Kara Darya 141, 142
Kara Sea 57, 128, 129, 145, 172, 260, 261
Karachi 57, 68
Karakaya Baraji 234
Karakaya Dam 234
Karakum 142
Karakum Canal 141
Karakoram Range 142
Karasu 233, 235
Karémirom 155
Karkamis Dam 234
Karlingerkees 252
Karlsruhe 110, 111
Karpatskiy 248
Kasai 118
Kasane 239
Kassala 212
Katanga Plateau 57
Katanning 223
Katima Mulilo 239
Katse Dam 198, 199
Katun 129
Kawasaki 262
Kazakh Steppe 57, 63
Kazakhstan 129, 142
Keban Baraji 234, 235
Keban Dam 234, 235
Kehl 110
Kelheim 108
Kelimyar 156
Kempen 110
Kendu Bay 149
Kenner 279
Kennett 94
Kenya 36, 58, 76, 115, 147, 148, 149
Kerguelen Islands 57, 176
Kerguelen Plateau 57
Kermadec Trench 56
Kevelaer 110
Khafr ash Shaykh 114
Khanty-Mansiysk 129
Khao Lak 272
Kharaulakhsk Mountains 156
Khartoum 54, 113, 114, 115
Khatanga 260
Khilgaon 202, 203
Kibali 148
Kibo 148
Kienstock 276
Kigali 115, 148
Kigoma 148
Kika 155
Kilimanjaro 57, 59, 148
Kiliya 109
Kimberley 199
Kimpoko 118
King Abdallah Canal (East Ghor Canal) 243
King Fahad Dam (Bishah Dam) 213
Kingston (Jamaica) 230, 278
Kinshasa 57, 68, 118, 119
Kintélé 118
Kirchberg am Wagram 277
Kirin 262
Kisangani 119
Kishinev 107
Kisian 149
Kiskore 248, 249
Kiskunsági 248
Kisumu 115, 148, 149
Kita-Kyūshū 262
Kitzsteinhorn 252
Klaipeda 244
Klammsee Reservoir 252, 253
Knielingen 111
Knielinger See 111
Knud Rasmussen Land 174
Ko Phuket 280
Kobe 262
Koblenz 110
Ködnitz 252
Kokaral Dam 143
Kola Peninsula 161
Kolyma 59
Kondul Island 281
Königswinter 110
Korea Strait 262
Kos 77
Kosciusko 57, 59
Kourou 28
Kousséri 153
Kout Kou 155
Kovancilar 234
Kowloon 186, 187
Koyna 272
Kraków 107
Krefeld 110, 111
Krems (river) 277
Krems a.d. Donau (city) 277
Krkonoše Mountains 276
Kroonstad 199
Krotz Springs 230
Krugersdorp 199
Kuala Lumpur 77
Kuba Bay 156
Kuba-Artyra Island 156
Kufra Basin 225
Kunder 222
Kunlun Shan 57, 122
Kunming 122
Kurbulik 144
Kuril-Kamchatka Trench 57
Kuta Raja 280
Kuwait (city) 212
Kuwait (country) 13, 36, 212, 235
Kwando 238
Kyoto 77
Kyōto 262
Kyrgyzstan 137, 141, 142
Kystyk Plateau 156
Kyūshū 262
Kyzylkum 142

L

L'viv 107
La Paz 136
La Plata 87
La Rochelle 165
La Roche-sur-Yon 165
Labrador Basin 56
Labrador Peninsula 56
Labrador Sea 172
Lac Débo 218, 219
Lac Fagiubine 218, 219
Lac Korientzé 218, 219
Lac Oro 218, 219
Lac Télé 218, 219
Laccadive Sea 273
Lafayette 230
Lafia 155
Lagash 74
Lago d' Idro 138
Lago d' Iseo 139
Lago di Ledro 138
Lago do Como 139
Lago Huinyaimarca 136
Lago Maggiore 139
Lagos 57, 68
Lahn 110
Lahr/Schwarzwald 110
Lake Albert (Mobuto-Sese-Seko Lake) 113, 115, 147, 148
Lake Alexandrina 220
Lake Aral 54, 55, 57, 73, 128, 131, 141, 142, 143, 218
Lake Assad/Buhairat al-Asad 233, 234, 235
Lake Baikal 57, 131, 133, 144, 145, 260
Lake Balkhash 128, 142
Lake Biddy (city) 222
Lake Canacari 101
Lake Chad 54, 59, 72, 73, 75, 153, 154, 155
Lake Charles (city) 230
Lake Chinocup 222
Lake Constance 106, 111, 131, 139
Lake Corangamite 220
Lake des Allemands 279
Lake Dorothy 222
Lake Edward 115, 147, 148
Lake Erie 133, 134, 135
Lake Eyre 150, 151
Lake Florence 150
Lake Frome 151
Lake Garda 106, 138, 139
Lake Grace (city) 222
Lake Grace (lake) 222
Lake Hills 222
Lake Hongze 189
Lake Huron 133, 134
Lake Itasca 93
Lake Kalamurra 150
Lake Kariba 282
Lake Kittakittaooloo 150
Lake Kivu 148
Lake Koolkootinnie 150
Lake Kyoga 113, 115
Lake Lefroy 223
Lake Lockhart 222
Lake Magenta 222
Lake Maracaibo 137, 256, 257
Lake Marituba 101
Lake Maurepas 279
Lake Mead 89, 90, 91
Lake Michigan 133, 134, 135
Lake Mulapula 150
Lake Mweru 118, 119
Lake Nakuru 131
Lake Nasser (Reservoir) 54, 113*ff.*
Lake Neusiedl 108
Lake Ngami 238
Lake Nipigon 134
Lake Nuba 114
Lake Ontario 133, 134, 135
Lake Pinatubo 131

Lake Pingarnup 222
Lake Pingrup 222
Lake Pontchartrain 279
Lake Poolowanna 151
Lake Poopó 137
Lake Powell 89, 90, 254
Lake Razazah 235
Lake Rei 100
Lake Salvador 279
Lake Sarykamysh 142, 143
Lake St. Clair 135
Lake Superior 133, 134, 135
Lake Taihu 189, 271
Lake Tana 113
Lake Tanganyika 118, 119, 131, 148
Lake Tharthar 235
Lake Titicaca 72, 136, 137, 257
Lake Torrens 220
Lake Tyrell 220
Lake Urmia 235
Lake Van 131, 235
Lake Victoria 57, 113, 115, 118, 131, 147, 148, 149
Lake Yalpuh 109
Lakhya 202, 203
L'Alzen 209
Lambert Glacier 179
Landau i.d. Pfalz 110
Langenlois 277
Lantau Island 186, 187
Laos 76, 77, 122
Laplace 279
Lappland 161, 172
Laptev Sea 57, 156, 168, 172, 260
Lapus 248, 249
Larsen Ice Shelf 176, 179
Las Vegas 90, 91
Latin America 54, 74, 77, 191
Lazarev Sea 176
Le Havre 167, 244
Le Porésur Vie 165
Lebanon 36
Lech 106, 274
Leeds 167
Leiden 111
Leipzig 276
Leiterbach 252, 253
Leitha 108
Leitha Mountains 108
Lek 111
Lena 57, 59, 129, 156, 260
Lena Delta 157
Lena-Angara-Plateau 144
Lens 111
León 236
Léré 218, 219
Lerma 192
Les Sables-d'Olonne 165
Lesotho 36, 198, 199, 282, 283
Leverkusen 110
Lhasa 122
Lhasa He 126
Li River 272
Liangduo 188
Liberia 36
Lybia 13, 36, 54, 70, 210, 211, 225
Liebenbergs Vlei 198, 199
Liechtenstein 106, 139
Liege 111
Ligurian Sea 106
Lille 111
Lilongwe 198
Lima (city) 56, 68
Lima (river) 236
Limberg Dam 253
Limburg a. d. Lahn 110
Limpopo 198, 199, 239, 282
Lincoln Sea 172, 260
Lindeman Group 250
Lindi 118
Linwu 187
Linyanti 238
Linz 106
Lippe 110
Lisan Peninsula 242
Lisbon 236, 244
Little Italy 222
Little River 94
Liuzhuang 188
Livingstone 282
Livingstone Falls 119
Livorno 244
Ljamain 128
Ljantor 128
Ljubljana 106
Llanos 56
Lockwitzbach 276
Logone 153, 154
Logroño 236
London 56, 68, 167
Long Beach 184
Long Island 185
Long Island Sound 185
Longxue Dao 187
Lonya 248, 249
Lorain 134
Los Angeles 56, 68, 90, 168
Louisiana 97, 229, 231, 246, 247, 271, 278
Lower Austria 277
Lower Guinea region 119
Lower New York Bay 185
Lower Rhine 111
Lowland of Surgut 128-129
Lualaba 118, 119
Ludwigshafen am Rhein 110
Lugo 245
Luhit 126, 127
Lusaka 198
Lützow-Hol-Bucht 176
Luxor 114
Luzern 139
Lysekil 244

M

Maas Delta 111, 259
Mabog 234
Mabopane 199
Macapá 101
Macau 186, 187
Machar Marches 114
Mackay 251
Mackenzie 56, 58
MacKenzie Bay 176
Macquarie Ridge 57
Madagascar 36, 57, 281
Maden 234
Madi Kimerom 155
Madigil 155
Madīnat ath Thawrah 234
Madrid 56, 68, 236, 237
Maemul-Sudo 265
Magadan 260
Magdeburg 167, 276
Magwegqana 238
Maiduguri 154
Main 86, 110, 111
Main-Danube Canal 108
Maine 135
Mainling 127
Mainz 110
Majia He 266
Makgadikgadi 282
Makkah 212
Málaga 210, 236
Malakal 114
Malaspina Glacier 81, 82
Malataya 234
Malatsi Dam 199
Malawi 36, 198
Malay Peninsula 280
Malcesine 138
Malebo Pool 118, 119
Maledives 167, 280, 281
Mali 36, 76, 210, 211, 218, 219
Malibamat'so 198
Mallee Hill 222
Malta 210, 211
Maluti Mountains 198, 199
Mamelodi 199
Manantali 76
Manaus 16, 85, 99, 100, 102
Manchal Island 281
Manchuria 57, 63, 168, 262
Mandalay 122
Mandeville 279
Manhatten (island) 175, 185
Manila 68
Manitoba 134
Mannheim 77, 110
Mantova 139
Manzini 199
Maputo 198, 199, 282
Mar del Plata 77
Maracaibo 256, 257
Marañón 99, 100
Marble Canyon 254
Margaret 150
Margaritze Dam 253
Margaritze Reservoir 252, 253
Mariana Trench 57
Mariani 126
Marie Byrd Land 56
Markala Dam 219
Marl 110
Marne-Rhine Canal 110
Maro-Hae 264, 265
Maros 107, 248
Marrakesh 77
Marree 151
Marrero 279
Marseille 77, 244
Martil 44
Mascarene Basin 57
Maseru 198, 199, 282
Mashai Dam 198, 199
Massachusetts 134-135
Matadi 119
Matamoros 230
Matelândia 255
Matsoku Dam 199
Maun 238, 239
Mauretania 36, 54, 76, 218, 219
Mauritius 36
Mautern a.d. Donau 277
Maximiliansau 111
Mazagão 101
Mbabane 198, 199, 282
Mbandaka 119
McMurdo-Sund 82, 176
Mechelen 111
Meckenheim 110
Medianeira 255
Mediterranean (Sea) 36, 53, 57, 87, 113, 114, 115, 117, 161, 210, 211, 225, 236, 243, 258, 259
Medok 127
Meekatharra 223
Meghna 126, 127, 201, 203
Mekong 57, 59, 73, 74, 76, 77, 122
Melanesia 57, 168
Melbourne 220
Melilla 236
Mellor Glacier 179
Mělník 270
Memphis 95, 278
Mendocino Fracture Zone 56
Mentawai Islands Regency 281
Meraux 231
Mérida 230, 257
Merilup 222
Merowe Reservoir 114
Merowedam 114, 115
Merredin 223
Mertz Glacier 179
Mesopotamia 9, 55, 74, 76, 235
Metairie 279
Metropolitan Area of Valley of Mexico 191
Mettmann 110
Meuse/Maas (incl. Oude Maas) 72, 110, 111, 259
Mexicali 91
Mexico (country) 76, 90, 91, 162, 191, 192, 230, 278
México (federal state) 194, 195
Mexico City 56, 68, 77, 168, 191, 192, 193, 194, 195, 278
Miami 230, 278
Michigan (federal state) 134
Micronesia 57, 168
Mid-Atlantic Ridge 56
Middle American Trench 56
Middle Rhine 111
Mid-Indian Basin 57
Mid-Indian Ridge 57
Midrad 199
Milano 106, 139
Milford Haven 244
Milwaukee 134
Minnesota 93, 134
Miño/Minho 236
Mira 236
Mirpur 202, 203
Miskolc 248
Missal 255
Mississippi (federal state) 96, 271
Mississippi (river) 56, 58, 72, 86, 89, 92, 93, 94, 95, 96, 97, 134, 229, 230, 279
Mississippi-(River-)Delta 86, 92, 93, 96, 97, 229, 230, 231, 246, 247
Missouri (federal state) 134
Missouri (river) 95
Mittelaletschglacier 83
Mittersill 47
Mituma Mountains 119
Moama 220
Mobile 230, 231
Moers 110
Mohale Dam 198, 199
Mohammadpur 202, 203
Mokp'o 265
Moldova 107
Möll 252
Molligoda 273
Mönchengladbach 110, 111
Mondego 236
Mongar 126
Mongolia 129, 145
Mongstad 244
Monroe 134
Mons 111
Mont de Marsan 165
Montabaur 110
Monte Baldo 138
Monte Pipalo 139
Monterrey 278
Montichiari 138
Montreal 134, 135
Mont-Saint-Michel 166
Mooroopna 220
Mooser Dam 253
Mopti 218, 219
Morava (Czech Republic/Slovakia/Austria) 106, 107, 108
Morava (Serbia) 248, 249
Morocco 36, 44, 206, 207, 210, 211, 236
Moscow 57, 68, 260
Moscow University Ice Shelf 176
Mosel 110, 111
Móstoles 236
Mount Boutmezguida 207
Mount Cook 57, 59
Mount Elbrus 57, 59
Mount Elgon 148
Mount Erebus 82
Mount Everest 57, 59
Mount Kailash 126
Mount Kenya 57, 59, 148
Mount Lofty Range 220, 221
Mount Minto 176
Mount Sheridan 222
Mount Sidley 176
Mozambique 36, 198, 199, 282, 283
Mozambique Basin 57
Mozambique Channel 57
Mt. McKinley 56, 58, 168
Muela Reservoir 198
Mugga 244
Müglitz 276
Mühlbach 252, 253
Mühlburg 111
Mühlheim a. d. Ruhr 110
Mühlviertel 277
Mui Wo 186
Mulhouse 110, 139
Mumbai 57, 68
Munich 106, 206
Mur 106
Murat 233, 235
Muray 220, 221
Murmansk 260, 261
Murray Fracture Zone 56
Myanmar 122, 271
Mys Shmidta 260

N

Naantali 244
Nāblus 243
Nagoya 262
Nahr al-Balīh 234
Nahr az Zarqā' 243
Nairobi 58, 68, 148
Najrān 212
Najran Dam 213
Nalón 236
Namib 57, 63,
Namibia 36, 37, 59, 198, 238, 239, 282
Namjagbarwa 127
Namur 111
Nanchang 123, 272
Nandagang Shuiku 266
Nanjing 85, 123
Nanning 123
Nansa 236
Nansha 187
Nanshentsao 188
Nantong 123
Nanyang 188
Naogaon 202, 203
Napier Mountains 176
Nares Strait 174
Narrogin 223
Naryn River 141, 142, 143
Nassau 230, 231
Nauta 99
Navajo Mountain 254
Navia 236
N'Djamena 59, 154
Neales 150
Neckar 86, 111
Neendaling 222
Neftejugansk 128
Negev 243
Netanya 243
Netherlands 28, 110, 111, 167, 259, 269
Neuburg am Rhein 111
Neuburgweier 111
Neuss 110
Neustift a.d. Donau 277
Neuwied 110
Nevada 89, 90
Nevado del Ruiz 271
New Brunswick 135
New England Seamounts 56
New Foundland and Labrador (federal state) 135
New Hampshire 135
New Jersey 134, 184, 185
New Mexico 90
New Orleans 93, 94, 230, 231, 271, 278, 279
New Providence Island 231
New Siberian Islands 172
New South Wales 220, 221
New York (city) 56, 68, 184, 185
New York (federal state) 134, 184, 185
New Zealand 57, 58, 66
Newark 184, 185
Newark Bay 1845
Newcastle (Australia) 221
Newdegate 222
Newfoundland 56
Newfoundland Basin 56
Ngalerom 155
Nhabe 238
Niagara Escarpment 135
Niagara Falls 134, 135
Niagara River 134, 135
Niagara Tunnel 134
Nicobar Island 280, 281
Nieuwe Maas 259
Nieuwe Waterweg 259
Niger (river) 56, 59, 72, 74, 75, 218, 219
Niger (country) 36, 153, 154, 155
Nigeria 36, 66, 153, 154, 155, 218
Nijmegen 111
Nile Basin 76
Nile 39, 54, 55, 57, 59, 72, 74, 76, 113, 114, 115, 116, 117
Nile Delta 87, 113, 114, 115, 117
Nile Valley 115
Nîmes 209
Ninety East Ridge 57
Nohwa-Do 265
Nongchang 187
Norco 230
Nordkap 164
Nordvik 260
Nordwijk 28
Noril'sk 260
Normanby Range 251
North Africa 211, 227
North America 31, 39, 55, 56, 58, 71, 89, 160, 162, 163, 168, 172, 173, 185, 271
North American Basin 56, 160
North Aral Sea 54, 143
North Atlantic 133, 264
North Burngup 222
North China Plain 123
North Korea 262, 271
North Lakhimpur 126
North Pacific 168, 169
North Pacific Gyre 168
North Pass 96, 97
North Sea 57, 87, 108, 111, 167, 244, 259, 260, 270, 276
Northam 223
Northeast Pacific Basin 56
Northwest Pacific Basin 57
Norway 54, 58, 164, 167
Norwegian Sea 56-57, 164, 172, 260
Nova Scotia (federal state) 135
Novara 139
Novaya Zemlya 57, 172, 260
Novi Sad 248, 249
Novosibirsk Reservoir 129
Nqugha 238
Ntoahae Dam 189, 199
Nuba Mountains 114

Nubia 55
Nubian Desert 114
Nullarbor Plain 223
Nürnberg 106
Nyeboe Land 174
Nyingchi 127
Nyíregynáza 248
Nynäshamm 244

O

Ob 57, 59, 73, 128-129, 143, 260
Oberaletschglacier 83
Oberhausen 110
Odense 167
Oder 72, 276
Odessa 107
Offenbach 110
Offenburg 110
Ogdensburg 134
Ohio 134
Okavango 72, 198, 238, 239, 282
Okavango Delta 86, 218, 238, 239, 282
Olenek 156
Olenek Bay 156
Olenek branch 156
Olkhon 144
Olt 106, 107, 248
Om el Tieur 210, 211
Oman 19, 36
Omdurman 114
Ontario 134
Ontario Hydropower Reservoir 134
Oostende 111
Oradea 248
Oran 210
Orange(-revier) 59, 72, 198, 199, 282
Oria 236
Orinoco 58
Orlando 77
Ōsaka 262
Oshawa 134
Ostrava 106
Oswego 134
Ottawa 134
Ötztal Alps 139
Ouargla 210
Ourense 236
Ouro-Guinndé 219
Oviedo 165, 236
Owen Falls Dam 149

P

Pacific Ocean 12, 31, 39, 53, 54, 56-57, 62-63, 159, 162, 163, 168, 169, 173, 176, 177, 178, 179, 230, 258, 260, 262
Padma 127, 201, 203
Pagai-Islands 281
Page 254
Pakistan 36, 75, 142, 271
Palermo 58
Pallabi 202, 203
Palm Springs 91
Pamir 142, 143
Pampas 56, 62
Pamplona (Iruña) 165, 236
Panama City 231
Pančevo 248, 249
Pangani 148
Pangin 127
Panjiapie 188
Paraguay 254, 255
Paran Autaz Mirim 100
Paraná 56, 58, 74, 87, 254, 255
Parana de Ramos 102
Paraná Ibicuy 87
Pareng 127
Parintins 85, 102
Paris 28, 57, 68, 77
Parry Islands 172
Pasadena 230
Pascagoula 231
Passau 276
Pasterze 252, 253
Patagonia 56, 167, 176
Paterson 184
Patkai Mountains 122, 126-127
Pato Bragado 255
Pavia 139
Peake 150
Pearl River Delta 186, 187
Pengtoushan 215
Peninsula de Copacabana 136
Peninsula de la Guajira 257
Peninsula Gydan 260
Peninsula Yamal 260, 261
Pennine Alps 139
Pennsylvania 134
Pensacola 231
Percy Isles 251
Persia 217
Persian Gulf 36, 55, 57, 212, 213, 233, 235
Perth 223
Peru 99, 136, 137, 162, 163
Peru Basin 56
Peru Trench 56
Peschiera del Garda 138
Petermann Glacier 174, 175
Pewek 260
Pfälzerwald 110
Philadelphia 184
Philippine Basin 57
Philippine Trench 57
Philippines 57, 168, 217, 271, 274f.
Piacenza 139
Piertermaritzburg 199
Pigŭm-Do 265
Pim 128
Pine Island Bay 178
Pine Island Glacier 179
Pingaring 222
Pingrup 222, 223
Pirmasens 110
Pitesti 248
Pittsburgh 77
Pjandz 141, 142
Plateau du Tademaït 210
Pleven 248
Plzeň 106, 276
Po 106, 139
Po Plain 139
Pochefstroom 199
Pogil-Do 265
Point Noire 59
Pojkovskij 128
Poland 55, 106-107, 276
Polar-Plateau 176
Polynesia 56
Ponevedra 245
Popa Falls 239
Popocatépetl 56, 58, 168, 191
Port Allen 230
Port Arthur 230
Port Elizabeth 282
Port Fouâd 258
Port Fourchon 97
Port Phillip Bay 220
Port Said 114, 258
Port Sudan 212
Portage (Burns Harbor) 134
Port-Au-Prince 278
Port-Cartier 135
Portel 101
Porto 77, 236, 245
Porto Torres 244
Portugal 11, 36, 236, 237, 245
Porvoo 244
Poyang 272
Poyang Hu 270, 272
Poza Rica 230
Prague 276
Pretoria 57, 68, 198, 199, 282
Primorsk 244
Prince Charles Mountains 176
Princess Elizabeth Land 57
Provideniya 260
Prudhoe Bay 260
Prut 106, 107
Prydz Bay 176
Pucara 136
Puerto Iguazú 255
Pungarancho 192
Puno 136, 137
Punto Fijo 257
Pusan 262
P'yŏsngyang 262
Pyramid of Chaba 117
Pyramid of Djedkare 117
Pyramid of Djoser 117
Pyramid of Merenre I. 117
Pyramid of Mykerinos 117
Pyramid of Neferirkare 117
Pyramid of Nuiserre 117
Pyramid of Pepi I. 117
Pyramid of Sahure 117
Pyramid of Teti 117
Pyramid of Unas 117
Pyramid of Userkaf 117

Q

Qa al Milh 226
Qin Ling 123
Qinā 114
Qionglai Shan 122
Quchan 208
Québec (city) 135
Québec (federal state) 134-135
Queen Elisabeth Islands 56, 172
Queen Maud Land 56-57, 176, 179
Queen Maud Mountains 176
Queensland 251

R

Rabak 114
Radebeul 276
Rakamaz 249
Rakka 234
Ram 248, 249
Ramallah 242, 243
Râmnicu Vâlcea 248
Ramstein 110
Rangia 126
Raritan Bay 185
Rastatt 110
Rattingen 110
Ravenna 244
Ravensburg 139
Razim 109
Reading 184
Recovery Glacier 179
Red Basin 122-123
Red Sea 36, 55, 57, 115, 205, 206, 212, 213, 243, 258, 259
Red Sea-Dead Sea Conduit 243
Regensburg 108
Reichenau 111
Remagen 110
Remoulins 209
Remscheid 110
Republic of Congo 36, 119
Repulse Bay 250, 251
Reservoir Mooserboden 252, 253
Reservoir Wasserfallboden 252, 253
Reshten-ye Alborz 142
Resolute 260
Retezat 248
Rhaetian Alps 139
Rhaetian Glacier 139
Rheinhafen 111
Rheinstetten 111
Rhine 72, 74, 86, 106, 108, 110, 111, 139, 259
Rhine Delta 111
Rhine Falls 111
Rhine-Main 111
Rhine-Main-Danube Canal 108, 111, 259
Rhine-Meuse Delta 111
Rhine-Ruhr 111
Rhône 139, 209
Rhône Delta 87
Riiser Larsen Ice Shelf 176
Riiser-Larsen-Peninsula 176
Rijeka 106, 244
Rimini 106
Rio de Janeiro 56, 68, 75, 77
Rio de la Plata 74, 87
Rio Grande 56, 58, 72, 230
Rio Grande Plateau 56
Rio Juruá 102, 103
Rio Madeira 100, 101
Rio Negro (Black River) 16, 99, 100
Rio Preta da Eva 100
Rio Solimões (Solimões) 16, 99, 100
Rio Tocantins 101
Rio Xingu 100, 101
Ríohacha 257
Riva del Garda 138
Rivoli Veronese 138, 139
Riyadh 212
Robeson Channel 174
Rochefort 165
Rockefeller Plateau 176
Rockhampton 251
Rocky Mountains 56, 62, 89, 93, 168
Rodna 248
Romania 105, 107, 248, 249
Rome 42, 77, 209
Rondônia 102, 103
Ronne Bay 176
Ronne Ice Shelf 56, 176, 178, 179
Roosevelt Island 176
Rosarito Reservoir 237
Rosetta branch 115
Ross Ice Shelf 82, 176, 178, 179
Ross Sea 82, 176
Rostock 244
Rotten 83
Rotterdam 111, 167, 244, 259
Roubaix 111
Roudnice nad Labem 270
Rovereto 138
Rub'Al Khali 18
Ruhr 110, 111
Ruhr Valley 111
Ruhrort district of Duisburg 111
Rundu 239
Rüsselsheim 110
Russia/Russian Federation 129, 142, 173, 262
Rustenburg 199
Rutford Glacier 179
Rwanda 36, 76, 115, 148

S

Sado 236
Sahara 56-57, 62,63, 153, 210, 211, 218, 225
Saharian Atlas 210
Sahel 54, 56-57, 62-63, 153, 211, 218, 219
Saidabad 203
Saint Elias Mountains 82
Saint Lawrence 58, 74, 135
Saint Lawrence Seaway 133, 134
Saint Rose 231
Saint-Gilles-Croix-de-Vie 165
Saint-Malo 166
Sakākah 212
Sala y Gomez Ridge 56
Salaberry-de-Valleyfield 134
Salamanca 236
Salar de Uyuni 137
Salechard 260
Saló 138
Salton Sea 89, 90, 91
Salzach 47, 106
Salzachtal 47
Salzburg 106, 276, 277
San 218, 219
San Antonio 77
San Cristóbal 257
San Diego 90, 91
San Francisco 169
San Juan 254
San Marino 106
San Roque 44
Şan'ā' 212
Sangha 118
Şanlıurfa 234
Sant' Ambrogio di Valpolicella 139
Santa Ana 257
Santa Clara 230
Santa Helena 255
Santa Rita 256
Santa Terezinha do Itaipu 255
Santander 165
Santarém 44, 102
Santiago 56, 68
Santiago de Compostela 245
Santiago de Cuba 230
Sanxia Dam (Three Gorges Dam) 124, 125
Sanzao 188
São Miguel do Iguaçu 255
São Paulo 56, 68
São Tomé and Principe 36, 70
Sapporo 262
Sarajevo 106
Saraland 231
Sargasso Sea 56
Sarnia 134
Săsar 249
Satu Mare 248
Saudi Arabia (Kingdom of Saudi Arabia) 18, 36, 49, 212, 213, 215, 225, 227, 235
Sava 106-107, 248, 270
Savannah 230
Savute 238
Sawa 155
Saxony 276
Sayan Mountains 57
Scandinavia 54, 55, 57, 63, 260
Scerencs 249
Schaffhausen 111
Schmiedinger Kees 252
Scotia Sea 56, 176
Sea of Galilee 243
Sea of Japan 57, 168, 262, 267
Sea of Ochotsk 57, 168, 260, 262
Sedom 242
Ségou 29
Segura 236
Selenga 144
Sélestat 110
Selvas 56, 62
Sendai 169
Senegal (country) 36, 76
Senegal (river) 73, 74, 75, 76
Seoul 57, 68, 168, 262
Seppeltsfield 221
Sept-Îles 135
Sequnyane 198
Serbia 107, 248, 249, 270
Serbian Carpathians 107
Seringueiras 103
Sévaré 218, 219
Severobaykal'sk 144
Sevilla 236
Seward Glacier 82
Seychelles 36, 167, 281
Sfax 210
's-Gravenhage 111, 259
Shabujbag 202, 203
Shackleton Ice Shelf 176
Shajiao 187
Shajing 187
Shaman Rock 145
Shammar 226
Shammar region 227
Shangbaomei 187
Shanghai 57, 68, 121, 123, 124, 168
Shatt al 'Arab 233, 235
Shatou 188
Sheffield 167
Sheikh Zayid Canal 116, 117
Shenyang 262
Shenzao 188
Shenzhen 186, 187
Shepparton 220
's-Hertogenbosch 111
Shikoku 262
Shilong 186, 187
Shiqiao 186, 187
Shiwei 187
Shunde 186, 187
Shyampur 202, 203
Siberia 22, 54, 128, 129, 157, 161, 172, 175, 260
Sibiu 107, 248
Sibsagar 126
Sichahe 188
Sidi Ifni 207
Sidi Zekri 207
Siegburg 110
Sierra de Perija 257
Sierra Leone 36
Sierra Nevada 56, 89, 236, 237
Sierra Leone Rise 56
Simeulue 281
Simmern (Hunsrück) 110
Simong 127
Simpson Desert 151
Sinai 114, 258
Sines 244
Sinn al Kadhdhab 114
Siret 106, 107
Sirmione 138
Siverek 234
Sivrice 234
Sizao 188
Skhirra 244
Skikda 244
Slagentangen 244
Slana 248
Slaná 248, 249
Slessor Glacier 179
Slovakia 106-107, 108, 248
Slovenia 106
Slyudyanka 144
Snowy Mountains 220, 221
Sobat River 113, 114, 115
Sobo-Sise Island 156
Sohâg 114
Sola 244
Solar Temple of Niuserre 117
Solingen 110
Somali Basin 57
Somali Peninsula 281
Somalia 36
Songhua 271
Sonnblickkees 252
Sonora Desert 89
Soo Locks 134, 135
Sorel 135
Sousse 210
South Africa 36, 39, 54, 59, 197, 198, 199, 282
South African Inland Plateau 197, 198
South America 31, 39, 53, 56, 58, 137, 160, 162, 163, 168, 176, 257
South Aral Sea 143

South Australia ...150, 151, 220, 221
South Australian Basin 57
South China Sea 57, 123, 169, 186, 187
South East Asia 162, 186, 217, 267
South East Point 220
South Korea 262, 263, 264, 265
South Orkney Islands 176
South Sandwich Islands 176
South Sandwich Trench 56
South Shetland Islands 176
South Sudan 36, 76, 113, 114, 115, 117, 148
Southeast Indian Ridge 57
Southeast Pacific Basin 56
Southeast Pass 96, 97
Southern Ocean 176, 177, 178
Southampton 244
Southwest Indian Ridge 57
Southwest Pacific Basin 56
Southwest Pass 94, 96, 97
Soviet Union 54, 55, 141
Soweto 199
Spain 28, 36, 44, 165, 210, 211, 236, 237, 244, 245
Spencer Gulf 220
Speyer 110
Spioenkop Dam 199
Split 106
Sri Lanka 57, 273, 280, 281
St. Clair River 135
St. Francis 94
St. George Branch 105, 109
St. George´s Channel 281
St. Lambert Lock 134
St. Petersburg (Russia) 57, 68, 260
St. Petersburg (USA) 230
Stanovoy Mountains 57, 168
Stara Palanka 248, 249
Starnberger See 139
Staten Island 185
Stein am Rhein 111
Sterkfontein Dam 199
Štětí 270
Still 210, 211
Stockholm 77
Straight Cliffs 254
Strait of Dover 259
Strait of Gibraltar 44, 161, 236
Strait of Magellan 176
Strasbourg 106, 110
Stub Ache 252
Stuttgart 106
Styria 277
Subansiri 126
Sub-Sahara 205
Suches 136
Sudan 36, 54, 57, 63, 76, 114, 115, 117, 137, 160, 212
Sudd 113, 114, 115
Suez 114, 258
Suez Bay 258
Sulina 109
Sulina Branch 105, 109
Sulzberger Bay 176
Sulzberger Ice Shelf 179
Sumatera 280, 281
Summom Voe 244
Sunda Trench 57
Superior 134
Surgut 128, 129
Sürüç 234
Suzhou 123
Svalbard (Spitsbergen) 57, 58, 172
Swain Reefs 251
Swaziland 36, 198, 199, 282, 283
Swenny 230
Swiss Alps 111
Switzerland 83, 106, 270
Sydney 57, 68, 221
Synevyr 248
Syrdar'ya 54, 141, 142, 143
Syria 36, 215, 233, 234, 235, 243
Szamos 248, 249
Szolnok 248, 249

T

Tabqa Dam 233, 234, 235
Tabūk 212, 227
Tacloban City 274, 275
Taegu 262
Tae-Hŭksan-Do 265
Tai Hu 123
Taipei 123
Taipingtang 188
Taiwan 123, 159
Taiwan Strait 123
Ta'izz 212
Taja/Tejo 236, 237
Tajikistan 142, 143
Taklamakan Desert 208
Tallahassee 231
Tambej 260
Tamil Nadu 280
Tampa 230
Tampico 230
Tana (river) 148
Tanger 44, 210, 236
Tangguka Shan 122
Tanţă 114
Tanzania 36, 76, 115, 147, 148, 207, 283
Tapajós 100
Târgu Mures 248
Tarifa 44
Tarim 59
Tarim Basin 57, 63, 142
Taring Rock 222
Tashkent 142
Tasman Basin 57
Tasman Sea 57, 151, 221
Tassili n' Ajjer 210
Tasso Plain 139
Tauernmoossee 252
Taunus 110
Taurus Mountains 233, 235
Tawa 155
Taymyr Peninsula 57, 172, 260
Taz 157
Tecolutla 192, 193
Teesport 244
Tehran 57, 69, 142
Tejgaon 202, 203
Tekija 248, 249
Tel Aviv 243
Tell Atlas 210
Tell Bazi 234
Tenlaa 281
Tennessee 94
Tétouan 44, 236
Texas City 230
Tezpur 126
Tezu 127
Thailand 76, 77, 183, 267, 271, 272, 281
Thaoge 238
Thar 57, 63
The Hague 77, 167
Theiß (city) 277
Thimphu 122
Three Gorges Reservoir 125
Thun 139
Thuner See 139
Thwaites Glacier 178
Tian Shan 57
Tibesti 57
Tibet 163
Tibetan Plateau 121, 122
Ticaboo 254
Tiétar 237
Tigris 9, 57, 73, 233, 234, 235
Tiksi 260
Tilburg 111
Timbalier Bay 97
Timis 248, 249
Timisoara 248
Timor Sea 57, 151, 168
Tinsukia 127
Tinto 236
Tirari Desert 151
Tishreen Dam 234, 235
Tishreen Reservoir 234
Tista 126
Tisza 106, 107, 248, 249
Tiszakeszi 248, 249
Tiszalök 248, 249
Tiszasziget 248, 249
Tiszavasvari 249
Tobol 128
Toch'o-Do 265
Togo 36
Tokaj 249
Toktogul Dam 142
Tōkyō 68, 168, 262, 263
Toledo 134
Toluca 192
Tom 128
Tonga Trench 56
Tongi Khal 202, 203
Tongshang 188
Tongyang Yunhe 188
Torrelavega 165
Torri del Benaco 139
Toronto 134
Toscolano-Maderno 138
Toshka 116
Toshka Depression 116, 117
Toshka Lakes 114, 116, 117
Totten Glacier 179
Touzao 188
Townshend Island 251
Traismauer 277
Transantarctic Mountains 56-57, 176, 178, 179
Transilvanian Alps (Carpatii Meridonali) 107
Traun 106
Trento 139
Trenton 184
Trieste 106, 244
Tripoli 210
Trois Rivières 134
Troisdorf 110
Tromegan 129
Tromsø 164
Trujillo 257
Tschardara Dam 142
Tsoelike Dam 198, 199
Tuamotu Archipelago 56, 168
Tuhai He 266
Tujamujun Dam 142
Tulcea 109
Tunceli 234
Tung Chung 186
Tunis 210
Tunisia 36, 210, 211
Tunyogmatocs 248, 249
Turag 202, 203
Turan Lowland 57, 63, 141, 142, 143
Túria 236
Turkey 36, 131, 233, 234, 235
Turkmenistan 36, 141, 142, 143
Tuxpan Dam 192

U

U.S. Snell Lock 134
Ubangi 57, 118, 119, 155
Ucayali 99, 100
Uganda 36, 76, 115, 147, 148
Ukraine 105, 107, 248
Ulan-Ude 144
Uleelheue 280
Ulla 236
Umma 74
Umtata 199
United Arab Emirates 13
United Kingdom (UK) 28, 161, 167, 197, 221, 259
United States of America 28, 54, 75, 76, 91, 95, 133, 134-135, 163, 167, 230, 254, 271
Upper New York Bay 185
Upper Rhine 111
Upper Rhine Plain 111
Upper Vallais 83
Ural (river) 142
Ural Mountains 57, 63
Uruguay 87
Usol'ye-Sibirskoye 144
Ust'-Kut 144
Utah 89, 90, 254
Utrecht 111
Uttara 202, 203
Uzbekistan 141, 142, 143
Uzès 209
Uzhhorod 248

V

Vaal 198, 199
Vaal Dam 198, 199
Vaalkop Dam 199
Vah 106
Vakhsh 141, 142
Val dei Molini 139
Valenciennes 111
Valera 257
Valkyrie Dome 179
Valladolid 236
Valle da Bravo Dam 192
Valley of Mexico 191, 192, 193, 195
Valsrivier 199
Várzeas 99
Vasarosnameny 248, 249
Vehlgast 274
Velbert 110
Venezia 106
Venezuela 257
Venice 96, 97
Venlo 110, 111
Venray 110, 111
Ventspils 244
Veracruz 230
Vereeniging 199
Verkhoyansk Mountains 57, 63, 168
Vermont 134-135
Verona 138, 139
Vetrivier 199
Victoria (Australia) 220-221
Victoria (Hongkong) 187
Victoria (USA) 230
Victoria Harbour 197
Victoria Island 56, 168, 172, 260
Victoria Land 57, 82,
Victoria-Nile 113, 147, 148
Vienna 76, 106, 108, 276, 277
Vienna Woods 108
Vierwaldstätter See 139
Vietnam 76, 77, 122, 271
Vigo 236, 245
Villa Victoria Dam 192
Villafranca di Verona 138
Villahermosa 230
Vincennes Bay 176
Vinsin Massif 176
Viseu 248
Vistula 72
Vitoria-Gasteiz 165, 236
Vladivostok 262
Vlissingen 77, 111
Vlitava 106, 270
Vobarno 138
Voges 110
Volga 57, 59, 72, 86, 105, 142, 143, 260
Volga Delta 86
Vorderrhein 111
Vouga 236
Vylkove 109
Vyzhenetskiy 248

W

Wad Medani 114
Wadduwa 273
Wādī al Jayb 242, 243
Wādī al Mawjib 242, 243
Wadi Bīshah 213
Wadi el Milk 115
Wadi Halfa 114
Wadi Kufra 225
Wadi Sidr 226
Wadi Toshka 117
Waldviertel 277
Walvis Ridge 56-57
Waranga Reservoir 220
Warburton Creek 150, 151
Warburton Grove 150, 151
Warginburra Peninsula 251
Warriners Creek 150
Washington Land 174
Weddell Sea 56, 176
Weiflsee 252
Weil Dongcun 188, 189
Weißeritz 276
Welkom 199
Welland Canal 135
Welland Canal Locks 134
Welland River 134
Wesel 110
Weser 111
West Australian Basin 57
West Bank 212, 242, 243
West Bay 96, 97
West European Basin 56
West Ice Shelf 176, 179
West Memphis 95
West Siberian Plain 57, 63, 129
Western Australia 223
Western Desert 114, 117, 224, 225
Western Sahara 36
Westlake 230
Westwego 279
White Island 176
White Nile 113, 114, 115,
White River 96
White Sea 161
Whitsunday Passage 250
Whitsunday Islands 250, 251
Wiesbaden 110, 167
Wilge 199
Wilhelmshaven 111, 244
Wilkes Land 57, 176, 179
Wilkins Ice Shelf 176, 179
Wilmington 184
Winam Gulf 149
Windhoek 59, 198, 282
Windsor 134
Wisconsin 134
Witwatersrand 197, 198
Wollongong 221
Woodmurra Creek 150, 151
Woodstock Dam 199
Worms 110
Wörth am Rhein 111
Wrangel Island 172
Wrocław 276
Wu Jiang 122
Wucheng 272
Wuhan 121, 123
Wuppertal 110
Wuxi 123
Wuyi Shan 57, 123
Wuyou 188
Wyoming 90

X

Xanten 110
Xi Jiang 123
Xi´an 123
Xiang Jiang 122
Xiaohai 188
Xiaolan 186, 187
Xinfeng 188
Xingwei 186, 187
Xituan 188
Xuanhui He 266

Y

Yaalup Laggon 222
Yablonoi Mountains 57
Yafo 243
Yakoua 155
Yakutsk 260
Yalong Jiang 122
Yamada Bay 169
Yamburg 260
Yanbu' al Bahr 212
Yangtze Delta 121, 122, 123, 124, 125
Yangtze(-kiang) 57, 59, 73, 85, 121, 163, 189, 217, 271
Yanshan 266
Yarkant He 142
Yarlung Tsangpo Grand Canyon 127
Yarlung Zangpo/Tsangpo 126, 127
Yarmuk 243
Yellow River 57, 73, 123, 271
Yellow Sea 123, 188, 265
Yellowstone River 11
Yemen 36, 212, 213
Yenisey 57, 59, 129, 145, 260
Yerushalayim 212, 242, 243
Yicang 188
Yichang 123
Yoakam 230
Yokohama 262
Yonkers 184, 185
Yorke Peneinsula 220
Ysyk-Köl 137, 142, 143
Yuhua 188
Yukon 58
Yuma 89
Yunnan Guizhou Plateau 122

Z

Zagazig 114
Zagreb 106
Zagros Mountains 57
Zambesi 37, 57, 59, 73, 198, 239, 282
Zambia 36, 37, 198, 282, 283
Zaragoza 236
Zeferetbach 252, 253
Zell am See 47
Zeller See 47
Zhangjiagang 123
Zhangwei Xinhe 266
Zhengzhou 123
Zhenjiang 85
Zhongshan 186, 187
Zhuhai 186, 187
Zi Shui 122
Zigui 124
Zimbabwe 36, 198, 282, 283
Ziro 126
Zixa Xinhe 266
Zürich 106, 139
Zürichsee 139
Zuurbekom Springs 198
Zwentendorf a.d. Donau 277

SUBJECT INDEX

A

AATSR 29, 41, 43
ablation zone 81
acacia 223
accident 76, 231, 244, 245, 249
accumulation zone 81
acidification 55
acropolis 185
active layer 157
ADEOS/OCTS [SST] 263
ADM-Aeolus 32, 33
aerial image 43, 46, 102, 211, 227
aerosol 32, 34
aerospace 27, 28
AfriGEOSS 37
age distribution pyramid 66
Agulhas Current 63
agriculture/farming 13, 34, 36, 43f., 48, 54f.f, 61, 65, 73, 90f, 102, 111, 113, 115, 124, 137, 141ff., 149, 155, 161, 185ff., 208, 211, 215, 217f., 221ff., 225, 227, 234, 237, 239, 251, 257, 263, 267, 272, 277
airport 185*ff.*, 202, 219
air current 163, 197
air pressure 35, 58, 279
air temperature 157, 171, 173
aircraft 33, 35, 46, 174, 177*f.*, 187
Akkadians 235
Albufeira Agreement 237
Alfred Wegener Institue (AWI) 177
algae 137, 149, 164*f.*, 229, 243, 251, 258,
algae bloom 121,149, 164*f.*, 267
algal growth 164*f.*, 229
allochthonous river 113, 117
alluvial fan 86, 87
alluvial plains 93
alluvial soil 124
ALOS 179, 245
alpacas 137
ammonium 165, 229
amphibians 239
Antarctic bottom waters (AABW) 177
Antarctic Circumpolar Current (ACC) 54, 62-63, 177
Antilles Current 160
anti-selection 275
Applied Analysis Inc. (AAI) 247
Apollo 8 12
Aqua 43
aquaculture 123*f.*, 165, 186*ff.*, 229, 264*ff.*
aqueduct 90*f.*, 192*f.*, 195, 208*f.*
aquifer 70, 74, 76, 192, 195, 208, 211, 213, 225
AQUIFER project 211
Arab Potash Company 242
Arctic creeping willow 157
Arctic wolves 173
Arctos 171
Argonautica 169
Ariane 26, 28
arid 9, 53*ff.*, 61, 65, 70, 89, 113, 117, 137, 198, 206*ff.*, 211, 213, 215, 218*f.*, 225, 227, 234, 238*f.*, 243, 254
Aristotle 275
Artemis 33
artesian wells/groundwater 54, 211
ASAR 29, 36, 41, 43, 82, 83, 102, 108, 126, 174, 178, 179, 224, 246, 259, 261
ASIRAS 177
Assyrians 235
astronomy 9
atmosphere 12*f.*, 26, 29*ff.*, 40*f.*, 43*ff.*,47*f.*, 56, 157, 159*f.*, 163, 174*f.*, 177, 247, 283
atmospheric motion 34
atmospheric properties 43
atmospheric transmittance 41
Austrians 139
AVHRR 43
AWF 211
Aymara 137

B

B-15A iceberg 82, 179
Babylonians 235
backlog of water 277
backwater floods 270
Baikal seal 145
ballast water 258
bananas 230, 251
bank 85*f.*, 93*f.*, 99, 107, 111, 117, 129, 202*f.*, 235, 270, 276
Baron Alvinczy 139
Barrosos no. 2 257
bathymetry 56, 57, 177
bear 171, 173
Beaufort Scale 279
bed of the glacier 81
bedrock 105, 133, 135, 177*f.*, 219
Benguela Current 63
BGIS2000 43
biodiversity 119, 155, 165, 223, 239
biogas 148
biomass 32*f.*, 48, 148
biosphere 12, 283
bird 23, 86, 145, 154, 239, 245, 263*ff.*
blizzards 178
blowout 246, 247
Blue Marble 12
Blue Planet 12
boreal coniferous forest 65, 129
boreal forest 129, 157
boreal tree line 173
bottle deposits 169
Boxing Day Tsunami 272, 281
brackish water 257, 267, 279
brash ice 172
Brazil Current 62
broadleaf forest 65
bromide salt 242
buoyancy 175, 245
buoys 35, 169, 178
bycatch 263

C

calcium 242, 243
Californian Current 62, 168
camera system 41, 43
carbohydrates 251
carbon 32, 102, 159, 164, 175, 177, 215, 217, 251
carbon dioxide 63, 71, 102, 157, 159, 164, 175, 177, 217
Carboniferous coal 54
CarbonSat 32
cargo hub 111
carnivores 239
carp 105, 267
cartography 39, 48
cataracts 113
catch basin 249
catchment area 102, 105, 111, 115, 117, 235, 237, 239
catchment basin 89*f.*, 93*ff.*, 99*ff.*, 105*ff.*, 111, 119, 121*f.*, 126*ff.*, 133, 149, 151, 155, 157, 201, 253, 276
C-band 27, 29, 43
Central European floods 2002 276
centre-pivot irrigation/systems 215, 224, 225, 227
CEOS 37
chemicals industry 115
chloride 242, 243
chlorophyll 43
cholera 149
Christaller, Walter 189
chrysophytes 164
circumpolar circulation 177
cirques 81
cisterns 206, 207
cities 70, 102, 106, 121, 137, 148, 175, 183, 185*f.*, 189, 191, 197*f.*, 205, 213, 244, 258, 273
citrus fruits 115, 230
climate 28, 30*ff.*, 34*f.*, 43, 47, 49, 81, 102, 129, 131, 133, 137, 139, 142, 147, 151, 154*f.*, 159*ff.*, 164*f.*, 171*ff.*, 175, 177*f.*, 189, 197, 201, 215, 217, 218*f.*, 221, 223, 225, 227, 238, 242*f.*, 269, 274*f.*, 283
climate change 28, 54, 81, 154, 163, 171, 175, 178, 219, 275, 283
climate graph 203
climate model(-ling) 32, 43
climate monitoring 30, 35
climate scenarios 47
climate system 175
climate zones 53, 62*ff.*
climatic energy transfer 12, 60
climatology 48
cloud (cover) 9, 11*ff.*, 26, 29, 32*ff.*, 36, 43, 45, 48, 53, 56, 59*f.*, 159, 205*ff.*, 238, 245, 261, 263, 272, 277, 279
cloud formation 56, 58, 205
CNES 169
coal 54, 129, 133, 221, 257, 274
coastal erosion 48, 49, 271
coastal protection 49, 166*ff.*, 267
coffee 65, 163
cold-water lake 145
colonisation 185
Colorado River Compact 90
colour images 41, 43
colour scale (range) 44
Columbus, Christopher 241, 258
communication satellites 49
condensation 11*f.*, 58*f.*, 206, 208
Congo Basin Forest Partnership (CBFP) 119
conservation areas 43, 48*f.*, 249, 255, 265
continental climate 63, 129
continental ice sheet 175
continental plate 57, 145, 272, 281
continental rift valley 145
Cook, James 241
Copernicus European Earth Observation Programme 29, 30, 34, 275
Copernicus Emergency Management Service of the EU Commision 274
COPUOS 76
coral bleaching 251
coral reef 231, 243, 251
Cordonazo 68
Coriolis effect 87, 160, 279
cotton 54, 115, 141, 143, 148, 189, 219, 230, 235
Counter Current 62, 63, 161, 168
crab 258
crocodiles 148
crop (cereal) 189, 230
crop (plant) 64, 115, 137, 189, 217, 218, 221, 223, 225, 227, 283
crop yield 34, 49, 143, 163, 215, 283
crude oil 245, 251, 257
cruise ship 231, 259
crustaceans 265
CryoSat 31, 33, 172, 174*f.*, 177*ff.*
cryosphere 12, 171
CSA 37
CSG 28
CSIR 37
currents 44*f.*, 82, 86*f.*, 101, 115, 160*ff.*, 168*f.*, 197, 247, 261, 267
cyanide 249
cyanobacteria 164
cyclone 68*f.*, 276, 271, 279

D

D'Annunzio, Gabriele 139
dam 47, 90*f.*, 107, 115, 117, 124*f.*, 149, 155, 192, 198*f.*, 201, 203, 206, 219, 221, 233, 235, 241, 249, 253*f.*, 270, 272
damage 49, 75, 148, 164, 201*f.*, 239, 243, 245, 258, 264, 270*f.*, 274, 276, 279
dam-break floods 270
Danube Commission 76
date palms 139, 227
Dead Sea Works Ltd. 242
debris 168, 169
debris flow 270
deciduous broadleaf forest 65
Decision Support System (DSS) 47
deep current 162, 177
deep sea 57, 160, 177, 257
deep-sea fishing 263
Deepwater Horizon 231, 246
Defense Meteorological Satellite Program 267
deforestation 55, 62, 85, 102, 119, 148, 201, 267
delta 21, 85*ff.*, 93*f.*, 96*f.*, 101, 105, 108, 113, 115, 117, 121*ff.*, 126*f.*, 145, 156, 167, 186*f.*, 189, 201, 218*f.*, 229, 238*f.*, 246*f.*, 259, 279
deposition 11, 12, 117
desalination plant 13, 71, 206, 213, 243
desert 49, 54, 58, 87, 89, 91, 113, 115, 117, 141*f.*, 151, 155, 208, 213, 215, 218*f.*, 224, 227, 269, 271
desert climate 49
desertification 49, 63, 65, 215, 219
Devonian 54
dew harvesting 206
diatoms 164
digital elevation model (DEM) 46, 47, 211, 277
dinoflagellates 164
disaster prevention 47, 49, 76, 269, 274
discharge hydrograph 253, 276
discharge properties 47
disease 54, 69, 99, 148*f.*, 162*f.*, 203, 241, 242
disposal 183, 192, 194*f.*, 203
diurnal climate 60
DMSP 66, 267
dolphins 264, 265
Doubková, Marcela 283
downpours 162, 201, 276
dragnet 264
drift nets 159, 264, 265
drilling platform 231, 246, 247, 256*f.*
drinking water 13, 56, 74, 81, 85, 107, 121, 131, 142, 145, 147, 153, 155, 183, 192*ff.*, 198*f.*, 203, 205*ff.*, 213, 225, 243, 249
drinking water production 207
drought 9, 90, 153, 162*f.*, 195, 198, 219, 237, 269, 271, 283
drumlins 81
dry season 155, 202*f.*, 207, 218, 238f., 283
duckweed 256, 257
dumping 244, 258
dunes 19, 155, 225
Dust Bowl 163
dykes 167, 241, 274, 276
dynamite fishing 265

E

EAC 28
Earth Explorer 31*ff.*, 283
Earth observation 25, 27*ff.*, 33*f.*, 37, 39*f.*, 42*f.*, 47*ff.*, 161, 165, 178
Earth observation satellites 37, 39, 40, 42, 43
Earth´s rotation 34
EarthCARE 32, 33
earthquake 44, 47, 68*f.*, 269, 271*ff.*, 281
Eastern National Water Carrier system 239
ecology 49
economy 149, 162, 241
ecosystem 49, 173, 229, 239, 244*f.*, 249, 251, 253, 257, 264*f.*, 267
ECSAT 28
eddies 15, 34, 164
EDRS 33, 34
Eduspace 28
EEA 30
EIGEN 6C2 31
El Niño 162, 163, 251
electromagnetic spectrum 41
elephants 239
embankments 93, 107, 274, 276
emergency plans 45, 47, 49
emission 63, 71, 213, 217
endorheic 55, 131, 151, 218
energy generation 47, 81, 85, 147, 166, 233, 237, 241
ENSO 162, 163
environmental protection 49, 251
Envisat 29*f.*, 33, 39*f.*, 41*ff.*, 82*f.*, 143, 167, 173*f.*, 179, 246, 251, 261, 279
Eocene 54
epicentre 281
equatorial trough 58
Eritrea project 206
erosion 9, 36, 37, 55, 87, 93, 97, 113, 115, 117, 121, 135, 157, 225, 235, 271
erosion risk map 36, 37
ERS 39, 41, 43, 179, 261, 276
ESA 26*ff.*, 37, 39, 82, 125, 161, 169, 172, 174*f.*, 178*f.*, 211, 245, 261, 275
ESA's Redu Centre 28
ESA's Space Situational Awareness Preparatory Programme 28
ESAC 28
ESOC 28
ESRIN 28, 33
ESTEC 28
estuary 85*ff.*, 101*f.*, 129, 166
ETM 41*ff.*, 260, 261, 276
EU Commission 169, 274
EUMETSAT 34
EUMETSAT´s Polar System (EPS) 34
Eurasian plate 145
European Union (EU) 27, 29, 267
eutrophication 55, 149, 164, 229
evaporation 11, 12, 13, 55*f.*, 61, 73, 117, 131, 137, 142, 151, 154, 159, 161, 208, 213, 215, 225, 227, 242*f.*
evaporation basins/ponds 242
evaporation rate 61, 154, 208, 215, 242
evapotranspiration 12, 13, 61

F

factory trawlers 265
false-colour image 41, 227, 256
famine 117, 163
FAO 77, 143, 215, 217, 263, 267
far infrared 41
farmed fish 267
fertile silt 117
fertile soil 87, 107, 115, 123*f.*, 147, 199, 217, 223
fertiliser 70, 91, 93, 117, 121, 148*f.*, 164, 229, 241, 251
FFEM (French Global Environment Facility) 211
firn ice 81
firn snow 81, 83
fish 159, 163*ff.*, 169, 230, 239, 245, 249, 251, 253, 257, 263*ff.*, 267
fish farm 267
fish stocks 117, 137, 147, 186, 263
fishermen 148, 153*f.*, 239, 245, 257, 264
fishing 49, 102, 141, 143, 147*f.*, 157, 159, 163, 168*f.*, 185*f.*, 229, 231, 239, 245, 247, 251, 263*ff.*, 267
fishing boats 263, 267
'Fishing for Litter' campaign 169
fishing industry 141, 251
fishing methods 263
fishing quota 263
flagellates 164
flash flood 183, 270*ff.*, 272, 276
FLEX 32
floating debris 169
floating glacier 174
floating ice 31, 171, 178, 179
flood control 195, 213, 273
flood damage 276
flood irrigation 143, 189, 215
flood retention 47, 274
flood wave 271, 277
flood(-ing) 9, 29*f.*, 37, 46*f.*, 69, 73, 81, 94, 99, 107, 117, 127, 151, 153, 162*f.*, 167, 183, 185, 195, 201, 203, 213, 215, 219, 238, 269*ff.*, 279, 283
flood(-ing) map 37, 270
flooded area 43, 218, 269*ff.*, 277, 279
floodplain 201, 203
floodwaters 238, 276
Florida Current 160, 247
flow conditions 43
fog collectors/nets (FOG|HARVESTER) 207
fog-harvesting 206, 207
FogQuest 206, 207
food(-stuff) 69, 73, 77, 117, 131, 137, 143, 183, 185*f.*, 215*ff.*, 233, 263*ff.*
food chain 163, 164, 169, 245
forest 29, 32, 36, 48, 65, 102, 129, 157, 163, 223, 255
forest fires 29, 163
forestry 48, 102
fossil water 211, 225
freezing 11, 12, 131, 157
freshwater 12*f.*, 53, 56, 70, 76, 81, 105, 107, 131, 133, 145, 147, 153, 161, 171*ff.*, 175, 178, 189, 199, 223, 229, 233, 235, 254, 257, 267, 272
frozen 171, 175
frozen soil 171
fruit bushes 157
fulvic acids 99

G

Galileo 27, 34, 39
Gallia Cisalpina 139
Gama, Vasco da 241
garbage patch 168, 169
gas 11*f.*, 29, 34*f.*, 159, 213, 229

GEF (Global Environment Facility) 211
GEO 37
geodesy 31, 48
GeoEye 43
geographic information system (GIS) 25, 28, 46
geographic North Pole 172
geoid 31, 33
geolocation 45, 261
geomorphology 85, 171, 225
GEOSS 30
geostationary 30, 33ff., 40, 43
Gilgamesh 235
giraffes 239
GIS (GeoEye Imaging System) 43
GITEWS (Tsunami early-warning system) 281
glacial advance 81
glacial ice 70, 81, 173, 177ff., 253
glacial lake outburst (floods) 81, 270
glacial lakes 131
glacial retreat 54, 81ff., 131f., 139
glacial striation 253
glacial valley 81
glaciation/glacial period 54, 139
glacier 12f., 46, 54, 56, 81ff., 105, 129, 131, 133, 135, 139, 141, 161, 167, 174f., 178, 253, 261
global (ocean) circulation 174, 177
global climate 62, 177, 219
Global Drifter Program 169
global population 217
global warming 69, 157, 161, 171f., 217, 271
GMES 30
GNSS 39
GOCE 31, 33
GOES 53, 159
Goethe, Johann Wolfgang von 139
gold deposits 54, 102, 197, 249
GOMOS 29
gorge 107, 119
GPS 39, 177, 178, 258, 264, 281
Gramp, Johann 221
grasses 157
gravel banks 85
gravity field 31
Great Barrier Reef Marine Park Authority 251
great egrets 105
Great Man Made River project 225
Great Pacific Garbage Patch (GPGP) 168
greek(-s) 86, 113, 164, 171, 185
Green Cross 75
greenhouse (effect) 62, 102, 159, 164, 175, 217
greenhouse gas 12, 159, 164, 175, 213
Greenpeace 263
Greenpeace Seafood Red List 267
ground control points 45
ground ice 171
ground resolution 29, 42, 261, 283
groundwater 12f., 19, 53f., 56, 73f., 76, 183, 191, 193, 195, 198, 203, 209, 211, 213, 215, 223, 225, 227, 239, 243, 270
groundwater level 19, 193, 209, 211, 215, 223, 225, 227, 243, 270
groundwater recharge 73, 195, 211, 213, 239
GSTB-V2/A 27
Guinea Current 62, 160
Gulf Stream 60, 62, 63, 160, 161, 247
Günz glaciation 139

H

Haq, Khondaker Azharul 203, 284
harbour 108, 111, 134, 185, 187, 213, 231, 258, 261
heavy metals 55, 142, 249
heavy rain 47, 151, 201, 218, 249, 276, 279
helicopter 178, 279
Helvetas 205
hemisphere 171, 174, 177
Herodotus 113
high mountains 54, 57, 137, 143, 167, 175
high mountains lake 137
high tide 87, 166
high water 137, 272, 276
hippos 238, 239
Holocene 54, 157
households 13, 148
HRV 42
humic acids 99
humidity 31, 35, 185
hunters 239
hurricane .... 68f., 163, 231, 271, 278f.
hurricane season 279
hydro(-electric) power (plant) .... 81, 107, 121, 124, 129, 134f., 141, 148f., 198f., 233, 235, 237, 241, 253f.
hydrographic basin 237
hydrological models 47
hydrology 48, 283
hydrosphere 12, 13, 283
hypoxia 164, 165, 229, 231
hypsographic curve 57

I

ice .... 9, 11ff., 171ff., 177ff.
ice age 54, 81, 83, 131, 133, 137, 139, 157, 227
ice caps 13, 171
ice cover 29, 33, 172, 173
ice desert 173
ice drift 15, 48, 261
ice extent 171ff., 177
ice loss 175
ice sheet .... 12, 31, 33, 133, 139, 171, 174f., 177ff.
ice shelf 56, 82, 177ff., 179
ice streams/tributaries 179
ice thickness 31, 48, 172, 175, 178
ice types 261
ice velocity 179
ice wedge polygons 157
iceberg .... 48, 82, 83, 160, 175, 178f., 260f.
Iceberg B-15A 82, 179
icebreakers 258, 261
ICL Fertilizers 242
IKONOS 41ff., 137, 244
image processing 28, 44
Incas 137
Industrial Revolution 55
industrialisation 241
industry 27f., 102, 115, 121, 129, 141, 143, 147f., 163, 185f., 189, 221, 237, 241ff., 249, 257, 259, 263, 266f., 274
infiltration 213, 261, 271, 274
infrared 29, 34f., 41, 44, 227, 277, 279
inland delta 86, 218, 219, 238, 239
inland ice sheet 178
inland lake 131, 137, 257
inland sea 70, 131, 161
inland shipping lane 111
inner bend 93, 95
InSAR 211
insurance 274, 275
integrated real-time irrigation scheduling system 221
Inter Tropic Convergence (ITC) 58, 198
interferogram 175
interglacial period 54, 157
Intergovernmental Panel on Climate Change (IPCC) 63, 173
International Charter Space and Major Disasters 245, 275, 277
International Conference on Freshwater 77
International Energy Agency 241
International Space Station ISS 9, 28, 40, 102, 263
interpretation 44
invertebrates 239
irrigated fields 48, 89, 91, 115, 215, 217, 221, 225, 227, 237
irrigation 9, 49, 53ff., 73, 76, 90f., 117, 121, 137, 141, 153ff., 189, 208, 211, 213, 215, 217, 219, 221, 223ff., 227, 233, 235, 237, 239, 243
irrigation systems 9, 141, 189, 208, 215, 219, 221, 225, 227
Isotope analysis 213
isthmus 258
IWAREMA 37
IWRM 37

J

jarrah forest (eucalyptus) 223
Jason 167
JAXA 32, 263
jellyfish 164
JERS 245
Johannesburg World Summit on Sustainable Development (WSSD) 37

K

katabatic winds 178
kerogen 251
Khanty 128, 129
krill 177
Kron, Wolfgang 275, 284
Kuro-Shio 63, 168

L

La Niña 162, 163
Labrador Current 62, 160
Lacrosse 45
Lake Chad Basin Commission 155
Lake Eyre dragon 151
lake level 137, 141, 143, 149, 151, 153f., 237, 243, 270
Lakers 133
land cover 36, 40, 48, 64f., 91, 108, 142f., 277
land degradation 65, 215, 233, 235
Land Monitor project 223
land reclamation 186, 187
land subsidence 44, 193, 195, 211
land surface temperature 30, 60, 157, 175
land use 37, 44, 47f., 64f., 91, 94, 184, 189, 195, 202, 255
land use classification (map) 44, 108, 142f., 185, 189, 219, 247
land use development 91, 274
land use policy 272, 274
Landsat .... 30, 39, 40ff., 149, 223, 227, 242, 260f., 276.
landslides 49, 69, 272
Late Medieval warm period 54
Lauer and Frankenberg 63
L-band 31
leeward sides 59
lemmings 173
lemna minor 256, 257
LEOWorks 28
Lesotho Highlands Water Project 198, 199
Lichem, Walther 77, 284
lichens 157, 161
lidar 32
lions 239
lithosphere 12, 56
litter 168, 169
Little Ice Age 54
Living Planet Programme 29, 31
llamas 137
lobster 264
Löffler, Heinz 55, 284
logging 48
Loop Current 246, 247
loss prevention 274
Loster, Thomas 207, 284
Louisiana Coastal Current .... 246f.
low tide 87, 166

M

Macondo oil field 246
Magellan, Ferdinand 241
magnesium 242, 243
magnetic field 32, 33, 172
magnetic North Pole 172
mangroves 231, 267
Mansi 128
map projection 45
mariculture 264, 265, 267
marine life 164, 169
marine park 251
Mars 53
Mayerhofer, Martina 207, 284
MDGs 37
meander 93ff., 111, 113, 129, 201
meat 221, 230
Medium Earth Orbit (MEO) 34
MEDSPIRATION 160, 161
Mekong River Commission 75, 77
melting 11f., 63, 81, 161, 167, 172, 175, 177, 179, 253, 179
meltwater 81, 131, 133, 135, 139, 141, 157, 253
MEO 34
Mercalli scale 68
MERCOSUR 77
Mercury 53
mercury 102, 249
MERIS 11, 29, 36, 40, 41ff., 143, 251
meteorology 33ff., 40, 48
Meteosat 30, 33ff., 40ff., 53
metropolitan area .... 11, 90, 124, 186f., 191ff., 198f.
methane 29, 157, 159, 175, 217
MetOp 30, 33ff., 43, 283
microplastics 169
microwaves 31, 41, 43, 44, 45
mid infrared 41, 43
mid ocean ridges 57
midnight sun 173
migratory birds 22, 145
Milankovitch cycles 54
mills 219, 241
Ming Dynasty 189
mining 13, 102, 157, 197, 211, 249, 251
Ministerial Council on Water (AMCOW) 37
Miocene 54
MIPAS 29
MODIS 43, 60, 179
molluscs 258, 265
monsoon 53, 60, 127, 163, 201ff., 217, 251, 269, 272
moon 40, 166
Moore, Charles 168
moose 157
moraine 81ff., 139
mosses 161
mountain glaciers 167
MSG 33, 40, 42, 43
MSS 43, 227
MTG 30, 33
mudslides 69, 271
multispectral 30, 41
multitemporal radar satellite image 102, 108, 119, 126, 156, 270, 272, 276, 281
Munich Re 271
Munich Re Foundation 206, 207
Munich Technical University 207
Murmansk Shipping Company 261

N

NAOMI 43
Napoleon 139
NASA 12, 172
natural catastrophes .... 269, 271, 274f.
natural disasters 69, 73, 127, 167, 270, 275
natural gas 128f., 148, 157, 231, 246, 257
natural harbour 184, 185
natural hazard 9, 49, 68f., 81, 269, 271, 274
natural phenomenon 101, 157, 162f., 173, 231, 251, 271, 281
navigable .... 89, 99, 108, 119, 121, 129, 148f.
navigation .... 27, 28, 33f., 39, 45, 49, 76f., 134, 231, 244, 258, 260f., 263f.
NDVI 237, 239, 282
near infrared 41, 43
near-real colour 45, 276
Nile Basin Initiative 76
Nile perch 147, 148
nilometer 39, 117
nitrate 149, 165, 229
nitrite 165, 229
nitrogen (oxides) .... 29, 55, 149, 164f.
NOAA 35, 169
Normans 185
North Atlantic Drift 62, 160, 177
North Equatorial Current 62f., 160, 168
North Pacific Current 62, 168
North Pacific Gyre 168
North Pole 172, 173
North-East Monsoon 60, 163, 201
Northeast Passage 260, 261
northern hemisphere 40, 54f., 87, 171, 177, 279
northern summer 40, 173
northern winter 40, 173
Northern Wastewater Treatment Works 199
North-West Monsoon 60, 163
Northwest Passage 260
nuclear-powered icebreaker 258, 261
nunataks 81
nutrient 55, 65, 99, 102, 117, 121, 149, 163f., 177, 229, 239, 251, 257
NWSAS 211

O

oasis 224, 225, 227, 235
ocean circulation 31, 43, 177
ocean colour 29, 30
ocean currents 54, 60, 62f., 160f., 163f., 168, 172, 177, 179, 247, 264
ocean temperature 175
ocean voyages 39
Office du Niger 219
offshore 30, 256, 261
oil .... 74, 128f., 157, 164, 193, 213, 229ff., 244ff., 251, 256ff.
oil disaster 244, 245, 247
oil (drilling) platform .... 231, 244, 247, 256f.
oil pollution 44, 244
oil shale 251
oil slick .... 245ff.
oil spill .... 11, 29, 45, 159, 231, 241, 245ff.
oil tankers .... 231, 244f., 256, 258f.
oil well 244f., 257
OKACOM 239
Okavango Delta Management Plan 239
OLI 43, 227
Olifantsvlei Wastewater Treatment Works 199
optical 29, 41, 44f., 47, 102, 108, 278
Ora 139
orbit 30, 33ff., 40f., 43
Ordovician Period 54
ore 230, 249
Organisation for the Development of the Senegal River (OMVS) 76
orographic precipitation 277
OSA 43
ospreys 239
OSS 211
outback 151
outlet glacier 82, 178
overfishing 263
oxbow lakes 85, 95, 111
oxygen 63, 102, 149, 164f., 229, 231, 243, 257
Oya-Shio 63, 168
oyster 230, 245
ozone 29, 35, 43

P

Pacific Ring of Fire 69
paddy field farming 215, 217
Palestine Potash Company 242
panchromatic 43
Pangaea 54
paper 145, 230
P-band 32
PDVSA 257
pedosphere 12
pelicans 105, 151
penguin 171, 177
permafrost 13, 56, 157, 161, 171, 173ff., 272
Permian 54, 55
Permian-Carboniferous ice age 54
Peruvian Current 62, 168
pesticide 54f., 70, 91, 141f., 148, 251
petroleum 246, 247, 251
phosphate 149, 164f., 229, 230
photodegradation 169
photosynthesis 164
phytoplankton (bloom) 44, 133, 149, 164f., 177, 229
piedmont glacier 81, 82
pike 105
pipe(-line) 128f., 143, 157, 192f., 198f., 203, 207, 209, 213, 215, 225, 227, 239, 249, 258
Piri Reis 39
plankton 163ff., 264
Plastic Age 168
plastic bottles 169
plastic soup 169
plastic (waste) 168, 169
plate tectonics 54, 57, 69, 85, 131
Pleistocene 54, 137, 139, 211
Pliny the Elder 139
pluvial period 54, 211
Polar -6 177
polar bears 173
polar ice cap 13, 63, 145, 167, 171
polar ice desert 173
polar orbit 30, 35, 40, 43
polar regions 12, 48, 52, 56, 58, 63, 67, 157, 160, 165, 170ff., 175, 178, 261
polar summer 177
pollutant (dispersion) 47, 55, 160
pollution incidents 249
pond aquaculture 265, 267

Pont du Gard 209
population 183, 185f., 187, 189, 191f., 195, 197, 201, 203, 205f., 208, 211, 213
population density/distribution 46, 66f., 71, 91, 127, 148, 185, 239
population growth 206, 213, 239
Pororoca 101
portolan map 39
ports 89, 111, 133, 185, 241, 243f., 256ff., 276
potassium carbonates (potash) 242
prawn 230, 231, 267
Precambrian ice ages 54
precipitation 12f., 34, 47, 56, 58f., 61, 65, 73f., 81, 89, 105, 113, 121, 137, 142, 149, 159, 161ff., 173, 211, 237, 253, 274f., 277, 283
precipitation distribution 48, 53, 58, 64f., 70f., 75, 117, 211, 233, 237
precision farming 48
Prestige 245
Proba 33, 125, 156
propagation speed (tsunami) 281
ptarmigans 173
pyramid 66, 117

Q

qanat 208, 209
Qing Dynasty 189
Quaternary period 54, 55
QuickBird 41, 43, 213, 216, 273

R

radar 27, 29f., 31ff., 41, 44f., 47f., 185, 207, 211
radar images 44, 119, 156, 174, 211, 225, 277, 281
radar interferometry 179, 193, 211
radar sensor/system 29, 207, 211, 245, 281
RADARSAT 175, 179, 245f., 277
radar-scattering 261
radiation 32ff., 41, 44, 58, 60f., 207, 243, 261, 279
radiolarians 164
radiometer 31
railway 119
rainforest 43, 48, 65, 70, 85, 101f., 119, 254f., 257
Ramsar Convention 153
Rand Water 198
RapidEye 43, 247
receiving station 28, 34, 40, 43, 47
red-breasted geese 105
reed islands 137
reindeer 157, 173
Reinhard, Dirk 207, 284
REIS 43
relief 47, 58, 60, 207f., 215, 242, 274, 277, 281
Roman (Empire) 54, 139, 209, 241
remote sensing 11, 37, 39f., 49
repetition rate 40, 43
reptiles 239
resource 11ff., 39, 48, 56, 70ff., 117, 141, 205, 227, 233, 239, 257, 283
reverse osmosis 213
Rhine Commission 76
rice cultivation 65, 121, 124, 153, 163, 189, 215ff., 267
rice terraces 216, 217
Richter scale 281
river basin 37, 72ff., 91, 192, 239
river floods 270ff.
river mouth 86f., 101
river system 85, 90, 93, 95,129, 199, 203, 225, 233, 235, 239
river-dominated delta 86
roches moutonnées 81
rockfalls 272
rockslides 81
Roman Empire 139
rubbish 168, 169, 231
run-of-river power plants 253

S

sabkhas 19
SADC 283
Saffir, Herbert 279
Saffir-Simpson scale 68, 278, 279
Saline Water Conversion Corporation (SWCC) 213
salinisation 49, 55, 211, 215, 221, 223, 225, 227, 235, 267
salinity 31, 33, 48f., 54f., 61, 70, 141ff., 151, 159ff., 164, 172, 177, 211, 223, 243
salmon 267
salt deserts 223
salt/saline lakes 137, 143, 223
salt marshes 19, 93
salt works 242
saltwater 12f., 56, 229, 243, 257, 259, 267
San 206
sand accumulation 143, 224, 225
sandbars 86, 87
sandstorms 142
Sandven, Stein 261, 284
sanitation 73, 163, 191, 193, 205
sardines 262, 263
SASS 211
satellite image map 45
satellite image mosaic 12, 44, 122, 173 ,177, 179, 289
savannah 54, 65, 155, 197f., 218
SCIAMACHY 29f.
scoop wheels 208, 215, 241
sea bed/floor 177, 244, 264, 267
sea ice 29ff., 45, 48f., 81, 171ff., 175,177f., 260f.
sea ice edge 177
sea ice extent 172ff., 177
sea ice thickness 31, 48, 172, 174f.
sea level 31, 55, 167, 171f., 175, 178f., 281
sea level rise 9, 31, 54, 81, 161, 166f., 175, 179, 270f., 281.
sea routes 241, 258
sea surface 12, 30, 49, 60, 162f., 173, 281
sea surface temperature 30, 43f., 60, 161f., 246, 263f., 279
sea surface topography 30
sea traffic 49
seafood 186, 263, 265, 267
seal 145, 169, 173, 177
sealed surface 49, 85
seasonal climates 60
seawater desalination 71, 213, 243
seaweed 265
sediment 11, 17, 81, 86f., 93f., 96f., 99, 101, 113, 115, 117, 121, 127, 145, 159f., 251, 257, 269
sediment load 48, 86f., 93, 99, 115, 117, 127, 269
semi-arid 89, 207, 218f., 234f., 239, 254
sensor 29, 32, 40f., 43f., 45, 207, 211, 221, 281
Sentinel 29, 30, 33, 37, 43, 169, 171, 178, 261
Seppelt, Joseph 221
septic tanks 194, 203
settlements 46, 49, 55, 67, 70, 85, 102, 111, 115, 137, 139, 184f., 189, 192, 197, 203, 208, 217, 223, 235, 276f.
seventh continent 168, 169
Seventh Continent Expedition 169
SEVIRI 41, 42, 43
sewage disposal 183, 194
sewage system 148, 183, 203, 205
sewage treatment plant 199, 258
sharks 263
shelf 57, 247
shellfish 251, 263
Shepparton Irrigation Region 221
shifting cultivation 102, 257
ship 29, 35, 49, 99, 108, 121, 129, 133ff., 141, 168f., 231, 244f., 257ff., 261
ship traffic 231, 258, 259
shipping 93, 115, 121, 135, 141, 229, 241, 244, 251, 257ff., 261
shipping lane/channel 9, 105, 111, 257ff., 259, 261
shipping routes 148, 185, 258ff.
shoals of fish 163f., 177, 263ff.
shrimp farming 231, 263, 267
shrub 64, 157, 202, 219, 221
silting (up) 49, 117, 253
Silurian period 54
Simpson, Bob 279
sisal 230
slash-and-burn 102, 119, 121
SMOS 31, 33, 283
snakes 148, 251
snow 11ff., 41, 49, 53, 56ff., 81, 91, 105, 133, 143, 156, 171ff., 179, 261
snowmelt 86, 94, 129, 201, 253
soda lakes 131
sodium 55, 242, 243
soil 9, 12, 30f., 41, 48f., 147, 157, 171, 175
soil degradation 65, 102, 129, 215
soil moisture 12f., 31, 33, 43, 48, 207, 221, 282f.
soil salinity 48, 49
soil subsidence 211
soil temperature 157
solar system 40, 53
sole 263, 264
Somali Current 63
sonar 263, 264
South Chad Irrigation Project (SCIP) 155
South Equatorial Current 62f., 160, 168
South Pole 54, 172, 177
South-East Monsoon 60
Southeastern Anatolia Project (GAP) 233
southern winter 53
South-West Monsoon 60, 201, 203
soya 230
Soyuz 30
space agency 27f., 37, 169, 211
space exploration/research 26, 27, 28
space industry 27, 28
space missions 27
space policies 27
space technology 28, 39, 75
space weather 32
spacecraft 27, 28, 33
spaceport 26, 28, 30
spectral bands 43
spectral reflections 41
SPOT 30, 41ff., 47, 213, 215, 276
Sputnik 40
squid 263, 267
SRTM 47
starfish (crown-of-thorns starfish) 251
steppe 57, 65, 143, 218f., 234f.
stereo pair image 47
storm surge 167, 259, 269ff.
strait (natural) 259
Stuart project 251
sturgeon 105
sublimation 11, 12
Subtropical Convergence Zone 168
sugar (cane) 148, 230, 251
sulfur (oxides) 55, 230
Sumerians 235
summer monsoon 163
sunlight 29, 44, 164f., 169, 229,242
Sun-synchronous 40, 43
suspended load 73, 208
swamp 13, 113, 127, 143, 155, 185, 202, 218f., 231, 271, 279
Swarm 32, 33
synthetic aperture radar (SAR) 29, 41, 43f., 47, 82, 211, 245, 261

T

Taiga 157
tanker 231, 244f., 256ff., 267
tanker accidents 231, 244, 245
tanker, double-hulled 244, 258
tanker, single-hulled 245
tea 127, 163
TECCONILE 76
tectogenic lakes 131
telecommunication 27, 28, 33f., 281
telecommunication satellites 40
temperature 11, 34f., 43f., 47, 53f., 57f., 60ff., 81, 154, 157, 159ff., 167, 169, 171ff., 175, 178, 185, 197, 206, 217, 237, 251, 258, 263, 267
Terra 43
terrace cultivation 216f., 217
TerraSAR-X 43, 47, 245
Tertiary lignite 55
Tertiary period 54, 151
thawing 81, 131, 156f., 173, 175
thermal erosion (thermokarst) 156, 157
thermal infrared 29, 41, 43, 44
thermal insulation 177
tide water glaciers 175
tides 87, 101, 115, 121, 166f.
TIGER initiative 36, 37, 211
TIGER-NET 37
TIRS 43
Titan 53
TM 43, 44, 149, 227
TOPEX/Poseidon 167
topography 30, 45ff., 56f., 65, 81, 86, 127, 198, 211, 242f., 247
Tortajada, Cecilia 195, 284
Toshka project 117
tourism 49, 121, 237, 239, 247, 251
toxic (substance) 142, 165, 169, 246, 249, 251
trace gases 29, 34, 35, 44
tracking 48, 172, 245
trade routes 49, 119, 154
trade winds 60, 162f., 197f., 238, 256
transboundary river system 74ff., 198, 201, 237, 239
transpiration 13, 61
transport routes 79, 119, 183, 185
Treaty of the River Plate Basin 77
tree 64, 139, 157, 219
tropical storms 53, 68f., 162, 279
Tsukiji fish market 263
tsunami 68f., 168f., 270ff., 281
Tulla, Johann Gottfried 111
tuna 263
tundra 23, 65, 67, 157, 173
turtles 251, 265
Turton, Anthony 199, 284
typhoon 69, 159, 271, 274

U

ultraviolet 41
UN 74ff., 77, 183, 205, 215, 263, 265
UNCED 77
undersea (earth) quake 68, 281
UNDP 37, 75, 77
UNDP Cap-Net 37
UNECE 74ff.
UNESCO 37, 74ff., 105, 145, 209, 239, 244, 251
University of Colorado 207
urban development 43, 49, 195, 197
urban population 91, 183
urbanisation 85, 183, 186
Uros 137
use of water 39, 71, 75ff., 141, 153, 237
U-shaped valley 81, 139
utilisation conflicts 74f., 233, 239

V

Várzeas 99
vegetables 218, 227, 237
vegetation cover 41, 44, 48, 60f., 64f., 115, 151, 218f., 256, 282
vegetation zones 65, 173
Venus 26, 53
Venus Express 26
Victoria perch 147, 148
Vikings 185
vine(-yard) 54, 139, 221, 237
Virgil (Publius Vergilius Maro) 139
virtual water 71
visible light 34, 35, 41, 43
volcanic ash 34, 43, 217
volcanic lakes 131
volcanoes 68f., 191, 271
V-track cyclone 276

W

wadi 114, 117, 213, 225ff., 227, 242f.
Wagner, Wolfgang 283, 284
Walker circulation 162
Wallace, Jeremy 223, 284
WasserStiftung 206
waste 157, 159, 164, 168f., 185, 213, 244, 257
waste disintegration 169
wastewater 11, 55, 71, 73f., 85, 121, 145, 147f., 159, 183, 192ff., 199, 203, 207, 213, 241, 257
wastewater disposal 73f., 121, 145, 148, 159, 183, 192, 194f., 202f., 207, 257
wastewater management 11, 195
wastewater treatment 71, 199
water agreement 72f., 75f., 90, 107, 235, 237
water authorities 37
water availability 53, 55, 70f., 73f., 185, 189, 191, 206
water balance 81, 131, 157, 175, 223
water conflicts 74, 75
water consumption 13, 30, 64, 70f., 192, 213, 221
water cycle 12f., 31, 48, 57, 61, 171, 274
water discharge 47, 53, 89, 99, 211, 253
water distribution 35, 75, 191, 195
water events/conferences 77
water extraction 155, 213, 243
water hyacinths 147, 148, 149
water information systems 37
water level 39, 49, 86, 90f., 111, 117, 124, 127, 129, 149, 161, 166, 187, 218, 235, 237, 238f., 243, 253, 259, 270, 272, 276f.
water law 73, 74, 75, 90
water management 25, 37, 74ff., 76, 91, 195, 199, 211, 237, 243
water mills 241
Water Observation and Information System (WOIS) 37
water pollution 11, 49, 55, 76f., 102, 107, 141ff., 148, 159, 164, 231, 244, 247, 249, 256ff.
water price 205
water quality 49, 55, 76, 91, 148f., 195, 208, 267
water reserves 12, 75, 208, 213, 225, 227, 239
water resources 12f., 37, 39, 53, 55f., 70ff., 155, 213, 229, 237, 274, 283
water scarcity 54, 71, 233
water stress 90, 205
water supply 9, 11, 30, 48f., 55, 73, 81, 121, 131, 142, 147, 183, 191ff., 198f., 203, 205ff., 208f., 213, 217, 225, 227, 233, 235, 239, 249, 267
water temperature 44, 49, 61, 69, 159f., 162ff., 175, 246, 251, 258, 263ff., 279
water treatment plant 71, 192, 199, 202f., 249
water usage rights 75, 76, 90, 233
water use 11, 55, 71, 73f., 76f., 141, 215, 235, 237, 253
water vapour (transport) 11ff., 34f., 41, 43, 56, 58f., 159, 276
water war 74
waterway 30, 108, 111, 121, 129, 133, 148, 184, 189, 223, 241, 259
wave height 29, 45, 272
wavebands 41
wave-dominated deltas 87
wavelengths 41, 43
weather conditions 45, 49, 167, 207, 237, 264, 267, 275ff.
weather forecasts 30ff., 34f., 40, 43, 47, 49, 162, 221, 261
weather map 35
weather satellites 34f., 40, 43f., 267
weevils 148
wells 203, 206ff., 225, 244f., 249, 257,
West Wind Drift 177
Westerlies 60, 133, 163
wet season 238
wetlands 36, 49, 55, 65, 86, 93, 151, 153, 185, 203, 223, 238f., 241, 244, 272, 279, 283
whales 159, 168, 177, 265, 267
white-tailed eagles 105
wind erosion 224, 225
wind farms 30, 229
wind profiles 29, 32, 43, 61, 166
wind speed 29, 35, 206f., 256, 278f.
windward side 59
wine 54, 221, 237
winter monsoons 163
wool 137, 221
World Bank 37, 74f., 183, 243
World Natural Heritage site 105, 145, 209, 239, 251
World Cultural Heritage site 209
World Water Development reports 76
World Water Forum 74, 76, 77
World Water Week 77
WorldView 43
Würm glaciation 139
WV10 43
WWF 168

X

X-SAR 43, 47

Y

Yuan Dynasty 189

Z

zander 105
zebra mussel 258
zinc 249
zooplankton 164
zooxanthellae 251

IMAGE CREDITS

Satellite images

Page	Satellite/Sensor	Date	© Provider
Cover	Envisat MERIS	26.08.2011	ESA
10/1	Envisat MERIS FR	19.02.2003	ESA
14/1	Landat MSS	08.10.1972	NASA
16/1	Landsat TM	06.07.1985	NASA
18/1	Landsat TM	Mosaic	NASA
20/1	Landsat ETM	17.11.2000	NASA
22/1	Landsat ETM+	19.07.2000	NASA
29/6	Envisat MERIS	20.08.2004	ESA
30/2	Sentinel-1	12.07.2014	ESA
34/1a	Meteosat-7 IR	31.03.2004	EUMETSAT
34/1b	Meteosat-7 IR	30.06.2004	EUMETSAT
34/1c	Meteosat-7 IR	30.09.2004	EUMETSAT
34/1d	Meteosat-7 IR	31.12.2004	EUMETSAT
34/2a	Meteosat-7 VIS	30.06.2004	EUMETSAT
34/2b	Meteosat-7 VIS	30.06.2004	EUMETSAT
34/2c	Meteosat-7 VIS	30.06.2004	EUMETSAT
34/2d	Meteosat-7 VIS	30.06.2004	EUMETSAT
34/3a	Meteosat-7 VIS+IR	30.06.2004	EUMETSAT
35/3b	Meteosat-7 VIS+IR	31.12.2004	EUMETSAT
35/4a	Meteosat-7 WV	30.06.2004	EUMETSAT
35/4b	Meteosat-7 WV	31.12.2004	EUMETSAT
39/2	Spot-4 HRVIR Veg./	.Global Mosaic	CNES-VITO/
	Terra MODIS/		ESA/NASA/
	SRTM SIR-C		NOAA/USGS
40/1	Envisat MERIS	12.08.2004	ESA
41/5	RapidEye	15.08.2009	BlackBridge
41/6a	Landsat ETM	Mocaic	USGS
41/6b	Landsat TM	Mosaic	USGS
41/6c	Landsat ETM	Mosaic	USGS
41/6d	Landsat TM	Mosaic	USGS
42/1a	MSG 1 Meteosat-8	15.08.2003	EUMETSAT
42/1b	MSG-1 Meteosat-8	15.08.2003	EUMETSAT
42/2a	Envisat MERIS FR	19.07.2003	ESA
42/2b	Envisat MERIS FR	19.07.2003	ESA
42/3a	Landsat ETM+	03.08.2001	USGS
42/3b	Landsat ETM+	03.08.2001	USGS
42/4a	Spot-3 XS/HRV	22.07.2000	CNES
	Distribution Astrium Services/Spot Image S.A.		
42/4b	Spot-3 XS/HRV	22.07.2000	CNES
	Distribution Astrium Services/Spot Image S.A.		
42/5a	IKONOS-2 PAN	12.07.2006	EUSI
42/5b	IKONOS-2 PAN	12.07.2006	EUSI
44/1	Landsat ETM+	22.08.2000	USGS
44/3	ERS-1 SAR	01.01.1993	ESA
45/6	Envisat MERIS	Mosaic	ESA
47/7b	Landsat ETM	28.07.2002	NASA
48/1	Envisat ASAR	15.07.2004	ESA
48/2	Landsat OLI	29.01.2014	NASA/USGS
49/3	Landsat OLI	27.08.2013	NASA/USGS
49/4	Landsat OLI	18.10.2013	NASA/USGS
52/1	GOES-9 EPS	01.07.2004	NASA/NOAA
53/2	GOES-12 EPS	31.12.2003	NASA/NOAA
53/3	Meteosat-5 VIS	18.07.2003	EUMETSAT
53/4	Meteosat-5 VIS	30.06.2004	EUMETSAT
67/3	DMSP OLS	Mosaic	NASA/NOAA
80/1	Landsat ETM+	08.06.2001	GLCF/NASA
82/1	Landsat ETM	04.12.2002	USGS
82/2	Envisat ASAR	15.04.2005	ESA
83/3	RapidEye	26.08.2010	BlackBridge
81/1	Landsat ETM+	Mosaic	USGS
84/2	Landsat ETM+	Mosaic	USGS
84/3	Landsat TM	Mosaic	USGS
86/1	Envisat MERIS	Mosaic	ESA
87/2	Landsat ETM+	20.12.2000	USGS
88/1	Landsat OLI	22.04.2013	USGS
90/3a	Landsat ETM	20.06.1991	USGS
90/3b	Landsat OLI	21.07.2014	USGS
91/4a	Landsat ETM+	27.04.1989	USGS
91/4b	Landsat OLI	15.05.2013	USGS
91/6	Landsat ETM	10.04.2000	USGS
92/1	Landsat TM	25.03.1984	USGS
94/1	Landsat ETM+	Mosaic	USGS
95/3	RapidEye	13.11.2013	BlackBridge
96/1	Landsat ETM+	Mosaic	USGS
96/2	Landsat MSS	09.04.1976	USGS
96/3	Landsat ETM+	Mosaic	USGS
98/1	Landsat OLI	Mosaic	USGS
100/1	Landsat TM	Mosaic	USGS
101/3	Envisat MERIS	Mosaic	ESA
102/1	Landsat TM	Mosaic	USGS
103/3	Envisat ASAR	multitemporal	ESA
103/4a	Landsat TM	25.07.1992	USGS
103/4b	Landsat ETM+	11.08.2001	USGS
103/4c	Landsat OLI	20.08.2013	USGS
104/1	Landsat OLI	22.07.2013	USGS
106/1	Envisat MERIS	Mosaic	ESA
108/1	Landsat ETM	Mosaic	USGS
109/3	Envisat ASAR	multitemporal	ESA
		(19.07./23.08./27.09.2010)	
109/4b	Landsat TM	Mosaic	USGS
110/1	Landsat ETM+	Mosaic	USGS
110/2	Landsat ETM+	Mosaic	USGS
111/3	Envisat MERIS FR	Mosaic	ESA
111/4	RapidEye	25.04.2011	BlackBridge
112/1	Landsat OLI	Mosaic	USGS
114/1	Spot-4 HRVIR Veg.	Global Mosaic	CNES-VITO
114/2	Spot-4 HRVIR Veg./	Mosaic	CNES-VITO/
	Landsat OLI		USGS
115/3	Spot-4 HRVIR Veg.	Mosaic	CNES-VITO
116/1	Landsat MSS	Mosaic	USGS
116/2	Landsat ETM	Mosaic	USGS
116/3	Landsat OLI	Mosaic	USGS
117/4	RapidEye	05.09.2012	BlackBridge
118/1	Landsat ETM	Mosaic	USGS
118/3	Landsat OLI	28.07.2013	USGS
119/4	Envisat ASAR WSM	multitemporal	ESA
120/1	Landsat TM	11.02.1989	USGS
122/1	Spot-4 HRVIR Veg.	Global Mosaic	CNES-VITO
123/3	Envisat MERIS	02.11.2004	ESA
124/1	Landsat OLI	15.09.2013	USGS
125/4a	Proba-1 CHRIS	30.07.2003	ESA
125/4b	Proba-1 CHRIS	18.11.2004	ESA
127/1	Landsat ETM	Mosaic	USGS
127/5	Envisat ASAR	multitemporal	ESA
		(20.01./24.02./31.03.2009)	
128/1	Landsat TM	Mosaic	USGS
128/3	Landsat TM	06.07.1987	USGS
129/4	RapidEye	12.08.2012	BlackBridge
131/1	Landsat ETM+	18.07.2002	USGS
131/2	Landsat TM	Mosaic	USGS
133/1	Envisat MERIS	06.03.2010	ESA
134/2	Landsat ETM+	15.03.2003	USGS
134/3	IKONOS-2	02.08.2004	EUSI
136/1	Landsat ETM	Mosaic	USGS
136/2	IKONOS-2	15.10.2004	EUSI
137/3	Envisat MERIS	Mosaic	ESA
137/4	IKONOS-2	15.10.2004	EUSI
138/1	Landsat OLI	10.08.2013	USGS
139/2	Envisat MERIS	Mosaic	ESA
139/3	RapidEye	23.09.2013	BlackBridge
140/1	Spot-4 HRVIR Veg.	Global Mosaic	CNES-VITO
142/2a	ARGON KH-4A	21.08.1964	USAF/USGS
143/4	Envisat MERIS	10.10.2011	ESA
144/1	Landsat TM	05.02.2001	USGS
146/1	Landsat ETM+	Mosaic	USGS
149/2	Landsat OLI	21.05.2013	USGS
150/1	Landsat ETM+	Mosaic	USGS
151/2	Landsat ETM+	11.07.2000	USGS
151/3a	Terra MODIS	11.07.2000	NASA
151/3b	Terra MODIS	02.11.2000	NASA
151/3c	Terra MODIS	20.02.2001	NASA
152/1	Landsat ETM	Mosaic 1999	USGS
155/4	Landsat ETM	Mosaic 1999	USGS
156/1	Landsat ETM+	Mosaic	USGS
156/2	Envisat ASAR	multitemporal	ESA
156/3a	Proba-1 CHRIS	22.04.2006	ESA
156/3b	Proba-1 CHRIS	29.06.2005	ESA
157/4	Landsat MSS	27.06.1973	USGS
157/5	RapidEye	27.06.2012	BlackBridge
158/1	GOES-9 EPS VIS	01.07.2004	NASA/NOAA
164/1	Aqua MODIS	19.07.2003	NASA-GSFC
165/4	Envisat MERIS	25.04.2004	ESA
166/1a	IKONOS-2	30.05.2004	EUSI
166/1b	IKONOS-2	07.08.2004	EUSI
169/3	WorldView-2	14.03.2011	EUSI/
			Digital Globe
170/1	Sentinel-1 HH/HV	13.04.2014	ESA
172/1	Spot-4 HRVIR Veg.	Global Mosaic	CNES-VITO
173/3	Envisat	14.06.2008	ESA
174/1	Sentinel-1 HV/HH	06.10.2014	ESA
175/4	Radarsat-2 TOPS	17.03.2014	ESA/MDA
176/1	Spot-4 HRVIR Veg.	Global Mosaic	CNES-VITO
178/3	Sentinel-1	27.11.2014	ESA
179/6	Envisat ASAR	Envisat ASAR	ESA
182/1	RapidEye	20.03.2013	BlackBridge
184/1	Envisat ASAR	12.11.2002	ESA
184/2	Terra MODIS	Mosaic	USGS
185/3b	Landsat ETM	Mosaic	USGS
186/1a	Landsat MSS	19.10.1979	USGS
186/2a	Landsat TM	24.12.1990	USGS
186/2b	RapidEye	24.10.2013	BlackBridge
187/1b	Landsat ETM	14.09.2000	USGS
187/5	Landsat ETM+	15.11.1999	USGS
188/1	Landsat OLI	23.10.2013	USGS
190/1	Landsat ETM+	Mosaic	USGS
196/1	Landsat ETM+	23.04.2000	USGS
199/6	QuickBird-2	18.04.2004	e-GEOS
200/1	Landsat ETM	28.02.2000	USGS
202/1	Landsat ETM+	01.02.2002	USGS
203/3	Landsat ETM+	24.11.1999	USGS
203/5	QuickBird-2	13.11.2004	e-GEOS
203/6	QuickBird-2	13.11.2004	e-GEOS
204/1	Landsat ETM	15.03.2000	USGS
208/1	QuickBird-2	30.10.2004	e-GEOS
208/3	QuickBird-2	30.10.2004	e-GEOS
209/6	Landsat OLI	31.08.2013	USGS
210/2a	Landsat OLI	Mosaic	USGS
213/2	SPOT-5	28.12.2013	KACST
214/1	Spot-4 XS	07.04.2004	CNES
	Distribution Astrium Services/Spot Image S.A.		
216/1	QuickBird-2	26.05.2002	e-GEOS
216/2	QuickBird-2	26.05.2002	e-GEOS
218/1	Envisat MERIS FR	06.06.2003	ESA
218/2	Envisat MERIS FR	12.10.2003	ESA
219/4	IKONOS-2	09.12.2003	EUSI
220/1	Terra MODIS	29.10.2002	NASA/GSFC
220/2a	Landsat ETM+	20.09.2000	USGS
221/3	Landsat OLI	15.09.2013	USGS
222/1	Landsat ETM+	Mosaic	
223/2	Landsat ETM	23.08.1999	USGS
223/4	Spot-4 HRVIR Veg.	Global Mosaic	CNES-VITO
224/1	QuickBird-2	29.07.2003	e-GEOS
224/2	Envisat ASAR	multitemporal	ESA
224/3	Landsat OLI	16.04.2013	USGS
225/4	QuickBird-2	29.07.2003	e-GEOS
226/1	Landsat ETM+	21.09.1972	USGS
226/2	Landsat OLI	10.02.2013	USGS
227/3	Spot-4 XS	07.04.2004	CNES
	Distribution Astrium Services/Spot Image S.A.		
228/1	Terra MODIS	Mosaic	NASA/GSFC
231/3	Landsat OLI	04.12.2010	USGS
232/1	Spot-4 HRVIR Veg.	Global Mosaic	CNES-VITO
234/1a	Landsat MSS	Mosaic	USGS
234/1b	Landsat TM	Mosaic	USGS
234/2a	Landsat MSS	21.08.1976	USGS
234/2b	Landsat ETM+	18.08.2000	USGS
235/3	Spot-4 HRVIR Veg.	Global Mosaic	CNES-VITO
237/3a	RapidEye	23.05.2013	BlackBridge
237/3b	RapidEye	18.08.2012	BlackBridge
237/3c	RapidEye	20.09.2012	BlackBridge
240/1	Landsat ETM+	08.03.2002	USGS
242/1a	Landsat MSS	01.01.1973	USGS
242/1b	Landsat OLI	06.09.2013	USGS
244/2	IKONOS-2	16.10.2001	EUSI
245/5	Envisat ASAR	17.11.2002	ESA
246/1	WorldView-2	15.06.2010	EUSI
246/2	Envisat ASAR WS	18.05.2010	ESA
250/1	Landsat ETM+	14.07.1999	USGS
251/2	Envisat MERIS	08.11.2010	ESA
251/4	Envisat MERIS FR	23.09.2004	ESA
253/2a	Envisat MERIS	16.03.2004	ESA
253/2b	Landsat ETM+	20.06.2000	USGS
254/1	Landsat ETM+	Mosaic	USGS
255/2	Landsat OLI	07.11.2013	USGS
251/3	Landsat MSS	23.02.1973	USGS
256/1	Terra ASTER	20.01.2003	NASA NIR/R/G
256/2	Aqua MODIS	26.06.2004	GLCF/NASA
256/3	Envisat ASAR	multitemporal	ESA
256/4	IKONOS-2	09.08.2001	EUSI
257/5	Envisat MERIS	07.03.2003	ESA
257/6	IKONOS-2	09.08.2001	EUSI
256/2	QuickBird-2	14.08.2002	e-GEOS
257/5	Envisat ASAR	27.07.2004	ESA
257/6	Envisat ASAR	27.07.2004	ESA
257/7	RapidEye	01.05.2011	BlackBridge
257/8	IKONOS-2	06.09.2004	EUSI
260/1	Landsat TM	14.07.1991	USGS
260/3	Landsat TM		USGS
262/2	ADEOS OCTS (SST)	26.04.1997	JAXA
264/1	RapidEye	28.02.2011	BlackBridge
265/2	Landsat ETM	23.11.2000	USGS
266/1	Landsat MSS	04.09.1979	USGS
266/2	Landsat OLI	24.07.2013	USGS
268/1	Terra MODIS	06.10.2002	NASA/GSFC
273/4	QuickBird-2	26.12.2004	EUSI
276/4	ERS-2 SAR	multitemporal	ESA
276/5	Landsat ETM/	28.07.2002/	USGS/
	SPOT-4	17.08.2002	CNES-VITO
278/2	Envisat MERIS	28.08.2005	ESA
278/3	Envisat ASAR	28.08.2005	ESA
280/2	IKONOS-2	10.01.2003	modified
	after © DLR/ZKI 2004, IKONOS/EUSI 2004		
280/3	IKONOS-2	29.12.2004	modified
	after © DLR/ZKI 2004, IKONOS/EUSI 2004		
281/5	ERS-1 SAR	multitemporal	ESA
282/1	Spot-4 HRVIR Veg.	Global Mosaic	CNES-VITO

Thematic maps and graphics

Page	© Data provider (in alphabetical order)
12/1	GlobeView/NASA
12/2	ESA/GlobeView/NASA
13/3	ESA/GlobeView
13/4	GlobeView/UN
26/2	AOES medialab/ESA
26/3	ESA
27/4	C. Donier/EADS-Astrium
29/5	ESA/Denmann production
29/7	ESA/NASA/University of Bremen
30/1	ESA/ATG Medialab
31/3	AOES medialab/ESA
31/4	AOES medialab/ESA
31/5a	eoVision/GlobeView/ ESA-GOCE High Level Processing Facility
31/5b	GFZ Geoforschungszentrum Potsdam-ICGEM International Centre for Global Earth Models
32/1	AOES medialab/ESA
32/2	ESA/DTU Space
33/3	eoVision/ESA/GlobeView
33/4	ESA/J. Huart
35/5	ESA/D.Ducros
35/6	ESA/EUMETSAT/ZAMG
36/1	CNES-VITO/ESA/GlobeView/NASA/NOAA
36/2a	ESA/gim
36/2b	ESA/gim
37/3	ESA
38/1	Bilkent University/Topkapi Museum Istanbul
39/4	ESA
40/0	ESA
40/3	ESA
41/4	ESA
43/6	ESA
44/2	ESA/USGS
44/4	ESA/NGA National Geospatial-Intelligence Agency
45/5	ESA
46/1	ESA
46/2a	ESA
46/2b	ESA
47/3	ESA
47/4a	CNES Distribution Astrium Services/Spot Image S.A.
47/4b	CNES Distribution Astrium Services/Spot Image S.A.
47/5a	ESA/USGS
47/5b	ESA/USGS
47/6	ESA/USGS

Page	© Data provider (in alphabetical order)
47/7a	ESA/USGS
51	ESA/Globeview
57/1	ESA/NOAA/USGS
58/1	ESA/USGS
59/2	ESA/ISCCP/USGS
60/1	ESA/NASA/NOAA/USGS-GSFC
60/2	ESA/NASA/NOAA/USGS-GSFC
61/3	ESA/IWMI/NASA/NOAA
61/4	ESA/IWMI/NASA/NOAA
62/1	ESA/NASA/NOAA/W.Lauer & P.Frankenberg
64/1	ESA/JRC Joint Research Centre/NASA/NOAA
66/1	eoVision/GlobeView/ East View Information Services/NASA/NOAA/ ORNL Oak Ridge National Laboratory/UN
66/2	ESA/U.S.Census Bureau
68/1	ESA/Munich Re Group/NASA/NOAA
70/1	ESA/GlobeView/NASA/NOAA/UNEP
70/2	ESA/NASA/NOAA/ WWAP World Water Assessment Programme
71/3	ESA/NASA/NOAA/ WWAP World Water Assessment Programme
71/4	ESA/NASA/NOAA/ WWAP World Water Assessment Programme
72/1	ESA/GlobeView/NASA/NOAA/ A.Wolf, OSU Oregon State University/ TFDD Transboundary Freshwater Dispute Database
72/2	eoVision/GlobeView/ TFDD International River Basin Register
75/2	ESA/NASA/Fiske&Yaffe/GlobeView/NASA/NOAA/ OSU Oregon State University/Ph.D. Associates Inc.
77/2	eoVision/ESA/GlobeView
83/4	BlackBridge/eoVision/GlobeView
90/1	CNES-VITO/ESA/NASA/NOAA
90/2	ESA/NASA/USGS
94/2	CNES-VITO/ESA/NASA/NOAA
97/4	ESA/USGS
100/2	CNES-VITO/ESA/NASA/NOAA
106/2	CNES-VITO/ESA/NASA/NOAA
109/4a	ESA/USGS
111/5	CNES-VITO/ESA/NASA/NOAA
115/4	CNES-VITO/ESA/NASA/NOAA
118/2	CNES-VITO/ESA/NASA/NOAA
122/2	CNES-VITO/ESA/NASA/NOAA
126/2	CNES-VITO/ESA/NASA/NOAA
128/2	CNES-VITO/ESA/NASA/NOAA
134/1	CNES-VITO/ESA/NASA/NOAA
139/4	BlackBridge/eoVision/GlobeView
142/1	ESA
142/2b	ESA/USGS
143/2c	CNES-VITO/ESA
143/2d	eoVision/GlobeView/NASA
145/2	ESA/NASA
148/1	ESA/NASA/ORNL Oak Ridge National Laboratory
149/4	ORNL Oak Ridge National Laboratory/USDA
151/4	CNES-VITO/ESA/NASA/NOAA
154/1a	ESA/Hugin
154/1b	ESA/Hugin
154/1c	ESA/Hugin
154/1d	ESA/Hugin
160/1	CNES-VITO/ESA/NASA/NOAA
160/2	CNES-VITO/ESA/GSFC/NASA/NOAA
161/3a	CNES-VITO/ESA/Millat & Robinson/NASA
161/3b	CNES-VITO/ESA/Millat & Robinson/NASA
161/3c	CNES-VITO/ESA/Millat & Robinson/NASA
161/3d	CNES-VITO/ESA/Millat & Robinson/NASA
161/3e	CNES-VITO/ESA/Millat & Robinson/NASA
161/3f	CNES-VITO/ESA/Millat & Robinson/NASA
162/1	eoVision/GlobeView/NASA/NOAA-NESDIS/PMEL/TAO
162/2	eoVision/GlobeView/NASA/NOAA-NESDIS/PMEL/TAO
163/3	eoVision/ESA
163/4	eoVision/ESA
163/5	eoVision/ESA
163/6	eoVision/GlobeView/NASA/NOAA-PMEL
164/1	ESA/NASA-GSFC
166/2	ARGOSS/ESA
167/4	ESA/NASA
167/5	ESA/NASA
167/6	ESA
167/7	ESA/NASA
168/1	ARTE/GlobeView/ NASA/NOAA-MDP Marine Debris Project
168/2	CNES-VITO/GlobeView/NASA/NOAA
169/6	GlobeView/ESA
173/2	ESA/F.Fetter et.al.-NSIDC National Snow & Ice Data Center Boulder/Globe View
174/3a	GlobeView/UCL University College London/A.Ridout
174/3b	GlobeView/UCL University College London/A.Ridout
174/3c	GlobeView/UCL University College London/A.Ridout
174/3d	GlobeView/UCL University College London/A.Ridout
175/5	ESA/GlobeView/IMBIE/NASA
177/2	ESA/F.Fetter et.al.-NSIDC National Snow & Ice Data Center Boulder/Globe View
177/5	CSIRO/ESA/GlobeView
178/1	AWI Alfred-Wegener-Institut, Helmholtz-Zentrum für Polar- und Meeresforschung, Bremerhaven-V. Helm et al.,/ESA/eoVision/GlobeView
178/2	CPOM Center for Polar Observation and Monitoring/ UCL Univ. College London/ESA/Planetary Visions
179/5	eoVision/GlobeView/GSFC-NASA's Goddard Space Flight Center Scientific Visualization Studio/ JPL Jet Propulsion Laboratory-Caltech California Institute of Technology CIT/Earth System Science Department-UCI University of California at Irvine
185/3a	ESA
187/3	ESA/USGS
187/4	e-GEOS/ESA
189/4	ESA/USGS
189/5	ESA/USGS

Page	© Data provider (in alphabetical order)
192/1	ESA/Third World centre for Water Management Mexico/CentroGEO-J.L.Tamayo-National Research Council for Science and Technology/USGS
193/2	ESA/GAMMA Remote Sensing Zurich/USGS
194/1	ESA/Third World centre for Water Management Mexico/CentroGEO-J.L.Tamayo-National Research Council for Science and Technology/USGS
194/2	ESA/Third World centre for Water Management Mexico/CentroGEO-J.L.Tamayo-National Research Council for Science and Technology/USGS
195/3	ESA/Third World centre for Water Management Mexico/CentroGEO-J.L.Tamayo-National Research Council for Science and Technology/USGS
198/1	CNES-VITO/ESA
198/2	CNES-VITO/ESA
198/3	CNES-VITO/ESA/Westermann
199/4	DWAF Department Water Affairs/ESA/NASA
202/2	ESA/USGS/Westermann
203/4	ESA
208/2	ESA/W.Wölfel
210/1	CNES-VITO/ESA
210/2b	ESA/SARMAP
211/3	ESA/Westermann
211/4	ESA/SARMAP
212/1	ESA/KSA General Commision for Survey
213/5	KSU King Saud University-PSIEWDR/USGS
219/3	ESA
220/2b	ESA/USGS
223/3	CSIRO/ESA/NDSP-Land Cover Project
230/1	CNES-VITO/ESA/ICLARM/WIR/WCMC
230/2	EIA/ESA/Petroatlas-Westermann
234/1c	ESA/GlobeView
236/1	ESA
236/2	ESA/NASA/TIEMPO
238/1	USGS
239/2	ESA/WDPA World Data Base on Protected Area
239/3	ESA/WDPA World Data Base on Protected Area
243/2a	ESA/NASA/Westerman
243/2b	ESA/NASA/Westerman
244/1	JRC Joint Research Centre//ITOPF/ESA/ European Commission/EuroStat/UN
245/3	GlobeView/ITOPF/ESA
245/6	CNES-VITO/ESA/NASA/NOAA/UICN/WDPA/ UNEP-WCMC
246/3	AVISO/CU University of Colorado/CNES/GlobeView/ ESA-GOES SST/Radarsat-2
247/7a	AAI/BlackBridge/eoVision/GlobeView
247/7b	AAI/BlackBridge/eoVision/GlobeView
247/7c	AAI/BlackBridge/eoVision/GlobeView
247/7d	AAI/BlackBridge/eoVision/GlobeView
248/1	IUCN Int. Union for Conservation of Nature/Env. Department Hungary & Romania/ESA/USGS/UNEP/ WDPA World Data Base on Protected Area
249/2	IUCN Int. Union for Conservation of Nature/Environ- ment Department Hungary & Romania/ESA/USGS/ UNEP/WDPA World Data Base on Protected Area
249/3	ESA/USGS
249/4	ESA/USGS
252/1	BlackBridge/eoVision/GlobeView
253/3	ESA/Verbund
253/5	ESA/University of Graz
255/2	ESA/USGS
258/1	ESA/NASA/NOAA-OSMC Observing System Monitoring Center
258/3	ESA/USGS
260/1	CNES-VITO/ESA/NERSC Nansen Environmental and Remote Sensing Center/ACIA Arctic Climate Impact Assessment
260/4	ESA/S.Sandven
261/5	ESA
262/1a	CNES-VITO/ESA
262/1b	CNES-VITO/ESA/JAXA Japan Aerospace Exploration Agency
263/5	ESA/ORI Ocean Research Institute/TODAI Tokyo
265/4	FAO
267/3	FAO
267/3	ESA/FAO
270/1	ESA/Research Center for Earth Operative Monitoring (NTsOMZ)
270/2	ESA
271/5	GlobeView/Munich Re NatCatService
271/6	GlobeView/Munich Re NatCatService
271/7	GlobeView/Munich Re NatCatService
271/8	GlobeView/Munich Re NatCatService
272/2	ESA
275/3	Copernicus GIO EMS/European Union; 1995-2004
276/1	DWD Deutscher Wetterdienst/ESA
276/2	BAFG/ESA
276/3	BOKU/ESA
277/7	CNES Distribution Astrium Services/ Spot Image S.A./ESA
277/8	CSA Canadian Space Agency/ESA
277/9	BEV/BWD/CSA Canadian Space Agency/ESA
278/1	ESA/NOAA/Universitiy Karlsruhe
279/4	ESA
279/5	BBC/ESA
279/6	ESA
280/1	CNES-VITO/ESA/NASA/NOAA
281/4	ESA/NASA
281/6	CNES-VITO/ESA/NASA/NOAA-PMEL Pacific Marine Environmental Laboratory
282/2a	ESA/NASA/USGS/USDA-GLAM Global Agricultural Monitoring Project
282/2b	ESA//EUMETSAT/NASA/TU-Wien
283/3	ESA/USGS
283/4	ESA/USGS
Back-/Endpaper	eoVision/ESA/GlobeView/CNES-VITO

Aerials and photographs

Page	© Data provider (in alphabetical order)
8/1	NASA
11/2a	L.Beckel
11/2b	L.Beckel
11/2c	L.Beckel
11/2d	L.Beckel
11/2e	L.Beckel
25/1	ESA/S.Corvaja
26/1	ARIANSPACE-Service & Solutions, Optique CSG/ CNES/ESA
28/1	ESA/A.Gonin
28/2	ARIANSPACE-Service & Solutions, Optique CSG/ CNES/ESA
28/3	ARIANSPACE-Service & Solutions, Optique CSG/ CNES/ESA
28/4	ESA/S.Corvaja
37/4	ESA
39/3	T.Crols
43/7	ESA/D.Ducros
43/8	ESA
51/1	iStock.com/pixonaut
54/1	L.Beckel
55/2	L.Beckel
74/1	W.Lichem
77/1	iStock.com/RobertDodge
79/1	iStock.com/MsLightBox
91/5	L.Beckel
102/2	NASA
107/3	Wikimedia/Cornelius Bechtler
108/2	L.Beckel
124/2	iStock.com/zjzpp163
124/3	L.Beckel
127/2	Rajan Simkhada, EARTHBOUND EXPEDITIONS
127/3	Stefan Skiba
137/5	iStock.com/geisha
142/3	iStock.com/DanielPrudek
145/3	Astrid Köpf
145/4	Astrid Köpf
149/3	iStock.com/debstheleo
1551/2	J.Baker Hill/UNEP
155/3	J.Baker Hill/UNEP
164/3	iStock.com/Firehorse
166/3	Wikimedia/Uwe Küchler
169/4	U.S.Navy
169/5	NOAA's Marine Debris Programme/ ORR Office of Response and Restoration
174/2a	M.Davidson
174/2b	Norwegian Polar Institute
177/3	UTAS University of Tasmania/J. Beardsley
177/4	ESA
179/4	ESA
181/1	iStock.com/kentuckyhanson
189/2	L.Beckel
189/3	L.Beckel
195/4	Wikimedia/Thelmadatter
199/5	iStock.com/deldew
199/7	iStock.com/mtcurado
206/1	WaterFoundation/Munich Re Foundation archives
206/2	WaterFoundation/Munich Re Foundation archives
206/3	WaterFoundation/Munich Re Foundation archives
206/4	WaterFoundation/Munich Re Foundation archives
207/5	WaterFoundation/Munich Re Foundation archives
207/6	WaterFoundation/Munich Re Foundation archives
207/7	WaterFoundation/Munich Re Foundation archives
208/4	M.Makki
209/5	M.Eisl
209/7	M.Makki
211/5	L.Beckel
213/3	KSU King Saud University-PSIEWDR
213/4	KSU King Saud University-PSIEWDR
217/3	H.Krause
223/5	CSIRO Land and Water/J.Wallace
227/4	L.Beckel
227/5	KSU King Saud University-PSIEWDR
239/4	iStock.com/pjmalsbury
243/3	iStock.com/HarryBin
245/4	Stf/EPA/PictureDesk.com
246/4	U.S. Coast Guard
246/5	NOAA-Office of Response and restoration/ NOAA's Ocean Service
246/6	NOAA-Office of Response and restoration/ NOAA's Ocean Service
251/3	iStock.com/npoizot
253/4	L.Beckel
258/4	iStock.com/HHakim
259/9	iStock.com/ictor
261/6	Murmansk Shipping Company
261/7	A.Glazovsky/RAS Russian Academy of Science- Institute of Geography
263/3	iStock.com/alvarez
233/4	NASA
263/6	Wikimedia/Geomr
263/7	Wikimedia/Marshall Astor
265/3	iStock.com/zorazhuang
267/4	Auburn University-Department of Fisheries
270/3	Munich Re/W.Kron
270/4	Munich Re/W.Kron
272/1	Munich Re/W.Kron
272/3	Munich Re/A.Allmann
274/1	L.Beckel
275/2	GEPS Green Energy Prognostic Systems/W.Lahmer
277/6	L.Beckel
283/5	USDA's Foreign Agricultural Service FAS/C.Reynolds

295

GLOSSARY

AATSR – Advanced Along Track Scanning Radiometer, a multispectral radiometer on the ENVISAT satellite (2002–2012).

Ablation – The melting of snow and ice.

Absorption – Conversion of radiant energy into another form of energy (e.g. heat) when it comes into contact with a material.

Active sensor (active system) – Remote sensing system that emits radiation and measures the amount reflected (e.g. radar).

ADM-Aeolus – Atmospheric Dynamics Mission, name of a three-year ESA satellite mission to launch in 2015, which will provide global data on the three-dimensional measurement of windfields.

Aerosol – A colloid of solid or liquid particles suspended in a gas (e.g. smoke, fog).

Allochthonous river – A river originating in areas with high rainfall and flowing through an arid region; also 'exotic'.

ALOS PALSAR – Phased Array type L-band Synthetic Aperture Radar, radar sensor on the Japanese satellite ALOS (Advanced Land Observing Satellite; launch 2006).

Altimeter – Active instrument to measure the height of a satellite above a reference plane, enabling the determination of topography using known orbit data.

Amplitude – Maximum deviation of a wave from a rest position.

Antarctic bottom waters (AABW) – Cold and saline, and therefore dense, water at the sea floor around Antarctica.

Antarctic Circumpolar Current (ACC) – Ocean current surrounding Antarctica.

Aqua – NASA satellite to determine precise oceanographic and atmospheric data with the aim of improving understanding of the global climate and how it is changing.

Aqueduct – A construction, often an arched bridge, used to transport water.

Aquifer – A body of rock with hollow spaces that can carry groundwater.

AQUIFER project – ESA project aiming to support institutions and governments with remote sensing in the field of water management, water resources and water resources management.

Ariane – Launch vehicles developed for ESA by a subsidiary of the European Aeronautic Defence and Space Company (EADS) and launched from the Kourou Space Centre in French Guiana.

Arid – Dry, desert-like.

Artemis – Advanced Relay and TEchnology MISsion, telecommunication satellite of ESA (launch 2001).

Artesian – groundwater layers that are under pressure and can feed artesian wells.

ASAR – Advanced Synthetic Aperture Radar, an active C-band radar sensor on board the satellite ENVISAT.

ASCAT – Advanced Scatterometer, sensor to measure wind speeds and wind direction across the oceans' surface and soil humidity on land.

ASIRAS – Airborne SAR/Interferometric Radar System is an airborne SAR-altimeter instrument for CryoSat validation.

ASTER – Advanced Spaceborne Thermal Emission and Reflection Radiometer, instrument on board the NASA satellites Terra and Aqua.

AVHRR – Advanced Very High Resolution Radiometer, scanner on NOAA satellites for the quantitative measurement of electromagnetic radiation in order to determine cloud cover, surface temperature and vegetation.

AWF – African Wildlife Foundation.

AWI – Alfred Wegener Intitute.

Axial tilt – Rotation of a satellite around its axis in order point to a special part of the Earth's surface.

Aymara – An indigenous South American people from the Andes.

Backscatter – Backscatter of electromagnetic energy from small particles towards the source.

Band – Limited range of frequencies on the electromagnetic spectrum to which the sensors of a remote sensing system respond.

Bathymetry – Mapping the topography of the ocean floor.

Biomass – Part of the Earth Explorer Mission of ESA, created to estimate the biomass of the world's forests using radar technology.

Blowout – an uncontrolled leakage of oil or natural gas from a borehole of a drilling or conveyor system.

Boreal tree line – Line around the poles, where the environment becomes too hostile for trees.

Brackish water – Mixture of saltwater and freshwater, e.g. at river mouths.

Brash ice – A patch of accumulated small fragments of ice floating on a water surface.

Buoyancy – Upward force on a body immersed or partly immersed in a liquid such as water.

C-Band – part of the electromagnetic microwave spectrum between 500 MHz and 1000 MHz.

CarbonSat – Planned Earth Explorer mission of ESA to monitor carbon dioxide and methane.

Centre-pivot irrigation – Irrigation system that sprays water as it travels in a circle.

CEOS – Committee for Earth Observation Satellites, committee comprising most civil space agencies, to coordinate Earth observation missions.

CET – Central European Time, time zone based on the mean solar time at the meridian at Görlitz (15° E).

Climate model – Computer model to calculate and project the climate for a specific period.

Climatology – Subdiscipline of meteorology dealing with climate patterns, i.e. the average conditions in the atmosphere in a given location and the processes at work there.

CNES – Centre national d 'études spatiales, the French space agency.

Continental climate (continentality) – Influence of the continents on the climate with increased temperature variations and extremes, as well as decreasing precipitation with increased distance from the sea

Copernicus – (see GMES).

COPUOS – United Nations Committee on the Peaceful Uses of Outer Space.

CryoSat – ESA research satellite mapping the Earth's cryosphere and collecting data in particular on the volume of the ice sheets in the Arctic and Antarctic (since 2010).

CSA – Canadian Space Agency.

CSIR – Council for Scientific and Industrial Research, South Africa.

CSIRO – Commonwealth Scientific and Industrial Research Organisation, Australian authority for scientific and industrial research.

Cyclone – Area of low pressure moving from west to east in the Westerlies zone.

Dead zones – Areas in the oceans and lakes where the oxygen concentration is no longer sufficient to support life.

Deepwater Horizon – Exploration oil rig in the Gulf of Mexico that sank following a blowout on 22 April 2010, triggering an environmental catastrophe.

Delta (river delta) – Triangular mouth of a river featuring a network of channels.

DEM – Digital Elevation Model, digital model showing topography, usually in the form of a regular microdot grid, in which the individual points represent elevations.

Differential Interferometry – Radar data evaluation method exploiting phase differences between two or more datasets to assess terrain movements.

Digital Elevation Model – (see DEM).

DMSP – US Air Force's Defense Meteorological Satellite Program.

Drainage basin (hydrological drainage basin) – All the water and substances in a body of water (e.g. a lake) resulting from physical, chemical and biological subprocesses.

Drift (ocean drift) – system of flows across the oceans.

Dry rice – A low-yielding subspecies of rice that is not adapted to flooding and needs high humidity, can be grown in the high mountains

EAC – European Astronaut Centre, Cologne; central ESA facility for training astronauts.

EarthCARE – Scheduled space mission to research aerosols and clouds and their impact on radiation in the Earth's atmosphere, as part of the Living Planet Programme of ESA. Launch date: 2016.

Earth Explorer – An ESA mission and part of the Living Planet Programme, which comprises the satellite missions providing new observation data on the Earth.

(Earth's) magnetic field – Magnetic field produced by the geodynamo.

Earth observation satellite – Satellites observing the Earth from space.

Eccentricity – Describes the form of an ellipse of an orbit using the ratio between the focii to the length of the principal axis. The eccentricity of a circle is 0.

Eddy – Turbulent currents resulting from obstacles such as islands or the convergence of two different currents.

El Niño – Anomalous, non-cyclic currents in the oceanographic and meteorological systems in the Equatorial Pacific with consequences for the climate over large parts of the Earth.

Electromagnetic spectrum – The range of all types of radiant energy or wave frequencies from the longest to the shortest wavelengths, usually divided into the categories of radiowaves, microwaves, infrared waves, visible light, ultraviolet waves, X-rays and gamma rays.

Endorheic – Describes rivers that do not drain into the ocean but into lakes with no drainage (e.g. basins).

ENSO – El Niño Southern Oscillation, complex coupled circulation system of the atmosphere and ocean in the Pacific.

Envisat – ESA's Environmental Satellite, whose primary task is to observe changes in the global environment.

Eocene – geologic period 56 to 34 million years ago.

Episodic (lakes, rivers) – Events with highly irregular repetition.

ERS – ESA's European Remote Sensing Satellite, significant for its radar data in particular (1991–2011).

ESA – European Space Agency.

ESAC – European Space Astronomy Centre, Villafranca/Spain; ESA's scientific operations centre for satellite data on astronomy and the solar system.

ESOC – ESA's European Space Operations Centre, Darmstadt/Germany.

ESRIN – ESA's European Space Research Institute, at Frascati near Rome/Italy.

ESTEC – ESA's European Space Research and Technology Centre, at Nordwijk/Netherlands.

Estuary – the tidal mouth of a large river.

ETM+ – Enhanced Thematic Mapper Plus, Landsat-7 sensor, which, compared to its predecessors, the MSS and TM, features an extra band with a pixel resolution of 15 m and, with 60 m, improved geometric resolution in the thermal band.

EU – European Union. Association of European states, with 28 Member States (2015).

EUMETSAT – European Organisation for the Exploitation of Meteorological Satellites, operator of Meteosat and MetOp weather satellites.

Eutrophication – Surplus of nutrients in a water body, causing intense plant growth and usually reducing dissolved oxygen.

Evaporation – Evaporation of water from bodies of water or the soil, not including transpiration.

Evapotranspiration – Amount of water evaporating from the land; comprises both evaporation and transpiration.

Exotic – Type of river that originates in a humid climate and flows through an arid region as an allochthonous river.

Exploration oil platform – oil platform to explore undersea oil fields.

False colour – Image processing method whereby an image is shown in colours other than those in which it is normally recorded.

FAO – Food and Agriculture Organization of the United Nations.

Far infrared – Electromagnetic radiation, with wavelengths of between 25 µm to 1000 µm, longer than those of thermal infrared.

Fauna – Describes the animal kingdom.

Firn – Compacted névé snow that has undergone a period of ablation (e.g. summer).

FLEX – Fluorescence Explorer, Earth Explorer satellite planned by ESA.

Flora – Describes the world of plants.

Floating glacier – Part of tidal glaciers floating on the sea.

Flow system – system of ocean currents with regional to global dimensions.

Fog Harvester – apparatus to extract water from the air using fog collector nets.

FOG QUEST – Canadian NGO devoted to water projects (mist collectors and effective rain collectors) in rural communities of developing countries.

Frequency – Number of events within a period of time.

Freshwater – The water from inland bodies of water with a salinity of less than 0.1 %.

Galileo – European civil satellite navigation system, compatible with existing American (NAVSTAR-GPS) and Russian (GLONASS) systems.

GAP – Güneydogu Anadolu Projesi, Turkish development project featuring a total of 22 dams, 19 hydroelectric power stations and irrigation systems along the Euphrates and Tigris rivers.

Garbage patch – collection of waste, dominated by plastics, accumulated in the ocean gyres by marine currents.

Genoa low (Ligurian Depression or V[5]-track cyclone) – Humid, warm weather system with a low pressure trough in the upper atmosphere above western and central Europe, generally developing in spring or autumn.

Geocoding – One element of georeferencing, where data with no georeference are translated into the desired reference system.

Geodesy – Mapping the Earth and its surface.

GeoEye-1 – US company selling satellite images and providing data for geoinformation systems.

Geoid – Equipotential surface in the Earth's gravitational field that roughly corresponds to the mean sea level.

GEOSS – Global Earth Observation System of Systems, an initiative by the ad hoc GEO-Group to promote closer cooperation in Earth observation.

GFO – GEOSAT Follow-On is the US Navy's initiative to develop an operational series of radar altimeter satellites to maintain continuous ocean observation (launched 1998).

Geostationary – A satellite on a geostationary orbit orbits at a height of 35,768 kilometres. The angular velocity of the satellite's orbit is synchronous with the rotation of the Earth.

GHz – Gigahertz, unit of frequency showing the number of repeating processes per second in a periodic signal.

GIS – Geographic Information System; system collecting, managing, processing, storing and displaying geographical data.

GITEWS – German Indonesian Tsunami Early-Warning System.

Global ocean current circulation – Global system of ocean currents, also called Ocean Conveyor Belt.

GMES – Global Monitoring for Environment and Security, former name of the EU's Copernicus Earth observation programme.

GOCE – Gravity field and steady-state ocean circulation explorer, an ESA geoscientific satellite that intentionally burned up in the Earth's atmosphere after running out of propellant in November 2013.

GOES – Geostationary Operational Environmental Satellite, a series of geostationary satellites developed by NASA and operated by NOAA.

GOMOS – Global Ozone Monitoring by Occultation of Stars, an instrument for observing the Earth's atmosphere on board the European Envisat satellite.

GPS – Global Positioning System, satellite-assisted positioning system to determine the position of a specific point on the Earth's surface. It comprises 25 satellites, orbiting at a height of 20,000 km, which provide precise data on position, speed and time.

Gravity field – Field transmitting gravitational forces, produced by a body of mass.

Great Pacific Garbage Patch – collection of marine debris particles in the central North Pacific gyre.

Greenhouse gas – Gaseous substances in the atmosphere affecting radiation and contributing to the warming of the Earth's atmosphere, known as the greenhouse effect.

Ground resolution – Describes the length of the side of a single square pixel in an image. The smaller this value is, the more precise and detailed the image.

Groundwater – Accumulation of water in the bedrock, which can be formed by the percolation of rainwater and water from rivers and lakes.

GSTB – V2/A – ESA satellite to measure radiation exposure in the Galileo orbit, now known as GIOVE A.

Gyre – (see Eddy)

Halophilic – Describes organisms capable of living in environments with high salt concentrations.

Helvetas – Swiss association for international cooperation.

High tide – High water levels due to tides.

Holocene – The latest epoch in Earth's history, comprising the end of the Quarternary to the present.

hPa – Hectopascal, unit for measuring air pressure

HRV – Haute Resolution Visible, sensors on board the SPOT satellites, which can be operated in panchromatic mode.

Hurricane – Tropical cyclone with wind speeds of over 12 on the Beaufort Scale and above 118 km/h.

Hydrology – Science dealing with the water on, above and below the Earth's surface.

Hypoxia – The concentration of dissolved oxygen in a body of water is so low (depending on salt content and temperature) that it limits the number of aquatic organisms able to live in the water.

Ice shelf – Large shelf of ice floating on the sea and connected to the land by a glacier.

Ice velocities – Rate at which ice bodies (glaciers, ice sheets and sea ice) are moving.

IEA – International Energy Agency, partnership for the research, development, market launch and use of energy-related technologies.

IKONOS-2 – A commercial Earth observation satellite.

Inclination – In satellite orbits, this is the angle at which the orbital plane of the satellite is tilted at the equatorial plane.

Infrared radiation (IR) – Electromagnetic radiation with a wavelength of between 0.7 µm and 1000 µm – above the visible range and below the microwave range. Subdivided into visible, near, mid-wavelength and far infrared.

InSAR – (see also SAR).

Instrument –(see also scanner instrument).

Interferogram – Result of interferometry method showing relative phase differences between two datasets.

Interferometry – A method of measurement that compares relative phase changes between two or more sources of electromagnetic radiation. Using the resultant interference pattern, changes in angles, distances and refractive indices can be calculated.

International Charter on Space and Major Disasters – Charter provides for the charitable retasked acquisition of and transmission of space satellite data to relief organizations in the event of major disasters.

IPCC – Intergovernmental Panel on Climate Change, institution that summarises the findings from the latest scientific research for political decision-makers.

ISS – International Space Station, a joint project between 16 countries designed as a scientific laboratory in space.

Isthmus – A narrow strip of land between two larger masses of land.

IWAREMA – A project from ESA's TIGER initiative to support African countries in solving water-related problems and to provide additional information about water using satellite data.

IWRM – Integrated Water Resources Management, measure to support successful technology and knowledge transfer in the field of sustainable water management in a selection of developing countries and emerging economies.

Jason – Jason-1 (2001–2013) and -2 (launched 2008) are two satellites dedicated to oceanography tasks.

JERS – Japanese Earth Resources Satellite, in operation from 1992 to 1998.

K – Kelvin, basic unit SI (International System of Units), which measures thermodynamic temperature. Also an official unit of temperature.

K–Band – Radar and microwaves ranging from 1.67 cm to 2.4 cm.

Katabatic winds – Cool and dense air sinking down, following the terrain towards sea.

Kilowatt (kW) – international unit for output (energy transfer for a given period).

L-Band –- Radar and microwaves ranging from 1.5 dm to 3 dm.

Lacrosse – A series of military reconnaissance satellites from the US National Reconnaissance Office (NRO).

Land cover – The land cover with forest or water, for example, over a certain area as determined by the spectral signature of satellite data.

Land Monitor – Australian research and development project project of the Western Australian Salinity Action Plan supported by the Natural Heritage Trust, looking into the salinity of dry regions and their causes, effects and options for combatting them.

La Niña – Ocean-atmosphere phenomenon as counterpart of El Niño accompanied with increased air pressure (see also ENSO), while the sea surface temperature across the equatorial Eastern Central Pacific Ocean will be lower than normal by 3–5 °C.

Landsat – American remote sensing system comprising a series of satellites (ERST-1, Landsat-2–8) with various sensors, primarily used to map natural resources (land usage classifications, forest condition, etc.).

Land use classification – evaluation of a remote sensing data set by which defined land use classes are mapped to individual pixels or regions.

Leeward – The side facing away from the wind (wind shadow).

Low tide – Low water levels due to tides.

MDGs – Millennium Development Goals, eight development goals set by the United Nations to be achieved by 2015 (drafted in 2001).

Meander – Loops in a river or valley with a river flowing in wide curves on flat land.

MEDSPIRATION – The Medspiration Project is a European intiative to collate data on the sea's surface temperature.

MERCOSUR – Common market and customs union in the south of Latin America.

MERIS – Medium Resolution Imaging Spectrometer, Envisat sensor primarily collecting data on the oceans and vegetation.

Meteorology – The science of physical processes and patterns in the Earth's atmosphere.

Meteosat – Meteorological Satellite, range of European geostationary weather satellites, launched into space before ESA existed and operated by EUMETSAT.

MetOp – Series of three European weather satellites with an orbit taking them close to the Earth's poles.

Microplastics – small plastic particles, sizes in the micrometre and nanometre range.

Microwave radiation – Electromagnetic radiation with wavelength between approx. 1000 µm and 1 m.

Mid-wavelength infrared – Electromagnetic radiation between near infrared and thermal infrared with wavelengths of approx. 2 µm to 5 µm.

Milankovitch cycles – periodic changes in the Earth's orbit around the sun.

MIPAS – Measuring instrument on board the European ENVISAT environmental satellite that researches the climate and atmosphere.

MODIS – Moderate–Resolution Imaging Spectroradiometer, instrument on board the Terra and Aqua satellites.

Monsoon – large-scale air circulation of the lower troposphere in the tropics and subtropics, where the trade winds blow.

Morphology – Study of the outer form or shape of an object and how it changes.

Mosaic – An image comprised of several adjacent digital remote sensing images used to create an overview.

MSG – Meteosat Second Generation, second-generation mission of the existing Meteosat satellite system.

MSS – Multispectral Scanner, sensor on the Landsat satellites 1, 2, 4 and 5 with four spectral bands in the visible range and in near infrared with a resolution of 80 m.

MTG – Meteosat Third Generation, planned third generation of European geostationary weather satellites.

Multispectral – Term to describe a sensor that is able to take images or measure data in several spectral ranges at the same time.

Multitemporal – Data that present the same region at various times.

Munich Re Foundation – non-profit foundation engaged with population development, environmental and climate change, disaster prevention and poverty reduction.

NASA – National Aeronautics and Space Administration, civil US Federal aerospace authority responsible for all American space projects.

Nautical mile (nm) – One nm corresponds to around 1.85 km.

NBI – Nile Basin Initiative to ensure mutual long-term positive development and to manage the water resources in the Nile.

Near infrared – Wavelengths in the electromagnetic spectrum ranging between 0.70 µm and 2 µm.

NOAA – The US's National Oceanic and Atmospheric Administration.

Nutrients – Components of water and soil utilized by organisms to survive and grow.

NWSAS – North–Western Sahara Aquifer System.

Ocean colour – Determined via the incident light interacting with substances or particles in the water. In various spectral ranges, phytoplankton can result in different colours due to its chlorophyll content.

Ocean currents – horizontal and vertical transport of water masses in oceans.

Ocean drift – (see Drift).

OKACOM – Permanent Okavango River Basin Commission, investigating the best possible usage of the natural resources of the Okavango.

OLI – Operational Land Imager, multispectral imaging sensor on board Landsat-8.

Orbit – Trajectory on which an object in space moves around another object under the influence of gravity.

Orbital plane – An imaginary plane desciped by the orbit of an Earth satellite and which passes through the centre of the Earth.

Ordovician – Geologic period 485 to 443 million years ago.

OSS – Observatoire du Sahara et du Sahel, platform for the African states neighbouring on the Sahara and Sahel to boost capacities for long-term, sustainable development perspectives.

Outlet glacier – Fast-moving glaciers at the end of ice shields, which generally flow into the sea.

Pack ice – Ice floes in the polar seas that, brought together by currents and wind, collide, sometimes forming towers of ice.

Panchromatic (PAN) – Sensor with a sensitivity level that matches the entire range of the human eye, from around 400 nm to 780 nm.

Pangaea – Supercontinent that existed in the period 300 to 200 million years ago.

Passive microwave radiometer (passive system) – Sensor system that collects natural microwave radiation emitted by the Earth's surface.

Passive system – A system sensitive to the electromagnetic radiation emitted or reflected by an object.

PDVSA – Petróleos de Venezuela S. A., the biggest oil company in Latin America and Venezuela's biggest exporter.

Permafrost – Soil that is frozen all year round and which occurs where the temperature remains below 0 °C for long periods of time.

Permian-Carboniferous – Covering the Permian (360 to 299 million years ago) and the Carboniferous (299 to 252 million years ago) periods.

Photodegradation – Decomposition of plastics by UV radiation.

Piedmont glacier – Glacier emerging from a mountain chain onto flat land.

297

Pixel – Term used to describe a single point in an image corresponding to a specific ground resolution.

Plastic soup – A concentrated collection of microplastics in the oceans.

Plate tectonics – Dynamics of the Earth's continental plates.

Platform – Where, for example, sensor systems for remote sensing or photogrammetry are installed (e.g. satellite).

Pleistocene – Epoch in Earth's history that started around 2.3 million years ago and ended around 10,000 years ago with the start of the Holocene.

Pluvial – Periods in the Earth's history characterised by relatively high humidity.

Polar orbit – Orbit of a satellite that passes above the polar regions and thus has a high inclination compared with the equatorial plane.

Precambrian – Geologic period from the Earth's birth to 541 million years ago.

Precession – Rotation of the Earth's axis around the poles.

PROBA – Project for On–Board Autonomy, ESA's experimental technology satellite for Earth exploration.

Qanat – Traditional method of transporting drinking water in arid regions in the forms of water tunnels transporting water from mountainous regions.

Quarternary – The most recent period in Earth's history, including the Holocene (the present).

QuickBird-2 – Ultra high-resolution satellite mission with panchromatic resolution, from the company DigitalGlobe.

Radar interferometry – (see also interferometry) Process used to evaluate radar data. Using the interference pattern, changes in distance can be calculated and used to create three-dimensional images of the Earth's surface.

Radar sensor – Instrument emitting and receiving microwave pulses.

RADARSAT – Canadian Earth observation satellite on a Sun-synchronous, polar orbit to monitor the environment.

Radiation (scattering) – Dissipation of energy in the form of waves or particles that give off energy when they are absorbed by an object.

Radiation (emissivity) – Ratio of the amount of energy emitted by an object at a certain temperature to the radiant energy of an idealised body (black body) at the same temperature.

RapidEye – Earth observation satellite constellation owned and operated by BlackBridge.

Reflectance – Coefficient between the amount of light reflected by an illuminated object and the intensity of the source of the illumination.

Reflected (terrestrial) radiation – All infrared radiation emitted by the Earth and its atmosphere.

Reflection – Reflection of electromagnetic waves or soundwaves by a surface. Depending on the direction in which the radiation is reflected, we can distinguish between specular and/or diffuse reflection.

Remote sensing – Process to obtain data and information about objects or phenomena without actually touching them.

Repetition rate (orbital period) – Also called temporal resolution, defined as time interval between two identical flights over the same area.

Sabkha – Flat basin, periodically filled with water, without surface outlets in a (semi-)arid zone.

SADC – South African Development Community, regional organisation for economic and political integration in southern Africa.

Saffir-Simpson scale – Five-stage scale to measure the intensity and danger level of a hurricane.

SARAL – Indian/French Earth observation satellite with a focus on ocean monitoring (launch 2013).

SAR – Synthetic Aperture Radar, imaging radar system that looks sideways to its flight path.

SASS – Système des Aquifers du Sahara Septentrional (NWSAS).

Satellite – Object orbiting the Earth, the Moon or another celestial body.

Satellite map – Map made using image data from satellites.

Satellite navigation system – System used to determine position and navigation on the Earth and in the air by receiving signals from navigation satellites.

Saxaul – Shrub growing on the arid steppes and in the deserts of Central Asia.

S-band – Range of frequencies from 4 GHz to 2 GHz within the microwave band of the electromagnetic spectrum. S-band radar is primarily used for meteorological purposes (e.g. for measuring precipitation).

Scanner instrument – Scanning system for recording image data.

Scatter – Process by which electromagnetic radiation from the molecules in the atmosphere, the ocean or the surface of the land deviates.

Scatterometer – High-frequency radar instrument to collect quantitative data on the backscatter coefficients of the terrain's surface.

Scene – Part of the Earth's surface as shown in a single satellite image.

SCIAMACHY – Scanning Imaging Absorption Spectrometer for Atmospheric Chartography, an atmospheric sensor on board Envisat.

Sensor – Describes an element on a satellite, aircraft, balloon or another remote sensing platform that carries out a specific task in remote sensing.

Sentinel – Multi-satellite project being developed by ESA under the Copernicus programme.

Sentinel (-1[A]) – ESA's series of operational satellites for monitoring tasks within the Copernicus programme; the radar satellite Sentinel-1A (launched 2014) is the first satellite in this series.

SEVIRI – Spinning Enhanced Visible and Infrared Imager, sensor on board MSG satellites.

Signature (radiation signature) – A characteristic pattern of radiation frequencies for a particular material or object.

Silurian – Geologic period from 443 to 419 million years ago.

SMOS – Soil Moisture and Ocean Salinity Mission, ESA's second Earth Explorer Opportunity mission to gather global observation data for the modelling of weather, climate and ocean currents.

Solar irradiation – Electromagnetic radiation, which is perceived by humans as sunlight.

Solar radiation – Electromagnetic radiation emitted by the Sun.

Space probe – Unmanned space probe sent into space for exploration purposes.

Spectral range – Describes the position of radiation within the electromagnetic spectrum and indicating the bandwidth for imaging by multispectral sensors.

SPOT – Systeme Pour l'Observation de la Terre, series of French Earth observation satellites located at a height of 822 km above the Earth on a polar orbit. The ground resolution is up to 2.5 m.

Sputnik – The Sputnik mission comprised the first ten Soviet satellites to orbit the Earth.

SRTM – Shuttle Radar Topography Mission; space shuttle mission that mapped the entire surface of the Earth (80 %) using radar interferometry (C-band, X-band) in order to generate a global terrain model.

SST – Sea Surface Temperature.

Stereo pair – Pairs of images suitable for stereoscopic evaluations consisting of partial images taken from different space parallax but with largely similar content.

Sun-synchronous – Polar, circular orbit of satellites crossing the Equator at the same local time, creating the same imaging conditions.

Swarm – Earth Explorer Mission of ESA, to observe the magnetic field of the Earth.

Swath width – Width of the strip on the Earth's surface that is monitored during an orbit of the Earth.

TDW – Deadweight tonnage, amount of weight a ship can carry.

TECCONILE – Technical Cooperation Committee for the Promotion and Development of the Nile, platform for the countries in the Nile catchment basin to discuss issues of water quality and environmental problems.

Terra – NASA Earth observation satellite to gather global data on the condition of the atmosphere, land and oceans.

TerraSAR-X – A German Earth observation satellite concerned with cartography, digital terrain models, collecting data on land cover and its classification, spatial planning and environmental monitoring.

Tertiary – Geologic period in the Cenozoic, characterised by the tectonic creation of mountain chains.

Thematic Mapper – MSS development, a multispectral scanner with seven spectral bands within the visible light range and within infrared radiation range on board Landsat-4 and Landsat-5. The resolution of the six visible and short-wave infrared bands is a pixel size of 30 m, or 120 m for the thermal infrared band (band 6).

Thermal infrared – Electromagnetic radiation of wavelengths from 3 µm to 25 µm.

Tidal range – The difference between low tide and high tide.

Tides – Periodic changes in the water movement of the oceans, driven by tidal forces.

Tide water glaciers – Glaciers flowing to the sea.

TIGER initiative – ESA initiative for the increased use of remote sensing for improved and integrated water resources management in Africa.

TIRS – Thermal Infrared Sensor on board Landsat-8 to record thermal radiation.

TM – Thematical Mapper, multispectral sensor on board the Landsat-4 and Landsat-5 satellites.

TOPEX / Poseidon – Former NASA and CNES (France) research satellite for measuring sea level.

Trace gas – Also trace elements, all natural and synthetic substances that make up a tiny proportion of the atmospheric composition of air.

Transpiration – Evaporation of water via the leaves (stomae) of plants and also, to a very small degree, sweat given off by humans and animals.

TRMM – Tropical Rainfall Measuring Mission, satellite programme launched in 1997 by NASA and NASDA with the aim of collecting data on tropical rainfall.

Tsunami – Enormous wave triggered by an undersea earthquake, shift in mass or volcanic eruption, which can reach the coast in the form of a wall of water several metres high.

Typhoon – Tropical cyclone in the East Asian Pacific.

Ultraviolet radiation – Section of the electromagnetic spectrum with wavelengths below the violet range. Comprises around 5 % of the radiant energy from the Sun and the primary source of energy in the stratosphere and mesosphere.

UN – United Nations / United Nations, intergovernmental association of 193 states.

UNDP – United Nations Development Programme.

UNECE – United Nations Economic Commission for Europe.

UNESCO – United Nations Educational, Scientific and Cultural Organization.

USGS – United States Geological Survey, American Federal authority providing and disseminating geographical information.

Venus Express – ESA space probe to research the atmosphere of the planet Venus.

VHR – Very High Resolution, remote sensing data with a ground resolution of 1 m or lower.

Visible light – The part of the electromagnetic spectrum visible to the human eye (0.4 µm to 0.7 µm).

Wadi – Dry valley in the desert or other arid region.

Walker circulation – air circulation parallel to the Equator, responsible for the El Niño and La Niña weather phenomena.

WasserStiftung – charitable foundation that supports people in regions with too little drinking water or polluted drinking water by helping them to help themselves.

Water vapour – Water in its gaseous state, the most important factor in the atmosphere's natural greenhouse effect.

Wave – Oscillation travelling through space and matter (e.g. electromagnetic field).

Wavelength – Distance between successive crests of a wave.

Weather satellite – Earth observation satellite that observes meteorological processes.

Windward – The side facing into the wind.

WorldView-2 – High-resolution commercial Earth observation satellite.

WWF – World Wide Fund for nature, one of the largest international conservation organisations in the world.

X-band – Radar frequency range between 12.5 GHz and 8 GHz (wavelength 2.4 cm to 3.75 cm).

µm – Symbol for micrometres, 10^{-6}.

Used abbreviations for countries by ISO

AM	Armenia
AZ	Azerbaijan
ARE	United Arab Emirates
BH	Bahrain
BZ	Belize
CMR	Cameroon
CYP	Cyprus
DOM	Dominican Republic
EGY	Egypt
ES	Spain
FR	France
GB	United Kingdom
GE	Georgia
GTM	Guatemala
ISR	Israel
JOR	Jordan
KWT	Kuwait
LBN	Lebanon
LU	Luxembourg
LS	Lesotho
MT	Malta
MOZ	Mozambique
MRT	Mauritania
MW	Malawi
PAK	Pakistan
PT	Portugal
QA	Qatar
RUS	Russian Federation
SZ	Swaziland
TKM	Turkmenistan
USA	United States of America

REFERENCES

Literature

Abeel, Z. (Hrsg.): New Approaches to Water Management in Central Asia. United Nations University, Tokyo, 2001.

Ahnert, F.: Einführung in die Geomorphologie. Verlag Eugen Ulmer, Stuttgart, 1996.

Albertz, J: Einführung in die Fernerkundung - Grundlagen der Interpretation von Luft- und Satellitenbildern. Wissenschaftliche Buchgesellschaft, Darmstadt, 2001.

Bamber, J.L. et al.: Widespread Complex Flow in the Interior of the Antarctic Ice Sheet, In: Science Vol. 287, No. 1248, 2000.

Barberis J.A.: International groundwater resources law. FAO Legislative Study No. 40, Rome, 1986.

Barlow, M., Clarke, T.: Blue Gold. The Battle against Corporate Theft of the World's Water. Earthscan Publications, London, 2002.

Beckel, L. (Hrsg.): Megacities. Geospace Verlag, Salzburg, 2001.

Beckel, L. (Hrsg.): The European Space Agency Schoolatlas – Geography from Space. Verlag Geospace, Salzburg, 2009.

Begni, G. (Hrsg.): Observing our environment from space. New solutions for a new millennium. A.A. Balkema Publishers, Lisse, Abingdon, Exton, Tokyo, 2001.

Beigelbeck, R., Paschke, F., Preisinger, A., Aslanian, S.: EGU, Vienna, April 2007.

Cano, G.J.: Survey of Existing International Agreements and Instruments: Transboundary Freshwaters. UNCED; Research Paper No. 40, 1992.

Caprara, G., Cheli, S.: Dallo Spazio per la Terra - Tutte le applicazioni utili all'uomo. Istituto Geografico De Agostini, Novara, 2003.

Chapagain, A.K., Hoekstra, A.Y. (Hrsg.): Water Footprints of Nations. UNESCO-IHE, Delft, 2004.

Couper, A. D. (Hrsg.): The Times Atlas of the Oceans. New York, 1983.

Elachi, C.: Spaceborne Radar Remote Sensing: Applications and Techniques. IEEE, New York, 1988.

Renger, J.: Wasserressourcen im Nahen Osten – Konfliktstoff oder Katalysator regionaler Kooperation?. In: Geographische Rundschau, No. 2, pp.51-56, 2002.

Emerton, L., Elroy, B.: Value. Counting Ecosystems as Water Infrastructure. IUCN, Gland, Switzerland and Cambridge, 2004.

Europäische Weltraumorganisation: The TIGER Initiative, 2006 Report. ESA, 2006.

FAO: Fishery and Aquaculture Statistics 2011. FAO, Rom, 2013.

FAO: The State of World Fisheries and Aquaculture, FAO Fisheries and Aquaculture Department, Rom, 2007.

Fetterer, F., Knowles, K., Meier, W., Savoie, M.: Sea Ice Index. [N_197903, N_197909, N_201403, N_201409, S_197903, S_197909, S_201403, S_201409]. Boulder, Colorado USA: National Snow and Ice Data Center, 2002 (updated daily)

Frater, H., Niedek, I. (Hrsg.): Naturkatastrophen. Springer-Verlag Berlin, Heidelberg, 2004.

Furby, S.L., Wallace, J.F., Cacceta, P., Wheaton, G.A.: Detecting and monitoring salt-affected land. Report to LWRRDC project CDM1, 1995.

Habersack, H., Moser, A. (Hrsg.): Plattform Hochwasser. Ereignisdokumentation Hochwasser August 2002. Zentrum für Naturgefahren und Risikomanagement. Universität für Bodenkultur, Wien, 2002.

Herschy, R.W., Barrett, E.C., Roozekrans, J.N.: The world's water resources: a major neglect; a study in remote sensing in hydrology & water management. EARSeL. Working Group 10, ESA, Paris, 1988.

Hofrichter, R. (Hrsg.): Das Mittelmeer. Fauna, Flora, Ökologie. Spektrum Akademischer Verlag, Heidelberg, Berlin, 2002.

Hölting, B.; Coldewey, W. G.: Hydrogeologie- Einführung in die Allgemeine und Angewandte Hydrogeologie. Spektrum Akademischer Verlag. 6. Auflage. München, 2005.

Hughes, T.J.: Thermal convection in ice sheets: New data, new tests, In: Natural Science, Vol.4, No.7, pp. 409-418, 2012.

Intergovernmental Panel on Climate Change: Climate Change 2007. IPCC, 2007.

Jevrejeva, S., Grinsted, A., Moore, J., Holgate, S.: Nonlinear trends and multiyear cycles in sea level records, Journal Geophysical Research, Vol. 111, No. 09012, 2006.

Johannesen, O.M., Muench, R.D., Overland, J.E. (Hrsg.): The Polar Oceans and Their Role in Shaping the Global Environment. American Geophysical Union, Washington, 1994.

Johannesen, O. M. et al. (Hrsg.): Polar Seas Oceanography, Remote Sensing of Sea ice in the Northern Sea Route: Studies and Applications, pp.472, Praxis Springer, 2007.

Jones, K. et al.: Monitoring and Assessment of Wetlands Using Earth Observation. In: GlobWetland: Looking at Wetlands from Space. ESA, Frascati, 2006.

Jørgensen, S.E., Löffler, H., Rast, W., Straškraba, M.: Lake and Reservoir Management. Developments in Water Science No. 54, Elsevier, 2005.

Jungfer, E.: Wasserpotenziale in Nordafrika. In: Geographische Rundschau, No. 6, pp. 56-61, 2001.

Kasperson, J.X., Kasperson, R.E. (Hrsg.): Global Environmental Risk. United Nations University Press, Tokyo, 2001.

Khondaker, A. H.: Water Management in Dhaka. In: Biswas, A.K. International Journal of Water Resources Development Vol. 22, No. 2, pp. 291-311, 2006.

Kiefer, R.W., Lillesand, T.M.: Remote Sensing and Image Interpretation. John Wiley & Sons, Inc., New York, 2000.

Knox, P.L., Marston, S.A.: Humangeographie - Spektrum Lehrbuch. Spektrum Akademischer Verlag GmbH, Heidelberg, Berlin, 2001.

Kramer, H.J.: Observation of the Earth and Its Environment - Survey of Missions and Sensors. Springer Verlag, Berlin, Heidelberg, 1996.

Kron, W.: Hochwasserschadenrisiko: Vorsorgestrategien und Versicherung. In: H.-B. Kleeberg und H. Nacken (Hrsg.): Hochwasser – Vorsorge und Schutzkonzepte. Forum für Hydrologie und Wasserbewirtschaftung, Vol. 18, No. 06, DWA, Hennef, 2006.

Levy, K.J., Gopalakrishnan, C.: Promoting Disaster-resilient Communities: The Great Sumatra-Andaman Earthquake of 26 December 2004 and the Resulting Indian Ocean Tsunami. Water Resources Development Vol. 21, No. 4, pp.543-559, 2005.

Löffler, H.: Die Weltwasservorräte – Ressourcen und Konflikte. Verlag der Österreichischen Akademie der Wissenschaften, Wien, 1997.

Marcinek, J., Rosenkranz, E.: Das Wasser der Erde. Eine geographische Meeres- und Gewässerkunde. Klett-Perthes Verlag, Gotha, 1996.

Meijerink, A.M.J.: Remote Sensing Applications to Groundwater, IHP-VI Series on Groundwater No. 16, UNESCO, 2007.

Mee, L.: Neuer Atem für marine Todeszonen. In: Spektrum der Wissenschaften, No. 4, pp. 50-57, 2007.

Münchener Rück: Überschwemmung und Versicherung, Münchener Rückversicherungs-Gesellschaft, München, 1997.

Oosterom, P.V., Zlatanova, S., Fendel, E.M.: Geo-information for Disaster Management, Springer Verlag Berlin, Heidelberg, 2005.

OMVS: Project for the Integrated Development of the Senegal River Basin, Dakar, 1977.

Pennwell: International Petroleum Encyclopedia 2005. PennWell Corporation, Tulsa, Oklahoma, 2005.

Rignot, E., Mouginot, J., Scheuchl, B.:Ice Flow of the Antarctic Ice Sheet, Science, Vol. 333, No.6048, pp.1427-1430, 2011.

Schmidt-Falkenberg, H.: Geophänologie - Wissenschaftliches Sachbuch Bd. I-III. Projekte Verlag 188, Halle (Saale), 2005.

Schuck, E.C. et al.: Adoption of More Technically Efficient Irrigation Systems as a Drought Response. Water Resources Development Vol. 21, No. 4, pp. 651-662, 2005.

Schultz, G.A., Engman, E.T. (Hrsg.): Remote Sensing in Hydrology and Water Management. Springer Verlag, Berlin, Heidelberg, New York, 2000.

Sommer, T., Ullrich, K., Luckner, L.: Auswirkungen der Augusthochwasserereignisse 2002 auf den Tal-Grundwasserkörper im Stadtgebiet Dresden. In: Schadstoffbelastung im Mulde- und Elbe-Einzugsgebiet nach dem Augusthochwasser 2002, UFZ Halle-Leipzig und TU Bergakademie Freiberg, No. 32, 2003.

Spektrum Akademischer Verlag (Hrsg.): Lexikon der Geographie. Bd. I - IV. Spektrum Akademischer Verlag, Heidelberg, Berlin, 2001.

Spektrum Akademischer Verlag (Hrsg.): Physische Geographie. Spektrum Akademischer Verlag, Heidelberg, Berlin, 2005.

Stani-Fertl, R.: Exonyme und Kartographie. Wiener Schriften zur Geographie und Kartographie Band 14, Institut für Geographie und Regionalforschung, Kartographie und Geoinformation, Wien, 2001.

Strozzi, T., Werner, C., Wegmüller, U., Wiesmann, A.: Monitoring land subsidence in Mexico City with Envisat ASAR interferometry, GAMMA Remote Sensing, Muri, 2004.

Szekielda, K.-H.: Satellite Monitoring of the Earth. John Wiley & Sons, Inc., New York, 1988.

Tortajada, C.: Who has access to water? Case study of Mexico City Metropolitan Area. In: Human Development Report Office – Occasional Paper 2006 No. 16 for Human Development Report 2006, United Nations Development Programme, 2006.

Turton, A. et al.: Gold, Scorched Earth and Water: The Hydropolitics of Johannesburg. In: Biswas, A.K. International Journal of Water Resources Development Vol. 22. No. 2, pp. 313-335, 2006.

Turton, A., Henwood, R. (Hrsg.): Hydropolitics in the Developing World – A Southern African Perspective. African Water Issues Research Unit, Pretoria, 2002.

UNDP: Beyond scarcity: Power, poverty and the global water crisis, Human Development Report 2006, UNDP, New York, 2006.

UNECA, OAU, ADB: The Africa Water Vision for 2025: Equitable and Sustainable Use of Water for Socioeconomic Development, UNECA, Addis Ababa, 2000.

UNECE: Convention on the Protection and Use of Transboundary Watercourses and International Lakes, United Nations, Geneva, 1994.

UNECE: Task Force on Monitoring & Assessment, Guidelines on Water-Quality Monitoring and Assessment of Transboundary Rivers, UNECE, Geneva, 1996.

UNECE: Sustainable Management of Transboundary Waters in Europe. Proceedings of the Second International Conference, UNECE, Geneva, 2003.

UNECE: Transboundary Water Cooperation in the Newly Independent States, UNECE; Geneva-Moscow, 2003.

UNEP: Africa's Lakes – Atlas of Our Changing Environment. UNEP, Nairobi, 2006.

UNEP: Atlas of International Freshwater Agreements. UNEP/DEWA/DPDL/RS.02-4, 2007.

UNEP: Global Environment Outlook 3, Earthscan Publications, London, 2002.

UNEP: Yearbook – Emerging Issues in Our Global Environment. UNEP Division of Early Warning and Assessment, Nairobi, 2011.

UNESCO: Water for People – Water for Life. The United Nations World Water Development Report. Paris, UNESCO-WWAP, 2003.

UNESCO: Water, a Shared Responsibility. The United Nations World Water Development Report 2. Paris, UNESCO-WWAP, 2006.

UNITED NATIONS: Institutional Issues in the Management of International River Basins: Financial and Contractual Considerations. United Nations, Natural Resources/Water Series No. 17, New York,1987.

UNITED NATIONS HUMAN SETTLEMENTS PROGRAMME: Water and sanitation in the world's cities: local action for global goals. Earthscan Publications Ltd, 2003.

Wagner, W. et al.: Soil moisture from operational meteorological satellites. Hydrogeology Journal Vol. 15, pp. 121-131, 2007.

WIR: World Resources 2000-2001. World Resources Institute, Washington, 2000.

WWF: Pipedreams? Interbasin Water Transfers and Water Shortages. WWF, 2007.

Zaag, P.v.d., Savenije, H.H.G. (Hrsg.): Water as an Economic Good: The Value of Pricing and the Failure of Markets. UNESCO-IHE Institute of Water Education, Delft, 2006.

Zepp, H.: Grundriss Allgemeine Geographie: Geomorphologie. Ferdinand Verlag Ferdinand Schöningh, Paderborn, 2002.

Web (30.06.2015)

http://dx.doi.org/10.7265/N5QJ7F7W (nsidc.org/data/G02135)
http://earth.esa.int/
http://emergency.copernicus.eu/
http://imbie.org
http://na.unep.net/atlas/
http://nilebasin.org/
http://nsidc.org/data/
http://oceanservice.noaa.gov/
http://ocid.nacse.org/tfdd/
http://response.restoration.noaa.gov/
http://taiga.net/acia/
http://worldoceanreview.com/wor-2/fischerei/
http://wwdrii.sr.unh.edu/
http://www3.gaf.de/aquifer/
http://www.britannica.com/
http://www.disasterscharter.org/
http://www.discover-aai.com/disaster.htm
http://www.dwaf.gov.za/iwqs/wms/Default.aspx
http://www.dwd.de/
http://www.earthtrends.wri.org/
http://www.eia.gov/energyexplained/
http://www.fao.org
http://www.fishbase.org/
http://www.grdc.sr.unh.edu/
http://www.greatbarrierreef.org/
http://www.grid.unep.ch/btf/maps/
http://www.gulfhypoxia.net/
http://www.hydrogeographie.de/
http://www.ipcc.ch/report/ar5/wg1/
http://www.marinedebris.noaa.gov
http://www.munichre.com/de/reinsurance/business/non-life/natcatservice/index.html
http://www.oekosystem-erde.de/html/wassernutzung.html
http://www.planet-wissen.de/natur_technik/fluesse_und_seen/
http://www.pmel.noaa.gov/tao/elnino/impacts.html
http://www.pol.ac.uk/
http://www.rev.net/~aloe/river/
http://www.transboundarywaters.orst.edu/
http://www.unep.org/
http://www.unesco.de/weltwasserbericht4_kernaussagen.html
http://www.usf.uni-kassel.de/wwap/results.htm#map1
http://www.wasserstiftung.de/
http://www.water-technology.net/projects/
http://www.worldmapper.org/display.php?selected=102
http://www.wri.org/

Europe